Putting People in Pigeonholes

Any history of homosexuality must begin by dealing with two related but quite distinct issues about sexuality in general. The first is the question of 'nature *versus* nurture'. Basically, is a preference for the opposite sex or the same sex the result of a genetic predisposition or upbringing? It is tempting and all too easy to reply that it is probably a combination of the two and then to move on. However, this is too simplistic and ignores the real questions posed (and assumed) by this debate.

Even if one were to argue that 'nature' (i.e. genetics) was the primary factor in sexual attraction, this does not necessarily mean that the individual will act on the 'genetic hard-wiring'. That is, a person might be genetically inclined to same-sex attraction but sublimate these desires, marry, have children and never have a same-sex encounter. In such a circumstance, the individual's culture, religion, laws and values might serve to short-circuit the hard-wiring.

Likewise, almost every individual in the developed West is raised in an environment that constantly and relentlessly portrays 'heterosexuality' as normative. Despite this overwhelming 'nurturing' by society at the macro level and by parents at the individual, micro level, from the earliest of ages, a significant minority of the population engages in same-sex activities. Thus, in this case, widespread socio-cultural

nurturing seems incapable of overriding same-sex feelings or stop-
ping same-sex activities. Does this suggest that the genetic drive is
stronger than the effects of upbringing? Alternatively, does it imply
that the general social and cultural context of an individual's upbringing is insufficient to reinforce or, more rarely in the case of a very 'liberal' household, overcome the specifics of the individual's upbringing?

Clearly, the question is more complex than just the opposition of
nature (genetics) and nurture (upbringing). It is also not just a 'mix of
both'. If there is a genetic disposition to same-sex attraction (and most
recent studies of humans and animals would seem to suggest that this
may be the case), then there is also more than enough evidence to
suggest that this genetic predisposition is not all-consuming. Nor is it
a case of either/or ('gay' or 'straight'). The range of sexual activities
between individuals at various points in their lives suggests that sexuality operates on a continuum. Also, individuals seem capable of
maintaining sex lives that seem at variance with their 'inclinations'
and, in some cases, have no sex lives at all (with others) out of choice.
Is there a gene for celibacy, one is inclined to ask?

Thus, the argument from the point of view of nature and genetics
is not compelling or complete. At the same time, the explanation of
non-normative sexuality through nurture also fails to explain the wide
range of human sexual activity. More importantly, much of the argument for nature or nurture presupposes that there is a normative type
of sexual activity (opposite sexual attraction) and that some 'explanation' must be found for 'deviation' from this norm. Were the question
turned on its head and scientists or sociologists asked to prove that
there was a genetic or socio-cultural 'explanation' for opposite-sex
attraction the reaction would be bafflement or amusement. Indeed,
the entire argument seems as much a social construct as anything else.
Western societies are trying to find all-embracing explanations for
why specific individuals have sex with other specific individuals. These
explanations are sought because they are crucial to ongoing social,
cultural, legal and political debates in Western societies. If these societies, for example, had little or no interest in individual sexual interaction and made no legal distinctions between types of sexual activities
or pairings, there would be little interest in the debate. Thus, the issue

of 'nature *versus* nurture' is very much a discussion arising from the specific context of debates in Western cultures about the appropriate social and legal reaction to non-normative sexual activities.

This leads us to the second and more important debate arising in any discussion of sexuality: essentialism *versus* constructionism. These two rather appalling words focus on the entire question of sexual 'identity'. Essentialists basically argue that there are such things as homosexuality, bisexuality and heterosexuality. Societies may use various labels and may respond in diverse ways to individuals who are homosexual, bisexual or heterosexual. However, the fundamental point remains that these are 'real' identities that are inherent (or essential) to individuals and the human condition.

Constructionists, on the other hand, would argue that such terms (homosexual) are simply categories created by cultures and societies. They do not really exist apart from these labels. Thus, a 'homosexual' is someone who understands who and what she/he is as 'homosexual' (or 'gay') because she/he lives in a society that labels her/his behaviour in a certain way. In cultures where no such labels exist there would be no inherent categories or boundaries. A person who engaged in same-sex relations in a society without these categories might not, in any way, perceive that they were 'different' from someone who never engaged in same-sex relations. In this model, describing someone as 'gay' is not the same as saying they are 'tall' or 'blonde'. 'Gay' is not an essential characteristic of the person but rather a way of defining and categorising (even pigeonholing) the individual by their behaviour. An analogy would be to suppose three categories: sporty (actively plays sports), spectator-sporty (likes watching sports) and non-sporty. In some cultures individuals might easily be defined by these terms. However, in cultures without extensive organised sporting activities such distinctions might be meaningless whereas 'competitively driven', 'consensual' and 'non-competitive' might be able to define similar personal traits and approaches to circumstances. These sets of categories would never match completely and would encompass a whole range of other social and cultural activities and values. They would, however, make sense in their own given culture. At its simplest, this is how constructionists view categories relating to sexuality. This distinction is *not* simply another version of the

nature *versus* nurture argument. Nature *versus* nurture is about the reasons *why* people engage in sex with certain people while the essentialist
versus constructionist argument focuses on how individuals and societies
identify, categorise and explain sexual behaviour. Or, put another way,
nature *versus* nurture seeks to understand *what* a person is doing while
the second debate looks at what that person *understands* she/he is doing.

If the question of 'nature *versus* nurture' is crucial to contemporary
debates about 'rights' and the law then that of 'essentialism *versus* constructionism' is even more important though largely unknown. 'Nature
versus nurture' is often used to argue that individuals engaged in non-
normative sexual practices should not be discriminated against any
more than a racial or ethnic minority (for their genetic or national
background) or a religious minority (for non-normative beliefs). Thus,
the argument is that 'homosexuals', for example, should not face discrimination because their sexual inclinations may be genetic (like
being black – the nature argument) or the result of upbringing *versus*
choice (like being Jewish or Catholic – the nurture argument). This
has proven to be a very powerful argument though it is hotly contested
by those who argue that same-sex activities are not about inclination
but are purely a matter of choice (i.e. like any other 'sin') and can be
resisted or overcome. As pure choice, same-sex activities no more
deserve special legal protection than skydiving or any other 'pastime'.

When one deploys the issues inherent in the 'essentialism *versus*
constructionism' the debate changes radically. This approach suggests
that there is no such thing as differing sexual categories (constructionism) and that all sexual behaviour is on a single continuum. The
most that one can say is that opposite-sex attraction has been 'more
common' historically though sex with both genders has been nearly
as 'common', especially in cultures without strong religious views on
sexual activities. Essentialism would imply that 'homosexuality', for
example, is not simply a genetic predisposition but something fundamental and key to an individual's identity (thus more like being Jewish
which has ethnic/genetic – and religious/upbringing – connotations).

One could use this debate to argue that seeing, defining, or prosecuting someone as a 'homosexual' is, in fact, historically *abnormal* and
unnatural. The sexual acts of such an individual are simply that – acts.

The other side of the debate could then respond that it might, therefore, be acceptable to criminalise the specific acts while making no assumptions about the individual (this is rather similar to the 'hate the sin, not the sinner' position of some Christian denominations). The point is that 'essentialism *versus* constructionism' is a debate that locates discussions about sex, sexuality and sexual activities in the realm of society and culture while 'nature *versus* nurture' locates the discussion largely within the individual and his/her own life experiences. Both can be used to argue for or against 'toleration', or 'decriminalisation'; neither allows one side or the other in current debates to win the day. However, they do focus the issues differently.

A few additional words need to be said about the structure of this volume. A broadly chronological approach is used which attempts to examine views on same-sex relations around the globe in roughly the same time periods. As such, there is a certain amount of 'jumpiness' geographically. Each chapter, though, serves as a snapshot of same-sex relations in a given period. Within the chapters there will be an attempt to treat geographical areas as more or less distinct. Thus, it should be possible for a reader interested, for example, in the Far East to move from chapter to chapter focusing on those parts of each chapter dealing with the Far East.

The ability to consider non-Western histories in detail is absolutely vital for any history of homosexuality. It is the intention of this book to be a history of same-sex activities around the world. It will *not* be a history of Western homosexuality to which some allusions about the rest of the world will be tacked. As a result, there is a lot of history here that will be unfamiliar to Western readers (by its nature the main target audience for this book). However, we are reminded by Dipesh Chakrabarty that one of the most peculiar aspects about history today is that non-Westerners are 'expected' to be familiar with large swathes of Western history but Western historians (amateur and professional) feel themselves perfectly free to be almost wholly ignorant of the history of non-Western societies and cultures. If there is to be any real hope of seeing the place of same-sex activities in the wider scope of human existence around the world and through history this Western-centrism cannot be tolerated.

It is to be hoped that Western readers will persevere and be genuinely attracted to seeing that homosexuality is not a Western phenomenon with some echoes in other cultures in the past and now. Rather, a real familiarity with, and exploration of, the history of non-Western cultures serves a number of purposes. First, homosexuality is seen as normative if uncommon both historically and geographically in humanity. Secondly, the presumptions and prejudices of Western Christian society will be seen to be truly bizarre in the wider context of human experience. Third, Westerners will be forced to confront the reality that their history is not 'History' and that major civilisations have developed and exist apart from the norms of Western Christian cultures. If the history of homosexuality remains a largely Western phenomenon then its critique by Western religious conservatives remains powerful – in effect, history simply shows an ongoing debate between the (various) Word(s) of God (Judaic, Christian and Islamic) and 'sodomites'. However, when treated as but one equal history in a wider global context one quickly realises how 'abnormal' is the monotheistic, anti-sex, anti-pleasure response to same-sex activities and attraction. Putting Western homosexuality in its global 'place' also well and truly puts the Western religious response to same-sex behaviour in *its* place – which is marginal, uncommon and, in the wider context of human history, abnormal.

The chapter divisions focus on the spread of monotheism arising from Judaism with its accompanying stress on sexual morals. Thus, the first chapter will look at the situation before the advent of Judaism. As the chapters proceed, the Judaeo-Christian-Islamic sexual mores spread across the globe and older, polytheistic (and polysexual) traditions are either replaced or heavily influenced by the sexual attitudes of these three great, intertwined monotheistic religions of the Middle East. By the height of European world domination (*c.*1900), these mores had become dominant across the world. The postscript will consider how the reaction to and rejection of this Western moral hegemony has arisen not from other cultures reasserting pre-existing social and cultural values and traditions but from within the very Western culture that swamped the world in the late nineteenth century. Thus, issues of sexuality are debated worldwide using the language – and constructs – of the West both 'for' and 'against' individuals who engage in same-sex activities.

Prior to the widespread acceptance of Judaeo-Christian-Islamic sexual mores, much of the world had little or no interest in same-sex activities and, in many cases, had a relatively positive (or broadly benign) view of them. The irony is that current debates about same-sex relations often see the most vociferously 'anti' views being expressed by members of cultures which have struggled long and hard to throw off the yoke of Western domination. Thus, what this specific discussion about same-sex activities highlights is that the West's rule of foreign lands was fairly short-lived; its control of the world's economy has proven to be more enduring; its impact on other cultures increasingly pervasive. However, its control of non-Western minds and morals has proven somewhat more resilient and so successful as to have been 'internalised'.

Many non-Western cultures have so effectively naturalised 'Victorian' values regarding same-sex acts and gender relationships (e.g. the role of women) that they deny these views to be alien and, indeed, reject aspects of their pre-colonial history which seem at variance with this moral identity. One crucial purpose of this volume will be to consider the impact that this adoption (by cultures previously colonised by the West) of Western sexual mores has had on debates about homosexuality in those cultures presently and historically.

one

Before Sodom and Gomorrah

(pre−1300 BCE)

Joined in life, joined in death

The tomb of Niankhkhnum and Khnumhotep (*c.*2430 BCE)

The most striking feature of the world before the advent of the Mosaic law (the laws, beginning with the Ten Commandments, that God gave to the Israelites through Moses) is how few cultures seem to have any significant 'moral' concern about same-sex activities. As we shall see, to the extent that there ever was an issue about the subject it related more to 'position' than 'partner'. That is, most cultures seemed to accept that males might have sexual relations with other males but thought that anyone assuming the passive position (in anal inter-course) was somehow less than male thereafter. However, even the issue of passivity became meaningless if the passive partner was an adolescent (say, fourteen to twenty years old).

Indeed, from a religious point of view, the feature that stands out most is how many of the non-monotheistic religions had gods and goddesses who engaged in same-sex acts (in various forms) in the mythology of the cults. For most of the religions before the rise of monotheism from the Middle East, the models (gods/goddesses) held up for adoration, emulation and worship presented an image of sexual ambivalence – in practice, bisexuality was the theological norm.

Where we have moral codes which pre-date and anticipate the Mosaic code there is little emphasis upon sexual activity in itself. The Code of Hammurabi (possibly the first written code of laws in human history, passed to the Babylonians by King Hammurabi in *c.*1700 BCE), for example, addresses land deals, money-lending, theft and a range of other crimes. It also discusses rape, prostitution, fornication and adultery. However, in all these latter cases the emphasis is not upon the sex act but the sense of 'loss of value' on the part of the female. Sex in the code can be something which robs a man (father or husband) of value. Beyond that, there is little interest in sexual activity (though to be fair there are some missing paragraphs, although these fall in a section distant from the passage relating to sexual activities).

Prior to the advent of Near Eastern monotheism (in the form of Judaism and, later, Christianity and Islam) religion in the East was replete with all varieties and permutations of sexual activity. More importantly, the gods were sexually active. For example, in Egypt, the god Osiris had an incestuous sexual relationship with his sister (Isis), which resulted in the god Horus. The great Babylonian god Ishtar seduced the mytho-heroic Gilgamesh, who himself was involved with another male hero; in Canaan, El (the chief god) had sex with Asherah. Further afield (as we will see in greater detail later) Hindu belief noted that the god Krishna was sexually active with his many wives while the god Samba, son of Krishna, seduced mortal women and men. In Greek myth, Zeus married Hera, chased women, abducted a beautiful young male (Ganymede) and masturbated; Poseidon married Amphitrite, pursued Demeter and raped Tantalus; Apollo was notoriously bisexual. This rampant and undifferentiated sexuality was also a feature of Roman beliefs about the gods and goddesses.

As believers saw their gods engaged in so many sexual acts it is hardly surprising that sex and sexual activity became an important feature not only of religious belief but also of worship and practice. People emulated their gods and goddesses. Thus, in many cultures, priests ritually deflowered virgins (sometimes at an extremely young age) before their arranged marriages, and sacred (ritual) prostitution was nearly universal. For example, in ancient Egypt, girls could be deflowered as young as six years old, which widespread practice partially underlies the 'humour' in Petronius's *Satyricon*. He has Quartilla, the priestess of Priapus (the phallic god) say, 'may Juno strike me down if I can remember when I was a virgin'. As the historian Sussman has explained:

male and female prostitutes, serving temporarily or permanently and performing heterosexual, homosexual oral-genital, bestial, and other forms of sexual activities, dispensed their [sexual] *favours on behalf of the temple.*

Sexual intercourse was almost universally seen as an aspect of worship. Male and female prostitutes had intercourse with male worshippers in the sanctuaries and temples of ancient Mesopotamia, Phoenicia, Cyprus, Corinth, Carthage, Sicily, Egypt, Libya, West Africa, as well as ancient (and, until 1948, modern) India. In ancient Egypt, Mesopotamia and Canaan, ritual intercourse took place annually between the ruler and a priestess.

Even in biblical Israel, there were repeated attempts to reintroduce temple prostitution, which had to be resisted (with violence and massacre) by the godly kings of Israel. The Bible records that king Asa 'expelled the male shrine prostitutes from the land' (I *Kings* 15: 12). His son, Jehosaphat 'rid the land of the rest of the male shrine prostitutes who remained there even after the reign of his father' (I *Kings* 22: 46). The situation remained so problematic even in the heart of monotheistic Israel that later, King Josiah (as part of his restoration of the Mosaic law) had to purge the land of various cults (Asherah and Baal) in which sex was a vital part (II Chronicles. 34: 3-8). These practices were not confined to the ancient Near East. In later chapters we will see the enduring nature of temple prostitution (male and female) in Hindu religious observance until it was outlawed, not under the British/Christian Raj but by India's first post-independence government in 1948. Likewise, in the fourteenth century, Chinese sources noted that Tibetan religious rites involving sex between men were being practised at the court of the Mongol emperor. Indeed, in Sri Lanka Buddhist worship of the goddess Pattini has long involved male, transvestite priests.

The key point is that sex was undifferentiated. The gender of the partner of a god or goddess (or of worshippers) was of little or no concern. Sexual choice was simply a matter of taste. What really mattered in the past was who was doing what to whom (not the identity or gender of the 'who'). As the historian Nussbaum has succinctly written:

Ancient categories of sexual experience differed considerably from our own... The central distinction in sexual morality was the distinction between active and passive roles. The gender of the object...[was] not in itself morally problematic. Boys and women [were] very often treated interchangeably as objects of [male] desire. What [was] socially important [was] to penetrate rather than to be penetrated. Sex [was] understood fundamentally not as interaction, but as a doing of something to someone.

Judaism, as we will see in the next chapter, introduced a profoundly different social construction for sex. In Jewish belief the gender of the individuals (and indeed the number of them and their familial relationships) were of utmost importance. As a small tribal group surrounded by hostile forces, the need to strengthen and increase the group placed an absolute premium on procreation. Sex was not and could not be an indifferent matter of sexual couplings of 'a doing of something to someone'. Sex was solely about procreation.

If Judaism was 'abnormal', as we will suggest below, in its views on sex, then what was normal? Greenberg, in his *The Construction of Homosexuality*, summarised the ubiquitous nature of homosexuality in the ancient world:

with only a few exceptions, male homosexuality was not stigmatised or repressed so long as it conformed to [socially constructed and culturally accepted] *norms regarding gender and the relative ages and statuses of the partners.*

Indeed, from evidence dating from 3000 BCE to the beginning of the Christian era it is clear that homosexual practices were an accepted part of the cultures of the Near East. This conclusion is confirmed by many literary and legal texts in which homosexual activity is mentioned.

Two laws from the Middle Assyrian period relate to male same-sex acts. The first involves a false accusation of passive homosexuality. Someone who accuses his neighbour of being involved frequently in such relationships and does not substantiate it is to be flogged, fined and have some mark of shame (branding?) inflicted on him. The second law – where a man is falsely accused of allowing his wife to be used as a prostitute – has similar repercussions. In both cases the accused man's *reputation* is at stake. He is being accused of being effeminate or unmanly in allowing his wife or himself to be sexually 'used'. This law makes sense in the context of the numerous texts which indicate that passive homosexuals (though not guilty of breaking the law) were despised. Thus, to accuse someone of effeminacy was a grave slur on his reputation.

The second Assyrian law initially seems to be very much like the Mosaic injunction in Leviticus (see later): 'If a man has intercourse with another and they indict him and prove him guilty, they will have intercourse with him and turn him into a eunuch'. However, this law differs in some interesting ways. It is the active partner who is punished; the passive partner is not mentioned. The biblical passages mention and punish both men. It also differs from the normal Assyrian punishment for adulterers, where both the man and the woman receive the same penalty (unless the woman was raped). This suggests that this law is dealing with a situation in which consent was not present. In other words, the law appears to be dealing with homosexual rape.

A thorough reading in the laws and customs surviving from the Near East has led historians to conclude that:

Homosexuality in itself is thus nowhere condemned as licentiousness, as immorality, as social disorder, or as transgressing any human or divine law. Anyone could practise it freely, just as anyone could visit a prostitute, provided it was done without violence and without compulsion, and preferably as far as taking the passive role was concerned, with specialists [i.e., men who were 'normally' passive].

It is certainly clear that there was no religious problem with homosexuality since there are texts in which blessings were asked for upon homosexual couplings. Thus, Israel's neighbours saw nothing intrinsically wrong with consensual homosexual acts.

It is equally important to stress that same-sex acts were not hidden; homosexuals in the cultures around Israel were not 'in the closet'. There were homosexual temple prostitutes who took part in public processions, singing, dancing, sometimes wearing women's clothes and carrying female symbols – even at times pretending to give birth. These 'ritual' homosexuals took the passive role in intercourse and for this reason were despised (being called 'dogs') as unmanly – in the context of societies which largely saw sex as penetrative and the 'manly' role as that of penetrator. Homosexuals (or men who engaged in genital contact with other men) were visible and tolerated, if not respected or liked. As one historian has concluded:

it therefore appears that these types of person, as in other places and periods including our own, formed a shady sub-culture where all sorts of ambiguities, mixtures and trans-formations were possible.

Sadly we have even less material for other Near Eastern cultures than we have for the Assyrians. A Hittite law (*c.*2000–1200 BCE) states that 'if a man violates his daughter it is a capital crime. If a man violates his son, it is a capital crime'. The context of the law is a list of inces-tuous relationships that are banned. Thus, male same-sex activity is not condemned unless it is incestuous. Or, as the eminent Hittitologist Hoffner has observed, 'a man who sodomises his son is guilty of *urkel* [illegal intercourse] because his partner is his son, not because they are of the same sex'. Later he added, 'it would appear that homosexuality was not outlawed among the Hittites'. The evidence is scant but it suggests that the Hittites shared with the Assyrians a general view of male homosexuality, which was probably no worse than ambivalent and mildly disapproving (of the passive partner).

When we turn to consider the evidence from the Near East's great-est civilisation, Egypt, the situation is less clear. Goedicke and, to a lesser extent, Westerndorf argue that consensual homosexual acts were not regarded as immoral. This interpretation has gained some support by the discovery of the grave of two men. Just as interestingly, in the iconography of the Amarna period:

the difference between the sexes appears to be almost obliterated… the ideal image of the body was virtually the same for men and women. It is the male image adapting to the female.

This androgyny need not necessarily imply same-sex activities but it does suggest an ambiguity about gender and sex. More conclusive evidence for Egypt's participation in the wider cultural presuppositions of the region comes from its religion and myths. To take but one example, a myth tells how the god Seth attempted to rape his younger brother Horus. He later bragged of his manly achievement to the other gods.

Other evidence suggests a more negative view of male same-sex acts. In the *Book of the Dead* the soul twice stresses that 'I have not had sexual relations with a boy'. A story of Pharaoh Neferkare (r.*c.*2300 BCE) having sex with one of his generals is almost certainly meant to prove the immorality of the pharaoh. The difficulty is that both of these texts involved relations which are inherently 'unequal' and, thus, may reflect more on specific views about consent and passivity than homosexuality more generally. One might therefore infer that the Egyptians were no less interested in, or concerned about, consensual male-male acts than other Near Eastern peoples. Apparently, though, they also shared a general distaste for the passive role.

Thus, the obvious context in which to read the biblical injunctions on sex, especially homosexuality, is that the ancient Near East was a world in which the practice of homosexuality was known and largely tolerated. Same-sex acts were an integral part of religious life in parts of Mesopotamia and, in the wider cultural setting, there appears to have been no scandal attached to its practice outside worship. Anyone who regularly took the passive role seems to have been despised for being effeminate and certain same-sex acts were banned as part of more general prohibitions against non-consensual or incestuous relationships. But, beyond these specific circumstances, homosexual relations and relationships seem to have been socially and culturally acceptable.

Before leaving the Near East, one specific example from Egypt needs to be discussed. As noted earlier, an interesting tomb of two men has been discovered in Egypt. A few preliminary comments need to be made about terminology before looking at the tomb in detail. There is a common word for eunuch in ancient Egyptian inscriptions – *hm*. The word is based on the word for female but lacks the feminine termination. It has a variety of definitions: in some circumstances it can mean 'coward', more generally it seems to mean a gender which is not male though the person was born biologically male. A text in the temple at Edfu says that in Sebennytus one must not have sex with a *hm* or a male. *Hm* is also a very common word in tomb inscriptions which is often translated as 'priest', because the *hm*s are depicted performing all kinds of sacrifices for the dead. The hieroglyphs for a *hm* as a priest differ slightly from those used for *hm* as a eunuch, but the pronunciation is exactly the same and the range of uses overlap in a more generic possible translation of *hm* as 'servant'. In general, the *hm* seems to be someone who is seen as being neither male nor female in gender who may be actually castrated (though perhaps not – castration may metaphorically refer to the transformation from male to *hm*) whose social and cultural roles include that of 'servant' with special associations with cultic rituals around death and burial.

In 1964 a tomb was discovered at Sakkara near Memphis. It was the burial place of two men who are depicted holding hands, feasting together and (in their sacrificial chamber) they are shown twice in very loving embraces. They both held the title of 'overseer of the manicurists in the royal place' and each is referred to as a *hm* – apparently in the sense of 'priest'. The tomb dates from the reign of Pharaoh Niuserre (2453–2422 BCE). The men, named Niankhkhnum and Khnumhotep, had their names decoratively intermingled at the entrance to their tomb: Niankh-Khnum-Hotep, which means 'joined in life, joined in death (or peace)'. Inside the tomb is an inscription authorising other priests (*hm*) to carry out their duties and forbidding the men's family members from impeding them. Reports on the excavation noted the extraordinary number of *hm* priests depicted in their tomb and that a large number of them were mentioned by name. This may imply that the men were of a high social status – which, as palace officials would not be surprising. Of course, it could also be a sign that they were considered *hm* themselves and, consequently, that their 'circle' might have been heavily involved in their burial. As we will see below, in a number of cultures individuals of 'intermediate' gender (strictly neither male nor female) play a significant role in life's transition moments (birth, marriage, death).

There are various other interpretations given for the tomb: the men were brothers, related by marriage, close relatives, business associates, or part of a specific 'guild'. Also, the paintings make it clear that both were married and had children. What is certain is that when calling them *hm* the inscriptions did not mean eunuchs – literally castrated. Most importantly, the unique nature of the iconography and the closeness of the two (especially in embracing) suggest a relational bond. That they were both called *hm* suggests a gender-ambiguity which would be more in keeping with an emotional tie between them than any of the other suggestions advanced.

When one leaves the Near Eastern Fertile Crescent to discuss the history of same-sex activities on other continents, one encounters an almost insuperable barrier. Africa, in particular (but also the Western Hemisphere) is lacking in written records. This means, in many cases, that little can be said before the arrival of Europeans and their accounts of the behaviour of 'native peoples'. Obviously, this is problematic. In most cases, Europeans were keen to justify their exploitation and/or conquest of these peoples and, thus, it served their purposes to portray them in the worst possible light. For Europeans this usually meant stressing the barbarity or primitivism of the peoples they encountered.

In the New World, this was expressed by charging the natives with cannibalism and human sacrifice. Also, great stress was laid on the nudity of New World inhabitants. This showed their lack of shame – and lack of civilisation. Although the Aztecs, Incas and Mayas of the New World had well-developed states and written records, sadly most of these were systematically destroyed by their European conquerors. This was done, it was argued, to rid the people of their evil, Devil-led histories thereby wiping the slate clean prior to their conversion to Christianity and, just as importantly, European socio-cultural, political and economic structures, practices and morals.

The situation in Africa, though, was more complex. The earliest European contacts with sub-Saharan Africa predated the discoveries in the New World. Initially the Portuguese (the first Europeans to explore Africa's coast extensively) were more concerned with finding a route *around* Africa to India and China. Africa itself was of little immediate interest. Western Africa was, however, important as a source of both gold and slaves. Here, though, Europeans encountered well-established, powerful indigenous states with which Westerners tended to negotiate and trade, rather than conquer. The lands beyond the immediate coast remained largely unknown to Europeans until the mid- to late nineteenth century.

By the time Europeans began to take note of Africa as a whole and began the process of exploration and conquest, the dynamics underpinning the way Europeans viewed other peoples were changing. Europe was now keen to stress the 'native purity' of Africans as opposed to the decadence of 'civilised' industrial societies. Also, the justification underlying conquest – the spread of Christianity – was no longer a strong driving force (though not wholly removed). Rather, Europeans articulated their 'mission' as one of paternalistic care and nurturing. They took over parts of the world which, they argued, were populated by 'children' and set about 'educating' them. In Africa this led European writers to stress the supposed purity of native peoples. The 'noble savage' became the recurring image used – to devastating effect. Of course, when confronted by 'childish' resistance to the 'chastising fatherly rod' of European rule, Europeans were more than willing to present their opponents as degenerates.

In all cases, as one might imagine, the sexual mores of non-Europeans figured prominently in European accounts of natives. In sixteenth-century accounts of the New World, the stress was more on the overall degeneracy (epitomised by nudity) of the natives. The seeming tolerance of sodomy was also attacked and held up as a proof of the satanic nature of New World societies (along with cannibalism and human sacrifice). In Africa (as elsewhere), polygamy was attacked along with the enforced seclusion of women (used effectively against Islamic cultures as well) – by a West hypocritically arguing that it treated its women with civility and courtesy. Although some mention was made of 'deviant' sexual practices in Africa, by and large, European writers were keen to stress the childlike, simplistic, in-harmony-with-nature aspects of African societies. A people closest to nature, to the minds of nineteenth-century Europeans, would be driven wholly by 'natural' inclinations with the need to procreate as the most prominent. Any evidence of non-procreative sexuality suggested a degenerate rather than simplistic state of existence. Consequently, European writers tended to gloss over perversion while stressing the simplicity and child-like qualities of African societies.

Of course, what this meant is that Europeans (and latterly Africans) had a vested interest in portraying Africans as 'natural', as the term was understood by Christian Westerners. The reality was much more complex – as common sense would suggest – and displayed a diversity of attitudes to sex, sexuality and gender that was as complex as that found in other non-Western, non-Christian societies across the globe. One example will suffice at this point in the discussion of African homosexuality. Although very much the result of modern investigations, it is clear that customs involving woman-woman 'marriages' (in which bride-price and dowries may change hands) is extensive. Such practices have been documented among a number of cultures: in the south (Sotho, Koni, Tawana, Hurutshe, Pedi, Venda, Lovedu, Phalaborwa and Narene Zulu), in the east (Kuria, Iregi, Kenye, Suba, Simbiti, Ngoreme, Gusii, Kipsigis, Nandi, Kikuyu and Luo), in the Sudan (Nuer, Dinka and Shilluk), and in the west (Dahomean Fon, Yoruba, Ibo, Ekiti, Bunu, Akoko, Yagba, Nupe, Ijaw, Nzemaa and Ganagana/Dibo). It would be ludicrous to suggest that a practice which is so widespread and yet differently constructed is anything but indigenous. To argue otherwise one might just as well assert that little if anything of pre-Arabic or pre-colonial African culture survives and that what exists today is wholly the result of non-native influences. In a non-African such a view would be racist; from an African it is simply pandering to traditional Western Christian values and mores.

This means that it is extremely difficult to view Africa and African societies other than through the jaded and prejudicial lenses of Western Christians. While cultures on the Indian subcontinent and in the Far East have extensive, independent histories and literatures which can be examined in a context untouched by Europeans, we have no such luxury when examining Africa. The New World, through its few surviving records and monuments does, fortunately, provide slightly more material for consideration. Despite this profound difficulty, one cannot and should not simply pass over Africa. More importantly, one cannot simply accept without examination the assertion of European conquerors and African nationalists that same-sex activities are merely the result of foreign influences – whether Arab-Islamic or, later, decadent Westerners.

The most that we can say about prehistoric Africa (which largely means pre-1400 BCE) is that certain traditional cures and legal codes suggest an awareness of same-sex activity. In addition, religious beliefs seem to allow a place for individuals failing or unwilling to conform to commonly accepted gender patterns. The one concrete example comes from the rock paintings done by bushmen several thousand years ago. The San people (bushmen) were the predominant ethnic group in southern Africa in the past but have been largely displaced both by black Africans and white European settlers. What has remained is a vast array of rock paintings. Many of these relate to religious rituals and beliefs with a heavy emphasis upon 'fertility' and 'sexuality' – in its broadest sense. Thus, paintings display menstruation and birth. Some, though, clearly display anal/intercrural sex between men. Beyond these singular yet compelling images we know little or nothing of Africa except from 'outside' sources.

Information relating to the history of the Indian subcontinent is much better. From their earliest surviving records the cultures of the subcontinent have shown an ambiguity towards sex and sexuality even more marked than that of the pagan Graeco-Roman world. It is, however, with this society that there are the most noticeable similarities. Unlike the Mediterranean, in India polytheism has survived to the present day in the various forms of Hinduism (and in the stories underlying Buddhism). The gods of India, as in Greece and Rome, took on many guises and showed a willingness to love and have sex with a variety of individuals without regard to gender. As we will see, though, this ambiguity and polysexuality is even more a feature of Hinduism. Hindu gods not only have same-sex relations, they alter their gender and, more interestingly, in some cases are explicitly seen as having manifestations both as males and females – and, in some cases, as both at the same time. Indeed, Tantric thought stresses the female element in every man and the male element in every female. The result is that sex, sexuality and gender are changeable through the cycle of reincarnation, generally, and, even, within a given incarnation.

One problem facing anyone studying sex and sexuality from a outsider's perspective is that many of the key texts were intentionally mistranslated (both into English and various Indian vernaculars) and bowdlerised to protect the sensibilities of nineteenth- and early twen-tieth-century readers. For example, when the medieval history work, *Murraqa*, refers to 'beautiful boys' the translator has supplied 'lads and lasses' – not only inaccurate but decidedly Burnsian! A recent transla-tion (1997) of the *Krittivasa Ramayan* describes the two widows of King Dilipa as 'living together *behaving* [emphasis mine] like husband and wife' while the original says 'in extreme love [*sampriti*]'. Their child is named Bhagiratha because he is born of two vulvas (*bhaga*) but the translation simply omits any reference to the explanation for his name.

Laying aside such problems, a general ambiguity and variability at the level of the divine has had and continues to have a profound impact on gender, sex and sexuality in the subcontinent. The lack of specific moral codes laid out in 'revealed' scriptures has also allowed for a more relaxed attitude to non-normative behaviour. Even the conquest of India by Islam failed to have a major impact on Hindu 'morality' with regard to sex. Indeed, it was not until the all-pervasive impact of Victorian Britain that India's cultures began to alter. The result is that today there is a heated and, at times, violent debate at all levels of Indian-Hindu society about sex and sexuality. At its most fundamental, 'conservatives', who find comfort in denying their own history in favour of a Western-constructed 'reality', reject the ambi-guities of the past. Socially constructed tolerance for non-normative behaviour – never universal – is increasingly denied as ever having existed. Instead, same-sex relations, despite their undoubted place and importance in the beliefs and stories underpinning and informing Hinduism, are seen as 'alien' imports from the 'liberal' West and, more often, from 'decadent' Islam. Thus, the Tantric focus on the anus as a centre for psychic energy and a way to energise artistic, poetic and mystical faculties, is embarrassing; that the god Krishna masturbates in many stories is just as problematic.

This desire to blame someone for homosexuality is profound and a feature of many societies, past and present. Arabs blamed the Persians, who in turn accused Christian monks. Anglo-Saxons saw sodomy as a by-product of the Norman conquest. Modern Indians do the same, blaming Mughal conquerors, British imperialists or – of late – American capitalists. This explains the plea by Vimla Farooqi, an Indian female politician, in 1994 that the state ban a gay men's conference in Bombay on the grounds that homosexuality was a result of Western decadence. Her call was, interestingly, as much about her rejection of homosexuality as 'the West' more generally – she spoke as a member of the National Federation of Indian Women, an organisation associated with the Communist Party of India.

Any understanding of ancient Hindu culture must begin, as with those of other non-monotheistic cultures, with a simple premise. It is a wholly modern belief that associates sex with emotional attachment – love. That is, being in love with someone, even of the same sex, will not necessarily have any bearing on one's ability to wed someone else and to procreate legitimate heirs by them. Indeed, most societies throughout history have seemed inclined to think that marriage was and remained primarily a means of securing legitimate progeny and *not* the focal point for emotion or love. This is hardly surprising when one remembers that most marriages were arranged. Thus, in India, marriages were familial contracts designed to construct or cement social bonds between families through the production of children. Spouses were expected to breed and even, over time, cherish one another and have affection for each other. However, there was no expectation that this attachment, legally or emotionally, would be to the exclusion of other more deeply held relationships. Spouses were free to love (and have sex) where they would as long as this had no substantial impact on the production, nurturing and eventual inheritance of the children.

This broader understanding of the objects of emotional and sexual attraction is equally evident in the Far East. The earliest known literature of China is a poetic collection called *Shi Jing* (*Classic of Odes*). These works were part of an oral tradition similar to the Homeric sagas of ancient Greece. They were memorised and recited; only later were they written down (in and about the seventh century CE). These suggest that beauty and eroticism were not gender-specific. Men were sexually attracted to both genders and romantic affection was also as likely to involve two men as a man and a woman. Thus, one finds the *Shi Jing* relating stories of attachments between noblemen (recalling Harmodius and Aristogeiton) and warriors (as in the *Iliad* with Achilles and Patroclus).

However, these male relationships were not to the exclusion of relations with women. The men routinely married and had children. As in many other early cultures falling just within the light of written history, marriage was expected and routine but almost wholly separated from emotion, love and affection. Husbands and wives were not expected, or required, to be united by bonds of romantic love. Again, these were socio-economic and political unions between families. Couples were free to express love and romance in other relationships with little or no regard for gender.

This 'ambiguity of affection' was a feature of the earliest known Chinese cultures. Terms of endearment, such as *mei ren* (beautiful woman/man), were gender neutral. Although no specific words appeared to describe homosexual relations the social emphasis on status and patronage is apparent in the term *chong* ('favour' or 'clientship'). *Chong* referred to a relationship that crossed status barriers. In Greece, same-sex relations were normally, thought not exclusively, transgenerational – a younger man was the passive partner of an older, active male. In China (and most of the Far East), the more common same-sex relationship was of a lower status man in the passive role with a higher status, active male. To the extent that it is possible to reconstruct the structure of same-sex relationships within a culture of arranged marriages, this seems to be a pattern that dates from the Zhou Dynasty (1122–1027 BCE). Sadly, little more can be said about same-sex relations in the East as most of the literature that survives is semi-mythical serving purposes (didactic, moralising, propagandistic) unrelated to the transmission of historical fact let alone socio-cultural norms. The key point is that the earliest literary material from the Far East evidences the same relaxed attitude to same-sex relations – if not relationships – that one sees in the semi-mythical writings of the West (e.g. the *Iliad* and *Odyssey*) and India (e.g. the *Ramayana* and *Mahabharat*).

Sadly, as we leave the Eastern Hemisphere for the New World, we return to the problem faced in Africa – the lack of records. Any discussion of homosexuality in the New World is extremely hampered by this lack of documents. Many of the cultures of the Americas left no written records at all. In those which had forms of writing and record-keeping (Aztec, Maya and Inca) most documents did not survive the post-conquest period. The Spanish systematically and intentionally destroyed as much of the 'history' of these societies as possible. The logic of this destruction was irresistible: these cultures were under the sway of the devil as evidenced by the presence of human sacrifice and deviant sexuality. As a result they needed to be cleansed of any association with the demonic as part of their conver sion to Christianity. The Spanish quickly realised that pre-existing histories, languages and traditional practices were likely to slow the process of Christianisation and Hispanicisation, and took steps to eliminate them. The consequence of this process of cultural eradication is that there is almost nothing that can be said about the societies and cultures of the New World before about 1450. Indeed, one only has some confidence in the historical record from the mid-1500s. Sadly, from that point, records were largely kept by Western colonisers or their supporters among the native populations, which further complicates any attempt to view sexuality through 'native' eyes as opposed to the eyes of Western Christians or indigenous converts to Christianity.

What we do see in a general way in this period is an approach to love and sex, which is relatively amorphous. The two were not necessarily connected nor was there a correlation between 'marriage' (however that was defined in a society) and love. Sex was certainly *about* procreation in some way – it was absolutely necessary to produce an heir. However, there was no sense in which marriage was the place in which sex or love were normally (or mostly) located. *Procreation* was located within the marital unit. Sex and love were able to take place in any number and varieties of couplings. From the gods and goddesses of pre-monotheistic religions to the common man all evidence suggests that men and women were as free (and as willing) to engage in same-sex acts as opposite-sex acts. There was no clear delineation of a concept of exclusive preference though there seems to have been an awareness that some individuals were likely to confine their sexual activities (almost) wholly to members of their own sex/gender. The chapters which follow will trace the alteration to this pattern, under the influence of Judaeo-Christian-Islamic thought, to one which locates love, sex and procreation in the same place (the marital unit) to the detriment of all others.

The Birth of Homophobia

(1300–100 BCE)

They must be put to death

(*Leviticus* 20:13 on sex between men – sixth century BCE)

In the previous chapter, we looked at the sexual activity of gods and goddesses in various cultures, and the impact this had on ideas of sex and sexuality. Judaism, with its stress on ritual purity and ethnic propagation, radically differed from other religions. Not only was it monotheistic but it also had a code (the Mosaic law) that placed an emphasis upon behaviour and 'being', which stressed the impact of acts in themselves. Thus, rape was not so much about the loss of value in a wife but the 'sin' of the act itself. It is always important to note though that Mosaic regulations about sexual activities are part and parcel of rules relating to diet, cleanliness and ritual activity.

While same-sex acts were completely condemned and death decreed as the punishment, the range of sins for which there was a similar punishment confirms that the emphasis was less upon sex *per se* and more upon purity of behaviour and character. One was supposed to be stoned or burnt for: being a spiritual medium; cursing one's parents; blasphemy or swearing; being a rebellious or drunken son; adultery; rape; and, in the case of a woman, not being a virgin when married. Moreover, the law also labelled as abominable making clothes out of two types of fabric or sowing two types of crop in a single field – as well as same-sex acts. Finally, the range of conditions or actions for which one would be excluded (temporarily or permanently) from the people of Israel was equally eclectic: having damaged testicles; being an illegitimate child; suffering from eczema; having a wet dream; living in a house suffering from damp or dry rot.

The gods and goddesses of the peoples around Israel and Judah engaged in sex for pleasure; so did their worshippers. The God of Israel did not have sex at all. However, he did give an explicit command in the Bible to procreate: 'God blessed them [the 'male and female' he had created] and said to them, "be fruitful and increase in number; fill the earth and subdue it" (*Genesis* 1: 27-28)'. Indeed, the first chapter of *Genesis* is replete with God's commands 'to increase' not only to man but also animals, fish and birds. There is no sense that sex is about pleasure; rather the emphasis is upon procreation and, after the Fall, sexual desire and childbirth are seen as punishments for Eve. 'I will greatly increase your pains in childbearing; with pain you will give birth to children. Your desire will be for your husband, and he will rule over you'.

Though later theologians (especially of the twentieth century) found scope for 'pleasure' and 'mutual comfort' or 'companionship' in biblical relationships it is fairly clear that the Bible takes a very utilitarian approach to sex itself. Every command in the biblical law which discusses sex, focuses on ensuring procreation from a large gene pool. Thus, incest and male homosexuality are explicitly condemned. However, one must stress that the focus is on procreation, not homosexuality. If the biblical law was truly concerned with homosexuality then the total silence on lesbianism seems inexplicable. Put into the context of a world view in which sex is about procreation *and* penetration then the absence of lesbianism makes sense. Judaism may have rejected the sexual free-for-all of the peoples and religions around them but it continued to view sex – the act – as primarily about 'a doing of something to someone'. Judaism was not attacking homosexuality *per se* but simply ensuring that penetration was procreative.

This may seem an obtuse and overly subtle distinction but it is nevertheless important. The biblical injunctions have a context of a wider world view in which sex is about penetration. Within that context,

Judaism placed a paramount importance on procreation. If the true purpose of sex is solely for procreation and is fundamentally an act of penetration (bereft of any real need for, or emphasis upon, pleasure) then the injunctions remain. However, in the modern world most monotheists (Jews, Christians and Muslims) who rely on these and similar injunctions, practice birth control and engage in sexual acts which are not always male-female vaginal penetration. The correct stress laid in the Bible would imply that these monotheists are violating the biblical injunctions in a manner identical to that of male homosexuals – a point made explicit in Catholic thought on the subject. Biblically, *any and all* sex which is not potentially procreative is 'unnatural' and condemned by God. Considering the prevalence of the use of contraceptives by most 'Scripture-believing' monotheists, the emphasis on the sexual activities of a few homosexuals seems an interesting focus on the 'mote' of homosexuality while ignoring the 'beam' of non-procreative, non-vaginal penetrative heterosexuality.

However, the important point for the discussion in this chapter is the dramatic impact of the Judaic view of sex as procreative, rather than procreative and pleasurable. Other than the Jews, 'none of the archaic civilizations prohibited homosexuality *per se*', as Greenberg notes. Judaism stands alone – indeed seems bizarrely uncommon – in condemning non-procreative sex (such as homosexuality). One must constantly stress that Judaism did *not* condemn homosexuality; rather it condemned sex that did not involve the penile penetration of a vagina for the purposes of procreation. The biblical stress is on defining what sex is supposed to be about and, thus, it was not essential to condemn every type of non-penetrative, non-procreative sex (hence the silence on lesbianism). Seen in this light the dramatic narrowing of the scope and range of sexual activity in Judaism becomes all the more obvious.

However, our focus is on homosexuality and the Judaic views on male-male acts could not be more dramatic: 'Do not lie with a man as one lies with a woman; this is detestable' (*Leviticus* 18: 22)…

If a man lies with a man as one lies with a woman, both of them have done what is detestable. They must be put to death; their blood will be on their own heads (Leviticus 20: 13).

This is clear enough. But, the important consideration is the place of Judaism's view on homosexuality in a wider historical, cultural and geographical context. The simple reality is that it is the biblical view on the purpose of sex and, consequently, sexual morality, *not* homosexuality, that has been historically 'deviant' in the sense of 'uncommon' and 'abnormal'.

The Levitical passage needs some careful consideration before looking at other biblical passages or the wider Near Eastern context. The exact terminology must be examined. *Leviticus* 18: 22 states: 'do not lie with a man as one lies with a woman; this is detestable'. There can be little doubt that this prohibits consensual sex acts between men in a Near Eastern context where this seems not to have been problematic. There is also no reading of this which would suggest that it is aimed primarily at pederasty (homosexual relations between men and boys) or, alternatively, same-age homosexuality – it is general enough to cover both situations. Clearly this very general term prohibits every kind of male-male intercourse. Finally, the use of 'detestable' ('abomination' in the Authorised Version of the Bible) is a very strong word with connotations of ritual and religious impurity, and separation from the body of God's people.

The second passage in *Leviticus* adds to the prohibition by demanding a specific punishment – death – which is not mentioned in the first. In some parts of the Levitical law specific human punishments are set out and, at other times, punishment is left to God (as the Koran would suggest for homosexuality). This means that homosexuality is treated the same as adultery (*Leviticus* 20: 10) and extreme forms of incest (*Leviticus* 20: 11-12). Israel's neighbours also condemned adultery and incest but they never put homosexuality on the same level. Secondly, both parties in homosexual intercourse are punished; the passive and active partners are both put to death. The use of the rather vague and neutral term to 'lie' along with equal punishment suggests that consent to intercourse is assumed. Although the Bible says nothing about homosexual rape, comparisons with the laws on adultery implies that only the rapist would have been executed (cf. *Deuteronomy* 22: 22-25). Thus, we can conclude that, in the context of a biblical understanding of sex as procreative, all forms of non-procreative sexual activity – including consensual homosexuality – are condemned. However, the key to the discussion remains the underlying argument set out in the Bible. The Judaic law is rejecting an approach to sex (common among Israel's neighbours) that sex could be pleasurable *and/or* procreative in favour of a view in which sex is, *first and foremost*, procreative. The Bible is not trying to list all of the types of illegal sex rather it is defining what limited – indeed singular – type of sex is actually acceptable to God: penile penetration of the vagina for the purposes of procreation.

The additional parts of the injunction in *Leviticus* also explain the concept of guilt: 'both of them have done what is detestable. They must be put to death; their blood will be on their own heads.' The second clause occurs only in this chapter (vv.9, 11, 13, 16, 27) and in *Ezekiel* (18: 13; 33: 5) and explains the use of the death penalty. It is simply the plural version of 'his blood shall be on his head'. In other words, anyone breaking the law knew the consequences and could not complain that the death penalty was unfair.

The Levitical laws are generic in their condemnation of homosexuality. However, as we have seen, ritual, cultic male homosexuality was well established in the ancient Near East. Therefore, it is not surprising that there are a number of laws aimed at this particular phenomenon and its associated practices. *Deuteronomy* (23: 17) prohibits male and female religious prostitution in Israel. The early historical books of the Bible note that when Canaanite religious practices were introduced into Israel so was temple prostitution and, as noted above, three Israelite kings attempted to abolish the practice.

Finally, male prostitutes were often castrated and took part in ceremonies in such a way as to highlight their androgyny and effeminacy. It may well be that an aversion to homosexuality (or, at least, its cultic version) partially explains the Bible's ban on eunuchs participating in public assemblies (*Deuteronomy* 23: 1) or on transvestism (*Deuteronomy* 22: 5). With regard to the latter the Bible says that 'God detests anyone who does this'. However, one must note that the Bible does not think of transvestism only as a man in drag – it also condemns women who wear male clothing. The latter point has become moot as Western Christianity and Judaism have largely accepted female 'transvestism' (the image of a priest, minister or rabbi railing against women in trousers or jeans is almost inconceivable even though the biblical injunction is as clear about that as it is about a man in a dress). While one might see these additional passages as attempts to ban anything smacking of homosexuality it is just as likely that they relate to specific associations with the cultic acts of Israel's pagan neighbours.

The story of Sodom, like the Levitical regulations, must be seen in this context. This is the main biblical account outside the law which seems to suggest views on homosexuality. Most commentators accept that the demand 'to know' the angelic visitors to Sodom was a demand to have sex with them – to sodomise them. That Lot offers his daughters instead (and, in the story of Gibeah, the Levite his concubine) shows that the demand was for sexual intercourse (*Genesis* 19: 5-8; *Judges* 19: 22-26). If we accept that sex by men with men was not socially rejected by Israel's neighbours, then the demand for sex, in and of itself, is not the key issue in the story. The truly repugnant feature of the behaviour of the men of Sodom is their total disregard for the accepted principles of hospitality. Visitors, whether anticipated or not, were to be treated with the utmost courtesy and kindness. What the story relates, then, is the demand by the men of Sodom that guests in their midst must submit to being degraded (as passive partners). The prophet Ezekiel (16: 49-50) makes it plain that this is the correct emphasis in the biblical account:

Now this was the sin of your sister Sodom: She and her daughters were arrogant, overfed and unconcerned; they did not help the poor and the needy. They were haughty and did detestable things before me. Therefore I did away with them as you have seen.

Thus, Sodom was destroyed primarily for its lack of concern, for its pride, for its gluttony, and for its inhospitable treatment of the weak and poor.

To argue that the main reason for the destruction of Sodom was homosexuality one would need to interpret Ezekiel's 'detestable things' as meaning only homosexuality and then ignore everything that Ezekiel listed first. Moreover, if one understands (as most commentators would) the Hebraic literary method of making a statement and then restating it for emphasis then one would read the first sentence as the main clause and the second as a rewording of the first. 'Haughty' becomes a shorter, pithier reworking of 'arrogant, overfed and unconcerned', while 'detestable things' restates 'they did not help the poor and needy'.

Having said this, the homosexual intentions of the inhabitants of Sodom simply makes the end of the story the more obvious to Jewish readers. The desire to rape guests just adds to the appalling image of the people of Sodom and makes their destruction all the more understandable. In this, the story of Sodom serves as a microcosmic tale similar to that other story of mass destruction at God's hand. Indeed, commentators often note that the destruction of Sodom parallels the destruction of the world in the Flood. In both stories there is a mass destruction of peoples by God and only one family saved by divine assistance. The explanations given for God's judgement are similar as well. The Flood was also partially explained by sexual acts. The only specific sin noted to explain why God had decided that 'every inclination of the thoughts of [men's] hearts was only evil all the time' was that the 'sons of God went to the daughters of men and had children by them'. As with the Flood, in Sodom a type of illicit sexual intercourse played some part in God's decision to destroy large numbers of men, women and children.

Unfortunately, there is little or nothing that can be said about Africa in this period. Obviously, North Africa was at this point part of the broader Hellenistic world. To that extent we can say that same-sex activities and individuals in northern Africa shared in the general cultural milieu of the Pharaonic, Hellenistic and Roman worlds which will be discussed in the next chapter. There is no doubt that some parts of sub-Saharan Africa (Nubia and parts of the Gold Coast) were in regular trading contact with the civilisations of the Mediterranean basin. This in no way proves or even suggests that same-sex practices were spread to the rest of the African continent from the Mediterranean, though the spread of Christianity (for example to Abyssinia/Ethiopia) highlights the ability of ideas successfully to migrate southwards. All that one can surmise is that black African societies and cultures on the southern border of the Sahara were in close contact with cultures that had a socially constructed place for same-sex activities and individuals. Or, put another way, Nubians and Abyssinians could not have been wholly ignorant of, for example, the sex life of the Emperor Hadrian whose lover Antinous drowned on a Nile cruise taken by the couple.

When we move eastwards from the Hellenistic world we confront the civilisations of the subcontinent briefly encountered by Alexander the Great. While Judaism was developing a view of sex and marriage which was emphatically procreative, the wider cultural context continued to see pleasure being as much a part of sex as procreation. More emphatically the focal point for emotional attachment and sex remained resolutely separate from procreative marriage. Love, friendship and sex were intertwined, and, occasionally, this might involve marriage.

This emphasis upon friendship over marriage is an even more marked feature in India. Thus, the *Jataka* tales of Buddhism (*c.*200–300 BCE), which are like Aesop's fables, recount stories surrounding the various incarnations of Buddha, as *bodhisatta*. The *bodhisatta* has no wife but almost always has a companion-friend who is usually identified as Ananda (Buddha's attendant and disciple). *Jataka* story 498 tells of three former births of the *bodhisatta* and Ananda. In the first they were both outcasts, in the last, ospreys. In the second, though, they lived as two deer who 'always went about together, eating and cuddling together, very happy, head to head, nuzzle to nuzzle, horn to horn'. As one scholar has noted:

Sex and marriage; love and friendship; there can be no doubt that this is the way in which the Jatakas, on the whole, see it. Sex and marriage on the whole are bad; love and friendship on the whole are good… this differs from the [traditional Buddhist] position [where] sex and marriage are bad, but so are love and friendship.

While it is tempting to infer that the primacy of friendship/love over marriage/sex mirrors the anti-sex bias of Christian asceticism, which values celibacy first and foremost – this would be a mistake. The stress in this scheme is not 'where sex takes place' but 'where love is located'. Christianity (along with Judaism and Islam) has traditionally valued procreation over (if not to the exclusion of) pleasure. Indian culture has not – seeing, rather, pleasure (*kama*) as finding 'its finality in itself'. Pleasure is an end in and of itself. Indian culture, in its myriad social and religious forms, seems more concerned with emotion and love and less about the mechanics of procreation.

Indeed, the divide between Indian thought (whether Buddhist, Hindu or Jain) and Judaeo–Christian-Islamic beliefs could not be more profound. In Indian philosophy there is an unreality and artificiality to the whole of the 'real' world – to nature. Thus, male and female are not ultimate distinctions but are created by society to perform certain roles. Individuals may be constructed as male or female based on role, dress, etc, as well as physical attributes. But these categories are fundamentally artificial and temporary constructs. As we will see, Indian thinkers without a 'revealed' moral-theological base advocating heterosexuality alone or a duality of existence (male/female) and lacking prescriptive moral codes were left free to try to understand and explain what was apparent in the world about them.

Clearly, though, the place to begin is the earliest Indian texts. The Puranic writings (epic, classical and early) date from *c*.200 BCE–800 CE. There is considerable debate about the dating of early Hindu literature but there is a general consensus amongst scholars (as opposed to devotees). Vedic literature is generally considered to include all *sruti*, that is the four *Samhitas*, the *Brahmanas*, *Aranyakas* and *Upanishads*. All other Sanskrit religious texts are *smrti* ('remembered not heard'). This category includes the *Vedanta Sutra*, the 'Epics' (such as the *Bhagavad Gita*) and the *Puranas*. Most of the major concepts in Hinduism (relating to duty, reincarnation, cause/effect, transmigration of the soul, enlightenment; or *varna*, *ashrama*, *karma*, *samsara*, *moksha*, etc) are detailed in what scholars define as 'Vedic literature' although most of these appear in the later literary compositions (such as the *Upanishads*) rather than earlier texts.

One of the best places to start is the relationship between Krishna and Arjuna, who are the most famous pair of male friends in the ancient texts, and their relationship forms the literary thread running through the *Mahabharata*. Krishna is divine but has human incarnations while Arjuna is human but also divine. They are both seen as reincarnations of the two primal sages (*rishis*): Nara (Narayana's 'prog-eny' and equal) and Narayana (creator of the universe). In their pre-vious (or eternal) form there was a mystical unity between them and this explains their closeness throughout the various stories – in which Krishna is primarily defined as a 'friend', warrior and king, not the lover of women as in later texts. Consistently, their relationship is placed above that of the ties with their respective spouses, lovers or children. Indeed, Krishna commits a number of 'dishonourable' acts in battle to save Arjuna (so great is Krishna's love for him). As Krishna explains in the *Drona Parva*:

I do not regard my father, my mother, yourselves [the other participants in the tale], *my brothers, yes, even my very life, so worthy of protection as* [Arjuna] *in battle. If there be anything more precious than the sovereignty of the three worlds, I do not, O Satwata, desire to enjoy it without Pritha's son,* [Arjuna], *to share it with me.*

This declaration recalls but surpasses the words (so well-known to Christians as they are frequently used in modern marriage cere-monies as an expression of the ultimate devotion between two lovers – happily forgetting the original exchange was between two widows) said by Ruth to her mother-in-law, Naomi:

Don't urge me to leave you or to turn back from you. Where you go I will go, and where you stay I will stay. Your people will be my people and your God my God. Where you die I will die, and there I will be buried. May the Lord deal with me, be it ever so severely, if anything but death separates you and me.

Compare Krishna to Arjuna:

You are mine and I am yours. All that is mine is yours also. Whoever hates you hates me, too. Whoever follows you follows me… O [Arjuna] *you are from me and I am from you.* Vana Parva

Indeed, Krishna makes his emotional love for Arjuna even more explicit in the *Saiptika Parva* placing it above his relations with his own family. When Aswatthama asks for Krishna's discus, Krishna replies saying Arjuna has never asked for such a thing: '[Arjuna] than whom I have no dearer friend on earth, that friend to whom there is nothing that I cannot give including my wives'.

Not only does the relationship between Krishna and Arjuna suggest that companionable emotion (love) exists between men and outside the marriage bond, but even some of the actions in the texts suggest that 'friendship' is similar to marriage. Thus, as with the Christian same-sex ceremonies discussed by John Boswell, the texts bind friends together by actions normally associated with marriage rituals. For example, Rama and Sugriva (in the *Ramayana*) swear an oath of friendship which is then solemnised by walking round a fire lit by Hanuman – perhaps even taking the 'seven steps' that constitute marriage. This idea of equality of value for friendship and marriage is also seen in the use of the theme of steps in proverbial phrases such as *saptapadam hi mitram* – 'seven steps taken together make a friendship (or marriage)' or 'seven words spoken together make a friendship'.

What the text suggests both in the tales of individuals (such as Krishna and Arjuna), and more widely, is that friendship is the focal point for emotional love. Marriage and procreation involve, by their very nature, sexual intercourse but not necessarily 'love'. Where emotional attachment is most often found and expressed is not only within the context of friendship but between individuals of the same sex. Admittedly, this does not necessarily require that this love be manifested in sexual acts – nor, however, does it exclude it. What is does imply, though, is that the Hindu texts accept and extol love between members of the same sex as the highest emotional bond between humans. Marriage, insofar as the texts imply, is *not* the 'tie that binds'; friendship is. The closest connections that humans can form are not between spouses solidified by sexual consummation but, rather, between men and men (or women and women) through the bonds of emotional attachment. Love is most frequently same-sex; sex is a means to a necessary end – procreation.

The best example of the conflict that can arise from the relationship of love with friendship *versus* marriage and sex comes from the most well-known Indian account of sex change, the story of Sikhandin(i). Born as a girl, she was granted transformation into a male. The wider context of the story, told in the *Mahabharata*, is that in an earlier life the girl, Sikhandini (then a woman named Ambi, 'mother') had her life ruined by men (in particular, Bhishma) and had been granted rebirth to avenge herself. While one might presume that the transformation from female to male (Sikhandin) was to allow her to kill Bhishma, in fact, the trigger was that she had become married to another girl. Thus, the sex change was to allow for love/friendship to function in the context of sex/marriage. Ovid recounted a similar story, from an ancient Greek account, about Iphis (a girl raised as a boy) who fell in love with Ianthe and whose sorrow at being unable to fulfil her love for the other girl so moved the gods that they transformed Iphis into a boy, they then married.

Indeed, Surya (god of light and life) when seducing the ever-virgin maiden Kunti articulates an attitude to sex that sets the tone for much of the early Hindu literature. Resisting his advances, Kunti says that to give in would be wrong – a 'sin' in Western parlance. But Surya replies:

how can I, who care for the welfare of all creatures, commit an unrighteous act? That all men and women should be bound by no restraints, is the law of nature. The opposite is the perversion of the natural state.

Desire, in Surya's 'chat-up line', should not be constrained by law or convention but should be expressed freely.

This desire for freedom in relationships takes an extreme form in Hinduism. Procreation, the bedrock of heterosexual activities, is not an insurmountable barrier to love. Hindu gods and mytho-heroic figures overcome the problems of procreation through a number of interesting methods. In some cases birth takes place involving only one person (human or divine) as with Zeus's generation of Athena (or the begetting of Jesus by Mary and the Holy Ghost). In other situations, same-sex couples procreate (hence, Bhagiratha – born of two vulvas). Many cultures (as just suggested) have variant approaches to procreation; Hinduism has more and gives them greater and more frequent prominence.

Other texts, especially those interested in linguistics, began a debate on the question of a 'third nature' which continues to the present day because of the presence of a third gender in Sanskrit grammar. For example, the *Mahabhasya* (third century BCE) says:

Q) What is it that people see when they decide, this is a woman, this is a man, this is neither a woman nor a man?
A) That person who has breasts and long hair is a woman; that person who is hairy all over is a man; that person who is different from either when those characteristics are absent is neither woman nor man *(*napumsaka*).*

This discussion would be developed in greater detail by Jain thinkers and became integral to an understanding of *hijras* – the 'third sex' of modern India.

As in the pre-classical, classical and Hellenistic world of the Greek Eastern Mediterranean of the same period, the pattern in China of culturally accommodating same-sex relations was not universal and did not exclude relations between men of the same status or age. These 'relationships of equality' might exist for extended periods of time and were largely accepted within Chinese society as long as they did not preclude the fulfilment of filial obligations to produce children, especially sons. Unwillingness or inability – let alone an outright refusal – to provide a subsequent generation to maintain the worship of ancestors and the integrity of familial inheritance was deplored and pitied regardless of the rationale. However, no specific social opprobrium was associated with same-sex relationships. Indeed, developments during the Zhou period are extremely important since they set patterns not only for attitudes to sexual relationships during this specific period but also more generally for much of subsequent Chinese history. Moreover, the foundations for Chinese thought were laid in this period in the writings associated with Lao Zu and Zhuang Zi.

Indeed, early Chinese literature (even more so than classical Greek literature) highlighted and extolled same-sex relationships as examples of romantic, emotional love. One tale, in particular, remains famous. Duke Ling of Wei (534–493 BCE) had a favourite, Mizi Xia. Mizi Xia displayed his devotion to his patron and lover by rushing to his side in the ducal carriage when the duke was ill. Using the duke's coach without explicit permission should have resulted in his feet being amputated; the duke, impressed by Mizi Xia's love, spared his favourite. Later, having tasted a wondrously sweet peach, Mizi Xia gave the other half to the duke. Eventually the relationship foundered and the duke used the 'theft' of the carriage and the gift of a 'half-eaten' peach as signs of Mizi Xia's *lack* of regard. Despite the end of the tale, the story gave China one of its two most common terms for same-sex romantic love – the 'love of the shared peach'.

The emphasis in Chinese tales on same-sex relationships is the cross-status nature of the affection. However, some tales highlight the ability of love to surmount the normal culturally accepted pattern of a socially superior active male and an inferior, passive favourite. For example, a minor official broke court and social etiquette in telling his master, Duke Jing of Qi, of his admiration. To proposition a ruler meant death – a reality underlying the courtier's reply when Duke Jing said, 'Why are you staring at me?'. The courtier replied, 'If I say, I will die. If I keep silent I will also die. I am entranced by the Duke's beauty'. Offended by this brazen affront, the duke ordered the immediate execution of the courtier. However, another official advised that it was not right to resist desire according to the best philosophy of the day. Moreover, anyone hating love invited bad luck. Duke Jing not only spared the admiring courtier but made him a servant of the royal bath.

This promotion of a favourite, though, was an example of a problem noted by many commentators during the Zhou dynasty. Too often a 'pretty face' was being given power and position without any evidence of ability: 'being wealthy and important, or beautiful and handsome does not mean the man will be intelligent and quick-witted', as one Chinese wag noted. However, the story of Duke Jing and his affectionate 'bather' also highlights the role of philosophy on Chinese attitudes to same-sex relationships. Unlike some pagan Graeco-Roman philosophies (e.g. Stoicism) or Judaeo-Christian theology, Chinese philosophy never developed an idea of 'natural' and 'unnatural'. Nor did it privilege sex as a means of procreation over sex as an act of pleasure. As will be discussed in greater detail in subsequent chapters, Chinese thought valued procreation (especially the production of sons) but also saw sex as a pleasurable act to be enjoyed.

In addition, instead of the 'natural/unnatural' debate, Chinese thought focused on the balance of *yin* and *yang* and the preservation of an individual's vital essence. Finally, Chinese philosophy stressed the sexual vitality of all people, including women, and never sought to develop a concept of 'sin' as an offence against divine law. To the extent that one could commit a sexual 'sin' is was to fail to produce offspring. However, the filial duty to provide sons did not, as already stressed, prevent a man from having sexual and emotional attachments to other men.

As we are preparing to turn to consider the spread of monotheism with the advent of Christianity it is important to pause and consider the situation worldwide regarding sex and sexuality. The Judaic stress on procreation as the sole significant and legitimate function for sex was peculiar and unique. Elsewhere across the globe – no less than in the lands immediately around Judaea – the pattern remained what it had been since the dawn of recorded history. 'Love' (which could be expressed through sexual contact) could and did have any object – regardless of gender or biological sex. Marriage was a separate 'institution', which was the focal point for procreation. It was most certainly *not* the linchpin of society or culture, nor was it the normal place in which people saw close emotional and loving relationships developing. Love, emotion and friendship remained closely intertwined and, more often than not, involved individuals of the same sex. This 'normal' pattern held the field until the spread of Judaism's unique ideas about sex, marriage and procreation. The change began in the centuries after the birth of the Christian faith.

three

Classical Civilisations and the Birth of Christianity

(100 BCE–600 CE)

Every woman's husband and every man's wife
Julius Caesar as described by Suetonius (75-160 CE)

This new faith, steeped in Jewish ideas about sex and 'God's design', broke into a world very 'un-Jewish'. The Graeco-Roman world was dominated by ideas about sex, which were considerably more multi-faceted than anything acceptable to Judaism of Christianity. The advent of Christianity began the transformation of the Mediterranean world from polytheism to monotheism and from sex-for-pleasure to (after a *very long* time) sex-for-procreation. Unlike Judaism, Christianity was a fervently proselytising religion. However, like Judaism, it placed a strong emphasis upon purity which, with the Gospel emphasis upon spirit, became less about physical purity and more about spiritual purity. Just as Christianity was more accessible to 'unbelievers', this spiritual emphasis allowed for a wider application of notions of purity especially in the area of sexual conduct. To cite but one example, Jesus in the Gospels stressed that adultery was not just an act of sex with a married person but also thinking about such an act.

Although we have some information on same-sex activities amongst the Greeks prior to the classical age, it is only with the abundance of sources from the classical period that we can speak with any authority. The picture that emerges then is of a range of acceptable same-sex activities, which almost certainly developed in the archaic period. William Armstrong Percy, in his *Pederasty and Pedagogy in Archaic Greece* has provided the most thorough overview and hypothesis of the roots of same-sex behaviour among the Greeks. Aristotle's explanation is probably the best summary of Percy's view:

The Cretan lawgiver regarded abstemiousness [from procreative sex] *as beneficial* [in overpopulated Crete] *and devoted much ingenuity to securing it, as also to keeping down the birth-rate by keeping men and women apart and by instituting sexual relations between males.*

While both an oversimplification and an anachronistic explanation, there seems to be some truth in the overall idea. What is clear is that pederasty (a young, primarily passive adolescent male having relations with an older, primarily active, adult male) originated among the Cretans and was diffused amongst archaic Greeks elsewhere. Certainly, that was the view of classical Greeks.

Nor was this meant to be a slur on the Cretans. Greeks almost universally held that some form of same-sex love was good and indeed intrinsic to what they saw as best in their civilisation. Thus, Greek thought repeatedly noted that the tyrants of the sixth century BCE tried to abolish pederasty out of a political fear of the heroic and freedom-loving bonds that were formed between the males. Athenian history specifically extolled the courage of the lovers Harmodius and Aristogeiton who assassinated Hipparchus (brother of Hippias, tyrant of Athens, ruled in 527–510 BCE), and tried to kill Hippias. Phalaris (ruled 570–544 BCE), tyrant of Agrigentum (Sicily), initially condemned his would-be assassins – another pair of lovers – but ended up freeing and praising them for their bravery and love. As Athenaeus (*c.*200 CE) noted:

Because of these love affairs, then, tyrants, to whom such relationships were inimical, tried to abolish entirely relationships between males, wiping them out everywhere.

Some even went so far as to burn down the athletic schools, regarding them as bulwarks in opposition to their own [power bases], *and so demolished them; this was done by Polycrates, the tyrant of Samos.*

Even as late as 200 CE, Greeks continued to regard male love and the heroic, brave bonds which it engendered as integral to the idea of Greek singularity and independence.

It is important to realise that love between men was so important a part of the whole of Greek culture. There has been a tradition of focusing on Athenian pederasty, which was fairly institutionalised or the system of male bonding in the Spartan military. Although important, these were not the only ways in which Greeks constructed and accepted love between men – and the Greeks constantly put the emphasis on the emotional bond though never to the exclusion of the sexual aspects of the relationship. As in other societies, the Greeks placed the bonds between men, based on love, emotion and friendship above those between spouses (which were often arranged by others) based on the desire for heirs. As Callicratidas says in the pseudo-Lucian dialogue, *Erotes* (Loves): 'marriage is a remedy invented to ensure man's necessary perpetuity, but only love for males is a noble duty enjoined by a philosophic spirit'.

The situation among the Eleans (who controlled the Olympic Games) is particularly interesting. Athenians and other Greeks considered the Eleans to be their less well-educated, rather simple relations. However, they were renowned both for their athletic prowess (leading the way in Olympic victories) and for their enthusiasm for male beauty – and the beauty of Eleans themselves. It is in this vein that one notes that Socrates (469–399 BCE) had his friends purchase the freedom of an Elean (Phaedo) from an Athenian brothel where Phaedo was a slave. Phaedo not only became Socrates' disciple but attended him at his enforced suicide and later founded a school of ethics in his native city.

The Eleans were famous, and infamous, for their appreciation of the male form and their indulgence in male same-sex activities. Athenaeus noted that 'Elis became famous for its male beauty contests… [which are] held with all solemnity… the winners receive weapons as prizes.' They were less well respected for their sexual athletics. The orator Cicero (106–43 BCE) said 'I say nothing of the Eleans and the Thebans among whom, in the loves of free-born young men, lust is actually allowed free rein.' The Jewish historian Josephus (c.37–c.100 BCE) revealed more about his own prejudices than Elean practices when he wrote of 'the unnatural vice so rampant among' them. Plutarch (c.46–c.120 BCE) preferred the type of same-sex love found at Athens and Sparta to 'the sort of love prevailing at Thebes and in Elis'. While many Greeks disapproved of the loves of the Eleans, their greatest sculptor (Phidias, b. c.500 BCE) chose an Elean, Pantarkes (victor in youth wresting at the eighty-sixth Olympiad in 436 BCE), as his lover and even represented him at the foot of his greatest sculpture – that of Zeus seated at Olympia (one of the seven wonders of the ancient world). If nothing else, this reminds us that every participant at the Olympics, and every worshipper and tourist at the temple to Zeus had a visual reminder of male-male love at the very heart of the Olympic temple.

Perhaps the most interesting example of male-male love comes from Thebes. Thebans, like Eleans, were not noted for their sophistication but where the Eleans were athletes, the Thebans (and their fellow Boeotians more generally) were renowned for their military prowess. The best instance of this in the context of this discussion is the Sacred Band. According to Greek legend, the Sacred Band of Thebes was an army of 150 pairs of homosexual lovers. To great renown, they successfully defeated the Spartans only to fall, some three decades later, to Philip of Macedon and his son Alexander the Great at the battle of Chaeronea (338 BCE). Refusing to surrender despite clearly being defeated, they were slaughtered by the Macedonians. Plato (c.428–c.348 BCE) wrote about the theoretical code which underpinned the success of the Sacred Band:

If there were only some way of contriving that a state or an army should be made up of lovers and their loves, they would be the very best governors of their own city, abstaining from all dishonour… For what lover would not choose rather to be seen by all mankind than by his beloved, either when abandoning his post or throwing away his arms… Or who would desert his beloved or fail him in the hour of danger?

Plutarch gave a similar explanation for the Sacred Band's existence:

For men of the same tribe or family little value one another when dangers press; but a band cemented by friendship grounded upon love is never to be broken, and invincible; since the lovers, ashamed to be base in sight of their beloved, and the beloved before their lovers, willingly rush into danger for the relief of one another.

Though there may have been a slight age difference in these pairs of lovers it does not seem that the Theban pattern was similar to that in Athens where the age gap was more pronounced. Indeed, it is more in keeping with the Athenian heroes Harmodius and Aristogeiton who were of similar age. Finally, one cannot help but note that the ancient Greeks, known then and now for their military abilities, did not consider homosexuality an impediment to good military order. Indeed, they saw it as an actual virtue and strength in battle.

One could continue to discuss city and region after city and region in the Greek-speaking world, spread from Black Sea coast to Sicily and Macedonia to Alexandria, noting the permutations in approaches to, and constructions of, socially acceptable male-male sexual relations. However, the key points have been made more generally by the few comments above and, briefly, below on Athens. Greek civilisation, the bedrock on which Western civilisation rests, not only tolerated but extolled – even institutionalised – male same-sex relationships.

Certainly by classical times, Athenian pederasty was an accepted part of life. It was closely associated with the education of young citizens in their duties. In many cases, the elder lover was, in part, selected for the younger beloved by the beloved's family. That is, the relationship also cemented ties between families. The athletic schools (*gymnasia*) were the focal point for courtship. The Athenians produced an extensive literature stressing the high-minded ideals associated with the relationships making clear that sex was only an incidental part of the affair. Indeed, the Athenian views on 'mere sex' were not at all complimentary, as Plutarch noted:

For friendship [the Athenian pederastic ideal] *is a beautiful and courteous relationship, but mere pleasure is base and unworthy of a free man. For this reason also it is not gentlemanly or urbane* [civilised] *to make love to slave boys* [a view *not* shared by the Romans]: *such love is mere* [sex], *like the love of women.*

For all the philosophical phrases and idealised expressions, sex did take place and was an accepted part of the relationships.

Throughout its pre-Christian history, male same-sex love remained an obvious and public feature of Greek civilisation. For example, it is interesting to note that ancient sources recorded that plays by Aeschylus, Sophocles and Euripides dealt with male-male love though this is not a feature of any that survive (one wonders to what extent one might see the hand of later Christians in this odd survival pattern). Thus, Aeschylus in his *Myrmidions* dealt with the love of Achilles and Patroclus, and closed with the death of the latter and Achilles' lament over their 'many kisses' and the 'holy union of their thighs'. Aeschylus's version is considerably truer to Homer than the one recently portrayed by Brad Pitt in *Troy*, where the heroes 'closeness' was 'explained' by making Achilles and Patroclus cousins – and not of the kissing variety! *Niobe* by Sophocles and Euripides's play about the rape of Chryssippus by Laius both dealt with same-sex love. Aristophanes often mocked older males who seemed addicted to male love but was basically supportive of what he considered 'traditional, idealistic' pederasty. At the end of his *Knights*, the hero is rewarded with a woman and an adolescent male.

Other classical works both of philosophy and history make the point just as emphatically. Plato, however, expressed contrasting views. For example, the 'Athenian Visitor' in the *Laws* advocates the banning of an 'unnatural' practice while Pausanius in the Plato's *Symposium* argues that love for the beloved is superior to heterosexual relationships. Aeschines (c.389–c.322 BCE) and Demosthenes (384–322 BCE), speaking before the Athenian assembly, showed no qualms about discussing their loves for other males. In his *Symposium*, Xenophon has his guests gossip openly and nonchalantly about same-sex affairs among members of their own set. Aristotle thought that the relationship between the lover and beloved should be sexually chaste (though emotionally intense) and considered the desire to be penetrated either a 'genetic' defect or the result of being sexually active with other males from too early an age. Overwhelmingly though, same-sex acts and relationships remained an important and accepted feature of Greek society.

Although the age of independent Greek city-states ended with their defeat by Alexander the Great (in 338 BCE), male same-sex relationships did not. Indeed, the Greek practice became even more widely diffused as a result of the Hellenising of much of the Near East and North Africa in subsequent centuries. There were frequent critics of Graeco-Hellenistic same-sex love but its supporters were even more vocal and Greek-speaking society simply would not relinquish the practice. It would later have an impact on Roman ideas, though perhaps less so than ideas native to the Italian peninsula. The simple reality, though, is that only the enforced Christianisation of the empire by the Romans managed to destroy the practice. Even then, as late as the *Dionysiaca* of Nonnus (dated anywhere in the period 390–500 CE) one can read a work extolling the love between a god and an adolescent male. However, by the time of the Roman emperor Theodosius (*c.*346–95 CE) things had begun to change. He closed the temples and banned paganism in 391 CE; two years later the last Olympics (begun in 776 BCE) were held, drawing to a close a significant element of Greek life, which had endured for over a thousand years. Pederasty and male same-sex love, also a Greek tradition for a thousand years, was equally doomed.

However, before writing off Greek practices it is important to consider their impact on Rome. The Romans had no native tradition of pederasty and, originally under the republic, made it illegal. At all cost, no Roman male was to be penetrated (regardless of age). Buggering an adolescent was *not* seen by the Romans are as an important part of the educational process. Instead, Roman emphasis lay on buggering anyone and anything else. Having said that, Romans had no problems with having sex with males (in the form of prostitutes or slaves) as long as the Roman remained the active partner. In time, this initial view on same-sex relations was modified by contact with the Hellenistic world. Romans might have initially disapproved of Greek pederasty and male same-sex love but they recognised a 'superior' civilisation when they saw it and were inclined to be culturally influenced by it. The result was a somewhat confused, and considerably more brutal, construction for same-sex relations than we have seen in Greece.

One of the best ways to appreciate both the polysexuality of Roman behaviour and the views of Roman culture about sex is to examine the lives of the rulers and emperors in the late republic and early empire. The best-known, though not unique, source is the writings of Suetonius, *The Lives of the Caesars*, written during Hadrian's reign (117–38 CE). Each biography contains a section on the sexual tastes of the given Caesar and, through the comments, makes apparent what was acceptable, what was not and what was barely conceivable.

Julius Caesar comes first and Suetonius made a clear distinction between Caesar's behaviour as *penetrated* (in his supposed and 'humorous' relationship with King Nicomedes of Bithynia) and as *penetrator* (as an adulterer). Suetonius stated that Julius Caesar (*c.*100–44 BCE) was 'notorious both for [being penetrated] and for adulteries'. Suetonius even included the extremely successful gibe at Caesar from a senator's speech that Caesar was 'every woman's husband and every man's wife'. Suetonius added a lengthy list of attributions for the stories about Caesar and Nicomedes, which served to underscore the public nature of the relationship, as well as seeming lack of concern with it. It certainly seems to have had no impact on Caesar's career beyond providing some opponents with easy jibes and some rather catchy jingles.

The basis of the joke to the Romans was that Caesar was nineteen years old when he took up his post in Bithynia. As such he was just on the borderline of the age at which it was acceptable still to act like a *puer* (adolescent youth) and be penetrated, and the age for becoming a *vir* (adult male). Much Roman humour revolved around playing with this borderline. In effect, Romans had an indistinct, 'reverse' age of consent – any underage youth was free to allow another (older, socially equal or superior) male to penetrate him. Over this unspecified age, the male was expected only to penetrate (other males or women – penetration, not gender, was the only real issue). Caesar engaged in his adolescent behaviour with the Hellenised Nicomedes at a time when Greek ideas had only begun to have an impact on Romans. Thus, the jibes against him may have been an attempt to paint Caesar as 'un-Roman'.

Youthful *impudicitia* (a word normally used of men to imply their taking the passive role) and grown-up adultery were likewise opposed in a similar section in the biography of Augustus (63BCE–14CE). Suetonius also provided extensive evidence for claims that Augustus (as Octavian) had been a *puer* to Julius Caesar's *vir*. Tiberius (42 BCE–37 CE), who followed Augustus, was even more bizarre in his tastes. Scandalous reports of his sexual proclivities are too numerous to mention but range from (basically unremarkable) adultery to having his penis suckled by young babies. Caligula (12–41 CE), if anything, outdid Tiberius. The more salacious reports of his reign have him forcing the wives of senators to serve in an imperial brothel, to deflowering both the bride and groom on their wedding day. As for Claudius (10 BCE–54CE), Suetonius noted that he was 'of the most excessively abundant lust toward women, but altogether uninterested in males'. Gibbon's passing comment that Claudius was the only early emperor who did not cheat on his wife by taking another woman or a male youth to his bed heightens the peculiarity of the emperor in Roman history. He was not only strangely chaste but also he was bizarrely limited in his tastes!

Suetonius then noted the swing of the pendulum with the arrival of Nero (37-68 CE; the last Julio-Claudian emperor) on the throne. Not only did he have sex with males (and women) but he also took both the passive and active role, which Suetonius advanced as evidence of his total moral depravity. He also married two men (in succession) in ceremonies identical to that used by men marrying women. One of the men was accorded the honours of an empress and Suetonius repeated a joke that said had Nero's father had 'that sort of a wife' (i.e. a male) the world would be a happier place (for the want of Nero). Galba (3 BCE-69 CE), who followed, preferred 'hardbodied and overripe' males or rather, males who were beyond boyhood and should not have been attractive to him. Of Domitian (51-96 CE), Suetonius wrote that there were stories that he had been 'corrupted' by his successor Nerva (*c.*32-98 CE) and that an ex-praetor (Claudius Pollio) always waved about a letter from the young Domitian, offering him a night of passion.

The early emperors, thus, allowed Suetonius to discuss much of the sexual continuum of Roman behaviour. He disapproved of some and seemingly had little comment on other elements. What is most interesting is how different Suetonius's compartments of 'depravity' and 'acceptability' are from those of the modern Western reader. The

Caesars were not boring but neither were they identical in their tastes. Each emperor had a set of preferences, of which Suetonius approved or disapproved in words he expected his readers to understand. To use modern parlance, Suetonius describes Claudius as 'heterosexual' and a 'good family man'. Julius Caesar and Augustus were 'heterosexual and promiscuous', but had 'experimented' with a 'homosexual phase' during adolescence. Galba was basically 'gay', being interested almost wholly in sex with other men (not youths). Nero was simply depraved having sex with anyone (and anything?) and submitting his body to the degradation of penetration by other men – even socially inferior men. Suetonius seems to have thought Claudius slightly peculiar for his chastity. Nero and Tiberius were depraved because of their unbelievable promiscuity for sexual experiences of any variety. Galba was as strangely limited in his tastes as Claudius but Suetonius thought Galba's preferences repugnant while Claudius was simply peculiar. Domitian, Nerva, Julius Caesar and Augustus were more or less normal for having been penetrated by men in adolescence but thereafter confining themselves to sex which was purely active and penetrative (though the passive, penetrated partner might be male or female).

This serves to highlight the point made elsewhere that Romans saw sex as being fundamentally about penetration. Pleasure and procreation were both equally acceptable reasons for sexual activities but, at its core, a 'man' penetrated someone or something. The man might penetrate to produce offspring, for simple sexual release, for reasons of state, or even for love – but the *man* penetrated. As long as that 'natural order' was maintained pagan Romans seem to have seen little to notice or criticise. However, breaking this correct order of nature and being penetrated – when an adult male – invited opprobrium and condemnation nearly as violent as modern homophobia. It is important, therefore, to consider the Roman cultural construction of 'natural' to get some idea of what was and was not socially acceptable.

The historian Amy Richlin, in an important article on Roman passive homosexuality, makes some crucial points, which serve to underline the different nature of the cultural niches devised by Roman society for sexuality. Romans, like the Greeks, did not separate sexual acts into 'same-sex (bad) *versus* different-sex (good)'. Adult (male)

Romans desired, loved and had sex with both women and *pueri* (boys). Indeed, Roman poetry frequently extolled the virtues of sex with adolescents males over that of sex with women (or adolescent females). However, Romans were explicit in making their own crucial distinctions: 'man+boy (good, at least for the man) and man+man (bad)'. The former was socially acceptable and is most correctly called pederasty – and has much in common with the situation in Greece. The latter, however, is a type of homosexuality as it describes (and dislikes) that adult male who *chooses* or *prefers* to be penetrated by another male. The Romans clearly understood that this was a matter of taste and preference but one which they disliked.

Richlin highlights the fact that discussions about Roman (and Greek) same-sex relations and relationships have become closely connected to modern political arguments. Two approaches predominate. In the first, any notion of Roman 'homosexuality' is rejected as an anachronistic reading placed on Roman realities. The other is to suggest that Rome was tolerant and accepting of homosexuality. The historian, John Boswell takes the latter view but Richlin rightly points out that much of his evidence actually relates to pederasty and *not* to sex between two adult males. On the other hand she also criticises those who focus on pederasty as behaviour, which is *not* homosexual (effectively the opposite of Boswell's approach) while ignoring the Roman reaction to adult same-sex acts:

The motive underlying Halperin's writing, and in part underlying Winkler's, is an activist one: to break out of the constraints imposed on sexuality by our own culture by arguing that they are not inevitable, but historical, and socially constructed. The result, though, seems to be that the material existence of the kinaidos [the passive adult] *fades from view; at the same time, insistence on a complete rejection of 'homosexual' nomenclature entails emphasising the issue of penetration while denying the issue of same-sex partners. Thus we lose sight of the fact that some forms of male desire for males in Greece and Rome were the object of extreme scorn, whatever they were called, and that any male who felt such desire would be in a lot of trouble.*

The effect of both approaches is to ignore the numerous examples of Roman adult male same-sex activities *and* the Roman reaction to it.

The point Richlin is making is that Roman society was different from our own in some important ways. First, Romans accepted sex between an adult male and an adolescent male youth, which most Western societies have criminalised as paedophilia. Romans had the concept of paedophilia (sex with a child) but had the additional category of sex with an adolescent – pederasty. However, the Romans expected that this behaviour was simply a phase and that no adult male would continue to want to be penetrated. They did think that adult males would continue to find adolescent youths attractive and have sex with them.

Just as importantly, Romans thought it perfectly reasonable to have sex with slaves and prostitutes regardless of their age or gender. One of the purposes of having slaves was to be able to have sexual release whenever it was desired. Prostitution was legal, and any free Roman male could penetrate his male or female slave or freed concubine, while slaves and freedmen were themselves so disdained that their sexual passivity would be condoned, encouraged, or even assumed (likewise, their assumed sexual penetrability contributed to the disdain in which they were held).

Clearly this is not our world. Having said that, there are similarities, which make the point that Romans did identify, and dislike, a certain type of same-sex behaviour which they considered inappropriate – the submission to penetration by an adult male Roman citizen.

While there was no word for homosexual in ancient Greek or Roman there were plenty of names for men who allowed themselves to be penetrated. Many of these resonate with modern derogatory terms for homosexuals. The most common was *cinaedus* (from the Greek *kinaidos*) or '*catamite*' – that is, 'a male who is penetrated by another male'. The range of other terms gives key insights into the Roman view of a *cinaedus*. Romans called a sexually penetrated male: *pathicus* (passive, 'bottom'), *exoletus* (mature, 'top'), *concubinus* (unmarried sexual partner, 'lover'), *sp(h)intria* (anal sphincter, male prostitute, 'hole-for-hire'), *puer* (boy, 'twink'), *pullus* (chick, 'chicken'), *pusio* (lad, 'twink'), *delicatus* (dissolute, 'spoiled'), *mollis* (soft), *tener* (dainty, 'camp'), *debilis* (weak, 'limp-wristed'), *effeminatus* (effeminate, 'queen'), *discinctus* (loose-belted, 'slut'), *morbosus* (sick, 'diseased'). Intrinsic to this negative view of the passive male is the Roman self-perception of the relationship between Rome and the empire:

Rome used to be, and should have kept on being, active in relation to the passive empire. The Roman projection of Rome as a male fucking the rest of the world is too large and depressing a topic to go into here. This is not something Juvenal has made up; he is drawing on a tradition that goes back at least to the time of Lucilius (second century BCE) and, I would argue, is probably intrinsic to Roman cultural identity.

Richlin's words remind us that there was more to the Roman reaction to the passive male than just individual (dis)taste. A passive Roman male was, in part, betraying the place and function of every Roman.

The verb *patior*, which has a range of meanings (suffer, undergo, experience), is used for being penetrated as in *vim pati* ('suffer force' or 'be raped'). Seneca said that women are 'born to be penetrated'. This explains the use of the phrase *muliebria pati*, 'to suffer womanish things' for male passives. The noun *stuprum* is often used; it can mean 'rape' but it also seems to mean any sexual act that is socially disliked – consent not being an issue. The word *impudicitia* (unchastity) is commonly used to refer to a male's willingness to have another male penetrate him. It has been shown that Roman medical thinkers considered the desire to be penetrated a pathology that could be diagnosed (a medicalisation of 'homosexuality' predating its supposed invention in the nineteenth century).

It is immediately apparent how difficult it is to find a modern equivalent for *cinaedus*. 'Gay' implies a range of sexual positions and relationships. 'Passive' and 'penetrated' are descriptive of the act but little else – and the former implies an inactivity that makes little sense in discussions about sexual relations. Moreover, the context of the idea of the *cinaedus* for Romans makes the concept very difficult to translate. From the Roman perspective, 'abnormal' sexuality was a man who continued to do into adulthood what he had done as a youth – allowed himself to be penetrated by another male. An adolescent male was assumed to be willing to be passive in anal intercourse and, perhaps less so, to fellate another man; an adult simply did not do such things. Or, more accurately, an adult *man* did not allow to be done to his person what was the role proper to adolescents (some not yet fully male), slaves, prostitutes, concubines, wives and women more generally. No matter how one understood it, being a *cinaedus* meant being less than a man.

The social disdain for the failure to make the full transition from adolescent (penetrated) to adult male (penetrator) was a frequent trope in literature occasioning much humour. It was also an effective weapon of invective and insult. For example, Martial wrote an admonitory (and humorous) epigram to an adolescent on preparation for marriage:

> *Use women's embraces, use them, Victor,*
> *and let your prick learn a job unknown to it.*
> *The wedding-veil is being woven for your fiancée,*
> *already the maiden is being readied*
> *soon the new bride will cut the hair of your boys.*
> *She will let her eager husband bugger her once,*
> *as long as she fears the first wounds of this strange weapon;*
> *but her nursemaid and her mother will forbid this to happen more often*
> *and will say, 'This girl is your wife, not your boy'.*
> *Alas, what perplexities, what labours you'll suffer,*
> *if a cunt is a thing foreign to you!*

The playing with gender and sexual roles is obvious. A *puer* (boy) is someone whose anus is penetrated while an *uxor* (wife) 'suffers' vaginal penetration. Because of the fear of the loss of virginity, though, a wife might submit to anal intercourse. The assumption is that this will also please the groom (clearly a virgin when it comes to vaginal sex with women) who already has a preference for anal intercourse as a result of his previous (and on-going) relations with youths. Older women will be needed to sort this confusion out and a prostitute is recommended as the ideal teacher to help make the groom fully into a man (*vir* – that is, someone who penetrates vaginas).

Roman ribaldry about the age of (quite literally) 'turning around' from being penetrated to penetrator was also key to insults. Tacitus, in his *Annales*, recorded the trial of Valerius Asiaticus (the association in the name of the individual with the 'soft-living' ways of the East is interesting) who was accused of being 'soft of body' (passive in sex).

Prosecution was a private, individual matter in Roman courts so Valerius attacked his accuser personally saying, 'Ask your sons, Suilius; they'll tell you I'm a man'. Valerius was saying that he was not only *not* passive but that he had made Suilius's sons (who were presumably no longer adolescents) *into* passives – the act of a true Roman, a conqueror.

On a more general level, specific stereotypes were associated with a *cinaedus*: lisping speech, hand-on-hip, scratching the head with one finger, using makeup, hair-plucking and wearing certain colours (e.g. light green and sky blue). The stereotypical figure is common enough in literature to suggest that the basic model of the *cinaedus* was relatively well known. In other words, there was almost certainly something approaching a sub-culture. However, it is just as clear that familiarity did indeed breed contempt. Sources from every period of the empire and from every social class that has left records associate the *cinaedus* with disdain and dislike – the term itself and its synonyms were universally seen as an insult.

Of course, it is important to remember that the accusation of being a *cinaedus* was not just a social slur – as the case against Valerius Asiaticus makes clear. It had actual social and legal repercussions. The impact of the Roman dislike of adult citizens submitting to penetration is something that must be examined in some detail. This social opprobrium highlights the fact that Roman society (though seemingly 'open-minded' sexually from the perspective of the modern, Christianised West) was 'homophobic' within its own cultural constraints and constructions. Having said that, it will become clear that any social consequences of passivity were not universal, and very much situational and individual. Thus, a cross-dresser was still able to make a will (an act of a *vir*). Governmental officials were able to have a reputation for passivity with little negative results. Military men might be tolerated although passive or they might, just as often, be given the equivalent of honourable discharges. On the other hand, one should avoid being indebted to a *cinaedus*. The overall picture is a society in which it was possible to be *cinaedus*, to socialise with the non-*cinaedus*, and to have an active (even public) sex life. However, the *cinaedus* always faced cultural disapproval and risked social exclusion.

One area where we can see this most obviously is in the class of *equites* (knights) in the republic and empire. On a regular basis, every male knight was required publicly to present himself with his horse before the censors. The censors, sitting in the forum at the very heart of the city and empire, then examined the knight for physical and moral defects. The scale of this 'census' is phenomenal. Augustus was said to have examined 5,000 knights when he sat in review. A man could be demoted from the class by the censors for physical and moral defects – and being morally 'soft' (*mollis*) was just such a defect. The public humiliation of being labelled *infamis* (notorious, disreputable, infamous) and a *cinaedus* was tremendous.

From imperial sources we get some idea of the other effects of *infamia*. Men could be excluded from holding office by the magistrates responsible for assessing eligibility. They might be removed from the *album iudicum* (the list of eligible jurors) or barred from the army. Anyone ruled to be *infamis* could expect a harsher punishment in a trial. They might also be prevented even from bringing certain types of cases to court or from giving testimony – purely at the judge's discretion. An *infamis* person might be refused permission to witness a will or to make a will (becoming *intestabilis* as well as *infamis*). However, none of these possibilities was fixed in law. They were only possible and depended on a given circumstance and the prejudice of the official (judge, magistrate) involved. No effort was ever made to identify or arrest *infames* or to prevent their sexual practices. When *infamia* went into the official public arena, though, it was perfectly possible that a very public humiliation would result.

Three specific types of *infamia* would almost certainly lead to the loss of status: anyone becoming a 'professional' prostitute (with a pimp); anyone taking any money for sexual favours; anyone labelled a *cinaedus* (or 'passive'). The first two were not seen as having any intrinsic 'fame' which would be impaired – the latter could and the imputation of *infamia* to a *cinaedus* was always a possibility but never a certainty. Moreover, once publicly labelled as *infamis* the individual joined the other two categories in being open to rape with impunity. In Roman thought, anyone who was 'notorious' for wanting to be penetrated was hardly in a position to complain when they *were* penetrated. As the jurist Paulus (fl. 200 CE) explained:

A man who rapes a free male against his will is punished by death. A man who of his own free will suffers stuprum [rape]... *is fined of the half part of his goods; neither is he permitted to make testamentary disposition of the remaining part.*

Male rape is punished (but not the passive 'victim'), consensual passivity is also punished (but not the active 'partner').

At the same time that Christianity began to have an impact on Roman society (in the 100s and 200s CE), Roman society was undergoing significant changes which altered views on sexuality. Emperors and much of the ruling elite were increasingly non-Roman and non-urban (at least not from large metropolitan centres). The growth of pagan philosophical systems (especially Stoicism), which placed an emphasis on 'family life' and 'moderation' (in sexual matters and more generally) created a society less willing to tolerate a sexual free-for-all. Moreover, the pagan imperial state's reaction to Christianity and other Eastern religions meant that the government was becoming much more involved in the beliefs and practices of its subjects and citizens at a time of a general expansion in the power and absolutism of the emperor. Finally, the emperors were increasingly former generals drawn from a military system, which had never adopted the Greek view that homosexuality was a benefit on the battlefield. This combination of 'provincialisation', Stoicism and absolutism began to effect the regulations of the empire in matters sexual.

Emperor Marcus Aurelius (born in Rome of Spanish ancestry; 121–180 CE) noted in his *Meditations* that he has learned 'from an early age... to suppress all passion for young men'. His personal views are most obvious in his refusal to list the deceased Antinous among the 'friends' of his predecessor Hadrian. No greater and more obvious a break with past Graeco-Roman traditions in so short a space of time can be imagined. Severus Alexander (born in Phoenicia; 208–235 CE) gave consideration to outlawing male prostitution but decided such a change would only drive the practice underground – and deprive the state of lucrative tax revenues. Philip the Arab (c.204–249) was supportive of Christianity (once doing penance to attend an Easter service) though almost certainly still a pagan. However, he did attempt to outlaw male prostitution in the Western empire which suggests a further Judaeo-Christianisation of imperial mores.

Some more general legal changes also occurred in the 200s and 300s CE. We have already met the jurist Paulus who believed that a *cinaedus* should lose half his estate. This view, among others, got him exiled by Emperor Elagabalus (203/4–222 CE) but, interestingly, recalled by Severus Alexander who wanted to outlaw male prostitution. As Hadrian was followed by the more austere Aurelius so Severus Alexander had his more licentious Elagabalus:

[Elagabalus] *had the whole of his body depilated, deeming it the chief enjoyment of life to appear fit and worthy to arouse the lusts of the greatest number* [of men]... *And even at Rome he did nothing but send out agents to search for those who have particularly large penises and bring them to the palace in order that he might enjoy their vigour.*

Change may have been taking place but the 'pagan pendulum' was never likely to swing entirely against a social and cultural attitude to same-sex acts that had endured in the Mediterranean world of the Greeks and Romans for 1,000 years.

However, once the emperors adopted Christianity, the situation changed dramatically. In 342 CE, the sons (Constans I, Western emperor, reigned 337–350 CE; Constantius II, Eastern emperor, reigned 337–361 CE) of St Constantine the Great, Rome's first Christian emperor (272/3–337 CE) abolished any *de facto* recognition of gay marriages. They also set in train the series of changes which would result in the Christianisation of imperial law and the abolition of paganism.

Those modern opponents who argue that gay marriage is a modern innovation should do well to consult Roman history along with the situation in any number of other cultures and societies – past and present – discussed in this volume. The reality is that same-sex marriages have a long historical tradition and have, at times, been widely and openly accepted on a par with monogamous and polygamous heterosexual marriages. More importantly, the imperial view on same-sex relations, although no longer benign, remained ambiguous even under Christian emperors. Indeed, it is a cautionary note on the impact of the forced conversion of the empire and social attitudes more generally that Rome's Christian emperors continued to collect the tax on legal male prostitution well into the 500s CE – two centuries after the empire's official 'conversion'.

By 390 and the reign of Theodosius the Great (379–395 CE) one saw the first recorded corporal punishment for homosexuality. Those condemned were involved in male prostitution, especially as pimps and procurers. Theodosius also introduced the death penalty (seemingly not enforced) for being a *cinaedus*. Despite this, officially sanctioned and legally enforced, Christianity was fighting an uphill battle. Literature and philosophy, on balance, continued to take the view that heterosexuality was necessary for the continuance of the species but that homosexuality (especially with an adolescent youth) was refined and civilised.

The *Affairs of the Heart* is an excellent example of the debate. Almost certainly written in the late 100s CE (and widely read for centuries thereafter), it makes a series of statements culminating in a conclusion, which attempts to be balanced but which still favours same-sex love:

Marriages were devised as a means of ensuring succession, which was necessary, but only the love of men is a noble undertaking of the philosopher's soul… For intercourse with women was necessary so that our race might not utterly perish for lack of seed… Do not then, Charicles, again censure this discovery [of male love] because it wasn't made earlier, nor, because intercourse with women can be credited with greater antiquity than the love of youths… Marriage is a boon and a blessing to men when it meets with good fortune, while the love of youths, that pays court to the hallowed dues of friendship, I consider to be the privilege only of philosophy. Therefore all men should marry, but let only the wise be permitted to love youths, for perfect virtue grows least of all among women.

If nothing else, this passage makes the point that exponents of male love strongly believed it to be a central feature of a 'civilised' society. An anonymous Greek poet made the same point:

All irrational animals merely screw females, but we rational ones
Are superior in this regard to all other animals:
We discovered screwing men. Men under the sway of women
Are no better than dumb animals.

Simpler, rustic, less advanced societies *had* to focus on procreation; a truly refined culture placed emphasis on *higher* things. Simper, sex-for-procreation-only cultures were more like flocks of animals than humans.

It is hard to imagine a more profound, or more explicitly articulated, challenge to the Judaeo-Christian spiritualising than the other-worldly ideas expressed by St Paul:

Finally, brothers, whatever is true, whatever is noble, whatever is right, whatever is pure, whatever is lovely, whatever is admirable – if anything is excellent or praiseworthy – think about such things (Philemon 4: 8).

Philosophers extolling male love might well have said the same but what they meant was the male form in all its beauty. St Paul meant something decidedly different – and wholly non-physical.

However, it is important to remember that words by ministers, theologians and even apostles are just that: words. Their impact on the actual behaviour of a culture long given to an acceptance of male love (especially pederasty) was certainly not immediate. Great preachers such as St John Chrysostom (*c.*347–407 CE) railed against the indifference of even Christians to the prevailing sexual mores of the empire:

Those very people who have been nourished by godly doctrine… these do not consort with prostitutes as [readily] *as they do with young men… None is ashamed, no one blushes, but, rather, they take pride in their little game; the chaste seem to be the odd ones, and the disapproving the ones in error… There is some danger that womankind will become unnecessary in the future, with young men instead fulfilling all the needs women used to* [fulfil].

This may simply be rhetorical exaggeration but there must be some truth underlying the complaint. Even St Augustine of Hippo (354–430 CE) confronted the complexity of the issue of male love in his own life because of his love for a friend:

For I felt that my soul and his were one soul in two bodies, and therefore life was a horror to me, since I did not want to live as a half; and yet I was also afraid to die lest he, whom I had loved so much, would die completely… Thus I contaminated the spring of friendship with the dirt of lust and darkened its brightness with the blackness of desire.

If nothing else, Augustine reveals himself to be a creature of a polysexual Graeco-Roman culture and reminds us of its enduring impact even amongst Christians.

The most important aspect of Christianity's interaction with pagan culture relates not to this period but the next. However, it is in this period when paganism and Christianity co-existed that those ideas about sex, the body and nature were formed, which then informed and shaped Christian thought from the Middle Ages to the present day. It is absolutely essential to realise that Christianity developed its ideas about sex within the context of the pagan Graeco-Roman world from the starting point of a Judaic tradition that considered procreation as the *paramount* reason for sex.

Boswell has carefully and brilliantly categorised early Christian thought into four basic ideas. He stressed that these arose largely from the ascetic and monastic wing of Christianity not the regular, parish clergy. These ideas, though, provided the intellectual and theological basis for the increasingly violent condemnation of homosexuality and homosexuals. He has noted that these early views did not explicitly relate only to homosexual behaviour but, rather, to all forms of nonprocreative sex. That is, as we have stressed elsewhere, Christian thought agreed with the Judaic view that any sexual contact (oral, anal, with contraceptive) which was not aimed primarily at procreation was 'unnatural', 'immoral', 'unbiblical' and 'sodomitical'. Boswell's four categories are: animalistic behaviour; unsavoury cultural associations; 'natural' and 'unnatural'; and gender norms.

Early Christian texts (especially the apocryphal *Epistle of Barnabas*) and teachers presented a view of animals theoretically (though, in fact, erroneously) based on the Mosaic law of Leviticus. Thus, Christians were told why Moses had condemned the eating of the hare, the hyena (not even mentioned in Leviticus), and the weasel. The hare engaged in anal sex and eating it would lead to child molestation. The hyena was believed to change its biological sex annually and this would lead to gender confusion, promiscuity and adultery. The weasel practiced oral sex since it gave birth through its mouth; contact with the weasel would lead to a preference for non-procreative fellatio (in women or men).

Clement of Alexandria (*c.*150–*c.*215 CE), whose *Paedagogus* was very anti-homosexual, used the *Epistle of Barnabas* to argue that 'fruitless sowings' (i.e. any non-procreative sex) was rejected and deemed unclean since it was like the behaviour of these unclean animals. He did reject the interpretation that hyenas were hermaphroditic but said that male hyenas regularly had sex with each other and, thus, what was being prohibited was male same-sex activities. The views of this decidedly Christian *Epistle* were buttressed by the *Physiologus*, which was a collection of anecdotes about animals that appeared about the same time and was to become one of the most popular books of the Middle Ages. In addition to Latin and Greek editions there were vernacular editions in every language from Arabic to Icelandic. In other words, the idea that same-sex and/or non-procreative activities were connected with strange and unclean animals had a very wide circulation indeed. This allowed men like the bishop of Pavia, Ennodius (473/4–521 CE), to mock a homosexual saying 'you are a hare' and St Bernard of Clairvaux (fl. 1100s) to say anyone engaging in same-sex acts was 'dishonouring his maleness… just like a hyena'.

In the longer tradition of opposition of homosexuality, this view is interesting. In effect, homosexuals (and anyone else engaging in non-procreative sex!) are being accused of being 'like beasts'. As we will see, in many ways, this is diametrically opposed to the idea that homosexuality is 'unnatural' in the sense of behaviour 'not found in nature'. There is an argument often advanced by anti-gay individuals that homosexuality is an aspect of deviant (or 'fallen') human conduct, which is perverse. So perverse in fact that it is not found elsewhere in nature. However, the idea that homosexuality is also 'animal-like' suggests exactly the opposite. Indeed, it is probably better to see this argument as saying that homosexuality is not 'civilised' or the correct behaviour for a human being. The Church long used a similar argument for explaining why a man should not mount his wife from the rear – clearly, by any stretch of the imagination, the most 'natural' sexual position. The

Church said the man-on-top, face-to-face was the only acceptable position *because* it was *not* like animals (i.e. the rest of nature).

Boswell's second category deals with the specific reaction of Christians to the pagan society in which they lived. They argued that same-sex relations should be avoided because they associated it with the 'sinful' pagan society around them. The first association was between same-sex acts and child abuse. Christians tended to see sex with adolescent youths as paedophilia not pederasty. Moreover, they observed that most (unwanted) infants who were abandoned by the roadside were sold into slavery and usually used as sex slaves until old enough to labour. Justin Martyr (*c.*100–*c.*165) noted that 'we have observed that nearly all [abandoned] children, boys as well as girls, will be used as prostitutes'. Although it was clear that young females were used as sex slaves, the Church never explicitly associated that with heterosexuality. The abuse of adolescent male youths was seen as simply part of a wider problem of same-sex acts. The same approach can be seen in modern society where the male abuser of a young (pre-sixteen) male is often called a 'gay' or 'homosexual' child abuser while another man abusing a young girl is called a child abuser but *never* a 'heterosexual' or 'straight' child abuser.

Christians also associated homosexuality – and many other forms of sexual licentiousness – with pagan religion. As Justin Martyr put is succinctly, 'we have dedicated ourselves to God, who was not born and does not suffer, and who we believe did not have sex with Antiope or other women… or Ganymede'. Homosexuality was seen as but the most obvious expression of the polysexuality and sexual licence of the pagan world. Christians expounded a different sexuality because they wished to be distinct from their pagan neighbours. Promiscuity, prostitution, adultery, homosexuality, sex with youths – all were part of the pagan sexual world rejected by the Church.

The third area identified by Boswell as developing in the early Church and crucially underpinning later Christian thought was the concept of 'nature' and '(un)natural'. Christians took from pagan philosophy, especially Stoicism, an idea of what nature was. Put simply, Stoics argued that it was 'obvious' that eating was to be moderate (for the needs of sustenance) and *therefore* excessive eating or eating overly rich food was unnecessary and, hence, unnatural. It is, of course, equally obvious that they could have said that eating had two purposes: sustenance and enjoyment. They did not and that has 'made all the difference' (to quote the American poet, Robert Frost).

Likewise, the 'obvious' purpose of sex was to procreate and any other use was, consequently, unnatural. As Clement of Alexandria said, 'to have sex for any purpose other than to produce children is to violate nature'. Augustine argued that 'in order to be sinless an act must not violate nature, custom, or law'. However, there were problems for Christian thinkers, especially monks, in this view. Celibacy – or the refusal to procreate – was also unnatural but it was just as clear that it was the 'ideal' according to the New Testament. It was as unnatural to masturbate as it was to remain married to and have sex with an infertile spouse – though this ran foul of Jesus's prohibition against divorce except for adultery (the Church managed to circumvent this by the introduction of the concept of annulment – in effect, declaring that the inability to consummate or procreate meant no 'real' marriage had taken place). The Jewish philosopher, Philo of Alexandria (*fl.* first century) made these very points. Both Judaism and Christianity, though, managed to ignore those aspects of nature highlighted by the Roman poet, Ovid (43 BCE–17 CE):

[nature] *does not consider it shameful for a heifer to be mounted by her father; his own daughter may become a stallion's mate, the goat goes into the flocks he has fathered.*

'Nature' was, and is, a very slippery theological peg on which to hang sexual mores.

Christianity modified this by placing the emphasis on what was 'normal' for 'natural'. Thus the issue was what was characteristic, native, or normal rather than any idea of an idealised or superior nature. This led Augustine to describe homosexuality as 'contrary to human custom'. To him, it was uncommon or abnormal in the sense of not frequent. Men having sex with men was simply odd for Augustine: 'every part which does not fit into its environment is wrong'. Christianity was never happy with a view of human morals, which advocated being *more* like nature (the animals).

The final way in which the early Church attempted to attack pagan sexual mores in general and same-sex acts in particular related to ideas advanced largely by Chrysostom about gender norms. His many homiletical fulminations against same-sex acts are often quite confused and contradictory though the general thrust is the same. He was appalled at passivity in a male:

If those who suffer it really perceived what was being done to them, they would rather die a thousand deaths than undergo this… for I maintain that not only are you made into a woman, but you also cease to be a man; yet neither are you changed into that nature, nor do you retain the one you had.

His basic complaint was that homosexuality produced a third type of gender, which was not one of the two created by God (male and female). Augustine could not imagine why any man would want to take the role of a woman: 'the body of a man is as superior to that of a woman as the soul is to the body'. Sex was also disliked – even procreation! A child was often said to be revolting as it was born amidst urine and faeces. Augustine, Jerome (*c*.342–420 CE), Tertullian (*c*.160–*c*.220 CE), Methodius (826–885 CE), Ambrose (*c*.339–397) and Arnobius (d.330) all thought sex was unclean, shameful, a defilement, filthy and/or degrading. Obviously, these and similar passages say as much about the early Church's views about women and sex as homosexuals – the misogyny is apparent as is the celibate's distaste for any type of sex.

Despite these various reactions to homosexuality, the Church largely accepted that it existed in a world in which same-sex acts took place and some men (and women) seemed to choose same-sex relationships to the exclusion of all others. This homosexuality was simply one feature of pagan Graeco-Roman sexuality that the Church observed and rejected. Most theologians and preachers in the large metropolitan centres (Rome, Alexandria, Constantinople) seemed also to have accepted that male-male attraction was 'natural' in the sense of 'normal' but acting on it should be resisted. Still, the one key idea coming from Judaism through the early Church and out of Christianity's triumph over the pagan Roman Empire was the idea that the *purpose* of sex was procreation *not* pleasure. While this precluded many types of heterosexual couplings it specifically ruled out *every* type of homosexual encounter.

Clearly the rise and triumph of Christianity in the Mediterranean, as well as the collapse of the Western Roman Empire, had an impact on Africa. North African provinces came under the rule of 'barbarians', trade links were severed and a new ideology was propagated. The increasing familiarity with monotheism and Judaeo-Christian ideas about sex (primarily for procreation) would have been more widely known. Sadly, one cannot find any evidence that this had a profound impact, during this period, on Africa − more generally. Clearly, the conversion of Abyssinia/Ethiopia to Christianity was important. However, the most important change − and the first to see a significant 'non-African' influence on Africa was to come at the end of the period we are currently considering. The rise and spread of Islam, especially along the east African littoral, is of great importance especially as many Africans take the view that sodomy was 'introduced by the Arabs'. As we will see in the next chapter, we have little historical information on this period but the view is important and will be more fully discussed in later chapters.

Although our study continues to be hampered by the lack of surviving documents for areas south of the Graeco-Roman world, we can always look to the East for the sort of detailed knowledge which we have for the Mediterranean world. Some of the most important documents are the *Shastras* and *Sutras*, which are manuals and treatises compiled largely in the period 100 BCE-400 CE. They explain how humans can attain the four goals of existence: *dharma* (fulfilling the law of one's being), *artha* (material success), *kama* (pleasure and desire; hence, *Kama Sutra* or *Treatise/Manual on Pleasure/Desire*), and *moksha* (liberation from reincarnation). The most important are: *Manavadharmashastra* (or *Manusmriti*, *c.*100 CE; a compendium of law codes); Kautilya's *Arthashastra* (on economics and statecraft − similar to Machiavelli's *The Prince*); Vatsyayana's *Kama Sutra*; and two medical texts (*Charaka Samhita* and *Sushruta Samhita*).

These texts all present an understanding of human psycho-sexual development (to use anachronistic phraseology) which demonstrates that the idea of a third sex 'has been a part of the Indian world view for nearly three thousand years'. This idea was so ancient that it had been incorporated into Sanskrit grammar by the sixth century BCE. Thus, medieval Jain thinkers argued that there were three types of *veda* (desire): male, female and third sex. The last was the most intense and any person, regardless of their biology, could experience any or all of the forms of desire. The Jain philosopher Sakatayan in the *Strinirvanaprakarana* (*c*.850 CE) said that a person could be sexually aroused by a member of the same sex, the opposite sex, or even a non-human animal.

Indeed, Jain thinking, especially in the area of medicine and gender (both in humans and grammar) is crucial for building an understanding of ideas about sex and sexuality in India. The Jains shared the pan-Indian acceptance of the idea of a third sex/nature, *napumsakam*. Working from this shared premise, they tried to understand what exactly such a person was like – what was his/her nature, *svrabhava*? This required that they engage with some of the ideas that underlie modern debates on sexuality.

First, it was important to decide if there was in fact a physiological difference. Thus, some medical texts said that a 'man' had 700 veins and 500 muscles; a 'woman' 670 and 470 respectively; and a *napum-sakam* 680 and 480 – hence, 'closer' to being female than male though still neither. Such an approach presages modern debates about the role of genes in sexuality. At times there was an attempt to differentiate between what would today be called 'gender' – by focusing on secondary sex traits (such as beards) – and 'sex' – stressing the ability to 'father' a child. Indian thought also engaged with essentialist ideas that some individuals were simply 'inclined' to same sex acts. In this they echoed debates in Aristotle (*Nicomachean Ethics*) and pseudo-Aristotle (*Problemata Physica*), as well as ideas about 'mental illness' as an explanation – as found in Caelius Aurelianus (the last great Latin medical authority, fl.400s CE, second only to Galen and author of *On Acute and Chronic Diseases*). Classical civilisations, despite the lack of 'scientific technology', were more than able to hypothesise about behaviour that to them was fundamental to human existence. They looked about their world and saw people who were primarily interested in the same-sex and having sexual relations with them. Eastern and Western philosophers and medical thinkers attempted to explain this.

Indian medicine, in particular, applied considerable thought to the issue of sexuality and formed the basis upon which Jain philosophy built its unique contribution to the discussion. Two major extant Sanskrit medical compendia survive from the first two centuries: the *Caraka* and the *Susruta*. Both discuss gender and sexual 'abnormalities'.

The *Caraka* lists eight:
    The true hermaphrodite, having both male and female genitalia
    The man with a 'windy organ' (no semen)
    Men who use aphrodisiacs
    The effeminate homosexual male
    The masculine lesbian female
    The man with a bent penis (erectile dysfunction)
    The voyeur
    The man born without testicles

The *Susruta* lists six:
    The fellator
    The man aroused exclusively by genital odours
    The anal-receptive male (passive male)
    The voyeur
    The effeminate homosexual male
    The masculine lesbian male

Buddhist thought, arising from these works, listed five types of men 'having no balls':
    The man born impotent
    The voyeur
    The man temporarily impotent (during the waning half of the
       lunar month)
    The fellator
    The man who reaches orgasm through special effort or artifice

What is certainly clear is that Indian thought did not shy away from discussing variant sexual attraction. It also saw such variations as in some way dysfunctional.

Jain thought, faced with these 'medico-scientific' ideas, developed a novel approach that, in time, largely rejected the dysfunctional interpretation of non-standard sexuality. Rather than trying to find a purely physical understanding for differences in sex, sexuality and gender, Jain thinkers hypothesised two factors that interacted: *veda* and *bhava* ('psychological' state). 'Male' sexuality was defined not in terms of genitalia but by object – male sexuality (*purumaveda*) desired a woman; 'female' sexuality (*striveda*) desired a man; 'third nature' (*napumsakaveda*) sexuality desired 'neither man nor woman'. These *veda*s had a hierarchy of intensity. Female desire was like a 'dung fire' (not too hot), male sexuality like a 'forest fire' and third nature sexuality like a 'burning city'. Thus, a third nature person is 'hyperlibidinous', which finds its echo in medieval Western ideas that a sodomite had a sex drive so strong that he could not be 'satisfied' with *just* a woman.

In this structure, we might be inclined to view Jain thought as constructing sexuality around straight men and women, and a third, feminised male (the 'camp gay man'?). However, later writings (*Bhagavati*) show that Jains were aware of another category, the man who behaved 'like a man' but still desired sex with men. This fourth category was called *purumanapumsaka*; it was indistinguishable from 'normal, gender-appropriate' men. Such men, unlike those of the 'third nature', were eligible for ordination since they 'looked' normal and the only thing that made them 'abnormal' was the object of their sexual desires (other men) rather than the host of behaviours which characterised and set-off *napumsaka* individuals.

It is tempting to consider these four groups as straight men and women, gay (camp) men and bisexuals – effectively reading the concept of *napumsaka* as midway between male and female. However, Jain discussions make it clear that third nature individuals (regardless of the other external characteristics) were *only* attracted to other men (lesbianism does not enter into the discussion). Where the distinction seemed to exist between *napumsaka* and *purumanapumsaka* was in sexual behaviour. Both desired sex with men; *purumanapumsaka* were normally active and the *napumsaka* passive (receptors in anal or oral intercourse).

Males (as in the Graeco-Roman world) were penetrators, females (or feminine males) were penetrated. In Jain thought, males who engaged in reciprocal penetration were basically masculine while those who were predominately passive were feminine. The important conclusion, though, is that the defining feature of both 'types' of third-nature individuals is involvement in same-sex activities. In effect, Jain thought proposed a third nature that was fundamentally 'homosexual'. As a result, by the fifth century Jains were able to differentiate between *dravyalimga* (biological sex) based on genitalia, etc., and *bhavalimga* (psychological gender/sexuality).

In time, this led to a widespread acceptance of variant sexuality amongst Jain thinkers and the possibility that these individuals could enter monastic orders and attain enlightenment. Ultimately this would allow Sakatayan (850 CE) to discuss the mutability of human sexuality. That some men, for example, in certain situations might have sex with another man or an animal when, previously, they had only had sex with women did not mean that that person had instantaneously changed his *svakaveda* (sexuality). Rather it simply highlighted the variability of human sexuality. He argued that sexuality was no more fixed than was any other emotional state such as anger, pride, or love (as opposed to sexual desire).

In the end, Jains struggled with biological sex, gender roles, sexual behaviour and orientation because they saw all of these interacting around them. Many were troubled with the simplistic views derived from ancient Indian thought, which simply overlay human sexuality on grammar (with its three 'genders'). This resulted in some unique ideas that sound very modern and remind us that 'modernity' is not an exclusive possession of the present day. Jain thinkers concluded that sexuality and sexual-object choice were separate from biological sex *or* gender roles. Biological males and females could be straight, gay or bisexual (to use modern terminology). Bisexuals were those with the highest, strongest sex drive unable or unwilling to be satisfied by any single sex. More fundamentally, Jains saw 'being attracted to the same sex' as an issue wholly detached from biology or social construction – neither nature nor nurture 'explains' (or predicts or causes) homosexuality; it just is.

While philosophy is interesting, one must wonder how third-nature individuals were treated in reality. One play, *Ubhayabhisarika* ('Both go to Meet') by Vararuci, set in a century either side of Christ's birth, has a character called *Sukumarika* (Pretty Girl). 'She' is of the third nature and is described as having wide hips but breasts so small they do not impede a close embrace – and in no danger of becoming pregnant so able to enjoy passion and pleasure without threat. *Sukumarika* is a high-class courtesan: vain, capricious, lustful and a 'drama queen'. The narrator of the play reviles and despises her, which suggests that, despite the seemingly 'tolerant' view of Jain philosophers, the dysfunctional stigma of the medical works was more in tune with the common view of the third nature. Other works suggest that these individuals faced not only social disapproval but also legal threats of punishment.

The *Arthashastra* is one of the earliest works to suggest any sort of punishment for same-sex relations. Sex between women is less severely punished than that between men though a woman 'forcing' another woman faces an even greater fine. In all cases, though, the acts are treated as misdemeanours. The text considers opposite-sex vaginal sex as the norm but makes no distinction between oral or anal sex regardless of the genders involved. More importantly, it considers vaginal rape a serious crime involving mutilation or death – not a simple fine. Indeed, the *Manusmriti* suggests that the traditional dictum that 'sexual union with a man [by a man] is said to cause loss of caste' was in the process of being replaced by a system of fines and ritual penance (mostly bathing to remove 'impurity'), which generally related to sex with anyone or anything other than a vagina. (The male-centric view of the texts is obvious.)

Two contemporary *puranas* suggest a more prosaic reaction to non-vaginal sex. The *Narada Purana* says that anyone (i.e. a man) who has sex other than in a vagina will end up in the hell called *Retobhojana* where he will have to feed on semen. The *Skanda Purana* simply suggests that this sort of behaviour will make its practitioners impotent. Terrifying perhaps, but these are considerably less threatening than the Romano-Christian approach of burning sodomites alive! Indeed, this contrast is all the more striking when we remind ourselves of the level of contact not only between the pagan Graeco-Roman world of the Hellenistic and later Roman Empires but also with the Christianised Roman and early Byzantine Empires. Throughout the whole of the period considered here, emissaries, trade and small-scale emigration

took place between the great centres of Eastern hemispheric civilisation: China, India and Rome. Bactrian and Indian ambassadors visited
the courts of Hadrian (r.117–138 CE – famous for his love for the youth
Antinous) and Antoninus Pius (r.138–161 CE). Moreover, from as early
as the great voyage east of Eudoxus (second century BCE), Hellenistic
merchants were present in India leaving not only trade goods behind
but also sculptors and architects. While these great civilisations may
not have been intimate, they were not at all ignorant of one another.
With the rise of proselytising faiths like Christianity, Islam and
Buddhism this interaction of Europe, India and the East became greater.

But let us return to the situation in India. The medical texts were less
concerned with attacking non-vaginal sexual practices and more interested in explaining (rather like early psychiatrists) the 'cause' of such
behaviour. For example, the *Sushruta Samhita* says that a man who can
only get an erection by sucking the penis of another man and swallow-
ing his semen was born of weak parental seed (in Indian thought both
parents contributed to procreation). A boneless child would result if the
seed of two females managed to unite in the womb of one of them.

More importantly for the discussions which follow, the plethora of
medieval texts that describe same-sex acts is crucial. They clearly demonstrate that same-sex acts were *not* imported into the subcontinent by
Mughal invaders. In the chronicles of the kings of Kashmir (*Rajatarangini*,
1148), King Kshemagupta (r.950–958 CE) is said to have been addicted
to anal, as well as vaginal, sex and to have had male favourites whom he
publicly caressed. The *Shilappadikaram* (*c.*200 CE) says that King Nurruvar
Kannar sent 'one thousand brilliantly dressed *kanjuka* – male prostitutes
with long carefully burnished hair' to King Shenguttuvan of Chera (the
brother of the work's author, Prince Ilango Adigal).

The key text though is the *Kama Sutra*, which is also the best-
known Hindu work in the West. The *Kama Sutra* is, basically, about
the pursuit of pleasure in a general sense and, in particular, in a sexual
sense. The text is composed of *sutras* or 'sayings', which are often
cryptic but are accompanied by quotations from literature giving
examples of the activity being discussed. The text discusses the sexual
activities of men (in the sense of sophisticated urban dwellers) and
women, as well as the role of friendship and how the latter often

excludes sexual intimacy even between members of the opposite sex. For example, a man may have a *snehamitra* (loving [female] friend) with whom he played as a child and with whom he should avoid sex.

The *Kama Sutra* also discusses the *tritiya prakriti* or 'third nature' from the very outset. The medieval commentator on the text, Yashodhara (*c.*1150) explained that the third nature is *napumsaka* – neither man nor woman – and added that these people get pleasure from oral sex. One should not infer that the *Kama Sutra* does not discuss anal sex (as those who associate this with the advent of Islam would like). In a descriptive, non-pejorative passage the text informs us that 'copulation below, in the anus, is practiced by the peoples of the South'.

Where the *Kama Sutra* is most explicit though is in its discussion of oral sex between men. Yashodhara describes two types of third-nature individuals: men who look and behave like women and those who do not (echoing the Jain distinction we have already seen). Both desire sexual contact with other men but it is simply more obvious in the former than the latter – and makes it easier for them to have sex. In particular, he illustrates the difficulties of two 'male-appearing' individuals of the third nature in having sex. He discusses a masseur and the techniques he uses to seduce his client including verbal innuendos, manual stimulation of the penis and, eventually, the eight types of oral sex that lead to orgasm for both men. Both the *Kama Sutra* and its commentator suggest that there is some impurity in oral sex but Yashodhara ended by suggesting that mostly it is a matter of local custom and one's own preferences.

In general, the text's author, Vatsyayana, and Yoshodhara took a very tolerant attitude to oral sex between men. Close friends may consummate a *parigraha* (marriage) by such acts or simply further cement their friendship, *maitri*. The act can be performed mutually and Yashodhara extrapolated that women can also pleasure one another orally. Vatsyayana concluded the chapter on oral sex by saying that the variability of the human mind (and desire) is such that no one can know when, how or why a person might want to have such types of sex. Although anal sex, including the use of dildos by women to penetrate men, is mentioned it seems clear that oral sex (unlike in the ancient Graeco-Roman world) was the 'normal' type of sex between men. Why and when anal penetration began to be understood as the 'normal' type of sex between men is not clear, though it may relate to the arrival of the Mughals. If so, then the latter did not introduce anal sex but were partially responsible for its supplanting oral sex as normative behaviour between men.

The picture of homosexuality that emerges from what we know about the Far East in this period differs in detail but not substance from that of India. The most common term in Chinese for same-sex relationships dates not from the Zhou (and Qin) dynasties but rather the subsequent Han dynasty (206 BCE–220CE). Official court chroniclers made no secret of the same-sex relationships of Han emperors. Their favourites are discussed along with their wives and concubines. At least ten emperors were so often involved in same-sex relationships that it is perfectly appropriate to refer to them as 'bisexual'. Although interesting to the modern historian, the important point to note here is that contemporaries made no negative references to these relationships. Indeed, same-sex relations by the emperors were no more noteworthy than their relations with members of the opposite sex. This more than anything else highlights the relaxed attitude in early Chinese society to same-sex relationships, which remained throughout this period despite the development of Taoist thought (as a philosophical system distinct from religion) and Confucianism (which secured in Chinese thought the emphasis upon one's filial duty to procreate). As we have seen, although Western classical, pagan historians and commentators were aware of the same-sex relations of their kings and emperors, there was often an implied distaste for, or disapproval of, the behaviour. No such stigma appears in Chinese accounts.

At the same time, the first accounts of same-sex activities are recorded in Japan. One of the most important stories relates to the reign of the Empress Jingu (170-c.270). During a visit to the Shinuno palace in Ki province, the empress was struck by the perpetual darkness in which the province lay. When she enquired, she was told that it was the result of events surrounding two Shinto priests. The priests, Shino and Ama were the closest of companions despite being attached to different temples. When Shino died, Ama was so distraught that he killed himself, his last wish being to be buried with his beloved Shino.

This was done but, from that point onwards, the sun failed to shine. The empress ordered the tomb opened and the bodies reburied separately. This done, day and night returned as before.

Many contemporary Japanese historians interpret this as a condemnation of the love of Shino and Ama. However, this is problematic for a number of reasons. First, it is just as possible that one might interpret this as a condemnation of suicide, which seems hardly likely in Japanese culture. Likewise, one might view the moral of the tale as a rejection of the burial of two priests from rival temples in one grave. Even if one sees the myth as a rejection of same-sex love one has to explain the commonplace nature of such sexual acts in subsequent literature and the apparent lack of any social opprobrium against any man having sexual relations with another man. More importantly, what is clear is that one of the most important myths in any culture – why day follows night – is, in Japanese mythology, intimately linked with the love of two men for one another.

While the mythology of Japan may present an ambiguous and complex attitude to same-sex relations, the situation in China at that time was much more straightforward. One of the last Han emperors, Ai, came to the end of his life without issue. He tried to arrange that his lover, Dong Xian, would succeed him. However, the political elite was unwilling to accept an heir whose attachment to the throne was not a blood-tie – a (dowager) empress would almost certainly have been tolerated. Dong Xian was forced to commit suicide.

A touching tale of their life together produced the phrase hinted at above. One day while taking a nap with Dong Xian, Emperor Ai awoke to find his lover lying across the flowing sleeve of his robe. Rather than wake Dong Xian, Ai cut off the sleeve so he could arise and go about the business of court. In tribute to this love imperial fashion changed; Ai's other courtiers began to wear their robes with a cut sleeve. Thereafter, love between two men was regularly referred to as 'the passion of the cut sleeve'.

Not only did the court not reject Ai's love for Dong Xian, it imitated an expression of that love. In most cases, the emperors were clearly 'polysexual' (bisexual seems an unfair term to use, implying as it does that there are two distinct types of sexuality – homosexuality and heterosexuality – with a third category 'in between'). Ai, though, was said 'by nature, not to care for women', which may explain the lack of issue and his desire to promote Dong Xian to the throne in his stead. While Dong Xian's accession was unacceptable there is no evidence of any accompanying condemnation of the relationship *per se*.

Nor was same-sex affection limited to those rejecting women or masculine 'roles'. As with the militarily successful Roman Emperor Hadrian, early Chinese history is replete with warrior emperors and their favourites riding into battle side-by-side (compare Alexander the Great and his general, Hephaistion). The quintessential example of this is Emperor Wu. His favourite, Han Yan, was as famed for his martial skills as the emperor. Historical accounts of their relationship stress not clothing and courtly politics (as with Ai and Dong Xian) but riding skills, prowess at archery and success on the field of battle. In this relationship one again sees the Chinese pattern of same-sex affairs based on ideas of status not age or 'active/passive'. Wu was 'dominant' because of his social status; both were, however, portrayed by contemporary chroniclers as 'men's men'.

It is important to note that as late as the end of this period (600 CE) even in Europe, the pattern we have long noted remained fairly widely accepted. Love, friendship, sex and pleasure were all interconnected, while marriage was largely an arranged affair specifically focused on procreation. However, the spread of Christianity and the powerful impetus it gained from imperial recognition was beginning to have an impact. Judaism and its ideas about sex-for-procreation within a recognised marital bond had remained almost wholly confined to the Jewish people. Christianity not only had a desire (indeed, a divine mandate) to spread its beliefs; it had also gained the weight and force of the law and the state. This would almost certainly have meant the further conversion of the peoples of Christendom (the Mediterranean littoral and northern Europe) to sex-for-procreation alone. The advent of Islam, which shared the Judaeo-Christian view and spread south along the East African coast and eastwards towards India, was to have an even more profound impact in the millennium to follow. The twin forces of Christianity and Islam ensure that primacy of place was given to sex-for-procreation. However, as we will see, this was not without resistance nor was it instantaneous or complete.

four

Closing Minds

(600 CE–1550)

The Amir wants to see what I look like when I'm sodomised

(Al-Dalal at his trial, *c*.1450)

Islam broke upon the Mediterranean stage in the late seventh and early eighth centuries, sweeping Romano-Byzantine authority from much of the Middle East and North Africa. As a monotheistic religion with a strong moral code, it differed little from Christianity or Judaism in relation to sex and sexual activities in general. Indeed, the Western inclination to refer to 'Judaeo-Christian values' could more accurately employ (as this volume does) the phrase 'Judaeo-Christian-Islamic values'. However, in one area, Islam differed in tone. Same-sex actions were largely seen as bad or inappropriate behaviour rather than as 'sin'. Same-sex activities could (and were) punished with death but they could also be 'repented'. Thus, for the most part, Islam took a slightly more lenient approach to the stray same-sex act and, in particular, preserved a more Graeco-Roman attitude to pederasty. Blatant, continual same-sex acts between adults usually resulted in death, wheras in the Jewish and Christian approach where a single same-sex act was likely to invite capital punishment.

However, the advent of Islam is not the place to begin this chapter. On the eve of the period we are considering the last great 'Roman' (Byzantine) emperor, Justinian (*c*.482–565) introduced the first specific laws aimed at proscribing *all* types of homosexual relations. In 533, he placed all homosexual acts under the law, which punished adultery (with death). Subsequent laws in 538 and 544 urged all homo-sexuals to repent their sins and do penance. Anyone who remained a 'practising homosexual' (to use the modern phrase) was to be handed over to the city prefect (magistrate). It is not clear what this meant but, presumably, the accused was then liable to the 533 law regulating adultery *and* homosexuality.

It is not clear that these new laws had any immediate impact. However, we do know that leading figures were punished under it, though the account by Malalas (*c*.491–568) presents a punishment which is at odds with the legal decrees:

Among [those punished] *were Isaiah of Rhodes, who had been the* prefectus vig-ilum [fire-chief; captain of the watch] *of Constantinople, and Alexander, the bishop of Diospolis in Thrace. They were brought to Constantinople by imperial order and were tried and deposed by the city prefect, who punished them, exiling Isaiah after severe torture and exposing Alexander to public ridicule after castrating him. Shortly after this, the emperor ordered that all those found guilty of homosexual relations be castrated. Many were found at the time, and they were castrated and died. From that time on, those who experienced sexual desire for other males lived in terror.*

After three centuries of official, state-enforced Christianity, at the very heart of the world's most powerful Christian state, homosexuality still existed at the highest social, political and religious levels. However, the approval of the Greek world had given way to the disdain of Rome, which had been replaced by Christian dislike – a new period was about to begin, of persecution and terror.

There is little reason to see this as a principled stance. Most chron-iclers said that Justinian and his wife, the Empress Theodora (*c*.500–548), were simply using the charge as a way to remove politi-cal rivals or to extort money. Procopius listed homosexuals among a long list of minorities targeted by the regime: Samaritans, pagans, unorthodox Christians, astrologers, and supporters of the 'Green' char-iot-racing faction. Theodora was able to prosecute one young Green enthusiast having him dragged from a church (where he had sought sanctuary), horribly tortured and castrated – all without the pretence of a trial. When she tried to have another Green tried in court she

was unable to stop the judges from dismissing the case despite brib-
ing witnesses and torturing a friend of the defendant into testifying
against him. The populace of Constantinople celebrated the acquittal
with an impromptu holiday.

A similar pattern is seen elsewhere of secular political authorities
passing laws against same-sex practices with little reference to theology and even less evidence of Church support. For example, the
Visigothic conquerors of Roman Spain attempted to ingratiate themselves with their Romanised subjects by passing laws against homosexuals and Jews. The Catholic Church showed little enthusiasm for
the measures and specifically opposed decrees to force Jews to convert
– under the leadership of St Isidore of Seville (c.560–636) at the Fourth
Council of Toledo (633). Eventually (c.675) the Church was forced by
direct royal order to enact ecclesiastical punishments for clerical and
lay homosexuality but, in both cases, attempted to lessen the penalties
though the state nullified the lesser penalties.

No other laws are extant. Indeed, although Charlemagne was
shocked by the revelation that some of the monks in his realm were
sodomites, he did no more than express his amazement:

The life and chastity of the monks is the greatest hope of salvation for all Christians…
[They must] *strive to preserve themselves from such evils…* [And he would] *not
permit such ills any longer in any part of* [his] *realm, much less among those who
should be especially chaste and devout.*

Additional decrees from the Carolingian court did no more than
deplore the existence of sodomites and exhorted Church leaders to
stamp out the practice.

Synods producing Church rules and states enacting laws during the
early medieval period seem to have had little interest in homosexuality.
This does not imply that they knew nothing about it. The 'peniten-
tials', which were guide books for priests assigning penance for specific sins, list just about every permutation possible – for just about
every sin imaginable. Homosexuality was not left out. However, one
can draw some conclusions about the Church's view by noting that
the penitential of Pope Gregory III (r.731–741) specified 160 days'

penance for lesbianism, 365 days for male homosexuality and three years for a priest who went hunting.

Indeed, the Carolingian court, in the form of Alcuin (732–804) saw a rebirth not only of Latin poetry but also pre-Christian sensibilities about male love. Alcuin's poetry was very homoerotic though the emphasis was mostly on the holy and idealised nature of such love. He was especially attracted and attached to his students, writing them fulsome 'love' letters. While it is perhaps convenient to see his writings as 'Platonic' (in the modern sense of the word) it is more difficult to see how one can reinterpret this letter to a bishop he admired:

I think of your love and friendship with such sweet memories, reverend bishop, that I long for that time when I may be able to clutch the neck of your sweetness with the fingers of my desire… how would I sink into your embraces… how would I cover, with tightly pressed lips, not only your eyes, ears and mouth but also your every finger and your toes, not once but many times.

It would require quite an interpretative flair to spiritualise such a letter. The simple fact is that the poetry of the time was replete with expressions of love between men (mostly monastics), and lay 'knightly' tales focusing on close male-male ties were also relatively common.

To the extent that one sees developments that relate to homosexuality, one must consider the spread of ideas about sex more generally. As noted in the last chapter, the great legacy of the early Church on this subject was the emphasis placed upon procreation as the *paramount* purpose for sex. It is this view that explains St Boniface's (*c*.680–*c*.754) condemnation of the English for 'sodomy'. He complained that his compatriots were 'despising lawful marriage and preferring incest, promiscuity, adultery, and impious union with religious and cloistered women'. Their 'sodomy' was non-procreative sex, incest and adultery, along with sexual relations with nuns. Hincmar of Reims, a leading German theologian and politician (*c*.806–882) was even more explicit:

therefore let no one claim he had not committed sodomy if he has acted contrary to nature with either man or woman [my emphasis] or had deliberately and consciously defiled himself by rubbing [masturbation], touching or other improper acts.

Indeed, Hincmar equated homosexual acts with simple fornication (sex outside a marital bond); when it involved (at least one) married person it was a type of adultery. He even added a discussion of lesbianism – something the Bible and most other Church writers and jurists never bothered to do. He wrote:

[Lesbians] *do not put flesh to flesh in the sense of the genital organ of one within the body of the other, since nature precludes this, but they do transform the use of the member in question into an unnatural one, in that they are reported to use certain instruments of diabolical operation to excite desire. Thus they sin nonetheless by committing* fornication *against their own bodies.*

Again, the crime is fornication. Hincmar also interpreted Paul's 'anti-homosexual' passage in *Romans* as:

whence it follows, as the Apostle says in Romans *(1: 26-27), that if any commit uncleanness in any way, whether men with men, women with women, men with women, or all by themselves, it is an indecency which separates the guilty party from the Kingdom of God.*

This is not quite what Paul wrote:

Their women exchanged natural relations for unnatural ones. In the same way the men also abandoned natural relations with women and were inflamed with lust for one another. Men committed indecent acts with other men, and received in themselves the due penalty for their perversion.

He also found not just homosexuality but also prostitution in Paul's Corinthian passage (6: 9):

Do you not know that the wicked will not inherit the kingdom of God? Do not be deceived: neither the sexually immoral nor idolaters nor adulterers nor male prostitutes nor homosexual offenders… will inherit the kingdom of God.

A general attack on prostitution is hard to find here.

Having said that, Hincmar seems unique in Church thought in seeing homosexuality in *Joel* 3: 3 ('They cast lots for my people and traded boys for prostitutes; they sold girls for wine that they might drink') and *Ephesians* 5: 12 ('For it is shameful even to mention what the disobedient do in secret'). Hincmar's views are somewhat confusing but what is clear is that same-sex acts for him were not fundamentally different from a whole range of possible sexual behaviour between a man and a woman or by individuals on their own. What we see by the 800s is a 'bedding down' in Christian thought of the correlation of 'nature', 'procreation', 'marriage' and valid sex. Every other sort of sexual act (from masturbation, through fornication, adultery and homosexuality to bestiality) is simply condemned as non-procreative, unnatural and sodomitical. There is no evidence of a hierarchy of sin with homosexuality at its apex. Rather, to the extent that one can discern it, adultery and incest seem to be the worst sexual sins imaginable.

Things began to change in the twelfth century, though moves against sexual immorality in general and sodomy in particular seem largely connected with attempts to enforce clerical celibacy amongst monastic communities (in the first place) and parish priests (later in the period). Thus, we see the Council of London (1102) specifically requiring that sodomy be confessed as a sin. Interestingly, St Anselm (1033–1109; Archbishop of Canterbury) simply refused to publish the decree, noting in a letter to one of his archdeacons and close personal friends: 'This sin has hitherto been so public that hardly anyone is embarrassed by it, and may have therefore fallen into it because they were unaware of its seriousness.' It may have been serious but St Anselm seems to have had little interest in making a specific move against it. Moreover, the decree of the council must be seen in context. Until the Fourth Lateran Council (1215) mandated annual confession, most Christians only confessed their sins once – from the safety of their deathbeds.

The First Lateran Council (1123) started the drive for the control of sexual mores. Pope Leo IX (reigned 1049–54) was an enthusiastic supporter of clerical celibacy and led the campaign to extend the vow of celibacy from the regular clergy (monks and nuns) to the secular clergy (parish priests). This culminated in the ruling of the First Lateran Council which nullified priests' marriages. The reality, though, was that not only were many clergy involved in sexual liaisons (and marriages) with women but also a significant number were public in their relationships with other men, so much so that it was a stock element in satires of the period. The famous poet, Walther of Chatillon (*fl.* early twelfth century) lampooned one bishop noted for his zeal in ending clerical marriage because the bishop himself had little interest in such things: 'the man who occupies the bishopric is Ganymedier than Ganymede'.

What is certainly the case is that sex between men was an open topic for discussion and some men were quite open in their love affairs with other men even when recognising that the Church disapproved. Therefore, we see Peter of Abano (*fl.* thirteenth century) explaining what sex between men actually meant:

Some exercise the wicked act of sodomy by rubbing the penis with the hand [masturbation; mutual or solitary]; *others by rubbing between the thighs of* [adolescent] *youths* [frottage; intercrural sex], *which is what most do these days; and others by making friction around the anus and by putting the penis in it the same way as it is placed in a woman's sexual parts.*

People knew what men did with men. That some leading men of the day were involved with other men (as well as women) was equally well known. Thus, there was extensive comment on the love affairs of King Richard the Lionheart of England (1157–99). His first notable love (while duke of Aquitaine) was with Philip, king of France (1165–1223):

They ate every day at the same table and from the same dish, and at night their beds did not separate them. And the king of France loved him as his own soul; and they loved each other so much that the king of England [Richard's father, Henry II] *was absolutely astonished at the passionate love between them and marvelled at it.*

No one seems to have been overly concerned with Richard's attachments even though it is clear that he was aware his behaviour was outside the Church's ideal of approved behaviour. He repeatedly repented himself of 'that sin'.

The key point is that the Church was beginning to take an interest in matters of sexuality. However, the primary focus for the Church was the sexual antics of the parish clergy and the need to extend clerical celibacy. For the most part this centred on ending the practice of priestly marriage (practised to this day amongst Orthodox parish priests and even Eastern-rite Roman Catholic priests). If there was any specific interest in homosexuality it was as a type of fornication and adultery. Sodomy was not an 'unpardonable sin'; it was simply a sub-category of sexual sins into which anyone might fall.

During the course of the 1100s the tone began to alter. The Third Lateran Council (1179) specifically forbade 'that [fornication] which is against nature'. Any priest caught in sodomy was to be defrocked or confined to a monastery for life, while laymen were to face excommunication and social exclusion. This same council also enacted decrees limiting the economic and social roles open to Jews and their interaction with Christians. Increasingly, a wholesale amalgamation of groups and practices was beginning to take place, which tended to lump heretics, Jews and homosexuals into a distinct (and threatening) category – when sorcery and contact with the demonic was added the mix became explosive. Secular legislation followed thick and fast – some of it gruesome in its viciousness.

A royal edict in Castile said that 'if any commit this sin, once it is proven, both [should] be castrated before the whole populace… then hung by the legs until they are dead.' The legal school in Orléans suggested castration for the first offence, dismemberment for the second and burning for the third. A law in Bologna (1288) replaced fines with burning – this may be part of a general revival in Roman laws, which under the late empire and early Byzantine period had prescribed burning. A statute in Siena ordered that sodomites be hanged by their genitalia. The simple fact is that the period leading up to the Black Death (c.1350) saw an increase in ecclesiastical and secular regulations aimed specifically at homosexuality as it became more and more associated with heretical movements. There is no reason to think that this was a response to any increase in male same-sex activities or indeed that they had much effect in practice (the structures of the state were normally too weak to enforce many laws). Nevertheless, the problem was prominent and had traditional acceptance (if not support) in many communities as evidenced by Pierre de la Palude's (fl. fourteenth century) spirited defence of why parish churches and priests should *stop* blessing homosexual unions as marriages.

In the wake of the Black Death, Europeans sought to explain why God had chastised them so horrifically. Numerous groups found themselves targeted as scapegoats. Jews were an obvious object to attack and across large swathes of France, Switzerland and the Rhineland, Jews and their communities were eradicated in a frenzy of anti-Semitism. Jews were accused of conspiring with Muslims, lepers and the devil (among others) to spread the plague and destroy Christendom. Heresy was also seen as a possible cause for God's divine wrath as expressed by the plague. Thus, the Church and state began to place a greater emphasis on belief and practice. That the Great Schism (1378–1417) occurred at this time, producing two and then three claimants to the Papal See, only heightened the sense that the Church was in chaos, and that the forces of heresy and evil were afoot. Of course, in any individual community there might be no Jews or heretics – and papal politics might be far removed. In most places, then, people had to identify causes for the disaster of the Black Death from *within* the community. Led by preachers and moralists it was easy to see that God had been angered by sexual immorality. Two groups tended to find themselves in the firing line (literally in the sense of the threat of being burned alive): sodomites and prostitutes.

This tendency to attack specific groups after the Black Death must be examined in detail for it constructed the panoply of legislation and cultural mindset which would largely determine Western European attitudes to Judaism, sexual immorality and unorthodox religious beliefs for the next half-millennium. Europe began to see, as Justinian had argued in his decrees, that 'sin' (specifically false religion, unnatural sex and heresy) was the cause of famine, plague, war and just about every other catastrophe. Jews were no longer just 'not Christian'; sodomites were no longer 'just fornicators and adulterers'; heretics were no longer just 'misguided brethren'. All three became the greatest threat to a society, the cause of all its evils and problems. The solution was eradication.

The first port of call in a crisis set the tone for what would follow. For obvious reasons, Europeans beset by the plague or languishing in its aftermath turned to the Church for an explanation and guidance. Since the clerics had a special relationship with the divine it was possible that they might be able to explain or alter the course of an epidemic. Their explanation was also considerably less cerebral than that of the physicians. There was an obvious reason for plague: God was angry with the community. It was absolutely essential that the sins that were inviting divine anger be identified and eliminated. Three key targets could be identified. First, the general piety or impiety of the entire community was examined. People were encouraged to avail themselves of the sacraments of the Church, to make pilgrimages, to pray, to participate in processions and to perform other pious acts. Second, the community might be guilty of harbouring impious and ungodly beliefs. Thus, heresy had to be rooted out and, coupled with this, the most obvious group of unorthodox worshippers, the Jews. Since the Jews rejected the 'truths' of the Christian faith they were seen as the enemies of God and, by extension, the followers of God's great enemy, Satan – as such they were heretics. Finally, societies were counselled to root out those sins that were most visible and likely to provoke God's wrath. Prostitution and same-sex acts were obvious targets.

In effect, the religious leaders were advising that the disease had a scientific as well as a theological explanation. The problems that caused epidemic diseases were environmental. Something in the region was infecting the community. Physicians looked to pollution in the air, in the natural sense, while religious leaders assumed that pollution was present (in the air) in a metaphorical and religious sense. To both, the plague was the result of factors already in existence in a locality and body politic. Plague was not 'caught' from someone or somewhere else. Plague 'broke out' because of the polluted conditions already present. Things, people and places did not carry and spread plague (by contagion) in a neutral sense. Rather, pestilence appeared because those factors that caused disease were already present. The way to prevent, curtail, or cure plague, for both physicians and religious leaders, was to change those environmental aspects that were sources of pollution. While magistrates were willing to accept that bad sanitation might worsen civic health they consistently held to the view that plague was a contagious disease not a fever caused by bad air. In addition, they were also willing to believe that God's wrath might be kindled against a city in the form of a contagious epidemic. The common people were especially inclined to agree that specific acts (especially those of others) were to blame. Whatever the theoretical reasoning,

one course of action was obvious: the community had to cleanse itself
of pollution and prevent recontamination.

As already noted above, attacks against Jews were the most obvious
and horrific example of this attempt to purify urban communities of
groups and individuals considered to be polluting and diseased.
Although outside the scope of this volume, the persecution of the Jews
in the aftermath of the plague must be considered in some detail
because it makes clear that subsequent attacks against homosexuals and
heretics were not isolated instances of 'morality'. Europe did *not* experience some moral revival against sexual sins in the 1400s, which
attempted to eradicate the last vestiges of classical polysexuality or Dark
Age licentiousness from Western Christendom. Seen in the wider context of anti-Semitism what becomes apparent is that Europe indulged
in a wave of scapegoating and embedded in the popular mind a theory
about disaster, which meant certain types of people were to be blamed.

By 1550, there were almost no Jews left in Western Europe as country after country had expelled or executed their Jewish people.
However, anti-Semitism did not start with the plague; Edward I
(1239–1307) had expelled England's Jewish population in the 1290s. In
1215, the Fourth Lateran Council had ordered that all Jews and Muslims
wear special clothes and distinguishing badges on their garments so
that everyone would be able to identify them with ease and at a distance. The council's requirement that belief in transubstantiation (the
bread and wine in communion actually become Christ's Body and
Blood) was a necessary article of faith also became important in subsequent accusations against Jews for supposed attacks on the Host.
Throughout the thirteenth and fourteenth centuries there had been
increasingly strong attacks on Jews especially (though not exclusively)
in the preaching campaigns of the Dominicans and Franciscans. The
appearance of plague and the accusation that Jews were intentionally
spreading the pestilence combined to accelerate the calls of the friars
for the complete expulsion of the Jews from the Christian West.

The accusations against the Jews were manifold. They were seen as
the group solely responsible for the crucifixion of Christ despite the
involvement of Pilate and the Roman (that is, Gentile) Empire. In
addition, rumours (called the 'Blood Libel') asserted that Jews used

the blood of Christian children in various religious ceremonies (for example, Passover). Their enemies accused them of stealing consecrated Hosts ('Host Desecration') for similar uses. Jews were frequently accused of conspiring with Muslims and heretical or Orthodox Christians against Western Catholics. Also, there were accusations that the seeming stubbornness of the Jews in refusing to accept the 'truth' of Christianity was a further sign of their intentional and conscious evil, which inevitably led to associating them with Satan and demonic practices. Even arson attacks (and other catastrophic events) were laid at their doors. Finally, during the plague outbreaks of the late fourteenth and early fifteenth centuries, the Jews were accused of working with, in turn, Muslims, lepers and the devil to poison wells and spread the plague. Many leading churchmen condemned these attacks following the teaching of St Augustine that Jews must be tolerated as an essential part of the cosmic history of Christendom. Indeed, Pope Clement VI (reigned 1342–52) and subsequent popes condemned attempts to blame Jews for the plague – they noted that Jews and Christians seemed to be dying in equal numbers from the pestilence.

As early as the 1100s, a Christian chronicler noted the impact of popular anti-Semitism and wrote that 'whether what I am relating is true or not is no concern of mine; it is told thus and thus must it be accepted'. In the decade immediately before the plague, parishioners in Deggendorf (Bavaria) dedicated a plaque on a church commemorating the fact that 'here were the Jews slain; they had set the city afire'. Other churches were raised as memorials to the destruction of Jewish ghettos and, especially, synagogues. In 1300, at Lauda (Würzburg), a massacre accompanying an accusation of Host Desecration saw a chapel built on the site of the demolished Jewish houses. Indeed, many of the churches dating from this period that are dedicated to the Body of Christ (*Corpus Christi*), the Holy Blood, or the Virgin Mary stand on ground formerly occupied by Jewish ghettos or places of worship.

Plague simply seems to have accelerated and intensified the persecution – and elimination – of Jews. In the 1340s, Jews were targeted as plague-spreaders in France, Italy, Switzerland and Germany. Some citizens cleansed their cities of Jews before the arrival of plague in an attempt to prevent the pestilence. Such preventative persecution

appeared at Strasbourg (900 Jews were burned alive), Nuremberg,
Regensburg, Augsburg and Frankfurt. The Holy Roman Emperor,
Charles IV (1316–78), even made laws arranging for the disposal of
Jewish property in the event of the elimination of a ghetto. Persecution
of Jews remained a consistent feature of plague outbreaks: Halle (1382);
Rappoltsweiler, Dürkheim, Colmar (1397); Freiburg-im-Breisgau
(1401); Cologne (1424); Schweidnitz (1448–53, 1543); Regensburg
(1472); Germany-wide (1475); Brieg (1541); Aix-en-Provence (1580);
Vienna (1679). Pre-existing accusations of (well-)poisoning seem to
explain this association of Jews with plague. As early as 877 a Jewish
doctor was accused of poisoning the Emperor Charles the Bold
(823–877) ; in 1161, eighty-six Jews were executed in a single massacre
as poisoners. Jews, along with Muslims and lepers, were subsequently
accused of poisoning in the Vaud (1308); Eulenburg (1316); Franconia
(1319); France-wide (1321); Provence, Germany-wide (1337) and
Provençal (1348). The move from persecution for poisoning to persecution for plague-spreading was virtually seamless.

There also seems to have been a connection between these accusations for poisoning and plague-spreading and the involvement of
Jews in medical work. The emphasis upon literacy among Jews, as
well as their prohibition from many trades (especially farming and
land-ownership) meant that Jews were concentrated in urban areas
and overrepresented in professions that required the ability to read. In
addition, Jewish familiarity with Hebrew and Arabic gave many Jews
access to the medical works of the ancients through the medium of
the Islamic world. Indeed, Jewish medical skills often allowed them to
work in areas otherwise closed to their co-religionists. For example,
despite the expulsion of Jews from England by Edward I, both Edward
II (1284–1327) and Henry IV (1367–1413) employed Jews as personal
physicians (a practice common among noble and wealthy families).
The power of Jewish physicians was a frequent concern. In the sixteenth century, Hans Wilhem Kirchhoff (1525–1603) noted that 'we
Christians are such brainless fools that when our lives are in danger
we turn to our archenemies [the Jews] in order to save [ourselves]'.
Friars in the late medieval period were especially keen to stop this
reliance on Jewish medical practitioners and were so successful that

many Italian cities were forced to get explicit papal permission (dispensation) to employ Jews as civic physicians.

The complex interaction between Jews as healers and as poisoners is obvious. Although Jews were clearly outsiders and suspect they were also essential to certain areas of life. Only with an increase in Gentile (Christian) involvement in medicine and finance (to name but two areas) was it possible to survive without a dependence upon Jews. However, a reliance on Jews in no way altered the overwhelmingly negative and suspicious image of them in the minds of most if not all Christians. As Peter the Venerable (1122–57), abbot of Cluny put it:

really I doubt whether a Jew can be human for he will neither yield to human reasoning [and accept Christianity], *nor find satisfaction in authoritative utterances, alike divine and Jewish* [in refusing to accept the Catholic interpretation of the books of the Jewish/Old Testament].

Shakespeare (*Merchant of Venice* II.ii.27) penned a more succinct and blunt assessment: 'Certainly the Jew is the very devil incarnal'.

While Jews were more easily identifiable, they were not the only groups in a society to be attacked after being blamed for causing a pestilential outbreak. Poor foreigners (those who would be called 'economic migrants' today) were usually expelled at the merest hint of plague. Refugees from wars and persecution (today's 'asylum seekers') were often seen as 'dirty' and, therefore, a potential source of disease. Tanners, leather-makers, butchers, fishmongers and gravediggers, whose professions produced bad smells or refuse, often saw their labours curtailed during plague outbreaks. Consistently, though, the emphasis was placed upon controlling any group or individual who was associated with dirt, pollution, refuse and illness. People involved in the sex trade or sexual deviance were, unsurprisingly, targeted as often as Jews and, after the expulsion of most of Europe's Jews, were one of the few groups of potential scapegoats remaining.

It is essential to realise that attitudes to sex and sexuality in the late medieval period differed quite dramatically from those of today. For example, until very late in the fifteenth century (and often a century later) brothels remained an accepted – and legal – part of the civic landscape. Brothels were built with public funds and overseen by a state-appointed or state-approved 'madam' (often called the 'abbess' or 'queen of whores'). Thus, in 1447, Dijon constructed a substantial building to serve as the city's brothel. There were rooms for the custodian, a spacious common room and nearly two dozen large bedrooms each with a stone fireplace. This city of 10,000 souls was well provided with over 100 legally recognised prostitutes.

Many publicly maintained bathhouses were used for prostitution and there were also small, 'private' brothels. Most of these establishments, and activities, were openly recognised, regulated and taxed by the city government. In addition to this licit activity, there were streetwalkers. The magistrates justified the provision of prostitutes (to their often censorious clergy) on the grounds of 'common utility' and 'in the interest of the public good'. They were meant to provide an outlet for the sexual appetites of the many single young men. Since artisans and workers were not usually allowed to marry until they became masters of their trade (that is, in their thirties), young men were a serious problem. Prostitutes were seen as an acceptable alternative to the gang-raping of 'respectable' young women (or boys) in the street, which happened not infrequently. In addition to providing societies with money (through taxes) and order (through the release of sexual tension), legal prostitution gave the city the chance to ensure that the sex-workers and the brothels were 'clean'.

Initially there seems to have been no clear identification of legal prostitution (in brothels) with plague. Indeed, 1350–1450 was the period of the construction and institutionalisation of public brothels. Rather than removing the sex-workers, the city governments seem to have been concerned to ensure that they were clean. The preaching friars, however, stressed that physical cleanliness and health were no cover for the moral dirtiness of the activity. They went further and asserted that legalisation inextricably tied the society, in general, with an unwholesome activity. The general populace seems to have agreed and prostitutes (who, like Jews, were often required to wear distinctive badges or clothes) were attacked in times of plague or harvest failure, or after especially successful and charismatic sermons. Still, until the 1480s, most single men went to brothels as a regular feature of their Sunday life – the brothels were only required to close during the actual time of religious services. In the later decades of the fifteenth century, prostitution came under increasing attack by preachers and, especially during the Protestant and Catholic Reformations of the sixteenth century, by society in general.

It is perhaps difficult to understand how the preachers were able to convince society that legal prostitution was so dangerous. Most men would, at some time prior to marriage, have visited brothels. Fathers sent their sons to them quite openly. Shame was not an effective tool. However, the preachers were able to accuse society of supporting behaviour that was unable to restore the population of Europe constantly devastated by plague. That is, prostitution (and illegitimacy) was unproductive and, therefore sinful. As such, it was unnatural. This theoretical approach to sexual sins is most evident in the accompanying attack on same-sex acts. Male homosexuality (normally grouped under the general term of sodomy) was an equally unproductive activity and, thus, denounced by the preachers – lesbian acts seem rarely to have been noticed. The depopulation of Europe as a result of the plague put a great emphasis on the production of legitimate children. Future workers (children) were needed to restore society and anything that worked against this was a social evil. The preachers now had a way of making the sinfulness of prostitutes (fornicators and adulterers) and sodomites understandable to the common folk. These sins were not just an affront against God but also a threat to society and likely to invite further divine wrath. As St Bernardino (1380–1444) preached to his fellow citizens of Siena: 'you don't understand that [sodomy] is the reason you have lost half your population over the last twenty-five years.' He claimed that God's (poetic) judgement against a society that seemed to despise children (by refusing to have legitimate offspring) was to deprive the people of the few children they did bother to produce. He claimed that he could hear, ringing in his ears, the unborn (not yet conceived) chanting for vengeance.

It is not surprising that population loss was a major concern for civic governments and their populations. For example, in the 1330s, Florence had about 120,000 people. The population finally stabilised in 1410–60 at 40,000. Moral rectitude and duty to the wider society became matters of the utmost concern to the state. Florence made attempts to control political views (1378), street-walking (1403), sexual immorality in convents (1421), malfeasance in officials (1429) and sodomy (1432). The creation of the *Ufficiali di Notte* (Officers of the Night) in 1432 to control sodomy led to seventy years of magisterial prosecution of men engaged in sex with other men (usually an older man and a youth in late adolescence). A similar institution (the *Collegium sodomitarum*) was established in Venice in 1418.

In the period 1432–1502, over 17,000 (240 per year, nearly five each week) men were accused and 3,000 (forty-three per year) were convicted of sodomy in a Florentine population of 40,000 people. If one takes a generation to be twenty years then in any generation about 12 percent of the male population was publicly and officially accused of sodomy and 2 percent actually convicted. The problem, it would seem, was not insignificant. The Florentine state even attempted to require that all magistrates aged 30–50 had to be married to avoid any secret sodomites from working in the courts to protect others like themselves. So common was the practice that Bernardino accused fathers and mothers of knowingly allowing their sons to engage in same-sex acts and relationships. He said that their sons should be locked up at home lest they be enticed into this behaviour (or raped). He preached that it was 'less evil' that their daughters be raped than their sons. He called sodomy 'this pestilential ruin' besetting the city. So close was the inter-relationship of sodomy, plague, pollution and sin that most Florentine laws and Bernardine sermons against sodomy occurred during or shortly after plague outbreaks.

What offended Bernardino and others the most though was the toleration of these sins at the highest levels of society. Nobles and the wealthy protected Jews for financial and medical reasons. Society's leaders legalised and protected prostitution. Worse, many of the greatest figures in Western Christian culture engaged in, or overlooked, sodomitical practices. For example, Poliziano (1454–94) who was a tutor to the children of Lorenzo de' Medici (1449–92) and a friend and teacher of Michelangelo (1475–1564) – and a further 500 men from all over Europe – was a leading Neoplatonist figure of the Renaissance. He was also (to use the contemporary term) a 'notorious sodomite' who never married. He, and others, wrote poems about their love of other men. For example:

If you would share in my society,
Do not discourse on female love to me...
I urge all husbands: seek divorce, and flee
Each one away from female company

Benvenuto Cellini (1500–71), in August 1545, while talking to
the duke of Florence, was attacked by an opposing artist, Baccio:
'Oh keep quiet, you dirty sodomite'. Stunned by this public accusation, Cellini amused (but did not shock) the gathered courtiers when
he replied:

You madman, you're going too far. But I wish to God I did know how to indulge in
[the] noble practice [of sodomy]... it is the practice of the greatest emperors and the
greatest kings of the world. I'm an insignificant humble man, I haven't the means or
the knowledge to meddle in such a marvellous manner.

His four arrests and two convictions for sodomy make his riposte all
the more pithy – and disingenuous.

It is hardly surprising that the Church and its clergy often attacked
sodomy not only as a great sin but also as an extreme threat to the
survival of society itself. However, the celibate clergy were not exempt
from this infection. On 1 November 1494, Savonarola (1453–98)
demanded of his fellow Florentine clerics that they 'abandon, I say,
that unspeakable vice, abandon that abominable vice that has brought
God's wrath upon you, or else: woe, woe to you!' Preachers, moralists
and, increasingly, magistrates became convinced that immorality (social
and cultural pollution) had to be eliminated. Clearly, it was impossible to eradicate prostitution or sodomy any more than foreigners or
refugee poor could be stopped at the border. However, society had to
be seen (by God) to be trying to purify itself if divine punishment was
to be avoided. In the course of the fifteenth century it became clear
to many that the 'toleration' of sinfulness and moral impurity was the
cause of God's anger. To prevent epidemic diseases being sent against
a society it was essential that everything possible be done to eliminate
the causes of pollution and defilement in the culture. However, this
drive for purity ran foul of the Renaissance (and, often, sodomitical)

sensibilities of the clerical hierarchy. For example, popes like Alexander (Borgia) VI were notorious for their appreciation of the male form.

The general populace, with its clergy and magistrates, could take comfort in seeing prostitutes, sodomites, migrants and the refugee poor driven from their streets and out of sight. Surely a society that moved harshly and strenuously against these sources of (metaphorical, metaphysical and religious) infection was less likely to suffer God's wrath. Lucy Hutchinson, in her diary of the early seventeenth century, could have spoken for most people even in the fourteenth century:

The face of the court was much changed in the change of the King [with the death of James VI & I], *for King Charles* [I] *was temperate, chaste, and serious; so that the fools and bawds, mimics and catamites* [sodomites] *of the former court* [of James VI and I] *grew out of fashion; and the nobility and courtiers, who did not quite aban-don their debaucheries, yet so reverenced* [feared] *the king as to retire into corners to practice them.*

Any society, cleansed of such vile pollution, could join her in breathing a collective sigh of relief. She may have written slightly outside the time period of this chapter but hers was a voice that simply echoed the demands of St Bernardino and Savanarola.

The important result of the Black Death and an increasing ecclesiastical emphasis upon clerical celibacy was twofold. The latter led to a greater focus on sexual immorality as a significant problem in the religious realm. The former created in the wider populace a connection between horrific disasters and specific groups of people. Since plague returned to most urban areas every fifteen to twenty years throughout the sixteenth and seventeenth centuries it is hardly surprising that opinions about same-sex acts became more and more ferocious. Once the Jews were largely expelled and heresy eclipsed by the splintering of Christendom into Protestantism and Catholicism, the groups who could be blamed became fewer, though no less obvious. The sexually immoral (fornicators, adulterers, and, especially, prostitutes and sodomites) were the people whose very existence threatened to bring ruin upon the community. No longer could Western Europe afford the luxury of ignoring and winking at same-sex acts. Homosexuality had to be punished swiftly and severely; the punishment had to be exemplary and visible. God's wrath had to be averted.

While Christianity was undergoing these changes the situation in the Islamic-controlled parts of the Mediterranean retained many of the cultural sensibilities about sex of the pagan Graeco-Roman world. One particular aspect of Arabic culture in this period which is of interest to any discussion of sexuality and Islam comes from Medina in the century immediately after the Prophet, Mohammed's death (632). In the 700s Arabic music and poetry moved from being dominated by women to men. These first male musicians/poets were often called *mukhannathun* (effeminate). By the time of the *Kitab al-Aghani* of al-Isfahani (d.967) these *mukhannathun* had dominated music circles in Mecca and Medina for two generations with exceptional visibility and prestige. Their position came to an abrupt and violent end under Caliph Sulayman (r.715–17) because of his supposed reaction to their licentiousness with women *not* men.

According to the Islamic grammarian, Abu Ubayd (d.838) the *mukhannathun* (derived from the word *khanatha* – compare, below, terms used in Mombasa/Zanzibar and Oman) were languid (*takassur*). By the time of the Islamic writer al-Ayni (1451) the term meant the passive partner in a homosexual act. One might infer from this that these individuals were considered depraved. However, at least as far back as the twelfth century, *mukhannathun* guarded the prophet's grave – a tradition maintained until the end of Ottoman rule in the twentieth century.

Mukhannathun is also only one of the Arabic words for men involved in homosexual acts. *Luti* (from Lot – recalling the destruction of Sodom) was the normal term for the active partner. The passive partner was known by a number of words: *mu'ajir* (rent-boy; passive for money); *mubadil* (who was both active and passive); *ma'bun* (passive). *Ma'bun* comes from *uban* which usually meant a 'pathological' desire to be a bottom and was a term mostly associated with medical treatises – i.e. being a *ma'bun* was a type of disease. If nothing else this serves to remind us that the Western-centric view that homosexuality was first 'medicalised' in nineteenth-century psychiatry is incorrect – on which, see chapter 6.

It is also noteworthy that another frequent term for a *luti* (pederast) was 'monk', which was clearly meant to be a slur on the morals found in the Christian monasteries scattered throughout the Islamic world. Lists of euphemisms for anal sex include sayings such as 'like a monk in his monastery' and insults such as 'more given to [sodomy] than a monk' were not uncommon. What these suggest is a lively discussion about, and awareness of, same-sex activities and individuals. The Victorian West may have had a 'love that dare not speak its name'; the Islamic world had a sexual practice that was freely discussed and, at times, openly practised.

While these individuals are, with the passing of time, difficult to describe precisely, we have accounts of individual *mukhannathun*, as well as comments about them as a group from other sources. For example, various *hadith* (or, sayings of the Prophet – Mohammed) such as the *Muwatta* of Malik bin Anas, the Islamic writer (d.797), and the *Musnad* of another Islamic writer, Ahmad bin Hanbal (d.855) give at least seven basic ideas about *mukhannathun*:

1. The Prophet cursed effeminate men (*al-mukhannathin min al-rijal*) and mannish women (*al-mutarajjilat min al-nisa*), thereby condemning cross-gendered behaviour (e.g. transvestism)
2. Calling someone a *mukhannathun* incurred twenty lashes as did saying someone had taken the active role (*luti*) in sodomy (Ibn Maja, d.886, and al-Tirmidhi, d.892)
3. Someone who dyes their hands and feet with henna (like a woman) was banished by the Prophet (who refused to execute him, though, saying, 'I have been forbidden to kill those who pray')
4. Banishment also related to a story about a *mukhannathun* who was among the women accompanying one of the Prophet's wives
5. Another version of (4) said that a certain *mukhannathun* was 'one of those lacking interest in women (*min ghayr uli l-irba*)'. This *mukhannathun* was allowed back into Medina twice a week to beg 'lest he starve in the desert'
6. The Prophet specifically condemned a *mukhannathun* who asked permission to continue acting as a musician
7. An opinion tied to a *hadith* by al-Zuhri (d.742) said that one should only pray behind a *mukhannathun* when absolutely necessary.

These *hadith* present a number of 'readings' of the *mukhannathun*. Clearly, they were individuals who were able to move between male and female spheres (number 4) and often acted as musicians (number 6; compare the situation in Mombasa and Zanzibar discussed later). They were rebuked by the Prophet (numbers 1 and 4) but with mercy being explicitly shown (numbers 3 and 5). Finally, a *mukhannathun* was considered, at best, socially 'dubious' if not actively disliked (numbers 2 and 7).

This gives us some ideas about the *mukhannathun* as a group. However, they were often attacked not so much for their effeminacy as their wit and an irreverence that bordered on the irreligious (even blasphemous). Al-Dalal – a famous *mukhannathun* – once farted during prayers and said 'I praise Thee fore and aft' and when the *imam* quoted the Koran and said 'And why should I not serve Him Who created me?' al-Dalal answered 'I don't know' causing most of the congregation to laugh. Al-Dalal, who was surely the most famous *mukhannathun*, had tales told about him giving some idea of the need to avoid the temptation to view the socially constructed 'niches' of other cultures as simply early versions of 'gay', 'queen', or 'drag'.

On another occasion al-Dalal had been to a party in the desert with a group of friends. They noticed his attraction to a youth in the party and arranged for them to be able to be alone. Unfortunately, the local constabulary arrived and al-Dalal and his young man, being too drunk to escape, were caught after the rest of their companions had fled. He was brought before the governor and this conversation took place:

Governor:	*'You wanton degenerate.'*
Al-Dalal:	*'From your lips to heaven.'*
Governor [to guards]:	*'Slap his jaw!'*
Al-Dalal [mockingly]:	*'And off with his head, too'.*
Governor:	*'Enemy of God, were you not comfortable enough at home, so that you had to go out into the desert with this boy and do your foul business there?'*
Al-Dalal:	*'If I had known that you were going to attack us, preferring that we do our foul business secretly, I would never have left my house!'*
Governor:	*'Strip him and give him the stipulated flogging.'*

Al-Dalal: *'That will do you no good, for, by God, I get stipulated*
                             floggings every day.'
Governor: *'And who undertakes to do that?'*
Al-Dalal: *'The penises of the Muslims.'*
Governor: *'Throw him on his face and sit on his back.'*
Al-Dalal: *'I suppose the amir wants to see what I look like when*
                             I'm sodomised.'

Clearly, the amir was as angry with al-Dalal's wit and irreverence as
he was with his sexual proclivities.

Indeed, al-Dalal is intimately connected with the supposed destruction of the *mukhannathun*. After arranging a marriage (the *mukhannathun*
often functioned as matchmakers – bringing to mind the connection of
Indian *hijras* and African transgendered people with marriage), he told
the bride she needed to have her excitement at the prospect of marital
bliss cooled – which he could do by having sex with her. He then told
her he would perform the same service for the groom (being the passive
partner for the groom). This tale is usually given by Arabic chroniclers to
explain the order by Sulayman to castrate all *mukhannathun*. However,
they all make it clear that his wrath was because of the corruption of the
woman. As with the Prophet, what worried Sulayman was the ability of
mukhannathun to cross into sequestered, female-only space.

The behaviour of al-Dalal and the association of *mukhannathun* with
song and sodomy finds an echo in the classical Arabic literature in the
centuries after the Prophet's death, and the massive geographical extension of Islam through the Middle East, North Africa and Moorish
Iberia. This Islamic-Arabic world of the caliphs witnessed one of the
greatest flowerings of literature, the arts and science – a period of
accomplishment and refinement to rival anything produced by Europe
during the Renaissance. Indeed, the Renaissance would have been a
much poorer thing (if it had happened at all) were it not for the
accomplishments of the classical Islamic world into which it tapped.

This sophisticated and urbanised Islamic world produced some fascinating poetry. A number of scholars have seen in this literature proof
of a society with relaxed and tolerant attitudes towards homosexuality. However, many scholars argue that much of the poetry seems to

have played a role in political and religious satire and protest that the former assumption must be considered with caution. Perhaps the safest thing to say is that the literature implies a social awareness of same-sex activities, which suggests that it was not unknown or hidden. Using 'gay' or 'homosexual' as derogatory terms or to make people laugh does not mean that the society accepts the behaviour. However, it certainly suggests that homosexuality is not an unspoken taboo. Thus, while the discussion that follows might lead to a view that classical Islamic society was homophilic (that is, either pro-gay or tolerant) it is perhaps better to think that it was more a society in which homosexuality was 'visible' if not especially 'liked'.

One of the key poets in this discussion is Abu-Nuwas (from Ahvaz, Persia; *c.*755–*c.*815), who was an Arab poet who spent most of his life in Baghdad. He was well-regarded by Harun al-Rashid (766–809; fifth caliph – reigned 786–809 – of the Abbasid dynasty) and Amin (787–813; sixth caliph – reigned 810–813) and lived a courtier's life. His poetry celebrated wine and the extravagance of this life. His poetry also used sexual imagery to shock, titillate and amuse while poking fun at the assumptions and morals of the day. For example, in the following poem he not only extolled wine-drinking but also homosexuality:

> *So if the wine comes round*
> *seize it and give it to me!*
> *Give me a cup of distraction*
> *from the Mu'adhdhin's call* [to prayer]
> *Give me wine to drink publicly*
> *and bugger and fuck me now.*

Even today, the verses have the power to shock. But do they make Abu-Nuwas or his listeners homosexual or exponents of 'gay rights'? Or do the verses simply suggest that the urban elite who patronised Abu-Nuwas were amused by the risqué and shocking – and, perhaps, more inclined to view such behaviour with indulgence and amusement in private (regardless of any public stance on drunkenness or same-sex acts)?

In some cases, though, one would have to suggest that the views expressed by the poet are perhaps more revealing when applied by the poet to himself. Thus, al-Badri (who wrote somewhat later than Abu-Nuwas) said he would prefer earthly pleasures over heavenly ones were God to give him a choice: '[give me each day of life] a handful of hashish, a pound of meat, a kilo of bread, and the company of a willing boy'. This may well be a joke but, if so, it is rather personal.

Other writers indulged in the conceit of comparing opposites or pairs of ideas and things that could be contrasted for the amusement of the reader and to provide a showcase for the wit of the writer. The fourteenth-century writer al-Safadi explained this genre:

Some have written works comparing the virtues of the rose and the narcissus… In the same way, excellent authors have written on debates about the sword and the pen… [the differences] between stinginess and generosity, between Egypt and Syria… between Arabs and [Persians], between poetry and prose, and between girls and beardless boys, for in all these cases arguments in favour of either side are possible… Al-Jahiz has written an original essay on the subject.

The sexual charms of adolescent males and females were, in this genre, treated as fit subjects for discussion. Moreover, both were seen as having merit and appeal. The treatise of the Islamic writer, al-Jahiz (776–869) mentioned is almost certainly his *The Mutual Rivalry of Maidens and Young Men*. A later essay (*Synopsis of All that is known about Pleasure* by al-Katib, 1036-1124 CE) developed al-Jahiz's theme and almost certainly made use of a (now lost) humorous, if coarse, piece on the subject by al-Saymari (828-888).

The basic premise is the same. There is a debate (in the form of a dialogue) between a *luti* (male homosexual) who takes the part of the *sahib* (boys) and a *zani* (fornicator) who defends the girls. The *luti* makes great and effective play with the tradition of *ghulamiyat* or girls who dressed like boys to excite men. Indeed, the *luti* opens the debate by reminding everyone that 'when one wants to describe a girl as beautiful, one says that she is like a boy'. The debate ends in a virtual draw though there is a sense that the refinement and beauty of the adolescent male might just perhaps win out.

Just as interesting, though, are some of the specific ideas within the debate. When questioned about Islam's anti-homosexual views, the *luti* responds that he 'does not know those *hadiths*', which implies they have no real value. It is also fascinating that every known poet of the early Abbasid period is mentioned and Abu-Nuwas takes pride of place. There are even quotations from pre-Islamic Arabic poets. Two key judges (al-'Awfi, d.*c*.816, and Yahya bin Aktham, d.857) are specifically noted for their favourable views about homosexuality. While the treatises (more or less part of a single on-going literary conceit) are amusing and witty there is every reason to suppose that they also contain some covert and implied attempts to suggest a tolerance of, and understanding for, homosexual attraction – especially the allure of the adolescent male.

Basically, this poetic tradition rests securely on an open and socially accepted appreciation of the adolescent male form by other men. The adolescent male was erotic and beautiful to other (older) men. Moreover, since most Islamic cultures of the time disapproved of any open discussion of the female as an object of sexual desire – at least any respectable female – the way one wrote 'love poetry' was largely confined to the discussion of the male form. By the end of the classical period (corresponding with the end of the West's Middle Ages) two genres of homoerotic poetry had developed. First, licentious and coarse poems (*mujun*) spoke in graphic detail about sex between men and suggest a rejection of societal norms in blunt terms. The second genre was of a 'romantic' variety and tended to ignore or sentimentalise the physicality of male-male attraction. This latter has much in common with the French chivalric poetry of the later Middle Ages in which knights and pages are deeply in love but seem never to manage to do much about it.

Thus one sees unrequited sentiments expressed by the Andalusian poet ibn Quzman (d.1160):

> *Should I love one who is hostile to me?*
> *Deliver me from such! Give me one who is compliant;*
> *[Who], when I drink, will fill and pour for me.*
> *What sort of beloved is one who won't [meet me],*
> *So that I can press him, all night long, to me breast,*
> *And remain with him thus, all my life?*

These represent the artistic end of the 'debate' about the male form
while other verses are just as homoerotic but much less refined. For
example, one reads ibn Rashiq's (d.*c.*1070) quotation of ibn al-Rumi's
(836–896) epigram:

> *He has a skilful groom*
> *Who rides upon his back,*
> *And pokes him in the ass,*
> *With thrust on piercing thrust*
> *Of what is longer than his horns*
> *And thicker than his wits.*

Both presuppose and, in their own way, extol homosexual attraction
– though ibn Rashiq was probably not too wrong in calling the second
poem 'the most malicious thing I have ever heard in this genre of
poetry'. The key point is that both are part of the larger genre of
erotic love poetry about the charms of homoerotic attraction.

Other literary forms echoed these poetic genres of licentious and
romantic homoeroticism. Two examples from Egypt in the period will
serve to stand for the rest. In a 'letter' by al-Safadi (d.1363), entitled
Plaint of the Lovelorn and Tears of the Disconsolate, as well as his poetic
anthology, *the Pure Beauty of One Hundred Handsome Boys* the author
treated the subject of homoeroticism. The story is simple, telling how
the fictional author of the letter saw a group of lovely youths, fell for
one, convinced him of his ardour and, later, shared a night of unbri-
dled passion with him. The lover then suffers great anguish as he wonders if and when he will next see his beloved. All of this springs from
the idea that falling in love is about the worst disaster that can befall
someone. The sheer pathos of love is best expressed by one tear-filled
interchange (and the work is bathed in tears of loving and longing):

Beloved: *'Why do you weep when I am here before you?'*
Lover: *'Only because of my certainty of our imminent parting.'*

Although the work is largely about the dangers and consequences of
love, it is also full of the actual joys of love. More importantly it deals

with the question of God's views on this love directly when the lover speaks to his beloved:

> I ask God for forgiveness for anything but my love for you,
> For it will be counted as my good deed on the day I meet Him.
> But if you claim that love is a sin,
> Love is surely the most trivial of ways that one can sin against God.

This is not a devil-may-care rejection of Islamic thinking about sex between men. Rather, it is an articulation of an idea that a loving God will surely not destroy someone for being in love or acting out of love.

The more blatant alternative view was to be found in a shadow play (for marionette-like flat figures moving behind a thin screen) by Ibn Daniyal (d.1310) who was much admired (if not imitated) by al-Safadi. Daniyal's play, *The Man Distracted by Passion and the Little Vagabond Orphan*, makes many of the same points about the dangers of love as the *Plaint* of al-Safadi but in crude rather than romantic phrases. Interestingly, the play opens with a debate on the relative merits of beardless youths (younger adolescents) and bearded youths (in their late teens and early twenties). Having established that there is nothing wrong in the lover longing for a beloved who is slightly older the play moves on to discuss the anguish of the lover in the throes of (somewhat) unrequited love.

Having seen his beloved in a bathhouse, the lover (al-Mutayyam) extols the beauty of his body at length and then rushes out after him only to fall flat on his face. The beloved, al-Yutayyim, stops to help him up and allows him to steal a kiss but when:

[al-Mutayyam] *put* [his] *hand on that gentle hill of his buttock, seeking a draught from that reservoir…* [the beloved] *said to* [the lover], *'Not so fast, Mutayyam! Not everything smooth is a pancake!'*

and departed leaving Mutayyam prostrate. Despite his best efforts Mutayyam gets nowhere and eventually attempts to entice his beloved to a feast to ply him with food and drink. However, his beloved fails to make an appearance and he is left entertaining a parade of men devoted to virtually every type of same-sex activity.

It is this last part of the play that is the most illuminating for us as it provides insight into the variety of social constructions for homo-sexual activity (whether approved or not) in Egyptian society in the period. Some we have already seen while others will be discussed in greater detail in subsequent chapters. The first to appear are Narjisa and Bashnina who are *mukhannath*. They sing a song which begins: 'If I should desire anyone other than al-Zubayri,/May my ass never enjoy a penis'. Narjisa then tells about 'giving birth' to a turd in the com-pany of other *muhkannath* and 'their men'. Mutayyam offers him wine and Narjisa dances and drinks until he passes out.

Next on the scene is Abu l-Sahl, a rather chubby fellow who tells of the 'wide welcome' (for cash) he gives everyone and laments the 'narrow' morals of the beloved. He also dances and drinks himself into insensi-bility (as does everyone else except the poor bereft Mutayyam). Al-Khannaqa then appears and says he is as narrow as l-Sahl was wide and will only allow intercrural sex. Before he passes out he indulges in some crude poetry about advances being made on his person by Mutayyam:

> *How big your thing is, Uncle! Slowly, slowly! Ouch! Mother!*
> *Be content with it outside! Not inside!*
> *Let it rub against the hair,*
> *Or put it in the gap,*
> *But don't tear open my ass with it!*

The next guest is called Baddal, who is famous for *bidal* – or taking turns being passive or active. His sage advice is that Mutayyam should just find someone else, especially someone like himself as his type of sex makes more sense.

The next set of guests remove love and sex even further from one another and, indeed, beloved and loved. Al-Qabbad appears to suggest that frottage or mutual masturbation is best while al-Jallad says self-masturbation is not only cleaner (than anal sex) but also avoids the law. He claims he can have sex with any youth whenever he wants – though only in his head. He says to Mutayyam, '[imagine] your beloved, despite his aloofness, and "whip 'Umayra" and say "this is in him"!'

The final three guests are nothing short of bizarre. Al-Dabbab explains that his method is simply to sneak up on sleeping youths and rape them. This causes Mutayyam to give him lots of wine and exclaim: 'No sleep for me tonight'. Al-Shashshi seems to extol the virtues of ascetic celibacy but succumbs to the wine too quickly to be clear. The final guest is al-Tufayli who has nothing to do with sex and is simply a glutton who gatecrashes parties. Although there is no food left by this point, Mutayyam manages to placate him with copious amounts of wine. The play closes with the arrival of the Angel of Death, Mutayyam's subsequent repentance and almost instantaneous demise.

Although these two works (a letter and a play) combine with the various types of poetry to give us some interesting insights into the way classical Islamic culture structured homosexuality, they must be treated with caution. These are fictional accounts in very stylised forms mostly aimed at amusing and titillating. They are not factual accounts of homosexual life in Damascus, Baghdad or Cairo in the period. However, they do suggest an easiness in the society with ideas of homosexuality and homoeroticism. In particular, they serve to reinforce the view that homosexual desire was seen as part of the human condition in Islamic society even when homosexual acts were sinful.

When we turn to Islamic jurisprudence (largely developed in this period) this important difference between the ideas of Islam and Western Christianity becomes even more apparent. Christianity takes the view that homosexuality is 'a sin contrary to nature' that is, against the natural predisposition of any and all 'natural' (normal) people. Islamic thought expresses something entirely different. It accepts that attraction to another male by a man is perfectly natural while disapproving of any resulting action. Thus the jurist ibn al-Jawzi (d.1200) said 'he who claims that he experiences no desire when looking at beautiful [adolescent males], is a liar, and if we could believe him, he would be an animal, not a human being'. In other words, only a mindless brute could be immune to the charms of a youth. Or, to make the contrast with Christianity more obvious:

same-sex attraction [was] *viewed as natural, surrendering to a natural temptation* [such as sodomy, wine-drinking, adultery] [could] *not make the individual abnormal – merely sinful.*

When one couples this view with the requirements for a conviction (either an outright confession – with three chances to retract – or four witnesses to a specific act of penetration) one senses that homosexuals had a fair amount of 'social space' for manoeuvre.

Though ambiguous, the situation for homosexuals in classical Islamic society is redolent with detail. Sadly, we know less about Africa south of the Sahara. As with earlier periods, it is almost impossible to speak about Africa during these centuries with any certainty. This period saw the spread of contact and trade with Islam and Arabia along the coast of East Africa leading to the conversion to Islam of some peoples (especially in Somalia and along the Kenyan coast). As already mentioned, some Africans would argue today that it was this contact with 'decadent' Muslims that led to the introduction of sodomitical practices into indigenous societies.

We can, however, hypothesise to some extent based upon extrapolations from religious beliefs later observed among African cultures largely untouched by outside influences. Religion is, by its very nature, extremely conservative and often preserves some of the oldest ideas, stories and views a people have about themselves. Where this specifically relates to our discussion is in the realm of cross-dressing and transgendered behaviour. Both refer to individuals adopting the costume, mannerisms and work of the opposite gender from their biological own. Before looking at such behaviour in Africa it is essential to remember that this does *not* imply same-sex genital contact. A person can rebel against gendered norms in their society without being sexually attracted to, or involved with, members of their own biological sex. A man can dress, act and work as a woman, and yet never have sex with another man. However, one also has to say that there is nothing which would preclude these individuals from engaging in homosexual practices. To imply that someone who cross-dresses is necessarily gay is as ludicrous as suggesting that a cross-dressing black African shaman could not engage in same-sex relations simply because he is black.

A number of African societies have individuals associated with magic, religion and the spiritual who engage in transgendered behaviour. For example, among the Kwayama of Angola many male spiritual leaders wear women's clothing, engage in 'female' work and even become the 'wives' of men who will almost certainly have other wives who are biologically female. Sex may form a part of this relationship (today and in the past) although it may also be that these husbands simply want a wife or two with the physical strength of a man. What is clear, though, is this traditional belief suggests that Kwayama culture has constructed a niche for transgendered individuals. More importantly, these people have been given a privileged place in the culture as spiritual leaders (compare with the North American *berdache* in chapters 5 and 6).

Zulu society also has mediums who cross-dress. Indeed, a medium – a person who allows the dead to give guidance to the living – is considered to be female. It is the work of a woman to be a medium. This does not seem to be contradicted by the fact that the medium may actually be a man in women's dress. In this construction, the man (man-woman) is accepted as a woman while performing the role of a medium – and called 'chief of the women' (*inkosi ygbatfazi*). This is similar to the sort of 'suspension of belief' that one sees in theatre and cinema (it would also suggest that we should take care in reading too much into the use of boys and youths to play women in Shakespearean plays). Again, there is no assumption that these mediums engage in sex with other men – nor is there any reason to assume categorically that they do not. It does stress that humans, when they wish, are able to reconstruct gender and biology in a way that simply ignores 'biological' reality – which is itself a subjective, socially constructed idea!

This point is made more effectively among some groups in Zimbabwe, for example, the Ila. Here, a cross-dressing male is assumed to be a medium (or prophet, *mwaami*), someone involved in the spirit-world rather than a homosexual involved in sex with other men. Westerners, in their own social construction, see a man in women's clothing and assume this implies information about the person's sexual practices. Africans in Zimbabwe would see the same man and infer information about the person's religious and spiritual behaviour. Admittedly, the Ila do seem to have been aware that a *mwaami* might be involved in pederasty but their only concern in such cases was based on the belief that the youth might become pregnant. The key point is that traditional practices suggest that some Africans, prior to outside influences, lived in societies in which transvestite males lived alongside men and women who conformed to more socially common gender identity roles. In these African societies the issue about these transgendered people was *not* their sex lives but rather their ability to perform specific, important spiritual roles.

The historian James Sweet has said that:

> *those scholars who have dismissed African homosexuality as aberrant behaviour or the product of European colonialism have failed to recognise the traditional religious importance of Africa's homosexual population.*

This perhaps overstates the case and makes inferences which say more about a modern construction of transgenderism than African history. It is perhaps safer to say that 'those scholars who have dismissed African homosexuality as aberrant behaviour or the product of European colonialism have failed to recognise the traditional religious importance' of non-normative and non-conformist patterns of gender identity amongst African societies. These patterns do not imply a prevalence of, or even familiarity with, same-sex behaviour. What they do imply quite clearly, though, is a nuance to African constructions of gender and sex, which would easily allow for same-sex acts to occur.

When one considers India, openness to same-sex relations are even more obvious. More importantly, India gives us even greater scope for an examination the social construction of gender, as well as cultural attitudes to homosexuality than Africa. The reality is that not only do many of the earliest texts refer to same-sex relationships but a range of words exist for this type of behaviour. Late medieval Urdu poets, referring to women 'clinging or sticking together', use *chapti*. The eleventh-century *Kathasaritsagara* uses the expression '*svayamvara* [self-chosen lover/bridegroom] *sakhi* [female friend]' to describe relations between two women.

The stories developed in the period about the gods are equally open and illuminating. One of the more interesting accounts relates to the birth of Kartikeya (god of war and leader of the armies of the gods – a more 'masculine' role is hard to imagine). He is usually depicted as a handsome young bachelor riding on a peacock. The three most common accounts of his birth are virtually identical. In the most common (from the *Shiva Purana*, *c*.750–1350 CE) Agni, the god of fire, swallows the semen of Shiva (god of destruction) and suffers from a 'burning sensation', which only goes away when he transfers the semen to the wombs of the wives of the sages from whose wombs it then falls into the Ganga, then onto the grass with the resulting 'creation' (birth) of Kartikeya. The two other most common accounts are similar (with minor variations at the beginning). In the *Skanda Parva*, Igni interrupts sex between Shiva and Parvati (daughter of the mountain, mountain goddess, etc) and catches Shiva's semen in his hands and swallows it. In the *Kathasaritsagara* (*c*.1000 CE) Shiva *forces* Agni to swallow his semen. All accounts accept that the act is 'impure', 'wicked' and 'improper' but it is also clearly not *uncreative* allowing for an alternative form of procreation, which produces a god.

Kartikeya's brother, Ganesha (the elephant-headed god; god of wisdom; remover of obstacles, etc.) is also generated in a non-normative fashion. He is the child of Shiva and Parvati. In some accounts he is produced by Shiva alone and elsewhere by the mingling of the generative fluids of Shiva and Parvati outside the womb. In most, though, Ganesha is produced by Parvati alone. In the *Shiva Purana*, Parvati tires of the constant invasion of her 'space' by her husband Shiva and rubs Ganesha from her body (rather as the Judaeo-Christian God fashions Adam from clay). In another version her bathwater (in the Ganga) is swallowed by Malini (an elephant-headed female) who gives birth to Ganesha. As with his brother, he is a bachelor.

In these two creation myths one sees the god Kartikeya created by a 'sexual' act (oral) between two men while his brother Ganesha is, at least in some versions, the result of a similar act between two females. What is interesting is that two of the most powerful gods in the Hindu pantheon, the god of war and the god of wisdom (who sits as the doorkeeper outside most Hindu homes) are the result of non-heterosexual procreation. While the gods of Greece and Rome may have indulged in parthenogenesis (generation by a single individual, e.g.

Zeus 'birthing' Athena) and Christianity has the generation of Jesus by incarnation without any actual sexual act, Hinduism has two of its greatest gods created by some sort of exchange of procreative power between individuals of the same sex. It is these images and stories, which give to Indian-Hindu culture an attitude to same-sex relations more ambiguous that that found in pagan Greece and Rome.

The relationship between Shiva and Parvati is even more complex than that suggested above. In the *Marsya Purana*, a certain King Ila enters Parvati's grove, where no man may enter and is transformed into a woman (and his stallion into a mare). Indeed, in the *Ramayana* account, even Shiva becomes female before entering the grove to make love to Parvati – the transformation all the more startling as Shiva is the 'absolute male' god worshipped across India in the form of the *lingam* (phallus). King Ila (now female) marries Budha (son of the moon). His brothers beg Shiva to change him back and Shiva, in part, relents decreeing that Ila become a *kimpurusha* – a man one month, a woman the next. Ila (thereafter called Sudyumna) produces children both as a father and a mother in subsequent relationships.

However, this period is most important for two major developments. The first was the arrival and dominance of Islam, which culminated in the establishment of the Mughal Empire in 1526 when Babur (r.1526–30) defeated Ibrahim Lodi, last Sultan of Delhi at the First Battle of Panipat. The Mughal position was further consolidated by Humayan (r.1530–56). However, the importance of the impact of Islam must await the next chapter.

The second major development of this period, which is extremely important for understanding the ongoing story of homosexuality in India, is its 'medieval' period. In the seventh century, at the very beginning of this period, a new form of religious devotion developed in, and spread from, south India. This is known as *Bhakti* and refers to a collection of movements centred around the mystical, loving devotion to a particular god or goddess. While some have seen this as a movement trying to overcome the problems both of the cycle of reincarnation and the 'damning' impact of caste, the reality is much more complex. Put simply and simplistically, *Bhakti* is a path to liberation that focuses on *perma* (love) more than *jnana* (knowledge). Love, desire

and sexual pleasure are not just a celebration of the human experience but also integral to attaining higher knowledge, and a means to
comprehending aspects of the profundity of the divine. As such it was
a means of escape (liberation) from the cycle of rebirth open to
anyone, of all castes – including not only untouchables in general, but
also women and even Muslims.

One major development associated with the *Bhakti* movement was
the completion of Puranic literatures (largely a product of the period
discussed in the previous chapters: most were composed *c.*200-100 BCE
with major redactions *c.*300–400 and *c.*600–700 – with the final form
achieved *c.*1200–1300). These produced the pantheon of gods and goddesses, which are now worshipped by Hinduism. The structure of
Puranic (literally, 'old stories') deities is considerably more complex
and multifaceted than that of the original Vedic writings from the
ancient period. Deities and stories associated with Vishnu and Shiva
came to the fore and the mother goddess, eclipsed somewhat in Vedic
literature, re-emerged in the worship of Shaktism and Tantrism.

As Ruth Vanita stresses, the development of the Puranic pantheon
and its ongoing importance plays a critical role in the story of sex,
sexuality and gender in India:

*The single most remarkable feature of the medieval stories of the deities is their mul-
tiplicity and variability. Almost any variation that can be imagined* [particularly in
the 'forms' assumed by the deities] *exists somewhere… The Puranic gods are not
just celebrated as omnipresent in a philosophical sense* [as is the Christian deity]*;
the stories of their doings represent them as taking all forms… including humans of
different ages, castes and genders* [as well as various animals, etc… This] *allows for
the deifying of all actions and every way of life.*

Thus, Shiva (as Ardhnarisvara – 'the Lord who is half woman') is represented as male on the right side and female on the left side; Arjuna
is frequently described in a similar way (*trtiyam prakrtim* – 'something
of a man, something of a woman' about him). As we have seen in the
Graeco-Roman pantheon, polytheism allows for a flexible view of
gender (and other forms of existence or incarnation) with a resulting
more holistic – and positive – view of sexuality in all its myriad forms.

Hinduism, if anything, presents an even more holistic and extreme view of 'deity in everything and everywhere' than the gods of Greece and Rome.

An excellent example of the impact of these permutations of divinity, as it relates to sexuality, is present in the story of Krishna's incarnation as the woman Mohini, which is told in Tamil versions of the *Mahabharata*. Arjuna's son, Aravan, offers himself as a sacrificial victim to the god Kali to aid his father and uncles in victory. Before death he is granted three wishes one of which is that he should marry. Since no family was willing to give a daughter to someone about to be killed, Krishna incarnated himself as Mohini and married Aravan for a night. This double 'sacrifice' is celebrated annually in Tamilnadu by *hijras* (on whom more below) portraying themselves as the sex-changing Krishna. Even at their most inventive, Graeco-Roman myths did not posit deity as so fluid and malleable!

A similar sort of loving devotion is visible to this day in the Ramanandis, an all-male community in eastern India. This group emerged in the 1400s as devotees of the monkey god, Hanuman (an incarnation of Shiva and servant of Rama). The celibate branch of the movement identifies itself with Hanuman and other men who became women to serve Sita (an incarnation of the goddess of wealth Lakshmi – consort of Vishnu) who married Rama (brother of an incarnation of Krishna). In their devotions to Sita these celibate males share in her union with Rama. In Ayodhya (scene of numerous clashes between Hindus and Muslims), these devotees take female names, dress as women and claim to experience menstruation as part of their 'transformation' into the female servants of Sita – by which they replicate the actions of Hanuman and the other males who originally took on female form to serve Sita. A similar devotion is apparent in some modern Vishnu cults (e.g. Sakhibhava) where male devotees take the role of Radha, Krishna's consort, and simulate menstruation. In northern Karnatak (south India), devotees of the goddess Yellamma (identified with Ranuka) adopt female names, clothing, occupations and ornaments, and call themselves *jogappa* ('sacred female men'). Paramahamsa Sri Ramakrishna (1836-86), dressed as a woman and so longed after Krishna that he was like the 'woman of Vrindavan' and 'sweat blood from the pores of his body'. Another commentator, discussing Krishna's beauty, mentioned 'the desire, on the part of men who see him, which takes the form of the thought, "If I were a woman, I would enjoy him sexually"'.

The two stories above of Mohini and Hanuman come together in the Puranas (c.850–950) relating to Shiva and Vishnu (both, technically, male gods). In the *Brahmanda Purana* Parvati, wife of Shiva, stands head bowed in embarrassment as Shiva chases lustily after Mohini (the female incarnation of Vishnu). In some versions, Shiva specifically asks Vishnu to take on the Mohini form as he had heard of its beauty. In these accounts, then, Shiva is knowingly lusting after a female 'form' of a male god whom he knows personally. The *Shiva Purana*, in one version of the Hunaman story, says that:

one day Shiva saw the Mohini form of Vishnu. He was struck by Kama's arrows and let fall his seed. The Seven Sages put the seed in a pot and they infused it into the daughter of Gautama through her ear. In time, Hanuman, the monkey-god, was born from it.

Again, the Puranic stories of Hindu gods and goddesses present an extremely fluid and ambiguous image of sex and sexuality among the deities. One can hardly imagine a religion having an extremely negative view of same-sex relations, transvestitism, transesexualism, etc, when two of its major gods (Shiva and Vishnu) are portrayed in sexual play while one 'pretends' to be female.

In the Ayyappa (celibate god, worshipped predominately in Kerala) legend, developed entirely in the medieval period, the relationship between Shiva and Vishnu is even less ambiguous. In this adjunct to the tale, Shiva (fully aware of the 'reality' behind the Mohini incarnation) has sex with Vishnu-Mohini who becomes pregnant and gives birth to Ayyappa – whom the medieval writers call *ayoni jata* (born of a 'not-vagina'). Eventually he becomes a great warrior defeating a powerful Muslim pirate, Vavar, who becomes his closest friend. In Ayyappa's temple in Sabarimalai, there is a shrine to Vavar (whom Ayyappa commanded should be seen as himself), which is managed by Muslims. Thus, in this south Indian story, through same-sex contact the followers of Shiva and Vishnu are united in their worship of Ayyappa-Hariharaputra (the son of Vishnu and Shiva) and Muslim and Hindus find union in the close

'companionship' of Ayyappa and Vavar. This complex story is further
enriched by Ayyappa's additional celibate relationship with Leela (as the
goddess Mallikapurathamma) whom he refused to marry but whom he
did accept as a life-long companion, *shakti*. Ayyappa's temples portray
him with Leela's shrine on his left, Vavar's on his right.

Thus, as the celibate god, he unites all major strands not only of
religion in the subcontinent but also of companionship – and his
celibacy is all the more potent as he shares it with his two brothers:
Kartikeya (god of war) and Ganesha (god of wisdom). Few elements
of Hindu religion can more effectively demonstrate the ambiguity of
attitudes to sex and sexuality. Companionship (love/friendship) is of
paramount importance but not to the exclusion of sex/marriage (Shiva
and Mohini-Vishnu). Both aspects of interpersonal relationships are
placed firmly within a context of same-sex and opposite-sex attraction, which presents both as valid and acceptable. The ambiguity at the
level of the divine, the 'model' for human existence, is nowhere more
clear than in hymns to Shiva: 'Homage to the one who is female and
male, to the *napumsakam* [third nature/sex]'; 'You are the Parusa whose
seed is golden, you are woman, you are man, you are *napumsakam*'.

However, at this point it is useful to return to the story of Arjuna
and Krishna, since a significant reworking of the story of their
relationship takes place in the medieval period as commentators
explained, amplified and reinterpreted the *Mahabharata*. In the *Padma
Purana* (c.1100s), Arjuna is so enamoured of Krishna that he begs to
see Krishna's 'dance of love' (*rasaleela*). His request is granted but he is
overcome with love and passes out. Arjuna's devotion to the goddess
Tripurasundari had allowed his initial glimpse of Krishna's dance and,
on her advice, he bathes in a lake and emerges as a woman, Arjuni. In
this form, she is loved by Krishna and, exhausted by 'all the sports in
the forest', Arjuni is told to bathe again in the lake and emerges as
Arjuna, the male. Desolate and disconsolate, he is mollified by Krishna
who touches him, revealing his nature and says:

*O [Arjuna], I bless you, my dear [male] friend. There is no one equal to you... as
you know my secret. O Arjuna, you will curse me if you tell anyone about the secret
which you... have experienced.*

In this manner the 'loving companionship' (*sakhya*) of Arjuna for Krishna seen in the *Mahabharata* of the classical period is, at times, transformed in medieval versions of the text into 'erotic love' (*madhurya*).

It is also at the end of this period that we can begin to move from the realm of the divine and mythic to that of the human and historic. Jagannath Das (1490-1550) was a poet-mystic, author of the *Bhagahata* famed throughout Orissa (on the Bay of Bengal). For our purposes, the important element is his relationship (as a disciple) with *Shri* Chaitanya, which began when Das was nineteen. The biographical *Jagannath Charitamrita* describes the meeting thus:

[Chaitanya] *was delighted to hear Jagannath Das's rendition* [of the Sanskrit *Bhagahata* into Orrissan]. *Overwhelmed with love he held Das in a tight embrace* [in which they stayed] *for two days and a half.*

These two men are seen as the products of the love between Krishna and Radha (Krishna's favourite 'cowherd maiden'). Their relationship was so close that Chaitanya referred to Das as his *sakhi* (female friend) and in some accounts Das is given female names (e.g. Tinkini). The men eschewed sexual liaisons though both were accused of immorality arising from their close relationships with each other and other young men.

In addition to the spread of literature, the growth of Islam (presaging the arrival of the Mughal conquerors) had a great impact on India. However, it was the advent of Sufism which, indirectly and unintentionally, had the greatest impact on the complex relationship of Islam, Hinduism and sex. Fundamental to Sufism (in either its more popular form − *ba shara*; within the *Shariah* − or the minority, less dogmatic form − *be shara*; without the *Shariah*) was the devoted and loving relationship between the *pir* (master), called 'friend of God' (*wali*) and his disciple (*murid*) which flourished in the monastic communities (*khanqahs*) of the various 'orders' (*silsillas*). The master educated his disciple and then sent him into the wider world to establish his own community. With an emphasis on the master-disciple relationship rather than dogma, Sufism appealed to many Hindu converts to Islam. A similar devotion is present in the relationship between the Baul teacher (*guru*) and his students, where the students are taught not only about the body and the universe but also led to the deity. Sufist devotion focused on songs, dancing and the mention of God's name in meditative chanting rather than the traditional, Arabic prayers of Islam. As such, both the structure and devotion were more familiar to traditional Hindu practices making conversion easier (if perhaps less 'complete' in the eyes of traditional purists). Moreover, this relationship very much followed the pre-existing Indian-Hindu model of same-sex love/friendship as the premier focal point for an individual's emotional life.

With the advent of papermaking (in the later medieval period) and the growth of urbanisation, other same-sex relationships – with a more explicit sexual component – become visible to us. In particular the Sufi mystic poets (in the same vein as Das) produced love poems (*ghazals*), which focused largely on the attractiveness of 'bazaar boys' and other male youths. Muslim poets (Mir, Madho Lal Hussayn, Ras Khan and Sarmad) all wrote not only of love for youthful males but, especially, Hindus. They even competed for the attention of an individual 'beloved' and were referred to as 'boy worshippers' (*amrad parast*), 'worshippers of beauty' (*husn parast*), 'professional lovers' (*ishq pesha*), or as having a 'colourful/amorous character' (*rangeen/ashiq mijaz*).

The writings of Islamic poets underline elements seen elsewhere in Arabic-Moorish culture (see above) though more starkly as a result of interaction with the more sexually ambiguous and charged Hindu environment. Amir Khusro (1253–1325) is generally hailed as one of India's greatest mystic poet-musicians and, as a saint, the anniversary of his death is one of the most popular Sufi religious celebrations. He wrote a number of verses extolling the beauty, and lamenting the danger, of beautiful Hindi youths:

> The Muslims have become sun-worshippers
> Because of these simple sprightly Hindu boys.
> I am desolate and intoxicated
> Because of these pure Hindu boys…
> Beloved, if at night I put my lips to yours,
> Pretend to be asleep – don't ask whose mouth this is…
> Oh lord, is this me with my shoulder next to my beloved?

Have I been in bed sleeping by his side?...
Don't tie a hand around your waist,
Let me wrap my hands around instead.

We will return to this type of Islamic love poetry later.

It is perhaps worth ending this discussion of homosexuality and India not only with the arrival of the first Mughal emperor (Zahiruddin Muhammed, called Babur; 1483–1530) but also with a brief account from his autobiography, the *Baburnama*, which echoes the thoughts of the poets already discussed:

In those leisurely days I discovered a strange inclination, nay! As the verse says, 'I maddened and afflicted myself' for a boy in the camp-bazaar, his very name, Baburi [Babur's], appropriate. Up until then I had had no inclination for anyone, indeed of love and desire, either by hearsay or experience, I had not heard, I had not talked... From time to time Baburi used to come to my presence but out of modesty and bashfulness, I could never look straight at him [let alone talk to him]... One day during that time of desire and passion when I was going with companions along a [road] and suddenly met him face to face, I got into such a state of confusion that I almost ran away... In that frothing-up of desire and passion and under that stress of youthful folly, I used to wander bareheaded and barefooted through street and lane, orchard and vineyard... sometimes like the madman, I used to wander alone over hill and plain... my wandering was not of my choice; I did not control whither I went or stayed:
Nor power to go was mine, nor power to stay;
I was just what you made me, O thief of my heart
[Turkish couplet]

Let us leave India then, with its images of gods and goddesses in various sexual permutations and its first Islamic ruler wandering confused, dazed by his love for a Hindu youth.

Though less confused and less ambiguous, the situation in China suggests parallels with India. Of course, China was not facing a religious and cultural invasion of the same magnitude in this period. Thus, continuity remained the hallmark of Chinese attitudes to sexuality. The open attitude to polysexuality at the highest level of Chinese society continued through subsequent successor states and pan-China dynasties. The continuity of views about same-sex relationships is all the more important as these views accompanied and survived the ongoing development of Chinese religion and philosophy. The First Intermediate period (220–581 – Sanguo, Jin, Shiliuguo and Nanbeichao), the Sui and Tang dynasties of the Middle Imperial period (581–907), and even the chaotic situation of the Second Intermediate period (907–c.965), and the predecessor states of the Third Imperial period (c.965–1277) saw the consolidation of Confucianism with its emphasis on filial piety, as well as Taoism and the integration of Buddhist ideas into the mainstream of Chinese thought. At no point did religion or philosophy begin to fixate on same-sex relationships or acts as a cause for concern let alone behaviour likely to invite divine retribution on society in general or to condemn individuals to any type of perpetual damnation.

Put simply, Chinese thought did not go down the route of a cosmology based on 'good *versus* evil' or 'grace or punishment' or 'natural/divinely decreed or unnatural/demonic'. Most importantly of all, through the various changes and developments in Chinese thought and belief, 'sex for pleasure' was never supplanted by 'sex for procreation'. In Chinese thought filial piety may have required procreation but it was not the expectation of a jealous god and was willing to accept other (pleasurable) expressions of sex and sexuality, as long as the duty to procreate was fulfilled.

These indigenous dynasties were brought to an abrupt end by the arrival of the Mongols and the establishment of the Yuan dynasty (1277–1367). There is some possibility that this foreign regime attempted to alter the native Chinese approach to same-sex relations. Certainly, there was a Mongolian law (predating the conquest of China) called the *Great Yassa* that decreed death for adultery and same-sex acts. However, there is no evidence from surviving legal codes passed under the Yuan emperors to suggest that this law was imposed in China. Moreover, some Western observers (e.g. the famed traveller, Marco Polo, 1254–1324) noted that the Mongolians were as accepting of – or given to – 'sodomy' as the Chinese.

Throughout the period of Chinese dynasties equivalent to Europe's medieval age, the classical stories of the 'shared peach' and the 'cut sleeve' remained fixed in the canon of Chinese literature and became part of the language itself. A similar situation in the West would have prevailed had the Roman Empire not fallen and had pagan culture not been superseded by Christianity. In such a situation, common parlance might have referred to participants in same-sex activities as 'Ganymedes' or such love as 'wearing another's armour' (*à la* Achilles and Patrolus). Indeed, classical Graeco-Roman literature would have provided a host of stories and role models for same-sex relationships.

China had such role models, stories, motifs and genres, all of which presented a positive view of same-sex relations within the context of the structure of society. This was not an approval of a modern view of gay relationships but rather an acceptance of polysexuality/bisexuality in a very socially stratified, specifically Chinese cultural setting. More importantly, Chinese culture continued to view procreation and enjoyment as equal elements of sexual activity. In addition, as with most other non-monotheistic societies, Chinese thought maintained a distinction between marriage (sex for procreation) and romantic affection (sex for pleasure and love).

So firmly embedded in Chinese culture were stories of same-sex relationships that they often formed part of the fabric of humour in popular literature as printing allowed not only for a wider familiarity with classical ideas but also the chance to hear the voices and views of a wider range of Chinese society. Consistently there is a total lack of animosity towards same-sex acts. One story, in particular, told of an interesting *ménage* of a husband, a wife and his male lover. During a visit, the mother-in-law asked her daughter who the young man was. The wife replied, 'my husband's husband'. Clearly, the male lover was an accepted part of the household and the story, widely read, presented the situation as simply amusing. If anything, the joke was on the mother-in-law. Likewise, one could say that the overriding cultural 'joke' was on the Mongols – as Islamicised Mughals they had a profound impact on India, as Mongols in China they became Chinese. The cultural stability of the Middle Kingdom remained intact.

The exploration of the African coast brought Europeans into contact with cultures with widely differing attitudes to gender, sex and sexuality from their own. However, the novelty of these new cultures was nothing compared to the shock European Christians received when they stumbled upon the societies of the Americas in the late 1400s. Columbus may have died convinced that he had arrived on the easternmost coasts of Asia but subsequent explorers quickly realised that the truth was much stranger. Europe had initiated contact with cultures so alien as to be almost unintelligible. These same Western explorers and conquerors also understood that these new civilisations were often extremely advanced technologically and socially. Despite the acceptance of the advanced nature of these societies, European Christians very quickly undertook their systematic destruction. Why?

In part, the violence wrought on the Americas was incidental to the arrival of Europeans. These new peoples brought with them diseases from which the inhabitants of the Western Hemisphere had been protected. In particular, smallpox wiped out entire populations and was, undoubtedly, the largest single factor in the collapse of these cultures in the face of European pressure. Hernando Cortés (1485–1547) and Francisco Pizarro (c.1478–1541) did not conquer with a handful of Spaniards, rather they occupied nations flattened by the catastrophic consequences of epidemic disease. However, the Americas were also subjected to a campaign of enslavement and forced labour that further depleted the populations of the Western Hemisphere.

These factors explain the demographic collapse of indigenous populations but they do not explain why so little is known of the histories, traditions, beliefs and cultures of civilisations such as the Aztec, Maya and Inca. When Europeans looked at the cultures they had 'discovered' they saw ideas and practices which they considered barbaric and demonic: human sacrifice, ritual cannibalism, polygamy, institutionalised sodomy and shameless nudity. These Western Christians concluded, on the basis of their pre-existing beliefs, that these new peoples were in the thrall of Satan, given over to the vilest practices imaginable as part of their service to the Prince of Darkness. It was essential that these people, converting to Christianity under threat and persuasion, should be cut off from their past. Being 'born again' was as much something for the society as the individual in the minds of missionaries trying to alter the cultures of the New World. Disease and mindless brutality destroyed the peoples of the New World, ideology and theology obliterated their histories.

What we have seen in this chapter is the slow spread of the idea of sex-for-procreation only from the Near East (its Jewish source) across the Mediterranean world down the coasts of West Africa (via Christianity) and East Africa (in Islamic thought). The Indian subcontinent fell under the rule of exponents of this idea (Islamicised Mughals). Finally, and catastrophically, this idea − once the possession of the small, inward-looking people of Israel − spread to the New World. The next two chapters will consider the lasting impact the spread of this idea has had. Before we turn to the 'modern' period one must pause to consider the situation on the eve of the explosion of Europeans onto the world stage. For the bulk of humanity, sex-as-procreation remained an important, even necessary, aspect of life but it was not the sole purpose for sex. Sex-for-pleasure as the focal point for love and emotion was still a type of sex which paid little attention to gender. Within the context of widespread and pervasive cultural impulses to procreate most societies managed to find niches for those whose tastes were for members of the same gender. More importantly, almost all societies seemed to have accepted that most men, in particular, would at some point in their lives have sexual contact and relationships with other men. That 'universal' norm was about to be placed under enormous pressure to give way to Judaeo-Christian-Islamic ideas that sex was about procreation, and pleasure was about sin.

five

Spreading Christian 'Values'

(1550–1800)

Because the White people thought it was evil
(Winnebago comment on the decline of *berdaches* – 1930s)

The disintegration of the Western (Roman) Church in the sixteenth century did not result in a lessening focus on sex or sexual activities. Indeed, with celibacy one of the key issues of debate between the papacy and nascent Protestantism, the issue of sexuality and sexual behaviour came to the fore. The sixteenth century, while disastrous for a unified ecclesiastical structure, proved to be a 'golden age' for moralists interested in controlling the interpersonal and sexual antics of their neighbours.

In the previous chapter we have seen how the rise of scapegoating after the Black Death and an increasing emphasis upon clerical celibacy had combined to move sexual issues to the fore both in popular and elite thought. Most of what we know of Europe between the fall of the empire in the fifth century and the mid-fourteenth century suggests a general disapproval of same-sex relations but a relatively relaxed response in practice. If couched in the terms of courtly romantic love and close (homosocial) friendships there was an even greater willingness to interpret behaviour and sentiments as non-sodomitical.

The situation in Europe on the eve of the sixteenth century was, as we have seen, altered. The religious crises of this new century would only make matters worse for homosexuals, Western Christianity splin tered into rival confessions, which confronted one another with violence and invective. Name-calling as a form of polemic – especially associated with attacking the morals of one's opponents – became a feature of the invective of the period. Protestants saw in Catholic celibacy a place for wanton promiscuity, concubinage, adultery and sodomy. Catholics looked on with horror as nuns, monks and priests converted and then married in violation of oaths they had taken before God and man to remain perpetually chaste. Sex was a stick with which to beat the other side throughout the Reformation period. And there was no doubt that the worst charge that one could level was to call an opponent a sodomite.

However, before the Reformation and throughout it, another movement held sway: Renaissance Humanism. Its emphasis upon recapturing the classical world with all its sophistication and civilisation worked to instil a different sentiment in the world from the Reformation to the Enlightenment. Italian art rejoiced in the male form in a way not seen since classical Greece. The great works of classical literature were recovered and widely translated into the vernacular languages of Europe – the drive for vernacular Bibles was simply part of the Humanist programme. The sensibilities of the ancients, including their love of the male form and the persons of adolescent youths, seeped into the Western cultural consciousness. Poets extolled male-male love. In theory, the love was spiritual in nature but most of the poetry (and some of the actions) are focused much more obviously on the physicality of lover and beloved. Even here, sex – in the form of physical beauty and intense emotional love – was a factor. Between the Reformation's use of sex as a confessional weapon and Humanism's interest in male love, relations between men were increasingly under scrutiny.

As we have seen with Richard the Lionheart, the behaviour of royalty was almost always exempt from censure. In the early modern period we have two similar and notorious cases: Henry III of France (1551–89) and James VI of Scotland (1566–1625) and I of England. While it would be historically inaccurate to focus exclusively on kings

alone they are worthy of some detailed discussion. Their behaviour
set the tone for their times and allowed others to engage in same-sex
relationships. Moreover, they allowed later moralists to react against
their reigns as periods of licentiousness as we have already seen in
Lucy Hutchinson's comments about the passing of James and his
catamites.

Henry III of France was born at the very beginning of this period.
At the age of eighteen he led France's Catholic armies in a brilliant
victory over her Protestant subjects. He was also noted for his love of
courtesans. However, he is most remembered for being the last of the
final three Valois kings (grandsons of Francis I) of France whose line
ended with his death in 1589 and the passing of the throne to the
House of Bourbon (Henry IV). In his day, though, he was mostly
notorious for his relationships with his *mignons* (darlings, dainties).

The *mignons* were an interesting group. They enjoyed causing scandal and their dandified and effeminate styles of clothing, deportment
and speech truly shocked French society (highly sensitised to religion
by the confessional strife of the Wars of Religion). Across the Channel
though, Englishmen with money rushed to copy this newest of French
fads (as they would the fripperies and fineries of Louis XIV's court)
which Pierre de l'Estoile (the famed diarist and commentator on
French politics and society, 1546–1611) described in his journal, 1576:

these pretty mignons *wore their hair pomaded, artificially curled and recurled, flowing back over their little velvet bonnets, like those of whores in a brothel, and the ruffs
of their starched linen shirts were half a foot long.*

Despite their appearances, Henry's *mignons* were known for their love
affairs with women each having not only a wife but usually a couple
of mistresses. The attachment of the king to some of his *mignons* was
real and emotional. When St-Megrin was killed in a duel, Henry had
him buried in his royal chapel which was, thereafter, nicknamed the
'temple of the *mignons*'. Thus, though effeminate, there is no reason to
assume that they engaged in same-sex practices nor is there any reason
to declare categorically that they did not. Effeminacy did not then (or
now) equate with sodomy.

In the case of James VI and I we have a much better sense of his (functional) bisexuality and have every reason to suppose that he was basically homosexual though he married and procreated for reasons of state. That James had heirs was integral to his chances of succeeding to the English throne upon the death of Elizabeth I; his strategy proved successful in 1603. Two particular studies have examined his life and loves in detail. The historian Michael Young (*King James and the History of Homosexuality*) located the king in the wider context of same-sex relationships and showed how a study of the man can be part of gaining a better concept of homosexuality in an historical context. David Bergeron (*King James and Letters of Homoerotic Desire*) focused on James's letters and his relationships with three royal favourites: Esmé (duke of Lennox, 1542–83), Robert Carr (earl of Somerset, *c.*1587–1645) and, most importantly of all, George Villiers (duke of Buckingham, 1592–1628).

James's first-known love was his thirty-three-year-old cousin, Esmé, with whom he formed a deep bond when only thirteen. This early love was especially strong but ended when Lord Lennox was exiled from Scotland for his supposed support for a Catholic restoration in the kingdom. In 1590, the Scottish king wed Anne, a Protestant Danish princess by whom he produced a number of children. Once in England, the two maintained wholly separate houses and households. James's court was noted for the large number of handsome young men kept on as retainers and courtiers. All James's favourites received noble titles and were given handsome presents. As with Henry and his *mignons*, James also saw to it that his favourites were wed to wealthy and/or well-established heiresses. On the occasion where some of his favourites followed their hearts and married when and whom they chose it was clear that the king was less than pleased.

The most important relationship that the king formed with a favourite was with the duke of Buckingham, George Villiers. We know a considerable amount about their closeness because of the large number of surviving letters that they wrote to each other over a ten-year period. The duke always called the king 'dad' and was, in turn, nicknamed 'Steenie' because James said Villiers resembled a picture of St Stephen he had seen in a stained-glass window of the Chapel

Royal. In addition to signing off his letters 'dad', the king also styled himself 'husband' and addressed Villiers as 'my sweet child and wife'.

It is not only from letters that we know about the affair between the two. Their public behaviour occasioned comment publicly and privately. One contemporary noted in his diary that:

In wanton looks and wanton gestures they exceeded any part of womankind. The kissing them after so lascivious a mode in public and upon the theatre, as it were, of the world, prompted many to imagine some things done in the tyring house that exceed my expression no less than they do my experience [in effect, 'I don't have the sort of background to let me talk about such things!']

In 1617, the Privy Council even debated the matter of royal favourites with the king. Another contemporary remarked that 'the king is wondrous passionate, a lover of his favourites beyond the love of men to women'. James's response still has the power to shock, making an allusion to Christ:

Jesus Christ did the same, and therefore I cannot be blamed. Christ had his son John [the 'beloved' – in a Graeco-Roman context the word resonates with meaning – apostle who rested his head on Christ's breast at the Last Supper], *and I have my George.*

alternatively he might have used the image of David and Jonathan so often advanced by modern gay rights' activists. This image of Christ and John was clearly of use to the king and the use he made of it almost certainly infuriated and annoyed his critics. Indeed, one wonders whether the unwillingness to show Christ and John cuddling on a dinner couch for the Last Supper (as was the custom of the day) in Mel Gibson's recent film *The Passion of the Christ* may, in part, stem from a concern about what might be read by today's audiences into the visual image.

The king may have had his favourites but he seemed never to associate his love for them – which was almost certainly, at times, physical and sexual – with the crime of sodomy. In his work, *Basilicon Doron*, which he wrote to advise his son about statecraft, James stated:

so is there some horrible crimes that yee are bound in conscience neuer to forgiue: such as Witch-craft, willful murther, Incest (especially within the degrees of Consanguinitie), Sodomie, poisoning and false coine.

How the king may have reconciled his own personal conduct with such advice is not clear. That he did, is obvious. That many of his courtiers and subjects were less than impressed with his apparent hypocrisy is just as plain. Although we have heard her in the previous chapter it is worth allowing Lucy Hutchinson to speak yet again with her pithy verdict on the court of King James:

The face of the court was much changed in the change of the King [with the death of James VI & I], *for King Charles* [I] *was temperate, chaste, and serious; so that the fools and bawds, mimics and catamites* [sodomites] *of the former court* [of James VI and I] *grew out of fashion; and the nobility and courtiers, who did not quite abandon their debaucheries, yet so reverenced* [feared] *the king as to retire into corners to practice them.*

Of course, it is worth noting that Hutchinson was a devout Puritan and ardent critic of all things Episcopal (or, as she saw it, crypto-Catholic).

What one can tentatively conclude from this brief discussion of the courts of Henry and James is that modern stereotypes simply do not find their mirror in the early modern period. That is, the courts do not have in mind a stereotype of a 'sodomite'. The men come from a range of professions and most are poorer artisans. Their activity seems either to be opportunistically associated with the sharing of a bed in a city crowded with male religious refugees or the result of long-term practices. However, the courts of the day show no evidence of believing that sodomitical acts were just one-off events. They wanted to know if any given defendant had had sex with a woman or produced children. They also assumed there might have been some contact with Italians or Italy (that is, classicised, Italian Renaissance culture). They also assumed that previous acts of sodomy were evidence of a predilection for the behaviour. In other words, they did seem to think that some people had 'appetites' that inclined them to one sex or another. Clearly though, they thought that 'giving oneself over' to these appetites was largely a matter of the will and habit.

This lack of a stereotype accompanied by certain assumptions about repeated behaviour seems to underlie the reports by a *conquistrador* in 1530. Writing of a recent battle with an Amerindian tribe in South America, he related that the very last soldier to surrender:

fought most courageously, was a man in the [clothes] *of a woman,* [who] *confessed that from a child he had gotten his living by that filthiness, for which I caused him to be burned.*

During the course of the seventeenth century one sees, at least in English drama, the emergence of the image of the 'fop' already commented on above. Still, the cases from this period seem to suggest that the earlier understanding of sodomitical acts survived. There was no assumption of a particular type of behaviour nor any necessary thought that a sodomite would, by definition, be wholly interested in his own sex.

Certainly, the trial and arrest of Mervin Touchet, Lord Audeley, earl of Castelhaven, in 1631 makes this point. He is displayed as a sexual libertine and pervert. Among his many perversions was sodomy. He was accused of (and later executed for) having had sex with a number of his adult male servants. His attentions then, in opposition to the fop of the stage, was not for adolescent males but full-grown men. He tried to argue that, under a strict interpretation of the law, the testimony against him only pointed to intercrural sex, not penetration. Thus, he had not committed buggery. The court ruled that the *sine qua non* of buggery was ejaculation not penetration. However, for most of his peers in the House of Lords sitting in judgment against him, the shocking aspect of his behaviour was not sex with servants (since that was simply an extreme extension of the hierarchical ordering of society). Rather, they were appalled that he had held down his wife, Catherine, while his favourite servant had obeyed his command to force her. In addition, he had helped the servant rape his twelve-year-old daughter-in-law so that he might have an heir by the servant rather than his son. As the girl was so young the servant related that the earl had had to apply lubricant to them to allow the rape to proceed. The diverse perversions of this case, of which sodomy was but one (and perhaps the least) were such that even Charles I was forced to abandon his good friend and favourite to the executioner.

The prevailing ambivalence to, and general toleration of, some sorts of sodomitical activity (most notably pederasty) as well as a more fluid understanding of the correct objects of masculine desire is evident throughout most of the seventeenth century. For example, Samuel Pepys wrote (in the 1660s) of the actor Edward Kynaston, who was known for his portrayal of women, that he was both 'the prettiest woman in the whole house' and 'the handsomest man'. That he was also widely rumoured to be the catamite of the duke of Buckingham seems not to have had any impact on his popular appeal. By the end of the century this situation was changing. One example of this alteration was the introduction of specific words for the passive (*berdache*) and active (sodomite) participant in sodomy. *Berdache* was considerably more pejorative than catamite and, more importantly, did not have the implicit association with pederasty. It also called to mind behaviour found amongst the 'savages' of the New World. So great had been the cultural shift that John Dennis in his *Usefulness of the Stage* (1698), which he wrote in response to Jeremy Collier's (clergyman and Jacobite) attack on the depraved morality of the theatre, said that 'that unnatural sin, which is another growing vice of the Age... [was] either never mentioned [by the Stage] or mentioned with the last Detestation'. The vice, of course, was sodomy and it was one of the 'four reigning vices' in England (along with, perhaps bizarrely considering the discussion, 'the love of women', 'drinking' and 'gambling').

For the purposes of this discussion, though, it does allow us to move rather quickly to an examination of the eighteenth century by which time, or so it has been argued for major metropoles such as London and Paris, attitudes had changed and an 'image' and stereotype of a sodomite had come into common parlance. This new image is obvious almost from the beginning of the century. In 1703, Thomas Baker in *Turbridge-Walks* had the foppish, male character Maiden say:

When I was at School... I lov'd mightily to play with Girls, and dress Babies, and all my Acquaintance now never quarell'd in their lives... Oh! The best Creatures in the World; we have such Diversion, when we meet together at my Chambers There's Beau Simper, Beau Rabbitsface, Beau Eithersex, Colonel Coachpole, and Count Drivel that sits with his Mouth open, the prettiest Company at a bowl of Virgin Punch;... Then we never read Gazets… like you Coffee-House Fellows; but play with Fans, and mimick Women, Skream, hold up your tails, make Curtsies, and call one another, Madame.

As well as,

Why, I can Sing, and Dance, and play upon the Guitar, make Wax-Work, and Fillagree, and Paint upon Glass. Besides I can dress a Lady up a Head upon Occasion, for I was put Prentice to a Milliner once, only a Gentleman took a fancy to me, and left me an Estate; but that's no Novelty, for abundance of People now-a-days take a fancy to a handsome Young Fellow… [Though] I can Raffle with the Ladies, Dance with them, and Walk with 'em in publick, I never desire any private Love-favours from 'em.

Baker is also assumed to be the author of *The Female Tatler* (1709) which mentioned a fashion boutique in Ludgate Hill. A noble customer noted that the shop assistants were the 'sweetest, fairest, nicest, dish'd out [male] Creatures; and by their Elegant Address and Soft Speeches, you would guess them to be Italians' while the three owners who sold their 'Gay Fancies' were 'positively the greatest fops in the Kingdon'. With an increasing emphasis on public morality and greater state control of the stage it became more difficult to portray sodomy (especially, pederasty) openly even to ridicule, it as this smacked of 'promoting' the vice (rather as any discussion of homosexuality became impossible with laws against 'promoting it in schools'). Thus, the effeminate character became a code for the sodomite much as Mr Humphreys in the television sitcom, *Are You Being Served*.

Moreover, the situation became very complicated for actors, as well as their characterisations. They now had to ensure no hint of 'unnatural' passions was attached to them. In the late seventeenth and early eighteenth centuries association with libertine interests was not a disability. For example, the assumptions underlying the scurrilous attacks on the actor James Noakes in a *Satyr on the Players* seems not to have harmed him.

> *You smockfac'd Lads, Secure your Gentle Bums*
> *For full of Lust and Fury See he comes!*
> *'Tis B[ugger] Nokes, whose unwieldly [Tarse]*

Weeps to be buryed in his Foreman's [Arse]
Unnatural Sinner, Lecher without Sense,
To leave kind [cunt], to live in Excrement.

Nor was actor and playwright John Leigh harmed by a reputation
that was later mentioned by William Chetwood, in *A General History
of the Stage* (1749) as a man of 'particular amiable Form, and genteel
Address...[who] might have been in the good Graces of the Fair-Sex,
if his taste had led him that way'.

However, by the latter half of the century, the situation had changed
dramatically. Isaac Bickerstaff, the close friend and collaborator of
David Garrick, was accused of making advances on a soldier. He fled
for France and was ruined. So terrified was Garrick of any of the
scandal touching him that he repudiated his friend and refused any
further contact with him. One attempt to defend Garrick's *volte-face*
said:

You rail at Bick[erstaff] *with all my heart:*
Think you I mean to take his part?
Think you I would one distich write
T'exculpate a vile s[odomit]e?
No, on him let thy rage be hurl'd;
No, – lash him naked thro' the world:
Expose in satire's keenest lays
This skulking, dam'd detested race.
Hang up to publick scorn each brute
Who dares Love's rite to prostitute.

So complete was Bickerstaff's disgrace that is it not known where or
even when he died.

The image of the effeminate sodomite moved from the stage to the
streets. However, the problem was that the image did not accord with
reality despite the apparent best efforts of both the 'sodomites' and
their villifiers. *The World* (1754) complained about 'these louts of six
feet high, with the shoulders of porters and the legs of chairmen,
[who] affect "to lisp, and to amble, and to nick name God's creatures"'.

Nathanial Lancaster, in *The Pretty Gentleman* (1747), presented the stereotype clearly:

Observe that fine Complexion! Examine that smooth, the Velvety skin! View that Pallor which spreads itself over his Countenance! Hark, with what a feminine Softness his Accents steal their Way through his half-opened Lips! Feel that soft Palm!... The whole System is of a finer Turn, and superior Accuracy of Fabric, insomuch that it looks as if Nature had been in doubt, to which Sex she should assign him.

Or, Garrick's description,

> *A* man, *it seems – 'tis hard to say –*
> *A* woman *then? – a moment pray; –*
> *Unknown as yet by sex or feature,*
> *Suppose we try to guess the creature;*
> *Whether a* wit, *or a pretender?*
> *Of* masculine *or* female *gender?*

While this characterisation is apparent and very decidedly a feature of the eighteenth-century English stage, one cannot be sure that it dates wholly from the period. For example, one might contrast these stereo-types with that implied by l'Estoile (as we have seen above) in his journal (1576) when he discussed the *mignons* of Henry III of France:

The name of the Mignons *began, at this time, to travel by word of mouth among the people, to whom they were very odious, as much for their make-up, and effeminate and immodest apparel, but above all for the immense and liberal gifts presented them by the King...*

Nevertheless, the sodomites seemed to have taken to the image in the eighteenth century at all social levels as one can hear in an overheard exchange between two mollies, 'where have you been saucy Queen? If I catch you strolling or caterwauling, I'll beat the milk out of your breast I will so'.

This comment returns us to practice from theory and stage. In 1726 a raid on molly-houses in London resulted in twenty places being discovered. The most famous was that of Margaret 'Mother' Clap. She was pilloried as a result – so badly that she fell off the pillory and fainted twice. It was during this period that sodomites were often seriously bruised or even blinded when in the pillory as a result of the dung (piled high in carts near at hand for the purpose) hurled by the crowd. Although the environment was changing the behaviour continued as the tour guide to St Paul's whispering galleries discovered when (in 1731) he chanced upon one William Hollywell buggering a certain William Higgins in the upper part of the cathedral.

Nor should one suppose that this sort of change in state interest was confined to England or London. In Paris as well, the authorities were increasingly interested in controlling the sexual activities of the sodomites or pederasts. However, they were more concerned about limiting acts of indecency in public than in actual prosecutions. Thus, they conducted patrols in well-known 'cruising' areas and kept copious records on any individuals suspected of 'unnatural' interests. The result is a fascinating amount of information on how men managed to find men in public places and how they then negotiated their particular desires.

In 1724, one man was approached by another. Both were clearly interested in sex but when the first man offered the other money for the encounter the second man huffily replied that 'he was not doing it out of interest... but only for his pleasure'. Another gentleman complained that 'as I was about to [piss], [he] asked me what time it was according to my cock and said that according to his it was high noon'. A later account, in 1737, noted that four men had been discussing their sexual exploits so loudly as they crossed the Pont-Neuf that passers-by had upbraided them for their indecency. Also, as one male prostitute made clear, the aversion to oral sex traditionally seen in most European cultures had changed: 'I perform the act with my mouth, in the same way as with my ass when I see that a man is clean and doesn't smell of women'.

Clearly, these men were understood by others and themselves as being a category rather apart. As the Marquis de Sade put it in a comment that also called for a more tolerant attitude and explicitly rejected the 'unnatural' charge levelled against sodomy: 'is it not clear that this is a class of men different from the other, but also created by nature?'

Even the Paris pederasts were more than able to identify one another. The police documents record overhearing two men, upon seeing another suspected sodomite, saying, 'there's somebody who looks like one. Let's split up and see what this sister is all about' and when another boy failed to respond to their banter at all 'they said to each other, "let's let him go, he doesn't speak Latin"'.

Moreover, many of these men not only clearly articulated their preferences but also demonstrated an acceptance of the prevailing view that relationships should be based on affection. Thus a certain Gallimard, a lawyer of the Paris *parlement* reported that he 'had a wife but hardly ever made use of her, that his marriage was a stratagem, cover-up, and that he had not a taste for women, that he preferred an ass to a cunt'. Reporting on another sodomitical relationship, an officer noted that:

Dusquenel and Dumaine had been sleeping together for two years. They were unable to fall asleep without having mutually touched each other and without having performed infamous acts. It was even almost always necessary for Dusquenel to have his arm extended along the headboard, under Dumaine's head. Without that Dumaine could not rest.

It may only be the survival of specific types of sources that have allowed us this sort of insight into the personal relationships and views of these men. However, this example and others suggest that some relationships were long standing and may well have involved deep feelings of mutual affection. All the more so as the maintenance of a sodomitical relationship (rather than one-night stands) under the threat of stake or gallows implies an amazing level of commitment.

According to the old chestnut, British legal reforms of the nineteenth century did not include lesbianism in laws against deviant sexual acts because Queen Victoria could not contemplate that such behaviour could take place. Indeed, as we shall see, there was a tradition emerging in late eighteenth- and early nineteenth-century English legal thought that 'good girls' (that is, educated women of quality) could not possibly engage in such vile acts. However, the period we are examining was under no such allusions.

Nevertheless, a number of problems confronted societies, judges and individuals when attempting to deal with same-sex acts between women. First and foremost, it was not clear what crime (if any) was being committed. Sodomy, by its very definition involved, at least, penetration and, more usually, anal penetration. Secondly, a male-dominated society was not really *au fait* with what women got up to at home amongst themselves and their maids. Also, because of traditional religious, medical and 'psychological' views about women, there was a real fear that publicising information about lesbianism might simply lead women to experiment – by their very nature they were ruled by their bodies in general and their sexual organs in particular. The last thing any male wanted to do was give them ideas. Or as one writer working around 1700 (Jean-Baptiste Thiers) opined: 'experience teaches us that often it is better not to explain in detail what is forbidden, in order not to suggest the possibility of doing it'.

One of the earliest codes to mention same-sex acts between women simply highlights the problems. In 1270, a French code, prescribed, bizarrely, that a man 'who has been proved to be a sodomite must lose his testicles and if he does it a second time, he must lose his member, and if he does it a third time he must be burned'. The same code said that 'a woman who [has sex with another woman] shall lose her member each time and on the third must be burned'. The law made no attempt to explain what exactly a woman must do to be a sodomite or precisely how she can lose her 'member' once, let alone twice. Even with this technical confusion in the letter of the law the spirit of the codes, the Bible and social norms were more than able to lead to the drowning of a girl in Speyer (Germany) for sex with another woman in 1477.

The reality is that little is known about lesbianism before the eighteenth century. There is some evidence from earlier periods which suggests there was a growing concern in the seventeenth century about female sexual activity and women's increasing knowledge of the body, and all things sexual through scientific and classical literature and, in particular, through novels and erotic writings.

The increasing availability of Greek and Roman writers in the Renaissance was facilitated by the spread of printing. Aristophanes' comedies, for example *Lysistrata*, with its ribald humour springing from the refusal of Athenian and Spartan women to have sex with their husbands (but not each other) until, and unless, they stopped fighting, could be read in original and in translations. For example, an original edition appeared in 1525 and there was a good French version in 1692. Juvenal's satires, which lampooned Roman sexual perversions, including lesbianism, were available from as early as 1486 and Martial's epigrams (of a similar nature) from 1482. As more women were taught to read both vernacular and classical literature this world became increasingly open to them. It may also explain why the expansion of female literacy in the mid-eighteenth century coincided with the increasing censorship and bowdlerisation of these and other classical authors.

Nor should one underestimate the impact of these works, accustomed as we are to dismissing the classics as boring. A few examples will show us the polysexuality of the Graeco-Roman world and how accessible it was through the works of major writers which survived from antiqu-ity. Peter Green's Penguin translation (1974) of Juvenal's sixth satire says:

> [Maura] *and her dear friend Tullia pass by the ancient altar*
> *Of Chastity? And what is Tullia whispering to her?*
> *Here, at night, they stagger out of their litters*
> *And relieve themselves, pissing in long hard bursts*
> *All over the Goddess's statue. Then, while the Moon*
> *Looks down on their motions, they take turns to ride each other*
> *And finally go home.*

A similar overt and easy sexuality is apparent in Stephen Halliwell's verse translation of Aristophanes' *Lysistrata* (1997):

Lysistrata:	*Warm greetings, Lampito, dear Spartan friend.*
	Sweetheart, you're looking simply ravishing.
	What gorgeous skin – and, oh, those muscles of yours.
	You could throttle a bull!
Lampito:	*By the Twins, I swear I could.*
	My exercise includes rump-stretching kicks.
Kalonike:	*I've never seen a finer pair of breasts.*
Lampito:	*Stop feeling my flesh; I'm not for sacrifice!*

Lysistrata:	*And what about this other girl—who's she?*
Lampito:	*A Boiotian—and a fine one, by the Twins.*
	She's come for the meeting too.
Myrrhine:	*A true Boiotian! Her belly's as flat as any Boiotian plain.*
Kalonike [peering]:	*And look at her little bush, how cutely trimmed.*
Lysistrata:	*This other girl?*
Lampito:	*A choice piece, by the Twins. Korinthian, what's more.*
Kalonike:	*A real 'choice piece'!*
	That's all too clear in front as well as behind.

One of Martial's epigrams (book 1:90) goes beyond the graphic in its depiction and mocking of lesbianism as Peter Howell's translation (1980) shows:

Since I never used to see you, Bassa, close to males, and since no rumour provided you with an adulterer, but a crowd of your own sex discharged every function around you, with no man coming anywhere near, I used to think you, I admit, a Lucretia: but you—shame on it, Bassa!—were a fucker. You dare clash together twin cunts, and your unnatural kind of love lyingly imitates [manliness].

The lasciviousness of this literature (almost wholly intended to amuse and titillate a male audience) was increasingly available to literate women of the aristocratic and upper middle classes.

The early modern period also produced its own erotic and pornographic literature. Again, the audience was mostly male but women increasingly had access to these works. Moreover, the erotica had a significant lesbian element. Indeed, the usual format for this literature was to have an older woman 'explaining' sex to an adolescent girl. These works took the pederastic sensibilities of the classical and Renaissance worlds (loaded with ideals of spiritual and non-sexual love) and replaced them with overtly pornographic lesbian physicality. For example, *A School for Girls* (1688, originally published in French as *L'Ecole des filles* in 1655) had chapters entitled: 'A discussion of mounting & various ways of riding, as well as others which can be imagined'; 'whether a man or a woman derives most pleasure from intercourse'; 'why it is wrong to toy with girls'. Nicolas Chorier's

Satyra Sotadica (1660) was widely distributed (in French as *Académie des Dames* and in English as *A dialogue between a married lady and a maid*). One small selection is enough to give the flavour of the genre:

Tullia:	*How I should like ye would grant me the power of*
[an older married woman]	*playing the role of* [your betrothed]…
Ottavia:	*I am well aware that no pleasure can accrue to thee*
[Tullia's younger, engaged cousin]	*from a maiden as I am, nor to me from thee either…*
	I should like thou wert [my betrothed]. *How*
	gladly would I then lay before thee all the fineries
	of my person… thy garden is setting mine on fire.

Despite their constant protestations against lesbian love they repeatedly have sex and their orgasms are especially highlighted in the text. Other books were in a similar vein as their titles imply: *The Wandering Whore* (1642); *Venus in the Cloister; or, the Nun in her Smock* (1683); *The Whores Rhetoric* (1683). Indeed, erotic literature almost always included lesbian acts either involving prostitutes or, more bizarrely and amusingly, aristocratic women (as Tullia and Ottavia above).

Although these works were increasingly common and more socially acceptable with the generally relaxation of morals during the Enlightenment, this situation did not continue. The period of the French Revolution and Napoleonic Wars produced a widespread conservative reaction across Europe. Just as the Reformation had brought to an end much of the social liberalism accompanying the Renaissance and classical Humanism, the Enlightenment became tainted with the excesses of the Revolution. No better example of the individual impact of this cultural shift can be found than in Mrs Keith of Ravelstone, an aged aunt of Sir Walter Scott (1771–1832). He related that she had decided to reread Aphra Behn's (1640–89) fiction, which had been a favourite of her youth. When asked for her impressions of the stories after so many years she said:

Is it not a very odd thing that I, an old woman of eighty and upwards, sitting alone, feel myself ashamed to read a book which, sixty years ago, I have heard read aloud for the amusement of large circles, consisting of the first and most creditable society of London?

This brief vignette serves as a cautionary note for all that follows. This discussion opened with the Renaissance, a period of relative openness, followed by the moralising of the Reformation and the liberalising of the Enlightenment. In the decades that follow the end of this work, morality was to come full circle ushering in the conservatism, which would culminate in the so-called 'Victorian values' lauded by many a modern politician. Anyone calling for a return to the values of the past might find be shocked by the result if the response was an enthusiasm for Renaissance or Enlightenment values rather than those of the Reformation or the nineteenth century.

While it is clear that literate men and (increasingly over time) women were able to read accounts of lesbian sexual acts, there were also women engaging in these same activities. The literature, though clearly meant to titillate and arouse (men), was also an expression of a reality that these early modern societies tried very hard to ignore. Lesbianism was more than a male fantasy. It was a reality for women and these women paid for expressing their desires with fines, the lash and the gallows.

It was this period that saw the first use of the term 'lesbian'. William King (1685–1763) wrote a satirical attack on the duchess of Newburgh after losing a debt case to her. In *The Toast* (1736) he referred to her as a 'lesbian'. Indeed, the use of the term brings to the fore, yet again, the question of the role of categories, words and definitions in shaping reality. Many scholars would hold that the 'category' cannot exist without a widespread acceptance of the idea of a lesbian and lesbianism as a distinct 'type' of person and lifestyle. However, the term clearly predates the psycho-sexual debates of the late nineteenth century (and thereafter). Also, this line of argument overlooks the existence of other early modern words for lesbians and lesbianism. For example, there are repeated references to tribades and tribadic women in addition to descriptions relating to specific sexual acts. One sees *fricatrices* (those who rub), *subigatrices* (those who work a furrow), or the more obvious *clitorifantes*. Thus, there were names for the individual women who engaged in same-sex acts with other women, as well as their actual acts. The overall behaviour was also named 'evil malignities', 'fouling' and 'sodomitical filthiness'.

In addition, there were discussions about the relationship of these tribades to the wider human species. How many genders were there? Some said there were three: male, female, and male sodomites. Others postulated a different three: male, female and hermaphrodites (who were most often seen as biologically female). Some placed the distinctions between male/female and effeminate males. All of which overlooked, as we have seen, attitudes to pederasty and most of which completely ignored lesbianism.

As attitudes began to change and lesbianism became more 'visible' in literature and among the social elites more lesbians appear in the records – and were prosecuted. This should not suggest an increase in the activity but rather an alteration in society's willingness to discuss the behaviour in public. Lesbians were no longer being executed for vague 'unnatural acts' but were being lampooned in print and drooled over in erotic literature. At the same time that historians have been able to identify the development of a subculture of 'gay' males, lesbianism seems to have become more socially acceptable as it moved from being a sin that threatened a male-dominated society to an activity that amused and aroused that same masculine world.

From the very top of society in the eighteenth century we see a greater openness to lesbianism. It was not accepted or approved, rather it was discussed with a certain censoriousness. Lesbianism was with gossip and giggles rather than gallows and gibbets. Thus, Queen Christiana of Sweden (1626–89) came to the throne as 'king' in 1650. She refused to marry her cousin Karl X Gustav, naming him, instead, crown-prince. She almost always dressed as a man and eventually abdicated in 1654 having tired of the restraints placed upon her as a female monarch. Likewise, rumours of the lesbian or bisexual activities and proclivities of Mary II (1662–94) and Anne (1665–1714) of England were rife. In Mary's case this seems only fair as William III (1650–1702) was widely rumoured to be more interested in adolescent males than women. Both women had multiple pregnancies, which seem in no way to have quieted the court gossips.

Similar charges were laid against Marie-Antoinette (1755–93). Clearly, there were political motives (not all from revolutionaries) for accusing the queen of sexual deviance. Nevertheless, there was also a widespread acceptance of the overall truthfulness of the queen's bisexuality. Thus, an English writer, Hester Thrale-Piozzi (1741–1821), said in 1789 that:

[she is] *at the Head of a Set of Monsters call'd by each other Sapphists, who* [follow] *her Example; and deserve to be thrown with the* [male sodomites who have the same tastes] *into Mount Vesuvius.*

Indeed, it is a historical irony that opponents of the *ancien régime* attacked the queen for her sexual libertarianism. The revolution that deposed her subsequently decriminalised sodomy – and then turned a few weeks later to outlaw female clubs.

However, this rather ironic end to the tale is taking us too quickly to the end of the period. The last half of the eighteenth century is rife with examples of lesbians both in court and in society more generally. This chapter brings us to the very threshold of an era in which the greatest monarch of the next century, Queen Victoria, could not even conceive of the activity. During the Enlightenment, lesbianism seemed to be coming into the wider public domain. Fifty years later it had become inconceivable.

When we look beyond Europe we see two features which move the world to 1800. In most places, pre-existing, ambiguous attitudes to homosexuality remain. However, the spread of Judaeo-Christian-Islamic ideas about sex-for-procreation-alone become more pervasive – and effective. The situation in early modern Egypt, ruled for the Ottomans by the Mamluks (slave mercenaries drawn from captured Christian children from the Transcaucus region), is particularly interesting in what it shows about an Islamic society in the eighteenth and even into the early nineteenth century, when European contact was still minimal. Egypt had been conquered by Islamic forces in 639–641 and, by this period, was almost wholly Islamicised.

The cultural 'rules' of Mamluk society worked to encourage non-procreative sexual relations. It was normal for a master to free a concubine when she bore a child and even take her as a wife thereby conferring inheritance rights on the child. To avoid a string of 'unwanted' pregnancies and an economically ruinous proliferation

of heirs, many elite Muslims practised *coitus interruptus* with their concubines – and perhaps, pederasty as well. We do know that male
homosexuality was accepted among the Mamluks and the Egyptian
middle classes, while lesbianism was seen as a direct threat to patriarchal control. Indeed, homosexual and homosocial ties were important
in counteracting the tendency to in-fighting and civil war in Mamluk
society in much the same way as arranged marriages were used in
medieval Europe to cement alliances and end conflict.

Moreover, despite an aversion to lesbianism, what we know of
Mamluk society makes it clear that, in practice, the situation was almost
as relaxed for lesbians as for homosexual males. For example, as early as
the 1300s, lesbians in the Mamluk harems of Egypt behaved like male
rulers, riding pedigree horses, hunting and playing *furusiyya* (chivalric)
games, debauching, drinking, becoming wealthy and owning land.
While there is clear evidence that this situation continued to the nineteenth century it is just as apparent that a double standard operated.
The most famous example of this is the case of Mehemet 'Ali
(1769–1849) who ruled Egypt (1805–49) as Ottoman viceroy. In reality he was the independent ruler of Egypt and the man who worked
tirelessly to 'modernise' Egypt in an effort to stave off European
encroachment. Once, Mehemet 'Ali sentenced his daughter Nazli to
death for lesbianism and only relented because of the intercession of
his grandson (and successor) Abbas I (r.1849–54) who was widely and
infamously known for his licentious debauchery and rampant homosexuality.

Not only do we know about Egypt, but our knowledge of Africa
more generally improves in this period. With the early modern period
one can begin to discuss Africa in greater detail. The increasing contact between Africans and, initially, the Portuguese – and latterly the
Dutch and British – means that Europeans began to write about the
societies and cultures they encountered. What they saw was very different from their experiences elsewhere and was made to fit into patterns relating to the way in which Europeans thought about Africans.
For Europeans, black Africans (perhaps more so than native peoples
elsewhere with the possible exception of Australia and Amazonia)
most epitomised 'primitive man'. This led to certain assumptions

about Africans. Since primitive man was supposedly closest to nature he was seen as 'ruled by instinct' and culturally unsophisticated. Such a person *had* to be heterosexual since his sexual energies and outlets would be the most 'natural'. That is, a primitive man, governed by the imperatives of nature, would be sexually driven – like an animal – to procreate. This recalls the Graeco-Roman ideal that civilisation was connected with male love. One must constantly remember that an early modern European did not conceive of being close to nature as a positive good; rather, it was bestial. Not only did this view have an impact on assumptions about sexual practices among the Africans but it also underpinned and 'justified' the control of Africans by 'civilised', 'sophisticated' and 'superior' humans – Europeans.

As ideas about race developed and became more 'scientific' in the eighteenth century this dichotomy between 'superior, civilised, normal' and 'inferior, uncivilised, depraved' became even more pronounced. Being superior became not only integral to the West but more importantly to the Western male, especially in the colonial context leading not only to the infantalisation of the African but also to the use of sex as a tool of control (through rape, etc. – a common method employed by whites dealing with black slaves). Part of the Western view of the role of paramount and 'normative' procreation can be seen in colonial views: David Gilmore, in his cross-cultural study of manhood, has noted that impregnating a woman was an integral part of 'male role-playing', as was the expectation that men 'tame nature' in order 'to reinvent and perpetuate the social order'.

Thus, not only did Westerners see sex with another man (especially in the passive role) as demeaning, but also that white men's sexual liaisons with 'native' women in the colony (or, often, with women of other races elsewhere) became viewed as unmanly, precisely because it undermined both the colonial endeavour and assumptions about white superiority. Thus, we see a white colonial ruler asserting that:

it is a known [fact], *that mixed race marriages between whites and coloureds pass the bad characteristics of the parents onto the children to a higher degree than the good… The woman and the offspring do not rise to the educational level of the man and father, but rather the man* [i.e., the father!] *sinks back to that of the woman.*

If nothing else, this should warn us against the easy acceptance of ideas of normality, scientific/natural 'rightness'. Behind much of what is said about sexuality is a very nuanced, powerful and (at times) dangerous mix of ideas about race, society, politics and power.

As early as 1781, in his *History of the Decline and Fall of the Roman Empire*, Edward Gibbon (1737–94) was articulating such a view – and fond hope: 'I believe, and *hope* [emphasis mine], that the negroes, in their *own country* [again, my emphasis], were exempt from this moral pestilence [of sodomy]'. Sir Richard Burton (1821–90), writing in 1885, said the same when he placed black Africa outside his 'sodatic zone' in which sodomy was practiced: 'the negro race is mostly untainted by sodomy and tribadism'. This wish to identify Africans with a 'pure', 'primitive' race meant forcing them *into* the preconceived notion of what such a race would be like. It also made it much easier to argue that they needed the heavy hand of Christian Europe to 'civilise' and 'care' for them.

One example of an African reality that would have reaffirmed Europeans in their beliefs that Africans were uncivilised would have been the *Iyoba* Idia (b. 1507) of the kingdom of Benin. In general, Europeans did not approve of women as sovereign rulers and often insisted that technically they were 'males'. This idea explains why women are banned from the Old Course Clubhouse in St Andrews except on St Andrew's Day even though the Queen may enter at any time – as sovereign, she is male.

Portugal and Benin (in present-day Nigeria) had been in contact since the late 1400s with ambassadors exchanged by the two kingdoms. Indeed, Portuguese mercenaries served in Benin's army in the sixteenth century and one of Benin's kings, Orhogbua (seventeenth *Oba*; r.1550–78), was trained at a Portuguese naval college. Benin slid into civil war at the end of the fifteenth century when *Oba* (king) Ozolua died (1481) leaving two powerful sons claiming the throne. One son (Esigie; r.1504–50) controlled Benin City while the other (Arhuaran) held the equally important city of Udo. Esigie ultimately defeated his brother, re-established the unity and military strength of the kingdom, and became Benin's sixteenth *Oba*. His mother Idia was seen as key to his triumph because of her wise counsel, her magical powers, and her medical knowledge. Esigie created a new position within the court

called the *Iyoba* (queen mother) to honour her. This post gave her significant political power, a separate palace compound, and her own staff.

Not only were Europeans amazed by Idia herself – known as 'the
only woman who went to war' – but also by the continuing strength
of the office of *Iyoba*. The distinct and separate palaces, staff and rental
properties guaranteed the *Iyoba* a large degree of political, social and
economic independence and power. As the biological mother of
the reigning *Oba* (as distinct from the other wives of the previous
Oba), the *Iyoba* continued to have a key role in Benin society. The
present *Oba* (Erediauwa; b. 1982) is thirty-eighth in a dynasty stretching back (apart from an interregnum 1897–1914 when the *Oba* was in
a British-imposed exile) to the 1100s while the present *Iyoba* traces
her office to its creation in the early sixteenth century.

However, the Benin court was also interesting to Europeans in
other ways. Court servants at the palaces of both the *Oba* and *Iyoba*
were seen as 'innocent', and lacking sexuality and maturity. As such, it
was expected that they would always be present in the nude (the
Benin symbol of immaturity and purity) as well as unmarried and
celibate. It also, more prosaically, ensured that no royal servant was able
to conceal a weapon! This practice continued until *Oba* Akenzua II
(r. 1933–78), acutely aware of the sensibilities of the British (who had
seized Benin, deposing and exiling his grandfather), introduced clothing for royal servants. One can well imagine that the British officials
in the 1930s would have found official visits to the palaces of the *Oba*
and *Iyoba* a rather interesting cross-cultural experience!

The kingdom of Dahomey (in modern-day Benin) was also difficult to fit into the European model of the 'primitive', 'naturalistic'
African. Sir Richard Burton, despite his assertion that sodomy was
rare among the Africans, noted that in Dahomey rulers kept eunuchs
who were secluded (as in a harem) and functioned as royal 'wives' – a
feature of the culture noted as early as the 1780s. While these biological Dahomean males were being 'reconstructed' as females a similar
pattern took place among some Dahomean women. From 1730 a
troop of about 2,500 women were raised and played an important role
in the military life and power of the state until the late nineteenth
century. In a complex cultural construction of gender these female

soldiers (often called Amazons by Europeans) said that they had
'become men' and mocked men that had defeated in battle for being
'women'. As late as 1851, Seh-Dong-Hong-Beh was a leader of the
Dahomey female corps under King Gezo (1818–58) She led an army
of 6,000 women against the Egba fortress of Abeokuta. Because the
Amazons were armed with spears, bows and swords while the Egba
had European cannon, only about 1,200 survived the battle.

One should not consider Dahomey an oddity – though the
transgendered understanding of female warriors does seem to be
unique. For example, Llinga, a warrior queen of the Congo (armed
with axe, bow and sword), fought the Portuguese in 1640. Moreover, women warriors were common in the Congo where the
Monomotapa confederacy had standing armies of women. Kaipkire,
warrior leader of the Herero tribe of south-west Africa in the eighteenth century, led her people in battles against British slave traders
and there are records of Herero women fighting German soldiers as
late as 1919. Nandi was the warrior mother of Shaka Zulu. She fought
slave traders and trained her son to be a warrior. When he became
king, he established an all-female regiment, which often fought in the
front lines of his army.

From the early modern period there is an increasing amount of
detailed information about African society, some of which touches
upon the sexual practices of these cultures. Not all of it, though, is
confined to Africa. One must remember that in the period 1450–1870
somewhat over 10 million Africans were forcibly transported to the
Americas as slaves, taking with them their own cultures and, in time,
producing various blends of African-American cultures in their new
homes. Thus, one sees (in 1591) a certain Matthias Moreira denouncing a black slave named Francisco for sodomy and cross-dressing.
Francisco had been brought to a Portuguese settlement in Brazil from
west-central Africa. He claimed that his behaviour was common
throughout the region from the Congo to Angola and that men who
cross-dressed and had sex with other men were known as *jin bandaa*.
Andrew Battel, an Englishman held for a while (in the 1580s) by the
Portuguese, made similar observations about the Dombe (Zambia):
'[They are] beastly in their living, for they have men in women's

apparell, whom they keep among their wives'. This account focusing on African terminology and practice may actually hide an indigenous practice more closely related to that of North American *berdaches*. For example, from other sources we know that the native Tupinamba of Brazil men took *berdache* wives as did Portuguese settlers (in the sixteenth century) after 'the custom of the land'. A report from 1587 talks of Tupi brothels with *berdache* whores.

Thus Francisco's account may suggest a non-Christian sexual categorisation, which helped unite and meld African and Amerindian cultures in Brazil. In any case, his case rather nicely echoes the earliest references from Angola in which Europeans noted that cross-dressing sodomites were called *quimbandas*. In modern-day Angola, medicine men (who also cross-dress and are frequently assumed to engage in same-sex acts) are called *kimbanda*. Not only does this give credence to Francisco's testimony in the 1590s but it also suggests that practices still visible in African societies have a lengthy history and that one can, with care and caution, extrapolate backwards especially from current traditional religious beliefs. On the other hand, Battel's account reminds one that it was also possible to construct a type of 'homosexual' who simply *became* a female without any apparent need to imbue them with a particular spiritual or religious function.

Captain Antonio de Oliveira Cadonega (in 1681) also commented on behaviour he had noted among Africans along the west-central coast, especially Angola:

There is also among the Angolan pagans much sodomy, sharing one with the other their dirtiness and filth, dressing as women. And they [call] them... quimbandas... And all of the pagans respect them and they are not offended by them and these sodomites happen to live together in bands, meeting most often to give burial services... This class of people is who dresses the body for burial and performs the burial ceremony.

Much of this recalls the role of Indian *hijras* in birth and marriage rituals. In addition, reports exist from 1719 of males, called *koetsire*, among the Khoi-Khoin (Kalahari desert) who had sex with other men. This suggests that societies in the area of present-day Angola (as in India with the *hijras* and the *berdaches* in the Americas) had constructed a place for individuals involved in same-sex and transgendered practices, which was intimately associated both with religion more generally, and key points of transition in life more specifically. One might hypothesise that some societies came to the conclusion that certain individuals, unable or unwilling to participate in the extension of the group via procreation, were intended (by nature or divinity) to perform other necessary functions for the group. That is, homosexuality had a purpose in the grander scheme of existence and, therefore, a place in the proper and successful life of the community.

However, one can also find African societies in which transgendered individuals had an even more significant role. For example, the Portuguese attempts to conquer the Ndongo kingdom (Angola) in the late sixteenth and seventeenth centuries were stymied until the overthrow of the kingdom in 1671. The leading force in this resistance was the ruling monarch, the *Ngola* (king). This 'king' was, in fact, a woman named Nzinga (1582–1663) who had succeeded her brother and executed her nephew to ensure her hold on power. This caused an interesting situation analogous to that we have already seen with the *Iyoba* of Benin. The new *Ngola*, Nzinga, was biologically female but had now assumed a 'male' role. For the Mbundu of the Ndongo kingdom gender was 'situational', as well as biological. A king was 'male' so the new *Ngola* was also male.

Everything in the structure (i.e., the social construction) had to conform to this reality. Consequently, as a Dutch military attaché noted in the 1640s, the new king (as was the custom) was surrounded by *his* harem of numerous wives. These 'wives' were, in fact, men dressed as women. Thus, biology was forced to submit to the realities of the Mbundu's social and cultural presuppositions and expectations. A king has wives. The new king happens to be female biologically but still must be supplied with wives. These wives must look and behave like wives just as the new king must look and behave – and be treated – like a male. On one level we can see this as the ultimate upholding of a heterosexual construction of society – there is no suggestion that Nzinga had wives who were biologically female. However, this is surely one of the most peculiar ways of maintaining a heterosexual reality. As with the visual image of the British officials being served by naked servants at the royal Benin courts, one cannot help but wonder how Portuguese and Dutch officials, functioning as ambassadors, coped with a female 'king' and *his* retinue of male 'wives' in drag!

Not only do these examples provide evidence of individuals interested in same-sex activities, as well as very complex social views about gender they also remind us that the history of Europe's contact with sub-Saharan Africa was not one of constant conquest and European domination. It is crucial to recall that Africa did not fall under European control until the mid to late nineteenth century. Before that, many African states maintained not only their independence but were treated as equals by European states. When the Portuguese first began sailing down Africa's coast to find a route to India they did *not* encounter primitive tribes – *pace* the desire of Europeans from Gibbon to Burton to portray the African as simplistic and simple. Instead they came across a number of established, powerful societies.

The Songhay Empire in Mali (centred on Timbuktu and Gao) was a rich and powerful Islamic state, which had succeeded, *c.*1470, the empire of Mali (successor to the empire of Ghana about 1300) but succumbed to Moroccan power around 1590. Of the Songhay, Islamic writer Leo Africanus (1485–1554) wrote:

In Timbuktu there are numerous judges, doctors and clerics, all receiving good salaries from the king. He pays great respect to men of learning. There is a big demand for books in manuscript, imported from Barbary. More profit is made from the book trade than from any line of business.

The Songhay Empire was also famed for the University of Sankore, founded *c.*1300 under the Mali Empire's greatest monarch, the legendary king Mansa Moussa (r.1307–37).

Even after initial contacts with an expansionist Europe, African states continued to develop. The Ashanti Union (centred around Ghana), founded in 1697 by King Osei Tutu (*c.*1660–*c.*1715) maintained its power until overthrown by the British in 1896. Europeans noted that male slaves were kept as concubines by leading officials of the Ashanti state. They were closely connected to their masters and were frequently sacrificed as part of the burial rituals accompanying the funeral of their owners.

Hausa city-states (e.g. Gobir, Katsina, Zamfara, Kano, Kebbi and Zaria) in northern Nigeria, developed in the late 1100s and were economically and militarily powerful into the late eighteenth century. Further south, Europeans encountered (in 1483) the powerful Kongo Kingdom (Congo) which had begun to develop in the late 1300s. However by 1665 and the battle of Mbwila, the Portuguese had ended the unity and power of the kingdom. Along the eastern coast of Africa, Swahili-speaking (a *lingua franca* mixture of Arabic and Bantu) Islamicised city-states (Mogadishu, Barawa, Mombasa, Gedi, Pate, Malindi, Zanzibar, Kilwa and Sofala) which came under Portuguese sway in the sixteenth century but then passed to the control of the Sultan of Oman in the eighteenth and nineteenth centuries.

The east African interior was dominated by a number of Bantu-speaking, non-Islamic states: Buganda, Bunyoro-Kitara, Toora and Ankole. One of the greatest kingdoms was the Shona Empire, which encompassed Zimbabwe and surrounding areas. It coalesced into a state in the 1200s and reached its apogee in the 1400s before beginning to decline around 1600. (The greatest lasting achievement of the Shona is over 300 walled settlements including the city of Great Zimbabwe, which housed nearly 20,000 in the fifteenth century when most European 'cities' had fewer than 5,000 inhabitants.) The Shona maintained trading links with China at a time when Europeans were desperately trying to discover new routes to the Far East. These Bantu speakers have left a number of words (some of which we have already encountered) relating to men (often considered spiritual leaders or shamans) who engaged in transgenderism, transvestism and same-sex acts: *chibadi*, *chibado*, *jimbandaa*, *kibamba* and *quimbanda*.

The Bantu were not alone in having words that have survived to the present day, which reveal a range of non-standard aspects of sexuality and gender. The Konso (who inhabit walled cities in southern Ethiopia) have words (e.g. *sagoda*) for men who never marry, wear skirts and are considered 'weak'. Among the Maale of southern Ethiopia are men who take on female roles and mannerisms, and are called *ashtime*. One *ashtime* (in the 1990s) explained himself this way: 'The Divinity created me *wobo*, crooked [because he could not or would not father a child but was not, as a female, able to birth a child]'. Among the Krongo and

Mesakin (non-Muslim Nubians in the Sudan) are men who temporarily become 'wives' (called *londo* and *tubele*, respectively) of (often) younger 'husbands' before marrying a biological female themselves.

The Islamicised Swahili-speaking cities of the east coast have a number of similar terms, though many are clearly of Arabic origin: *mumeke* (man-woman from *mume*, man and *mke*, woman); *hanithi* (passive sodomite presumably from the Omani word for a 'man-woman', *khanith*); *mke-si-mume* (woman-not-man); and *mzebe* (impotent). These highlight non-standard gender identification, same-sex activities and non-procreativity. Indeed, it is worth noting that the Omani *khanith* refers to someone of a 'third gender category', which is wholly natural 'within the rubric of Islamic cosmology'. As early as 1860, the American ambassador to Zanzibar for the installation of Sultan Bargash (1837–88; soon after the transfer of the sultanate's capital from Muscat) noted that 'numbers of sodomites have come from Muscat, and these degraded wretches openly walk about dressed in female attire, with veils on their faces'.

One interesting aspect of any discussion of homosexuality in Africa is best highlighted while considering the Islamicised city-states of the east coast. Many African societies, especially those which have adopted Christianity, point to the cities as proof that homosexuality was an import from Islamic Arabia and not native to Africa. Even groups (such as the Wganda of Uganda) which were noted, in 1899, as 'totally given to pederasty' now claim that sodomy was an Arab importation. Interestingly though, Wgandans also claim that such behaviour is just 'fooling' or 'playing around', which would seem to imply another construction to explain (and allow) same-sex contact, distinct from the supposed Arab influence.

The reality is that such an historical explanation for homosexuality in Africa says more about the present than the past. For example, it very effectively allows Christianised Kenyans of the interior to define their Islamicised countrymen of the coastal region as 'the other' on the basis not only of their attachment to Islam but also, and more negatively, their sexual proclivities. The implication is that by becoming Muslim and adopting Arabic mores these peoples have become in some way 'less' authentically and historically African. The same type of mechanism is involved in Mugabe's assertions that he is standing up for

Zimbabwe in the face of an imperialist and capitalist Britain dominated by a 'sodomite Mafia'. Calling one's opponent a Muslim, imperialist or capitalist is not necessarily simplistic enough to make them a despised 'other'; labelling them a 'sodomite' is considerably more effective.

Let us now move from linguistics and return to the historical records. The cultures of West Africa were the earliest to come into contact with Europeans and, unlike the rest of Africa, the abundance of gold and slaves lured Europeans inland. The result is much greater information on societies away from the coastline. For example, from the early modern period to as late as the early 1900s, the Mossi courts (in Burkina Faso) had male pages (*sorones*) who were aged seven to fifteen and chosen for their physical beauty. They were dressed as women, did women's work and, on Fridays when the Islamic rulers were meant to refrain from contact with women, were available to service the sexual needs of their masters. They were checked annually to ensure that they had not had sex with women and when they were old enough to marry the kings provided them with wives with the understanding that their firstborn children were to be the property of the kings: if male then as *sorones*, if female, as wives.

Among the Dagara, also of Burkina Faso, one sees a pattern more reminiscent of what has already been noted in Angola and the Congo. Dagara men who were gender-ambivalent or attracted to other men were considered spiritually important. Before birth certain 'souls' chose to be gatekeepers ensuring that universal balance and harmony were maintained. These people were gender or sexually ambiguous. The sociologist Malidoma Somé (himself a Dagaran with PhDs from Brandeis and the Sorbonne) reported on these spiritual beliefs and that among the Dagaran as 'everywhere else in the world [except Christendom] gay people are a blessing'.

While Somé's assessment of the religious beliefs of non-Christians with regard to homosexuality are (as we have seen) somewhat over-generous, it is certainly true that other faiths do have quite distinct opinions on sexuality from the three monotheistic faiths (Judaism, Christianity and Islam), which arose in the Middle East. In Africa, the Bafia (Cameroon) are a prime, indeed extreme, example. They had had little if any outside contact when they were studied by Tessman in the 1920s. In their cosmology, all life originated from a primal egg. They had no concept of a deity or an afterlife. Sin, to the extent that the idea existed, related to acts which harmed others. As such, there was no specific stigma attached to sex though he did note some ideas about 'punishment' among the Bantu-speaking Fang (Gabon and Cameroon) whom he also studied. They believed that a passive male could sexually transmit 'medicine for wealth' to another man but that both partners risked contracting yaws as a result. However, it is important to realise that Tessman was using his observations to influence political debates in Germany about the legalisation of homosexuality (through the repeal of paragraph 175) among 'born inverts'. Thus, he had a vested interest in identifying an acceptance of same-sex behaviour in a 'primitive society'. This does not invalidate his information but it does suggest that his interpretations of what he observed may have been mediated by his own political agenda.

In addition, the Bafia posited a threefold development of men and women. In the first stage a male was a *kiembe* (having had no sex with a woman) and females were *ngon* (not having had sex with a man). Males (*ntu*) and females (*tsobo*) then entered a subsequent stage in which heterosexual intercourse had taken place but no children had been produced. In the final stage of maturation men (*mbang*) and women (*gib*) had procreated. During the first stage boys and girls 'played' physically with one another with no objection from their parents.

However, as males became older a more mature relative would take the youth as a sexual partner. Sex took place during daylight hours and in the home with little if any regard for the sensibilities of those who might come upon the males in the act. Parents, stumbling upon the scene, would simply laugh at the two males 'playing around' even when this involved anal intercourse, *ji'gele keton*. The males (the pubescent youth and the slightly older relative) referred to one another as 'bosom buddies' – *lexan*. The relationship, which was not always or necessarily sexual, continued throughout life and it was the custom to name children (regardless of gender) after the *lexan*. This stresses the closeness of the ties but it also suggests that there was more to the relationship than just sex – social bonding between families was also important.

One must admit the evidence for same-sex activities is limited; this largely relates to the lack of records in general. It might equally be argued that there is little evidence for a strict adherence to heterosexuality. The simple fact is that any discussion about Africa prior to 1800 risks being an argument from silence. Sadly, any analysis thereafter is complicated by the biases of European colonial administrators and settlers. Despite these various problems, there is more than sufficient evidence from a variety of sources, including surviving beliefs and practices which clearly have a long history, that individual Africans engaged in same-sex acts and relationships. In addition, their societies did not adopt negative responses to such people or practices. While one may not be able to say much with complete assurance there is no doubt whatsoever that the assertions by some that homosexuality is totally alien to Africa and was unknown prior to contact with Islam and the West are wholly incorrect.

Attempts to 'blame' Islam for the arrival of homosexuality play a part not only in modern African politics but also in the conflicts of the Indian subcontinent. The most important historical trend in this period of Indian history is the consolidation and decline of the Mughal Empire and, in time, its replacement by the forces of the English East India Company. The early empire was ruled by a succession of brilliant emperors: Akbar (r. 1555–1605); Jahangir (r. 1605–27); Shah Jahan (r. 1627–58); and Aurangzeb (r. 1658–1707). After 1707 and a series of disastrous military setbacks, the empire went into decline with subsidiary governors breaking away and establishing successor states as (semi-)independent princes.

While the discussion on Arabic-Moorish Islamic society has made it clear that there was considerable cultural ambiguity about same-sex acts and attractions, one must not forget that the Koran is fairly clear on the subject. In the Koran (*Sura* 7: 80–81), Lot says to the people of Sodom:

Do ye commit a wickedness, wherein no creature hath set you an example? Do ye approach lustfully unto men, leaving the women? Certainly ye are a people who transgress all modesty.

1 *Above left:* Ishtar, a Phoenician goddess, seduced the mytho-heroic Gilgamesh, who himself was involved with another male hero. Note the blatant physicality of her sexuality. All early religions (apart from Judaism, which developed rather later) accepted the sexual activity of deities. Gods and goddesses had sex and they usually had sex without any regard to gender.

2 *Above right:* The relief (from Nineveh) shows a eunuch going into battle as a warrior on a chariot. This image reminds us that individuals who might otherwise be considered effeminate or unmanly were, in some societies, very active in battle and other 'manly' pursuits. There are numerous examples of North American *berdaches* taking the role of a warrior.

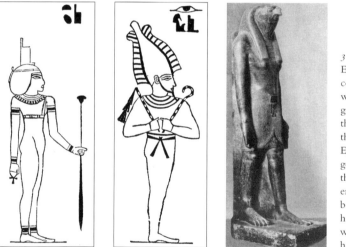

3 *Far left:* Osiris, an Egyptian god, committed incest with his sister, the goddess Isis, who then gave birth to the god Horus. Egyptian gods and goddesses, as with those in India, engaged in incest, bestiality and homosexuality, as well as heterosexuality.

4 *Above centre:* Seth, another Egyptian god. A myth tells how Seth attempted to rape his younger brother Horus and later bragged of his manly achievement to the other gods. One would not normally associate male rape with a god, even less being proud of it. However, as with other polytheistic religions and non-Judaeo-Christian cultures, sex was as much about power and penetration (as well as pleasure) as it was an attempt to procreate.

5 *Above right:* Although Horus was the product of an incestuous relationship and the victim of rape by Seth, neither fact had any impact of attitudes to the god and he was seen as extremely powerful. Indeed, the pharaoh was considered to be the Living Horus, the temporal stand-in for Horus in the earthly domain – hardly the sort of person with whom one would expect a godlike ruler to identify.

6 *Above left:* Apollo, the Greek god, was not only seen as an ideal male beauty but also renowned for his sexual prowess (with males and females). The emphasis upon the male form and male sexuality is evident in Greek representations of their gods. Graeco-Roman gods were not just sexually active, they were the very embodiment of the male ideal – being able to take pleasure (sex) and when it suited and with whomever the male desired.

7 *Above right:* Harmodius, with his lover, Aristogeiton, was famous for attempting to rid Athens of its tyrant, Hippias (r.527–510 BCE) by assassination. They became martyrs to Athenian democracy. Thus, all Athenians (and the city-state, which is usually seen as the very basis of Western civilisation) looked to two male lovers as their greatest national heroes.

8 *Right:* Alexander the Great (Greece). Though married with more than one wife, he was famous for his close relationship with his comrade-in-arms, Hephaistion. This relationship with another man is variously denied or ignored in modern, popular representations of Alexander the Great.

9 Top: This statue of Hermaphrodite sleeping highlights the feminine form from the back but the front of the statue has full male genitalia along with nascent female breasts. This fascination with androgyny, as Freud noted, was central to Greek aesthetics and sexual desire: 'Among the Greeks... it is quite obvious that it was not the masculine character of the [adolescent] which kindled the love of man; it was his physical resemblance to woman as well as his feminine psychic qualities...'

10 Above left: Physical exercise in the nude was part of the life of the gymnasium, which was the place where a 'lover' (older male) would be most likely to meet and seduce his 'beloved' (adolescent male).

11 Above right: In this bronze statue we see the Greek ideal of the 'beloved'. The focus on the perfection of the adolescent male form is obvious. A small, thin penis was fashionable among the Greeks and Romans; a large penis was considered vulgar and animalistic. Even mighty Hercules was always portrayed with an adolescent's genitals.

12 Left: Augustus, emperor of Rome, although known for his strict morality, was also famous for being the beloved (passive) partner in a relationship with Julius Caesar. As his passivity was during his adolescence no one was remotely concerned, nor was it thought ironic that in his later life, he would exile his own family members for adultery.

13 *Left:* Tiberius, emperor of Rome, was famed for his polysexuality and depravity. He was said to have had infants suckle his penis. Most Roman writers and historians considered him depraved not so much for the objects of his desire as for his sexual insatiability.

14 *Below left:* Claudius, emperor of Rome, was considered peculiar for his devotion to his wife and the fact that he did not cheat on her – with another woman or an adolescent youth. The Romans considered such monogamy slightly bizarre. In particular, no Roman would have thought it odd for a man to make sexual use of his slave (of either gender).

15 *Below right:* Hadrian, emperor of Rome, was inconsolable when his lover, Antinous, drowned during a cruise on the Nile. Indeed, he renamed a number of cities of the empire for his beloved.

16 Right: Antinous, the beloved of the Emperor
Hadrian. As Camille Paglia has noted (in her
Sexual Personae): 'The adolescent dreaminess of
the Antinous sculptures is not true inwardness but
a melancholy premonition of death. Antinous
drowned, like Icarus. The beautiful boy dreams
but neither thinks nor feels... His face is a pale
oval upon which nothing is written.'

17 Below left: Elagabalus 'had the whole of his
body depilated, deeming it the chief enjoyment of
life to appear fit and worthy to arouse the lusts of
the greatest number [of men]... And even at
Rome he did nothing but send out agents to
search for those who have particularly large
penises and bring them to the palace in order that
he might enjoy their vigour'. Roman writers
considered his behaviour shocking only because
he wished to take the passive role – a 'true man'
(to the Romans) penetrated anyone and anything
but was never penetrated.

18 Below right: St Constantine the Great was
Rome's first Christian emperor and began the
process which eventually saw the forced
conversion of the empire to Christianity and the
slow changing of its culture from an acceptance
of 'sex-for-pleasure-and-procreation' to 'sex-for-
procreation-only'.

19 *Above left:* Krishna, a Hindu god, and Arjuna are the most famous pair of male friends/lovers in ancient Indian texts and their relationship forms the literary thread running through the *Mahabharata*. In various guises and incarnations their relationship is portrayed as intimate and physical.

20 *Above right:* Shiva, Hindu god/goddess of destruction, has various incarnations and sexual relations with both males and females. Hindu stories about gods and goddesses are replete with sexuality in a myriad of forms and permutations. The gods present to the average believer a variety of sexual roles as acceptable. What is clearly lacking in the stories of Hinduism is any sense that sex is 'wrong' and solely about procreation.

21 *Right:* Shiva and Parvati (a masculine-looking mountain goddess). Their love is connected with the birth of the god, Ganesh. Shiva washes herself, in one tale, and eventually the water finds its way to a woman (or women) and impregnates her (or them), resulting in Ganesh.

22 Right: Shiva *linga* note the phallic nature of
the bust. The worship of the phallus (*lingam*;
erect male penis) is an important part of Hindu
religion. It is hard to imagine a greater contrast
with the Judaeo-Christian emphasis upon sex as
a purely utilitarian act designed to procreate.
Hindus may worship the phallus as a sign of
fertility but their understanding of sex is
considerably more complex and liberal than
that found in the great monotheistic faiths
(Judaism, Christianity and Islam).

23 Right below: Ganesh, Hindu god, He was
born of sexual contact between two female
deities. As his statue is frequently placed at the
entrance to homes and businesses, every Hindu
is regularly presented with the image of a god
with 'two mommies'.

24 Below left: Agni, a Hindu god, swallowed
the semen of Shiva as the beginning of the
process which led to the birth of Kartikeya
(god of war and leader of the armies of the
gods). Although the stories make it clear that
this act was ritually impure, there is no sense
of revulsion, and the result – the god of war –
puts an extremely positive 'spin' on the tale.
One does not normally associate a god of war
with a peculiar type of 'homosexual' oral sex!

25 Below right: Where the West often
associates male-male love with effeminacy, the
Hindu accounts of the birth of Kartikeya in no
way lessen his 'manliness' or ferocity – he is,
after all, the commander-in-chief of the armies
of the gods.

Clockwise from top left:

26 Nadir Shah (1688–1747), emperor of Persia,.was famous for his military skill, as well as his appreciation of the adolescent male form. He was a contemporary of the last Mughal emperor of India, Aurangzeb, to whom he once sent a large troupe of beautiful adolescent male slaves as a present.

27 A *Samurai* and his *wakashu* (page). The Japanese warrior was expected to train his page in the art of chivalry but it was also assumed that they would be romantically and sexually involved. This relationship was similar to the 'instructional' or didactic type of pederasty found in Athens, as well as the emphasis on male warrior-bonding in Sparta. It helps explain why early Christian missionaries found it so difficult to convince Japanese converts to give up the 'unnatural vice'.

28 Iyeyasu, first Shogun of Japan, brought stability to the country. Under his successor Tsunayoshi, the Korean ambassador reported that 'King, noble, or rich merchant, there is no one who does not keep… beautiful young men'.

The most explicit passage (which does not deal with the issue of same-sex acts in the context of the Lot-Sodom story) comes from *Sura* 4: 19–21: 'And if two of you commit the like wickedness [fornication], punish them both: but if they repent and amend, leave them both alone; for God is easy to be reconciled and merciful'.

Of course, most commentators are aware that this latter verse is somewhat problematic coming as it does in the *Sura* 'on women' and in prescribing a much milder punishment for this sin than for female fornicators. Moreover, the ambiguity of the text relating to the gender of the 'two' has been debated: the Islamic writers Al-Zamakshari (1075–1144) and Al-Beidawi (d.1286) assumed fornication, not sodomy was meant while Jallalo'ddin (*fl.* thirteenth century) interpreted the passage as anti-sodomy. This confusion is further increased by the Koran's appreciation for the male form more generally and, especially, from the male perspective. *Sura* 52: 24 describes Paradise as a place where 'young boys... as fair as virgin pearls' will wait on Muslim men. *Sura* 76: 19 says the same: 'They shall be attended by boys graced with eternal youth, who will seem like scattered pearls to the beholders'.

There is less ambiguity, though, in the *hadith* (traditions/sayings) from which the *Shariah* (unwritten law of Islam) is derived. Quotations from the Prophet are clear in condemning same-sex acts. The chief compiler of the Prophet's sayings, Al-Nuwayri (1279–1332), argued that both the active and passive participants should be executed by stoning. He reported that the first caliph, Abu Bakr (r.632–634), had a wall pushed on top of a sodomite (the punishment famously preferred by the Taliban in Afghanistan). Other sources prescribed burning, stoning, or throwing an offender headfirst off a minaret. Jurists such as Ibn Hambal (780–855) supported stoning.

However, in the context of Mughal India it is crucial to realise that the juridical school which came to predominate there, the Hanafi, was considerably less severe. Historically, Hanafi (one of four schools of Islamic law) has been the most popular and most open to outside ideas. Moreover, in practice, the need for either a confession or four eyewitnesses (to actual penetration) meant that cases were exceedingly difficult to prove. The reality, though, as we have seen when considering the situation in the Arabic-Moorish world was more complex and less restrictive. Islamic culture, especially in an urban and/or courtly setting, remained enamoured of youthful male beauty. In the sexually ambiguous cultural milieu of Hindu India, over which the Mughals found themselves masters in the sixteenth century, this trait in their own culture was encouraged rather than discouraged. Nevertheless, this ambiguity was not without its detractors and Muslim theologians in the 1600s and 1700s – such as Abdul Haq Muhaddis Dehlavi and Shah Walliullah (1703–81) – were firm in demanding harsh punishments for same-sex acts.

In the light of this theological demand for harshness it is interesting that only Emperor Akbar (r. 1555–1605) made any serious attempt to impose a strict reading of Islamic sexual law on India. Similarly to Augustus in Rome, he was determined to instil moral values and familial duties in his subject, especially at court. All courtiers were to marry and at an age that would produce children. No one was allowed to marry a barren woman. Moreover, homosexuality was proscribed. Interestingly, in the context of the Indian-Hindu dichotomy of love/friendship and sex/marriage, Akbar said homosexuality was 'the wicked ways of Transoxiana (Uzbekistan), which are neither consuming nor melting, neither love nor friendship'.

This enthusiasm for 'law and order' in the Koran, the *Shariah* and at Akbar's court seems to have had little impact on the behaviour of the ruling Islamic princes. Sultan Mahmud of Ghaznah (held up as an ideal ruler by Islamic political theorists such as Ziauddin Barani; fl. 1300s) loved his slave Ayaz. Mubarak Shah Khalji (r. 1316–20) loved Khurso; Alauddin Khalji (r. 1296–1316) loved one of his eunuchs, Malik Kafur and made him his deputy ruler; Mira Nathan (a Mughal nobleman) also loved a eunuch, Khwaja Mina; Adil Shah (d. 1618; ruler of Bijapur) was stabbed by one of his eunuchs when he made advances on him in 1580. According to one English visitor to the court of Jahangir (Akbar's son), the emperor kept 'little boys' for his 'wicked use'.

Lest one think this merely the slander of a Christian, Western visitor to the court, we should consider the poet-scholar 'Mutribi' (musician) from Samarkand who visited the court in the latter years of Emperor Jahangir's reign. Mutribi kept a record of his conversations with the emperor. The emperor asked if he thought light-complexioned or dark-complexioned youths more comely. Mutribi tried to side step the issue by giving the balanced opinions of others. Jahangir demanded a more personal response and placed examples to the poet's right and left. Overcome with desire, Mutribi could only conclude that the most attractive colour was 'verdancy' (youth itself). The emperor applauded this response and added a quatrain that echoes the sentiments we have already encountered in his illustrious predecessor, Babur:

> He who is altogether attractive
> His attractive vitality [youth]
> Infused with life
> Has created this wonderful appearance.

No less than Babur, Jahangir not only appreciated the youthful male form but was not averse to making his opinions – or desires – known.

When we return to consider the *ghazals* (love poems) of the period we see that this emotional attachment was not only ambiguous but had a highly charged sexual element to it. Most importantly of all, unlike the assumptions that underlay much of the reading of homosexual erotic poetry from the Arabic-Moorish world, *ghazals* occasionally refer to real-life affairs. For example, the poet Maulvi Mukarram Baksh wrote extensively of his love for Mukarram who observed *iddat* (the period of widow's mourning) following Maulvi's death. He also inherited the poet's property. A similar relationship formed between Jamali (d.c.1535), a Sufi poet in Delhi, and his beloved disciple, Kamali. Jamali's *khanqah* (monastic community) and its mosque still remain with two graves in Jamali's tomb – one his, the other Kamali's. Here again, we see evidence of the primacy given to love/friendship in Indian (even Islamic-Indian) culture. Also, the place of men over women and male friendship over relationships with women helps one to understand the importance given to love/friendship. In the Hindi poetry of the Brahmin Tulsi Das (1532–1623, in his *Ramcaritmanas*) there is little room for, or consideration of, women, whom he groups with donkeys, drums and low-caste Hindus as 'things which need to be beaten'.

A similar relationship is seen between the Sufi mystic Shah 'Madho Lal' Hussayn (c.1539–c.1600) and his beloved Hindu youth, Madho. When Hussayn heard his master reciting the *Sura* 'the life of the world is nothing but play and pleasurable distraction' (compare *Sura* 29: 64 and *Sura* 47: 36) he resolved to throw off the constraints of piety and to live like a child at play disdaining social opinion and ambition and avoiding hypocrisy. Over a half century after his death, his biography, in the form of a lengthy Persian poem (entitled *The Truth of those Impoverished by Love*) appeared detailing not only his life but, more importantly, his love for Madho. The biographer recounts that on his first sight of Madho Hussayn cried out to his friends:

> *That young man has just stolen away my heart!…*
> *I'm dazzled with passion for this youth…*
> *I'm a captive to the sorrow of being separated from him*
> *I can't bear the burning fever of not seeing him for an instant!*

Later, the poem recounts the consummation of their courtship:

> *Hussayn and Madho sat together in one room…*
> *Hussayn was kneeling in respect,*
> *His eyes and his heart focused only on Madho*
> *Madho took from his hand a glass of deep-hued wine –*
> *He drank from it, and Hussayn kissed his wine-sweet lips*
> *Then Madho gave him a glass filled to the brim*
> *And kissed Hussayn in answer on his reddened lips…*
> [The exchange of sips and kisses continued]
> *Hussayn rose again to give of himself more generously*
> *And Madho graciously accepted his advances.*
> *In this way, the lovers engaged in a play of passions,*
> *Demanding and acceding, teasing and refusing.*
> *Each enticed the other, stirring his desire,*
> *Mingling wine and kisses like sugar dissolved in milk…*
> *In this duet of beseeching and tenderly replying*
> *The two friends made love with each other*

This erotically charged encounter though is wholly absent from the more popular translations from the Persian. One author distils the entire scene of shared wine and kisses into:

so the saint, while drinking wine, embraced Madho and made him arrive at the Truth, making Madho into a complete and perfected saint himself without any rigors or strenuous labors!

Some Urdu discussions of Hussayn make no mention at all of Madho and the 1865 Persian version reduces Madho to a single mention, *en passant!* The same desire to distort and deny same-sex relationships of the past is apparent in the 1975 Urdu translation of the biography (*Blooming Garden of the Righteous*) of Shaikh Makhu, a Gujurati Sufi contemporary with Hussayn. The original Persian tells how the forty-year-old saint fell in love with a handsome young man, Hansu; the translation says Hansu was a woman.

Undoubtedly many Indians, both Muslim and Hindu, would complain that restoring the prominence of Hussayn's relationship to Madho to its rightful place is the result of the same 'political correctness' that stresses the same-sex relationships of Alexander the Great, Hadrian, James VI and I, various Chinese emperors, and a host of other 'famous dead (white and otherwise) males'. Here, as in other cultures, the erasure and misrepresentation of the sexual liaisons of famous historical characters is seen as acceptable even necessary – the discussion of them in full, contrived and artificial and 'politically correct'. And yet, reading the words of Babur, Jahangir and, here, Hussayn, it would be hard to believe that these individuals would share the sense of shame about their loves, which so pervades many contemporary historians and politicians.

The Ming period (1368–1644) and the subsequent Qing dynasty (1644–1911) continued the practices of the classical and 'medieval' period. However, as we will see, the Qing dynasty – of Manchurian origin – associated the decay and decline of China under the Ming dynasty with sexual licentiousness. Before looking at the reaction of Qing China to same-sex relations it is important to consider, in some detail, the situation in Ming China. The Ming period is the earliest period to leave substantial records and an extended literature giving insight not only into elite culture but also the behaviour of people at most levels of society.

In the northern heartlands of the empire, same-sex relationships were referred to as the *southern custom*. However, historical and literary accounts from the northern province of Fujian provide evidence of a ceremony in which an older, socially superior man 'adopted' a younger, socially inferior male as a 'younger brother'. Various animals and fish were sacrificed in the ceremony and the two swore eternal loyalty to each other. After a celebratory feast, the younger man moved in with his 'elder brother' and was accepted into the household as a 'son-in-law'.

Chinese writer, Shen Te-fu (1578–1642), in particular, discussed the relationship between an older man (*ch'i-hsiung*) and his younger lover (*ch'i-ti*). The elder undertook the care and maintenance of the younger and, in return, was treated as a son-in-law by the younger man's parents. Some of these relationships lasted until the men were in their thirties. If they had sufficient funds, it was not unknown for them to 'adopt' boys as their own children. In addition, he noted that prisoners often paid money to pay for another man to live with them in prison. Furthermore, the work *Wu-tsa-tsu* said that contrary to popular belief, same-sex behaviour was not especially 'southern'. Rather it was common across China with males, *hsiao-ch'ang*, taking the place of (illegal) female prostitutes in Beijing. Regardless of any 'geographical' locus for same-sex relations it is clear that in reality it was an accepted part of Chinese culture.

However, it is in the literature and erotica of the late Ming and early Qing period that one gets the most detailed view of same-sex relationships and acts at this time. Some specific anthologies of novellas and short stories (*Bian er chai*; *Yichun xiangzhi*; *Longyang yishi*) were published in the mid-seventeenth century that were wholly based on same-sex relations. The more common works of romance and erotica centre on sex between the genders and present two opposing views of sexual relations between men and women, which serve further to highlight the divergence between 'sex for procreation' (perforce, between men and women) and 'romantic involvement' – which was just as likely to involve someone of the same sex as the opposite. One stressed that sex was fulfilling and worthy while the other warned of the dangers of love. In the latter, sex was an act of battle in which men and women struggled to conquer and (rather vampire-like) 'steal' the vital essence (*yin* or *yang*) of the other.

These works present a number of key terms which, as with *mei ren* above, could be used regardless of the gender of the participants. *Jia jing*, the 'beauteous realm', was the state of pure sexual arousal and bliss. To give but one example of how gender-complex these stories can be one can consider *Prefect Qiao re-orders the Lover Register* by Lang Xian. A young man, Yulang, impersonates his sister and moves in with the family to which she has been betrothed. While in this transvestite disguise (which would normally face prosecution as a type of fraud), he shares a bed with a daughter, Huiniang, of the family. He suggests that they pretend to be 'girl husband and wife' and, like a married couple, sleep under the same coverlet. They then engage in wild and joyous love-making despite some initial resistance by Huiniang. In addition to the transvestism and oblique reference to lesbianism, this story also strays into a negative view of sex between genders in which the man overcomes, by the sheer force of his sexual prowess, the resistance of the woman who, despite protests, really does want sex.

What is most interesting is that this concept of sex-as-battle is *less* evident in the stories about same-sex relationships. Men and women 'make war' in bed; men make love to other men. For example, in the *Hairpins beneath his Cap* (four stories of five chapters each), the author Zui Xihu makes clear that he feels that only in sex between men can one find true love. The stories lay no stress on passive or active roles; the characters assume either with equanimity. There is a spiritual element to the affairs that surpasses anything possible between a man and a woman. Indeed, 'true love' overcomes rigid ideas about sex and gender roles. To be true and complete love must be not only spiritual but fully and joyfully sensual (contrast this with chivalric and 'platonic' concepts of love in the West).

In the first story, 'A Chronicle of True Love', a teacher disguises himself as a student to court a student he has admired from afar. Most of the story is about the seduction itself and the bond which unites the two throughout the remainder of their lives (during which they marry and have children). Filial piety is preserved but the youth forms a 'true love', which endures to the end of his life. The story also serves as a sex manual, giving details on anal intercourse and it is during this discussion that the story's association with sex between genders is most apparent. The elder partner explains that the boy's 'beauteous realm' is the seven inches of his rectum. After sex, when asked if he had enjoyed the experience, the student replied, 'if I had not felt it myself, how would I have ever known that I possessed within me a nest of such pleasure?' Soon thereafter, the relationship is brought to an end and, thus, the student learns not only the meaning of true love but also how to face the loss of it. Any idea that these affairs could continue to the exclusion of a procreative relationship is rejected in a later story when, in reply to the suggestion of a permanent situation, a beloved says, 'in all history when has there ever been a precedent for two men to live out their lives together?' There may be an exultation of the bonds formed through same-sex acts (as in classical Greek thought – Plato's *Symposium*, for example) but these tales do not present or promote a modern 'gay lifestyle'.

In another story in the collection ('Chronicle of Knightly Love'), a man Zhong Tunan, seduces his beloved, a military hero named Zhang Ji, while the latter sleeps. Initially outraged at being penetrated while in a drunken stupor, Zhang Ji falls for Zhong Tunan and, after numerous triumphs on the battlefield, returns to make love one last time:

Zhong began slow and gentle, giving tight thrusts and cautious pulls. In a short while waves of passion gushed forth from Zhang's cave of sin and sprayed out like a jade mist. The waves of passion, rich and milky, flowed against the current and, wending past his tailbone, wetted the bamboo mat below. The waves of passion, frothing and surging, first streamed forth along the length of Zhong's member, then soaked downward along his body.

Thereafter the two (as with the teacher and student above) remain close friends and their descendants intermarry for generations eventually uniting the two into one blood through their children. Once again this story makes clear that Chinese thought places no disapproval on same-sex acts, in general, or the passive role in particular. Indeed, the author bluntly and humorously states that 'even a great hero cannot resist the romance of a "boy meets girl" story'.

While the role of same-sex attachment and military prowess was but a part of Chinese culture, during this period it was integral to Japanese society. When the Jesuits first arrived in Japan in the 1540s they were shocked by the behaviour of the *Samurai*. When St Francis Xavier (1506–52) visited Kyoto to have an audience with the emperor, he was appalled by the acceptance and openness of 'sodomy' at the Zen monastery he was shown. He reported that:

the abominable vice against nature [is] *so popular that* [the monks] *practice it without any feeling of shame. They have many* [adolescents] *with whom they commit wicked deeds.*

A Portuguese missionary, named Valegnani, wrote to the head of the Jesuit order that:

the gravest of their sins is the most depraved of carnal desires, so that we may not name it. The young men and their partners, not thinking it serious, do not hide it. They even honour each other for it and speak openly about it.

How did the Japanese respond to the shocked morality of the saint and his fellow missionaries? They laughed!

During their early successes in Japan, the Christian missionaries found that attempts to convert the ruling warrior class, the *Samurai* and the *Shogun*, were hampered by their 'addiction' to same-sex relations. They preached against sodomy describing it as 'something so abominable that it is more unclean than the pig and more low than the dog' in an effort to convince their *Samurai* hosts to reject it. However, they found that the result was that they were often expelled from the warlord's realm or simply ridiculed for their bizarre views. One of their few successes among the ruling elite was Lord Otomo Yoshikata (1530–87) who was baptised in 1576, aged forty-six. It is clear though that he found it almost impossible to relinquish his attachment to other males.

This syncretic and ambiguous reaction to foreign religious influences is a response seen repeatedly in Japanese history. According to tradition, Confucianism spread to Japan in 284 from China as did Buddhism in 552. The latter, as with Christianity, had some strong patrons in the royal family and nobility A number of orders of Buddhism managed to gain a foothold in Japan: Tendai and Shingon (ninth century) and Zen (eleventh century). More importantly, two Japanese sects (Shinran and Nichirin) began to found Buddhist orders which were uniquely Japanese. For example, Monto-Shin Shu allowed monks to marry. Both Confucianism and Buddhism had an impact on general thinking and culture in Japan but neither was able to dislodge native Shintoism and, in the long run, proved to be minority interests. The Japanese have seen this basic resistance to foreign ideas as a positive aspect of their culture. Thus, in 1896, Tokiwo Yokoi would write that Buddhism had 'made Asia mild' but it had failed in Japan; had Buddhism succeeded, Japan would have become like 'Sodom and Gomorrah'. While it is interesting to note, as elsewhere, the close connection being made between 'the other' and sexual deviance, what is most importance here is the failure of external religions to make much headway in Japan.

The brief flirtation with Christianity proved as unsuccessful as that with Buddhism. By the 1590s, a significant minority of Japanese had converted, albeit less than 5 percent. The Shogun and his fellow *Samurai* was increasingly concerned about the cultural impact of the missionaries with they 'foreign' ideas. The missionaries were ordered to leave the country and, in 1637, a widespread persecution resulted in the massacre of most Japanese Christians. Thereafter, apart from a Dutch enclave in Nagasaki, Japan closed itself to foreign contact until the nineteenth century. Christianity and Western values had been rejected in favour of traditional Shinto and Buddhist ideas. Japanese culture also rejected the morals of the missionaries. Same-sex relationships became a regular feature of Japanese society under the label of *shudo*. Monks, *Samurai* and merchants – in all groups and classes there was an acceptance of romantic and physical love between men. Nevertheless, as in China, there was still a cultural obligation laid on all men to procreate.

So entrenched and accepted was love between men that foreign observers noted it in the behaviour of various Shoguns. In the early seventeenth century, François Callon of the Dutch company in Nagasaki, discussed Iemitsu (third Shogun, 1604–51) and that the 'low opinion in which he holds women and the shameful inclination he has towards youths have always kept him from marriage'. About the court of the fifth Shogun, Tsunayoshi (1646–1709) the Korean ambassador reported

There are many male favourites who surpass young girls in beauty and attractiveness; they much exceed them, in their toilet especially, painting themselves with false eyebrows, making themselves up, dressing in coloured robes decorated with designs, dancing with fans; these beautiful young men are like flowers. King, noble, or rich merchant, there is no one who does not keep these beautiful young men.

Not only can one see the widespread and public acceptance of same-sex relations, it is also important to contrast the Western views in the disparaging comments of the Dutch and the Jesuits with those of the Korean ambassador. He displays a typical 'Eastern' view – clearly he thinks the young men are beautiful and expresses no surprise or condemnation at their popularity among the elite.

Moving away from the views of outsiders, it is important to consider the Japanese idea of *shudo*. It arose from the philosophical milieu that swirled around Buddhist monasticism and *Samurai* chivalry. Ijiri Chusake, in his *The Essence of the Jakudo* (1482) recorded the first written use of the word when discussing the love affairs amongst the monks of monasteries in Kyoto and Kamakura. The lovers swore eternal devotion to one another with no regard to rank or wealth. In this, *shudo* stands in stark contrast with what we have seen in China. The emphasis in Japan was upon an eternal, enduring, spiritual love that *transcended* the barriers of society and culture. In *shudo* love truly conquered all. Chusake stressed that the love of one man for another must be about loyalty and care, giving no regard to any consequent loss of status or power.

The poet Sogi (1421–1502) composed poems based on the ideals of *shudo* giving specific advice to the beloved (*wakashu*) who was – as in classical Greece – usually an adolescent male. (Unlike classical Greece or China of the same period, the Japanese situation placed no importance on social status.) Sogi stressed that the youth must be pure in heart, gentle, noble and always responsive to the love of an elder – one wonders how old Sogi was when he wrote this. This courtesy to elders was important as it reminded the *wakashu* that he too would grow old and having been the desired object of so many men would provide the older *wakashu* with happy memories. Buddhists writers likewise wrote of the importance of the *wakashu* being courteous and kind. Even when love would not grow from the sexual relationship, there was still a duty of decency to the lover. Finally, it is worth noting that throughout the Togugawa era (1603–1868; from the first Shogun, Iyeyasu, to the Meiji Restoration of the Mikado/emperor) Japanese poets, in particular, held that there was an entire category of men who were exclusively interested in other men – the *onna-girai* or 'women-haters'.

In time, *shudo* developed into a philosophical and practical system for regulating same-sex relationships in Japanese society. Yamamoto Jocho (1649–1719) wrote that 'you (the *wakashu*) must have only one lover in your life, otherwise there would be no difference between you and prostitutes'. He also advised the elder *Samurai* lover that '[this] pleasure must never be pursued at the same time as pleasure with women'. The advice was that the *wakashu* would be given up when the *Samurai* married in his early thirties and his *wakashu* would, in turn, take a young lover. In practice, it is clear that many relationships continued after marriage and the fulfilment of the obligation to procreate. As one character in the *Five Women in Love* by Ihara Saikaku (1642–93) says, 'between the pleasure one has in a man and that which one obtains with women there is no difference'. That such views were expressed by Saikaku (who also wrote *The Life of an Amorous Man* and *Glorious Tales of 'Homosexuality'*) is unsurprising. More interesting is that Saikaku is still revered as one of the leading prose and poetic writers of his day and an innovator in both fields of Japanese literature. Of course, about the same time (1684) John Wilmot (1647–80), the earl of Rochester was writing *Sodom; or, the Quintessence of Debauchery* with its *dramatis personae* of Queen Cuntigratia, General Buggeranthos, a Buggermaster-General, as well as Fuckadilla and Cunticula (maids-of-honour) – and the court was enjoying a one-off presentation of the play! The difference, of course, is that the court enjoyed the play in private; Saikaku was enjoyed publicly and continues to be extolled as a great Japanese poet.

Even more surprising for Western readers, Jocho also gave extensive advice to the *Samurai* about dress and appearance, as well as love and sex. A *Samurai* was always to have powder and rouge close to hand. If pale, one should pause and apply rouge. During the Sengoku period (*c.*1300–*c.*1600) they perfumed their hair and applied make-up before going into battle. Dressed for the event, each *Samurai* then went to fight and perhaps to die taking with him his young *wakashu* so that he might teach the youth the skills of war as well as chivalry. In this, the relationship between *wakashu* and *Samurai* mirrors that of page and knight in the West. However, while Western society placed a strong emphasis upon the spiritual, non-physical love between page and knight, Japanese culture considered the physical to be just as important and integral to the relationship as the spiritual.

The Japanese approach while different in caring little for social barriers was still fairly similar to the situation in China. In both societies, the key point was that the indigenous approach to sex and love between men was intertwined with, and fully developed within, the context of sexual relations between the genders. Even the erotic when specifically focused on sex between men and women was not without an attitude to sex that most of the Christian West would find uncomfortable, at best, and, at worst, depraved.

For example, in the anonymous, late medieval *Expanse of Passion* a group of young men, carousing for the night, are walking home. One grabs another and they begin to have sex. The friends laugh and suggest that they are stuck together like rutting dogs and someone needs to splash them with cold water so they can be pulled apart. In another, a man, Dongmen Sheng, has become so addicted to masturbation from his youth that he cannot have sex with his wife so he invited a friend to his wife's bed to provide him with an heir. He watches through a window and spatters the wall with his seed. More bizarrely, Dongmen Sheng's penchant for self-abuse did not prevent him from penetrating his friend before sending him into his wife! In a third story, two monks have sex with a woman staying in the monastery's inn. The elder monk usually has sex with the younger but, on this occasion, he ejaculates too quickly and can only watch as the younger monk and the woman have wild sex. However, he does try to rejoin

the activity by fondling himself and the other two 'at the place where
they [were] interlocked'. In these romantic and erotic stories, as so
many others, sex in all its myriad of forms (same-sex, transvestism,
masturbation, group, etc.) is presented without disapproval or scandal.
Interestingly, self-abuse (when totally alone), bestiality, lesbianism and
cunnilingus are almost wholly absent from the literature. Despite these
absences, sex throughout is about pleasure. In most, though, there is a
resolution as the actors marry and have children – though sex in these
myriad forms can quite legitimately continue after the marriage.

But the records of the period can be even more 'bizarre'. Gender
appears to be a very fluid idea indeed. There are eunuchs, 'stone-maid-
ens' (with hymens incapable of penetration), men who give birth or turn
into women, and people capable of being either male or female as the
whim takes them (rather recalling the gods of ancient Greece and classical India). Chinese medical accounts discuss 'hermaphrodites' (which
differ from those of Thailand) as those having 'two forms' who are the
result of disordered *ch'i* – 'human anomalies'. Some are both male and
female; some are for one half of the month and the other for the rest of
the month; some have both genitalia but can only 'function' as females.
What is interesting about these fantastic beings is that they are seen as
'over-sexed', capable of amazing erotic feats. They had too much sex
drive, in modern parlance, and recall the medieval Western view that a
sodomite was someone who was so driven sexually as to be incapable of
being satisfied *only* with women rather than *only* attracted to other males.

Although the literature of the period presents a wholly positive (or,
more accurately, neutral) view of same-sex relations, medical treatises
are more ambiguous. Sex between men is not seen as perverse or
unnatural. Rather, it was a 'waste' of male seed, which should be con-
served at most times (as 'vital' essence, a key to good health) or only
'spent' on procreation. Anyone who refuses completely to fulfil his
filial duties is seen as a coward; the other category contains those males
incapable (impotent or castrated) of procreative sex. Indeed, the lack
of a concept of the 'natural' in the sense of Divine Law, is crucial.
Unique events (in the sense of abnormal) – like snow in summer – are
noteworthy and strange but will simply resolve into a greater, intelli-
gible whole. This view had been propounded as early as the Song

dynasty (960–1279) and was never repudiated. While scientists and thinkers of the Ming dynasty were less willing to accept 'strange' events without question their interest in them was to understand them not to categorise them into 'natural' and 'unnatural'. Abnormality or the uncommon occasioned no fear for the Chinese who overlay them with no ideas of 'right and wrong' or 'good or bad'. That which was 'normal' was not, *ipso facto*, good; that which was rare was not, alternatively, bad. Where Western thinkers drew logical conclusions about right and wrong based on the generalities and 'normality' of the natural world, the Chinese saw permutations of *yin* and *yang*.

However, medical accounts and literary ideas about same-sex relations were not completely divided nor were medical treatises wholly negative. Rather, they tended to present same-sex relations in a context that resolved them into socially acceptable patterns. Thus, in 1567 imperial chroniclers reported on Li Liang Yu and Pai Shang-hsiang. Yu had previously married but then abandoned his wife to move in with his elder sister. He became ill and was nursed by another bachelor, Pai, who also shared Yu's bed. Over a period of months, Yu's genitals gradually withdrew into his body to become female. He – now she – began to menstruate and dress like a woman.

His brother-in-law became curious about what was going on and after an examination by Yu's elder sister the matter came to official notice. Yu was arrested – abnormalities in gender were seen as omens by the state and carefully scrutinised – and examined by a midwife. Yu's ex-wife confirmed that he had been male and that they had had regular if issue-less sex. A report was sent to the court and Yu was released and allowed to live out his live as she now was, a female. While strange, one must remember that Taoist thinking taught that a male, triumphing over his own sex drive, would see his genitals shrink and wither. Indeed, the Buddha is often said to have his penis 'sheathed' within his body as a sign of his victory over his own flesh. Clearly, the complete transformation of a male to a female is a step beyond but well within the tradition of Chinese philosophy, medicine and science.

What Chinese thought most frequently rejected was a type of same-sex relationship which became permanent to the exclusion of procreative sex. The late Ming story, *A male Mother Mencuis teaches the*

Three Removals, presents two male lovers sympathetically, when one castrates himself and takes on the accoutrements of a woman. The relationship is still non-procreative but at least it conforms to the social norms of the day. The same tale modifies this rather harsh model by allowing a 'homosexual' male (*dragon yang*) to list the seven unpleasant things about a woman and a typical speech by a 'moralist' ends with the satirical plea to men to:

cast your vital essence in a useful place (womb). Isn't it beautiful to increase the Emperor's household registers and produce progeny for your ancestors? Why would you take you 'golden fluid' and throw it away in some filthy receptacle?

These suggest an ambiguity about same-sex relationships in late Ming thought but this appears to centre on the issue of the filial obligation to procreate rather than any idea of depravity or sin. What writers, moralists and officials feared was that same-sex relationships would exclude procreative ones to the detriment of the empire – that the 'whole country [would go] crazy'. They were not, however, averse to criminalising sexual relations when these impinged upon the socio-economic unit of the family. Thus, adultery (more in theory and practice) was a crime in Ming China and female adultery was worse. Still, the stories and records would imply that, at least for men, sexual freedom was common as long as filial duties were fulfilled.

A possible solution to this was the widespread idea that men would become pregnant. Indeed, the increase in same-sex acts would see more male pregnancies as nature strove to restore the balance being lost through non-procreative acts. Apparently, changing fashions at the Ming court meant that such long-term relationships were not only more common but socially prominent. At the highest levels of society, this threatened a breakdown in the elite as fewer leading families reproduced. Moreover, the increasing power of eunuchs was considered a threat to the empire. China was coming under the sway of feminine males: graceful, refined, sophisticated, intellectual – long the ideal of masculine beauty in the Far East.

It is hardly surprising that the in-coming Qing dynasty from Manchuria took the view that part of the explanation for the decline in Ming power was the debilitation at the top of society. For the first time in Chinese history laws were passed to limit same-sex relations and laws against rape (of either gender) became much harsher. The new wind of change from the north rejected pre-existing ideas extolling the beauty of the androgynous (sexless) male. However, the model of the sexless female (rather as in Victorian Britain) remained and became even stronger. The difference between the two models is important. The androgynous male is a male capable of performing sexually with either gender; the 'sexless' female is not seen as sexual at all. The Manchus, in effect, limited the acceptable sphere for male sexual activity (more and more to procreative sex) while proscribing it for women almost wholly. Despite this 'puritanical' approach to the restoration of Chinese power, the reality is that the Manchus very quickly adopted the mores of Ming culture. Indigenous Chinese ideas about gender and sex, developed over two millennia, proved more resilient than Qing moral 'cleansing'. As we will see, the next great assault – under the Communists and the proponents of Western values – proved much more successful.

Indeed, it is during the early modern period that Westerners began to play a role in the Far East at first as observers and, by the eighteenth century, as active imperialists. In the sixteenth century, though, Westerners, especially the Spanish and Portuguese were in regular contact with China through trade with their colonies. Europeans were keen to expand their knowledge of Eastern civilisations having identified them as wealthy and powerful societies capable not only of generating income but also posing a very real threat to European expansion. One feature of Eastern culture that Europeans found most noteworthy was the very differing attitudes to sex.

In 1588, the attorney general of the Spanish Philippines, Gaspar Ayala, wrote to the king of Spain commenting on the incidence of same-sex activity among Chinese merchants resident in Manila. He reported that rumours of sodomy had been investigated and over a dozen men arrested. However, the Chinese culprits and their acquaintances had defended their actions by saying the behaviour was common in China. This availed them nothing; two were burnt at the stake and the rest condemned to the galleys. The archbishop at the time (c.1590–1600),

Friar Ignacio de Santibáñez, said the Chinese were not content to confine their vices to their own kind but had also 'introduced' the practice
to the native Filipinos. Chinese sources of the time provide a Chinese
perspective on the European response to same-sex relations. The *Tung
Shih* notes that sodomy was illegal in Luzon and severely punished as
a crime against 'heaven'. The tone suggests that the Chinese considered
this a surprising response to something of little importance.

On the other hand, the Chinese were not above looking askance at
practices of their Asian neighbours in their far-flung trading network.
Indeed, one must remember that the Chinese were present in large
numbers across much of Southeast Asia, and regularly commented
and judged the cultures with which they had contact and in which
they often had sizeable merchant colonies. Not only did this mean the
Chinese had the chance to examine other cultures but it also meant
that Europeans often came into contact with a distinct type of
Chinese: merchants, mostly male, living in often enclosed canton-
ments in foreign cultures.

The early modern period in Southeast Asia saw a growth of urban
centres, where foreign men were disproportionately represented.
Whereas Chinese women rarely left their homeland, the migration of
Chinese men to Southeast Asia increased markedly after 1567, when
the imperial court lifted its prohibitions against maritime travel. A
modern scholar has described Spanish-ruled Manila in the seventeenth century as 'indubitably' a Chinese town, and, she might have
added, a male Chinese town at that. Between 1602 and 1636 the
Chinese population rose from 2,000 to 25,000 people. Dutch-con-
trolled Batavia was another magnet; in 1625 alone, five Chinese junks
arrived, each carrying around 400 men. By the 1730s, the Chinese
community accounted for about 20 percent of Batavia's inhabitants,
with the result that there were twice as many males as females. This
may explain European perceptions of the 'rampant' sodomy amongst
Chinese merchants – a combination of 'situational sodomy' and a
more relaxed cultural attitude to same-sex activities.

This extensive network of Chinese, sending regular reports back to
the homeland, provides some interesting insights into the relaxed
views about sex and sexuality in part of Southeast Asia during the

early modern period. For example, one notes that the female 'promiscuity' that so displeased early Chinese observers reflected not merely relaxed ideas regarding interaction between men and women but the use of sexual relationships to welcome traders into the community. Chinese travel-writer, Ma Huan's (*fl.* 1400–30) description of Siam in the fifteenth century nicely captures these attitudes:

If a married woman is very intimate with one of our men from the Middle Kingdom [China], *wine and food are provided and they drink and sit and sleep together. The husband is quite calm and takes no exception to it; indeed, he says, 'My wife is beautiful and the man from the Middle Kingdom is delighted with her'.*

Moreover, the accumulation of gifts was a customary means of enabling a woman to increase her resources. According to a fourteenth-century law code from northern Siam, it was quite acceptable for a husband or parents to 'have [a woman] go and live with another man in order to get money and goods from him, with a limit on the period'. This was less prostitution and more a time-specific 'marriage' arranged for economic advancement for the woman and her family.

The result was that, as both the Chinese and Europeans noted, far from being condemned 'loose' or amoral, a woman who had been passed from one European to another was in her own society 'rather the better lookt on, [because] she has been married to several European husbands' as a certain Alexander Hamilton (East Indiaman) observed. At the bottom end of the social scale this did lead to a form of 'relationship prostitution' but even then there was still the recognition that casual sex with strangers, while certainly not desirable, was an acceptable way for the very poor to make a living, as long as all parties agreed. A ruler in east Sumatra stressed that his concern to prevent Dutch men from 'dishonouring' local females was not intended to stop consenting women from receiving payment for sexual services, since these must be considered a wage (*loon*). While commenting on these practices (and occasionally condemning them), merchants, both Chinese and Western, were more than willing to accommodate themselves to the indigenous cultural realities and make use of the relaxed sexual practices of these societies. Westerners were perhaps more condemning as their views were coloured by religious presuppositions about the sinfulness of sex-for-pleasure and sodomy; the Chinese were simply more likely to be shocked by the 'easy virtue' of the womenfolk – they seem to have had little concern about sodomy.

Indeed, what is most clear is that from the earliest recorded periods of Chinese history to the end of the eighteenth century, sexual relations between men were commonplace enough to pass almost without comment. They were integral to the literature, history, humour and mythology of China. The great civilisations of the Far East, as with India, were heirs to a continuous historical and cultural development from prehistory to the modern. Cultures based on ideas of balance derived from indigenous philosophies, such as Confucianism and Taoism, had borrowed extensively from Buddhism to produce attitudes to sex that were substantially different from those which had developed in Europe and the Near East under the influence of the three great monotheistic religions (Judaism, Christianity, Islam). Sex remained a multifaceted activity. Procreation and pleasure were *both* important. The 'flesh' was never repudiated as inherently dangerous or evil. 'Nature' was not an expression of divine will or decree. Without the strictures of revealed religion, sexuality was able to express itself within the socio-culturally proscribed boundaries of filial piety. As long as males were produced, those same males were relatively free to have sexual relations or romantic attractions with whomever they pleased.

Once we arrive at the sixteenth century it becomes possible to discuss the peoples of the Western Hemisphere with some confidence. However, as with comments about Africa, one must always bear in mind that information about indigenous peoples has been interpreted by, and filtered through, Christian Western European sources. Thus, the very use of words by early modern Europeans can be misleading. For example, the Inquisition (working in Portuguese Brazil) was interested in eradicating 'sodomy'. This mostly meant 'perfect sodomy', which was anal penetration *and* ejaculation involving two men. However, the term also included unconventional sexual positions, masturbation and (as the historian Elizabeth Kuznesof has noted) 'even a focus on pleasure rather than procreation'. The result is that European sources, which condemn a New World culture for 'sodomy' may or may not be observing, talking about and condemning same-sex acts. While this is problematic, in some circumstances the variety and quantity of sources is such that we can begin to reconstruct some of the cultural and social norms relating to sexuality that existed in the period of initial contact between groups in the New World and Europeans.

The most obvious example of this is the person of the *berdache* in North American Amerindian societies. The word '*berdache*' or '*bardache*' was first used by the French in New France and originates from the Persian *bardah* 'kept-boy' or 'male prostitute', via the Italian *bardascia* from the Arabic word *bardaj*. There are numerous accounts of *berdaches* going back to the sixteenth century and these provide a picture of Amerindian society (in part) which has echoes of the *hijras* of Indian and various 'third gender' constructions in Africa. For the most part, though, the phenomenon became rarer the longer the contact with Westerners and accounts mentioning *berdaches* became less common and, in some cases, were hidden under vague or even Latin expressions.

Before considering the early modern Amerindian *berdache* (and, in the next chapter, the more modern phenomenon) it is possible to say some things in general. The *berdache* may be defined as a person (usually male) who was anatomically 'normal' but assumed the dress, occupations and behaviour of the other sex to effect a change in gender status. Literal translations of the term often indicate its intermediate nature: halfman-halfwoman; man-woman; would-be woman. A *berdache* did not necessarily engage in same-sex acts. Although some did, this was usually only with a non-*berdache*. It is better to say that a *berdache* was 'directed' socially and culturally to bisexuality. Moreover, there is plenty of additional evidence of accepted same-sex activities which did not involve *berdaches* at all. There is no evidence to suggest that they were viewed as anatomically/biologically intersexed (hermaphroditic). The issue was behaviour *not* biology. In this sense the *berdache* was, as suggested above, very similar to the *hijras* of India and various shamans/mediums in Bantu-speaking south/south-western Africa.

When we turn to the specifics relating to individual Amerindian groups the widespread nature of the phenomenon becomes immediately apparent. Generally though, *berdaches* do not seem to have been universal in North America. Rather the behaviour was prevalent in a

large area from California to the Mississippi Valley and to the upper
Great Lakes. Over 100 Amerindian groups present direct evidence of
berdaches. Indeed, only nine groups in this extensive region present
denials with no contradictory evidence: Cahuila, Chimariko, Cochiti,
Karok, Maidu, Serrano, Walapai, Wappo and Yavapai. However, even
some of these are doubtful and may have more to do with a general
reticence to discuss sexual matters and lack of specific data than early
modern cultural realities.

Among those better known Amerindian groups with *berdaches* were
Arapaho, Blackfoot, Cheyenne, Choctaw, Crow, Hopi, Illinois, Iowa,
Lipan Apache, Miami, Mohave, Natchez, Navaho, Nez Perce, Omaha,
Pawnee, Pima, Santee Dakota, Shoshoni, Ute, Winnebago, Western
Apache, Yumi and Zuni. There are vague references suggesting there
may have been *berdaches* among the Creek, the Delaware and the
Tuscarora. There is enough evidence to infer it did not exist among
the Iroquois – or in the East more generally (except along its southern fringe). *Berdaches* would also appear to have been absent in some
of the southern Plains Indians (most notably the Comanche who had
a strong prohibition against cross-dressing – perhaps a reaction and
way of setting off themselves from neighbouring 'other' tribes who
had *berdaches*). Only thirty Amerindian cultures have provided any
evidence of female *berdaches*, among which the best known were
Crow, Mohave, Navaho, Ute, Western Apache and Yuma. Interestingly,
among the Kaska and Carrier only female-to-male *berdaches* are noted.

Later references state that *berdaches* were rare but the earliest
accounts suggest the opposite. For example, Cabeza de Vaca (writing
on the Coahuiltecans, 1528–33) and Le Moyne du Morgues (on the
Timucua, 1564) said they were common. Miguel Costanso noted
(1769–70) that there was at least one *berdache* in every village of the
Chumash while Gerónimo Boscano (on the Yuma, 1822) and Prince
Maximilian zu Wie (on the Crow, 1832) spoke of them as relatively
common and a 'normal' feature of society. Indeed, sixteenth-century
Yuma were reported (1565) to have had a rule that there always had
to be four *berdaches*. However, there was a clear decline in the phenomenon over time. For example, among the Crow, Maximilian noted
many while the sociologist, Holder, later counted only five (in 1889),

a later sociologist, Simm, three (in 1902) and another sociologist, Lowie, only one (in 1924). The last Cheyenne *berdache* died in 1879. Two explanations are possible. As Indian populations declined (through war, dislocation and disease) the number of *berdaches* would also have dropped while, perhaps, remaining statistically constant. However, it is much more likely that there was actually a decline in the number of berdaches in relative terms as their social role changed – with the collapse of indigenous cultural, social and religious systems.

With some idea of what a *berdache* was and how widely spread was the practice, one must now consider how this socially constructed 'gender' worked in the given cultures. Transvestitism was the major hallmark of a *berdache* but it was not universal. For example, the Pima forbade cross-dressing although their *berdaches* imitated the speech, behaviour and posture of women. Moreover, Crow female *berdaches* were armed and fought as men but dressed as women. Among the Navaho it was even more complex. The Navahos insisted that 'married' *berdaches* wear women's clothing while their non-*berdache* 'husbands' dressed as men. However, unmarried Navaho *berdaches* of either (biological) sex dressed as they pleased.

The clothing might also change based on a specific function regardless of the length of time involved. Thus, as just noted, the Navaho 'male' in a marriage had to dress as a man regardless of the gender of his 'wife'. Miami and Osage *berdaches* had to dress as men when in a war-party but reverted to female dress upon their return from battle. This might suggest that these individuals who changed dress were not fully 'acclimatised' as *berdaches* but were in mid-transformation. Unfortunately, there is insufficient detail to draw specific conclusions other than that cross-dressing, though a major feature of the *berdache*, was not universal in time or place in any or all cultures that had *berdaches*. Finally, the impact of Westerners (Americans) tended to limit cross-dressing. For example, the last known Winnebago *berdache* (cited in 1953) wore a mix of gender-specific clothing until his brothers threatened to kill him unless he wore male-only attire.

Another hallmark of the *berdache* was the sort of occupations that interested the person – and there is an argument that boys who showed a propensity for, or interest in, female occupations were assumed to be

headed for 'berdachehood'. Coupled with this was the frequent assertion that male berdaches were actually better at female work (compare
the Western distinction between a cook – usually female – and a chef
– usually male). Female berdaches were also often seen as better than
men at male tasks (compare the myth of the Amazons). As late as 1961
Edwin Denig noted that Woman Chief was as good a hunter as any
other Crow and able to support her four female wives. Linked to this
idea of skill and expertise was the notion that a berdache in a marriage
or an extended family (or even a berdache alone) was 'good luck' in the
sense that wealth would follow. For example, the Navaho said a family
with a berdache (by birth or marriage) was 'assured of wealth'.

The third hallmark (after transvestitism and transgendered occupations) was supernatural powers – often validated by their economic success. Of course, a berdache could undertake the labour of either sex – a
distinct advantage in allowing one person to combine the work, which
would otherwise require two individuals. Indeed, some Plains tribes
mocked men who sought male berdaches as wives saying they were
trying to 'have their cake and eat it too' – by having a 'wife' who could
hunt and keep house. However, this ability to be lucky was simply part
of the manifold powers and 'blessings' often associated with berdaches.

Among the Teton, berdaches conferred secret names on newborns
(compare the hijras's role at births in India). Among many Californian
cultures they were involved in burial and mourning rituals (compare
shamans among various Angolan groups) and were able to mediate
between men and women as they could move between the groups
(rather like the mashoga of Mombasa and various transgendered groups
in Islam elsewhere). An interesting similarity was observed among
Chileans in the sixteenth century. The Spanish reported that their
mediums (and medical practitioners) were cross-dressing men called
machis. These European conquerors viewed them as witches in league
with Satan and worked to eradicate them. They were partially successful; today, the machis still exist but are all biological females.

A number of explanations have been advanced to explain the
presence of berdaches. For example, in upper Midwest tribes, men who
displayed cowardice in battle were forced to wear women's clothes
but could redeem themselves. Some have seen this as the 'principle'

underlying the *berdache*; the *berdache* was a 'failed' warrior. However, this practice was temporary, shaming and imposed. Being a *berdache*, on the other hand was permanent, positive/neutral and voluntary. Indeed, there is little evidence to suggest that *berdaches* were 'failed warriors' or 'failed men'. *Berdaches*, for the most part, were identified at a relatively young age and many seem to have taken part in hunting and fighting. In addition, while a number of societies punished cowardice with cross-dressing, it was clearly quite distinct from being a *berdache*. With *berdaches*, the emphasis seems to have been less on the individual's ability or propensity for warfare and more on assumptions about what was 'right and proper' to their (assumed and socially constructed) 'gender' status. There seems to be no evidence for the assertion made in a few sources that war captives were forced into *berdache* status though some may have been humiliated by being made (as with the cowards noted above) to don female attire.

Thus, Illinois *berdaches* fought but were denied the use of the bow while Miami *berdaches* dressed as men for battle. As late as 1897, an American travel writer knew an Ojibwa *berdache* who had fought as the rearguard – hardly the role for a 'coward' – while his fellow warriors retreated from a Dakota attack. Another late account records that a Hidatsa chief wanted to count coup among three Dakota women but was driven off when one was revealed to be a *berdache* and fought with 'his' digging stick.

Two probable explanations have been advanced for a person 'becoming' a *berdache* (these are *not* mutually exclusive). The first is sexual, functional and pragmatic: the person showed interest in the occupation of the other gender and associated with the other biological sex. The second says there was a supernatural revelation of some sort, which directed the individual to assume the accoutrements of the 'other' sex and become a *berdache*. Thus, in some cases, children were selected from infancy and 'gendered' opposite from their biology (e.g. Kaska, Luiseno and Kaniagmiut). Others were directed into a certain gender when they demonstrated an interest in, or propensity for, characteristics associated with the 'opposite sex'.

Visions seem to have been involved in some transformations. The best evidence for this comes from the Dhegiha and Chiwere Siouans, the Pawnee and some Algonquian tribes (e.g. Omaha, Winnebago, Iowa, Kansas, Pawnee and Miami). Normally, the change related to lunar deities or female supernaturals. Indeed, the Ponca term for *berdache*, *mixuga*, is best understood as 'instructed by the moon'. These supernaturals have a variety of names in various Indian cultures: Double-Woman; Village-Old-Woman; Woman-Above; Holy Women; and Old-Woman-Above. In other cultures, *berdaches* were associated with spiritual/mythological hermaphrodites: Sxints (Bella Coola); twins born to First-Man and First-Woman (Navaho); the Elk – as first transvestite (Oto).

The importance of supernatural or divine revelation is paramount. In many cases, the surviving sources suggest that individuals actively resisted the divine vocation as a *berdache*, only relenting after repeated revelations or as the result of social and familial pressure to 'accept their calling'. Moreover, it is also clear that in some tribes *berdache* status was not open to everyone: among the Oto one had to be from the Elk clan to receive the supernatural call. As one might imagine, the important part played by religious belief in assuming *berdache* status changed over time. Thus, although *berdaches* declined and became contemptible after their tribes had lengthy contact with European-Christian ideas, there is a fairly consistent amount of evidence suggesting that originally they were seen as holy, sacred and mysterious, as well as fortunate and lucky.

Before leaving *berdaches* to look at non-normative sex and sexuality elsewhere in the New World, it is perhaps worth considering a 'case study' of *berdaches* in this period. The Illinois word for berdache was *ikoneta*. The Illinois (stretching from southern Wisconsin to northeastern Arkansas) spoke a central Algonquian language and were related to other Prairie cultures such as the Miami, Sauk and Fox. They first entered European historical accounts with the Louis Jolliet (1645–1700) and Jacques Marquette (1637–75) expedition of 1673. According to Marquette (1673) *berdaches* fought as warriors but were never armed with bows (which were seen as male 'attire'). A member of René La Salle's (1643–87) expedition (1682) said Illinois *berdaches* were chosen at a young age and grew up speaking their language with the 'accent' reserved for women. Although it is not clear that all Illinois shamans were *berdaches* or all *berdaches* were shamans, the evidence suggests that both were thought to possess – or to be – *manitous* (possessing the generalised essence of spiritual power). In other words, the Illinois *berdaches* display – in these contemporary European accounts – all the features one generally associates with *berdaches*. They also demonstrate (in their fighting as warriors) why it is difficult to make assumptions about the 'meaning' of this status in early modern Amerindian cultures.

Finally, a comment from a later expedition among the Illinois highlights the greatest danger in reading these accounts as sources on early Amerindian culture and society. Pierre Deliette (who has left an account of his travels with La Salle's expedition of 1698) wrote that 'the sin of sodomy prevails more among [the Illinois] than any other nation'. Deliette and others made the simple assumption that men who assumed female roles and attire were homosexual in their sexual practices. However, as we will see in the next chapter when we consider the *berdache* in the modern period, this is a dangerous and misleading assumption. Suffice it to say here that the 'average' *berdache* was complex both with regard to gender (socio-cultural behaviour) and sexuality (in choice of sex-partner).

One last point remains to be made about North America and sexuality. Europeans of the early modern world worked with a set of presuppositions about 'civilisation', which radically affected their view of other peoples. Societies (in the New World, Africa, and elsewhere) that wore little clothing were not only seen as barbarous but also licentious. Contact with these people – or even living in 'luxuriant' tropical climes – could taint even the hardiest European Christian. Thus, British elites had a view of their settlements in the New World as depraved and depraving. In particular, the sexual appetites and morals of the colonial societies were questioned:

they are such who have been Scandalous *in* England *to the utmost degre, either* Transported *by the* State, *or led by their* Vicious Inclinations; *where they may be* Wicked *without* shame, *and* Whore *on without* Punishment... *In short,* Virtue *is so* Despis'd, *and all sorts of* Vice Encourag'd *by both* Sexes, *that the* Town *of* Port Royal *is the very* Sodom *of the Universe'.* [1700]

Inhabitants of the New World were 'assumed' to be depraved because they lived in wilderness as 'wild men'. Virtue was expected to be little prized and rarely present. New World hypocrisy was seen as having a long and honoured history. As Samuel Johnson noted (in 1775) America's revolutionary leaders (e.g. Jefferson and Washington) were 'drivers of negroes', who presented themselves as 'lovers of liberty'. The moral, of course, of these tirades is that we must view early modern European sources, which talk about sexuality, especially that which they viewed as immoral, as slightly suspect. They may well have supplied (scandalous) behaviour because they *assumed* it had to be present in the given society and climate.

In South and Central America, Europeans encountered societies that they *knew* had to be immoral. Human sacrifice and ritual cannibalism were but the tip of depraved cultures given over to the worship of Satan. That they found and noted a whole range of (to them) depraved behaviour should not surprise us. Thus, we turn to early modern European accounts of Aztec, Maya and Inca civilisations, and cultures elsewhere in Central and South America, with some caution and trepidation.

The situation in the Portuguese colony of Brazil not only exemplifies this Christian European tendency to force diverse and divergent indigenous cultural norms into their own ideas about, and 'niches' for, sexuality but also to use sexual practices as rhetorical and ideological tools to justify conquest and intra-European rivalry. Thus, a Scottish (Protestant) commentator on (Catholic) Brazil was even more scathing of the behaviour of the settlers (who he felt had *more* than 'gone native') than the natives themselves.

In his *In colonias brasilienses, vel sodomitas, a Lusitanis missos in Brasiliam* (On Brazilian colonists or the sodomites sent from Portugal to Brazil; 1568), George Buchanan said that 'native' cannibalism was as nothing compared with the 'perversity of the degenerate settlers' and their 'accursed filthiness' – *execranda spurcitia*. He went on to pray to God, saying,

Come down from the sky in flaming whirlwind, armed, angel, with avenging anger, long since known as the scourge of lust in the destruction of Sodom the wicked city. May it perish once more at thy hands! The progeny of the Syrians [Portuguese] calls up a sacrificial offering to rival Gomorrah, and it renews an arena for accursed and unspeakable filthiness.

He called the settlers 'filthy sodomites' (*impuris cinaedis*) and could not resist a dig at (Catholic) clerical homosexuality. From top to bottom, he condemned Portuguese (Catholic) society by suggesting that it had been completely 'infected' by the lascivious ways of the New World:

and [the cleric] *who formerly defiled the boys,* [now] *defiles the fields* [in Brazil], *and* [King João I] *who takes away land* [in Morocco] *from his own soldiers, gives it* [in Brazil] *to the sodomites.*

Buchanan tells us much about his views on Catholics and sex but little about the actual practices of the Portuguese settlers or their indigenous subjects.

Another example of this use of 'history' and 'proto-anthropology' for political and confessional reasons comes from the Aztec. According to a post-conquest Franciscan account the Texcoco (one of the three ruling nations of the Aztec Triple Alliance) had a number of sexual crimes punishable by death: raping a virgin; adultery; incest and homosexuality (active and passive). When one turns to consider Aztec beliefs as we know them this seems difficult to accept and may be more of an attempt by the Franciscans to present the Indians in the best possible light to other Spaniards. As great advocates of the Indians pleading for their better treatment, the Franciscans had a vested interest in downplaying their 'deviant' past.

The reality is that wider aspects of Aztec belief and culture would suggest that same-sex acts were not viewed as wholly evil. In Aztec cosmology, the highest celestial level was the realm inhabited by Ometeotl, a female/male god of duality. The goddess, Tlazolteotl (Filthy Deity) – also called Tlaelcuani (Eater of Foul Things) – was patroness of dust, filth, adulterers and loose women. Her 'pair' was the god Tezcatlipoca (The Mirror's Smoke), a trickster who usually punished people for behaviour he had instigated. A number of gods could be male or female (e.g. the god/goddess of earth and water) while some were gender-twinned, existing as male-female pairs. Xochipilli had various incarnations (as god of flowers, song, dance and love) and was also associated with hallucinogenic substances.

Although of a much later date, some aspects of a similar 'New World' cosmology are echoed in the syncretic religions that have developed in Brazil where a mixing of Christian, African and indigenous Amerindian ideas have produced some extremely complex beliefs. One of these religions (Condomble), for example, is polytheistic with sexual ambiguity as a mark of the most powerful gods. Thus, Oxala (Creator God) is a male with a feminine half who lives under a cotton plant with a young boy as a lover. Oxumare (God of Life) is male for six months of each year and female the next six months. This ambiguity has created a range of views about same-sex activities. One is always loathe to use very modern examples to provide insight into past cultures about which we know little. Nevertheless, the complexity of views in Brazil today does perhaps give us the chance to speculate, at least, about how very different earlier views about sexuality might have been in the Western Hemisphere before the arrival of Christian Europeans. In contemporary north-eastern Brazil there are three gender roles: male (who penetrates a woman or a man – there is *no* stigma attached to being a 'top'); a woman (a biological female – who is penetrated); and a *bicha* (a biological male who is passive – but still widely seen as male in social interactions). A *bicha* who penetrates another *bicha* is considered 'deviant' and such behaviour is called 'lesbianism'. What this modern-day situation suggests is the difficulty of mapping Western Christian categories of sexuality onto a totally alien culture. This at least implies that what we know about New World sexuality from the Christian and Christianising language of post-conquest sources may hide a much more complex reality.

When we return to Central America we see that aspects of Aztec culture, especially drawn from linguistics associated with the dominant language of the area, Nahuatl, tell another story. The word for harlot/whore in Nahuatl gives an interesting insight into ideas about sex: *ahuiani* – 'one who habitually has a good time'. Nahuatl has no word for 'virgin' rather the terms used were for the phases between adolescence and the acceptable age of marriage (adulthood): *ichpochtli* (female), *telpochtli* (male) when a person was neither a child nor part of a marital unit. Moreover, as Rebecca Overmyer-Velázquez has argued that:

Sexual pleasure in moderation was openly valued [among the Aztecs] *as one of the gifts given to humanity to sweeten an otherwise sorrowful life. Moderation in sex, as in all things, was indicative of someone who honoured herself and himself, which resulted in praise.*

None of this would seem to suggest a prurient attitude to things sexual. Indeed, taken together one sees a society with a mythology and culture very different from Christian Europe of the time.

When looking specifically at same-sex activities, other evidence from post-conquest Mexico (New Spain) also undermines the very Christian-sounding laws of the Texcoco. In colonial sources from New Spain the sodomite is described as one who 'talks like a woman, [or] takes the part of a woman', which places the emphasis on characteristics of effeminacy. Such an understanding of same-sex individuals is not normative to Europe of the sixteenth century. Indeed, one does not see any European association of, or discussion about, effeminacy and sodomy until the late seventeenth and early eighteenth centuries. This would seem to imply that this represents an Aztec understanding of 'sodomy' based on Aztec norms of behaviour.

We do know that the Maya also had an interesting if ambivalent attitude to same-sex behaviour. Moreover, as they borrowed words from Nahuatl for active and passive homosexual activities (*tzintli* and *cuiloni*, respectively) their ideas may have been borrowed as well – or at least shaped by contact with the Aztec. In Maya thought two constructions of homosexuality seem to have been apparent. In the first (largely negative) one, an enemy might be denigrated or mocked as a homosexual in the sense of 'taking the role of a woman'. This shows a gender-structured type of homosexuality. However, we also know that Maya had rites of passage, which seem to have involved same-sex acts in an age-based structure (older man with an adolescent youth). Indeed, where Maya used their own language for sodomy they simply replaced the 'male' signifier (*ah* as in *ah pen*) with that for a female – *ix pen*. This seems to imply that, in a general sense, they viewed same-sex acts as simply related to the biology/gender of the partner and little more. There certainly seems to have been no negative connotation to the word. On the other hand the Nahuatl word, *cuiloni*, for the passive partner may have had negative meanings. The Aztecs chanted it at the Spaniards as they retreated from

Tenochtitlan (Mexico City) after the murder/assassination of
Moctezuma. Alternatively, they may simply have been giving the Spanish
an idea of the fate that awaited them before their sacrifice to the gods.

While the Spaniards faced the dangers of being ritually sodomised
and then sacrificed, the problems faced by European explorers elsewhere was more prosaic – and even amusing. Captain Cook's
(1728–79) crew were shocked by the cultural practices they observed
in Hawaii. Members of the Hawaiian royal family (the *ali'I*) maintained a category of male concubines (*aikane*) for use in same-sex acts.
The log of the ship's surgeon, David Samwell (1751–98), surely
recorded the bemusement and consternation of the entire crew:

*Of this Class [aikane] are Parea [Palea] and Cani-Coah [Kanekoa] and their busi-
ness is to commit the Sin of Onan [masturbation] upon the old King. This, however
strange it may appear, is fact, as we learnt from the frequent Enquiries about this curious Custom, and it is an office that is esteemed honourable among them & they have
frequently asked us on seeing a handsome young fellow if he was not an Ikany [aikane]
to some of us [29 January 1779].*

As we have seen elsewhere, cultures with socially constructed 'niches' for
same-sex practices were completely confused by the Christian European
response. Hawaiians thought it perfectly reasonable that their male royals
would have men close to hand to masturbate them, especially in old age.

Cook and his men, unlike the Spaniards, were rarely in a position
to do more than record their shock. On the other hand, on the Western
Hemisphere landmass Europeans had the power to attack those cultural elements of which they disapproved. For example, two days
before Vasco Balboa (1479–1519) saw the Pacific he conquered a
Panamanian village in which he killed the leader of the Quarequa
Indians along with 600 of his warriors and then fed forty more Indians
to his war-dogs – for being sodomites. The 1555 English translation of
Peter Martyr's *Decades* (1516), which contains the story says:

*[He] founde the house of this kynge infected with most abhominable and unnaturall
lechery. For he founde the kynges brother and many other younge men in womens
apparell, smoth & effeminately decked, which by the report of such as dwelte abowte*

hym, he abused with preposterous venus [lust]. *Of these abowte the number of fortie, he commaunded to bee given for a pray to his dogges.*

The account portrays the 'noble savages' in the village (who are not the 'nobles and gentlemen') as offended by sodomy and affirming (as the historian, Jonathan Goldberg has noted), pre-conversion, 'the universality of the Judaeo-Christian condemnation of "unnatural" sexuality' when in fact the presence of sodomy so openly suggests just the opposite. While we can draw little from this account we must ensure that we avoid being as blinkered as Balboa. Cross-dressing *cannot* mean the same thing in all Indian societies; to ignore this would be to amalgamate them into one racial *lump* as crude and unrealistic as that of 'noble savage' or 'depraved worshippers of Satan'.

Moreover, although not necessarily part of a discussion about the New World, we must not forget that Captain Cook and Balboa were not the same type of Christian. The Reformation, which broke Western Christendom just at the point of exploration and discovery introduced a level of confessional violence and competition in the European mindset. It also had a direct impact on issues of sex, sexuality, marriage and procreation. As Alexandra Walsham has succinctly put it:

Protestantism led [as argued by Roper in *Oedipus and the Devil*] *to a reconceptualisation of the relationship between sexuality and holiness; by repudiating clerical celibacy and elevating the institution of marriage on a pedestal the reformers severed the medieval connection between sanctity and ascetic abstinence from the pleasure of the flesh. But the effects of this shift were complex and double-edged: on the one hand it encouraged the emergence of a stricter code of marital ethics, on the other it carried the Anabaptists along a path towards licensed promiscuity and polygamy.*

That is, at the very point that Europeans were coming into contact with many diverse cultures they were acutely aware of issues of sex in the midst of an atmosphere of religious hatred and warfare. If medieval Europeans had been concerned with the pleasures of the flesh, their post-Reformation successors were even more aware of a relationship between sex, Satan and chaos. This was clearly *not* the best time for a non-Christian culture to be overrun by Europeans!

six

Colonising Minds

(1800–2000)

They had grown from childhood in their own natural way

(Herero tribesman to a Christian missionary – Namibia, 1906)

There is always the temptation to see the Enlightenment as an age of toleration and growth in personal liberty. In many ways it was. However, one must always remember it was also an age of slavery. Moreover, it is absolutely essential to recall that the eventual defeat of Revolutionary-Napoleonic France led to an extreme conservative 'backlash' across the European continent. The European nations that entered the nineteenth century expanding into all areas of the globe where not driven by the ideology of '*liberté, égalité, fraternité*'. Rather, post-Napoleonic France and the Britain of the nineteenth century were reacting against Enlightenment and Revolutionary ideologies, and becoming increasingly conservative, moralistic, supremacist and *bourgeois* as the century progressed.

In many ways the history of homosexuality in the Christian West is a history of enormous change and contrast. As we have seen, previous centuries were largely hostile, in theory, but also quite often unconcerned in practice. Indeed, coming from a tradition of Graeco-Roman ambivalence and toleration, which was substantially revived in the Renaissance and continued through the fads and fashions of the seventeenth and eighteenth centuries, one might have expected the nineteenth century to have been an age of greater openness and tolerance. This was most definitely not the case.

Although outside the scope of this volume, one cannot afford to underestimate the impact of the Enlightenment, French Revolution and Napoleonic Wars on the Europe of the subsequent century. Many rulers and elites in Europe looked back on the excesses and violence of the years surrounding the French Revolution and concluded that liberalism was the problem. The period of the French Revolution and Napoleonic Wars produced a widespread conservative reaction across Europe. Just as the Reformation had brought to an end much of the liberalism accompanying the Renaissance and classical Humanism, the Enlightenment became tainted with the excesses of the Revolution. No better example of the individual impact of this cultural shift can be found than in Mrs Keith of Ravelstone, an aged aunt of Sir Walter Scott. As we have noted in the previous chapter, Scott related that she had decided to reread Aphra Behn's fiction, which had been a favourite of her youth. Her response, when asked for her impressions of the stories after so many years, are worth repeating:

Is it not a very odd thing that I, an old woman of eighty and upwards, sitting alone, feel myself ashamed to read a book which, sixty years ago, I have heard read aloud for the amusement of large circles, consisting of the first and most creditable society of London?

This brief vignette serves as a cautionary note for all that follows. The last chapter opened with the Renaissance followed by the moralising of the Reformation and the liberalising of the Enlightenment. In the following decades morality was to come full circle ushering in the conservatism, which culminated in the so-called 'Victorian values', lauded by many modern politicians.

Anyone calling for a return to the values of the past might be shocked by the result if the response was an enthusiasm for Renaissance or Enlightenment values, rather than those of the Reformation or nineteenth century. However, for this discussion, one of the most important historical realities (not lost on reactionaries in the early decades of the nineteenth century) was that one of the first acts of the French Revolutionary parliament was the decriminalisation of sodomy. Across Europe (semi-)absolutist states tried to reconstruct the world of the *ancien regime*. That world was gone but the conservative alternative built in its place – an alternative based on the middle-class, *bourgeois* morality of 'respectable' families – had every intention of rolling back the dangerous liberalism of the Revolution and Enlightenment.

This period also marks the apogee of European global dominance. While the West still dominates the world economically and its (especially American) culture seems to be carrying all before it, we shall see that the greatest result of this period was the inculcation and naturalisation of nineteenth-century Western *bourgeois* values in cultures across the globe. The colonial armies of Europe swept across the world, like a tide waxing strong and then, by the end of the Second World War, waning on every front. They left in their wake a heady mixture: post-colonial resentment, technological feats, legal systems, languages, artificial borders and religion, to name but a few. Also, and most importantly, they left behind a cultural mindset and system of values, which profoundly altered almost everything they touched. This globalisation of 'Christian' and Western values is most obvious in changing attitudes to homosexuality in societies whose deities, historical heroes, mythological figures and common people had previously been largely benign about same-sex relationships.

In England, the century opened with the execution of a number of sodomites. Five men were hanged in Lancaster (1806), the judge lamenting that:

such a subject should come before the public as it must do, and above all, that the untaught and unsuspecting minds of youth should be liable to be tainted by such horrid facts.

Mathusalah Spalding and Joshua Archer were hanged in 1804 and 1808 respectively. So widespread was the behaviour – and so concerned was the state to keep it 'in the closet' that (in 1808) the Home Secretary, later Prime Minister, Lord Liverpool (1770–1828) ordered Hyde and St James's parks closed at night to 'prevent these scandalous practices in such a way that the public is *kept ignorant* [emphasis mine] of the disgrace of them'. In 1815, four sailors of HMS *Africaine* were hanged for sodomy.

The most famous case in early nineteenth-century England was the Vere Street scandal of 1813. So public was it that the lawyer Richard Holloway produced a volume about it entitled *The Phoenix of Sodom, or The Vere Street Coterie* (1813). The authorities uncovered a molly house (a place where men interested in men could meet). Mock marriages were celebrated in the house and consummated often in front of other men or other couples also engaging in sex. Most of the men seem to have been married and almost all were from working-class trades. Lack of any real evidence against specific individuals resulted in few prosecutions (though the men almost certainly had their names ruined by the publicity). In the end, six were pilloried with extreme violence by the crowd. One journalist reported the scene: 'it is impossible for language to convey an adequate idea of the universal expressions of execration which accompanied these monsters on their journey'. Being pilloried was horrific and often resulted in permanent mutilation (especially blindness) and even death. The men were placed in the pillory and the mob hurled faeces, urine, rotten produce (fruit, vegetables and eggs) and, even, decaying cats at their heads and faces. The acid and bacteria could blind and, if enough of the refuse actually coated the face, suffocation was a distinct possibility.

From the Home Secretary to the common man in the street, sodomites were hated and attacked as never before. Of course, this is not the entire picture. If there are two things the nineteenth century is known for it is Victorian values and Victorian hypocrisy. European rulers and politicians wanted to wipe sodomy and sodomites not only from their world but their past and even their consciences. Yet, at the same time, one finds Benjamin Disraeli (1804–81; later Prime Minister) in his novel *Coningsby* (1844) writing about the relationships between boys in England's private, all-male boarding schools:

At school friendship [emphasis mine] *is a passion... All loves of after-life can never bring its rapture, or its wretchedness; no bliss so absorbing, no pangs of jealousy... so keen!... what bitter estrangements and what melting reconciliations; what scenes of wild recrimination, agitating explanations, passionate correspondence... what earthquakes of the heart... are confirmed in that simple phrase, a schoolboy's friendship.*

Charles Metcalfe (1785–1846; later governor-general of India) wrote to his sister in 1824 about the:

joys... in the pure love which exists between man and man, which cannot I think, be surpassed in that more alloyed attachment between the opposite sexes, to which the name of love is in general exclusively applied.

One Victorian clergyman, Edward Lefroy, wrote of his admiration for adolescent males in terms that would not have out of place in an Athenian gymnasium:

I have an inborn admiration for beauty, of form and figure. It amounts almost [emphasis mine] *to a passion, and in most football teams I can find one Antinous*[!]... *some folk would say it was... sentimentalism to admire any but feminine flesh. But that only proves how base is the carnality, which is now reckoned the only legitimate form* [of love]. *The other* [love] *is far nobler... Platonic passion in any relationship is better than animalism.*

Yet this same society, as Sir Robert Peel (1788–1850; later Prime Minister) said in parliament, thought *actual* physical and genital love between men was a crime '*inter Christianos non nominandum* [which must not be named among Christians]'.

   Across the Atlantic Americans were treated to the same sort of unconscious hypocrisy though usually the context was the frontier wilderness with men braving the elements together rather than the boarding school. In *John Brent* (1862) Theodore Winthrop tells of the meeting of Brent (who had lived long in the wilderness) with a former school chum (Richard Wade). Wade, initially, does not recognise his old friend. His first impressions are fascinating and, despite the obvious homoeroticism, perfectly acceptable to the readers:

[Brent is an] *Adonis of the copperskins* [Indians]... *a beautiful youth!... There are a dozen romances in one look of that young brave... What a poem the fellow is! I wish I was an Indian myself for such a companion; or, better, a squaw, to be made love to by him.*

Later Wade said he had come to love the man John Brent, 'as I had loved the boy; but as mature man loves man. I have known no more perfect union than that one friendship, nothing so tender in any or my transitory loves for women' [this in the context of their joint search for Wade's kidnapped sweetheart, Ellen!].

Of course, the same sort of people who read such literature, produced at the height of that ultimate of male-bonding experiences – a war (the American Civil War in this case) – could be just as scathing about the reality of such love. As one medical doctor (George Napheys, who ironically happens to be a relative of this author) said when considering the physical expression of male love in his *The Transmission of Life: Counsels on the Nature and Hygiene of the Masculine Function (1851)*:

Sufficient to say, that every unnatural lust recorded in the mordant satires of Juvenal, the cynical epigrams of Martial, or the licentious stories of Petronius, is practiced, not in rare and exceptional cases, but deliberately and habitually in the great cities of our country. Did we choose to draw the veil from those abominable scenes with which our professional life has brought us into contact [emphasis mine], *we could tell of the vice which called vengeance from heaven on Sodom practiced notoriously; we could speak of restaurants frequented by men in women's attire, yielding themselves to indescribable lewdness; we could point out literature so inconceivably devilish as to advocate and extol this utter depravity. But is it enough for us to hint at these abysses of iniquity. We cannot bring ourselves to do more; and we can only hope that the fiery cautery of public denunciation will soon destroy this most malignant of ulcers.*

'Victorians' on both sides of the Atlantic could talk (endlessly) about love between men but when confronted with its physical expression they turned to the hangman or hard labour, or public humiliation and ruin to 'cauterise' the malignancy.

But, as Napheys suggested, the reality was that the malignancy was widespread and, in its own context, quite brazen. Prostitution was rife in Victorian England and included brothels catering to men with a taste for other males, especially youths. Obviously, there were more female prostitutes and the numbers mid-century are truly staggering: Norwich, 888; the City of London, 2,000 (in 360 brothels); Liverpool, 200 children aged under twelve. In 1837, a brothel specialising in boys just reaching puberty was closed in Spitalfields (London). The youths simply moved in Piccadilly, the parks and railways stations as freelance rent-boys.

However, the situation across the Western world was mixed. The Anglo-Saxon, English-speaking peoples of the British Empire and the United States saw laws and punishments become harsher and more frequent. In the period 1800–34, eighty men were hanged in England for sodomy (over two per year). In 1828, the burden of proof was lessened by Peel's bill to make conviction easier – previously the Crown had had to prove penetration *and* ejaculation; henceforth, only penetration. Even liberal reformers could not bring themselves to repeal the death penalty. When, in 1836, the Criminal Law Committee (which saw capital punishment dropped for burglary and robbery) considered sodomy it could only say, '[it is a] nameless crime of great enormity we, at present, exclude from consideration'. As a result in the period 1836–56 a further 200 men were hanged (ten per year).

On the continent, the situation was different – something well known to the leaders and elites of Britain and America. The restored French monarchy and later Republics made no attempt to recriminalise sodomy. Where states had been freed from the Napoleonic Code sodomy was often recriminalised though harsh penalties were dropped. By 1833 four states (Russia, Austria, Prussia and Tuscany) no longer used capital punishment in sodomy cases. Of course, one must be cautious about thinking this a sign of leniency. After the 1871 unification of the German states into the Prussian-dominated German Empire, Bismarck (1815–98) imposed the Prussian legal code across the empire. Paragraph 175 of the code (re-)criminalised sodomy in many Rhineland states where it had been legal since the time of Napoleon. Indeed, the German 'gay rights' movement (the first organised attempt *by homosexuals* to obtain legal protection for homosexuals and decriminalisation of sodomy) came into being largely as a reaction to the imposition of the 'liberal' Prussian code.

While continentals were engaged in arguments about the decriminalisation of sodomy, English-speakers were trying to uncover its cause so that it could be eradicated at its source. George Beard (1839–83), an important neurologist (the first to describe 'nervous exhaustion'), spoke for much Anglo-Saxon popular and scientific opinion in the nineteenth century when he said (in 1884) that 'long-standing masturbators of either sex care little for the opposite sex; are more likely to fear than to enjoy their presence, and are terrified by the thought of a sexual connection'. The situation in all-male boarding schools was a breeding ground for masturbation leading to sodomy. The novelist, William Thackeray (1811–63) recalled that nearly the first thing he heard upon entering his boarding school was having a school friend say, 'come and frig [masturbate] me'. The historian, J.A. Symonds (1840–93) said that at Harrow (in 1854) attractive boys were given female nicknames and were either 'public prostitutes [slept with any and everyone] or some bigger fellow's "bitch" [passive partner in a more stable relationship]'. The simple fact is that most of the politicians and judges sending men to the gallows and hard labour for sodomy had, during their school days, engaged in genital contact and passionate, emotional relationships with other males. If nothing else one can say that when they railed against sodomy they knew 'whereof they spoke'.

Despite the enthusiasm of the leading officials of society to control sodomy, the sentiment of the age was moving against the death penalty. In addition, the possibility of death meant the burden of proof was extremely high and juries frequently less willing to convict. In 1861, the state finally abolished the death penalty for sodomy in England and Wales and replaced it with ten years' hard labour (penal servitude) with the passage of the Offences Against the Person Act, which replaced Henry VIII's sodomy act. However, the new act resulted in few prosecutions. It was not until the passage of the Criminal Law Amendment Act (1885) that a new definition of the crime was found, which opened the floodgates to prosecution (and to blackmail). The act was actually aimed at the protection of young girls and raised the age of consent for women from thirteen to sixteen years old (amendments suggesting eighteen and twenty-one were defeated by the Commons). One single, vague amendment was passed, though:

Any male person [note, lesbianism is not mentioned or criminalised] *who, in public* or private [emphasis mine], *commits, or is a party to the commission of, or procures or* attempts [emphasis mine] *to procure the commission by any male person of any act* of gross indecency [emphasis mine] *with another male person, shall be guilty of a misdemeanour, and being convicted thereof shall be liable at the discretion of the court to be imprisoned for any term not exceeding two years, with or without hard labour.*

This marked an enormous change in the legal status of same-sex acts. The previous law had required clear proof of penetration (and, before that, penetration *and* ejaculation) for conviction. Now one needed only prove 'gross indecency' (whatever that was!).

This change needs to be set in the legal context of the early nineteenth century. Not until 1817 (in England) was a man convicted and sentenced to death for 'sodomising' a seven-year-old boy by forcing the child to fellate him – and he was acquitted on appeal. At the same time, most American states were also altering their sodomy laws to include mutual masturbation and oral sex. The lower threshold of proof and the expansion of the types of genital contact defined as sodomitical combined to make prosecutions and convictions considerably easier. Just as importantly, the English law meant that anyone so much as making a pass at someone might find themselves threatened with exposure and prosecution. Blackmail and entrapment became a regular feature of the 'homosexual scene'.

The best and most notorious example of the impact of this change in the law was the case of Oscar Wilde (1854–1900). Wilde was a great dramatist, wit, classicist and intellectual. A star of the Oxford world, he was a leading light of the aesthetic movement. Although he married (in 1884) and fathered two children, Wilde was also involved with a number of men throughout the 1880s and 1890s until, in 1892 he met and fell in love with Lord Alfred Douglas (1870–1945; youngest son of the marquis of Queensberry – the compiler of the famous boxing rules). They met when Lord Douglas asked for help to recover an indiscreet letter he had written and about which he was being blackmailed. The men became attached and Douglas introduced Wilde into the seedier side of London's homosexual underground where both men pursued their taste in young working-class men. Their involvement with a sixteen-year-old son of an army colonel almost ended in a prosecution but the colonel relented under legal advice that his son, too, would face prison. This highlights the amazingly bizarre effect of the vague wording of the amendment – the boy almost certainly would have been deemed to have been 'party to the commission of' the crime.

Disaster struck in 1894 when Lord Douglas's father sent a note accusing his son and Wilde of being in a 'most loathsome and disgusting relationship'. Douglas's telegram in reply ('what a funny little man you are') appalled Wilde and incensed the marquis. His riposte threatened to 'make a public scandal in a way you little dream of'. After a shouting-match in Wilde's home between Wilde and the marquis, Douglas warned his father that Wilde might sue him for libel and slander. Wilde finally resolved to end the affair and remove himself from what was becoming a very dangerous situation – the pawn in a battle between father and son.

However, in October, the marquis's eldest son and heir killed himself. Although the papers reported that it was a hunting accident most were certain it was because of Lord Drumlanrig's equally homosexual relationship with Lord Roseberry (1847–1929; Minister for Foreign Affairs and later Prime Minister). The marquis now resolved to force the issue but was told by his lawyers that letters from Wilde to Douglas would not suffice. The marquis left a malicious and insulting note for Wilde at the Albemarle Club where both men were members: 'To Oscar Wilde, Posing as a Somdomite [*sic*]'. Finally Wilde had had enough and, under goading from Douglas, Wilde sued for libel. The result was disastrous for Wilde (though Douglas was untouched – protected as he was by his father's power and status).

The first of three trials ended when Wilde withdrew his libel action having realised that the marquis's agents had amassed enough evidence to defeat him. Wilde had seen the evidence that the marquis had prepared and knew he could be cited for sodomy with at least ten named youths. As soon as this civil trial ended, Wilde was arrested along with Alfred Taylor, who had provided a box containing the names and addresses of youths Wilde had been with. Despite Taylor's penchant for cross-dressing and sharing his rooms with a string of young men, the jury failed to convict either man. A second trial was convened, focusing on 'gross indecency' rather than the more technical charge of sodomy (anal penetration). At the end of this trial Wilde was convicted and sentenced to two years' hard labour.

The consequences of the trial were dramatic. The presses in America and Britain were ecstatic to see such sin punished. French and other continental presses were simple bewildered having to explain to their incredulous readership that the English seemed to think sex between men was almost as bad as murder. Douglas began a campaign of press interviews and letter-writing insinuating that he could name scores of other 'homosexuals' (to use a word only just then coined). The novelist Henry Harland (1861–1905) wrote to the poet Edmund Gosse (1845–1928) that 'six hundred gentlemen' left for France the night the conviction was announced when one might normally expect only sixty to make the crossing.

Despite the overwhelming enthusiasm for the conviction amongst most of the British ruling elite, some voices were raised in support of Wilde. Max Beerbohm, writer and caricaturist (1872–1956), was stunned by the verdict as he thought Wilde's speech in his own defence had been:

quite superb. His speech about the Love that dares not tell its name was simply wonderful and carried the whole court right away, quite a tremendous burst of applause. Here was this man, who had been for a month in prison and loaded with insults and crushed and buffeted, perfectly self-possessed, dominating the [courtroom] with his fine presence and musical voice. He has never had so great a triumph.

But it was not a triumph, it had been a disaster. The journalist, W.T. Stead captured the whole hypocrisy of the trial when he publicly wrote:

If Oscar Wilde, instead of indulging in dirty tricks of indecent familiarity with boys and men, had ruined the lives of half a dozen innocent simpletons of girls, or had broken up the home of his friend by corrupting his friend's wife, no one could have laid a finger on him… Another contrast… is that between the universal execration heaped upon Oscar Wilde and the tacit universal acquiescence of the very same public in the same kind of vice in our public schools. If all persons guilty of Oscar Wilde's offences were to be clapped in gaol, there would be a surprising exodus from Eton and Harrow, Rugby and Winchester.

Despite the obvious truth of these observations, Wilde was not spared. He languished in jail and died a broken man soon after his release. His

plays were pulled off stages and his name removed from polite conversation. The message at the turn of the century was clear.
Homosexuals could, and would, be jailed and destroyed in public.

However, one cannot help but note from the discussion of previous chapters that this was a novelty. Sodomy, of a specific character,
had been prosecuted before. This new act, and the new idea of a
person as a 'homosexual' ('the entire, vaguely disconcerting nexus of
effeminacy, leisure, idleness, immorality, luxury, insouciance, decadence and aestheticism, which Wilde was perceived, variously, as representing, was transformed into a brilliantly precise image'), crystallised
in people's mind that a danger existed and needed to be stamped out.
Indeed, using the 1898 Vagrancy Law Amendment Act, a magistrate of
the London Sessions of 1911 brought back the birch and in October
1912 nearly two dozen men received fifteen lashes each for indecency!
A whole range of behaviour never specifically associated with same-
sex activities now became seen as 'queer'. Thus we see the irony that
the very century which saw the West take the hardest stance not only
against same-sex acts but homosociability and homoeroticism eventually saw the decriminalisation of most acts between consenting
males. Sadly, though, it was this image and hatred of the homosexual
that were firmly planted across the world by the forces of European
– especially British – colonialism.

While the case of Wilde remains etched in popular memory it was
only one of a dramatic number in the opening decades of the twentieth century, which rocked Western societies. In Germany, the Kaiser
was implicated in the so-called Eulenburg Affair, while in England the
case of Hector MacDonald (1853–1903) became front-page news
across the globe. He was the hero of the battle of Omdurman (1898)
outside Khartoum, where his troops massacred the forces of the Khalifa
(successor of the Mahdi who defeated Gordon) with modern
weaponry. However, MacDonald was the son of a crofter who had
risen through the ranks from private to commander-in-chief of imperial forces in Ceylon (Sri Lanka). As such, he could not expect the
protection afforded to men like the Lords Douglas, Kitchener
(1815–1916) and Baden-Powell (1857–1941; the notorious pederast
who founded the Boy Scout Movement).

MacDonald had been discovered in a private railway carriage with four Sinhalese youths engaged in mutual masturbation. Reports circulated and more 'witnesses' came forward. Kitchener (who was himself noted for his deep, lasting affection for his aide-de-camp, Oswald FitzGerald) wanted MacDonald court-martialled and shot. The governor of Ceylon (whose son was implicated with MacDonald) wanted things kept quiet. The case circulated in rumour throughout the upper echelons of the empire. Eventually MacDonald was recalled from Britain for court-martial in Ceylon after the entire matter was publicised in the *New York Herald*. Before leaving he had a private interview with the king, Edward VII (1841–1910), who said that it would be best for all if MacDonald were to shoot himself – the hapless general complied with his sovereign's wishes two days later in a Paris hotel. The state then destroyed the entire file on MacDonald.

In the course of the nineteenth century, it was not only the law that was changing in its approach to same-sex acts. The most important area of development was science and medicine. In 1848, the psychologist, Karoly Maria Benkert (1824–82) coined the term 'homosexual', which he defined by saying, 'in addition to the normal sexual urge in men and women, Nature in her sovereign mood has endowed at birth certain male and female individuals with the homosexual urge... This urge creates in advance a direct horror of the opposite sex'. In 1892, J.A. Symonds seems to have been the first English-speaker to use the term in a private letter; it appeared that same year in the American translation of the German-authored *Psychopathia Sexualis* (1886; *Sexual Psychopathology*). It was popularised in the works of Magnus Hirschfeld (1868–1935) and Havelock Ellis (1859-1939).

Magnus Hirschfeld was the homosexual German Jewish physician and sex researcher who founded the Scientific Humanitarian Committee in 1897, whose many books and publications made him a leading sexologist. The committee led a campaign to repeal the anti-sodomy laws of the German Empire (Paragraph 175 of the Prussian Code) though, in the end, they were unsuccessful. In 1919, his reputation as one of sexology's founding fathers was secured when he opened in Berlin the world's first sexological institute, the Institute for Sexual Science. Hirschfeld was also a promoter of his research and he was hailed as an expert in the American press during a 1930–32 world speaking tour that marked the apex of his career. Although he was never a systematic thinker, Hirschfeld supported some hormonal theories of homosexuality that ultimately led others unsuccessfully to attempt to cure homosexuality with hormone injections. In 1935, Hirschfeld died in exile in France two years after his institute had been closed by the Nazis. In contrast to Hirschfeld, the Englishman Havelock Ellis never practised medicine. Instead, he devoted his life to the scientific study of sex. His most controversial book (co-written with J.A. Symonds), *Sexual Inversion*, was suppressed in England because it advocated tolerance. Eventually, it attracted a wide following in England and the US, though not before Symond's family had bought and destroyed almost every copy of the first edition and got agreement that Symond's name would not appear on any further copies. His interest in homosexuality was, at least partly, motivated by his wife's lesbianism and a circle of intellectual friends who were themselves homosexuals. A retiring individual, Ellis never gained the fame of his contemporary Sigmund Freud (1856–1939), but his collected work on sex, *Studies in the Psychology of Sex*, was influential through its many editions.

However, Ellis's book was not a plea for toleration. It opened with three case studies of lesbianism. The first two end with one woman killing her lover and the third was about attempted murder. It stated unequivocally that lesbianism was almost always at the heart of female suicide. The books, in common with many others of the day, took the view that homosexuality was congenital and hereditary. Richard Krafft-Ebing (1840–1902) explained that although one could rarely find evidence of homosexuality (or bisexuality) in the parents of homosexuals:

in almost all cases where an examination of the physical and mental peculiarities of the ancestors and blood relations has been possible, neuroses, psychoses, degenerative signs etc. have been found in the families.

In other words, the prevailing scientific, medical and psychiatric view was that homosexuality was a congenital *disease* arising from some genetic abnormality associated with mental problems in the family.

This view of homosexuality combined in the 1930s with emerging ideas about racial purity and eugenics with disastrous consequences. While one might normally expect to see such a statement followed by a discussion of Germany and the Nazis, the appalling reality is that some of the earliest and strongest exponents of these ideas were in America. In 1893, a certain Dr Daniel gave a paper to a conference on eugenics in New York entitled, 'Should Insane Criminals or Sexual Perverts be allowed to Procreate?' He argued that such degeneracy was more common in the 'lower' orders – especially African-Americans – and lumped together: alcoholism, insanity, criminality, rape, sodomy, masturbation and paedophilia. His conclusions were that the law was ineffective and that the individuals involved showed no desire to change. He asked that:

rape, sodomy, bestiality, pederasty and habitual masturbation should be made crimes or misdemeanours, punishable by forfeiture of all rights, including that of procreation; in short castration, or castration plus penalties, according to the gravity of the offence.

He also was amazed at a society that 'will break a criminal's neck, but will respect his testicles'.

A most pathetic example of this 'treatment' was popularised by Havelock Ellis in a 1896 publication in the *British Journal of Mental Science*. It told of a Guy T. Olmstead who had been arrested for shooting his estranged lover (William L. Clifford) and then trying to shoot himself. Prior to the attempted murder and suicide, he had voluntarily had himself castrated to be cured of his deviant desires (the hospital, interestingly, made no record of the operation). While recovering he wrote to a doctor:

My vileness is uncontrollable and I might as well give up and die. I wonder if the doctors know that after emasculation it was possible for a man to have erections, commit masturbation and have the same passion as before. I am ashamed of myself; I hate myself; but I can't help it. I am without medicine, a big, fat stupid creature without health or strength and I am disgusted with myself. I have no right to live and I guess people have done right in abusing and condemning me.

He was eventually confined in the Cook Insane Hospital in Chicago. Although the American Psychiatric Association finally removed homosexuality from its official list of mental disorders in 1973(!), as late as 1993 a doctor still castrated a man in a prison (at his request) to cure him of deviant lust. Indeed, in 1953, the *Journal of Social Hygiene* published an article by Karl Bowman and Bernice Engle called 'The Problem [*sic*] of Homosexuality', which argued for more research on the positive value of 'therapeutic castration'.

Another common treatment for sexual dysfunction (notably homosexuality and female nymphomania) was lobotomy. Lobotomies of gay people stopped in Western Germany in 1979. In Norway, lobotomy victims (of whom there were 2,500) eventually got compensation (eighteen of the first thirty-five operations in Norway were fatal). In Sweden more than 3,300 were lobotomised; the Danish number was 3,500. Indeed, Denmark was the world leader in proportion to its population and the last operation took place in 1981. Lobotomy operations were pioneered by the Portuguese Dr Egas Moniz (1874–1955) for which he received a Nobel prize in 1949. In the US the number of individuals (male and female) lobotomised for sexual 'disorders' of various kinds ran into the tens of thousands.

It seems pointless to prolong this litany of woe. Throughout most of the twentieth century science, religion and politics combined to degrade and persecute homosexuals and same-sex activities. The range of 'theories' was ever-changing from hypnosis and castration through to reparative and aversion therapy. The goal remained, and remains, the same: to alter a person's private desires and preferences to the culturally constructed norms of the society. Many may see this as 'helpful' and 'kind' in societies where homosexuals face dislike, hatred and discrimination. But, the lunacy of the position is most obvious if one were to say that many of the same arguments could be deployed in relation to African-Americans. Who would argue for medical and psychiatric treatment to turn 'blacks' into 'whites' through altering their skin tone, physical features, accent, or cultural values and behaviours? Not only would such a suggestion be ludicrous it would almost certainly be criminal in many societies with hate-crimes legislation. Alternatively (if one prefers to see homosexuality as purely a matter of personal choice resulting from upbringing and other 'environmen-tal' factors), one might suggest the same approach to Judaism or Catholicism in (Protestant) Christian societies.

One cannot, though, pass through the twentieth century without considering the apotheosis (or nadir) of ideas about eugenics and the improvement of the human race. Most research suggests that over 20,000 homosexual men were murdered in concentration camps by the Nazis. Under the Kaiser and the Weimar Republic, homosexuals had gained a measure of protection since they were suffering from a recognised 'mental disability'. They needed only register with the state to be protected from discrimination. Obviously, this made the Nazis' task all the easier. The Nazis simply removed the protections and then used paragraph 175 (only finally repealed in 1969 – indeed, the post-war German government required some 'convicted' homo-sexuals to finish their prison sentence, simply counting their time in concentration camps as part of the sentence!) to great effect. Homosexuals (with their pink triangles) found themselves part of a rainbow of colours in the camps marked for total extermination (Jews, yellow; gypsies, brown) or lengthy incarceration (political prisoners, red; criminals, green; anti-socials, black; emigrants, blue; Jehovah's Witnesses, purple). Only in the opening years of this century has the German government finally agreed to provide limited compensation to homosexual victims of the Nazis and to quash their convictions.

In the last half of the twentieth century change has come quickly and dramatically. In 1967 there was a partial decriminalisation of homo-sexuality in England and Wales (between consenting adults aged over twenty-one in private – all other acts remained criminal) followed by Scotland (1980) and Northern Ireland (1982). The Sexual Offences Act currently progressing through the Westminster Parliament (which will be incorporated into Scottish law under a Sewell motion of the devolved Holyrood Parliament) will finally make sexual legislation more or less non-specific (that is, heterosexual and homosexual acts will be treated exactly the same). Early in 2004, the US Supreme Court threw out all remaining state sodomy laws though it is unclear what effect this will have in practice – and it may not apply in the US military at all. The legalisation of marriage for same-sex partners under 'equal protection' clauses of the Massachusetts constitution promises to cause a furore for at the least two years before the citizens of the state will be asked to approve an amendment specifically discriminating against same-sex couples (one wonders if conservative lawmakers might secretly wish to add mixed-race couples while they are at it!).

Numerous other countries have seen enormous changes. Across Europe civil partnerships are being legalised and most Scandinavian countries now recognise same-sex marriages, as does the Netherlands. More importantly to the US debate, the whole of Canada looks set to follow Ontario and a few other provinces in legalising same-sex marriages in 2005. The Human Rights Act of the European Union specifically forbids discrimination on the grounds of sexual preference or orientation, though numerous groups (especially religious bodies) have received exemptions (similar to the exemptions from equal-opportunities legislation the Catholic Church has to allow it to continue to discriminate against women in posts of leadership and power – that is, the priesthood). Despite these few caveats, the trend is decidedly towards the removal of all legislation which differentiates between citizens on the basis of sexual preference or orientation. It is this change that is causing such profound consternation in other non-Western countries. Increasingly, the acceptance of homosexuality is able to be portrayed in other parts of the world as a type of Western decadence.

No matter what some may claim, though, same-sex acts and cultural accommodation of them is *not* a Western phenomenon. One of the best case studies of Islamic ideas about sexuality and the social construction of categories for non-normative, non-procreative sex comes from modern-day Oman. Unni Wikan, in a study of institutionalised transexualism (*xanith*) in Oman, looked at male homosexual prostitutes who, despite being classified as 'females' for rules of segregation, retained male names but were treated as women. In one Omani coastal town (Sohar, the reputed home of Sinbad the Sailor) of approximately 3,000 adult males, about sixty were *xanith*. That is, they were men who behaved and were treated as women.

Women interacted with *xanith* publicly and privately in a way they would not with other men – even close male relatives. *Xanith* also sang with women at weddings (recalling the role of *hijra*s in weddings

and what was noted above in Zanzibar and Mombasa). Most male servants (not slaves) were *xanith* and *xanith* functioned also as male prostitutes − at least according to Wikan's female informant. The *xanith*
was often admired for his beauty (judged by concepts of female beauty)
and his facility as women's work (compare the *berdache* of North
America). Thus, at weddings women sing and men are musicians but
xanith are usually seen as the *best* singers − and weddings are the public
occasions at which *xanith* often 'come out' by being seen singing with
the women and thereby publicly declaring their gender transformation. Most *xanith* support themselves (as all *men* are expected to do)
though as servants − which no woman or freeman would do. Clearly
one sees a mix of gender-status and identity. The *xanith* may be female
in most socio-cultural ways but is still expected to conform to that
most male of all virtues − independence.

A similar mixture is seen in the appearance of a *xanith*. The *xanith*
is *not* a transvestite − his clothing is androgynous or effeminate but he
does not wear a veil. Men wear white, women patterned bright
colours, *xanith* unpatterned bright colours. Men wear their hair short,
women long and *xanith* medium length. Men and women cover their
heads but not *xanith*. The *xanith* makes no attempt to present himself
as a women rather, he is intermediate but treated *socially* as a woman.
Indeed, where *xanith* have tried to appear in female dress they were
flogged − but being the passive partner in same-sex acts was not punishable. Nor did being the active partner have any impact on the
gender/sex construction of the person − he remained a male. A
woman (regardless of the sex of her partner) is always a female because
she can *never* penetrate. Just as importantly, being a *xanith* need not be
permanent. Any man may:

1   be a 'woman' for some years and then revert, permanently, to
    being male
2   may be a 'woman' into old age
3   alternate repeatedly between being male and female

However, only men seemed to be able to move between genders −
women were *always* women.

This last point is crucial for it brings into sharp relief the role of gender-identity (how one acts) and biological sex (the genitalia one is born with). *Xanith* are legally males and adults while women are always minors. The *xanith* retain male status. A *xanith* can become 'male' as a result of successfully consummating a marriage and is thereafter treated as a man by women (i.e. segregation will happen) though he may still retain the characteristics (clothing, etc) of a *xanith*. Thus the defining feature of biological sex is *not* the possession of certain anatomical organs but rather the ability to use them. A man is someone who has sex with a woman. A man who assumes the passive role is *socially* a woman as that is the role of a woman (the female gender) in sexual relations.

One must immediately wonder how such a group can exist in a strict, traditional Muslim society. In part this is because the laws of tactfulness and hospitality are such that an Omani would not dream of acting in a way, which would suggest criticism of someone else's behaviour – especially someone outside the immediate family group. In addition, the basic structural unit is the family with the head of the family having most of the 'power'. This results in some seemingly strange legal realities. Public female prostitution is unlawful and punished by the state. Discreet female prostitution by married women – though known to all and sundry – is sinful (i.e. adultery) but only the husband can complain. Male prostitution is sinful but not unlawful and so no one can complain as no one is 'harmed' (i.e. has a direct cause for complaint) in their property or person (honour, as with the case of adultery). Thus, most Omani simply take the pragmatic view that:

no stigma attaches to the man who seeks the company of a [xanith] for sexual purposes, though both men and women agree that the act itself is shameful. But the world is imperfect, and shameful acts [are] an inherent part of life.

This relatively sensible view, which also preserves familial and neighbourly relationships in a tight-knit society, is not the norm. Despite earlier ambivalence, Islamic countries are today extremely anti-gay. All seven countries where homosexuality is punishable by death are Muslim and of the eighty-two where it is a crime, thirty-six are predominately Muslim. This seems strange considering the situation (noted above) in earlier ages when, for example, the Caliph of Baghdad (in the 800s) 'gave himself over entirely to dissipated pleasure in the company of his eunuchs and refused to take a wife'. Moreover, although the Koran spells out clear, specific punishments (e.g. number of lashes) for most crimes there is no explicit punishment for sodomy except notations that 'the people of Lut' (Sodom and Gomorrah) *had been* punished. Where there are punishments is in the *hadith* (sayings of the Prophet) and *Shari'a* (legal codes based on tradition, the Koran and the *hadith*).

As we have noted above, this repressive reaction to same-sex acts is not universal. Oman, as with many of the more traditional, hospitality-orientated, family-based Islamic societies is more relaxed. As late as the 1930s a similar situation existed at Siwa (an oasis community in the Libyan desert of western Egypt famous in ancient times as an oracle second only to Delphi). Anthropologist Walter Cline (in the 1930s) noted:

all normal Muslim Siwan men and boys practise sodomy. Among themselves the natives are not ashamed of this; they talk about it as openly as they talk about love of women and many, if not most, of their fights arise from homosexual competition.

The archaeologist Count Byron de Prorock (*c.*1930) made much the same report. He noted 'an enthusiasm that could not have been approached even in Sodom. Homosexuality is not only rampant, it was raging'. Moreover, men married other men with great ceremony – a practice only ended by the British authorities.

Nor should this come as a great surprise in extremely close communities that strictly sequester women and put a premium on premarital female virginity, female marital fidelity and late ages of marriage for men. These cultures must, almost of necessity, accept some same-sex activities if for no other reason than as an outlet for male sexuality. That this favours the acceptance of those men who *prefer* homosexual activities is obvious; that it requires some social constructions to allow for homosexual acts is perhaps less obvious but no less necessary.

While this is certainly the case, the situation in most of the rest of the Islamic world – especially amongst urbanised Muslims is very different. Modern Islamic leaders are much harsher than those of the past. Dr Muzammil Siddiqi, director of the Islamic Society of North America has said, 'homosexuality [*being* homosexual not a homosexual *act*] is a moral disease, a sin, a corruption… no person is born homosexual'. Sheikh Sharkhawy, a cleric at London's Regent's Park Central Mosque has said, 'we must burn all gays to prevent paedophilia and the spread of AIDS'. Perhaps most surprisingly of all in a nation with laws banning incitement to violence and hatred, the Muslim Education Trust (London) has produced literature for schoolchildren, which suggests the death penalty for homosexuality.

Moving back to Africa, despite the numerous problems we have had with discussing this continent in the past one is on much surer ground when considering homosexuality in Africa from 1800. However, problems still exist. Sources from the nineteenth century are the production of European colonial rulers, who had an inherent interest in portraying Africans in a light which would justify continuing colonial control. Sources from the post-colonial period can suffer from a similar defect. Many modern African leaders are determined to deny past events, which they see as casting 'slurs' on their ancestors. Effectively, both colonial and post-colonial leaders accept a Western Christian understanding of homosexuality as 'sinful' and 'evil'. Colonial rulers used the presence of sexual deviance as an argument for the subjugation of 'inferior' Africans. African leaders deny these acts and individuals for the same reason – they too consider any such society to be 'inferior'.

The reality, though, is that African cultures traditionally had ideas about sex, sexuality and gender that simply were not part of the Judaeo-Christian models that took shape in Western Europe. Saying this is simply to state an historical fact. To attempt to label such a difference as inferior or deviant is to accept that Western-developed models are the 'correct' yardstick by which societies should be measured. That is pure subjectivity. This subjectivity – or bias – has led to many societies denying history. It produces an Alexander the Great who only had sex with women, Indian rulers, Chinese emperors,

North American medicine men and African individuals who likewise
were wholly heterosexual.

Distinctive constructions of sexuality were not confined to homosexuality. For example, among the Akan of the Gold Coast there was a
tradition relating to prostitution Two types of prostitution historically
existed. Leaders in rural communities would purchase women as sex
slaves. The women charged for their services but the money went to
the local elite who had paid for the woman. In return, the woman was
fed and housed and, later in life, supplied with a 'retirement pension'.
A second type of prostitution involved women who entered into prostitution as a profession giving them financial freedom. Public women
were a despised albeit pragmatic solution to the problem of scarcity of
women caused by the accumulation of wives by the very rural leaders,
who then supplied the public women. Those women who became
'professional' prostitutes did not face social disapproval and were often
able to parley their incomes into other successful businesses.

Across the continent, one finds a similar attitudes towards male
prostitutes. Writing about Zanzibar in 1899, the sociologist Michael
Haberlandt noted that the locals made a distinction between male
prostitutes and men who engaged in sex with other men out of choice.
His European prejudices meant that he could not understand why
this distinction existed:

In outward appearance, inborn contrary men [homosexuals by 'birth' or 'choice'] *are
not distinguishable from male prostitutes* [slaves forced into same-sex acts], *but the
natives make a sharp distinction between them: the professional catamite* [sic] *are despised,
while the behaviour of the inborn-contrary is tolerated as* amri ya muungu *(the will of
God).*

What Haberlandt seemed unable to infer was that in Zanzibar social
disapproval was directed against enslaved prostitutes rather than homosexuality. Interestingly, though he did not investigate the phenomenon, he also noted that there were a number of terms for lesbian sex
acts which were in common use, seemingly without social opprobrium: *kulambana* (cunnilingus), *kusagana* (frottage), *kujitia mbo ya
mpingo* (using an ebony dildo). A similar view was noted a half-

century later by Simon Messing among Coptic (Christian) Amhara peasants. They had words for female-men (*wändarwäräd*) and male-women (*wändawände*). Despite their Christianity, these peasants largely tolerated these individuals considering them to be 'God's mistakes'.

Haberlandt's reports from Zanzibar simply begin a string of observations. He also reported on non-masculine men among the Wganda (Uganda) who were 'totally given to pederasty' though more recent reports say that the Wganda claim that such behaviour is of Arabic origin and 'foolish': 'why fool around with a man when women are freely available'. Around the same time Simon Ambrogetti noted that some Eritrean men entered into homosexual relationships when adolescents, though they normally moved on to heterosexual marriages. However, he noted that some of the youths (whom he called 'little devils', *diavoletti*) continued to have sex with other men later in life even when married.

In 1909 Friedrich Bieber recorded same-sex relationships among the Muslim Harair (in Ethiopia) as well as the Galla (also in Ethiopia) and the Somalis. He could identify no age distinctions in the relationships (i.e. they were not pederastic) or assumption of specific gender roles (i.e. one did not 'become a woman'). He also noted that same-sex mutual masturbation was common amongst both sexes. Another Islamic group (river-dwellers in northern Sudan) were studied by Pamela Constantinides who observed that effeminate men (*zaar*) were key to a local healing cult and that most other people in the culture assumed that these men also engaged in same-sex acts.

Of course, the presence of same-sex acts can be interpreted in a number of ways – which may be accurate or may just give more insight into the observers' presuppositions. One further example of the early twentieth century comes from the work of Melville Herskovits in the 1930s. He noted homosexual activities amongst adolescent Dahomeans (called *gaglgo*) but viewed it as 'situational' since he argued it occurred because of lack of access to women (as with same-sex acts in a prison). David Livingstone (in 1865) noted same-sex acts between adolescents but put it down to the polygamous monopolisation of most available women by a few powerful chiefs.

A century after Haberlandt, Deborah Amory conducted a study of Zanzibar and Mombasa more specifically focused on homosexuality.

Her report considered *mashoga* men — who have much in common
with Indian *hijras*. *Mashoga* men (from *shoga* and the plural prefix *ma*)
take on the accoutrements of women at certain social and ritual events.
She noted that these men (also called *makhanith* and *mahanisi*) were
stigmatised and assumed to be sexually passive. The active partner is
called the *basha* (boss, master) or *haji* (a reference to someone who has
managed to afford a *haj*). The *shoga* is normally *juko wazi* (open, 'out')
while the *basha* will normally — at least officially — be *anajificha* (hiding,
'closeted'). Most people she met tolerated but really disapproved of
mashoga. What is interesting is that the general view was that the
homosexuality of a *shoga* was part of that person's basic *roho* (spirit) or
umbo (nature), which reminds us that believing that homosexuality is
fundamental to one's being (i.e. genetic) does not necessarily lead to
toleration, acceptance, and equality.

One of the most important studies, though, was conducted by
Edward Evans-Pritchard in the 1930s among the Zande (a group
spread across Sudan, the Central African Republic and the Congo).
One gains some interesting insight not only into modern African
homosexuality but also into the views of Western sociologists in this
study. In his original published work Evans-Pritchard made no references to same-sex activities. It was only in the 1970s, near the end of
his career and life, that he shared his observations on homosexuality
among the Zande with the wider academic world. Clearly, he was
uncomfortable with the information he found and seems to have
assumed that it would be considered inappropriate for publication.

In particular, he reported on the warrior-pagess (similar to the
samurai and his young apprentices) behaviour that was described to
him. An elderly Zande noted that in pre-colonial days:

Men used to have sexual relations with boys as they did with [their] *wives. A man
paid compensation to another if he had relations with his boy. People asked for the
hand of the boy with a spear, just as they asked for the hand of a maiden of her
parents. All those young warriors who were at court, all had boys* [ndongo-techi-la].

As far as Evans-Pritchard could discover the sex that took place was
intercrural. He also heard rumours (from male informants) about

lesbian activities. Supposedly, women in the royal harems made strap-on dildos of root vegetables or bananas. The Zande tolerated and even accepted male–male (age-based) sex but had a horror of lesbianism considering it 'highly dangerous'. One cannot conclude from Evans-Pritchard's study (or others mentioned) that age-based sex (pederasty) was the sole or normative model. At the same time (late 1930s) as he was studying the Zande, studies of the Nkundo (Congo River) noted that younger males tended to penetrate their older partners.

Among the various ethnic groups (Rundi, Hutu and Tutsi) in Rwanda a number of words were noted in the early twentieth century for sodomites (*umuswezi; umukonotsi*) and sodomy (*kusweana nk'imbwa; kunonoka; kwitomba; kuranana imyuma; ku'nyo*) as well as trans-gendered, 'hermaphrodite' traditional spiritual leaders (*ikihinu; iki-maze*). However, the mere presence of words does not imply tolerance for the activity or even an understanding of the behaviour along Western lines. For example, physical acts between women in South Africa which Westerners would consider sexual are not perceived as sexual. This is the same sort of rationale that underpinned President Clinton's assertion that he had not had 'sexual relations with that woman' though many people, including Monica Lewinsky, were just as certain that he *had* had sexual relations. Recent studies have also suggested that the large number of unmarried American evangelicals who have taken oaths to remain 'virgins' are applying an interpretation of the word that only excludes vaginal penetration – heavy petting, mutual masturbation and even oral sex, in such a view, would not alter one's virginal status. In other words, what counts as sex, sexual relations, sodomy, etc, can vary dramatically from culture to culture, over time and even within cultures at specific times.

The situation among the Hausa illustrates the African context of this idea of cultural relativism very nicely. For Hausa males, marriage is not a matter of emotional attachment, love, or even choice; it is a fundamental moral and social obligation to the family and the wider community. Among the Hausa there are men who are called *'yan daudu* which can be translated as 'homosexual', 'transvestite', or 'pimp'. Obviously these are not synonyms! 'Homosexual' implies same-sex activities; 'transvestite' focuses on gender-assigned clothing, while

'pimp' is someone involved in the sex industry but almost certainly
not as a participant. In most cases, the word seems to refer to gender-
specific aspects of behaviour. That is, a *'yan daudu* takes on women's
work and considers himself 'womanlike' but does not normally cross-
dress and is still addressed and treated as male by other members of
the community. To complicate the matter, when the focus is on actual
sexual activity the terminology becomes even more culturally specific
and confusing. Two men who engage in reciprocal penetration (rather
than one being active and the other passive) or who are of the same
social, economic and age background are said to be practising *kifi* –
lesbianism! It would almost certainly be more accurate to refer to a
'yan daudu as an effeminate man doing tasks normally associated with
women while *kifi* would suggest something more along the lines of
same-sex acts in an 'equal', versatile relationship.

The fact that English has no specific word for either of these two
concepts brilliantly highlights some of the problems of assuming that
same-sex acts – or behaviour which seems to imply same-sex acts to
modern eyes – are homosexual or gay. Each culture we have examined has, almost from the beginning of history, had various categories,
places, or niches for individuals whose behaviour does not conform
to the most socially common constructions of sex, gender and sexuality. However, as the Hausa example illustrates, these categories rarely
coincide with those of other cultures and times – and almost never
with the modern Western construction of 'gay'. Saying that, though,
does not mean that men did not have sex with men or women with
women in the past across the planet. Clearly they did and, just as
surely, their cultures (with the exception of monotheistic societies,
especially Christianity) tended to tolerate or disregard such acts.

One can also look to the Ghanaians for one further example.
Androgynous males are called *kojobesia* (man-woman) though this need
not imply any actual comment on the man's sexual activities. It is a
remark about gender roles and traits. Indeed, the rejection by Ghanaians
and other Africans of terms such as 'gay' and the idea of 'homosexuality' as native to Africa can be a more complex comment on these words.
It is in part a rejection of the Western cultural construction, which
these words label rather than an explicit repudiation of same-sex acts

or behaviour. The latter seems to be almost universally tolerated as long as it is discreet and, as we have seen elsewhere, it does not negate procreative responsibilities to the wider community. Even when procreation is problematic, individuals are often 're-interpreted' as fulfilling a spiritual or religious role which is mostly antithetical to procreation.

Thus, the Hausa and others remind us that, no matter how inventive and perplexing, most human societies have historically managed to construct a viable place for people who are 'different' (in the sense of 'not like most others'). Western Christian societies seem to have won the unique distinction of deciding that, as champions of freedom and democracy, it is for them to spread homophobia worldwide. Through the 'colonised' acceptance of Western cultural hegemony and prejudices, other societies have begun the eradication of as many of these pre-existing niches for the sexual non-conformist as possible.

What is even more interesting is the extent to which a number of modern African cultures evidence a cultural construction we have encountered elsewhere: sex-for-pleasure as distinct from sex-for-procreation. The latter is, perforce, heterosexual but the former may involve any number of couplings. In some cases, this view has been articulated forcefully and unequivocally. Not every assertion of the validity of same-sex acts and loves is Western and post-Stonewall (that is, after 1969 and the rioting at the (largely gay-frequented) Stonewall Bar in lower Manhattan, which is usually seen as leading to the birth of the 'gay-rights movement'). In 1923 a Nguni (South African) soldier was punished for sexually assaulting another soldier one night in the barracks (this may have amounted to no more than making a very explicit pass). When he was punished he defended himself by saying:

Doesn't the Sergeant know that there are men who from youth on desire women, and others, who are attracted only to men? Why then should he be punished now? After all, he knows not why, God created him like this – that he can only love men?

A similar assertion was found among the Herero (Namibia and Botswana), who recognised special male-male friendships called *oupanga*, which included anal intercourse (*okutunduka vanena*; 'mounting a youth'). When criticised for tolerating such disgusting practices by the missionary Johan Irle, they replied that 'they had grown from childhood in their own natural way'.

Similar same-sex relationships were noted among the Naman (South Africa) in the 1920s (called *soregus*); the emphasis was on economic benefits from the bonds but sex was not an unknown component. In 1951, reports on the Nyakyusa (Tanzania) discussed homosexual acts between adolescent males, as well as younger and slightly older males. Intercrural sex was most common and anal sex was possible but oral sex was disapproved of. The Herero, already noted above, also remind us that one cannot rule out sex in male-male relationships by pretending that the men are 'just close friends' or that sex is infrequent and not really part of the cultural construct of same-sex friendship bonds. The Herero not only have the idea of the *oupanga* (sexual friendship) with an *epanga* (erotic friend) but also that of a relationship with an *omukueta* (non-erotic friend; comrade). These words are also used for female relationships. Interestingly though, the normal reaction to attempts to enquire about such things is that 'the act is allowed but speaking about it is forbidden' – 'do but don't tell'. Thus the social disapproval lies with the discussion of sex rather than its practice.

Because of the prominent stance taken by Mugabe and his regime in Zimbabwe it will be necessary to discuss the situation there at some length. As such, Zimbabwe can serve as a 'case study' for the rest of the continent. Before turning to Zimbabwe, though, it is worth pausing for a moment to consider same-sex acts and persons among one of Africa's best-known groups – the Zulus. The Zulus merit discussion if for no other reason than that they inflicted the greatest defeat of European troops (British) ever suffered at the hands of a non-European army, in January 1879 at Isandhlwana. (Perhaps not surprisingly, the West preferred to make the lesser engagement at Rorke's Drift, which the British won, the subject of the movie *Zulu*).

The great warrior king and founder of the Zulu nation, Shaka Zulu (1785-1828), certainly behaved in a way that, as one scholar has put it, would imply that he was a latent homosexual. It is not quite clear why 'latent' is used. Although Shaka Zulu had a large harem of 'wives' he specifically refused to call them wives, preferring 'sisters'. He also let it be known that he thought children were best left until a warrior was too old to fight and, in the meantime, he practised *ukuHlobonga* (intercrural sex/frottage). He ordered his soldiers to remain celibate unless they were already married and grouped them into communal, same-sex barracks. The majority of his time was spent not in his harem but in the company of the regiment of youngest bachelors, the *uFasimba*.

Subsequent accounts of other Bantu-speakers closely related to the Zulus support the idea that same-sex relations were a recognised part of the culture. In 1883, the Basotho (Lesotho) chief Moshesh said there was no punishment for 'unnatural crimes' in traditional law and that the behaviour was 'rare'. One notes the use of Christian-Western legalese (unnatural crime) and the vague word 'rare' (how rare is rare?). Around 1900 another Zulu leader followed Shaka Zulu in ordering his soldiers to refrain from sex with women. 'Nongoloza' Mathebula (1867-1948), also called 'King Nineveh' led a resistance movement against whites in South Africa. The older soldiers (*ikhela*) were to take adolescent males (*abafana*) as boy-wives (*izinkotshone*). When he was arrested and tried he reported that homosexual acts were common among his warriors. Moreover, he made it clear that this was not the (situational) result of the lack of women: 'even when we were free on the hills of south Johannesburg some of us had women and others had young men for sexual purposes'.

However, situational homosexuality was most definitely a feature of the mining communities of South Africa where women were scarce (wives and girlfriends were left in home villages) and prostitutes were considered a significant health risk. In these circumstances though the relationships were not surreptitious and informal; they were public and ritualised. Most relationships were age-differentiated with the older male (*nima*, 'husband') paying bride-price (*lobola*) for the youth (called a variety of names: *nkhonsthana, amankotshame, izinkotshane* – as were Mathebula's warriors – or *tinkonkana* – 'mine-wife'). Clearly this was strongly related to the availability of women but as an aged miner, Philemon, said in 1987, 'mine-wives' entered the relationships 'for the sake of security, for the acquisition of property and for the fun itself'. So public were these arrangement that as late as 1988 black mine authorities enforced a code of practice (*mteto*) on these relationships.

Even when women were available such relationships existed. For example, in Mkumbani (a settlement near Durban) in the 1950s male-male weddings took place at the rate of one a month. The rituals used for male-female weddings were the same and in most cases the new 'male-bride' entered a family unit in which there was already a female wife who welcomed the new 'bride' as an ideal subordinate wife – she/he was unable to produce children to threaten the inheritance of the first wife's progeny. The husband (of both types of wives) was called *iqgenge* while the male-wife was *skesana*.

These examples from South Africa might suggest that the situation in present-day Africa is relatively tolerant. On one level this is the case. South Africa took the lead with its post-apartheid constitution, which was the first national constitution to prohibit discrimination based on sexual orientation. The clause passed parliament with the support of the African National Congress, the Pan-African Congress, the National Party and the Inkatha Freedom Party. Moreover, despite the homophobic rhetoric that one so often associates with African religious leaders, it also had the enthusiastic support of Archbishop Desmond Tutu. This positive stance, resting securely on a historic tradition of indigenous toleration of non-normative sexual and gender behaviour, has not been followed by that other nation to free itself from apartheid, Zimbabwe.

In 1995 when opening the Zimbabwe International Book Fair whose theme that year was, ironically, 'Human Rights and Justice', President Robert Mugabe said:

I find it extremely outrageous and repugnant to my human conscience *[emphasis mine] that such immoral and repulsive organisations* [a lesbian and gay group had its literature stall banned], *like those of homosexuals who offend both against the law of nature* [note: a concept developed by pagan Graeco-Roman philosophers *not* Africans] *and the morals of religious beliefs* [also note: imported by European colonial rulers] *espoused by our society, should have any advocates in our midst and elsewhere in the world…* [and in a subsequent press conference] *I don't believe they should have any rights at all* [a sentiment which, by changing the target, Ian Smith could have uttered].

These sentiments are the extreme version of those heard repeatedly from many African religious and political leaders. In addition, it is a stance taken up by Africans of the diaspora – for example any number of rap artists whose lyrics are frequently homophobic take the view that there is no word in any African language for 'homosexual'. Laying aside what we have already seen – words aplenty – one also notes, for example, that there is no word in Shona (Zimbabwe) for 'orgasm'. Should one conclude that there is no such physiological phenomenon?

However, the best way to counter the Victorian, Christian, European-derived colonial mentality of Mugabe is to let the history of Zimbabwe speak for itself. The contemporary historian Marc Epprecht has demonstrated conclusively that same-sex acts and individuals were a part of pre-colonial, traditional society. His findings are well worth rehearsing in some detail. In 1890, the British South Africa Company occupied Mahonaland and began the process of bringing the area under British colonial control. By 1892, a structure of colonial courts was in place and, in that year, 1.5 percent of cases tried were homosexual while there were *no* cases of heterosexual rape (or assault) or bestiality. Following Mugabe's line of argumentation one might conclude that traditional Zimbabwean society (two years after the arrival of European administration) was bereft of bestiality and heterosexual sexual violence – but one cannot argue that there is no evidence of same-sex activities.

The years that followed (1892-1923) produced a continuing stream of same-sex cases, in all about 300. Primarily, these were cases of homosexual assault. In these cases, 90 per cent of the accused were African; 8.7 per cent European and about 3 per cent Asian or 'coloured'. Most of the cases were concentrated in the earlier part of the period and suggest that over time judges became less interested in prosecuting same-sex acts except when committed by Europeans. A clear bias developed among the colonial white judges, which seems to have been based on the assumption that such crimes amongst whites endangered their 'superior' standing in the colony (much like the attitude we will see below among the British in India to sodomy among European troops).

Just as importantly, from very early in the colony's history, judges took the view that *consensual* homosexual acts were not criminal – decriminalisation by judicial act rather than legislative initiative. For example in 1913, a magistrate, L.F.H. Roberts, threw out a case saying, 'it seems to me no offence has been committed'. The prosecution's witness had complained that he had been assaulted anally but admitted that he had received money for repeated acts of intercrural sex. In effect, the judge seems to have been taking the view that the victim 'asked for it'. While this is not uncommon in cases of heterosexual assault it is amazing to find it here. The judge seems to have been unconcerned that the defendant had been trying to have sex with another man. Two years later, the attorney-general ruled in another case that 'as complainant was old enough to appreciate what was being done, and consented, no crime was committed'. In 1922 the solicitor-general Clarkson Tredgold overturned a conviction on the grounds that the evidence 'points almost directly to a case of consent'.

These cases suggest a number of important points. First, the judges took the view that consensual homosexual sex (especially among Africans) was not a criminal offence. Second, Africans were not less noticeable proportionally than one might expect considering the colony's overall demography (and the circumstances to be discussed below make this point even more strongly). Third, the pattern suggests that the white colonial administration was fairly unconcerned with African sexual practices but was determined to maintain a 'good example' among whites.

Two features of the colonial mentality further complicate attempts to identify the prevalence of homosexuality in Zimbabwe. First, although wanting to control white sexual behaviour to avoid scandal, the British also tended to avoid open discussions about sodomy trials in general. For example, in 1929, James Noble was convicted for nineteen counts of (quite lurid) sexual assaults on boys and teachers at Thabas Unduna Mission School where he had been superintendent. The *Bulawayo Chronicle* chose not to report the trial or its result and no mention was made of the case in the 'official' annual report of the British South African Police.

The second aspect of colonial thought that tended to hide African sexuality was the assumption that Africans were 'children'. African men remained 'boys' in the eyes of their white colonial rulers and, as such, their behaviour was viewed as immature. The debate for whites was whether Africans were 'immoral' (by nature) or 'perverse' (by choice). In either case, they were perceived to be immature, less civilised and 'closer to nature'. Obviously, this latter idea had none of the modern concept of 'organic' and 'conservationism' rather it meant that Africans were understood as animalistic, bestial – driven by their basest instincts. While Zimbabwean Africans never accepted this stereotype, they shared with their colonial masters a desire to avoid any open discussion of sex.

This reticence is a traditional feature of African society in Zimbabwe. The best example of this is the practice of *kupindira* or *kusikira rudzi* (raising seed). When a couple have trouble producing a child it is acceptable to come to an arrangement in which a close relative or friend would impregnate the wife with the resulting child accepted as the legitimate and natural offspring of the couple. Everyone would be 'aware' of what had happened but no one would ever refer to it. In general, the functionalist understanding of what sex is, is even stronger among traditional Zimbabweans than most European Christians. 'Sex' is what produces children – thus the *point* of homosexuality as 'sex' is baffling.

This pragmatic yet unspoken approach applies in same-sex cases as well. Many Africans would argue that 'playing' with someone of the same sex was not sex since orgasm (from frottage or manual manipulation) was purely 'accidental' and, indeed, incidental to the play. Even local words which might refer to homosexuals rely not on clarity but inflection and implication (as with the old English euphemisms of 'confirmed bachelor' and 'spinster' – it would all depend on *how* one said it – with a 'nod and a wink'). Thus, Shona has *tsvimborume* (someone who has a penis but nowhere to put it – unmarried) and *sahwira* (close male comrade). Where there are explicit references to homosexuals the words used are 'foreign' borrowings (*ngotshana* from Zulu or Shangaan and *manayero* from the Chewa of Malawian immigrants). This is used by Mugabe and his supporters to imply that homosexuality itself is an import. In actuality what this suggests is a different cultural approach to discussing (or not discussing) sexual activities generally. Moreover, the fact that the words are borrowings from other African languages would simply suggest that these cultures were more open in talking about sex – not that homosexuality was alien to all Africans.

More importantly, the colonial judicial structure adopted in Zimbabwe masked the behaviour of Africans. Most urban areas (centres of white, Asian, coloured and immigrant/urbanised African population) were tried under a Romano-Dutch system developed in South Africa. The bulk of the African population, though, lived in rural areas and were overseen by the native commissioner applying a type of 'customary' law. Within this rural context the native commissioner focused on crimes against persons and property leaving most of the rest of justice in the hands of local 'headmen'. Very little of the justice actually administered at the headman level produced written records except when appealed to the native commissioner.

It is in the context of appeals that one gains some insight into what was happening at the local, traditional level and why so few sodomy cases appear in the written sources. In 1921, headman Mbata (from Bindura) said:

In native custom we should require a beast [as a fine] *if a native attempted sodomy. If however, it was done while sleeping* [a defence of unconscious nocturnal emission in a shared bed] *we would still require reparation but only a small amount. I was satisfied there was nothing* deliberate [emphasis mine] *about the act.*

Unsurprisingly, awareness that any act of sodomy or attempted sodomy could be defended by claiming that it occurred while sleeping or semi-awake was likely to produce a more lenient response from the headmen's courts meant most simply made this claim and were dealt with by means of a small fine at the headman's discretion.

However, in the urban areas there is a 'paper-trail' of homosexuality. In the period 1897–1921, Salisbury was about 33 percent European but only 10 percent of sodomy trials involved whites. Although the rest of the population (over 60 percent) was non-white, the majority of these individuals were also non-native immigrants (black Africans from elsewhere, Asians, coloureds, etc). This non-native, non-white population was not, however, the majority in same-sex trials. Thus, although native Zimbabweans (Shona) were only about 20 percent of the Salisbury population, they accounted for over half of the cases tried. What Mugabe and his supporters stress, though, is that whites and Asians predominate in the appellate level. This is hardly surprising. Whites and (to a lesser degree) Asians were more likely to be able to afford the appeals process. When one looks at the totality of surviving cases it is clear that native Zimbabweans were as likely to commit homosexual acts as anyone else.

Why then the assertions by Mugabe and, to a lesser degree, by other black African leaders elsewhere? Clearly, Mugabe's political interests are served by his ability to portray himself as the moral bulwark against foreign perversity. Moreover, one has to remember the impact of the arrest of Canaan Banana in 1997 for sodomy – it can hardly be coincidence that Mugabe's campaign began in 1995 paving the way for the arrest of Banana. The disgrace of the country's first President, a close friend and supporter of Mugabe meant it was essential that Mugabe distance himself from Banana and his activities. However, even the Zimbabwean ruling class had little stomach for widening and publicising the scandal. The *Herald* paper mentioned the trial but spilt much ink attacking the enthusiasm of the South African press for details. The *Sunday Mail* simply refused to mention the case.

It is, however, in the realm of foreign affairs that 'sodomy as import' is most useful. Mugabe regularly accuses the former colonial power, Britain, of being dominated by a 'gay Mafia'. Dr Ken Mufuka, a historian, who has lived in the American Bible Belt for years, has written his own Alistair-Cooke-esque 'Letter from America' for the *Sunday Mail*. Railing against the power of 'homosexuals and feminists' (whom he treats as one and the same), he frequently portrays America (the centre of world capitalism and globalisation) as a country overrun by gays. Thus, for internal and external political reasons, Mugabe has a vested interest in promoting a campaign of homophobia – 'family values' are a potent political tool in more places than the United States.

However, the Zimbabwean campaign is especially virulent because the assertion that homosexuality is 'foreign' allows attacks against African homosexuals and 'gay-rights' activists to be couched in the language of racism and race-betrayal. This explains how one Zimbabwean parliamentarian was led to speak of Archbishop Desmond Tutu and Nelson Mandela (when they condemned homophobia) as 'pseudo Nobel Peace Price winners'. The campaign also has the support of many leading churchmen. For example, Dr Michael Mawema (a minister of the African Reformed Church) has said that homosexuals should be castrated, publicly whipped and stoned as 'perverts'. His full-page advert in *The Herald* (a state-controlled paper) was explicit in its homophobia and hate:

Crusade Against Rapists And Homosexuals
God commands the death of sexual perverts.
Our culture and traditional justice system condemns them to death.
Our religion condemns them to death.
Rape, incest, homosexual victims want the sexual molesters to die.
Why does the law condone these evils and save sexual perverts from
    death?
All those concerned about the lack of justice for the sexually molested
    are invited to the meeting.

Agenda:
To debate proposals required for the enactment of laws that will protect
    the sexual victims and prescribe effective punishment for the culprits.
Set up committees to mobilise Zimbabweans against sexual perverts.

What is most amazing about this advert and the general campaign led by Mugabe is the almost total lack of international condemnation. If such a campaign were being waged against any other minority groups (blacks in America; Jews in Germany; though perhaps not women in a strict Muslim society) there would be comment and action.

As Marc Epprecht has shown, the simple fact is that the assertions underlying the Zimbabwe campaign are incorrect, indeed, deceitful. From the earliest surviving records there is evidence of same-sex activities among native Zimbabweans. The system of justice implemented by the British, as well as underlying assumptions about black Africans tended to marginalise their place in the historical records. Nevertheless, homosexual Africans were present in pre-colonial Zimbabwe and elsewhere on the continent. More importantly, African societies evidence a diversity of cultural reactions to same-sex activities, which directly undercuts racist attempts to generalise about these cultures and to lump them into an amorphous mass of 'primitives'. Sadly, some Africans' political and religious leaders would prefer a view of their pre-colonial societies created by Europeans (to justify imperialism) to an honest acceptance of their diversity, uniqueness and creativity in constructing, and sustaining, cultural niches for individuals with non-standard sexuality.

Before leaving Africa one must confront constructionism and social relativism head-on. Many Africans today, taking their lead from those Europeans, who wrote much of the literature justifying the European exploitation and conquest of Africa, simply assert that same-sex activities were unknown to Africans prior to influences from outside the continent. Homosexuality is, in this view, an alien import and an infection. From Mugabe to Afro-American rap stars, there is the almost constant refrain that Africans, in their 'native state', knew no such behaviour.

This is problematic on a number of levels. First, what does Africa mean? It seems clear that men like Mugabe, blaming homosexuality on Arab-Islamic or Western influences, mean sub-Saharan Africa – 'black' Africa. This would seem to imply that the Muslim inhabitants of the northern third of the continent are somehow interlopers, not *really* Africans. Second, it falls into the dangerous trap of homogenising all African societies and cultures into a single amorphous *thing*. Surely this plays into the hands of racists, who want to lump masses of humanity into a few, single undifferentiated groups.

An additional problem is that the issue is really one of definitions. If African leaders and others are arguing that Western, socially constructed, late twentieth-century homosexuality was unknown in Africa then, in that simplest and narrowest of senses, they are right; it was equally unknown in the West, too. In effect, this is a non-argument! One might just as effectively argue that 'modern' views about heterosexuality (partners choosing one another for love with no regard to socio-economic status or other hierarchical concerns) is alien to Africa, an infection in native society – which would be just as true. Such a view is misleading, pointless and, ultimately, a deceit.

The real question is whether or not same-sex, genital relations occurred between men or between women in African societies prior to the arrival of Arab and European influences. Every scrap of

evidence suggests that this is the case. Men had genital contact with
men and women with women. To be fair, it is not always clear that
their societies would have understood this 'physical' activity as 'sexual'
activity. It is equally certain that the construction in Africa consistently presupposed that marriage and procreation would take place
regardless of any other sexual, physical, or emotional bonds.

One can certainly argue that men did not *love* one another but it is
even easier to argue that most husbands did not *love* their wives – in a
modern, Western sense of the word. Such an argument, in either case,
is patently ridiculous. One can assert that it was the universal expectation in African societies that the great bulk of men and women would
'marry' and procreate. However, it is clear from any fair reading of the
historical, cultural and linguistic sources that not everyone conformed
to this pattern and that most African societies found some way to construct a *niche* in which these 'non-conformists' could exist. More importantly, as we have seen elsewhere, African societies seem to have accepted
that sex-for-procreation and sex-for-pleasure were not directly connected and one was not better than the other. Nor did they assume that
the focal point for emotions and love was the marital bond.

Where does that leave us as we prepare to leave Africa to consider
other parts of the globe? Africa appears to be *normal* in the sense of the
wide, global sweep of attitudes to same-sex relations and relationships.
African societies, in common with those of the Indian subcontinent
and the Far East, have assumed that almost everyone would procreate
while leaving room for sex-for-pleasure to have a number of diverse
outlets. These societies also constructed ways of normalising and
tolerating those who never married or procreated. If some Africans
wish to assert that this is not the case then they must accept that they
are implying that Africans are historically and globally *abnormal*. If they
wish to cling to a model of *normality* and *morality* constructed by their
Western conquerors that is, of course, their choice, but their own histories, cultural heritage and linguistic record, as well as the testimony
of all other non-Western/Christian societies suggests that this would
be aberrant – *abnormal*. African societies, in finding a place for same-
sex activities and individuals, prove that they were part of the normal
behaviour of human communities across the world throughout time.

Why would Africans and others wish to align their histories with cultural patterns which are the least *normal* in an historical, global sense? As we have seen, consistently negative and violent responses to homosexuality are a reaction peculiar to Judaism, Islam and, especially, Christianity. Homosexuality, while never the behaviour of the majority and also never historically seen as a life-long alternative to procreative relationships, has in almost all cultures across the globe and throughout time been accepted and 'fitted into' the structures of society. Indeed, the virulent homophobia of Western Christianity has been shown to be a feature that came to fruition only in the past 500 years and was never consistent. More importantly, the spread of the negative Christian view of homosexuality became worldwide only as a result of the nineteenth-century global hegemony of Europe, and the cultural and economic dominance of the United States in the last century. In effect, the West's 'colonisation of the mind' continues apace aided and abetted by non-Westerners, who seem bent on sacrificing their own histories and traditions in an effort to emulate all aspects of what even they seem to consider the 'successful' cultures of the West.

The West dominated large parts of the globe and altered pre-existing cultural patterns. It is left to those leaders and societies, who threw off Western political and social domination and who strive to resist Western economic and cultural hegemony to decide if they wish to do what the West never managed to do despite its best efforts – that is to eradicate their histories. One can either affirm what appears to be the historical reality across the globe – that same-sex behaviour and individuals had a place in non-Western and pre-Christian societies – or strive to erase these Africans, Indians, Chinese and others from history. Westerners are rightly criticised by other peoples for holding to a history that largely erases the slave trade, genocide, etc., from the wider popular consciousness in favour of 'dead, white males'. It would be truly sad, though, if it were the hands of non-Westerners that whitewashed 'dead, black, Indian, African, and Asian men and women' from their own history simply because they engaged in same-sex activities.

With the arrival of the British and the replacement of Mughal dominance with the power of the East India Company, the situation in India began to change (as it would in Africa). Two trends are discernible. First, negative attitudes to same-sex activities became louder, more strident and more common. As we have seen, there had always been an attitude to sex between men, which had seen it as distasteful and ritually impure. However, this had been more than balanced by the ambiguity towards sex in the Hindu stories of the gods and goddesses, as well as the prevailing realities of historical figures and the sentiments in literature, especially poetry. The English/British, especially after the assumption of direct rule following the 1857 Great Rebellion/Mutiny, increasingly imposed the legal and moral codes of Christian Victorian Britain on India.

The second trend is, in some ways, even more fascinating. Increasingly in the nineteenth and twentieth centuries literature and other popular media have turned towards lesbianism as the primary form of same-sex behaviour represented. Traditionally, male-dominated Indian society (both Hindu and Muslim) had focused on the sexual activities of men – even with other men. Same-sex when discussed and portrayed was *male*. However, in modern India this has been replaced by an increasing focus on, and interest in, female same-sex behaviour. A number of hypotheses might be advanced to explain this. Heterosexual men are considerably less threatened – and too frequently titillated – by lesbianism. In India, as we have seen elsewhere, sex between women is not really considered as 'sex' and therefore viewed differently. Here the recurring issue of whether sex without penetration is sex is again visible. For whatever reasons, sex and love between men is considerably less visible than historically was the case, while lesbianism (whether sexual, emotional, or both) has become the socially acceptable (or tolerated) face of same-sex activities.

As in Europe though, one must be careful when discussing representations of lesbianism. Too often these are for and by men: lesbianism as male erotica rather than any accurate depiction of same-sex relations between women. This is perhaps the case in one of the best-known representative forms for lesbianism in modern India: Rekhti poetry. This is a form of poetry in Urdu developed (largely) in the nineteenth century by male poets based in the princely state of Avadh (capital, Lucknow) writing in the female voice. The poets, writing as women, depicted explicit female sexuality, especially lesbianism. In many cases, Rekhti poems by leading poets have been excised from their published works as too obscene. For our purposes, it is crucial to remember that the poems were by men writing about what they thought (or would like to think) female sexuality and lesbianism was like. On the other hand, there is no reason to assume that these court poets did not have regular contact with courtesans and were, therefore, able to 'speak for' these women through their poetry.

What one sees is an overlap between Rekhti poetry and the earlier *ghazal* forms, for example in *Bustani-I Khayal* by Siraj Aurangabadi (1715-63). Desolate after the loss of his male beloved, the poet turned to his female friends, courtesans, for comfort. He described them as one another's *aliyan* (close 'girlfriends') and one commentator has explained they had a 'colourful character' (the *rangin mijaz* we have seen above referring to those given to same-sex loves). Elsewhere, such women – who were frequently dancers and musicians, as well as courtesans – called themselves *chapathaz* (given to sex between women) and mocked marriage and heterosexual relationships in satirical songs. While these women may not have written about their loves in Rekhti poetry they were certainly not averse to articulating their tastes and it would seem the male Rekhti poets listened occasionally. Four of the five words (*dugana, zanakhe, sa'tar, chapathai, chapatbaz*) identified in the late nineteenth century by pioneering sexologist Havelock Ellis as referring to lesbians appear in the genre.

Not only have these poems been dismissed as obscene but they have also been attacked for their base sensuality and physicality in comparison with *ghazal* poetry, which is presented as being all about mystical, spiritual love. As we have seen, *ghazal* poems are not only explicit in gendering the lover and beloved as males but also fairly 'physical'. This same attempt to divide what is fundamentally Muslim cultural forms of poetry into mystical, spiritual, male-male poetry (read good) and base, physical, female-female poetry is replicated in the Hindu tradition as well. Reeti poetry is denounced as base and erotic, while Bhakti poetry is refined and devotional (though in both genres relationships are normally male-female). The point in both cultural forms is that there is an attempt to reinterpret some literary forms as mystical and devotional, devoid of any eroticism and sensuality, especially where this involves same-sex activities. Same-sex portrayals are *either* rejected as obscene (Rekhti) *or* reinterpreted as spiritual (*ghazal*). The same sort of approach rereads Shakespeare's sonnets (largely written to men) as non-physical and rarifies or allegorises the blatant sensuality of the *Song of Songs/Solomon* in the Bible.

Just as importantly, the rejection by Victorian British culture and some elements of modern India's socio-political elite may have as much to do with the genre's connection with Lucknow as with its supposed obscene content. While Avadh was the focal point for the fiercest resistance to the British in 1857-58, this strength was later denigrated by the British who portrayed Avadh as decadent and 'Eastern'. The behaviour of the rulers and elite of Avadh allowed the British to emasculate their staunchest military and political opponents by, in effect, accusing them of being feminine and unmanly – in modern parlance, calling them 'gay'. One of the last kings before the Rebellion, Nawab Nasirudin Haider (r.1827-37) not only kept eleven women at his court to represent the wives of the last eleven Shia imams (as had his mother) but, on the birthdays of the imams, he pretended to go into labour and give birth to them! Moreover, court officials imitated his adoption of female attire and characteristics during these birthdays – and at other times. The British must have been particularly galled to find that their most difficult battles, their fiercest military opponents in 1857-58 were led by men who spent some of their time in drag and whose king mimicked childbirth as a form of religious observance. That Indian nationalists have often accepted the British view of Muslim-ruled Avadh as decadent simply highlights the extent to which Indian history has fallen prey to the post-colonial inculcation and assimilation of the values and morals of the imperial power: Christian Victorian Britain.

These values, though, were of a variety and shape peculiar to the 'Brit abroad'. In India, the British developed a type of 'hypermasculinity'. In particular, the British became increasingly concerned to ensure that their image in the eyes of the 'native peoples' remained extremely 'virile' and 'warlike'. The image of the 'warrior' became crucial. Thus, by 1839, it was made explicit that 'conduct unbecoming an officer' had come to encompass 'conduct tending to lower the character of British officers in the opinions of the Natives'. In this context it was critical to maintain an attitude to sex and sexuality that, from the British perspective, was as 'manly' as possible but also 'controlled' – a 'real man' was in control of himself.

This was no small concern as it involved trying to control the sexual behaviour of the large number of European troops in the subcontinent. Part of this was trying to ensure that these troops did not 'go native' by becoming entangled in permanent liaisons with native women. This, of course, was problematic. If the men were not to 'marry' (via concubinage) local women, the obvious alternative – or the one most feared by British officers and officials – was to engage in sex with each other. As nearly a third of European troops were hospitalised with venereal disease at any given time in the early nineteenth century the problem was critical. Rejecting the acceptance of concubinage (favoured by the Dutch in Indonesia and the French in Africa), the British chose 'regulated' prostitution – concubinage would endanger the effective homosocial bonds among the troops while total segregation would lead to sodomy.

Aggressive, violent, non-emotional (just sex, no love) heterosexuality along with heavy drinking produced a 'masculinity' which kept European soldiers cut off from native society and the 'superior, self-controlled' officer culture. Underlying this was a host of elite British beliefs about the enervating, degenerate threat of Eastern culture and the sex-driven, uncontrolled behaviour of Europeans of the 'lower orders'. In this context, to counter any hint that the British were anything but strong-willed, 'masculine' men, the British strove to ensure that *any* sexually abnormal behaviour – any slippage in the mask of hypermasculinity – was kept secret so as not to undermine the self-cultivated image of masculinity and manliness in the face of the 'luxuriousness and sensuality' of the East.

In this context of image-projection, trials for rape and sodomy were largely prosecuted in secret. The judge-advocate general's office in Bengal recommended that rape trials where the girl was aged under ten should be conducted *in camera*. In 1835 the same office decreed that trials for 'unnatural acts' (bestiality and sodomy) should also be behind closed doors. In Britain, public trials for sodomy (e.g. Oscar Wilde's) were extremely effective in reinforcing social strictures against same-sex acts. However, in India, the trials were in secret and the guilty were transported to Australia since any publicity might undermine the masculinity of Europeans in the eyes of *sepoys* (native troops), in particular, and, more generally, in the wider 'native' culture. So conscious was this policy that (in 1846) a legal authority said, 'transportation has no other recommendation as a punishment for soldiers, but that it gets rid of offenders'.

Within a few years of the incorporation of India into the British Empire in the aftermath of the 1857 Rebellion, British law was imposed on the new imperial territories in the form of the 1861 Indian Penal Code. This code, effectively, translated the English legal code to India. As such, the timing could not have been more interesting. In 1860, a new anti-sodomy law had been passed into British law. At home, this was a progressive act replacing imprisonment for death as the normal punishment for sodomy. It also provided a definition for same-sex acts, which could, with some ingenuity, apply to lesbianism. Further it made prosecutions easier in defining sodomy as merely penetration rather than, as the technical situation before, as penetration *and* ejaculation. The act passed into Indian law as Section 377 of the Indian Penal Code – and is still in force:

Whoever voluntarily has carnal intercourse against the order of nature with any man, woman or animal, shall be punished with imprisonment, or with imprisonment of either description for a term which may extend to ten years, and shall be liable to fine.

There was an accompanying 'explanatory' note: 'penetration is sufficient to constitute the carnal intercourse necessary to the offence'.

It is interesting that this law meant that 'sodomy' was not, necessarily, an act between consenting adults. Rather, a male rapist (or indeed a woman forcing another person with some sort of implement) was a 'sodomite' not a rapist. Also, the lack of any reference to anatomy (penis) with penetration meant that lesbianism was not excluded from the act although was unlikely to be punished. More importantly, the act itself, in its Indian context, was rarely used. Only thirty-six prosecutions occured from 1861 to 2000 and the majority of these relate to male rape. However, the law remains in force and can be used, effectively, to intimidate, harass and blackmail anyone engaged in same-sex practices. More bizarrely, it has also been used (in 1998) to prosecute the Population Service International for 'promoting homosexuality' in its sex-education programme.

The Victorians did more than change India's legal structures, though. They also justified their occupation and control of the sub-continent by defining a paternalistic and civilising mission for them-selves in India. In this model, India was a childlike culture badly run by decadent, sensualist elites, who wallowed in a depraved eroticism. Hindu religion came in for particular criticism with the sexual ambi-guity of its gods and goddesses. Victorian Orientalists tended to divide Hindu writings into two categories: a 'Greater Tradition' and a 'Lesser Tradition'. The Brahmin writings of the classical period (which are considerably less 'sensual') were the core of the former and presented a male-dominated, heterosexual view of history and myth (*Mahabharata*; *Ramayana*; and some legal codes, *dharmashastras*, such as the *Manusmirti*). The latter tradition contained much of the Puranic literature of the medieval period with its myriad of stories about the lives – and sex lives – of the gods (for example the *Kama Sutra*; folk-tales; traditional practices such as female marriages, *maitri karar*; and the same-sex iconography of some temples, Tara-Taratini in Orissa).

The British also provided a reading of India's political history to mirror its critique of Hinduism. India's medieval and Mughal rulers were presented as decadent with their harems, eunuchs, temple and court prostitution, polygamy etc.; Islamic rulers were particularly tar-geted. The new Western rulers also divided the elite of Hindu society by making common cause with the 'martial' castes and groups and denigrating the upper, Brahman caste as decadent and hedonistic. Wherever possible, the ancient classical cultures of the subcontinent were held up as more moral – a reading of history largely sustained by post-colonial nationalists. Wherever necessary, even 'Great Tradition' texts were altered to make the model work. The process began early: Sir William Jones (1746-94) in his eighteenth century translation of the *Gita Govinda* omitted 'passages which are too luxu-rious and too bold for an *European* taste'. He also rendered Hafiz' eighth *ghazal* in such a way that the gender-neutral Persian (strongly implying the beloved was a young male) became, in the English, most definitely a young girl.

Victorian values, which were anti-sex and, especially, opposed to sex–as/for–pleasure had a profound impact. Indians were increasingly presented with a model for men/husbands, women/wives, and children that was Victorian, British and Christian. So effective was this that monogamous heterosexual marriage has become the model for acceptable, natural, moral and religious sexual coupling. Thus, one saw the creation of 'Protestantised' Hindu movements (such as Arya Samaj, founded in the early 1900s by Dayananda Saraswati, a Brahmin scholar), which opposed polytheism, idolatry and polygamy as 'accretions to' and 'corruptions of' the Vedic tradition and tried to find the 'modern' (i.e. Western) in ancient India. The British may have left but their lasting success has been in the reshaping of pan-Indian culture along Victorian, Christian lines. The promiscuity and matrilineal culture of *devdasi* communities and some Vishnu groups in eastern India, as well as the matrilineal inheritance systems used in parts of Kerala and temple prostitution (male and female) – all of which were regarded with some disdain in pre-colonial India and which the British strongly disliked – were only outlawed by an 'independent' India supposedly freed from the forces of Western imperialism (both political and cultural).

The real problem for Indian society (then and now) is that, having accepted the Western Christian idea of a 'man's man' at the top of a hierarchy with inferior women, monogamy, heterosexuality, etc, every incidence of a culture that did not conform to this model was both embarrassing and, potentially, helped buttress British claims that Indian culture was decadent and 'needed' the firm hand of British paternalism – a Western, Christian, Victorian father-figure. Thus, when Katherine Mayo in her *Mother India* (1927) connected nationalist, anti-imperial militancy with sexual deviance:

Bengal is the seat of bitterest political unrest – the producer of India's main crop of anarchists, bomb-throwers and assassins. Bengal is also among the most sexually exaggerated regions of India; medical and police authorities in any country observe the link between that quality and 'queer' minds – the exhaustion of normal avenues of excitement creating a thrust and a search in the abnormal for gratification.

the response was not to defend the right of men to be free not only politically but also sexually from the British, but rather to claim that Hinduism was as anti-sodomitical as Christianity and, in any case, such behaviour was an alien (for which read, Muslim) infection in India.

In this context it is easy to see why the state and many contemporary political leaders (especially the more extreme nationalists) continue to denounce homosexuality as a 'foreign' import while trying to eradicate or cleanse 'traditional' practices, which still exist in India: same-sex environments (*ashram* and *khanqah*), male prostitution, concubinage and domestic servants as sexual objects. The alternative approach, to value traditional norms above Western ones, is not without some adherents: in 1897, Indian author and Muslim apologist, Muhammad Abdul Ghani argued that polygamy had kept India relatively free of prostitution unlike the Christian, monogamous West.

The most obvious and shocking effect of the British 'reading' of India's past and sex is the response of Muslims to the charge of importing sodomy into the subcontinent. In 1882, the Indian Islamic scholar, Altaf Hussain Hali (1837-1914) led a campaign to eliminate 'boy-love' from Urdu poetry (*ghazal*). A similar sentiment underlies the plea from Andalib Shadani (1904-69; a scholar of Urdu literature) that any references to 'boy-love' are 'an insult to 'that pure emotion' (love): 'Wouldn't it be great if all well-wishers of Urdu destroy whatever they can of such poetry so that this ugly blot on Urdu's reputation is washed away'. In his 1965 treatise *Nasl Kushi* (Race Suicide), the Islamic author, Mufti Muhammed Zafiruddin added a twist to the charge against Muslims by saying that sodomy was introduced by Persians (that is, Shi'ites *not* Sunni Muslims). The alternative view was voiced by the Indian poet, 'Firaq' Gorakhpuri (born Raghupati Sahay, 1896-1982) who accused those attacking the homosexuality of Indian history and poetry of 'slavish mentality and pedestrian prejudice'. Homosexuality, he argued, was at the core of Urdu *ghazal* poetry not incidental – the 'most sensitive vein of their life'.

Time and again one sees the history of homosexuality becoming an integral part of polemic *against* the 'other'. Indeed, the historian Suleri has argued that 'homoeroticism forms the fundamental dynamic of colonial interaction' – imperial overlords necessarily emasculate and 'feminise' (or infantilise) those they wish to subjugate. In this scheme, any imputation of same-sex activity is an insult and a justification for control. This preconception (based on accepting Western Christian ideas of masculinity) that a 'man' would not have sex with another man and that such behaviour is enervating and degenerate explains the general view of Indian academe, as well as the more popular view in other parts of the world. For example, recent films portraying Achilles-Patroclus and Alexander the Great-Hephaistion either go to vast lengths to re-interpret same-sex relationships (Achilles and Patroclus are 'close' *because* they are cousins) or simply ignore them in favour of a heterosexual romance (Alexander 'loves' his Persian princess-bride and has only a 'professional', man's-man, comrade-in-arms relationship with his general).

The simple reality is that India, a place with a complex socio-cultural historical relationship with sexuality, is a perfect place to examine the successful spread of Christian and Western values about sex. Both ends of the political spectrum denounce homosexuality, exposing their indebtedness, and submission, to Western ideas both secular and religious. The enthusiasm for the social constructions of the former colonial culture and the rejection of previous cultural norms as decadent and despised could not be more extreme or more obvious. A leading Indian Marxist, denouncing calls to repeal Section 377, said homosexuality is 'backward and reactionary' like sati (widows throwing themselves on their husbands' funeral pyres), polygamy and the caste system. Being ancient and widespread (in Indian culture) no more makes homosexuality moral than it would incest or bestiality. He concluded by saying 'gay liberation' is:

decadent bourgeois… encouraging all deviant forms of sexual relations… Marxists stand for heterosexual, monogamous relations and proscribe all deviant forms of sexual relations, including homosexuality… Marxists try to change [emphasis mine] *sexual behaviour through education… if some people, much against public conscience, take to the streets on the plea that they have the right to gratify their sexual urges in any way they like, Marxists do not hesitate to use force against such homosexual activists.*

Right-wing activists, such as Swapan DesGupta, admit that 'lesbianism is part of our heritage' but add:

thievery, deceit, murder and other [Indian Penal Code]-*defined offences have a long history. That doesn't elevate them to the level of heritage… Homosexuality may have found mention in* some [emphasis mine] *ancient manuals and even depicted in a temple carving* or two [again, my emphasis], *but as in the pre-promiscuous* [i.e. Victorian, Christian] *West, it was a preference that was greeted with tolerant disapproval. It was always an alternative to marriage and family but never a socially acceptable option.*

Where same-sex activities cannot be whitewashed from history the alternative is to repudiate them as either alien or depraved (unsuitably for a vibrant, 'manly' society) – sex-as-pleasure is impure; 'pure' sex is for procreation.

Of course, one is just as likely to see opponents of the right accusing them of being 'fascists' *and* 'homosexuals'. For example, political opponents of the RSS (Rashtriya Swayamsevak Sangh) and its political wing, the BJP (Bharatiya Janata Party) ignore the fact that both associate same-sex relations with 'anti-(Hindu)-national Otherness'. For their part the RSS and BJP see homosexuality as either a British or Muslim import – rather as the British saw sodomy in their midst as the result of becoming 'too oriental', too Indian!

Where the mix of post-colonialism and sexuality is seen at its most destructive and interesting is the reaction of the Parsi community to independence. In the 'divide and rule' culture of British India, the British had long relied on and encouraged the minority Parsi community (descendents of Persia's Zoroastrians). The Parsi were major participants in the opium trade to China. This high profile saw the elevation of the famous Parsi merchant Jamsetjee Jeejeebhoy (1783-1859) to a knighthood and, later, a baronetcy (the first for an Indian). His life overlapped with that of another great Parsi merchant, Jamsetji Nusserwanji Tata (1839-1904) whose Tata Group companies remains one of India's largest commercial conglomerates. In an environment in which colonial authorities saw 'natives as passive, ignorant, irrational, outwardly submissive but inwardly guileful, sexually unrestrained and emotionally demanding' the Parsi were keen to identify themselves with the self-defined image the British projected as 'hypermasculinised' males.

During British rule, the Parsi community saw itself, in the words of a 1906 Parsi publication, as 'the one race settled in India... that could for a moment be called white'. The year before, *Stray Thoughts on Indian Cricket* noted that 'many a wealthy and educated Parsi now-a-days takes an annual holiday to England, just as a Mahommedan or a Hindu goes to Mecca or Benares'. This view of themselves was predicated on an identification of Parsi values (truthfulness, purity, charity, industry and progressive improvement) with Victorian 'manly' values. However, with independence, the Parsis were now in the position of being 'white' in India but no longer in control. The community has been beset with a sense of self-doubt and anguish about its place in independent India. This introspection has led some to conclude – though only rarely to say – that the Parsi 'fall' is the direct result of the 'degeneration' (feminising) of Parsi males. The young of today are frequently accused of being 'effeminate', 'impotent', 'inadequate', 'gay' and 'Mama's boys'. Not only does this say much about attitudes towards men and women, gays and straights, but also how these ideas are being worked out in a non-Western society heavily reshaped by years of cultural imperialism.

None of this general trend, however, can change history. Same-sex relationships existed and were tolerated even under British rule – especially in the princely states where the heavy hand of British law rested more lightly. For example, the novelist E.M. Forster wrote in detail in his personal papers of his affairs with men and youths when he visited Dewas and the court of Maharaja Vishwanath Singh Bahadur (r. 1866-1932) in 1912 and 1921. During both visits his liaisons enjoyed the friendly, if amused tolerance of the maharaja and was well-known among the staff and wider community.

Just as importantly, modern voices in India argue for a traditional, *laissez-faire* approach to non-standard sexual relationships. Jiddu Krishnamurti (1895-1986), a spiritual leader, has rejected celibacy and said that unnecessary suffering has been caused by making any distinction between types of sexual expression: 'not [to] condemn one or the other or approve one and deny the other, but [to] enquire why sexuality has become so colossally important?' Spiritual and political leaders who extolled celibacy (Swami Prabhavananda and Mahatma Gandhi) did so by treating homosexuality and heterosexuality as identical expressions of lust and desire. Srinivasa Raghavachariar, Sanskrit scholar and priest of the Vishnu temple at Shri Rangam (and father of thirteen), simply explains that same-sex lovers must have been opposite-sex lovers in a previous life – the sex may change but the souls remain in love. He added an explanation for homosexuality, which rivals that of Plato in the *Symposium*:

Homosexuality is also a design of Nature. Earth is overpopulated by the human species and the Earth Mother – Bhooma Devi – is no longer able to carry the burden. So this is one of Mother Nature's way[s] of combating the population explosion… [this has created an overbalance and homosexuality, along with man's drive to other planets] *are all Mother Earth's plans to relieve herself of the burden of the mass of humanity. All we can do is to sit back and wonder at the divine tricks of the Almighty.*

In the discussion of nature *versus* nurture, this view is certainly unique.

The most interesting aspect of the situation in modern India is the *hijra*s. As early as the end of the eighteenth century, James Forbes, a merchant in the East India Company reported that he and a surgeon-major examined a number of 'hermaphrodites', who worked as cooks in the Maratha army. He and others considered these people to be 'disgusting' and their 'practices, revolting'. In 1817, a junior officer in Poona noted the presence of 'hermaphrodites', who wore a mixture of male and female clothing. As the British became more aware of these their revulsion only increased and they lumped *hijra*s together with other 'degenerate' aspects of Indian culture. As the subcollector of Poona said in 1836, it is 'lamentable to think that we are living amongst people who look upon infanticide, suttees, tuggee and hijeras without apparently a feeling of horror'.

For nineteenth-century British officials in India, the *hijra*s were extremely problematic. Not only did they exist but moreover they had an important role in society. The presence of a *hijra* at a wedding or birth was, and still is, important. A bride, to avoid infertility, must ensure that her face not be seen by a *hijra*; a male newborn blessed by a *hijra* will be healthy and produce many (male) children. The British were also extremely confused about what exactly a *hijra* was – a question that still exercises scholars who study them to this day. From as early as 1836, officials described *hijra*s as men who were completely

castrated by a *hijra* 'midwife' (*dai*). However, it is clear that this ceremony did not, and does not, necessarily lead to any physical alteration
– that is, it is often a symbolic castration.

Likewise, the assumption that the *hijra*s were male prostitutes or
zenana ('men given to sodomy') has been consistently questioned by
scholars and rejected by the *hijra*s themselves – especially in recent years
with the establishment of the All-India *Hijra Kalyan Sabha* (Welfare
Organisation) as a pro-*hijra* pressure group. Finally, British officials were
equally confused by the terminology often used by *hijra*s to discuss their
'transformation'. It was (and is) usually described as 'becoming Muslim'
with some taking Muslim names (though 'new' Hindu names seem just
as common). In addition, the main religious focus of *hijra* culture centres on worship of the Hindu goddess Bahuchara Mata and various sexually ambivalent representations of Shiva (especially as male-female).

The officials did what any Victorian did when faced with a mys-
tery; they investigated. However, there was a serious danger in becoming 'too familiar' with *hijra*s. The British assumed (presaging the sort
of comments coming from modern Indians) that *hijra*s were just a
barbarous practice – such as *sati* and infanticide – that needed to be
wiped out as part of Britain's civilising 'mission' in the subcontinent.
To most, *hijra*s were just transvestite male prostitutes. However, when
the Poone official, again in the mid-1830s, interviewed seven *hijra*s he
found they all adamantly denied any knowledge of the 'passive abomination' claiming they were simply 'legally-recognised' beggars who
only 'beg with decency and character'.

What the British quickly realised was that *hijra*s occupied a very
marginal place in most villages. *Hijra*s could curse or bless and often
used this power to extract alms from neighbours. They were not feared
or despised because of any association with sexuality. Rather their
caste status (they needed attendants, *mamara-mundas*, to act as go-
betweens when begging from upper caste Brahmins), their ability to
curse, their accepted right to beg and, in many cases, their legal permission (*sanad*) to certain rights of revenue (*vatam*) from lands granted
to them by Indian princes made them dangerous and powerful.
Research in legal documents, for example in Poona, demonstrated
that such protections had been granted by King Sahu (r.1708-49).

What the British were determined to do was to eliminate any economic rights that might make being a *hijra* attractive. They believed that this would end the practice as it withered on the vine. In 1854 the Bombay presidency, therefore, ruled on the legal question of rights granted under previous regimes (of which the British claimed to be heirs): 'the right of begging or extorting money, *whether authorized by former governments or not* [emphasis mine], has been discontinued'. A year later, the *hijra* right to beg was ruled to be 'a notion of course wholly erroneous'. Unfortunately, many *hijra* had legal documents entitling them to pensions (*varsasans*) from the state, as well as access to rent-free land (*inam*) heritable to their heirs (in practice a younger *hijra* disciple rather than, for obvious reasons, a blood relative).

One case in particular forced the British to deal with this issue. At stake were a number of fundamental points. As 'heirs' of the Mughal Empire the British were keen to ensure that they honoured the legal situation before them – the securing of property rights was, in particular, extremely important to Victorian British officials. On the other hand, they did not want to perpetuate those aspects of Indian culture that they considered degenerate or uncivilised. The place of *hijra* rights to land and pensions brought these two issues together and to the fore. Victorian Christian males had no desire to continue to sustain – officially – the welfare and status of men they deemed to be degenerate, transvestite sodomites!

In 1842, the collector of Poona forced the issue when he seized about twenty hectares of *inam* (rent-free land) from a *hijra*. The resulting investigation proved that the land had been passed (by a grant dated before 1730) from master to disciple for six 'generations'. An 1845 ruling made the 'inheritance' of the *inam* null and void but returned the then-incumbent *hijra* to his land as a lifetime grant. In 1849, the *hijra* died and his disciple (Saguni) petitioned against being dispossessed of his inheritance. He accepted that blood inheritance was impossible for *hijra*s but argued that inheritance via disciples was a well-accepted principle and produced three Maratha (pre-British) kingdom documents to support his claim and the legal, state acceptance of the principle of inheritance via discipleship. He lost his case in 1852 when the British ruled that 'supposing the title to be valid [which was never really in doubt], the conditions could not be observed without a scandalous breach of public decency'. Thus, the British accepted that the pre-existing grants were legal but invalidated them because continuing officially to support *hijra*s would be indecent.

In 1852 a new law stated that no *inam*, no matter its legal basis, could be inherited where this would recognise, publicise or institute a 'breach of the laws of the land [despite the legal basis for the *inam*!], or the rules of public decency'. In particular the British thought that these economic benefits were attracting disciples. Two years later the British further explained the situation to make clear that they were acting against *hijra*s:

the very fact of a man transforming himself [note the acceptance of the voluntary nature of the change] *into a Hijera [sic] and appearing in public* [note desire to avoid scandal] *in the garb of a woman should be held to constitute a breach of condition i.e. such a breach of public morality and of the rules of public decency as to justify the present Government in at once withholding their continuance and active support of the institution.*

However, the obvious breach of natural justice in depriving incumbents of pensions and lands was too profound for Victorians obsessed with property. In 1855, the British converted all *inam* holdings and pensions into lifetime, non-heritable grants (without prejudice to the state). The result of this action was catastrophic for *hijra*s. Deprived of their main means of subsistence (begging, rent-free lands and pensions) they abandoned the villages and moved to the cities. Thus, what had been a widespread rural phenomenon before the mid-nineteenth century became, as it remains today, a largely urban minority group. The British believed that, with the wisdom of Solomon, they had: eliminated the power of *hijra*s to extort; upheld the semblance of property rights (within their cultural views of inheritance); and made the life of a *hijra* so unbearable (that is, destitute) as to be undesirable. To the immense surprise of the British, the behaviour did not disappear – the *hijra*s refused to stop multiplying.

Since the power of Europeans never extended to direct rule in large parts of the Far East, the situation there differs from India. However, the power of Western, Christian ideas have proven almost as powerful and pervasive in the Far East as elsewhere. Nevertheless, despite the vicissitudes of changing dynasties and fashions, a tolerant, open attitude to same-sex relations and relationships remained a feature of Chinese and Japanese societies into the twentieth century. Both, however, maintained a social structure to these relationships, which had much in common not only with other cultures but, more specifically, with the classical civilisation of the Mediterranean. Relations between men were largely based on a subtle mix of class and age distinction. This should not be taken to imply that this was the sole, socially acceptable model for same-sex acts. Working alongside and overlaying this social construct was a belief that sex was to be enjoyed with any and all partners, as long as one's filial duty to produce an heir was met.

It was this *laissez-faire* approach to sexual pleasure that so shocked Westerners moving in and about the Far East during the heyday of Western imperial power. Male brothels in Shanghai and Tokyo, male concubines amongst the shoguns and mandarins, and the obvious lack of social disapproval (let alone any concept of the 'unnaturalness' or sinfulness of these sexual activities) stunned many – though not all – Westerners. This pattern was only broken by the adoption, for diverse reasons, of Western social mores about sex in the twentieth century. The Chinese and Japanese Empires may have avoided the yoke of Western imperialism but they were not immune to the puritanical morals of the West – or its political ideologies.

A similar impact is apparent in the Thai situation. As with Japan and China, Thailand maintained its independence throughout the colonial period. However, again like Japan and China, Thailand has not been able to avoid the impact of Western cultural and economic – or moral – imperialism. Thai has a number of expressions that relate to same-sex relations. Sex between 'masculine' men (*phu-chai*) was usually described as 'playing with a friend' (*len pheuan*). The same term was used for sex between women. However, Thai society had and has another category with its own set of terms – the *kathoey*. While villagers often referred to sex between *phu-chai* as an omen of bad luck (*heng suay*) or sheer insanity (*ba*), which might bring droughts or death by lightning, sex involving *kathoey* was different.

Although literature relating to *kathoey* dates as far back as the 'medieval' *Law of the Three Seals* it is their treatment in the present that is of most interest to us. Throughout Thai history, *kathoey* were seen as a 'natural' phenomenon, the result of karma from a previous existence. However, from the time of King Mongkut Rama IV (r.1851–68) there have been attempts to amalgamate aspects of Buddhist karmic philosophy with Western scientific ideas. In the twentieth century, this took the form of attempts to correlate karma with genetics. As such, the *kathoey* remains someone who is the way they are for purely 'natural' reasons.

Interestingly, this tolerant view of the *kathoey* has become problematic as Thai society has tried to fit 'masculine' gay men into the pre-existing cultural scheme. In Thai thought, the *kathoey* is a transgendered individual – effectively a man who lives and acts in a 'feminine' manner – who engages in sex exclusively with men. Originally – for centuries – *kathoey* was a 'catch-all' term that applied to all same-sex activity. *Phu-chai*, as a category and *len pheuan*, as a behaviour, may have attracted greater social disapproval than transgendered *kathoey* but they remained types of *kathoey*. Modern commentators have tried to re-define same-sex behaviour. In this interpretative model, transgendered *kathoey* are 'physically' (or, more accurately, genetically) 'disabled' while *phu-chai* (gay men in a more Western sense) are 'mentally disabled'. The former are, thus, correctly afforded rights and protection under the law; the latter should and can be 'treated'.

However, not all Thais are happy with this restructuring of traditional views. The adoption of genetics for karmic ideas and Freudian psychology has not been without resistance. For example, a leading psychologist of the early twentieth century, Ari Saengsawangwatthana, wrote:

It would be quite interesting if we were to follow Freud's ideas… but only from the point of an amusing topic to chat about. If we Thai psychiatrists hold to Buddhist teachings and follow the Buddhist path we do not need to be too concerned about sexual matters, no matter whether it is homo-, hetero-… transvestism, or whatever. This is because in Buddhism we have more than these categories, namely, kamatanha [desire for pleasure], bhavatanha [desire for being] *and* vibhavatanha [desire for separation]. *Homosexuality may be* [any of these three]. *A person with a spouse who no longer wants to live together with their partner* [exhibits] vibhavatanha [desire for separation]. *When he is not pleased with a partner of the opposite sex it is normal* [thammada] *for him to seek pleasure with a person of the same sex because by this he will, to some extent, be able to lesson his suffering, tension and anxiety. It is also normal for a* [young] *single person or someone who must live a single life, because of their occupation or because they are too old too marry, to find happiness with the same sex. I don't see that we need to go placing too much importance on Freud's ideas at all.*

This did not remain the majority view, though. Thai psychologist, Somphot Sukwatthana's view expressed in the 1970s still found acceptance among many Thai psychiatrists in the 1990s:

the sexuality of every human being expresses both homosexual and heterosexual constitutive factors, but people whose sexual development is normal repress the homosexual factors. These repressed factors are then expressed in the form of [same-sex] *friendship and socialising, sport, music and other artistic pursuits.*

While this expresses a relatively negative view of 'homosexuality' is it worth noting that it is a Western view rather heavily reinterpreted by Thai thought. Even when Western psychology and psychiatry defined homosexuality as a mental illness it was never likely to stress that such tendencies were inherent in all men and their repression was best expressed in such male-bonding, homosocial behaviour as sport!

Likewise, the Thai rereading of Freud on mothers and fathers is fascinating. In the West, 'pop psychology' suggests that boys become gay because of fathers who are absent and/or not really 'manly' enough and over-protective mothers. The Thai version suggests that fathers who work away from home (i.e. 'normal' jobs) 'may lead to children viewing their mother as being more skilful, industrious, persevering and as having more ability than their father'. Thus, in Thai Freudianism, the father as 'bread-winner' is not a good role model. Rather, the father working from home at traditional activities is the best image for a young boy. Indeed, Thai writers advise against too great a stress on sexual prowess (macho culture) among men as this might lead to anxiety and, thus, to premature ejaculation, impotence, fear of sex with women and, ultimately, homosexuality. Most importantly, the 'blame' lies with the parents for 'gay' children as it does (genetically) for their *kathoey* children.

As in the other Eastern societies we have examined, same-sex relationships were not accepted in a modern 'gay lifestyle' sense. Thai society structured patterns in which same-sex behaviour was accept-able – largely *kathoey*, transgendered males with other, more 'mascu-line' males. China and Japan had similar indigenous structures based on status and philosophical ideas within a context of procreation and filial piety. These traditional structures came under increasing criti-cism with the introduction of Western morality and science (espe-cially psychiatry). Moreover, as the indigenous cultures of the Far East rejected, in part, their traditional socio-economic structures in a drive to 'modernise' political, social and economic critiques were also applied to pre-existing ideas about sex. On a diversity of fronts, Eastern sexuality came under pressure from Western ideas and mores.

In some parts of the Far East, though, same-sex behaviour has been so integral to social structures as to have proved remarkably resist-ant to Western (and other external) forces for change. The most surprising attitude to same-sex behaviour is found in the ritu-alised homosexuality in most indigenous cultures in Melanesia. Outside the 'civic' pederasty of Athens and the enforced 'military' sodomy of Sparta, few societies have given sex between males a ritual place in the maturation and acculturation of men. In Athens, sex between a young man and an older male was part of educating the youth in the respon-sibilities of citizenship; in Sparta sex between men was part of creat-ing a close military unit. In Melanesia, sex between men (of the pederastic variety) played – and in some places still plays – an integral part in a man passing from boyhood/adolescent into adulthood.

For example, in Malekula, when a father decides it is time to circumcise his son he finds an older man to become the boy's husband. A monogamous bond is then formed until the youth, in turn, becomes old enough to become the husband of another youth. A chief, unlike other men, may have more than one boy-wife. Moreover, a man may continue to have a string of boy-wives (in a series of monogamous relationships) throughout life while also marrying a woman and father-ing children. With the exception of chiefs, male-female relationships are also monogamous though they may be contemporaneous with a monogamous relationship with a boy-wife.

In the Marind-Anim coastal chain, a six-year period of initiation starts when the boy is aged between seven and fourteen, and will involve sex with his maternal uncle, as well as other youths his own age. Similar behaviour springs from ideas about the power of male seed among various societies in Papua New Guinea. The Kaluli believe semen has magical qualities, which encourage physical growth and mental development. The Etoro say that semen transfers life-force through same-sex acts while, in opposite-sex acts life is created (through combining with female blood). At ten years old males in Sambia society are removed from their mothers and subjected to painful initiation rites meant to purge them of female contamination. They are then encouraged to ingest sufficient semen to make them strong warriors. At the age of fifteen the same youth will begin to inseminate other younger youths, as well as allowing his pre-menstrual wife to fellate him – though vaginal sex will not take place until she has begun to menstruate.

It is clear that ritualised homosexuality in these communities performs a number of key roles. Institutionalised homosexuality and monogamy reinforces patriarchal control of women. It also controls males, through age-based hierarchies and effectively excludes women from power entirely. Men are made to be distinct (through secrecy and seclusion) and superior (by subordinating and excluding women). However, men merely delude themselves into believing that women are 'unnecessary' and the strict control of women – and their exclusion – may simply be an overreaction to the perceived threat posed by women without whom the society cannot and will not continue. So extreme can be the reaction to this that some societies, as in the Sambia creation-myth, believe that even women were initially created through male same-sex acts. Just as importantly as controlling women these hierarchies of age and sex keep vibrant young males from threatening the position of elders in the power structure. Youths are slowly initiated into 'knowledge' and 'power' through secret ceremonies and insemination. Interestingly though, it does not yet appear that the alteration of hierarchies (through labour migration, cash economies, 'democratic tribal' councils, the end of violent blood-feuding, 'warrior recreation' and Christianity) has meant the end of these rituals and, in time, they may be invested with new prominence in the cultures.

The mixing of Western political thought, in the form of Communism, with a critique of late imperial China, led Chinese

Communist leaders after 1949 to conclude that the sexual 'debauchery' of Chinese society was largely responsible for the weakness of China before both the West and Japan. China's Communists were determined to eliminate from China all vestiges of what they considered to be *bourgeois* decadence.

For somewhat similar reasons, Japan after its defeat in the Second World War embraced many of the values of the West, especially America. In particular, *Samurai* and imperial culture were increasingly seen as anachronistic and debilitating. This view was not solely the result of the experiences of the 1940s. Indeed, late nineteenth-century Japan had chosen to embrace many Western values and methods in an effort to throw itself into the great imperial race against the West. This rejection of many elements in traditional Japanese society not only included production methods and political structures but also social and culture attitudes to sex. Both China and Japan, for different reasons, perceived Western *Puritanism* as an integral part of Western 'success'.

Ironically, just as many in the East rejected their pre-existing cultural constructs as 'weaknesses', almost as many Westerners were keen to embrace the sensuality and sexual libertinism of the East as 'liberating'. For many, it was one of the most appealing features of Eastern cultures. 'Sexual tourism' was attractive and drew to China some leading lights of Western culture between the two world wars. The actor Noel Coward (1899-1973) and his companion, Jeffrey Amherst delighted in visiting Shanghai's 'gayer haunts' in the company of British naval officers. The playwright Christopher Isherwood (1904-86) and the poet W.H. Auden (1907-73) made full use of the city's bathhouses during their 1937 visit. The 'scene' in Beijing was less about rampant sex and more focused on the aesthetic culture of China. Westerners delighted in Beijing as a 'sunlit haven difficult to describe, superb for the enjoyment of the mere sweetness of existence'. The majority of resident Westerners were tolerant of their compatriots' behaviour though, as Alastair Morrison (a long-term resident in Beijing during the 1940s) put it, 'one wouldn't necessarily invite them to dinner'. For the Western traveller, though, same-sex relations produced a separation from their own culture. For the Chinese, it remained part of their culture: same-sex acts were 'widespread and of no concern to society as a whole'.

The attitude was one of polite indifference – 'you can take anyone you like to bed. Just don't talk about it'. Some Westerners embraced the 'gay' aspects of Chinese society without understanding or adopting the context in which they had been nurtured and flourished for 2,000 years. These foreigners 'knew much about Chinese civilisation, they studied it with love and learning, but they did not succeed in interpreting it to the world at large'. But then, the West had no great desire to know that one of mankind's longest enduring, and arguably most 'successful' civilisations accepted same-sex relations.

In the end, even the Chinese, under the puritanical morals of the atheistic Communists (whose morals would be much at home with the views of the rampant capitalists of America's religious right), wished to hear less of the sexual traditions of their own history and culture. Homosexuality became a crime under the wider umbrella of 'hooligan' activity. However, as with the Mongols and Manchus, China's rulers imbued with the 'foreign' ideology of Communism and 'puritan' sexual mores soon accepted in private many of the trappings and behaviour they derided, criminalised and prosecuted in public. Thus, one reads of Mao enjoying 'groin massages' administered by adolescent youths. Regardless of what went on (as in centuries past) behind the gates of the Forbidden City, the reality is that Communism had succeeded in making China Western and Christian in its sexual values and assumptions.

All of which produced a statement that from the historical perspective could not have been less Chinese or Eastern. In 1993, the *Beijing Review* contained an article stating that 'in China, from the view of public morals, homosexuality is synonymous with filth, ugliness, and metamorphosis'. It is hard to imagine a more 'Western' and 'Christian' comment than this or to place it in a more surprising place than a Chinese publication. The 'conversion' of Chinese society (which never bowed to direct Western control and still strives officially to avoid Western cultural imperialism) to European values could not be made more explicit. Or as Bret Hinsch put it succinctly and tragically in *Passions of the Cut Sleeve* (1990):

The long duration of tolerance allowed the accumulation of a literature and sense of history that in turn enabled those with strong homosexual desires to arrive at a complex self-understanding. In many periods homosexuality was widely accepted and even respected, had it own formal history, and had a role in shaping Chinese political institutions, modifying social conventions, and spurring artistic creation. A sense of tra- dition lasted up until [the twentieth] *century, when it fell victim to a growing sexual conservatism and the Westernisation of morality.*

The *passion of the cut sleeve* and the *shared peach* are being 'air-brushed' from the earlier histories of the East with the same enthusiasm as sim- ilar tales and histories are from the cultural inheritance of India and Africa. This same zeal led to the bowdlerisation of Graeco-Roman history in the West. So thorough has this been in the West that attempts to reunite Alexander and Hephaistion, Harmodius and Aristogeiton, Achilles and Patroclus, Hadrian and Antinous, or to discuss Athenian pederasty, or to explain what 'platonic' love (*à la* the *Symposium*) actu- ally means are all seen as 'politically correct' attempts to distort the past into a 'gay' history. In the West, and increasingly elsewhere, dis- cussions of same-sex relationships of the past and social toleration of them is seen as the a-historical glosses of a 'politically correct gay mafia'. Thus, it seems perfectly acceptable to deny the male lovers of Emperors Hadrian and Wu or, at least, confine any discussion about this to academia. Most historians, pundits and the public agree that it is embarrassing to admit that Henry VIII, the founder of Anglicanism, was a serial divorcee with six wives, some of whom he executed. Therefore, is it acceptable to present him to most students below the doctoral level as having only one wife?

This process of airbrushing same-sex relations and relationships from history has been as prominent in the New World – where the Indian is increasingly held up as the virtuous, at-one-with-nature victim of European greed. In the previous chapter we considered the *berdaches* of North America's Amerindian groups. Although informa- tion is relatively sparse about them in the earlier period there is con- siderably more available in the nineteenth and, especially, the twentieth centuries. However, earlier European accounts present a snapshot of the situation at the time of first contact between Amerindians and Europeans, albeit one interpreted through the lenses of European pre- suppositions about cross-dressing, effeminacy and sodomy. Records from the period under consideration in this chapter provide us with more detail but only of a cultural pattern seriously disrupted by European and Christian contact. More importantly, in the twentieth century, when the *berdache* phenomenon first attracted scholarly interest amongst historians, sociologists and anthropologists, there were almost no *berdaches* left. What survived were vague memories often coloured by embarrassment at a cultural practice which many twentieth-century Amerindians considered inappropriate or sinful (under the influence of Christianity). Despite these enormous difficulties in trying to examine the *berdaches* in great detail there is still a wealth of information. While little more than the ghost and shadow of the *berdache* remains the image formed is substantial and fascinating.

One of the greatest problems in trying to understanding the *berdache* phenomenon in this period continues to be the problem noted in the last chapter – the assumption by Europeans that cross-dressing men were *necessarily* involved in same-sex practices. The extent to which this is true must be tested at length. However, in this later period and, especially, in discussions with interested scholars another significant hurdle is apparent: the reticence of many Amerindians in speaking about sex, especially to outsiders.

Some cultures seemed to have accepted or assumed that homosexual activities were a part of being a *berdache* (e.g. Crow, Mohave, Ojibwa and Santee) while others clearly did not (Potawatomi). Where there is any explicit discussion of same-sex acts it clearly involved a *berdache* and a non-*berdache* in a relationship ranging from the promiscuous to the marital. Navaho, Mohave, Ojibwa, Yuma and Hidatsa (among the latter, male-*berdache* couples could adopt) had stable same-sex relationships. Indeed, among the Mohave there was a distinct fourth gender status called *hwame* (lesbian). A Cheyenne or Luiseno *berdache* could only be an auxiliary wife in a polygamous setting while Crow female *berdaches* would certainly marry other biological females. The types of sex reported were as varied as the types of relationships allowed: anal (Arapaho, 1902); oral on the non-*berdache* (Crow, 1889); anal and oral – in both homosexual and heterosexual relationships (Mohave, 1937). The general view seems to have been that long-term sexual relationships with a *berdache* were not problematic when they involved a man who was already married to a biologically female wife; or who had already had children; or who was too old/young to be producing children. Short-term relationships and casual sex which had no impact on the procreative responsibilities of the non-*berdache* male or female were of no concern.

This was not the case with all Amerindian groups. Santee and Teton Dakota forbade *berdaches* from long-term same-sex relationships or marriage, though they did allow casual homosexual liaisons with non-*berdaches*. In some cases asexuality/celibacy seems to have been the pattern: Pima, Plains Cree, Chiricahua Apache and Bella Coola. In other cultures the *berdaches* were either wholly heterosexual or bisexual: Haisla, Quinault, Bella Bella, Osage and Bella Coola. Illinois and Navaho *berdaches* seem to have been mostly homosexual although they were known to have sex with women – though the Navaho restricted *berdaches* to men for long-term sexual relationships. Indeed, we know for certain that some *berdaches* engaged in heterosexual sex. In 1941 a Shoshonean told an anthropologist that his great-grandfather had been a *berdache*; another study (in 1935) noted that the grandfather of a certain Navaho had also been a *berdache*.

In other words, *berdaches* simply do not conform to Western Christian presuppositions about cross-dressing, effeminacy (e.g. 'being camp') or same-sex acts. This is especially apparent when considering the *berdache* as a 'man in drag acting like a woman'. Westerners 'see' this person in a specific way, which emphasises the camp, female-like characteristics. Compare that image with the reality. Many *berdaches* were not necessarily 'gentle' or effeminate. Yellow Head (an Ojibwa warrior who won fame as the rearguard in a battle with Dakota) lost an eye in a fight (noted in 1897) yet was a *berdache*; Mohave *berdaches* would assault unfaithful husbands and men who made fun of them (from a 1937 report) and Wewha (a Zuni *berdache*) was jailed for a year (as noted in a 1939 account) for resisting three policemen trying to make an arrest.

How then are we to reconstruct the cultural niche that was the *berdache*? The obvious place to begin is by looking at how a person became a *berdache*, and then how they moved and lived in their given cultures. Most men (and it is mostly men we are talking about) became *berdaches* in adolescence but in some case the transformation occurred when they were adults with some men having been previously married in a 'normal' gender structure. For example, a female Kutenai *berdache* had had a husband, transformed and married other women (1935). Mohave women might transform after a difficult delivery (1937). Two Klamath men *stopped* being *berdaches* (1930).

The case of one female *berdache* is especially fascinating. A woman noted among the Kutenai (of Montana, Idaho and British Colombia) in 1811 acted as a courier, guide, prophetess and warrior. She was also regarded as a Kutenai leader in 1825 and as a mediator between the Flathead and Blackfoot in 1837. She dressed as a man and assumed the role of a 'husband' in a number of relationships with women. Clearly, as a *berdache* she was a very successful 'man'. What we know of her transformation from European sources is also interesting. In about 1808 she had left her tribe and lived with European fur traders and explorers and 'married' a French-Canadian man. She was sent back to her people for her 'loose morals' and, upon her return, claimed that her husband had transformed her into a man and that, thereafter, she would live as a man. She now took a new name, Kauxuma Nupika (Gone to the Spirits). The explanation for this transformation makes little sense in the context of normal *berdache* transformations. However, her new name suggests that her change was motivated by a supernatural revelation, as does her subsequent role as prophetess and medium.

Another case study will make some necessary points and provide focus to this discussion of the *berdache* – or what might appear to be the *berdache* – in the modern age. The Dene Tha of Chateh, a Northern Athapaskan tribe in Alberta, have 'cross-sex reincarnation', which an outside, might consider a version of the *berdache* phenomenon but which is actually much more complex. More importantly, the Dene Tha example gives us the sort of detail missing from accounts amongst other tribes and warns us that behind every supposed *berdache* there may be a whole complex set of beliefs, presuppositions and cultural practices that make the '*berdache*' something entirely different.

Among the Dene Tha (as among the Tlinkit tribe – and in Hindu thought), 'biological sex' is not an unchangeable attribute of the individual but can be changed at reincarnation. A person's soul/spirit does not have a sex/gender. This unfixed attitude to biological sex and the person is not unique to the Dene Tha. It is worth noting that most Indian languages do not have gender-specific pronouns nor do they assign gender to objects, which means that gender is less intrinsic to something when speaking about it/him/her. Even 'biological sex' can be 'socially constructed'. For example, the Navajo stress that *everything* is male *and* female. As Guolet notes, 'even the [sexual] organs are male and female, inseparable and distinct. At the tip of the penis is a little vagina, while on the vulva there is a little penis'.

The indeterminate nature of biological sex in relation to that which makes individuals fundamentally themselves (call it soul or spirit) is crucial in Dene Tha thought. If a person 'chooses' (and *choice* is key to Dene Tha reincarnation) to come back as another sex, no attempt is made to *force* the person to assume the 'previous' gender since this would contradict their free choice in reincarnation but there is still an awareness and acceptance of their previous gender. Thus, at times, family members and friends may ask that a reincarnated person temporarily assume some of the attributes of their former life, sex and gender.

The best example of this is the case of Paul (aged twenty-seven) who said he was the reincarnation of Denise (a sister of his cousin Mary; Denise had died as an infant). He related his story:

I am Denise, Mary's sister, I came back, that is what I was. One day, all of a sudden, Denise [a ghost] and her sister [Rose, also a ghost, another of Mary's sisters] came to my mother [in a dream/vision]. Rose said: 'My big sister, I bring her [Denise] with me, that is what I am doing'. After Rose went, I (Denise) stayed. My mother says: 'Denise grabbed me and I fell unconscious'. It will be a baby girl they thought. But I was [born a boy]. Now, they knew I had come back, and they loved me very much. If I put my hair behind, from a distance I am as a woman, and they tell me I am a girl. I colour my eyes and my mouth, and sometimes they ask me to put my hair behind, like this, and they tell me: 'Yes, you look like a woman'.

No more complex situation could be imagined by Western Christians – and one can only wonder how an early European explorer would have recounted Paul's tale in a chronicle.

What Paul's story highlights though is something we have seen time and again in culture after culture. Gender, sex, sexuality and preferences are not fixed and static. They are not 'natural' like a rock or the sun. Sexual attraction to opposite-sex individuals seems to be most common but same-sex attraction is certainly 'universal' in the human condition. An interest in assuming the roles culturally and traditionally assigned to the other biological sex also seems a recurring feature throughout history. Finally, some cultures (especially those with beliefs in reincarnation) simply do not see sex or gender as intrinsic aspect of a person's true 'being' – a soul is not male or female. This echoes the biblical passage which says that in Christ there is neither 'male nor female' (*Galatians* 3: 28) and that in heaven the saved 'will neither marry nor be given in marriage… for they [will be] like angels [which have no gender or sex]' (*Luke* 20: 35). Indeed, this idea of sex and gender as earthly only and not spiritual explains why the marital bond is sundered by death – and will not be rejoined in the afterlife. There will be no males or females in the Christian heaven and certainly no heterosexual couples.

The brief Dene Tha case study reminds us that the situation in non-Western cultures is complex and can be distorted when 'seen' only through Western eyes. Still, we must try to draw some conclusions about *berdaches*. The best insight comes from explicit statements of the Navaho that they believed that their prosperity and very existence as a people depended, in some way, on the presence of *berdaches*. The *berdache* does not 'cross-gender' but 'mixes gender' since she/he moves relatively freely between the two genders, never losing his/her biological sexual identity but attaining a redefined cultural gender status. And, as in the Navaho case, the *berdaches* 'enjoy more opportunities for personal and material gratification than the ordinary individual'.

Neil Whitehead argued in 1981 that:

North American Indian definitions of gender emphasised occupational pursuits and social behaviour rather than choice of sexual object, which in itself was not sufficient to change gender status.

Thus, gender was about occupation and actions rather than sex – people were relatively free to have sex as they pleased, as long as (if they were not *berdaches*) they procreated. To the extent that sex acts entered into the discussion it was to free *berdaches* from social pressures to procreate. This is not the whole picture, for Mircea Eliade in 1965 noted that for Siberian shamanism homosexuality 'is believed to be at once a sign of spirituality, of commerce with gods and spirits, and a source of sacred power'.

The simple reality is that the *berdache* is so complex as to be almost impossible to speak about as a single phenomenon. Indeed, the berdache can only give a limited insight into Amerindian attitudes to homosexuality. For example, the Tewa (in the American Southwest) as late as the 1960s recognised a range of gender identities: *quethos* (not *berdaches* but inter-gendered in some way), homosexuals, women, men and those who cross-dressed for ceremonial occasions. This confusing and confused picture is primarily due to cultural change resulting from contact with Westerners and Christianity. Thus, an account of *berdaches* in the 1940s (a half-century after the death of the last known Winnebago *berdache*) gives insight into the confusion of sex and gender. An older Winnebago said:

Yes, I used to hear about [berdaches], but I don't know much about it. Once there was a man who fasted and he learned that if he dressed like a woman he would be the richest person in the world, but if he wore men's clothing, he [would] die soon. She [sic] wore earrings, and bracelets, and necklaces and a shirt like a woman, but his [sic] brothers told him [pause] her? [pause] if he [pause] she? [pause] put on a skirt they would kill him [sic]. There used to be people like that, not just that one. I think siange is the word for them but I don't know, now it's just a slang word that means 'no good'. Those people did women's work, and they did it real good, better than even women could.

In 1953, Nancy Lurie who studied these same Winnebago noted:

Most informants felt that the berdache *was at one time a highly honoured and respected person, but that the Winnebago had become ashamed of the custom because the white people thought it was amusing or evil.*

But this decline into shame, embarrassment and discomfort is not the end of the *berdache*. Though their 'role' in society has largely ended they have not disappeared. Interestingly, Amerindian cultures that still have *berdaches* are slowly reconstructing their niche into that of a Western homosexual. For example, *berdaches* still exist among the Lakota though they rarely cross-dress, preferring the unisex dress of modern Western Americans. Older Lakota respect them as *berdaches* though younger Lakota tend to see them as homosexuals. These *wink-tes* are, however, still *wakan* (sacred).

It is important to reiterate that socially constructed roles like that of the *berdache* are not unique to the Western Hemisphere. The *hijras* of India and various shamans and mediums of Africa (especially southern Africa) share many features with the *berdaches*. We have already touched upon the complex situation in many Pacific Islands (for example the 'imparting' of 'manliness through ingesting semen in Papua New Guinean cultures, as well as the brief remark about Hawaii from Cook's surgeon). In this context it is worth considering briefly the *fa'afafine* of Samoa and their similarity to *berdaches*.

In Samoa, as elsewhere in the Pacific, a male can take 'the way of women' and become a *fa'afafine* and be, thereafter, included in female activities (for example, wedding showers – note the connection with weddings among *hijras*, Omani *xanith* and transgendered people in Zanzibar and Mombasa). Considering the early references to *berdaches,* it is intriguing that there are no references to *fa'afafine* in early accounts of Samoa though these same accounts do comment on various sexual practices at length. By the early twentieth century, though, we have more information and the picture that emerges is quite interesting. Samoans did not (and do not) categorise sexual acts as heterosexual or homosexual. Thus, boys 'play' homosexual games and casual lesbian relationships were noted by outsiders (but ignored by Samoans) in the 1920s. Samoan society seems to have operated on a principle of 'don't tell, don't notice' for what one did in private did not define a person – rather one's *persona* in public (one's public *face*) did. In this context one can see the clear importance of the dramatic and public nature of transvestism.

However, in practice the situation is extremely complex. While the role of *berdache* seems, for the most part, to have been viewed favourably it is clear that, in some Amerindian groups, there was resistance to someone becoming a *berdache*. Thus, on occasion, individuals seem to have been loath to accept the transformation from the roles and characteristics of their biological sex to that of their opposite. In Samoa a similar reticence is discernible but the dynamic is different. A family, especially the mother, may decide that a boy (if there is no daughter) will be brought up as a girl with little or no opposition. However, male relatives will usually try to stop an adolescent male from 'choosing' to be a *fa'afafine* while, on the other hand, the mother and female relatives will most often be supportive. There is some suggestion that the female family members may see this as a way of redressing a gender imbalance in a given family group (that is, too few girls to help with the important work of the household). While there may be a pragmatic element one notes that the Samoan situation places the initiative, in most cases, with the *choice* of the adolescent male. That is, there may be good reasons for supporting or resisting the choice but it is still a choice and seen as one.

This idea of choice in gender-status becomes even more complex in those rare cases where a person is born inter-sexed (having genitalia – in part or in whole – of both sexes, or being indeterminate biologically or genetically). This is not common (perhaps 1-2 percent of births) though this idea of hermaphroditism was widely used in the past to explain individuals who did not seem to conform to the 'correct' gender status. The most recently studied example of this in a society (Dominican Republic) which accepts the phenomenon and has a socially constructed category for it offers some fascinating insights into gender-identity and, perhaps more importantly, modern Western inflexibility in the face of the diversity that is the human condition.

The starting point for this brief discussion must be assumptions about biological sex and gender as they currently exist in the West. As Ruth Hubbard explains in the beginning of her article about the Domincan Republic,

I accept the usual distinction between these concepts by which sex – whether we are male or female, men or women – is defined in terms of chromosomes (XX or XY), gonads (ovaries or testes), and genitals (the presence of a vagina or a penis – or, more usually, merely the presence or absence of a penis). Gender, specified as masculine or feminine, denotes the psychosocial attributes and behaviours people develop as a result of what society expects of them, depending on whether they were born female or male.

It is this categorisation, accepted as 'natural' and scientifically fixed, which underlies the discussion about sexuality and gender.

Indeed, Western doctors suggest that ambiguous children be 'fixed' to conform to the sex they most resemble – which is usually female since it is easier to fashion female genitals. If the doctors later change their minds about the 'gender-assignment', the doctors attempt to ensure that parents believe that the new 'suggestion' was the right one all along – so there is no doubt in the parents' mind about the sex/gender of the child. 'The belief that gender consists of two exclusive types is maintained and perpetuated by the medical community in the face of incontrovertible physical evidence that this is not mandated by biology' – or indeed a necessity of socio-cultural realities. As we have seen, it is the West alone, which seems to have fixated on the idea of only two sexes and, more crucially, only two genders – and then insists that every person be forced into one or the other, rigidly, without alteration for life.

An examination of the Domincan Republic shows how inflexible and unnecessary these Western presuppositions are. In 1979, a study in the *New England Journal of Medicine* reported on 'males' born in the Dominican Republic, who did not visually 'look male' until puberty when what appeared to be 'female' genitalia changed appearance. These 'boys' had all been reared as girls but then changed their gender identification with seemingly no difficulties for them or their neighbours. The villagers (who do not live in a world of binary sex differentiation; i.e., *only* male and female) actually have names for these types of people: *guevedoche* (balls at twelve) or *machihembra* (male-female). As we have seen there is a similar acceptance of a third sex among the Sambia of Melanesia; the Navajos and Zunis (with *nadle* or *berdache*), and the *hijras* of India.

Despite the enormous impact of Western cultural constructions and values, pre-existing traditions remain in almost every corner of the globe. Nevertheless, a subtle reworking of social constructions for same-sex activities and individuals is taking place, moulding them to the modern Western niche of 'gay'. We are, as a result, fast losing the *real* value of comparative studies – the obvious lesson that gender and sex, sexuality and preference are not fixed categories but are culturally malleable. That some people have decided preferences does not seem to be in doubt. What is now fast disappearing is the myriad of ways in which various human societies have managed to cope with the fact. We are also in danger of losing much of the history of same-sex acts as their place in the history of individuals, events and societies become victim to the socio-political battles being fought about deviancy and equality. So politicised has this become that in many countries even suggesting that someone in the past had a sex life other than resolutely heterosexual is seen as an *entirely* political statement.

Rediscovering Diversity

What this book shows is that throughout history and across the globe homosexuality (same-sex attraction and acts) has been a feature of human life. In that sense, it cannot be called unnatural or abnormal. It is certainly true that homosexuality is and has been less common than heterosexuality (opposite-sex acts and attraction). However, homosexuality is clearly a very real *characteristic* of the human species taken as a whole. The presence of gay people is, in other words, a *natural* part of humanity – it is a *normal* feature of the human condition. Most societies throughout history have accepted this with varying degrees of toleration albeit with similarly varying degrees of disapproval. Most cultures have found some way to construct sexual interaction between members of the same sex in a way that allows some scope for sexual activity and real emotional bonding. Usually, this has been within the context of an expectation that individuals, regardless of their 'tastes' and 'preferences', will still participate in the procreative activity of the general society – they will have children. Once this obligation, though, has been fulfilled the bulk of these societies throughout history have had little concern about the *other* sexual activities of individuals. Indeed, some societies have embedded homosexual acts and attraction into the processes by which an individual becomes an adult. In these cultures, same-sex acts were not simply tolerated; they were encouraged or even expected and demanded.

Where one sees a stark difference, historically, in this pan–global human reaction to homosexuality is in the three great monotheistic religions: Judaism, Christianity and Islam. As we have seen, though, the Islamic reaction has been less harsh and more accommodating of same-sex acts and attraction, as long as the requirement for procreation is fulfilled. This is largely because of the paramount Muslim concern for segregating the sexes – effectively, the trade-off is that some same-sex activity is ignored in order to maintain the sexual cloistering of women. Judaism and Christianity, on the other hand, have taken a much less compromising attitude towards homosexuality. The reality, though, is that Judaism has not been in a position to regulate individuals for nearly two millennia and, in these circumstances it has largely fallen to Christianity to regulate sexuality in the 'Judaeo-Christian world'. However, the important point to remember in evaluating the Christian response to homosexuality is that Christianity has had a largely negative attitude to sex generally. Because of the Christian dichotomy between *spirit* and *flesh* coupled with an explicit desire to 'mortify' the flesh, the Christian response to non-procreative sexual activities has been (and remains) more severe, in a historical context, than that of other religions in the world. Since Christianity takes the view that sex must *only* be for procreation and *not* pleasure *and* that the *only* acceptable context for sex is within a monogamous, life-long relationship, the reaction to other forms of sexual expression (homosexual or heterosexual) has been extreme.

This Christian 'extremism' must be placed in a wider historical and global context. Most other human cultures have not valued procreation *to the exclusion* of pleasure. Other societies have stressed procreation over pleasure but, in reality, have largely supported a social structure in which procreation is 'accomplished' and pleasure 'enjoyed'. Sex in a historical and global sense has had a twofold purpose – to increase the race (procreation) and to provide emotional and physical satisfaction (pleasure). Christianity has largely rejected the latter in favour of the former. Over time this negative attitude to sexual enjoyment has been adopted, assimilated and 'naturalised' by most non-Western cultures who, whether implicitly or explicitly, have associated Western sexual norms (sex only within marriage for purposes of procreation) with Western socio political and economic 'success'. Thus, the worldwide adoption of 'Western Christian' sexual mores is simply one extreme example of the imperialistic spread of Western values and culture more generally. In so doing, cultures that have historically constructed sex and sexuality in a broader context of procreation *and* pleasure with varying degrees of acceptance of less common expressions of sexual attraction (homosexuality) have acquiesced in the Westernisation of their cultures. Ironically, this has tended to be integral to the agenda of post-colonial movements claiming to 'protect' their societies from – or purge them of – Western influences.

When one considers the long sweep of historical attitudes towards, and socio-cultural constructions of, sex and sexuality in general and homosexuality in particular one is struck by the wide variety of 'methods' adopted for accommodating less common sexual acts and preferences in the wider community. One also notes the overwhelming 'uniformity' of the end result – same-sex acts and attractions are tolerated, accepted and even, at times, embraced. In most cultures throughout history, homosexuality has been allowed 'space' to exist in public while facing little or no actual intolerance. Engaging in homosexual acts may, in these societies, attract indifference or ridicule and, when conducted to the exclusion of procreation, face disapproval. The reality, though, is that the vast majorities of cultures have accepted that same-sex attraction is simply a facet of the human condition. Christianity, on the other hand, has chosen to construct sex, sexual acts and sexuality in a manner that is wholly at odds with the pattern, which has adopted by almost all other human cultures throughout recorded history. In other words, in the context of human history and culture, it is the (Judaeo)-Christian response to homosexuality that is *abnormal* and *unnatural*.

Bibliography

Adam, Barry D., 'Structural Foundations of the Gay World', *Comparative Studies in Society and History*, 27 (1985): 658–71

Akyeampong, E., 'Sexuality and Prostitution among the Akan of the Gold Coast c. 1650–1950', *Past and Present*, 156 (1997): 144–73

Altman, Dennis, 'Rupture or Continuity? The Internationalization of Gay Identities', *Social Text*, 48 (1996): 77–94

Andaya, Barbara Watson, 'From Temporary Wife to Prostitute: Sexuality and Economic Change in Early Modern Southeast Asia', *Journal of Women's History*, 9 (1998): 11–34

Anderson, Richard, 'Hindu Myths in Mallarmé: Un Coup de Des', *Comparative Literature*, 19 (1967): 28–35

Atwood, Craig D., 'Sleeping in the Arms of Christ: Sanctifying Sexuality in the Eighteenth–Century Moravian Church', *Journal of the History of Sexuality*, 8 (1997): 25–51

Bacchetta, Paola, 'When the (Hindu) Nation Exiles Its Queers', *Social Text*, 61 (1999): 141–66

Banner, L., 'The Fashionable Sex, 1100–1600', *History Today*, 42 (1992): 37–44

Beinart, William, 'Men, Science, Travel and Nature in the Eighteenth and Nineteenth–Century Cape', *Journal of Southern African Studies*, 24 (1998): 775–99

Bell, R.M., 'Renaissance Sexuality and the Florentine Archives', *Renaissance Quarterly*, 40 (1987): 485–511

Bergman, David, 'Race and the Violet Quill', *American Literary History*, 9 (1997): 79–102

Binhammer, Katherine, 'The Sex Panic of the 1790s', *Journal of the History of Sexuality*, 6 (1996): 409–34

Blasius, Mark, 'An Ethos of Lesbian and Gay Existence', *Political Theory*, 20 (1992): 642–71

Bond, R.B., '"Dark deeds darkly answered": Thomas Becon's Homily against
    Whoredom and Adultery', *Sixteenth Century Journal*, 16 (1985): 191–205
Boswell, John, *Christianity, Social Tolerance, and Homosexuality* (Chicago, 1981)
—, *The Marriage of Likeness: Same-Sex Unions in Pre-Modern Europe* (1995)
Brackett, J.K., 'The Florentive *Onesta* and the Control of Prostitution,
    1403–1680', *Sixteenth Century Journal*, 24 (1993): 273–300
Brackett, John K., *Criminal Justice and Crime in late Renaissance Florence, 1537–1609*
    (Cambridge, 2002)
Bray, A., *Homosexuality in Renaissance England* (1982)
Breitenberg, Mark, 'Anxious Masculinity: Sexual Jealousy in Early Modern
    England', *Feminist Studies*, 19 (1993): 377–98
Bremmer, Jan, 'Scapegoat Rituals in Ancient Greece', *Harvard Studies in Classical
    Philology*, 87 (1983): 299–320
Brown, Carolyn E., 'Erotic Religious Flagellation and Shakespeare's *Measure for
    Measure*', *English Literary Renaissance*, 16 (1986): 139–65
Brundage, J., *Law, Sex, & Christian Society in Medieval Europe* (1990)
Bullough, V., *Handbook of Medieval Sexuality* (1996)
—, *Sexual Practices & the Medieval Church* (1984)
Burg, B.R. (ed.), *Gay Warriors: A Documentary History from the Ancient World to the
    Present* (2002)
—, *Sodomy and the Pirate Tradition: English Sea Rovers in the Seventeenth-Century
    Caribbean* (1995)
Burns, Catherine, '"A Man is a Clumsy Thing Who does not Know How to
    Handle a Sick Person": Aspects of the History of Masculinity and Race in
    the Shaping of Male Nursing in South Africa, 1900–1950', *Journal of Southern
    African Studies*, 24 (1998): 695–717
Caldwell, John C., Pat Caldwell and I.O. Orubuloye, 'The Family and Sexual
    Networking in Sub-Saharan Africa: Historical Regional Differences and
    Present-Day Implications', *Population Studies*, 46 (1992): 385–410
Callender, Charles, and Lee M. Kochems, 'The North American Berdache',
    Current Anthropology, 24 (1983): 443–70
Chajes, J.H., 'Judgments Sweetened: Possession and Exorcism in Early Modern
    Jewish Culture', *Journal of Early Modern History*, 1 (1997): 124–69
Chakrabarty, Dipesh, 'Postcoloniality and the Artifice of History: Who Speaks
    for "Indian" Pasts?' *Representations*, 37 (1992): 1–26
Citarella, Armand O., 'The Relations of Amalfi with the Arab World before the
    Crusades', *Speculum*, 42 (1967): 299–312
Clark, Anna, 'Anne Lister's Construction of Lesbian Identity', *Journal of the
    History of Sexuality*, 7 (1996): 23–50
Cohn, Sam, *Women in the Streets: Essays on Sex & Power in Renaissance Italy*
    (1996)
Cook, Blanche Wiesen, '"Women Alone Stir My Imagination": Lesbianism and
    the Cultural Tradition', *Signs*, 4 (1979); 718–39

Cott, Nancy F., 'Marriage and Women's Citizenship in the United States,
    1830–1934', *The American Historical Review*, 103 (1998): 1440–74
Coward, D.A., 'Attitudes to Homosexuality in 18th Century France', *Journal of
    European Studies*, 10 (1980): 231–55
Crain, Caleb, 'Lovers of Human Flesh: Homosexuality and Cannibalism in
    Melville's Novels', *American Literature*, 66 (1994): 25–53
Das, Rahul Peter, 'Problematic Aspects of the Sexual Rituals of the Bauls of
    Bengal', *Journal of the American Oriental Society*, 112 (1992): 388–432
David, Alun, 'Sir William Jones, Biblical Orientalism and Indian Scholarship',
    Modern Asian Studies, 30 (1996): 173–84
Davis, D.L., and R.G. Whitten, 'The Cross-Cultural Study of Human
    Sexuality', *Annual Review of Anthropology*, 16. (1987): 69–98
De Welles, Theodore, 'Sex and Sexual Attitudes in Seventeenth-Century
    England: The Evidence from Puritan Diaries', *Renaissance and Reformation*, 12
    (1988): 45–64
Dekker, Rudolph M., 'Sexuality, Elites, and Court Life in the Late Seventeenth
    Century: The Diaries of Constantijn Huygens, Jr.', *Eighteenth-Century Life*, 23
    (1999): 94–109
Desens, M., *The Bed-Trick in English Renaissance Drama: Explorations in Gender,
    Sexuality & Power* (1994)
Dimock, Edward C. Jr, *The Place of the Hidden Moon: Erotic Mysticism in the
    Vaisnava-sahajiya Cult of Bengal* (Chicago, 1966)
Douglas-Irvine, Helen, 'The Landholding System of Colonial Chile', *The
    Hispanic American Historical Review*, 8, 4 (1928): 449–95
Dundas, Charles, 'The Organization and Laws of Some Bantu Tribes in East
    Africa', *The Journal of the Royal Anthropological Institute of Great Britain and
    Ireland*, 45 (1915): 234–306
Edwards, R. & Spector, S. *The Olde Daunce: Love, Friendship, Sex, & Marriage in
    the Medieval World* (1991)
Edwards, Clara Cary, 'Relations of Shah Abbas the Great, of Persia, with the
    Mogul Emperors, Akbar and Jahangir', *Journal of the American Oriental Society*,
    35 (1915): 247–68
El-Gabalawy, Saad, 'The Trend to Naturalism in Libertine Poetry of the Later
    English Renaissance', *Renaissance and Reformation*, 12 (1988): 35–44
Ellrich, Robert J., 'Modes of Discourse and the Language of Sexual Reference in
    Eighteenth-Century French Fiction', *Eighteenth-Century Life*, 9 (1985): 217–28
Epprecht, Marc, 'Gender and History in Southern Africa: A Lesotho
    "Metanarrative"', *Canadian Journal of African Studies*, 30 (1996): 183–213
—, 'The "Unsaying" of Indigenous Homosexualities in Zimbabwe: Mapping a
    Blindspot in an African Masculinity', *Journal of Southern African Studies*, 24
    (1998): 631–51
—, 'Women's "Conservatism" and the Politics of Gender in Late Colonial
    Lesotho', *The Journal of African History*, 36 (1995): 29–56

Erauso, Catalina de, *Lieutenant Nun: Memoir of a Basque Transvestite in the New World* (Boston, 1996)

Erlmann, Veit, 'Migration and Performance: Zulu Migrant Workers' Isicathamiya Performance in South Africa, 1890–1950', *Ethnomusicology*, 34 (1990): 199–220

Faderman, L. (ed.), *Chloe plus Olivia: An Anthology of Lesbian Literature from the Seventeenth Century to the Present* (1994)

Fernandez, André, 'The Repression of Sexual Behaviour by the Aragonese Inquisition between 1560 and 1700', *Journal of the History of Sexuality*, 7 (1997): 469–501

Feroli, Teresa, 'Sodomy and Female Authority: The Castelhaven Scandal and Eleanor Davies's *The Restitution of Prophecy* (1651)', *Women's Studies*, 24 (1994): 31–49

Fleischer, M., '"Are Women Human?" – The debate of 1595 between Valens Acidalius and Simon Gediccus', *Sixteenth Century Journal*, 12 (1981): 107–20

Folbre, Nancy, '"The Improper Arts": Sex in Classical Political Economy', *Population and Development Review*, 18 (1992): 105–21

Frank, David John, and Elizabeth H. Mceneaney, 'The Individualization of Society and the Liberalization of State Policies on Same-Sex Sexual Relations, 1984–1995', *Social Forces*, 77 (1999): 911–43

Fudge, Erica, 'Monstrous Acts: Bestiality in Early Modern England', *History Today*, 50 (2000): 20–25

Garber, Marjory, *Vested Interests: Cross-Dressing and Cultural Anxiety* (New York, 1992)

Gardner, Jared, '"Our Native Clay": Racial and Sexual Identity and the Making of Americans in The Bridge', *American Quarterly*, 44 (1992): 24–50

Gerard, Kent, and Gert Hekma (eds), *The Pursuit of Sodomy: Male Homosexuality in Renaissance and Enlightenment Europe* (London, 1989)

Ghani, Muhammad Abdul, 'Social Life and Morality in India', *International Journal of Ethics*, 7 (1897): 301–14

Gilbert, Arthur N., 'Buggery and the British Navy, 1700–1861', *Journal of Social History*, 10 (1976); 72–98

Gilfoyle, T.J., 'Prostitutes in History: from Parables of Pornography to Metaphors of Modernity', *American Historical Review*, 104 (1999): 117–41

Goldberg, Jonathan, 'Sodomy and Society: The Case of Christopher Marlowe', *Southwest Review*, 69 (1984): 371–8

—, 'Sodomy in the New World: Anthropologies Old and New', *Social Text*, 29 (1991): 46–56

— (ed.), *Reclaiming Sodomy* (London, 1994)

Goldman, Robert P., 'Transexualism, Gender, and Anxiety in Traditional India', *Journal of the American Oriental Society*, 113 (1993): 374–401

Goodich, M., *The Unmentionable Vice: Homosexuality in the later medieval period* (1979)

Goulet, Jean-Guy A., 'The "Berdache"/"Two-Spirit": A Comparison of
    Anthropological and Native Constructions of Gendered Identities Among the
    Northern Athapaskans', *The Journal of the Royal Anthropological Institute*, 2
    (1996): 683–701

Gowing, L., *Domestic Dangers: Women, Words & Sex in Early Modern London*
    (1996)

Grant, J.A., 'Summary of Observations on the Geography, Climate, and Natural
    History of the Lake Region of Equatorial Africa, Made by the Speke and
    Grant Expedition, 1860–63', *Journal of the Royal Geographical Society of
    London*, 42 (1872): 243–342

Greenberg, David F., and Marcia H. Bystryn, 'Christian Intolerance of
    Homosexuality', *The American Journal of Sociology*, 88 (1982): 515–48

Grierson, George A., 'The Popular Literature of Northern India', *Bulletin of the
    School of Oriental Studies*, 1 (1920): 87–122

Griffiths, Paul, 'Meanings of Nightwalking in Early Modern England',
    Seventeenth Century, 13 (1998): 212–38

Grunzinski, Serge, 'La Mère dévoranté: Alcoolisme, Sexualité et Déculturation
    chez les Mexicans (1500–1550)', *Cahiers des Ameriques Latines*, 20 (1979):
    5–36.

Guicciardi, Jean-Pierre, 'Between the Licit and the Illicit: The Sexuality of the
    King', *Eighteenth-Century Life*, 9 (1985): 88–97

Gutiérrez, Ramón, *When Jesus Came, the Corn Mothers went away: Marriage,
    Sexuality, and Power in New Mexico, 1500–1846* (Stanford, 1991)

Gutmann, Matthew C., 'Trafficking in Men: The Anthropology of Masculinity',
    Annual Review of Anthropology, 26 (1997): 385–409

Hall, Martin, 'The Legend of the Lost City; Or, the Man with Golden Balls',
    Journal of Southern African Studies, 21 (1995): 179–99

Hansen, Kathryn, '*Sultana the Dacoit* and *Harishchandra*: Two Popular Dramas of
    the Nautanki Tradition of North India', *Modern Asian Studies*, 17 (1983):
    313–31

Hari, Johann, 'The Crusaders', *Attitude*, 122 (2004): 68–72

Hartman, Janine C., 'The Modernization of the Bourgeois Erotic Imagination
    in the 18th Century', *Proteus*, 6 (1989): 16–21

Hatem, Mervat, 'The Politics of Sexuality and Gender in Segregated Patriarchal
    Systems: The Case of Eighteenth- and Nineteenth-Century Egypt', *Feminist
    Studies*, 12 (1986): 250–74

Hauser, Raymond E., 'The Berdache and the Illinois Indian Tribe during the
    Last Half of the Seventeenth Century', *Ethnohistory*, 37 (1990): 45–65

Hayden, Corinne P., 'Gender, Genetics, and Generation: Reformulating Biology
    in Lesbian Kinship', *Cultural Anthropology*, 10 (1995): 41–63

Hazareesingh, K., 'The Religion and Culture of Indian Immigrants in
    Mauritius and the Effect of Social Change', *Comparative Studies in Society and
    History*, 8 (1966): 241–57

Herdt, Gilbert (ed.), *Third Sex, Third Gender: Beyond Sexual Dimorphism in Culture and History* (New York, 1994)

Hester, M., 'The Dynamics of Male Domination using the Witch Craze in 16th and 17th Century England as a Case Study', *Women's Studies International Forum*, 13 (1990): 9–19

Higgs, D., *Queer Sites: Gay Urban Histories since 1600* (1999)

Hiltebeitel, Alf, 'Siva, the Goddess, and the Disguises of the Pandavas and Draupadi', *History of Religions*, 20 (1980): 147–74

Hinsch, Bret, *Passions of the Cut Sleeve: The Male Homosexual Tradition in China* (Berkeley, 1990)

Hitchcock, T., 'Redefining Sex in 18th Century England', *History Workshop Journal*, 41 (1996): 72–90

Hollibaugh, Amber, and Nikhil Pal Singh, 'Sexuality, Labor, and the New Trade Unionism', *Social Text*, 61 (1999): 73–88.

Holmes, Rachel, 'Queer Comrades: Winnie Mandela and the Moffies', *Social Text*, 52/53 (1997): 161–80

Hopkins, E. Washburn, 'The Social and Military Position of the Ruling Caste in Ancient India, as Represented by the Sanskrit Epic', *Journal of the American Oriental Society*, 13. (1889): 57–376

Hopkins, L., 'Touching *Touchets*: Perkin Warbeck and the Buggery Statute', *Renaissance Quarterly*, 52 (1999): 384–401

Hotchkiss, V., *Clothes make the Man: Female Cross-Dressing in Medieval Europe* (1996)

Hubbard, Ruth, 'Gender and Genitals: Constructs of Sex and Gender', *Social Text*, 466 (1996): 157–65

Hurl, Jennine, '"She being bigg with child is likely to miscarry": Pregnant Victims Prosecuting Assault in Westminster, 1685–1720', *London Journal*, 24 (1999): 18–33

Hurteau, Pierre, 'Catholic Moral Discourse on Male Sodomy and Masturbation in the Seventeenth and Eighteenth Centuries', *Journal of the History of Sexuality*, 4 (1993): 1–26

Huussen, A.H. Jr, 'Sodomy in the Dutch Republic during the Eighteenth Century', *Eighteenth-Century Life*, 9 (1985): 169–78

Jacques, T. Carlos, 'From Savages and Barbarians to Primitives: Africa, Social Typologies, and History in Eighteenth-Century French Philosophy', *History and Theory*, 36 (1997): 190–215

Jaffrey, Zia, *The Invisibles: A Tale of the Eunuchs of India* (New York, 1996)

Kahr, Brett, 'The History of Sexuality: From Ancient Polymorphous Perversity to Modern Genital Love', *Journal of Psychohistory*, 26 (1999): 764–78

Kelly, Joan, 'Early Feminist Theory and the *Querelle des Femmes*, 1400–1789', *Signs*, 8 (1982): 4–28

Kloppenberg, James T., 'The Virtues of Liberalism: Christianity, Republicanism, and Ethics in Early American Political Discourse', *The Journal of American History*, 74 (1987): 9–33

Kowalski-Wallace, Beth, 'Shunning the Bearded Kiss: Castrati and the Definition of Female Sexuality', *Prose Studies*, 15 (1992): 153–70

Krekic, B., '*Abominandum Crimen*: Punishment of Homosexuals in Renaissance Dubrovnik', *Viator*, 18 (1987): 337–45

Kritzman, L., *The Rhetoric of Sexuality & the Literature of the French Renaissance* (1991)

Krysmanski, Bernd, 'Lust in Hogarth's *Sleeping Congregation* – Or, How to Waste Time in Post-Puritan England', *Art History*, 21 (1998): 393–408

Kuznesof, E.A., 'Sexuality, Gender, and the Family in Colonial Brazil', *Luso-Brazilian Review*, 30 (1993): 119–32

Labalme, P.H., 'Sodomy and Venetian Justice in the Renaissance', *Tijdschrift voor Rechtsgeschiedenis*, 52 (1984): 217–54

Lal, Vinay, 'Not This, Not That: The Hijras of India and the Cultural Politics of Sexuality', *Social Text*, 61 (1999): 119–40

Larson, Pier M., 'Reconsidering Trauma, Identity, and the African Diaspora: Enslavement and Historical Memory in Nineteenth-Century Highland Madagascar', *The William and Mary Quarterly*, 3rd Series, 56 (1999): 335–62

Lehfeldt, Elizabeth A., 'Ruling Sexuality: The Political Legitimacy of Isabel of Castile', *Renaissance Quarterly*, 53 (2000): 31–56

Leinwand, Theodore B., 'Redeeming Beggary/Buggery in *Michaelmas Term*', *English Literary History*, 61 (1994): 53–70

Leites, Edmund, 'The Duty of Desire: Love, Friendship, and Sexuality in Some Puritan Theories of Marriage', *Journal of Social History*, 15 (1982): 383–408

Lester, Alan, 'Reformulating Identities: British Settlers in Early Nineteenth-Century South Africa', *Transactions of the Institute of British Geographers*, New Series, 23 (1998): 515–31

Link, Matthew, 'Hawaii's Surprising Homo History', *The Out Traveler* (Summer 2004): 68

Lochrie, K., McCracken, P., & Schultz, J., eds., *Constructing Medieval Sexuality* (1997)

Loughling, M.H., '"'Love's Friend and Stranger to Virginitie": The Politics of the Virginal Body', *English Literary History*, 63 (1996): 833–39

Luhrmann, T.M., 'The Good Parsi: The Postcolonial "Feminization" of a Colonial Elite', *Man, New Series*, 29 (1994): 333–57

Lurie, Nancy Oestreich, 'Winnebago Berdache', *American Anthropologist*, New Series, 55 (1953): 708–712

Mageo, Jeannette Marie, 'Male Transvestism and Cultural Change in Samoa', *American Ethnologist*, 19 (1992): 443–459

Markham, C.R., 'Travels in Great Tibet, and Trade between Tibet and Bengal', *Proceedings of the Royal Geographical Society of London*, 19 (1874–5): 327–47

Maurer, Shawn Lisa, 'Reforming Men: Chaste Heterosexuality in the Early English Periodical', *Restoration: Studies in English Literary Culture 1660–1700*, 16 (1992): 38–55

McFarlane, Cameron, *The Sodomite in Fiction and Satire* (New York, 1997)

McGeary, Thomas, '"Warbling Eunuchs": Opera, Gender, and Sexuality on the London Stage, 1705–1742', *Restoration and Eighteenth Century Theatre*, 7 (1992): 1–22

Meem, Deborah T., 'Eliza Lynn Linton and the Rise of Lesbian Consciousness', *Journal of the History of Sexuality*, 7 (1997): 537–60

Merrick, J., 'Sodomitical Inclination in early 18th Century Paris', *Eighteenth Century Studies*, 30 (1997): 289–95

Merrick, Jeffrey, and Bryant T. Ragan, Jr (eds), *Homosexuality in Early Modern France* (Oxford, 2001)

Merrick, Jeffrey, 'Commissioner Foucault, Inspector Noël, and the "Pederasts" of Paris, 1780–3', *Journal of Social History*, 32 (1998): 287–307

Mitchison, Rosalind and Leah Leneman, *Sexuality and Social Control: Scotland 1660–1780* (1989)

Morrell, Robert, 'Of Boys and Men: Masculinity and Gender in Southern African Studies', *Journal of Southern African Studies*, 24 (1998): 605–30

Morrissey, Lee, 'Sexuality and Consumer Culture in Eighteenth Century England: "Mutual Love from Pole to Pole" in *The London Merchant*', *Restoration and Eighteenth Century Theatre*, 13 (1998): 25–40

Mourão, Manuela, 'The Representation of Female Desire in Early Modern Pornographic Texts, 1660–1745', *Signs*, 24 (1999): 573–602

Murray, J., 'Agnolo Firenzuola on Female Sexuality and Women's Equality', *Sixteenth Century Journal*, 22 (1991): 199–213

Murray, S.O., and W. Roscoe (eds), *Boy-Wives and Female Husbands: Studies in African Homosexualities* (1998)

Murray, Stephen O., 'Explaining Away Same-Sex Sexualities: When They Obtrude on Anthropologists' Notice at All', *Anthropology Today*, 13 (1997): 2–5

Mutongi, Kenda, '"Dear Dolly's" Advice: Representations of Youth, Courtship, and Sexualities in Africa, 1960–1980', *The International Journal of African Historical Studies*, 33 (2000): 1–23

Nanda, Serena, *Neither Man nor Woman: The Hijras of India* (California, 1990).

O'Flaherty, Wendy Doniger, *Asceticism and Eroticism in the Mythology of Siva* (Oxford, 1973)

Otis, L. L., *Prostitution in Medieval Society* (1985)

Overmyer-Velázquez, R., 'Christian Morality revealed in New Spain: The Inimical Nahua Woman in Book 10 of the Florentine Codex', *Journal of Women's History*, 10 (1998): 9–37

—, 'Christian Morality revealed in New Spain: The Inimical Nahua Woman in Book 10 of the *Florentine Codex*', *Journal of Women's History*, 10: 2 (1998): 9–37

Pacheco, Anita, '"A mere cupboard of glasses": Female Sexuality and Male Honor in *A Fair Quarrel*', *English Literary Renaissance*, 28 (1998): 441–63

Parker, Graham, 'Is a Duck an Animal? An Exploration of Bestiality as a Crime', *Criminal Justice History*, 7 (1986): 95–109

Peers, Douglas M., 'Privates off Parade: Regimenting Sexuality in the Nineteenth-Century Indian Empire', *International History Review*, 20 (1998): 823–54

Percy, W. A. III, *Pederasty and Pedagogy in Archaic Greece* (1996)

Perdue, Danielle, 'The Male Masochist in Restoration Drama', *Restoration and Eighteenth Century Theatre*, 11 (1996): 10–21

Perry, Ruth, 'Colonizing the Breast: Sexuality and Maternity in Eighteenth-Century England', in *Eighteenth-Century Life* 16 (1992): 185–213

Pincheon, Bill Stanford, 'An Ethnography of Silences: Race, (Homo)Sexualities, and a Discourse of Africa', *African Studies Review*, 43 (2000): 39–58

Pool, Ithiel de Sola, and Kali Prasad, 'Indian Student Images of Foreign People', *The Public Opinion Quarterly*, 22 (1958): 292–304

Porter, Roy, '"The Secrets of Generation Display'd": *Aristotle's Master-piece* in Eighteenth-Century England', *Eighteenth-Century Life*, 9 (1985): 1–21

Poska, Allyson M., 'When Love goes Wrong: Getting out of Marriage in Seventeenth-Century Spain', *Journal of Social History*, 29 (1996); 871–82

Poster, M., 'Patriarchy and Sexuality', *Eighteenth Century: Theory and Interpretation*, 25 (1984): 217–40

Prakash, Gyan, 'Science "Gone Native" in Colonial India', *Representations*, 40 (1992): 153–78

Preston, Laurence W., 'A Right to Exist: Eunuchs and the State in Nineteenth-Century India', *Modern Asian Studies*, 21 (1987): 371–87

Restall, Matthew, and Pete Sigal, '"May They not be Fornicators equal to these Priests": Postconquest Yucatec Maya Sexual Attitudes', *UCLA Historical Journal*, 12 (1992): 91–121

Rey, Michael, 'Parisian Homosexuals Create a Lifestyle, 1700–1750: The Police Archives', *Eighteenth-Century Life*, 9 (1985): 179–91

Richlin, Amy, 'Not before Homosexuality: The Materiality of the Cinaedus and the Roman Law against Love between Men', *Journal of the History of Sexuality*, 3 (1993): 523–73

Richter, Simon, 'Wet-Nursing, Onanism, and Breast in Eighteenth-Century Germany, *Journal of the History of Sexuality*, 7 (1996): 1–22

Risman, Barbara, and Pepper Schwartz, 'Sociological Research on Male and Female Homosexuality', *Annual Review of Sociology*, 14 (1988): 125–47

Roberts, A., *Whores in History* (1993)

Roper, L., *Oedipus & the Devil: Witchcraft, Sexuality & Religion in Early Modern Europe* (1994)

Roscoe, Will, 'Strange Craft, Strange History, Strange Folks: Cultural Amnesia and the Case for Lesbian and Gay Studies', *American Anthropologist*, New Series, 97 (1995): 448–53

Rose, M., *The Expense of Spirit: Love & Sexuality in English Renaissance Drama* (1991)

Rossiaud, J., *Medieval Prostitution* (1998)

Roulston, Christine, 'Separating the Inseparables: Female Friendship and its
    Discontents in Eighteenth-Century France', *Eighteenth-Century Studies*, 32
    (1998–99): 215–31

Rowland, J., *Swords in Myrtle Dress'd: Towards a Rhetoric of Sodom* (1998)

Rowse, A. L., *Homosexuals in History* (1977)

Rowson, Everett K., 'The Effeminates of Early Medina', *Journal of the American
    Oriental Society*, III (1991): 671–693

Rozbicki, Michal J., 'The Curse of Provincialism: Negative Perceptions of
    Colonial American Plantation Gentry', *The Journal of Southern History*, 63
    (1997): 727–52

Ruggiero, G., *The Boundaries of Eros: Sex Crimes & Sexuality in Renaissance Venice*
    (1985)

Saikaku, Ihara, *The Great Mirror of Male Love*, Paul G. Schalow, trans. (Stanford,
    1990)

Santesso, Aaron, 'William Hogarth and the Tradition of Sexual Scissors', *Studies
    in English Literature 1500–1900*, 39 (1999): 499–521

Saslow, J., *Ganymede in the Renaissance: Homosexuality in Art & Society* (1986)

Schaeffer, Claude E., 'The Kutenai Female Berdache: Courier, Guide,
    Prophetess, and Warrior', *Ethnohistory*, 12 (1965): 193–236

Schleiner, Winfried, 'Male Cross-Dressing and Transvestitism in Renaissance
    Romances', *Sixteenth Century Journal*, 19 (1988): 605–619

Schlindler, Stephan K., 'The Critic as Pornographer: Male Fantasies of Female
    Reading in Eighteenth-Century Germany', *Eighteenth-Century Life*, 20
    (1996): 66–80

Seligmann, C.G., 'Some Aspects of the Hamitic Problem in the Anglo-Egyptian
    Sudan', The *Journal of the Royal Anthropological Institute of Great Britain and
    Ireland*, 43 (1913): 593–705

Senelick, Laurence, 'Mollies of Men of Mode? Sodomy and the Eighteenth-
    Century London Stage', *Journal of the History of Sexuality*, 1 (1990): 33–67

Siena, Kevin P., 'Pollution, Promiscuity, and the Pox: English Venerology and the
    Early Modern Medical Discourse on Social and Sexual Danger', *Journal of
    the History of Sexuality*, 8 (1998); 553–74

Sigal, Pete, 'The Politicization of Pederasty among the Colonial Yucatecan
    Maya', *Journal of the History of Sexuality*, 8 (1997): 1–24

Skrine, C.P., 'The Highlands of Persian Baluchistan', *The Geographical Journal*, 78
    (1931): 321–38

Smith, B.R., *Homosexual Desire in Shakespeare's England* (1994)

Sommerville, M., *Sex & Subjection: Attitudes to Women in Early Modern Society* (1995)

Soper, Alexander C., 'The Roman Style in Gandhara', *American Journal of
    Archaeology*, 55 (1951): 301–19

Spear, Gary, 'Shakespeare's "Manly" Parts. Masculinity and Effeminacy in Troilus
    and Cressida', *Shakespeare Quarterly*, 44 (1993): 409–22

Spencer, Colin, *Homosexuality: A History* (London, 1995)

Spencer, Colin, *Homosexuality: A History* (London, 1995)

Stewart, A., *Close Readers: Humanism & Sodomy in Early Modern Europe* (1997)

Stone, Donald Jr, 'The Sexual Outlaw in France, 1605', *Journal of the History of Sexuality*, 2 (1992). 597–608

Stone, Lawrence, 'Libertine Sexuality in Post-Restoration England: Group Sex and Flagellation among the Middling Sort in Norwich in 1706–07', *Journal of the History of Sexuality*, 2 (1992): 511–26

Suleri, S., *The Rhetoric of English India* (Chicago, 1992)

Tannahill, R., *Sex in History* (1980)

Teasley, David, 'The Charge of Sodomy as a Political Weapon in Early Modern France: The Case of Henry III in Catholic League Polemic, 1585–1589', *Maryland Historian*, 18 (1997): 17–30

Terraciano, Kevin, 'Crime and Culture in Colonial Mexico: The Case of the Mixtec Muder Note', *Ethnohistory*, 45 (1998): 709–45

Texler, Richard, *Sex and Conquest: Gendered Violence, Political Order, and the European Conquest of the Americas* (Ithaca, 1995)

Thorner, Daniel, 'Hindu-Moslem Conflict in India', *Far Eastern Survey*, 17 (1948): 77–80

Tóth, I.G., 'Peasant Sexuality in 18th Century Hungary', *Continuity and Change*, 6 (1991): 43–58

Traub, Valerie, 'The Perversion of "Lesbian" Desire', *History Workshop Journal*, 41 (1996): 19–49

Trautmann, Thomas R., 'Length of Generation and Reign in Ancient India', *Journal of the American Oriental Society*, 89 (1969): 564–77

Trumbach, Randolph, 'London's Sodomites: Homosexual Behaviour and Western Culture in the 18th Century', *Journal of Social History*, 11 (1997): 1–33

Trumbach, Randolph, 'Sex, Gender, and Sexual Identity in Modern Culture: Male Sodomy and Female Prostitution in Enlightenment London', *The Journal of the History of Sexuality*, 2 (1991): 186–203

Turley, H., *Rum, Sodomy, and the Lash: Piracy, Sexuality, and Masculine Identity* (1999)

Turner, J., *Sexuality & Gender in Early Modern Europe* (1993)

Ucko, Peter J., 'Penis Sheaths: A Comparative Study', *Proceedings of the Royal Anthropological Institute of Great Britain and Ireland*, 1969 (1969): 24a–67

Van der Meer, Theo, 'Tribades on Trial: Female Same-Sex Offenders in Late Eighteenth-Century Amsterdam', *Journal of the History of Sexuality*, 1 (1991): 424–45

Vanita, R. and S. Kidwai (eds), *Same-Sex Love in India: Readings from Literature and History* (2000)

Vicinus, Martha, 'Lesbian Perversity and Victorian Marriage: The 1864 Codrington Divorce Trial', *The Journal of British Studies*, 36 (1997): 70–98

Wall, Wendy, '"Household Stuff": The Sexual Politics of Domesticity and the Advent of English Comedy', *English Literary History*, 65 (1998): 1–45

Walsham, A., 'Witchcraft, Sexuality, and Colonization in the early modern World', *Historical Journal*, 42 (1999): 269–76

Walther, Daniel J., 'Gender Construction and Settler Colonialism in German Southwest Africa, 1894–1914', *The Historian*, 66 (2004): 1–18

Warnicke, Retha M., 'The Eternal Triangle and Court Politics: Henry VIII, Anne Boleyn, and Sir Thomas Wyatt', *Albion*, 18 (1986): 565–79

Webb, James L.A. Jr, 'The Horse and Slave Trade between the Western Sahara and Senegambia', *The Journal of African History*, 34 (1993): 221–46

Weed, D.M., 'Sexual Positions: Men of Pleasure, Economy and Dignity in Boswell's London Journal', *Eighteenth Century Studies*, 31 (1997/98): 215–34

Wikan, Unni, 'Man Becomes Woman: Transsexualism in Oman as a Key to Gender Roles', *Man*, New Series, 12 (1977): 304–319.

Willen, D., 'Gender, Society and Culture, 1500–1800', *Journal of British Studies*, 37 (1998): 451–60

Williams, Walter, *The Spirit and the Flesh: Sexual Diversity in American Indian Culture* (Boston, 1987)

Williamson, Arthur H., 'Scots, Indians and Empire: The Scottish Politics of Civilization 1519–1609', *Past and Present*, 150 (1996): 46–83

Wilmsen, Edwin N. Denbow, and R. James, 'Paradigmatic History of San-Speaking Peoples and Current Attempts at Revision', *Current Anthropology*, 31 (1990): 489–524

Wright, J.W., and E.K. Rowson (eds), *Homoeroticism in Classical Arabic Literature* (1997)

Yang, Alan S., 'Trends: Attitudes Toward Homosexuality', *The Public Opinion Quarterly*, 61 (1997): 477–507

Yarbrough, Anne, 'Apprentices as Adolescents in Sixteenth Century Bristol', *Journal of Social History*, 13 (1979): 67–81

Yohannan, John D., 'The Persian Poetry Fad in England, 1770–1825', *Comparative Literature*, 4 (1952): 137–60

Yokoi, Tokiwo, 'The Ethical Life and Conceptions of the Japanese', *International Journal of Ethics*, 6 (1896): 182–204

Young, M.B., *King James and the History of Homosexuality* (2000)

Zabin, Laurie Schwab, and Karungari Kiragu, 'The Health Consequences of Adolescent Sexual and Fertility Behavior in Sub-Saharan Africa', *Studies in Family Planning*, 29 (1998): 210–32

Zorach, R.E., 'The Matter of Italy: Sodomy and the Scandal of Style in 16th Century France', *Journal of Medieval and Early Modern Studies*, 28 (1998): 581–609

Zwilling, Leonard, and Michael J. Sweet, '"Like a City Ablaze": The Third Sex and the Creation of Sexuality in Jain Religious Literature', *Journal of the History of Sexuality*, 6 (1996): 359–84

—, 'The First Medicalization: The Taxonomy and Etiology of Queerness in Classical Indian Medicine', *Journal of the History of Sexuality*, 3 (1993): 590–607

List of Illustrations

All illustrations are reproduced by courtesy of the Aberdeen University Library.

1   Ishtar, a Phoenician goddess, seduced the mytho-heroic Gilgamesh, who himself was involved with another male hero. Note the blatant physicality of her sexuality. All early religions (apart from Judaism, which developed rather later) accepted the sexual activity of deities. Gods and goddesses had sex and they usually had sex without any regard to gender.

2   The relief (from Nineveh) shows a eunuch going into battle as a warrior on a chariot. This image reminds us that individuals who might otherwise be considered effeminate or unmanly were, in some societies, very active in battle and other 'manly' pursuits. There are numerous examples of North American *berdaches* taking the role of a warrior.

3   Osiris, an Egyptian god, committed incest with his sister, the goddess Isis, who then gave birth to the god Horus. Egyptian gods and goddesses, as with those in India, engaged in incest, bestiality and homosexuality, as well as heterosexuality.

4   Seth, another Egyptian god. A myth tells how Seth attempted to rape his younger brother Horus and later bragged of his manly achievement to the other gods. One would not normally associate male rape with a god, even less being proud of it. However, as with other polytheistic religions and non-Judaeo-Christian cultures, sex was as much about power and penetration (as well as pleasure) as it was an attempt to procreate.

5   Although Horus was the product of an incestuous relationship and the victim of rape by Seth, neither fact had any impact of attitudes to the god and he was seen as extremely powerful. Indeed, the pharaoh was considered to be

the Living Horus, the temporal stand-in for Horus in the earthly domain – hardly the sort of person with whom one would expect a godlike ruler to identify.

6   Apollo, the Greek god, was not only seen as an ideal male beauty but also renowned for his sexual prowess (with males and females). The emphasis upon the male form and male sexuality is evident in Greek representations of their gods. Graeco-Roman gods were not just sexually active, they were the very embodiment of the male ideal – being able to take pleasure (sex) and when it suited and with whomever the male desired.

7   Harmodius, with his lover, Aristogeiton, was famous for attempting to rid Athens of its tyrant, Hippias (r. 527-510 BCE) by assassination. They became martyrs to Athenian democracy. Thus, all Athenians (and the city-state, which is usually seen as the very basis of Western civilisation) looked to two male lovers as their greatest national heroes.

8   Alexander the Great (Greece). Though married with more than one wife, he was famous for his close relationship with his comrade-in-arms, Hephaistion. This relationship with another man is variously denied or ignored in modern, popular representations of Alexander the Great.

9   This statue of Hermaphrodite sleeping highlights the feminine form from the back but the front of the statue has full male genitalia along with nascent female breasts. This fascination with androgyny, as Freud noted, was central to Greek aesthetics and sexual desire: 'Among the Greeks… it is quite obvious that it was not the masculine character of the [adolescent] which kindled the love of man; it was his physical resemblance to woman as well as his feminine psychic qualities…'

10   Physical exercise in the nude was part of the life of the gymnasium, which was the place where a 'lover' (older male) would be most likely to meet and seduce his 'beloved' (adolescent male).

11   In this bronze statue we see the Greek ideal of the 'beloved'. The focus on the perfection of the adolescent male form is obvious. A small, thin penis was fashionable among the Greeks and Romans; a large penis was considered vulgar and animalistic. Even mighty Hercules was always portrayed with an adolescent's genitals.

12   Augustus, emperor of Rome, although known for his strict morality, was also famous for being the beloved (passive) partner in a relationship with Julius Caesar. As his passivity was during his adolescence no one was remotely

concerned, nor was it thought ironic that in his later life, he would exile his own family members for adultery.

13 Tiberius, emperor of Rome, was famed for his polysexuality and depravity. He was said to have had infants suckle his penis. Most Roman writers and historians considered him depraved not so much for the objects of his desire as for his sexual insatiability.

14 Claudius, emperor of Rome, was considered peculiar for his devotion to his wife and the fact that he did not cheat on her – with another woman or an adolescent youth. The Romans considered such monogamy slightly bizarre. In particular, no Roman would have thought it odd for a man to make sexual use of his slave (of either gender).

15 Hadrian, emperor of Rome, was inconsolable when his lover, Antinous, drowned during a cruise on the Nile. Indeed, he renamed a number of cities of the empire for his beloved.

16 Antinous, the beloved of the Emperor Hadrian. As Camille Paglia has noted (in her *Sexual Personae*): 'The adolescent dreaminess of the Antinous sculptures is not true inwardness but a melancholy premonition of death. Antinous drowned, like Icarus. The beautiful boy dreams but neither thinks nor feels... His face is a pale oval upon which nothing is written.'

17 Elagabalus 'had the whole of his body depilated, deeming it the chief enjoyment of life to appear fit and worthy to arouse the lusts of the greatest number [of men]... And even at Rome he did nothing but send out agents to search for those who have particularly large penises and bring them to the palace in order that he might enjoy their vigour'. Roman writers considered his behaviour shocking only because he wished to take the passive role – a 'true man' (to the Romans) penetrated anyone and anything but was never penetrated.

18 St Constantine the Great was Rome's first Christian emperor and began the process which eventually saw the forced conversion of the empire to Christianity and the slow changing of its culture from an acceptance of 'sex-for-pleasure-and-procreation' to 'sex-for-procreation-only'.

19 Krishna, a Hindu god, and Arjuna are the most famous pair of male friends/lovers in ancient Indian texts and their relationship forms the literary thread running through the *Mahabharata*. In various guises and incarnations their relationship is portrayed as intimate and physical.

20 Shiva, Hindu god/goddess of destruction, has various incarnations and
sexual relations with both males and females. Hindu stories about gods and
goddesses are replete with sexuality in a myriad of forms and permutations.
The gods present to the average believer a variety of sexual roles as acceptable.
What is clearly lacking in the stories of Hinduism is any sense that sex is
'wrong' and solely about procreation.

21 Shiva and Parvati (a very masculine-looking mountain goddess). Their love
is connected with the birth of the god, Ganesh. Shiva washes herself, in one
tale, and eventually the water finds its way to a woman (or women) and
impregnates her (or them), resulting in Ganesh.

22 Shiva *linga* note the phallic nature of the bust. The worship of the phallus
(*lingam*; erect male penis) is an important part of Hindu religion. It is hard to
imagine a greater contrast with the Judaeo-Christian emphasis upon sex as a
purely utilitarian act designed to procreate. Hindus may worship the phallus as
a sign of fertility but their understanding of sex is considerably more complex
and liberal than that found in the great monotheistic faiths (Judaism,
Christianity and Islam).

23 Ganesh, Hindu god, He was born of sexual contact between two female
deities. As his statue is frequently placed at the entrance to homes and
businesses, every Hindu is regularly presented with the image of a god with
'two mommies'.

24 Agni, a Hindu god, swallowed the semen of Shiva as the beginning of the
process which led to the birth of Kartikeya (god of war and leader of the
armies of the gods). Although the stories make it clear that this act was ritually
impure, there is no sense of revulsion, and the result − the god of war − puts
an extremely positive 'spin' on the tale. One does not normally associate a god
of war with a peculiar type of 'homosexual' oral sex!

25 Where the West often associates male-male love with effeminacy, the Hindu
accounts of the birth of Kartikeya in no way lessen his 'manliness' or ferocity −
he is, after all, the commander-in-chief of the armies of the gods.

26 Nadir Shah (1688-1747), emperor of Persia, was famous for his military skill,
as well as his appreciation of the adolescent male form. He was a
contemporary of the last Mughal emperor of India, Aurangzeb, to whom he
once sent a large troupe of beautiful adolescent male slaves as a present.

27 A *Samurai* and his *wakashu* (page). The Japanese warrior was expected to
train his page in the art of chivalry but it was also assumed that they would be

romantically and sexually involved. This relationship was similar to the 'instructional' or didactic type of pederasty found in Athens, as well as the emphasis on male warrior-bonding in Sparta. It helps explain why early Christian missionaries found it so difficult to convince Japanese converts to give up the 'unnatural vice'.

28 Iyeyasu, first Shogun of Japan, brought stability to the country. Under his successor Tsunayoshi, the Korean ambassador reported that 'King, noble, or rich merchant, there is no one who does not keep... beautiful young men'.

Index

The multiplicity of proper names for places, individuals and, even, gods/goddesses has meant that this index has, perforce, been kept very brief. Emphasis has been placed on locating 'places'. As a global history it seemed most reasonable to devise an index which would allow the reader to locate and focus on specific places. A few important 'case studies' involving individuals and key ideas have also been indexed.

If you are interested in purchasing other books published by Tempus,
or in case you have difficulty finding any Tempus books in your local bookshop,
you can also place orders directly through our website
www.tempus-publishing.com

New Directions in
Educational Evaluation

New Directions in Educational Evaluation

Edited and
Introduced by

Ernest R. House

The Falmer Press

(A member of the Taylor & Francis Group)
London and Philadelphia

UK	The Falmer Press, Falmer House, Barcombe, Lewes, East Sussex, BN8 5DL
USA	The Falmer Press, Taylor & Francis Inc., 242 Cherry Street, Philadelphia, PA 19106-1906

First published 1986

Library of Congress Cataloging in Publication Data

Main entry under title:

New directions in educational evaluation.

1. Education—United States—Evaluation—Addresses, essays, lectures. 2. Education—Research—United States —Addresses, essays, lectures. 3. Curriculum planning— United States—Evaluation—Addresses, essays, lectures. I. House, Ernest R.
LA217.N48 1985 370'.973 85-6742
ISBN 0-85000-047-6 (pbk.)
ISBN 0-85000-048-4

W 32474 /15.95. 3.87

Typeset in 10½/12 Plantin by
Imago Publishing Ltd, Thame, Oxon

Printed in Great Britain by Taylor & Francis (Printers) Ltd, Basingstoke

Contents

Contents

For Tom Hastings
who saw the flaws and
pioneered a new beginning

Acknowledgements

The Publishers are grateful to the following for permission to reproduce copyright material:

Review of Educational Research for Nevo, D. 'The conceptualization of educational evaluation', Vol. 53, No. 1, 1983; and Darling-Hammond, L., Wise, A. and Pease, S. 'Teacher evaluation in the organizational context: a review of the literature', Vol. 53, No. 3, 1983.

Jossey Bass for House, E. (1983) 'How we think about evaluation' from *New Directions for Program Evaluation*, No. 19; Weiss, C. (1983) 'The stakeholder approach to evaluation' from *New Directions for Program Evaluation*, No. 17; Farrar, E. and House, E. (1983) 'The evaluation of Push/Excel: a case study' from *New Directions in Program Evaluation*, No. 17; and Weiss, C. (1983) 'Toward the future of stakeholder approaches in evaluation' from *New Directions in Program Evaluations*, No. 17.

Australian Educational Research Association, publishers of Australian *Educational Research*, for 'Evaluation as a paradigm for educational research', Vol. 00, No. 00, 1983.

Taylor and Francis Ltd, publishers of the *Journal of Curriculum Studies*, for 'Three good reasons for not doing case studies in curriculum research', Vol. 15, No. 2, 1983; and 'Seven principles for programme evaluation in curriculum development and innovation', Vol. 14, No. 3, 1982.

General Editor's Preface

Measuring the outcomes of educational practices is a modern pheno-menon. Valuing their worth is as old as philosophy itself. It is the singular value of this collection of papers set in context and introduced by Ernest House that it holds in dynamic equilibrium both the measurement and the valuing sides of educational evaluation.

There are few more fitted by experience, cool-tempered intellect and humane sensitivity than Ernest House to provide the conspectus of the educational evaluation scene that this book offers. Within its covers the student will find the theoretical analysis of educational evaluation in its several meanings, suggested practices, cautionary tales and the new frontier, nor is the controversial issue of the evaluation of teaching avoided. The specialist will also find much, not least a critical and challenging appreciation of educational evaluation theory and practice as it faces the problems of the final decades of the twentieth century.

There can be little doubt that educational evaluation is here to stay. It has not only entered the academic bloodstream, it has become a tool of government policy and decision-making. It is these twin facts that make this book a primer for all concerned with education. They could not be better served.

Philip Taylor
Birmingham
July 1985

1
Introduction:
Evaluation and Legitimacy

Evaluation and Legitimacy

Ernest R. House

Over the past two decades or so, education evaluation has evolved as a field of intellectual endeavor complete with its own theorists, controversies, journals, and conferences. For example, at the 1984 annual meeting of the Evaluation Conference in San Francisco, 600 people attended, and this was only a fraction of the total number engaged in evaluating educational programs. Most of this activity has centered on the United States, but there is considerable interest in Britain, Canada, Australia, some northern European countries, and a nascent interest in Latin America and Asia.

There was, of course, formal evaluation of education prior to the 1960s, embodied primarily in the regional accreditation organizations in the United States and the Inspectorate in Britain. In the late 1950s and early 1960s, however, the development of the so-called new curricula, such as the new maths and new science, generated an interest in social science evaluation of these curricula. The Elementary and Secondary Education Act passed by the US Congress in 1965 required that all Title I (economically disadvantaged student) programs be evaluated. This requirement engendered a flood of evaluation activities.

Eventually, an evaluation mandate was placed upon most federal social programs in the United States. In other countries evaluation has not been mandated across the board but has been initiated for particular programs. As a result a sizable evaluation establishment has come into being with its own organizations, publications, institutions, and ways of behaving. The purpose of this book is to bring the reader up to date with some of the most pressing issues and controversies in this rapidly developing field, although no single book could possibly do justice to all the evaluation developments now underway.

As I have indicated, the overwhelming number of evaluation activities are in the United States, and the Reagan administration has had a strong influence on evaluation, indirectly by cutting back the funding of social programs. Since evaluations have been tied directly to social programs, this has meant a significant decline in the number of evaluations

5

undertaken. The field of evaluation is no longer permeated by the boom town atmosphere that it once was, and this decline has led to a more sober and pessimistic view of the future, perhaps the inevitable outcome of all recessions. One can say unequivocally that evaluation is intimately tied to the initiatives of governments, and that shifts in government policies can result in significant changes in evaluation practices in a particular country or region. To put it another way, if evaluation is the watchdog of the public welfare, as some would have it, then it is a securely leashed watchdog.

A second significant development is in the social role that evaluation is expected to play. In the United States, at least, public education is being subjected to yet another round of industrialization. The immediate pressure stems from the harshly critical reports of several national commissions and the actions of state governors and legislators. American education is being transformed by so-called scientific management techniques, also called Tylorism. This trend is most clearly manifested in a massive employment of standardized tests — tests to promote students from one grade to another, to certify graduation from high school, to allow older students to enter teacher training, and to certify teachers when they finish training. In addition, experienced teachers are being evaluated to determine their competency and to assign them merit pay. In this social transformation evaluators are often designing, implementing, and monitoring the necessary evaluation machinery. This monitoring role is akin to the role of efficiency engineers in the scientific management movement, and I believe is a further extension of that movement. Of course, this shift in the role of what evaluators do also changes the content of evaluation.

I do not perceive this trend towards strong accountability policies in other countries at this time. In fact, in some parts of Australia there is movement in the opposite direction, towards action research and teachers controlling their own evaluation. Whether the industrialization of American education spreads to other countries or remains another manifestation of the American mania for technology, I do not know. It does seem to me that we may witness in the United States, at least, the industrial transformation of vast sectors of society, such as education and health care, that have never been fully rationalized in the industrial sense, and evaluation is playing an instrumental role in that transformation and is being transformed itself in the process.

Several of the chapters in this book reflect this social transformation. For example, in the first chapter Nevo tries to order the issues now current in the evaluation literature and finds that there is a lack of consensus among evaluation theorists concerning the social-political role of evaluation. In the second chapter I analyze the conceptual structure of one of the most widely-used evaluation textbooks and find it to be based extensively on deep-seated metaphors of industrial production so that the criteria for judging social programs are efficiency and effectiveness. In the last chapter in the book, which deals with teacher evaluation, the authors contend that the evaluation of teachers differs depending upon whether one sees teaching as labor, craft, profession, or art. If one sees teaching as labor, as a set of standard operating procedures planned and programmed by administrators, then evaluation becomes direct monitoring of teacher performance according to set standards. This is the direction American evaluation is currently taking.

The reader interested in evaluation would do well to keep this developing drama in mind since evaluation will be affected differently in countries where this trend is and is not occurring. Perhaps I should add that the industrialization of education is not a trend of which I approve nor a use of evaluation which I endorse. But my resistance to these events seems to have no bearing upon their realization.

An issue of long standing in the study of evaluation is the connection between fact and value. The traditional position of positive social science, of course, is that fact and value are quite separate and that it is the evaluator's job to ascertain the facts and the clients and the sponsors and the public will place value upon these facts. Hence, the evaluator is in a value-free or a value-neutral position. This value-neutral position is manifested in many different ways in the extant approaches to evaluation. The distinction between fact and value is one of the most fundamental to evaluation, and to social science, and it is now under serious attack.

At least two of the papers here directly reflect dissatisfaction with the traditional fact-value dichotomy and the consequent role for the evaluator. Scriven asserts that all social science is in fact value-based and that researchers had best adopt the evaluation paradigm for all educational research. According to Scriven, ascertaining the value of something is quite analogous to ascertaining a fact about something and can be accomplished just as objectively as the determination of fact. The determination of the worth of various approaches and teaching techniques is precisely what the educational researcher should be doing.

For her part Kirkup claims that she has tried various approaches to evaluation and has found them wanting, particularly when she deals with a controversial and value-laden area like women's studies. Her radical solution is to abandon the burden of objectivity altogether and to join with the program developers in a collaborative effort to determine the worth of what they are doing. The evaluator becomes in part an advocate rather than a judge or a neutral broker of information.

These are only a few of the possible positions along the fact-value line, and I expect considerable intellectual activity and controversy in the future as traditional evaluators try to defend their own objectivity, and hence legitimacy, by claiming their approaches are value-neutral, while other evaluators disengage from this position and attempt more radical approaches. Few issues are as fundamental to evaluation.

Several new evaluation approaches have been tried over the past two decades and we now have enough experience to see how some have turned out in practice. One of the hottest controversies has been the use of qualitative as opposed to quantitative evaluation techniques. Quantitative techniques have long been considered the *sine qua non* of modern social science, largely because their advocates believe that quantitative techniques ensure a degree of objectivity that any science must possess. This position has been assailed by advocates of qualitative studies, who have been successful in establishing qualitative approaches as more or less legitimate ways of evaluating. The more or less qualification is advisable because qualitative studies are still not considered quite up to par with proper quantitative techniques, the reason being, of course, that qualitative approaches are considered too subjective by many. Nonetheless, qualitative studies have been established as a legitimate minority approach and the warfare between the camps is diminishing in intensity, although skirmishing continues.

Some qualitative evaluators work under the banner of naturalistic evaluation and the two primary centers for naturalistic evaluation have been the Centre for Applied Research in Education (CARE) at the University of East Anglia and the Center for Instructional Research and Curriculum Evaluation (CIRCE) at the University of Illinois, the former founded by Lawrence Stenhouse and the latter by Tom Hastings. The ties between the two centers have been close ones since the early 1970s, although the ideas and context of each center are different. Although the boundaries of naturalistic evaluation extend far beyond East Anglia and Illinois, it seems appropriate that the chapters here are from personnel at those centers. Stake presents the fullest rationale he has yet attempted of the nature of naturalistic generalization, which he sees as the basis for naturalistic evaluation, while Walker struggles with the ethical problem of actually trying to employ naturalistic techniques. As his article demonstrates, these approaches are not panaceas but have formidable difficulties of their own. The final chapter in this section is by Kemmis, who was educated at CIRCE and employed at CARE for several years before returning to Australia. Kemmis proposes several principles for naturalistic studies, although there is some question whether he has not extended the principles to the point where his approach should be labeled a new one together. In any case, having achieved a measure of legitimacy for their approaches, the naturalistic evaluators now face the problem of refining and explicating naturalistic studies. One would expect to see differences emerge among them now that the common goal of legitimizing naturalistic studies has been reached.

Another effort in evaluation has been to encourage non-evaluators to participate in evaluations, in other words to democratize evaluations somewhat. This has not been very successful. As Weiss notes in her chapter, there have been several attempts, one of the most ambitious being to apply the stakeholder notion to two large, highly politicized programs.

What happened in one of them is documented here in detail. It is clear that evaluation is a highly political activity which can even affect politics at the national level. It is also clear that participatory approaches have a very long way to go and face an uphill struggle against evaluation conceived as a purely technical act conducted by experts. I expect renewed attempts at participatory evaluation and renewed controversy.

Finally, I would like to note a structural shift that has long-range implications for the practice of evaluation. This is the shift towards moving evaluators inside the organizational structures. That is, organizations such as state education agencies and local school authorities now have their own offices of evaluation. In earlier days evaluation studies were usually contracted out to other agencies, such as universities, and almost all the evaluation literature assumes that evaluation will be conducted by an outside agency on a contractual basis. Increasingly, however, evaluation has been moved inside the organization. This means that the evaluators are now subject to the internal administrative structure, and the authority relationships inside their own organizations. This has profound implications.

Evaluation has become so important a function that major government agencies cannot afford to be without their own experts. Hence, many organizations establish units inside to perform this task. In modern liberal society there are few deep-seated beliefs shared by everyone. Legitimating ones policies and decisions has become a major difficulty. One way of doing this is to appeal to formal evaluation studies, which presumably are premised upon scientific techniques. Evaluation seems to be a necessity for modern governments, and too important a function not to be brought under some government control.

2
New Analyses:
Issues and Metaphors

Introduction

The first two chapters in this book provide recent analyses as to the status and nature of the field of educational evaluation. Nevo's chapter assesses the current status of the field by defining the key issues. My own chapter investigates the internal workings of how we actually develop ideas about a field like evaluation. One chapter attempts to be comprehensive, the other in-depth.

Nevo's chapter orders the vast evaluation literature by focusing upon ten critical questions that he believes determine the shape of actual evaluations. These questions include who should do the evaluation, to whom the evaluation should be addressed, and how the evaluation should be done. On some of these questions he finds a considerable degree of consensus among evaluation theorists. On other questions there is little consensus.

For example, there is considerable consensus on the definition of evaluation, the objects of evaluation, who should do the evaluation, and on standards for judging an evaluation. On the other hand, there is not much consensus upon what the functions of evaluation are, who should be served by an evaluation, or what the criteria for judging an evaluation object should be. Nevo contends there is an emerging consensus upon the issues of what kinds of information should be collected and what methods of enquiry should be used, but no consensus as to the socio-political function of evaluation or the role that evaluation should play in society. Overall, Nevo's brief chapter provides a quick entry into the voluminous evaluation literature and his ten key questions provide an update on the current status of the field. Some of the questions he has posed will receive rather different answers from other authors in this book.

My own chapter provides a rather different kind of analysis. Rather than surveying the entire field of evaluation and seeing how different theorists address key questions, my chapter takes one prominent evaluation work and examines the conceptual structure of this work in detail. The purpose is to discover what fundamental ideas lie beneath a particularly elaborate and systematic theory of evaluation. I contend in this chapter that the conceptual base of one of the most widely used evaluation textbooks is in fact composed of several highly elaborated, overlapping metaphors. In particular, these are metaphors of industrial production and sporting contests. The industrial production metaphors include concrete images of the machine, the assembly line, and the pipeline. In other words, social and educational programs are *seen as* machines, assembly lines, and pipelines.

These metaphors are not merely casual, adventitious uses of imagery to enliven the narrative of the textbook occasionally, but are rigorously and systematically developed analogues for educational programs: in fact they comprise the fundamental cognitive structure of the work. Furthermore, the evaluation of the program is based upon these systemic metaphors. That is, the criteria for the program emerge directly from the metaphorical transformation of the program into industrial production and the other metaphors.

If my analysis is correct, it raises a number of questions about evaluations of educational programs. Are all evaluation approaches based upon implicit metaphors? How does this change the nature of evaluation? Where do these metaphors come from? Does this make evaluation arbitrary? Unscientific? Some of these issues are addressed in the chapter.

The Conceptualization of Educational Evaluation: An Analytical Review of the Literature

David Nevo
Tel-Aviv University

Many attempts have been made in recent years to clarify the meaning of evaluation and expose the distinction between evaluation and other related concepts such as measurement or research. The literature contains many approaches regarding the conceptualization of evaluation and the determination of its countenance in education. Many of those approaches have been unduly referred to as 'models' (for example, the CIPP Model, the Discrepancy Model, the Responsive Model, or the Goal-Free Model) in spite of the fact that none of them includes a sufficient degree of complexity and completeness that might be suggested by the term 'model'. Stake (1981) rightly suggested that they be referred to as persuasions rather than models.

For the benefit of those of us who lost their way among the various evaluation models, approaches, and persuasions, several attempts have been made to put some order into the growing evaluation literature through classifications of evaluation approaches. Such classifications (for example, Guba and Lincoln, 1981; House, 1980; Popham, 1975; Stake, 1976; Stufflebeam and Webster, 1980; Worthen and Sanders, 1973) made a significant contribution through their critical reviews of the evaluation literature denoting similarities and differences among the various approaches. Those classifications were based on a somewhat holistic approach by placing each evaluation model as a whole in one of the labeled categories with some other models. Trying to do justice to each evaluation model as a whole they sometimes ignored the major issues underlying the agreements and disagreements among the various evaluation approaches.

Stufflebeam (1974) suggested eight questions to be addressed in any attempt to conceptualize evaluation. Nevo (1980) revised Stufflebeam's list of questions and extended it to ten major dimensions in a conceptualization of evaluation. These ten dimensions represent the major issues addressed by the most prominent evaluation approaches in education. They will be used here as an organizer for an analytical review of the literature on educational evaluation.

The ten dimensions for our analysis are expressed by the following questions:

1 How is evaluation defined?
2 What are the functions of evaluation?
3 What are the objects of evaluation?
4 What kinds of information should be collected regarding each object?
5 What criteria should be used to judge the merit and worth of an evaluated object?
6 Who should be served by an evaluation?
7 What is the process of doing an evaluation?
8 What methods of enquiry should be used in evaluation?
9 Who should do evaluation?
10 By what standards should evaluation be judged?

We shall review the literature seeking the various answers to those questions provided by the various evaluation models, approaches, and persuasions. The significance of such a review for evaluation practitioners as well as evaluation theorcticians and researchers will be pointed out at the conclusion of the chapter.

1 How is evaluation defined?

Many definitions of evaluation can be found in the literature. The well-known definition originated by Ralph Tyler perceives evaluation as 'The process of determining to what extent the educational objectives are actually being realized' (Tyler, 1950, p. 69). Another widely accepted definition of evaluation has been that of providing information for decision making suggested by various leading evaluators such as Cronbach (1963), Stufflebeam (Stufflebeam *et al.*, 1971), and Alkin (1969). In recent years considerable consensus has been reached among evaluators regarding the definition of evaluation as the assessment of merit or worth (Eisner, 1979; Glass, 1969; House, 1980; Scriven, 1967; Stufflebeam, 1974), or as an activity comprised of both description and judgment (Guba and Lincoln, 1981; Stake, 1967). A joint committee on standards for evaluation, comprised of seventeen members representing twelve organizations associated with educational evaluation, recently published their definition of evaluation as 'the systematic investigation of the worth or merit of some object' (Joint Committee, 1981, p. 12).

A major exception to that consensus regarding the judgmental definition of evaluation is represented by the Stanford Evaluation Consortium group who defined evaluation as '[a] systematic examination of events occurring in and consequent of a contemporary program — an examination conducted to assist in improving this program and other programs having the same general purpose' (Cronbach *et al.*, 1980, p. 14). Cronbach and his associates (1980) clearly reject the judgmental nature of evaluation advocating an approach that perceives the evaluator as 'an educator [whose] success is to be judged by what others learn' (p. 11) rather than a 'referee [for] a basketball game' (p. 18) who is hired to decide who is 'right' or 'wrong'.

A definition that points to the judgmental character of evaluation might create considerable anxiety among potential evaluees and raise resistance among opponents of evaluation. Obviously, a non judgmental definition of evaluation, such as 'providing information for decision-making,' might be accepted more favorably by evaluees and clients. However, it may be unrealistic to create positive attitudes toward evaluation by ignoring one of its major features. Another approach intended to develop positive attitudes toward evaluation might be to demonstrate its constructive functions within the various domains of education.

2   What are the functions of evaluation?

Scriven (1967) was the first to suggest the distinction between 'formative evaluation' and 'summative evaluation,' referring to two major roles or functions of evaluation, although he was not the first to realize the importance of such a distinction. Later, referring to the same two functions, Stufflebeam (1972) suggested the distinction between proactive evaluation intended to serve decision-making and retroactive evaluation to serve accountability. Thus, evaluation can serve two functions, the 'formative' and the 'summative.' In its formative function evaluation is used for the improvement and development of an ongoing activity (or program, person, product, etc.). In its summative function evaluation is used for accountability, certification, or selection.

A third function of evaluation, the psychological or socio-political function, which has been less often treated by evaluation literature (Cronbach *et al.*, 1980; House 1974; Patton, 1978), should also be considered. In many cases it is apparent that evaluation is not serving any formative purposes nor is it being used for accountability or other summative purposes. However, it is being used to increase awareness of special activities, motivate desired behavior of evaluees, or promote public relations. Regardless of our personal feelings about the use (or misuse) of evaluation for this purpose, we cannot ignore it.

Another somewhat 'unpopular' function of evaluation is its use for the exercise of authority (Dornbusch and Scott, 1975). In formal organizations it is the privilege of the superior to evaluate his or her subordinates and not vice versa. In many cases a person in a management position might evaluate someone to demonstrate his authority over that person. We may refer to this as the 'administrative' function of evaluation.

To summarize, evaluation can serve many functions: (a) the formative function for improvement; (b) the summative function for selection, for certification, for accountability; (c) the psychological or socio-political function for motivation and to increase awareness; and (d) the administrative function to exercise authority.

Some evaluators (Alkin, Daillak, and White, 1979; Cronbach *et al.*, 1980) express a clear preference for the formative function of evaluation, but the general perception seems to be that there are no 'right' or 'wrong' roles of evaluation, and that it can serve deliberately more than one function. However, different functions can be served in various ways and by different evaluation methods. It is therefore important to realize the existence of the various evaluation functions and to determine the specific function(s) of a concrete evaluation at an early stage of its planning.

3   What are the objects of evaluation?

Students and teachers have always been popular objects of evaluation in education. Almost all the measurement and evaluation literature in education up to the mid-sixties dealt with the evaluation of students' learning. Up to that time one could hardly find in the educational literature any substantial guidance regarding the evaluation of other objects such as educational projects or programs, curricular materials, or educational institutions. Various developments in the educational system of the United States (for example, the Elementary and Secondary Education Act of 1965) led to a significant shift of focus regarding the objects of educational evaluation from students to projects, programs, and instructional materials, which have been since then most common in the writings of the major authors in the evaluation literature in education (Alkin, 1969; Provus, 1971; Scriven, 1967; Stake, 1967; Stufflebeam, 1969; Stufflebeam *et al.*, 1971).

Two major conclusions can be drawn from the review of contemporary evaluation literature: (a) almost everything can be an object of evaluation, and evaluation should not be limited to the evaluation of students or school personnel; and (b) the clear identification of the evaluation object is an important part of the development of any evaluation design.

In planning an evaluation it seems to be important to determine what is 'the thing' (or 'the evaluand,' to use Scriven's, 1980, term) that has to be evaluated. It helps to determine what kind of information should be collected and how it should be analyzed. A clear object identification helps keep an evaluation focused. It also helps to clarify and resolve value conflicts and potential threat among stakeholders and others likely to be affected by the evaluation (Guba and Lincoln, 1981).

4 What kinds of information should be collected regarding each object?

After an evaluation object has been chosen, a decision must be made regarding the various aspects and dimensions of the object that should be evaluated. Information pertinent to such aspects must be collected. Earlier approaches to evaluation focused mainly on results or outcomes. Thus, to evaluate an educational object (for example, a new curriculum) would mean to evaluate the quality of the results of its functioning (for example, students' achievements). In recent years some interesting attempts have been made to extend the scope of evaluation variables is various evaluation models (Alkin, 1969; Provus, 1971; Stake, 1967; Stufflebeam, 1969 and 1974; Stufflebeam *et al.*, 1971). Stufflebeam's CIPP Model suggests that evaluation focus on four variables for each evaluation object; (a) its goals; (b) its design; (c) its process of implementation; and (d) its outcomes. According to this approach an evaluation of an educational project, for example, would be an assessment of (a) the merit of its goals; (b) the quality of its plans; (c) the extent to which those plans are being carried out; and (d) the worth of its outcomes.

Stake (1967) in his Countenance Model suggested that two sets of information be collected regarding the evaluated object: descriptive and judgmental. The descriptive set should focus on intents and observations regarding antecedents (prior conditions that may affect outcomes), transactions (the process of implementation), and outcomes. The judgmental set of information is comprised of standards and judgments regarding the same antecedents, transactions and outcomes.

Guba and Lincoln (1981), expanding Stake's Responsive Education Model (Stake, 1975) and applying the naturalistic paradigm, suggest that the evaluator generate five kinds of information: (a) descriptive information regarding the evaluation object, its setting, and its surrounding conditions; (b) information responsive to concerns of relevant audiences; (c) information about relevant issues; (d) information about values; and (e) information about standards relevant to worth and merit assessments.

Thus, the evaluation literature seems to suggest that a wide range of information should be collected by evaluation regarding the evaluated object. It should not limit itself to the narrow scope of evaluation regarding outcomes or results. This does not mean that each single evaluation must always collect all possible kinds of information; it may focus on some of them according to identified evaluation priorities or practical constraints.

> 5 *What criteria should be used to judge the merit and worth of
> an evaluation object?*

To choose the criteria to be used to judge the merit of an evaluation object
is one of the most difficult tasks in educational evaluation. Those who
think that evaluation should attempt to determine whether goals have
been achieved (Provus, 1971; Tyler, 1950) make this task easy for
themselves by partially ignoring the issue of evaluation criteria. What they
actually do is use 'goal achievement' as the evaluation criterion without
having justified its being an appropriate criterion. What about trivial goals
or all kinds of 'stated objectives' that aren't worth achieving? Should they
be used as evaluation criteria?

Another way to avoid the issue of evaluation criteria is to ignore the
judgmental nature of evaluation. Those who defined evaluation as an
information collection activity to serve decision-making or other purposes
(Alkin, 1969; Cronbach, 1963; Stufflebeam, 1969) did not have to deal
with the problem of choosing evaluation criteria.

Apparently, the achievement of (important) goals is one possible basis
for evaluation criteria. Alternative bases for evaluation criteria suggested
by the literature might be: identified needs of actual and potential clients
(Joint Committee, 1981; Patton, 1978; Scriven, 1972b), ideals or social
values (Guba and Lincoln, 1981; House, 1980), known standards set by
experts or other relevant groups (Eisner, 1979; Guba and Lincoln, 1981;
Stake, 1967), or the quality of alternative objects (House, 1980; Scriven,
1967).

Most evaluation experts seem to agree that the criterion (or criteria)
to be used for the assessment of a specific object must be determined
within the specific context of the object and the function of its evaluation.
While in many cases the evaluator does not have the authority to choose
among the various alternative criteria, it is the evaluator's responsibility
that such a choice be made and that he be able to provide a sound
justification for the choice, whether it is made by him or by somebody else.

> 6 *Who should be served by an evaluation?*

Those who define evaluation as providing information for decision-
making (Alkin, 1969; Cronbach, 1963; Stufflebeam *et al.*, 1971) seem to
have a clear opinion as to who has to be served by evaluation. They
identify the relevant decisionmakers and attempt to determine their
information needs. Others (Cronbach *et al.*, 1980; House, 1980) reject the
notion of serving 'decision-makers' because of the threat of co-optation or
oversimplification of social and organizational processes. Cronbach and
his associates (1980) are inclined to serve the 'policy-shaping community'
rather than some kind of managerial decisionmaker. Many authors refer to

'evaluation clients' or 'evaluation audiences' as those who have to be served by evaluation. Guba and Lincoln (1981) suggested the term 'stakeholders' or 'stakeholding audience' for the whole group of persons having some stake in the performance of the evaluand and therefore should be served by the evaluation.

If evaluation is to be useful at all, it has to be useful to some specific client or audience. The evaluation literature does not suggest which is the 'most appropriate' audience for evaluation, but three important propositions can be found in writings regarding this issue. They are: (a) an evaluation can have more than one client or audience; (b) different evaluation audiences might have different evaluation needs; and (c) the specific audiences for an evaluation and their evaluation needs must be clearly identified at the early stages of planning an evaluation.

Differences in evaluation needs might be reflected in many ways: for example, the kind of information to be collected, the level of data analysis to be used, or the form of reporting the evaluation results. Sometimes it is impossible to serve all identified evaluation needs at the same time, and some priorities have to be set regarding the specific evaluation needs to which the evaluation will respond.

7 *What is the process of doing an evaluation?*

The process of doing an evaluation might differ according to the theoretical perception guiding the evaluation. A theoretical approach perceiving evaluation as an activity intended to determine whether goals have been achieved (Tyler, 1950) might recommend the following evaluation process: (a) stating goals in behavioral terms; (b) developing measurement instruments; (c) collecting data; (d) interpreting findings; and (e) making recommendations.

According to Stake's Countenance Model (Stake, 1967) the evaluation process should include (a) describing a program; (b) reporting the description to relevant audiences; (c) obtaining and analyzing their judgments; and (d) reporting the analyzed judgments back to the audiences. Later on, in his Responsive Evaluation Model Stake (1975) suggested a continuing 'conversation' between the evaluator and all other parties associated with the evaluand. He specified 12 steps of dynamic interaction between the evaluator and his audiences in the process of conducting an evaluation.

Provus (1971) proposed a five step evaluation process including (a) clarification of the program design; (b) assessing the implementation of the program; (c) assessing its in-term results; (d) assessing its long-term results; and (e) assessing its costs and benefits.

The Phi Delta Kappa Study Committee on evaluation (Stufflebeam *et al.*, 1971) presented a three-step evaluation process. It included (a) delineating information requirements through interaction with the decision-making audiences; (b) obtaining the needed information through formal data collection and analysis procedures; and (c) providing the information to decision-makers in a communicable format.

Scriven (1972a) has suggested nine steps in his Pathway Comparison Model. Guba and Lincoln (1981) suggest in their recently published book that a naturalistic-responsive evaluation be implemented through a process including the following four stages: (a) initiating and organizing the evaluation; (b) indentifying key issues and concerns; (c) gathering useful information; and (d) reporting results and making recommendations.

While there seems to be no agreement among evaluation experts regarding the 'best' process to follow when conducting an evaluation, most of them would agree that all evaluations should include a certain amount of interaction between evaluators and their audiences at the outset of the evaluation to identify evaluation needs, and at its conclusion to communicate its findings. Evaluation cannot be limited to the technical activities of data collection and analysis.

8   *What methods of enquiry should be used in evaluation?*

While challenging the usefulness of various research methods for evaluation studies (Guba, 1969; Stufflcbcam *et al.*, 1971),recent years have also introduced various methods of enquiry into the field of educational evaluation. In addition to traditional experimental and quasi-experimental designs (Campbell, 1969; Stanley, 1972; Cook and Campbell,1976), naturalistic methods (Guba and Lincoln, 1981; Patton, 1980), jury trials (Wolf, 1979), case studies (Stake, 1978), art criticism (Eisner, 1977 and 1979), journalistic methods (Guba, 1978), the modus operandi method (Scriven, 1974), and many others became legitimate methods for the conduct of evaluation. Some methodologists still advocate the superiority of certain methods such as experimental design (Boruch and Cordray, 1980; Rossi, Freeman and Wright, 1979) at one extreme, or naturalistic methods (Guba and Lincoln, 1981; House, 1980; Patton, 1980) on the other extreme, but overall there seems to be more support for a more eclectic approach to evaluation methodology. At the present state of the art in evaluation it looks like 'the evaluator will be wise not to declare allegiance to either a quantitative-scientific-summative methodology or a qualitative-naturalistic-descriptive methodology' (Cronbach *et al.*, 1980, p. 7). It might be also true that for a complicated task such as the conduct of evaluation an approach is needed that seeks the best method or set of methods for answering a particular evaluation question, rather than assuming that one method is best for all purposes.

9 Who should do evaluation?

Becoming a professional group, evaluators devoted much attention to identifying the characteristics of 'good' evaluators and appropriate ways to train them (Boruch and Cordray, 1980; Cronbach *et al.*, 1980; Guba and Lincoln, 1981; Stufflebeam *et al.*, 1971; Worthen, 1975). To be a competent and trustworthy evaluator one needs to have a combination of a wide variety of characteristics. These include technical competence in the area of measurement and research methods, understanding the social context and the substance of the evaluation object, human relations skills, personal integrity, and objectivity, as well as characteristics related to organizational authority and responsibility. Because it is difficult to find one person possessing all these qualifications, it often becomes necessary to have a team conduct an evaluation or to choose the person with the most appropriate characteristics for a specific evaluation task.

The evaluation literature also suggests two important distinctions that should be taken into account when deciding who should do an evaluation. The first is the distinction between an internal evaluator and an external evaluator (Scriven 1967 and 1975; Stake and Gjerde, 1974; Stufflebeam *et al.*, 1971). An internal evaluator of a project is usually one who is employed by the project and reports directly to its management. Obviously, the internal evaluator's objectivity as well as external credibility might be lower than those of an external evaluator, who is not directly employed by the project and/or enjoys a higher degree of independence.

The second distinction is between a professional evaluator and an amateur evaluator. This distinction, suggested by Scriven (1967), refers to two different foci of training and expertise rather than to a value judgment regarding the quality of an evaluation. An amateur evaluator is usually one whose major professional training is not in evaluation, and involvement in evaluation represents only part of his or her job description (for example, the associate director of a new maths curriculum development project conducting the formative evaluation of the project, who has an MA in maths education and some on-the-job training in evaluation). A professional evaluator is one with extensive training in evaluation and whose major (or even only) responsibility is conducting evaluation (for example, the internal evaluator of a special education project, who has an MA in measurement and evaluation and five years' experience evaluating special education projects). While the amateur evaluator's technical evaluation skills might be lower than those of a professional evaluator, he or she might have a better understanding of the project's unique evaluation needs and be able to develop better rapport with the members of the evaluated project.

These two distinctions are independent; there may be an internal-amateur evaluator, an external-amateur evaluator, an internal-profession-al evaluator, and so forth.

10 By what standards should evaluation be judged?

Several attempts have been made in recent years to develop standards for evaluations of educational and social programs (Evaluation Research Society, 1980; Joint Committee, 1981; Stufflebeam *et al.*, 1971; Tallmadge, 1977; US General Accounting Office, 1978). In spite of the fact that some writers (Cronbach *et al.*, 1980; Stake, 1981) have criticized the rationale for the whole standard-setting effort as being premature at the present state of the art in evaluation, there seems to be a great deal of agreement regarding their scope and content.

Boruch and Cordray (1980) analyzed six sets of such standards and reached the conclusion that there has been a large degree of overlap and similarity among them. The most elaborate and comprehensive set, and the one based on the largest amount of consensus, is probably the set developed and published by the Joint Committee on Standards for Educational Evaluation (1981). These standards have been developed by a committee of seventeen members, chaired by Dr. Daniel Stufflebeam, which represented twelve professional organizations associated with educational evaluation. The committee suggested thirty standards, which are divided into four major groups: utility standards (to ensure that evaluation serves practical information needs), feasibility standards (to ensure that evaluation is realistic and prudent), propriety standards (to ensure that evaluation is conducted legally and ethically), and accuracy standards (to ensure that evaluation reveals and conveys technically adequate information).

Summary

Risking oversimplification, one could summarize the review of the literature with the following most common answers to our ten questions. This could be one way to describe briefly the state of the art in the conceptualization of educational evaluation.

1 How is evaluation defined?

Educational evaluation is a systematic description of educational objects and/or an assessment of their merit or worth.

2 *What are the functions of evaluation?*

Educational evaluation can serve four different functions: (a) formative (for improvement); (b) summative (for selection and accountability); (c) sociopolitical (to motivate and gain public support); and (d) administrative (to exercise authority).

3 *What are the objects of evaluation?*

Any entity can be an evaluation object. Typical evaluation objects in education are students, educational and administrative personnel, curricula, instructional materials, programs, projects, and institutions.

4 *What kinds of information should be collected regarding each object?*

Four groups of variables should be considered regarding each object. They focus on (a) the goals of the object; (b) its strategies and plans; (c) its process of implementation; and (d) its outcomes and impacts.

5 *What criteria should be used to judge the merit of an object?*

The following criteria should be considered in judging the merit or worth of an educational object: (a) responding to identified needs of actual and potential clients; (b) achieving national goals, ideals, or social values; (c) meeting agreed-upon standards and norms; (d) outdoing alternative objects; and (e) achieving (important) stated goals of the objects. Multiple criteria should be used for any object.

6 *Who should be served by an evaluation?*

Evaluation should serve the information needs of all actual and potential parties interested in the evaluation object ('stakeholders'). It is the responsibility of the evaluator(s) to delineate the stakeholders of an evaluation and to identify or project their information needs.

7 *What is the process of doing an evaluation?*

Regardless of its method of enquiry, an evaluation process should include the following three activities: (a) focusing the evaluation problem; (b) collecting and analyzing empirical data; and (c) communicating findings to evaluation audiences. There is more than one appropriate sequence for implementing these activities, and any such sequence can (and sometimes should) be repeated serveral times during the life span of an evaluation study.

8   *What methods of enquiry should be used in evaluation?*

Being a complex task, evaluation needs to mobilize many alternative methods of enquiry from the behavioral sciences and related fields of study and utilize them according to the nature of a specific evaluation problem. At the present state of the art, an a priori preference for any specific method of enquiry is not warranted.

9   *Who should do evaluation?*

Evaluation should be conducted by individuals or teams possessing (a) extensive competencies in research methodology and other data analysis techniques; (b) understanding of the social context and the unique substance of the evaluation object; (c) the ability to maintain correct human relations and to develop rapport with individuals and groups involved in the evaluation; and (d) a conceptual framework to integrate the above-mentioned capabilities.

10   *By what standards should evaluation be judged?*

Evaluation should strike for an optimal balance in meeting standards of (a) utility (to be useful and practical); (b) accuracy (to be technically adequate); (c) feasibility (to be realistic and prudent); and (d) propriety (to be conducted legally and ethically).

Conclusion

As stated at the beginning of this chapter, a critical analysis of the various theoretical approaches to educational evaluation might have important implications for practitioners of evaluation as well as for theoreticians and researchers who are concerned with developing new concepts and better methods. All of them could benefit from the analytical scheme of the ten questions, which guided our analysis, as well as from the review of the answers contained in the evaluation literature.

Evaluators could use the ten questions to organize their own perceptions of evaluation using the evaluation literature to develop their own sets of coherent answers of the ten questions rahter than adopting piously one evaluation model or another. Understanding what others mean when they refer to evaluation could be another use of the ten question. Evaluators may encounter considerable difficulties if their perceptions of a concrete evaluation differ from those of their clients and audiences. It is appropriate before one starts planning an evaluation or even decides to do it all to find out what is meant by evaluation by the various parties involved in the evaluation, what purpose it is intended to serve, what is to be evaluated, what are some feasible alternatives for doing it, and by what standards the evaluation is to be judged if it is to be conducted at all. In other words, addressing the ten questions discussed in this chapter might help evaluation problems before they get themselves into all kinds of dubious evaluation adventures.

Discussions among theoreticians of evaluation can be a fruitful contribution to the advancement of evaluation theory and practice. It could be even more so if those discussions focused on issues in disagreement rather than on competing models and paradigms. The contribution would be even more robust if the various theoretical propositions were substantiated by some research findings. The ten questions reviewed here could provide a framework to delineate research variables for an empirical study of evaluation. Data on the actual relationships among those variables as well as their relationships with other variables (for example, evaluation utilization or variables reflecting the context of evaluation) would be very much appreciated by the evaluation profession.

References

ALKIN, M.C. (1969) 'Evaluation theory development', *Evaluation Comment*, 2, pp. 2–7.

ALKIN, M.C., DAILLAK, R. and White, P. (1979) *Using Evaluations: Does Evaluation Make a Difference?*, Beverly Hills, Calif., Sage.

BORUCH, F.R. and CORDRAY, D.S. (1980 *An Appraisal of Educational Program Evaluations: Federal, State, and Local Agencies*, Evanston, Ill, Northwestern University.

CAMPBELL, D.T. (1969) 'Reforms as experiments', *American Psychologist*, 24, pp. 409–29.

COOK, T.D. and CAMPBELL, D.T. (1976) 'The design and conduct of quasi-experiments and true experiments in field settings' in DUNNETTE, M.D. (Ed.) *Handbook of Industrial and Organizational Psychology*, Chicago, Rand NcNally.

CRONBACH, L.J. (1963) 'Course improvement through evaluation', *Teachers College Record*, 64, pp. 672–83.

CRONBACH, L.J., AMBRON, S.R., DORNBUSCH, S.M., HESS, R.D., HORNIK, R.C., PHILLIPS, D.C., WALKER, D.E. and WEINER, S.S. (1980) *Toward Reform of Program Evaluation*, San Franciscio, Jossey-Bass.

DORNBUSCH, S.M. and SCOTT, W.R. (1975) *Evaluation and the Exercise of Authority*, San Francisco, Jossey-Bass.

EISNER, E.W. (1977) 'On the uses of educational connoisseurship and educational criticism for evaluating classroom life', *Teachers College Record*, 78, pp. 345–58

EISNER, E.W. (1979) *The Educational Imagination*, New York, Macmillan.

Evaluation Research Society (1980) *Standards for Program Evaluation*, Evaluation Research Society.

GLASS G.V. (1969) *The Growth of Evaluation Methodology*, research paper No. 27, Boulder, Laboratory of Educational Research, University of Colorado, mimeo.

GUBA, E.G. (1969) 'The failure of educational evaluation', *Educational Technology*, 9, pp. 29–38.

GUBA, E.G. (1978) *Metaphor Adaptation Report: Investigative Journalism*, Research on Evaluation Project, Portland, Ore, Northwest Regional Educational Laboratory, monograph.

GUBA, E.G. and LINCOLN, Y.S. (1981) *Effective Evaluation*, San Francisco, Jossey-Bass.

HOUSE, E.R. (1974) *The Politics of Educational Innovation*, Berkeley, Calif., McCutchan.

HOUSE, E.R. (1980) *Evaluating With Validity*, Beverly Hills, Calif., Sage.

Joint Committee on Standards for Educational Evaluation (1981) *Standards for Evaluations of Educational Programs, Projects, and Materials*, New York, McGraw-Hill.

NEVO, D. (1981) 'The evaluation of a multi-dimensional project' in LEWY, A., KUGELMASS, S., BEN-SHAKAR, G., BLASS, N., BORUCH, R.F., DAVIS, D.J., NEVO, B., NEVO, D., TAMIR, P. and ZAK, I. *Decision Oriented Evaluation in Education: The Case of Israel*, Philadelphia, International Science Services.

PATTON, M.Q. (1978) *Utilization Focused Evaluation*, Beverly Hills, Calif., Sage.

PATTON, M.Q. (1980) *Qualitative Evaluation Methods*, Beverly Hills, Calif., Sage.

POPHAM, W.J. (1975) *Educational Evaluation*, Englewood Cliffs, NJ, Prentice Hall.

PROVUS, M.M. (1971) *Discrepancy Evaluation*, Berkeley, Calif., McCutchan.

ROSSI, P.H., FREEMAN, H.E. and WRIGHT, S.R. (1979) *Evaluation: A Systematic Approach*, Beverly Hills, Calif., Sage.

SCRIVEN, M. (1967) 'The methodology of evaluation' in STAKE, R.E. (Ed.), *AERA Monograph Series on Curriculum Evaluation*, No. 1, Chicago, Rand McNally.

SCRIVEN, M. (1972a) *The Pathway Comparison Model of Evaluation*, Berkeley, University of California, January, mimeo.

SCRIVEN, M. (1972b) 'Pros and cons about goal-free evaluation', *Evaluation Comment*, 3, 4.

SCRIVEN, M. (1974) 'Maximizing the power of causal investigations: The modus operandi method' in POPHAM, W.J. (Ed.) *Evaluation in Education*, Berkeley Calif., McCutchan..

SCRIVEN, M. (1975) *Evaluation Bias and its Control*, occasional paper No. 4, Kalamazoo, Western Michigan University.

SCRIVEN, M. (1980) *Evaluation Thesaurus* (2nd edn) Inverness, Calif, Edgepress.

STAKE, R.E. (Ed.) (1967) 'The countenance of educational evaluation', *Teachers College Record*, 68, pp. 523–40.

STAKE, R.E. (1975) *Evaluating the Arts in Education: A Responsiveness Approach*, Columbus, Ohio, Merrill.

STAKE, R.E. (1976) *Evaluation Educational Programmes: The Need and the Response*, Washington, DC, OECD Publications Center.

STAKE, R.E. (1978) 'The case study method in social inquiry', *Educational Researcher*, 7, pp. 5–8.

STAKE, R.E. (1981) 'Setting standards for educational evaluators', *Evaluation News*, 2, 2, pp. 148–52.

STAKE, R.E. and GJERDE, C. (1974) 'An evaluation of TCITY, the Twin City Institute for Talented Youth' in KERLINGER, F.N. (Ed.) *AERA Monograph Series in Curriculum Evaluation*, No. 7, Chicago, Rand McNally.

STANLEY, J.C. (1972) 'Controlled field experiments as a model for evaluation', in ROSSI, P.H. and WILLIAMS, W. (Eds) *Evaluating Social Programs*, New York, Seminar Press.

STUFFLEBEAM, D.L. (1969) 'Evaluation as enlightenment for decision making' in BEATTY, W.H. (Ed.) *Improving Educational Assessment and an Inventory for Measures of Affective Behavior*, Washington, DC, National Education Association.

STUFFLEBEAM, D.L. (1972) 'The relevance of the CIPP evaluation model for educational accountability', *SRIS Quarterly*, 5, pp. 3–6.

STUFFLEBEAM, D.L. (1974) *Meta-evaluation*, occasional paper No. 3, Kalamazoo, Western Michigan University.

STUFFLEBEAM, D.L., FOLEY, W.J., GEPHART, W.J., GUBA, E.G., HAMMON, R.L, MERRIMAN, H.O. and PROVUS, M.M. (1971) *Educational Evaluation and Decision-making*, Itasca, Ill., Peacock.

STUFFLEBEAM, D.L. and WEBSTER, W.J. (1980) 'An analysis of alternative approaches to education', *Educational Evaluation and Policy Analysis*, 2, 3, pp. 5–20.

TALLMADGE, G.K. (1977) *Joint Dissemination Review Panel Ideabook*, Washington, DC, US Government Printing Office.

TYLER, R.W. (1950) *Basic Principles of Curriculum and Instruction*, Chicago, Ill., University of Chicago Press.

US General Accounting Office (1978) *Assessing Social Program Impact Evaluations: A Checklist Approach*, Washington, DC, US General Accounting Office.

WOLF, R.L. (1979) 'The use of judicial evaluation methods in the formation of educational policy', *Educational Evaluation and Policy Analysis*, 1, pp. 19–28.

WORTHEN, B.R. (1975) 'Competencies for educational research and evaluation', *Educational Researcher*, 4, 1, pp. 13–16.

WORTHEN, B.R. and SANDERS, J.R. (1973) *Educational Evaluation: Theory and practice*, Belmont, Calif., Wadsworth.

How We Think
about Evaluation

Ernest R. House
University of Illinois

Much of our everyday thinking is metaphorical in nature. That is, we experience one thing in terms of another, according to such theorists as Lakoff and Johnson (1980). They present the following metaphor about argument as an example:

Arguments Are Wars

- Your claims are *indefensible*
- He *attacked every weak point* in my argument
- His criticisms were *right on target*
- I *demolished* his argument (p. 4).

Underlying these separate metaphoric statements is a deep-seated metaphor: *Arguments Are Wars*. This generative metaphor is the basis for a number of expressions, and these expressions constitute a systematic, recognizable pattern. Based primarily upon such evidence, some linguists and philosophers contend that such extended metaphors, which occur in our ordinary thinking, are not haphazard or idiosyncratic: All of us employ them in a systematic fashion to structure the way we think about the world. Thus, these metaphoric concepts are extended, conventional, and intersubjective — much like language itself. Moreover, in structuring our thinking about argument in terms of concepts about war, we do more than just express ourselves colorfully We actually win or lose arguments, attack and defend positions, and gain or lose ground. We live and experience arguments in these terms. The metaphor — *Arguments Are Wars* — shapes our actual behavior.

Until recently, the employment of metaphor was thought to be merely ornamental. Metaphor was used to make an expression more poetic or to emphasize a point rhetorically. However, novel experiences usually are structured in terms of more familiar ones, abstract concepts in terms of more concrete ones, and cultural notions in terms of physical ones. Metaphor is essential to our most complicated thought processes and a vital intellectual tool that we use to understand the world. For example, argument as war reflects aspects of our concept of *argument*. The metaphor highlights how participants in an argument relate to each other, how they treat one another, and how the argument might progress. However, argument as dance would indicate quite a different set of relationships between participants — that is, opponents would be partners. Therefore, *Arguments Are Dances* is not a common metaphor in our culture.

Complex concepts also can be structured by more than one metaphor. For example, the concept of argument is shaped not only by *Arguments Are Wars* but also by other metaphors:

Arguments Are Buildings

- The argument is *shaky*
- *We need to construct a strong* argument
- The argument *collapsed*
- Is that the *foundation* of your argument? (p. 46)

Arguments as building indicates other aspects of our concept of argument that we consider to be important. *Arguments Are Buildings* highlights how arguments are put together, based, and constructed — quite different aspects than those conveyed by *Arguments Are Wars*. We might refer to how arguments proceed in waves, are calm or stormy, and appear on the surface as opposed to what is beneath the surface — that is, *Arguments Are Oceans*. But we do not.

The images of wars and buildings are quite different. But neither are they incompatible with one another. In emphasizing two distinct aspects of our notion of arguments, the two metaphors do not present a single, consistent image but they are coherent. This fundamental coherence is demonstrated by the fact that we mix *Arguments Are Wars* and *Arguments Are Buildings* in our thinking:

- When I *attacked* his argument, it *collapsed*
- The *foundation* of his argument is the *weak point*
- We need to *construct* an argument that is *defensible*
- Your *defense* is a *shaky* one

As the last statement indicates, even a strange mix of metaphors makes sense to us, since these two aspects of argument are used and associated with one another so commonly. Coherent metaphors often fit together by being sub-categories of a major category and sharing a common entailment. For example:

Love Is a Journey

- It's been a long, bumpy road
- We're just spinning our wheels

- We've gotten off the track
- Our marriage is on the rocks (p. 44)

Although all of these statements concern journeys, they are based on different kinds of journeys: a car trip, a train trip, and a sea voyage. The concrete images in each sentence define a more general category and, in that sense, are coherent rather than consistent. They fit together but do not compose a single image.

Quite a number of other metaphors also shape our conception or argument, usually in terms of familiar, concrete, and physical experiences like wars and buildings. Abstract, complex concepts are usually shaped by a number of metaphors that are coherent because the ideas themselves are too complex to be conveyed by one single, consistent image. Whether argument commonly is seen as a war or a dance is culturally determined, and the user of the concept ordinarily is not aware of the underlying metaphor that shapes his or her experience of the actual phenomenon. The user believes that arguments naturally happen that way. Thus, arguments follow certain social patterns because of the common conception that the participants have (Turner, 1974). These fundamental metaphoric concepts are essential to our understanding of the world because they form coherent systems of thought that we use extensively in everyday life (Lakoff and Johnson, 1980).

Metaphors Underlying Social Policy

Schön (1979) contends that social problem-setting is mediated by the stories people tell about troublesome situations. The framing of the social problem depends on the metaphors underlying the stories, and how the problems are framed is critical to the solutions that emerge. For example, a pervasive description of the social services is that they are 'fragmented,' and the implicit solution to this problem is that they be 'coordinated.' But services seen as 'fragmented' could also be seen more benignly as 'autonomous.' Therefore, the underlying metaphor gives shape and direction to the problem solution.

Schön maintains that we are guided in our thinking about social policy by pervasive, tacit images that he calls *generative metaphors*, in which one frame of reference is carried over to another situation. These metaphors generally are used because the user is immersed in the experience of the phenomenon. Thus, these guiding images are necessary to his or her thinking. For example, urban renewal can be viewed in different ways. The slum can be seen as a once healthy community that has become diseased. A social planner with such an image envisions wholesale redesign and reconstruction as the cure to urban blight. However, the slum can also be viewed as a viable, low-income community, which offers its residents important social benefits. The second view obviously implies strikingly different prescriptions for improving the community.

The predominant image of the slum in the 1950s was that of a blighted community. However, in the 1960s the slum as a natural community arose as a countermetaphor that vied for public and expert attention in social planning. Each image features certain themes — taken from a reality that is ambiguous and indeterminate — that define the phenomenon of the slum (Schön, 1979). In the first vision, terms like *blight, health, renewal, cycle of decay*, and *integrated plan* are highlighted in descriptions of social planning. In the second vision, *home, patterns of interaction, informal networks*, and *dislocation* represent key ideas about what should be done with slums. Each overall image presents a view of social reality by selecting, naming, and relating elements within the chosen framework. According to Schön, *naming* and *framing* are the key processes in such conceptualization. By selecting certain elements and coherently organizing them, those processes explain what is wrong in a particular situation and suggest a transformation. Data are converted to recommendations.

Naming and framing proceed by generative metaphor. The researcher sees the slum as a blight or as a natural community. In seeing A as B, the evaluation implicit in B is carried over to A. The first metaphor is that of disease and cure. The second is that of natural community versus artificial community. The transferred evaluations are based on images deeply ingrained within our culture, and once we define a complex situation as either health and disease or nature and artifice we know in which direction to move. Seeing A as B greatly facilitates our ability to diagnose and prescribe. On the other hand, it may lead us to overlook other important features in the situation that the metaphor does not capture. Since generative metaphors usually are implied rather than expressed openly, important features may pass undetected. Schön argues that we should be more aware of our generative metaphors, and that this is best done by analyzing the problem-setting stories we tell. The 'deep' metaphor accounts for why some elements are included in the story while others are not, some assumptions are taken to be true in spite of disconfirming evidence, and some recommendations seem obvious. It is the metaphor of the slum as diseased — or as a natural community — that gives shape to the study and direction of a social planner's actions.

Industrial Production as a Metaphor for Social Programs

Evaluation concepts are often derived from fundamental, generative, and deep-seated metaphors that remain hidden. These metaphors guide one's thinking in certain directions. In this sense, evaluative thinking is no different from the metaphoric thinking in other areas. To illustrate this point, I turn to an examination of the ideas presented in Rossi and others' book, *Evaluation: A Systematic Approach* (1979). This book is one of the most widely used textbooks in the teaching of evaluation, and the authors' work is exemplary of thinking in the field of evaluation — and pervasively metaphoric.

The most fundamental metaphor that the authors use is that of the delivery of social services as industrial production. In their conceptualization, social services are utilities or commodities that are required by the public, and it is the duty of a social program to supply these services. The notion that services are produced by social programs and that they are to be delivered to a clientele manifests the production metaphor. For example, related ideas taken from the book include:

Social Service Delivery Is Industrial Production

- Program elements are defined in terms of *time, costs, procedures,* or a *product*
- A delivery system consists of organizational arrangements that provide program services
- These services are delivered to a target population
- Program development is equivalent to designing the system
- There are production runs
- Services can be calculated in terms of service units delivered
- One should monitor the delivery of these services
- There are operational indicators of success
- A *monitoring evaluation* is an assessment of whether the program conforms to the design and reaches the target.

Even more specifically, social programs as conceived in the preceding examples not only as industrial production in general but as a particular kind of industrial production — that is, an assembly line. At other times within the book, social programs are viewed as machines:

Social Programs Are Machines

- A program consists of elements
- Program elements are discrete intervention activities
- Programs may be broad, complex, but also have component parts
- They are implemented
- They operate according to a design
- They produce benefits, effects, and outcomes
- They can be replicated and replaced
- They can be tested
- They can be fine-tuned
- Accountability means conformity to program specifications
- A major failure is unstandardized treatment
- Variables can be manipulated to achieve results

Rossi and others employ yet a third specific metaphor of industrial production — that of a pipeline or conduit:

Social Delivery Systems Are Conduits

- A delivery system is a combination of pathways that allow access to services
- A major failure in systems is dilution of the treatment to an insufficient amount
- Outcomes always represent changes in the level of measurable variables
- Contaminants may either enhance or mask true changes
- Assessing net intervention effects requires purification of outcomes by purging contaminating elements
- The point of assessing the magnitude of effects is to rule out causal links between inputs and outcomes
- The unreliability of measuring instruments may dilute the difference in outcomes

Social programs as machines, assembly lines, and conduits all fit the overall metaphor of social programs as industrial production. But each metaphor emphasizes a slightly different aspect of the nature of social programs. That is, in thinking about social programs, one may emphasize the way social programs are put together and operate to produce benefits. Or the inputs and outputs, the raw material, and labor that go into programs may be emphasized — or the way benefits or services are delivered to the program recipients. Therefore, social programs can be conceived as involving all of these aspects, and the various separate metaphors are used to emphasize different ones.

Different conceptions of what evaluation entails follow from these different metaphors of social programs: conformity to program design, monitoring of production processes, and measuring of purified outcomes. The evaluation of the program corresponds to the perceived nature of social programs. Sometimes the emphasis is on design specifications and the parts of the program; sometimes it is on the inputs and outputs, and other times the emphasis is placed on the outcomes — the latter metaphor being that of a pipeline with certain substances that issue from it and the corresponding evaluation resembling a chemical analysis from which the evaluator seeks to ascertain the results, purified of possible contamination. Of course, the overall metaphor is that of industrial production but there is no single, consistent image for all of the metaphors. Taken together, the three images present a coherent picture of social programs as industrial production (see Figure 1). The internal coherence among these metaphors is demonstrated in the mixed metaphors that make sense within this conceptual structure and used throughout the book. For example, delivery systems are said to deliver programs or program elements or treatments.

Programs may produce benefits or outcomes or outputs. These terms are used interchangeably.

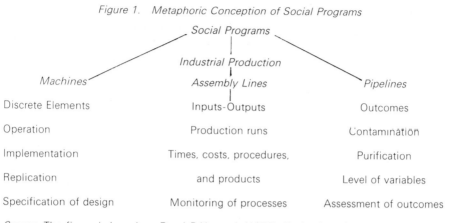

Figure 1. Metaphoric Conception of Social Programs

Source: The figure is based on Rossi P.H. *et al.* (1979) *Evaluation: A systematic approach,* Beverley Hills. Calif, Sage.

The internal coherence of these metaphors is derived from their shared entailments. That is, the better the discrete elements of the program fit together,the more efficiently the time, costs, and procedures are converted into products, and the more outcomes the program delivers. Hence, the design of the programs, the inputs of the program, and the delivery of outcomes are linked together, though by no means synonymous with one another. There is a sequentiality that underlies all three: a sense in which a social program must be created, made, or produced, and in which it must reach the people for whom it is intended. The concept of industrial production is not the only way in which this process can be conceived and made coherent, but it is one way of doing so. Of course, such an overall metaphor entails certain types of evaluations.

The ubiquitous metaphoric nature of these concepts is illustrated further by a detailed examination of the concrete images. For example, the assembly line is a fundamental image in our culture, and it is not surprising that Rossi and others apply this notion to social programs. Raw materials come in one end of the assembly line, labor is performed in stages, and products come out the other end. Underlying the assembly line concept are deeper metaphors that define both labor and time as material resources. A material resource is a kind of substance that can be used in a manufacturing process, quantified precisely, assigned a monetary value per unit of quantity, serve a purposeful end, and used up progressively as it serves its purpose. If time and labor are material resources, they also can be quantified, assigned a value per unit, serve a purposeful end, and be used up (Lakoff and Johnson, 1980). In addition, in our society labor is seen as an activity — and an activity is defined as a substance. Hence, labor can be treated as a substance and a material resource; likewise, time commonly is viewed as a substance — defined in units. Conceiving of labor and time as substances and material resources permits them to be measured, used up, assigned monetary value, and used for various ends. Thus, in conceiving of social programs as assembly lines, Rossi and others can state '*Program elements* may be defined in terms of *time, costs, procedures,* and *products*' (p. 137). Doing a cost-benefit analysis of how time and labor are used in social programs is a logical next step and an important part of the authors' ultimate thinking.

In such a metaphoric framework, efficiency quite naturally looms large as a criterion for successful social programs. Social programs are expected to be efficient just as industrial production is expected to be. In the Rossi and others' conceptualization a comprehensive evaluation must include monitoring, impact assessment, and cost-benefit or cost-effective analysis, and one chapter is entitled 'Measuring Efficiency.' Production functions and econometrics are an extension of this type of analysis, although these authors do not go so far, choosing instead to emphasize both the desirability and difficulty of measuring the benefits and costs of social programs. However, other theorists have been less reticent in setting up equations for social programs that model the production processes, and the discovery of such production functions has at times been the object of considerable federal effort such as the evaluations of Title I of the Elementary and Secondary Education Act of 1965 (McLaughlin, 1975).

Rossi and others also repeatedly speak about social programs as being *effective, efficient, adequate,* and *useful.* This language suggests that there is a job to be done and that the program must accomplish this job. The notion of particular job or task to be performed is congruent with the entire industrial production metaphor. Within the world defined by the fundamental metaphor, these terms become major evaluative terms. They indicate that the program is good if one can apply these terms and also suggest where to look to see if the program is good. They become major criteria of evaluation, criteria that are entailed by the general metaphors.

Targets and Goals as Metaphors

Although the industrial production metaphors dominate Rossi and others' view of evaluation, other metaphors also play a key role in their thinking. These are the metaphors of *target* and *goal.* The target metaphor is used extensively in the book in reference to *target problems, target populations,* and *impact.* The social program has impact on the targets. Presumably, the targets are social problems that social planners attack or alleviate.

Social Problems Are Targets

- Programs and projects are *aimed* at the target problems
- The program can be *misguided*
- The problems are located *in* the target population
- Problems are distributed and have location, extent, type, scope, and depth
- A needs assessment determines the nature, extent, and location of social problems
- Targets have boundaries and rules of inclusion and exclusion
- Programs have *impact* on the targets
- Impacts vary in magnitude
- An *impact evaluation* assesses the extent to which the program causes changes in the desired direction in the target population (Rossi *et al.*, 1979, p. 16).

The underlying metaphoric conception is that social problems are targets, and that the social program is aimed at the target. Hitting the target results in the impact, and the magnitude of the impact is an indicator of how effective the program has been. The evaluator must measure the impact of the program on the target. The target population must be defined, and social services are directed not *to* the target population but *at* the target problems. The targeting metaphor entails quite a different image than the industrial production metaphors but one coherent with these. The target metaphor is employed when the authors discuss the ultimate effects of the program, and the industrial production metaphors are used in discussing the monitoring of the program itself. They use the pipeline or conduit image when discussing outcomes and the target image when discussing impact, which is the ultimate result.

Once again, the metaphors can be mixed to a certain degree. Interventions can be delivered to the target or directed to the target population. *Coverage* is defined as the extent to which the program reaches the target population, combining the notions of both delivery systems and targets. The targeting metaphor maps out a particular aspect of social programs and their evaluation. And, according to Rossi and others, a comprehensive evaluation includes monitoring, impact assessment, and cost-benefit analysis.

A third possible metaphor employed extensively in the book is that of the *goal*. However, there is some question as to whether it should still be called metaphor. That is, goal is used literally to mean *purpose*. The notion of goals appears to be derived originally from sports or games, but it has lost much of its metaphoric connotation. Concepts can be derived from metaphors and gradually transformed into literal meanings, thus losing their metaphoric meanings. The more the concepts are used, the more they take on the meaning of their new application. For example, the *foot* of the mountain is clearly metaphorical in origin but is close to meaning literally the bottom of the mountain. On the other hand, most of the terms and concepts of industrial production applied to social programs are clearly metaphorical, though some are more so than others. A term like *outcomes* is well on its way to literal usage in the evaluation community. Thus, there seem to be degrees of metaphoric meaning for particular concepts, and these meanings change over time. In a few years we may see literal dictionary definitions for terms that we now consider metaphoric. Their metaphoric nature will then reside only in their etymology. With that caveat I will proceed to a metaphoric analysis of *goal* and its connection to the other concepts, bearing in mind that these notions may have passed into literal usage.

The original definition of goal seems to be that of a physical distance, in which a goal is set along a course — such as a race course, a game, or a sport. In the course of the race, game, or sport, the player is supposed to reach or attain that goal.

Program Activities Are Goal-Directed Movements

- Goals are unattained standards
- Goals and objective can be *set* and measured
- There are *gaps* between the goals and reality, between *where* one wants to be and where one is
- The intervention *closes* the *gap* between the two
- One seeks *convergence* between the program design and its implementation; there is *distance* between them
- Evaluations can *direct* the *course* of social life
- Evaluation can be a firm *guide*
- Surveys assess whether the target has been *reached*.

The latter statement is derived from a mixing of the goal and target metaphors and indicates the coherence between the dominant metaphors. This mixing of metaphors can be seen clearly in Rossi and others' definition of impact evaluation: 'impact evaluation-assessment is the extent to which the program causes change in the desired direction in the target population' (p. 16). Although the basic metaphor is that of impact and target, impact is defined in terms of direction and physical distance, which is essentially goal language. Often in the assessment of goals and objectives, a land surveying metaphor of marking off the landscape, triangulating, and measuring distance is used. So again, even though these various metaphors do not present a single consistent image of evaluation, they form a coherent conception. Rossi and other's conceptualization of evaluation is so complex that several metaphors are necessary to highlight different aspects. No single metaphor will do, but both the target and the goal metaphors highlight the aim, direction, and purpose of the program.

Target is ultimately derived from war and sport. Originally a target was a light round shield used in combat, and this came to be the object one aimed at in target practice. The etymology of *goal* is less clear. Apparently, the term was derived form an ancient rustic sport *(Oxford English*

Dictionary). In Old English it meant an obstacle, boundary, or limit. Eventually goal came to mean the terminal point of a race or the posts between which a ball is driven in a game or sport, as in football or soccer. And in archery the goal is the mark aimed at — that is, the target. But the notion that a game is non-serious, or just for fun, has not carried over from goal's original meaning. The goal metaphor has been stripped of its non-serious side and is used to mean a serious striving for achievement, or an earnest contest that is perhaps akin to war. Even though sports language is employed, social program evaluation is at least as serious as a game in the National Football League, which is serious indeed. Within this context, the player attains a goal in a sport or a game by scoring. Originally a score was a cut or a mark on something to keep count and eventually came to mean a line drawn for runners or marksmen to stand at. Ultimately, to *score* as a verb came to mean to make points in a game or contest *(Oxford English Dictionary)*. Score also means one's performance on a test, as in a test score. Scores on outcome measures are very important in Rossi and others' framework: For example, net effects are measured in differences in scores on outcome measures. Apparently, both the target and goal metaphors, which are so pervasive in social program language, are derived from equating social programs with sports or games, or, more generally, contests (see Figure 2). Yet many of the metaphoric meanings are now lost, especially for goals.

In general, there is a strong directionality within all of these diverse yet coherent metaphors. Industrial production, such as in an assembly line or conduit, moves from one point to another, as does the trajectory traced by a missile as in archery, by a runner in a race, or the throwing of a ball through the goal as in a sport. Implicit in these metaphors is the movement of a physical object from one place to another. As more services are produced by the assembly line, more are delivered to the target population. As more services hit the target, there is more impact from the program. The more goals that are attained, the higher the scores and the more successful the program. Beneath these fundamental metaphors are the rather abstract notions of linearity and directionality — movement from one point to another. All of the basic metaphors share this abstract property and serve the purpose of indicating a certain kind of movement that is correlated with program success. Greater production, stronger impact, and more goals attained are all correlates of program success. Underlying the coherent metaphors, then, is a shared topological concept, a concept that remains invariant across metaphors.

The Building Metaphor in Program Evaluation

Yet another set of terms is applied directly to the evaluation itself rather than to the program. The evaluation must be a *firm assessment*, be a *firm guide*, produce *firm estimates of effects* and *solid information*, and not result in *faulty conclusions*. The construction terminology in evaluation is derived from such conventional metaphors as *Arguments Are Buildings* (Lakoff and Johnson, 1980). Evaluations, like arguments and theories, are conceptualized as physical structures, quite possibly because evaluations are recognized tacitly as arguments themselves. The building and construction metaphor is quite commonly applied to evaluations, regardless of the particular metaphors applied to social programs. Evaluations are expected to be firm, solid, well-constructed, and so on. They share the same basic societal metaphors as arguments, and these terms are applied not only in Rossi and others but in much of the evaluation literature.

Figure 2. An Extended Metaphoric Conception of Social Programs

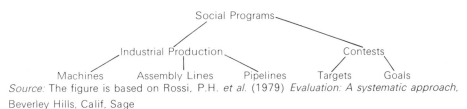

Source: The figure is based on Rossi, P.H. *et al.* (1979) *Evaluation: A systematic approach,* Beverley Hills, Calif, Sage

Thus, some aspects of evaluation are derived from particular metaphors about what social programs are. In conceiving of social programs as industrial production, the evaluation takes shape from the nature of the object evaluated. However, other aspects of evaluation are rendered by more general metaphors, such as *Arguments Are Buildings*. These aspects of evaluation seem to be independent of notions of what social programs are supposed to be. And there are even more fundamental metaphors employed in the articulation of programs and evaluation. These include metaphoric structurings of time and labor as material resources, events as objects, and activities as substances. Although these ideas fit well into the overall conceptual scheme, they are not dependent upon it. They are readily available in everyday thought. Hence, the metaphors employed in evaluations of social programs are both special ones drawn specifically for this purpose and common ones used in many other settings.

Even this does not exhaust the metaphoric structure of the book by Rossi and others. The discussion of cost-benefit analysis draws upon the economic and accounting literature, which has its own metaphoric structure. But, although the metaphoric structure is pervasive and extremely important in shaping the ideas in the book, it is difficult to discover and make explicit. We share so much of the common experience of assembly lines, goals, and targets that the discussion seems literal rather than metaphoric. In this sense, the metaphoric structure is nearly invisible.

Ernest R. House

The Metaphoric Nature of Evaluation

The realization that a great deal of evaluative thought is metaphoric in nature will no doubt surprise and disturb many evaluators. Many see evaluation of social programs as applied social science and may wonder how metaphors could be so crucial to their thinking. The metaphoric analysis raises a number of questions: To what degree does metaphor characterize all evaluative thinking? How does it work? Where do these metaphors come from? Are there conflicts between different schemes, depending upon one's underlying metaphors? Are all metaphors equally good? What is the scientific status of evaluation if this analysis is correct? Does such an analysis lead to relativism? Unfortunately, discussion of these issues is beyond the scope of this chapter. And, in general, the role of metaphor in thought is not well understood. (For further philosophical discussions of metaphor, see Sacks, 1978; Ortony, 1979; Johnson, 1981). This section briefly touches upon the origins of these metaphors, the values they embody, the purposes they serve, their scientific status, and their appropriateness.

Industrial production and sporting contests are often used as metaphors in evaluation because they are pervasive experiences in our society, and production and competition are primary values. Taken together, they entail winning. It is not surprising that we should evaluate our social programs from frameworks derived from such central experiences, and that these structural metaphors embody core values of American society. In employing these metaphors to evaluate social programs, we bring those values to bear upon social programs, sometimes explicitly but often tacitly.

Faced with the new task of evaluating social programs in the past two decades, evaluation theorists have turned to areas of their own experience that seem better defined. Evaluations therefore have been conceived and structured through concepts derived from other domains of experience. Differences in conceptions of evaluation often reflect differences in underlying metaphors, which are in turn derived from certain cultural experiences. The ultimate purpose of this metaphoric structuring is to tell us how to act as evaluators. In spite of the often expressed skepticism about the role of evaluation theory, without such conceptions to guide us we would not know how to act as evaluators. 'In all aspects of life, not just in politics or in love, we define our reality in terms of metaphors and then proceed to act on the basis of the metaphors' (Lakoff and Johnson, 1980, p. 158).

The metaphors discussed to this point substantially define the reality of the evaluator's world. Once an evaluator has accepted the basic metaphors, certain entailments follow. Of course, our thinking is not entirely determined by the metaphors we use, and we are not enslaved by our own concepts. The relationship between metaphors and thinking is more one of likelihood — of probability — than one of determination. For example, it is very likely that an evaluator will be led to certain types of evaluations if he or she sees social programs as industrial production. Furthermore, evaluators are taught certain metaphors as part of their training; it is part of their enculturation. Although they might conceivably overcome a particular way of viewing the world, as defined by certain metaphors, the pressure to be consistent is more likely to make them follow through with particular types of evaluations — to elaborate the metaphor, as it were. Such metaphoric structuring enables us to do a number of things in our evaluations and prevents us from doing others. Every way of viewing the world eliminates alternative possibilities. Metaphors highlight some things and shadow others, and the predominant views we have are necessarily partial and particular. Furthermore, metaphoric structures are derived from domains of our experience that are seldom logically consistent and fully coherent. This lack of consistency and coherence often carries over into our conceptions of evaluation.

Many evaluators and social planners see social programs as industrial production, targeting, and goal attainment and cannot see programs in any other way. Other theorists employ similar metaphors in their articulation of what evaluation is. In fact, these metaphors underlie one of the dominant views of social programs among professional evaluators in the United States, not because people adopt Rossi and others' point of view but because theorists draw upon common experiences and a common intellectual framework. However, as common as this point of view is, there are yet other evaluation theorists and planners who adopt different views of social programs and evaluations. They employ different metaphors — with different results in their conceptualization of evaluation. For example, responsive, illuminative, and stakeholder-based evaluation suggest different metaphors at work.

Not just any metaphor will do in structuring the concept of an evaluation. A former student of mine once wrote a paper in which she developed an evaluation system based upon the beliefs of a tribe of Plains Indians. Such a scheme is intriguing but unlikely to have much application in contemporary America, just as metaphors of industrial production would not have much appeal to the Plains Indians. Appropriate metaphors must be rooted in the experiences of the culture to be applicable. Metaphors used to evaluate social programs necessarily will be close to our core social values, although some theorists have attempted to create new evaluation approaches by deliberately developing different metaphors (Smith, 1981).

Embracing a particular set of metaphors not only expresses certain values but also promotes them. It is in the nature of metaphor that certain things are emphasized and others de-emphasized. Efficiency, effectiveness, goal seeking, and values of industrial production are promoted in the Rossi and others framework. The authors explicitly advocate these values which are embodied in their conceptual apparatus. Conceptions of evaluation are not value-neutral, and much of this inherent evaluation is embedded within the metaphoric structure. Different conceptions emphasize different values or weight the same values differently. Also the more common the metaphors employed to structure evaluation, the more persuasive and invisible the metaphors will be. Unusual metaphors are creative, but conventional metaphors shape most of our thinking and therefore seem natural.

Employing certain metaphors allows us not only to promulgate certain values but to do a number of other things as well, such as to refer and identify causes. For example, the employment of ontological metaphors, such as defining labor and time as substances, allows us to quantify things (Lakoff and Johnson, 1980). Defining a territory or putting a boundary around something is an act of quantification. Bounded objects, like social programs and social problems, have scope, dimension, and size. Within such a framework; an evaluator can locate social problems and measure them. This is usually accomplished through a *survey,* the original purpose of which was to determine the form, extent, and situation of parts of a tract of ground by linear and angular measurement *(Oxford English Dictionary).*

Other entities can be thought of as containers. For example, the participants are *in* the program, but they cannot be *in* the problem, although they can be *part* of the problem. Containers define a limited space, with a bounded surface, a center, and periphery, and can be seen as holding a substance, which may vary in amount. If one sees the program as a container object, it can be measured.

Programs Are Containers

- That is *not much* of a program.
- The program *does not have any content.*
- The program *lacks substance.*
- That is the *core* of the program.

Machines, assembly lines, and pipelines can all be viewed as container objects. Things can be located in them or be part of them. The notion of a container object is abstract and deeply embedded in our thinking. In addition, one can conceive of the outcomes of a program as substances — which issue from the program container. The program has outcomes (a substance). For example, when discussing the outcomes of programs, Rossi and others often switch to their *Social Programs Are Conduits* metaphor. Contamination and purification are of primary concern, so that one can measure the net outcomes: 'An outcome is always a change in the level of a measurable variable' (Rossi and others, p. 164). The *gross* outcome effects are the measures of overall impact but the *net* outcome effects are those left after confounding effects have been removed (a mixing here of the conduit metaphor and an accounting metaphor, which they also use).

Both social programs and program outcomes can be quantified and measured via their metaphorical conversion into objects and substances, but the nature of their measurement differs. As metaphorical objects, programs have size, scope, and dimension, and require different methods of measurement than does the metaphorical substance of the outcomes. Objects may be described, and program description has received much attention. But, measurements of programs themselves have been limited compared to measurement of outcomes. Therefore, social programs normally must be converted into other categories, such as the time, costs, and procedures of the assembly line, before measurements become possible. In contrast, outcomes lend themselves more easily to direct measurement. An object may be dissimilar in its different parts but any quantity of a substance is like any other part of the substance. Hence, conceiving of outcomes as substances permits *cardinal* measurement — that is, the use of an interval scale. To be measurable in this way means that every instance of a commodity is a sum of perfectly identical parts or units. This is not literally true of the outcomes of social programs, but they often are treated that way in order to be quantifiable. In any case, quantification of programs and their outcomes is greatly facilitated by their metaphorical conversion into concrete objects and substances.

If outcomes are quantifiable we can define them as members of a particular statistical distribution, such as a normal curve. We might infer from the degree of overlap between the pre- and post-measured distributions the likelihood of the post-measure coming from a different statistical population. Hence, we begin employing statistical models, in which one treats the outcome scores as member of particular populations. A statistical treatment of impact data is a logical next step for Rossi and others to take, but the preliminary conceptual apparatus for doing this resides in the fundamental metaphors that they employ. For certain purposes, programs and activities are treated as if they were objects and substances. Obviously such conversions are useful.

The statistical model might be called a metaphor, but there is a significant difference between it and the overall metaphoric framework of Rossi and others. The statistical model is internally consistent: There is a single representation from which one can draw logical inferences that do not contradict each other. This is more similar to a scientific or mathematic model than the overall evaluation conceptualization of Rossi and others. But, there is no question that metaphoric thinking plays an important role in scientific thinking. For example, Kurt Lewin's theories draw heavily on analogies with physical theories in the use of certain concepts, such as *field, sector, force,* and *fluidity* (Black, 1962). More recently, cognitive psychology has conceived of the human mind as a computer, employing such concepts as *information processing, feedback, encoding,* and *memory storage* (Boyd, 1979). Metaphors play a constitutive role in scientific theories, although exactly how this role is performed is a matter of dispute (Kuhn, 1979). Of course, the use of metaphors does not mean that a conception is nonscientific. The traditional view of science as a clear, unambiguous, testable rendering of external reality in literal language has given way to a view of knowledge as based upon mental constructions (Ortony, 1979). Perhaps the significant difference between scientific theories and conceptions of evaluation is their internal consistency. Formal scientific theories can be seen as attempts to extend a set of metaphors consistently, whereas metaphors underlying evaluation are rarely consistent (Lakoff and Johnson, 1980).

However, there is another important difference between conceptions of evaluation and scientific theories — a difference of purpose. One might imagine that *minds are computers* and investigate the way in which information processing is done by the mind. According to Boyd (1979), a term like this provides 'espistemic access' to the phenomenon being investigated. Other investigators may extend the concept until it becomes descriptive of how the mind functions — and eventually far removed from what the term means in the study of computers. But metaphors in conceptions of evaluation are not quite like this. The purpose of *Social Programs Are Conduits* is not to arrive at a finer definition of social programs (though one may do so). The researchers in the field do not investigate the extent to which social programs really resemble conduits. Rather, the main purpose is to impose the metaphor so that one knows how to act — that is, how to evaluate. Given the fundamental metaphors, certain investigations and judgments become possible. The judgments are about whether the social programs are any good, not about whether the metaphors fit and not even about finer descriptions of the programs themselves. The difference is between describing and evaluating: these are fundamentally different acts. In both cases metaphors are employed but to different ends.

Perhaps this difference can be seen more clearly if the roles are reversed. Suppose that the *Minds Are Computers* metaphor is used for evaluation purposes. One can imagine trying to assess the information processing capacity, the memory storage, and the encoding processes of the mind — even comparing different minds on these dimensions. No doubt various criteria for evaluating would emerge from our experience with computers, and no doubt one could develop reliable procedures for assessment. One might end up saying that the information processing of a particular mind was very strong but the feedback mechanisms were poor. One would use concepts similar to those in cognitive psychology, but the purpose would be quite different than that of trying to describe the mind by computer analogies or judging the goodness of it. In the act of evaluating, the metaphor is used to generate criteria for making judgments of worth. Conversely, if one used the metaphor *Social Programs Are*

Assembly Lines in a descriptive investigation, one would investigate the degree to which social programs actually resemble assembly lines, modifying one's notions of industrial production to fit the operation of social programs. This is not what evaluation theorists or evaluators do.

In general, these underlying metaphors provide some of the basic concepts that instruct us on how to proceed. If one sees arguments as wars, one will argue in a certain fashion. If one sees social programs as industrial production, then one will evaluate in a certain fashion. Once one is committed to a particular metaphor, certain entailments arise for both thought and action. Thus, the dominant metaphors shape our actions. But not all metaphors are equally good for the purposes they are supposed to serve. There can be good and bad and appropriate and inappropriate metaphors, just as there can be good and bad social programs (Binkley, 1981; Booth, 1978; Loewenberg, 1981). The sense in which a metaphor is true, correct, or appropriate is beyond the limits of this chapter, but what can be said briefly is that the underlying metaphors must be considered within the context of the overall conception of evaluation. That is, one must judge the consequences of the overall conception. These judgments must be based upon criteria broader than being simply true or false as the notion is commonly understood. Evaluators of social programs must embrace comprehensive notions of correctness, including rightness and wrongness. The obligation of the evaluator is broader than that of the describer.

In retrospect, perhaps it is not so surprising that metaphoric thinking is important in evaluation. Black (1962) has explored the similarity between scientific models and metaphors and concludes that both models and metaphors play an indispensable role in scientific thinking. In fact, all intellectual pursuits rely upon such 'exercises of the imagination .... Perhaps every science must start with metaphor and end with algebra; and perhaps without the metaphor there would never have been any algebra' (Black, 1962, p. 242).

Acknowledgements

I would like to thank Lee Cronbach, Robert Ennis, Don Hogben, Mark Johnson, Sandra Mathison, James Pearson, and Paul Silver for providing helpful comments.

References

Binkley, T. (1981) 'On the truth and probity of metaphor' in Johnson, M. (Ed.) *Philosophical Perspectives on Metaphor*, Minneapolis, University of Minnesota Press.

Black, M. (1962) *Models and Metaphors*, Ithaca, NY, Cornell University Press.

BOOTH, W.C. (1978) 'Metaphor as rhetoric: the problem of evaluation' in SACKS, S. (Ed.) *On Metaphor*, Chicago, University of Chicago Press.

BOYD, R. (1979) 'Metaphor and theory change: What is "metaphor" a metaphor for?' in ORTONY, A. (Ed.) *Metaphor and Thought*, Cambridge, England, Cambridge University Press.

JOHNSON M. (Ed.) (1981) *Philosophical Perspectives on Metaphor*, Minneapolis, University of Minnesota Press.

KUHN, T.S. (1979) 'Metaphor in science' in ORTONY, A. (Ed.) *Metaphor and Thought*, Cambridge, England, Cambridge University Press.

LAKOFF, G. and JOHNSON, M. (1980) *Metaphors We Live By*, Chicago, University of Chicago Press.

LOEWENBERG, I. (1981) 'Identifying metaphors' in JOHNSON, M. (Ed.) *Philosophical Perspectives on Metaphor*, Minneapolis, University of Minnesota Press.

McLAUGHLIN, M.W. (1975) *Evaluation and Reform*, Cambridge, Mass, Ballinger.

ORTONY, A. (Ed.) (1979) *Metaphor and Thought*, Cambridge, England, Cambridge University Press.

ROSSI, P.H., FREEMAN, H.E. and WRIGHT, S.R. (1979) *Evaluation: A Systematic Approach*, Beverly Hills, Calif., Sage.

SACKS, S. (Ed.) (1978) *On Metaphor*, Chicago, University of Chicago Press.

SCHÖN, D.A. (1979) 'Generative metaphor: a perspective on problem-setting in social policy' in ORTONY, A. (Ed.) *Metaphor and Thought*, Cambridge, England, Cambridge University Press.

SMITH, N.L. (Ed.) (1981) *Metaphors for Evaluation*, Beverly Hills, Calif., Sage Publications.

TURNER, V. (1974) *Dramas, Fields, and Metaphors*, Ithaca, NY, Cornell University Press.

3
Radical Propositions:
Fusing Fact and Value

Introduction

Michael Scriven has long been one of the most provocative thinkers in evaluation. He has produced some of the classic papers of this still-young field of endeavor and has taken some of the most unusual and controversial positions on various issues. This chapter follows in that tradition.

Scriven contends that most educational research is virtually worthless since it does not address the practical problems of the field faced by practitioners. The reason for this is that educational researchers have adopted the basic research paradigms of social sciences like psychology, which leads them to produce knowledge of little relevance. Rather than addressing problems of how children process knowledge, educational researchers should determine what teaching approaches work best in teaching children to read, a practical problem. Such problems are best addressed by studying successful teachers not by developing theories. Hence, evaluation is a better model for educational research than are the models of the basic sciences.

Evaluation very much involves values, according to Scriven. The value-free stance adopted by many researchers and evaluators — such as merely collecting information and letting administrators value it as they will — is completely wrong. The making of value judgments can be as objectively accomplished as the determination of fact, and in truth scientific investigations cannot proceed without evaluative judgments. As a result of these considerations, Scriven calls for a far-reaching reform of how research is conducted and of how educational researchers are trained. In Scriven's mind the separation of fact and value, a heritage of the logical positivist tradition, was ruinous for the practice of educational research and predicated upon the false dogma of value-free science.

Almost as an illustration of the inadequacy of value-free research, Kirkup begins her chapter by lamenting the inadequacy of 'straight' research to help her in her job of evaluating the women's studies courses at the Open University — she simply could not account for the critical interpersonal relationships and institutional politics that counted for so much. Faced with practical problems she has evolved her own theoretical position on evaluation, drawing upon both the feminist and evaluation literature to do so.

Kirkup claims that the experience of individuals and groups must be respected so much that one should not evaluate another's work unless one is thoroughly familiar, even sympathetic, to the other's experiences. This raises the question of whether men have any business evaluating women's studies at all, since men are too far removed from women's experiences and too biased.

Kirkup's solution was to adopt a collaborative research strategy in which she would rely heavily upon the students' experiences and in which she would also share responsibility for the evaluation with the students and staff. She then tried out her approach in an actual evaluation and found her strategy partially blunted by the institutional framework in which she worked. Although she was not satisfied with the results, all duly reported in the chapter here, her chapter and Scriven's demonstrate the dissatisfaction and questioning of the split between fact and value in the traditional educational research paradigm.

Evaluation as a Paradigm for Educational Research

Michael Scriven
University of Western Australia

Education is a field like medicine in that its name simultaneously refers to a practice and to a field of disciplined enquiry. In fact, both fields of enquiry have a number of very different sub-fields — there is the history of medicine or education; the area of medical ethics corresponding to one part of the philosophy of education; medical jurisprudence corresponding to the law of education, and so on. The paradigm of research in the area of the philosophy of education, to take one example, is surely the paradigm of philosophical research in any area — and the same for the history of education (or medicine) and for the law of education or medicine.

But that leaves open the area of research that we normally think of as the domain of scientific research in medicine or education. Traditionally, and I think rather carelessly, we have tended to suppose that in this area of medical or educational research the correct model is that of the related sciences. That is, for example, educational research has modelled itself on social science research. Now in medical research that approach has brought us some problems because it seems to lead to results that conflict with the practical wisdom of physicians and the economic realities of patients. The search for ever-more-perfect diagnoses (surely the correct model of scientific research) leads us to the CAT scanner 'race' and the latest magnetic resonance scanner, possibly costing more than a million dollars a year to maintain. The heart-lung machines, in vitro fertilization, artificial joints and hearts, and amniocentesis have all plunged us into raging controversies to which the scientific model of research provides no answer and no methodology for finding an answer. The same can be seen in education with the refined development of IQ tests, norm-referenced testing, teaching machines and token economies for classroom management. The conventional 'scientific paradigm' way of dealing with all this is to refuse to deal with it, that is, to say that these problems are not the business of science — they are values issues, and must be sorted out by the citizenry.

Most readers will probably feel a good deal of sympathy — perhaps complete agreement with this answer. But I think this answer is one we have been conditioned to accept by the wide acceptance of a certain paradigm of scientific research, a paradigm which crucially misrepresents the relation between pure science and practical science. In my view, the very idea that the problem of what to do with the internal combustion engine is a social problem, whereas the problem of how it works (or how to make it work better) is a scientific one, is a sign of three undesirable conditions:

- Social irresponsibility by scientists, due to the use of a wrong paradigm, and insensitivity to that fact.
- Laboratory science dominating field science instead of vice versa.
- A model of practical scientific research which excludes several crucial elements that the practitioner sees as defining the problem.

While it's clear that the traditional paradigm of scientific research in the social sciences does apply to many of the special problems that the academic scientist addresses, it's equally clear that it's a very poor model for most of what I'll call practical scientific research, by contrast with basic research. Of course, practical research is often done in the laboratory and in the academy, so I don't want to persist with the terms 'laboratory science' or 'academic science' as the antonyms to 'practical science' but the ease with which those terms come to mind for the task reminds us that the usual model, which after all emanates from the prestigious labs and academies, has ignored or misrepresented the practitioner. And the widespread use of the term *'applied science'* as a synonym for *'practical science'* nicely epitomizes this set of implicit values, because it presupposes that practical problems are to be handled by applying some more general or abstract principles uncovered by 'pure' or 'basic' science. The simple truth is quite different; practical problems are defined by reference to several parameters concerning which the basic scientist gathers no data and rarely has any competence. These include the not-entirely-independent parameters of cost, ethicality, political feasibility, the set of practicable alternatives, system lability, and overall practical significance. What I am proposing here is simply a model or paradigm for practical research — and hence for the central core of educational (and medical) research — that includes these parameters and regards them as absolutely crucial, while acknowledging the frequent but not universal importance of finding general laws, determining statistical significance, modelling deep structure, and hypothesis-testing — the processes that characterize various aspects of the traditional scientific model and comprise a fine model for basic research. To suggest that the basic research model is appropriate as a model for scientific research is either to suggest that the practical is unimportant, a self-contradiction, or to suggest that science is necessarily incapable of dealing with the dimensions of the practical, an allegation without evidence though attractive to many academics. The true situation is simply that the traditional scientific paradigm represents an extremely narrow conception of science, a conception that includes maths and physics and lab psychology but excludes half the subjects that we have been painstakingly raising to the status of science in more recent years, such as ergonomics and cost-analysis, policy studies, methodology and needs assessment. My general thesis is that practical science involves all of these (and more), and is dominated by a paradigm that integrates them all in a way analogous to the way in which experimental design integrates the other — the paradigm is the most general paradigm for scientific research so that pure science should be seen as a special case of limited interest.

The consequences of this proposal may be so serious as to force people to treat it as a joke. Let me illustrate two of its consequences briefly.

1   Consequences for training of educational researchers competent to handle practical problems. Given a relatively fixed amount of time for doing this, the two necessary consequences are first that a good deal of the time currently spent on statistics and traditional experimental design will have to be put into cost analysis, side-effect search techniques, external validity analysis, and gen-eralizability analysis. Second, the existing sections of the as-sociated curriculum, for example on philosophy of education, will have to cover the conceptual analysis of practical choices, and their presuppositions, the ethics of testing, affirmative action, etc., while the unit on sociology of education will have to develop political feasibility and systems analysis, the history unit will have to teach the use of history to develop projections, lability estimates and overall perspectives, the educational psychology component will have to teach needs assessment — and so on. Only a co-ordinated and massive effort from every faculty member in a department of education, combined with massive retraining of that faculty, can turn out professional educational researchers competent to handle practical problems in education.

That's a radical prescription, but the alternative to it is worse — and, I believe inevitable if we do not adopt the prescription. The alternative is the continued dismissal of the educational researcher and his or her work as irrelevant, an extravagance, not responsive, not reliable. This will mean the continued loss of necessary funding, social respect and influence. And, in my view, much though not all of that loss to date has been fully deserved. Which brings us to the second consequence of taking the new paradigm seriously — consequence for the content of research itself.

2   The first research consequence of the evaluation paradigm is that it is self-referent. One might say 'Evaluation begins at home'; evaluators have to be evaluated. To put it in other terms, practical research is itself an allegedly useful practical activity and hence must be subject to the same scrutiny for cost-effectiveness, ethicality, etc. that it will apply to the things that it studies. I invite you to apply these standards to the dissertation proposals and professional journal articles that you see. Are they economically justified expenditures of the author's time, and yours — and the taxpayer's money? Is there any way, by minor change or completely new choice of topic — that they could be more valuable? If so, why not make that change? Exactly what has research contributed to today's educational practice? It is not easy to say. Is that because the problems are so intransigent — or is it because the paradigm was pure research, not practical investigation? The research on classroom teaching, on school management, on discipline, on audiovisual, on special education, on computer-assisted education — in all these cases, and many more, much of the research, often nearly all of it, has been designed on the *'quest for knowledge'* model rather than the *'improvement of practice'* model. And has been wasted, trivial, unremembered as a result; as a result of not looking at itself as an activity to be ruthlessly evaluated.

Notice that this is in no way an attack on basic research. We need some basic research in order to solve practical problems, and some because of the great intellectual payoffs it promises — 'pure' research. And pure research often has unintended practical payoffs. It is nevertheless true that much and probably most education research has no possible justification within a practical field, which is what education is. All too often, people think that pure research is justified within education because it's part of the traditional package of scientific research — some pure and some applied. That's a non-sequitur. If you want to do pure research on learning, you get into psychology not education, and not educational psychology. Educational research is not, I am suggesting, to be defined as 'all research that in any way involves concepts related to education', because that's too broad (it includes learning theory), but as *'research that contributes to the facilitation of education'*, just as medical research should not be defined as 'all research that involves concepts related to medicine', since that brings in all physiological and haematological research, but simply as research contributing to health. The fact that pure research in related fields often surprises us by paying off for practical problems provides no justification for educational researchers to do it, since such results are accidental side effects and less frequent than payoffs from well-designed research aimed at problem-solving. (At least this is true as far as we know, when done by researchers of comparable talent. Certainly it has to be the operative assumption until disproved.)

Whether or not we tidy up the definition of the field of educational research in this way, however, is much less important than the need to tidy up our efforts to select and solve problems that really pay off for practitioners, rather than those that catch the interest of a researcher who was trained only to look at the narrowly conceived 'scientific' component of practical problems. We have to change our vision of ourselves, I believe, into service-researchers rather than pure-scientific-researchers — though what we should serve is not the whims of the Australian Federation of Teachers or of the Minister, but the needs of the student and the professional needs of those others who help students.

In case you think this is coming too close to platitudes, let's pick up a couple of the more striking consequences of this aspect of the position.

First, it relegates the search for explanations, i.e. for the theoretical understanding, to a secondary position by comparison with the search for improvements. It is policy-oriented rather than theory-oriented. It is part of the traditional mythology of ivory tower research that you can't improve something without understanding it, though the most naive student of the history of serendipity or folk medicine or pharmacy or the crafts knows of a dozen famous fixes whose mechanism was and often still is unknown, from aspirin and the boomerang up and down. (And others where an explanation is trivial.) The correct view is that the search for understanding sometimes yields solutions to practical problems; and it's sometimes worth a try because the alternatives seem unpromising and the prospect of either practical or intellectual payoff justifies the effort and cost. Without careful thought about that justification, however, we spend far too much of our time mimicking what we think pure scientists do instead of doing something worthwhile; searching for deep causes when fixes will do. Additionally, we often think that 'understanding' requires a theory: but understanding why a child is upset today, or struggling to cope with easy material, may only require knowledge of a simple fact about the home situation and the usual trivia about human nature known to our palaeolithic forbears.

So the first search for understanding, as for fixes, should eschew theory. The model to keep in mind is the Toll Bridge Model. You can save millions a year on the three San Francisco Bay toll bridges by collecting twice the toll in one direction; more, if you realize that before building the toll plazas. But that suggestion, though widely publicized, was ignored for nearly twenty years, apparently because it didn't come from the staff of the Bridge Authorities or traffic engineers in their consultancies. Even the beauty of solutions to practical problems is in the eye of the beholder and may be ignored if that eye has been conditioned to look only towards the heights for insights.

Consider another practical consequence of the evaluation paradigm's

self-reference. In my view, the time for public defense of a dissertation is
when the proposal has been formulated, not when the research has been
completed. Some huge though unknown proportion of doctoral — let
alone lower-level dissertations — simply lack justification of the effort
involved, either because of design errors or because of failures to take
account of the factors that matter in practice, such as cost or support
requirements. And I do not mean to suggest — as one might suppose from
what I've just said — that we need more complex or sophisticated studies,
something for which we may well lack the time and talent. Not at all.
Valuable studies of practical problems are often far simpler than the ones
usually proposed. The practitioners, like psychological patients, need
fixes not 'deep understanding — or at least they need to know when a
supposed and popular fix is not a fix. How often in the literature does one
find a distinguished educational researcher saying something like 'without
an adequate theory of learning, it's impossible to evaluate teaching'! What
nonsense! One might as well say that if you don't have an adequate theory
of the operation of automobile engines, you can't tell whether your car is
running well; or that without understanding the causes of illness one can't
identify its presence. Here we have the confusion of theoretical understanding with the very identification of a problem, let alone with its
solution.

Evaluation is sometimes just as instant and certain as any observation
or measurement; it is, for example, part of the database, not the set of
conclusions of a study that a particular student composition is badly
organized though it makes a good point. Only an ideological block makes
us think that evaluation must be arbitrary, capricious, subjective, idiosyncratic, unscientific; those who thunder to their introductory educational
psychology courses about the empiricist paradigm of value-free research
in the social sciences do not even notice the schizophrenia with which they
grade — that is, evaluate — those same students, using tests designed and
marked with all the considerable sophistication that educational psychology can contribute. Evaluation is not an add-on to true scientific
research, it is part of all serious scientific activities. We'll come back to
that point in a moment. First, let me pursue one step further the effects on
educational research of what I am now saying.

Let us consider for a moment the difference between the ivory-tower
research approach to particular problem and the practical research
approach. The problem, or family of problems, is of unparalleled importance to education. It is the problem of how to improve the teaching of
handicapped children; or of normal children; or the problem of how to
maintain order in an unruly classroom or school. I have frequently posed
this problem to groups of educational researchers or post-grad social
scientists in education or even to educational administrators. In all cases,
the results are about the same. What one must do, they suggest, is find out
— from the literature or by developing a theory — which variables control

the outcomes in question and then modify those variables. I ask: Is there any way to find that out besides the ways that researchers have been trying for decades? Well, basically, No, they say; except to do it better; the literature search, the design, the run, the data crunch. But there is a much better way, and the fact they do not think of it immediately shows how far we have come from commonsense. You must begin by identifying a number of practitioners who are outstandingly successful at the task in question; you must then use all the tricks in the book to identify the distinctive features of their approach (possibly but not necessarily by discrepancy comparisons with unsuccessful practitioners); you then teach new or unsuccessful practitioners to use the winning ways and retest until you get an exportable formula. If we'd done that 30 or 50 years ago with teachers, we could have saved most of the wasted efforts between then and the 'refined time on task' approach which we in fact reached by macro-analysis of relative success data. And in the administrative area we would almost certainly have a fix for many of the discipline problems that we still lack. It goes contrary to the very spirit of the traditional model to think that the practitioner knows more than the researcher about teaching or discipline; but the simple distinction between *knowing how* and *knowing that* could save one's self-respect and facilitate getting on with the job. You don't disregard successful prospectors because you can't understand how diamonds could possibly be found in the Pilbara, you rush out and start finding out where exactly to find them.

So the effects on training researchers and on selecting research problems and on research designs and on administering research, of the move to the evaluation model are substantial. It's time to summarize what's been said so far and perhaps say a little more about the model.

Evaluation research can be a far more complex business than hypothesis-testing, which is only part of some evaluations. Many evaluations involve no traditional experimental design and no quantitative analysis at all; but even those that do, involve many more dimensions such as cost and ethics. Yet it is completely wrong to conclude from this design complexity that evaluation is of its nature epistemologically or inferentially complex. The same mistake was made about causation — because it often takes a complex study to determine causation it was thought that causation was a logically complex notion. It is not: 'He moved the block across the table' reports an observation, not infallible but highly reliable, just like an evaluation of an answer in a maths test as wrong, or an evaluation of the organization of a presentation like this one. The traditional analysis of evaluation, then, like that of causation, was based on fear of the unknown rather than the common-sense uses of the terms. Reading the efforts by Bertrand Russell fifty years ago, and by recent writers in the *Educational Researcher* to dispense with the notion of causation in scientific research is just as clear an indication of contempt for the practitioner as the attempts to rule evaluation out of bounds. Those are the two key concepts of practice, in science and outside it, and it takes only moments of looking through the most austere writings of paradigm mathematicians or physicists, let alone social scientists, to find hard-core, rock-solid straight forward uses of *causation* and *evaluation*.

Our ideology misleads us more than we know. Description, classification, explanation, generalization, causation, prediction, evaluation — these are the key basic notions of scientific research, and they are highly independent; for example, prediction is just as independent of explanation as evaluation is, a fact still denied by many in the grip of an oversimplified philosophy of science. One might like to have a simpler world, and keep evaluation out of the scientific bed, but then of course you wouldn't have science itself, not because evaluation is too important to exclude, but because the difference between good and bad hypotheses, predictions, classifications, observations and so on is itself evaluative. Science needs methodology, and methodology is a normative subject. Economists often wish to dump welfare economics because it's such a tiresome subject, just as many political scientists would like to dump policy studies or political theory and statisticians would like to cut off evaluation — but when they get to the surgery, they find it is their own heart that they have condemned. It is often true that we detest part of ourselves, but it is no basis for surgery, only for therapy.

Let me finish this study of our defences against recognizing the importance of evaluation with a reference to the 'apples and oranges' argument.

One very often hears it said, by someone objecting to an attempt at a 'bottom-line' evaluative conclusion about the comparative merit of two rather disparate entities such as programs or products, that such an attempted comparison is 'like comparing apples and oranges'. And so it is. And so, of course, we can do it, in just the sensible ways that everyone does when shopping for fruit. That is, we use some of the cross-cutting criteria of quality, cost and consumer needs or preferences to help us pick a winner. The irony is that the very simile that the academic uses to justify eschewal of comparative evaluation needs only a little closer examination to be seen as containing the opposite message. It is of the essence of evaluation to compare what is different and, in particular, things that are different in more than one dimension. Differences along one dimension are completely handled by mere measurement. That measurement may comprise evaluation as when we evaluate runners by timing them over a fixed distance, or weightlifters and high jumpers analogously. But differences in more than one dimension, although they can be described by measurement, require a further process of weighting and combining those measurements in order to reach an evaluative conclusion. That further process is quite complex even in decathlon, where the events are equally weighted, because the intervals between the performances of competitors on each event (and not just their ranking) are converted to a common metric. In the yachting equivalent, the Admiral's Cup, by contrast, the events are differentially weighted but only the rankings in each count, and the ranking provides an easy common currency. But in gymnastics or diving, each individual performance is evaluated by considering it as a multi-dimensional achievement with certain pre-determined weights for the dimensions. How can one possibly compare a three-and-a-half forward somersault with a reverse gainer including a double twist, one might say — surely that is like comparing apples and oranges? Indeed it is — which means it's easy enough — and in fact we can do it quantitatively and with high reliability.

Thus evaluation of the simpler kinds can be thought of as a generalization of measurement; yet, at the other extreme, it extends far into the non-quantitative domain without losing its objectivity and reliability. Even the simpler kinds, however, are different from most measurements in that they involve an immensely important pair of decisions as to what performances are relevant and how they should be weighted. Those decisions require detailed justification, although they are rarely accorded it. No better example could be given than the evaluation of intelligence; but there are other good examples such as the evaluation of candidates for a teaching job or for college admission; of essays in an English examination or of whole exam papers; or of patients for sanity in court certification procedures or of prisoners for rehabilitation at parole board hearings. In each case a good deal is at stake and quite sophisticated methodology is involved. Yet little scholarly literature is devoted to the detailed procedure — by contrast with the semi-popular literature about IQ which merely reacts to certain overall features of the test and its results. And by contrast with the literature on the finer points of statistical analysis. And we find a similar backwardness in discussing the evaluative applications of statistics for example in assessing the significance of a hypothesis or the difference between statistical significance and educational significance. Few statistics texts even today contain a halfway decent discussion of either issue, and yet virtually no use of statistics in education can avoid them.

It is hard to avoid the impression that there is a reluctance to confront the practical issues. Indeed, as we look closer at, for example, the primitive state of the evaluation of teaching or research or applications for research funds, we begin to see the influence of a deeper reluctance, indeed a fear, of evaluation in particular. 'Judge not that ye be not judged' is a great approach to anxiety reduction but incompatible with the scientific mission — which requires that one judge, critically and constantly, the hypotheses, designs, experiments and analyses of oneself and others.

I do not believe one can reconcile the widespread support for the doctrine of value-free social science with the continued, indeed inescapable, practice of evaluation by social scientists — of the work and worth of students, subordinates, peers and selves — except by invoking a kind of phobia which made them blind to the contradiction between their doctrine and their practice. This phobia, which I call valuephobia, blocked us for nearly a century from addressing explicitly the methodology of evaluation and the systematic evaluation of our own practices in social science research. For educational research this was particularly unfortunate because these were years when vast resources were available for research, when vast new systems of education were developed, and when at last our supporters gave up on us. Opportunities on that scale may never come again. Certainly they will not be justified until we show that we understand, better than we have so far, ourselves and what we are doing and how to make it useful to others. The key to that understanding is understanding first, that science is essentially an evaluative process and hence that the value-free doctrine is nonsense; second, that very little educational reasearch that is not evaluative is justifiable, and whatever evaluative research is done must itself be evaluated; third, that the two previous points mean that our track record to date is appalling and we almost have to start justifying our existence from scratch, not because we lacked tools or talent, not because the problems were overwhelmingly difficult but principally because we worshipped false gods in order to disguise the truth from ourselves.

This is a terrible indictment, and it oversimplifies matters a little. A small part of recent research on teaching, for example, has been serious practical research. In Rosenshine's words: 'In the past five years our knowledge of successful teaching has increased considerably. There have been numerous successful experimental studies in which teachers have been trained to increase the academic achievement of their students.' ('Teaching Functions in Instructional Programs', *The Elementary School Journal*, March 1983, p. 335) The significance of this remark lies chiefly in the implied contrast, which is with the years prior to 1978. But the continued emphasis on the trivia of interaction analysis, for example, makes clear that no wholesale reform has occurred.

Perhaps the simplest demonstration of the still-desperate state of educational research is the lack of critical analysis or evaluation studies of computer assisted instruction. Here we have all the earmarks of social mania — vast amounts of money being spent on hardware without software, demands that a new subject be incorporated in a hard-pressed curriculum without needs assessment or with absurd suggestions about the need for it (to train programers, an essentially non-existent job market), with the added spice of pronouncements by heads of state or surgeons-general about the wickedness of arcade games. In this maelstrom, which has been raging for several years, can one detect the steadying influence of the educational researchers and their findings? Scarcely. One's fingers are not all needed to count the valid studies of CAI plus the press releases of our professional associations. Are such matters beneath contempt? Are our other research projects so much more important? The track record suggests otherwise. There was a time when the medical profession and associations thought it beneath their dignity to make announcements about the evils of smoking or the ineffectiveness of laetrile. Fortunately, they have changed and it is time for us to follow suit.

Unpacking the Evaluation Paradigm

When social scientists, apparently contrary to their religion, started accepting evaluation contracts in the late 1960s, the rationalization was embodied in what we can call the Naive Social Science Model of evaluation. On this approach, it was possible to do evaluations without actually making any judgments of value. One simply had the clients tell you what facts they lacked, for example, about program outcomes, you provided these facts and they then attached whatever values they liked to these facts. Ergo — evaluations without valuing!

You could even begin by finding out what they valued, investigate to see if any such things had emerged, score these results against the clients' values profile and report back. This variation would give a conditional evaluative result; 'If one values X more than Y, the program was a good one.' The scientists could still avoid any commitment to specific values.

A third variation exploited the marginally evaluative part of language which refers to 'success' and 'achievement' rather than 'good' and 'valuable'. If the program's goals are achieved, it is successful — and that, presumably, was what the client wanted to know.

These moves, which preserved the value-virginity of the investigator, ran afoul of several problems of which perhaps the leading ones were:

1   What to do about side effects; since nobody expects these, the evaluator hasn't been given any standards by which to judge them. Should they be disregarded; referred back to the client for evaluation; sought for; not sought for too assiduously; regarded as of potentially greater importance than the intended effects, and hence their discovery regarded as possibly the most important — and normally the most difficult — part of the investigation?
2   What to do about a number of obviously important issues like cost or extremely promising decision-alternatives if they happen not to have been included in the goals (the problem of missing factors) although it is obvious that they should have been taken into account by any rational decision-maker
3   What to do about a variety of possible errors in the values or goals of the client, such as inconsistency or factually false presuppositions or the failure to have detected serious ambiguities
4   What to do with clients who can't combine the results of a multidimensional report in a way that is consistent with their ends

5   What to do about ethics, an issue not always independent of the precending[1]

The tough-minded value-free disciple tried to treat as many as possible of these problems as not part of the job, but this obviously showed a lack of concern with professional ethics (which seemed immune to the value free prohibition), and a lack of concern for the client's needs which was rather more worrying than the ethics for someone interested in further contracts.

The next move is to try to handle these problems by referring them back to the client for answers. But evaluators' clients are not the only people with a stake in education, should not the stakeholders be consulted too? It's not good professional ethics to assume that just because someone wants another person or group investigated, one is entitled to undertake the investigation without consulting with the other group (one of the key differences between product and program evaluation). In deciding whether to go ahead, and also in deciding what to weigh to what extent, it seems appropriate to be at least consulting with and influenced by even if not controlled by the service providers (teachers, school administrators etc.), the parents, the taxpayers, the local authority or school board, and the students — rather than just with the funding or supervisory agency that is the usual client. Even if you ignore ethics, considerations of politics and of mere efficiency require more than a cosy client-consultant treatment of these problems.

But bringing everyone in on the act does not generate a solution in itself — though there are one or two evaluators who sometimes sound as if they think so — it merely makes the problem more complicated.

One way to think of evaluation as a discipline is to see it as the accumulation of ways to handle these and a number of related problems. What is characteristic about it is not the area of common ground that it shares with traditional social science research, much of which it frequently needs, but the differentiae. Amongst these one would have to list the intrusion of ethics, cost analysis and problem redefinition, especially the way in which the nature of whatever is being evaluated and the nature of a sound evaluation of it depends on very complicated social interactions.

Another way to see evaluation is simply as the effort to answer questions that require you to find out what the merit, worth or value of things are, rather than their size, weight or number. It is obvious to anyone who has ever read serious product evaluations that there is no difficulty of principle in applying scientific research to find out such answers. It's equally obvious to anyone who has done a few program evaluations, that product evaluation isn't all there is to evaluation; but its existence is an existence proof of the feasibility of the general type of enterprise since there are many cases of program evaluation that princip-ally consist of product evaluation. For example, there are reading programs that cannot be justified for any school; there are others that are live options in some types of school and not in others; there are some that should be considered in almost any school. We don't have all the data and syntheses of the data that we need in order to list every current reading program under one or the other of those headings, but it isn't particularly hard to do the research that makes that listing possible. It's just that nearly all of our research on reading, all those millions of hours of work, has gone into studies that do not tell us the answer — or even moves us far towards an answer — to the basic question of what materials to use in teaching it. It's easy to find research-oriented rationalizations of this fact; but no excuse that should cut any ice with parents or teachers or taxpayers. They want consumer reports on the products they pay for, and there is no reason why they shouldn't get them. Of course, there will remain questions about how best to use the materials, train the teachers, group the pupils and so on, just as there are similar questions about every drug that comes on the market. But that doesn't mean we shouldn't be doing drug outcome studies, in which we standardize the environment of treatment for the sake of getting one answer at a time.

I would be inclined to say that it is now pretty obvious how to deal with the above problems, from the point of view of someone who accepts evaluation as one if not the most important type of research. It is even more obvious that one can hardly ignore such problems. Yet current texts in educational research more often than not produce a version of the Naive Social Science model that cannot deal with these problems at all; it usually reads something like this . . .

'In order to evaluate a program, you
1   Identify the goals of the program
2   Convert them into behavioural objectives
3   Identify tests (or construct them) that will measure these objectives
4   Run these tests on the target population
5   Crunch the data
6   Report whether or not, or to what degree, the goals have been met.'

It will be obvious that this approach runs into all the problems listed above. It is also of some interest that the same problems apply to a slightly reworded version of the above that is sometimes called the Managerial Model of evaluation that is to be found in most texts on program and personnel management.

This is not the place to set out in detail how one goes about handling all these problems and many others; a concise treatment will be found in the entry 'Key Evaluation Checklist' and the cross-references from it, in the present author's *Evaluation Thesaurus* (3rd Edition, Edgepress, 1981). There is a standard set of about fourteen questions that need to be investigated in most evaluations, of which only one is the traditional investigation of alleged or hypothesized effects so familiar in social science research. The only points that need to be made are that these questions, be they concerned with cost or alternatives or ethics or unexpected effects or historical background, cannot be ignored; and that a systematic approach to them is possible, with about the same chances of getting an answer as we can expect in the usual scientific or criminological hunt for explanations and theories. The search is sometimes easy, sometimes close to impossible but still possible in principle and frequently, though not always successful, in practice with the help of searches for new information, more computing power, fresh minds, new models from other areas and so on.

In the end, then, the correct evaluation of some thing or person is just as objective a matter as the correct explanation of the behaviour of some thing or person, no more and no less. The latter is our standard of scientific objectivity, and evaluation can meet it, obviously in product evaluation but equally well in the evaluation of personnel and programs, plans and projections, schools and students. This is one place where we feared to follow the physicists, but partly because we believed the physicists who said that the path they trod led to no value judgments; while the same week they stood in front of their classes evaluating historical and contemporary physical theories and theoreticians, designs and instruments.

The attempt to do what the physicists said they were doing rather than what they did, has done us much harm in education. The other great harm besides the denial of the legitimacy of the evaluative heart of science (and history and literature was to take us away from the practitioners in a field where, unlike physics, they define the important problems and usually have better solutions than the scientists.

The fact that the practitioners define the problems that should be dealt with is unlikely to change in education; certainly not until the researchers have re-established credibility. The fact that the best — not the average or most — practitioners have much better solutions than the researchers will also only change when the researchers change and begin to work on problems whose importance is clear to someone besides themselves. There was a time when engineers thought that designing cars with reduced emissions was nothing to do with real automobile engineering, but an irritation interruption to the progress of engineering science forced on them by a political intrusion. On the contrary, it is the real problem, just as the real problems with atomic energy are the disposal of wastes and the safety factor. The fates have even been kind enough to arrange that solutions to the emissions problem have in fact improved the specific power production of all engines, regardless of emissions controls. Whether we get that lucky in education remains to be seen. First we have to accept a redefinition of the problems for educational research; not how do children process information nor how do their intellectual capabilities develop with age, but what books — or other materials or teaching approaches — work best in teaching what children in what school circumstances to read. Psychologists as such can address the first problem; educational psychologists have other and more practical agendas, from diagnosis to test analysis to determination of the variables that explain the success of great teachers or administrators by analysis of the performance of those people not by developing a general theory.

Traditional social science/educational research is sometimes important. But even to determine that is to do an evaluation. Evaluation is what distinguishes science from random bottletop-collecting, and to deny its legitimacy or primacy is to deny science its essence. We should not further delay our recognition of that fact and its implications for educational research.

Note

1 Ethics has an irritating way of coming into evaluations — irritating for the value-free protagonist, at least. For example, it is a little implausible to suppose that one can evaluate a program without any consideration of the way in which the staff of the program are treated; and one can hardly do that without checking for the absence of improper discrimination; and one can hardly determine what is improper discrimination without having worked out a legally and morally sound position on affirmative action; and not too many social scientists who do program evaluation can pass a serious examination on that.

The Feminist Evaluator
Gill Kirkup Open University

Introduction Educational Evaluation

Evaluation plays an increasingly important role in the development of educational projects and courses, and it is, therefore, important to examine evaluation models to see how they may be refined to make them appropriate to a particular educational situation. My own problem has been to carry out an evaluation of an undergraduate women's studies course, at a distance teaching university: the Open University of Britain. The aims of the course and its content material are grounded in value-based theories of sexual equality and liberation, values which I share. In a most obvious way this evaluation was one where attempts at value 'neutral' evaluation would have at worst been dishonest, and at best simply incapable of exploring some of the more problematic issues faced both by students and staff on the course. However, this is not an unusual situation in the context of educational evaluation, because education is not a value free activity, and those of us involved in it: professional educationalists and educators, researchers and evaluators, subscribe to its values. I believe, therefore, that the evaluation model I describe here has applications outside the area of women's studies, in situations where the evaluator has a commitment to the values of the educational programme, and where the purpose of the evaluation is to explicate these and to contribute to the success of the programme based on them.

Adelman and Alexander (1982) give the following general definition of educational evaluation:

> the making of judgments about the worth and effectiveness of educational intentions, processes and outcomes; about the relationship between these; and about the resource, planning and implementation frameworks for such ventures. (p. 5)

In terms of this definition we, at the Open University, have, in the past, concentrated mostly on processes and outcomes. Evaluation is a major activity of members of the Institute of Educational Technology at the University: evaluation of the effectiveness of course materials and teaching strategies, and more recently of the appropriateness of materials to community needs and potential markets. However, we are beginning to question whether our evaluations are really getting close to understanding the students' experience of the course and also how successful we are at measuring the produced course against its original intention.

In any evaluation project the role of an evaluator is often a complicated and confused one. Many of us come to evaluation from 'straight' research, and it takes some time before we appreciate that we can't operate in the same way in the new context. During the time that I have worked as an evaluator I have become less concerned about fulfilling the criteria for objective research and more concerned to negotiate methodological criteria to take account of interpersonal relationships and institutional politics. I had one experience of working on a project where problems over role definition, status of evaluation findings and even disagreements over the purpose of the evaluation after the event, caused enough controversy to swamp the findings (Kirkup, 1981). Since then I have begun to redevelop my role and to do so I have re-examined evaluation literature and criticism of research. I have been especially interested in the new feminist critique of research methodology, which is presenting a consistent and constructive criticism of research practice in both the arts and social sciences (see various collections, for example, Gamarnikow, *et al.* (Eds) 1983; Spender 1981; and articles in journals such as *Feminist Review*). Since evaluation is a branch of research practice, ethical and methodological issues that are of concern to social researchers in general are also of concern to evaluators.

Suchman (1967) argues that evaluation is better described as 'evaluative research' with the major emphasis

> upon the noun 'research' and evaluative research refers to those procedures for collecting and analyzing data which increase the possibility for 'proving' rather than 'asserting' the worth of some social activity. (p. 7)

However, in practice I have not found this a useful model. There are many points of difference between evaluation and 'pure' social research and the major ones have been summarized by Fife (1980) as being about

> the intent and type of criteria against which judgments are made. The intent of research is to know something in a generalizable way, while the intent of evaluation is to make a choice between options in a given situation. While both research and evaluation must have internal validity (measure what they are supposed to measure), external validity is much more important for research than evaluation. However, the data collected for evaluation must be considered believable by its users. (p. 1)

I have found that a flexible Illuminative Evaluation model has been more useful. I have taken this model as my base and redeveloped it to give a more expressive and value-bound role to the evaluator. I have called that role 'feminist' to identify the ideological context of my ideas and to acknowledge my debt to feminist theory.

Illuminative Evaluation has been a successful strategy in use in higher education for some years now (Parlett and Dearden, 1977) and is only one of a family of 'naturalistic' enquiry models (Guba, 1978). With these models it is possible to study both the process the evaluator is interested in, as well as the process of the evaluation and how it is used. They free the evaluator to be responsive to both the subjects and the clients of the evaluation. However, naturalistic enquiry is a very broad concept and as it stands a rather vague term, which serves mainly as a useful umbrella for a number of different evaluative models. The two most influential of these models have probably been Responsive Evaluation (Stake, 1967) and Illuminative Evaluation (Parlett and Hamilton, 1977). Responsive evaluation is an iterative process by which the evaluator presents and represents her findings to the various clients, each time attempting to increase their understanding of the issue and her understanding of their needs. It is a model which stresses the relationship between evaluator and clients. It also recognizes that clients' needs sometimes change, or are sometimes not clearly understood at the beginning of a project, and provides for ways in which an evaluation can take account of this and still provide useful results. Illuminative Evaluation begins with a general anthropological sort of data gathering and progressive focusing in upon general principles and special incidents. It is a type of responsive evaluation, in which the evaluator is most responsive to the setting and the activity occurring there.

> The research worker contributes to decision making by providing information, comments, and analysis to increase relevant knowledge and understanding. Illuminative Evaluation is characterized by a flexible methodology that capitalizes on available resources and opportunities, and draws upon different techniques to fit the total circumstances of each study. (Parlett, in press)

However, both models can be criticized in the ambiguous role they assign to the evaluator. The evaluator is to be committed to producing a clear and 'fair' report but is *not* to be committed to the process or product she is evaluating. I suspect that this is impossible in educational evaluation, as well as undesirable. House (1977), whose model of evaluation is that of evaluation as argument rather than evaluation as proof, comments on the notion of the objective evaluator:

> People being evaluated do not want a neutral evaluator, one who is unconcerned about the issues. A person on trial would not choose a judge totally removed from his own social system.
> Being disinterested does not give one the right to participate in a decision that determines someone's fate to a considerable

degree. Knowledge of techniques for arriving at objective findings is inadequate. Rather the evaluator must be seen as a member of, or bound to the group being judged, just as a defendant is judged by his peer. The evaluator must be seen as caring, as interested, as responsive to the relevant arguments. He must be impartial rather than simply objective. (p. 8)

New Models For Evaluators

The role of the researcher in the research process has concerned feminist and humanist social scientists greatly over the last few years. I believe that there are two major reasons why the role of researcher has concerned feminists so much. One of these is to do with the fact that as women in a society which privileges men and their view of the world, women have been able to demonstrate bias in research that was claimed as objective, and bias at all sorts of different levels: the choice of topic, the choice of method and the interpretation of results. Many, therefore, no longer believe in the possibility of unbiased enquiry and they are instead concerned that bias should be recognized and acknowledged because that way it becomes accessible to scrutiny.

The other major theme of feminism is signalled by the slogan: 'The personal is the political'. This is a philosophy which denies any separation between individual experience and intellectual theorizing and has much in common with phenomonological theory (for example, Schutz 1967), although its origins do not lie there. One advantage of feminist theory is that its language is simpler and more grounded in ordinary speech than the more abstract social theories it has much in common with. Like phenomenology it claims that the basis for all understanding is one's own personal experience of life and that all experiences have validity. Alongside it there has been a rejection of the scientific method and positivistic forms of theory building (Arditti, 1979) and attempts have been made to build theory through group activity, sharing and validating experience (Evans, 1982). Recognition is also given to the fact that theories so built will have limited generalizability that is, that because the black experience is different from the white, male from female, middle class from working class, it is impossible for one group of people to produce theories which adequately describe the experience of others. General descriptions and theories need to be produced collectively, if they can be produced at all, and the researcher or scholar has no particular monopoly of knowledge.

There are connections between this position and that of Habermas and the critical social theorists. He argues that social enquiry cannot use the same method as enquiry in the natural sciences. Social action depends on the individual's understanding of her situation, an understanding which is not idiosyncratic, but has intersubjective meanings which are part of the social context in which she operates, and these meanings embody value. The whole purpose in pursuing knowledge in this area is to emancipate (Habermas, 1972).

Two British feminists, Stanley and Wise (1981), make strong assertions about the implications such a position has for the researcher and her methods:

> Feminism either directly states or implies that the personal is the political; that the personal the everyday are important and interesting and must be the subject of feminist enquiry; that other people's realities mustn't be downgraded, sneered at or otherwise patronized; that feminists must attempt to reject the scientist/person dichotomy and, in doing so, must endeavour to dismantle the power relationships which exist between the researchers and researched . . .
>
> . . . But of course in order to examine 'the Personal' in this way it's necessary to locate not only the researched but also the researcher thus making her extremely vulnerable in ways usually avoided by researchers like the plague. (pp. 101 and 103)

In their later writing (1983), they have developed an ethnomethodological model of research where the researcher is the pivot of the enquiry. In common with many researchers who want to either humanize or politicize research practice they find scope for doing this if they adopt qualitative rather than quantitative research techniques, although such methods are not inherently less sexist than 'hard' methods.

The researcher's experience, argue Stanley and Wise, should be the core of the research. They go so far as to suggest that the researcher should not attempt to explain other people's views of the world because she risks misunderstanding them or presenting them as deficient. Instead she should present only her own understanding.

> . . . researchers should present analytic accounts of how and why we think we know what we do about research situations and the people in them. The only way we can avoid overriding other people's understandings as 'deficient' in some way is not to attempt to present these within research. Instead, we should be much more concerned with presenting *ourselves* and *our* understandings of what is going on, by examining these in their context. We must make ourselves vulnerable, not hide behind what 'they' are supposed to think and feel, say and do. (p. 168)

Reinharz, an American sociologist, has developed a similar model which she calls 'experiential analysis' (Reinharz, 1979 and 1981). Her model is also an ethnographic one but it lays stress on the commitment and involvement of the researcher. Before beginning research, she writes, it is necessary that:

The research question be of sincere concern to the *researcher* and that it be of sincere concern to the subject(s) (Reinharz, 1981, p. 80)

Next the trustworthiness of the researcher has to be established. A new model of the relationship between researcher and subjects has to be built based on collaboration at all points during the project:

It begins with shared topic formation — the participants acting as partners or consultants in shaping the research focus, selecting research procedures and their implementations; collaborating in data analysis and publication, or at least monitoring publications before their distribution. (Reinharz, 1981, p. 86)

This collaboration and value-based planning is the core of her model, she's less worried about methods of data collection and analysis except 'that the analysis draw heavily on the language of the persons studied i.e. that it is grounded.' She claims, along with some writers on evaluation (Guba) that there is never a final correct conclusion: 'there is no final interpretation which is endowed by participants, conjured by readers and cognitively satisfying the researcher.' (Reinharz, 1981, p. 87)

Such models are not restricted to feminist research. For example, a humanistic psychologist Heron (1981) also uses the term experiential research to describe a similar relationship. He describes how he sees the basic difference between experiential research (cooperative enquiry) and the usual social science research method:

But there are two quite different ways of interacting with persons in research. One way is to interact with them so that they make no direct contribution to formulating the propositions that purport to be about them or to be based on their sayings and doings. This, of course, is the traditional social science experiment or study in which the subjects are kept naive about the research propositions and make no contribution at all to formulation at the stage of hypothesis — making, at the stage of final conclusions, or anywhere in between. In the extreme, and still popular form of this approach, the enquiry is all on the side of the researcher, and the action being enquired into is all on the side of the subject.

The other way — the way of cooperative enquiry — is for the researcher to interact with the subjects so that they do contribute directly both to hypothesis-making, to formulating the final conclusions, and to what goes on in between. This contribution may be strong, in the sense that the subject is co-researcher and *contributes* to creative thinking at all stages. It may be weak, in the sense that the subject is thoroughly *informed* of the research propositions at all stages and is invited to assent or dissent, and if there is dissent the researcher and subject negotiate until agreement is reached. In the complete form of the approach, not only will the subject be a fully fledged co-researcher, but the researcher will also be co-subject, participating fully in the action and experience to be researched. (pp. 19 and 20)

These writers agree that the researcher can only do research on issues and with people with whom she shares certain defining characteristics. The researcher herself is the instrument rather than the questionnaires, interviews etc. which are more usually seen as such, and as the instrument she must be appropriate to the task. Appropriateness is defined through group membership or ideological commitment, rather than professional expertise. Reinharz (1979) argues that experiential analysis 'can be produced concerning any condition which would permit a researcher to be a temporarily affiliating insider' (p. 356)

It therefore follows that there will be issues and groups that it will be impossible for the researcher to do work on. In discussions about feminist research, male researchers frequently ask whether they could do such research. This is the wrong question. Anyone is free to adopt the model described as long as they accept the restrictions it imposes on the range of possible projects. Men, for example, would have to accept that it would be almost impossible for them to do work on mainly female situations. They could never fulfil the criteria to be a 'temporarily affiliating insider'. It also follows that you cannot do research on unwilling subjects. The researcher as a person is acknowledged to be crucial in interpreting the situation. Reinharz (1979) recommends that the researcher has some form of personal analysis.

If the researcher's self is the instrument by which the investigation proceeds, then that instrument must be well understood. For this reason I have urged the social researcher to undergo some form of systematic self-analysis as part of training. If the researcher's 'biographical presence' (....) participates in a context to create perceptions or interpretations, then the biography of events, relationships and ideas that the researcher has experienced demands clarification. (p. 356)

The reports etc., produced by such a worker would be personal documents. Stanley and Wise (1983) compare such work to literature.

We see all research as 'fiction' in the sense that it views and so constructs 'reality' through the eyes of one person. We accept it because much literature is concerned with such an exploration of 'society' through the eyes of particular characters, but ultimately and frequently explicitly through the eyes of the writer. If this is the kind of literature that our kind of research is compared with then we accept the comparison and feel flattered .... If this kind of research can open people's eyes, can influence them and change them, to the extent that literature has done, then it will do better than any other social science research that has appeared to date. (p. 174)

However, this causes practical problems for an evaluator, who is often assigned a topic of investigation rather than being free to choose it. She also has clients whose needs, wishes and biases it is important to take into account. She is accountable to these clients for her final findings. Is it possible to resolve, honestly, the different needs and requirements of the client-sponsor and the client-subject?

I found an example of a different approach to research/evaluation in a Trades Union sponsored investigation into the stress involved in working on buses. The aim of the project was to locate the 'potential sources of stress in the working environment and in the work process' (TGWU, 1981, p. 6).

The investigation was initiated by union members and Worker's Educational Association[1] tutors involved in teaching Trades Union Congress[2] day-release courses. They felt that the common view of stress as a product of individual personality problems made it difficult for workers to argue for improvements to conditions in the workplace. There was also disagreement over what constituted evidence and who was expert about the problem. The workers felt, with some justification, that they were experts in knowing what caused stress in their workplace since they *experience* it. Therefore the form of investigation they wanted was a workers' investigation, that is 'not only one carried out by the workers themselves for themselves, but is also one that insists on the legitimacy of their "own way of experiencing and understanding the problem".' (TGWU, 1981, p. 7)

The rationale of such an enquiry was expounded further by two of the people involved in the investigation:

> Any workers' investigation must develop methods that can be understood by the workers and used by them on their own in other situations. The methods chosen must therefore involve learning transferable skills and not require expert control, for whatever reason, for example, accessibility, comprehensibility, cost, etc. (Forrester and Thome, 1981)

The areas of investigation were determined by the workers, and where they needed more information it was brought to them. For example, it was important to do an ergonomic survey of the cab of the bus so a seminar was held for the workers involved to explain the basic principles of ergonomics and to discuss how it might be used in the project. Another of the methods used was a questionnaire, designed by the workers and administered by certain trusted members. The questionnaire was also analyzed collectively. In this sort of approach the researched is also the researcher and the ordinary role of researcher is transformed into technician or resource. It is part of a process known as 'demystifying' expertise (as in Irvine *et al.*, 1979). 'Above all, a workers' investigation must attempt to challenge what is commonly accepted as science and to minimize/eliminate the mystique attached to the "expert".' (Forrester and Thome, 1981)

The researcher/evaluator becomes a resource and a facilitator whose job it is to develop the skills and confidence of all collective members of the project and to provide whatever support services are necessary to enable them to achieve what they want. This enabling role lends itself more obviously to evaluation situations where the declared purpose is to inform action and policy. It is a role that requires the researcher/evaluator to place the needs and experience of the researched first. It is least problematic when the researched and the client are both the same as in the busworkers enquiry.

There is no reason why the concerns and the methods of the feminist researchers quoted earlier could not be incorporated into such a workers' investigation. The remarkable and rare thing about this investigation is that the workers had the confidence to define the research problem and to control the research strategy. It could be seen as an example of strong cooperative enquiry.

With these models in mind I negotiated an evaluation of the first year of a women's studies course at the Open University, Course U221: *The Changing Experience of Women*. The circumstances, I felt, were ideal for me to explore the possibility of feminist evaluation since there was a convergence between the ideology contained in the course and held by the course writers, and that which I wanted to manifest in my role as evaluator. In negotiating a role for myself in evaluating the course I wanted to incorporate aspects of the models discussed above by developing a collaborative and reflexive way of working which was also flexible and responsive to the needs of the groups involved in the evaluation.

A Feminist Evaluation

Before I describe the evaluation I will briefly describe the course and its context. Women's studies is now an established academic area in Britain, with courses at all levels of education: school and post-school, formal and informal. It is still a developing area and there are debates over what constitutes women's studies and what its defining characteristics should be. (See Spender 1981; Bowles and Duelli Klein, 1980; and *Women's Studies International Forum*, Vol.6, No.3, 1983.)

Women's studies is a heterogeneous subject; courses which come under its protective umbrella can look very different from each other. What they all have in common is that they are part of the academic arm of the Women's Liberation Movement, to which they are accountable and whose aims they are intended to further. This is done through three activities and any women's studies course will be engaged in one, if not more, of these. One activity is that of presenting materials to compensate for bias and omission in courses as they presently exist. Another is to engage in consciousness raising activities which both validate the personal experience of the student as well as providing a base from which to develop theory in an experiential way. Finally, students on such courses are engaged in developing and extending feminist theory in all areas of knowledge.

Within the constraints of an academic institution and particularly one which teaches 'at a distance', *The Changing Experience of Women* contains some of the features of other women's studies courses. It is concerned with affective learning and developing non-hierarchical ways of teaching/ learning as well as a commitment to personal and social change within the political context of feminism and the women's movement. I have been closely involved with the development of this particular course as an educational technologist and a feminist academic, and then as the evaluator of the course. I was concerned that strategies which I adopted for the evaluation take general criticisms of evaluation practice into account, as well as examine the special features of a women's studies course, and incorporate some of these features into the evaluation methodology. Indeed, an innovatory course which is involved with personal development and social change lends itself well to an evaluation where the role of the evaluator is to be closely involved with the experiences of the students.

I adopted a role that was experiential in a weaker sense than that used by Reinharz and Stanley and Wise, a sense closer to that of Heron, and which incorporated a commitment to cooperative working and to demystifying the evaluation process as in the workers' investigation. I would not claim that merging the different models produced a coherent final model but it provided me with a base from which I feel able to operate.

There were four major aims to the evaluation:

1　To provide insights into what students' expectations about this course are and how far the course fulfils them.
2　To identify particular aspects of course material which are not teaching effectively and to make recommendations for change and improvements.
3　To provide other people involved in women's studies courses with an evaluation of aspects of the course that are common to other women's studies courses.
4　To examine the special features of a distance teaching women's studies course to discover whether its distance teaching aspects detract from the success of the course.

One of the first problems was that of defining the clients of the evaluation. In an educational evaluation there are usually at least two groups of 'clients': one group is the sponsor and the people to whom the evaluator is accountable, the other group are the powerless, those whose interests the educational evaluator has at heart in being involved in the programme at all. I had three major clients: the central course team who wrote the course, the students and tutors who were using the materials, and the University. Although, in a loose sense the course team commissioned the evaluation, the greater body of the University was also a client because it *requires* that certain aspects of a new course must be evaluated and obliges the course team to use academic members of the Institute of Educational Technology as evaluators. This equalizes the power relationship between course team client and evaluator so that the evaluator has much more scope for negotiating the form of the evaluation and the strategies it incorporates. Therefore, in my first memo to the course team I outlined how I would like to operate and I also suggested that I saw my prime responsibility as being towards the other set of clients — the students on the course. I also briefly outlined the concerns that I felt would be central to the evaluation, the relationships involved, and the sort of qualitative methods I might use.

The memo was well received and negotiations with the course team were enthusiastic, although muted since the course was in the final throes of course production, struggling with tasks which were much more critical at that time than a projected evaluation study. Some members were enthusiastic *because* I was attempting a more unusual research strategy and because as feminists they were interested in being part of an evaluation which took account of a feminist critique of research.

There were 708 students from all over Britain on the course, of this 8 per cent (fifty-six) were men. Their ages ranged from the mid 20s to the mid 60s, the largest age range, 41 per cent, being between 30 and 40. The majority of students, 76 per cent (494), were studying the course as part of their undergraduate programme. The remainder were doing it simply out of interest. I chose to study in depth only two tutor groups, a total of forty students, one group in Kent, one in Oxford. They were not chosen as representative in any way, they were chosen so that they were within reasonable travelling distance and because the tutors were enthusiastic about an evaluation. Over the year my relationship with one tutor group was excellent and I developed a role that was completely integrated with the functioning of the group. With the other group my relationship was just satisfactory, but for much of the time I felt an outsider, and was not privileged to share the group's experiences. I believe that this was due to the different point at which I was able to first meet the groups, and the fact that I had already established a relationship with the tutor of group A.

My first meeting with group A students was at their first tutorial, we were all strangers together. I explained the aims of the evaluation and asked people to raise any doubts they had. There was overwhelming enthusiasm. In response to my request for people who wanted to talk or write to me to put their names and addresses on a piece of paper everyone did so. Many of the group wanted to talk to me during lunch in the nearest pub. From then on my position was fully accepted in tutorials and outside of them. I received letters from most of the group in which they wrote in great detail about their personal histories and their reasons for doing this particular course. I felt privileged to have had so much personal experience recounted to me. I believe no questionnaire could have elicited such a wealth of material, and I suspect that the form in which it was given — that of a letter — allowed the considered expression of personal details even better than an interview. I believe the use of unstructured personal letters as a form of data gathering and a way of explicating meaning has not been explored enough by social researchers. I also believe that my acceptance was helped by the fact of my membership of the course team and my identity as a woman (only five of the students in the sample are men and only one of these has ever written to me). This supports the arguments of Reinharz and Heron that it is only where the researcher is seen as a member of a group will she be allowed access to important information, and only as a group member will she be able to make sense of it. For various reasons, to do with the timing of my visits and my relationship with the tutor, I was unable to set up such good relationships with so many of the students in the second group.

My original intention had been to engage in as little written data collection: questionnaires, checklists etc, as possible. I had hoped that I would have enough personal contact or contact by phone to elicit as much data as I needed. However, this was not possible. Finding time to visit people in their homes in Kent was not feasible and women at home frequently have so many demands made of them that it is very difficult to choose a good time to phone them. I found that I wanted more detail about specific aspects of course material than I could get during and after tutorials and I resigned myself to writing letters. That in itself is also time consuming. Experiential research techniques, even with a sample as small as mine, demand a large amount of time from the researcher.

The original commitment to flexibility over data collection techniques proved very worthwhile. I tailored my needs for information to the students' need for privacy and for a technique which would not increase their workload. I have less sense of imposing on a student's good nature in this project compared to my previous experiences. I was also able to respond to the course team's changing needs for information and this increased their trust in the evaluation because of its responsiveness.

In order to involve people in evaluation they must feel that they are receiving some return to compensate for their time and energy. It is possible to get high levels of cooperation in situations where the researcher provides friendship, information, or support to the research subject. A powerful example of this is given by Ann Oakley (1981), in a discussion of interviewing women in a study of the transition to motherhood. She found that it was impossible to remain a detached interviewer and she resolved to be as involved with the women in her sample as they invited her to be. This engaged her in answering questions, being willing to talk about her own experiences, staying for dinner, and developing friendships. She considered that her behaviour was the major reason why she had such high levels of cooperation from her sample of women during the project.

I found I was able to involve those students who I could meet face to face at tutorials. And, although the response to my initial letter was very good (85 per cent), I was disappointed in the number of comments I received on draft reports that I circulated. Ultimately students were less involved in the final reports than I would have liked. It is important to realize when engaging in experiential research that, although the project is close to your heart and taking up the majority of your time, even if it interests the other people involved it is probably one of their least important activities. People must be free to have a limited involvement and therefore the researcher, since she has the prime responsibility for producing the goods, must be willing to exercise more control than she would ideally wish to do.

I was able to achieve the four aims I had set for the evaluation, although I cannot here go into any detail. The students' expectations of the course fell into three parts that can be loosely classified as academic, personal, and political. Academic expectations were referred to by expressions such as: 'getting a greater awareness and insight into women's position.' The personal expectations were to do with making sense of their own experiences as women. The political expectations where that the course would provide the student with language and the terms with which to argue the case for women with their friends or at work. This group saw themselves as already in agreement with feminist arguments, but needing to consolidate their understanding.

The evaluation suggested that the course was better at fulfilling the academic and personal expectations and less successful at fulfilling the political ones. One of the great successes of the course appeared to be that it introduced feminist ideas and arguments to women who very strongly did *not* identify themselves as feminists when they began, and to introduce these ideas in a way that the students felt was thought provoking and exciting without being threatening.

The evaluation, as well as raising some of these general issues, also identified weaknesses in parts of the course and contributed to suggestions for change. For instance, I was able to report strong feelings of annoyance from both tutors and students about the structure and wording of assignments. This was then backed up by personal conversations that members of the course team had with each other. The structure of assignments for the following year, as well as the examination, was redesigned in the light of this feedback. I feel that the power of the material I was able to give the course team in terms of reports of anger, despair over completing assignments and extended verabatim comments from students about exactly what they thought was wrong, gave an urgency to the issue that would not have been felt in questionnaire responses alone. The flexible way of working with verbal reports to the course team also made evaluation data available quickly and the course team were able to respond soon after the details were known. There were other areas of the course, such as a particular audio-visual programme, which was not perceived as very relevant, and a textual component which was very difficult. Changes have been made to these for following years.

Teaching this type of course at a distance has proved difficult. The impact of the material is lessened somewhat when it is studied by the isolated individual. Those times when students were together, such as during the summer school, were experienced as the most powerful part of the course but were not always enjoyed. The course has retained its popularity in following years and has been studied by more people than any other women's studies courses in Britain.

Assessing the Potential of Feminist/Experiential Strategies for the Evaluation of Educational Programmes

It seems necessary, to me, that those of us who hold any ideological world view which is critical of the one commonly in operation in our own society, need to apply our criticism to our work. It has been argued that ideological commitment can change the choice of topic for evaluation and can influence the interpretation of evaluation results but not the methods by which data are collected; these will either be appropriate or inappropriate, well done or badly done. Feminists critics of research, as well as critical theorists, have argued that this is not the case and that particular methods of enquiry are inherently biased. For those of us who have political as well as methodological reasons to suspect that this is true, the time has come to stop throwing rocks at the 'patriarchal paradigm' and to begin building an alternative, feminist paradigm and see what the results look like.

However, attempting to do evaluation which is based on an ideal of cooperative non-hierarchical working in an educational situation that is both hierarchical and individualistic as is the Open University, resounds with contradictions. The ethos of the educational experience runs counter to the aims of the evaluation. The Open University has a model of the student as the isolated individual who has contact with a tutor and through the tutor with the university; a type of linear chain of command. It has been a problem to teach a women's studies course with this model since such courses have stressed the importance of the group learning environment and the educational value of students working cooperatively and sharing experiences, and the role of the tutor has been one of a resource rather than a pedagogue. The effect of the evaluation has been to open channels of communication which don't normally operate in the Open University. For example, I provided a channel between the central academic course team and the student groups so that some sort of dialogue could occur between them. My draft report which was sent to all the students and tutors involved in the evaluation allowed communication between students about themselves and their experience of the course. I therefore feel that those students involved in evaluation had an enriched experience which rubbed off in their enthusiasm for the course. However, the educational structure remains hierarchical and as the evaluator I have been placed in a position along that chain of command.

The attempt to re-negotiate accountability also contains contradictions. I tried to make myself and the evaluation accountable to the students much more than would be usual. But I had to recognize that in making myself more accountable to them I did little to change their power in the University structure. The freedom to renegotiate relationships at all is one, in a sense, only allowed by the central course team.

One of the main drawbacks of experiential research, as defined by Reinharz (1979) and Heron (1981) and feminist research as described by Stanley and Wise (1983), is that it is unrealistic in its expectations of the level of involvement of the co-researchers (the subjects). Even when problems are of major concern to people, they have work and private lives which usually take priority, whereas research *is* work for the researcher and evaluator. I suspect that frequently the evaluator will end up with more responsibility and power than she planned for. The TGWU model of a workers' investigation has great potential for involvement of the co-researchers in all aspects of the work, but it is unlikely that the majority of people have the confidence or the contacts to initiate such products, and it must be recognized that the Leeds busworkers' investigation was initiated by people made powerful by their membership of a union.

I also recognize that I am still undecided about the nature of generalizability of an evaluation. Stanley and Wise argue that generalization from research is impossible and an unrealistic aim. I do not feel as strongly as they do, but I recognize that all research design bargains validity against generalizability, and agree with Fife (1980) quoted earlier, that for evaluation validity is the more important measure. The assumption contained in the evaluation I have done, using indepth qualitative data from a small sample, is that if I am able to understand the experience of the sample and describe it in appropriate language it will resonate with the experience and understanding of others involved in women's studies. It will be 'meaningful' rather than 'true', and although perhaps not generalizable in the research sense it will allow others access to the experience of those in my sample in such a way that will contribute to such others gaining insight into their own situations. In phenomenological research the exploration of meaning to uncover truth is the primary aim of social research, although the methods I have used could be open to criticism for not probing meaning deeply enough. Despite these draw-backs, I believe that the models I have described, perhaps in a less pure form than presented by their original authors, offer ways of approaching both practical and ethical research problems.

I approached the task of evaluating course U221 *The Changing Experience of Women* from the position of identifying myself as a feminist and seeing the course as a feminist course. I am also a professional evaluator engaged in resolving problems inherent in the evaluation process. I have adopted strategies for this particular task that address both the problems of the evaluation process as well as the particular issues raised by the nature of the women's studies course. However, these experiential strategies can be used equally well in the evaluation of other educational programmes, as long as the necessity of the evaluator being a 'temporarily affiliating insider' is recognized, and in doing so the evaluator can honestly subscribe to the values of the programme.

The strategies have given me the opportunity to explore some of the contradictions I feel between my work and my ideological commitments. These contradictions have not been resolved and I doubt whether they can be as long as I accept work as an evaluator within the educational system. And, since I intend to carry on doing so, I put myself in the position of arguing that it is, in fact, the tension caused by these contradictions which provides the impetus for a more creative personal development of my role. I would also argue that there is some benefit to be gained by all groups involved in an evaluation in bringing these contradictions to the surface and examining them more closely.

Notes

1 WEA (Workers' Educational Association) *Aim*: 'to interest men and women in their own continued education and in the better education of their children' (*Directory of British Associations*, CBD Research, 1982). It does this by organizing and support-ing a national system of adult evening classes.
2 TUC (Trades Union Congress) *Aims*: 'the promotion of interests of affiliated organizations; improvement of economic and social conditions of workers in all parts of the world; assistance in the complete organization of workers eligible for its affiliated membership and settlement of industrial disputes.' (*Directory of British Associations*, CBD Research, 1982).

References

ADELMAN, C. and ALEXANDER, R.J. (1983) *The Self-Evaluating Institution: Practice and Principles in the Management of Educational Change*, Methuen.

ARDITT, R. (1979) 'Feminism and science' in ARDITTI, R. BRENNAN, P. and CAVRAK, S. (Eds) *Science and Liberations*, South End Press.

BOWLES, G. and DUELLI-KLEIN, R. (1980) (Ed.) *Theories of Women's Studies*, Berkeley, University of California.

EVANS, M.(1982) 'In praise of theory: the case for women's studies', *Feminist Review*, 10, spring, pp. 61–75.

FIFE, J.D. (1980) in FEASLEY, C.E. *Programme Evaluation*, American Association for Higher Education.

FORRESTER, K. and THOME, C. (1981/82) 'Stress on the buses', *Science for the People*, 50, winter.

GAMARNIKOW, E. *et al.* (Eds) (1983) *Gender, Class and Work*, Heinemann.

GRAHAM, H. (1983) 'Do her answers fit his questions? Women and the survey method' in GAMARNIKOW, E *et al.* (Eds) *The Public and the Private*, Heinemann.

HABERMAS, J. (1972) *Knowledge and Human Interests*, Heinemann.

HERON, J. (1981) 'Philosophical basis for a new paradigm' in REASON, P. and ROWAN, J. (Eds) *Human Inquiry A Sourcebook of New Paradigm Research*, John Wiley and Sons.

HOUSE, E. (1977) *The Logic of Evaluative Argument*, CSE Monograph Series in Evaluation No 7, Centre for Study of Evaluation, UCCLA.

IRVINE, J. MILES, I. and EVANS, J. (Eds) (1979) *Demystifying Social Statistics*, Pluto Press.

KIRKUP, G. (1981) 'Evaluating and improving learning materials: a case study' in PERCIVAL, F. and ELLINGTON, H.I. (Eds) *Aspects of Educational Technology XV*, Kogan Page, pp. 171–6.

OAKLEY, A. (1981) 'Interviewing women: A contradiction in terms' in ROBERTS, H. (Ed.) *Doing Feminist Research*, Routledge and Kegan Paul.

PARLETT, M. (in press) 'Illuminative education', *International Encyclopaedia of Education: Research and Studies*, Pergamon Press.

PARLETT, M. and DEARDEN, G.J. (Eds) (1977) *Introduction to Illuminative Evaluation: Studies in Higher Education*, Washington DC, Council of Independent Colleges.

REINHARZ, S. (1979) *On Becoming a Social Scientist*, Jossey-Bass.

REINHARZ, S. (1981) 'Experiential analysis: A contribution to feminist research' in BOWLES, G. and DUELLI-KLEIN, R. (Eds) *Theories of Women's Studies II*, Berkeley, University of California.

SCHUTZ, A. (1972) *The Phenomenology of the Social World*, Heinemann. 'So far, so good — so what? Women's studies in the UK, (1983) *Women's Studies International Forum*, 6, 3.

SPENDER, D. (Ed.) (1981) *Men's Studies Modified: The Impact of Feminism on the Academic Disciplines*, Pergamon Press.

STANLEY, L. and WISE, S. (1981) 'Back into the personal or: Our attempt to construct feminist research' in BOWLES, G. and DUELLI-KLEIN, R. (Eds) *Theories of Women's Studies II*, Berkeley, University of California.

STANLEY, L. and WISE, S. (1983) *Breaking Out: Feminist Consciousness and Feminist Research*, Routledge and Kegan Paul.

Stress at Work (1981), an investigation carried out by shop stewards of the Transport and General Workers Union (TGWU) 9/12 Branch, final report, March.

SUCHMAN, E.W. (1967) *Evaluative Research*, Russell Sage Foundation.

4
Naturalistic Evaluation: Acting from Experience

Introduction

One of the significant events in the development of the evaluation field over the past twenty years has been the emergence of naturalistic evaluation. Led by such people as Barry MacDonald, Lawrence Stenhouse, David Hamilton and Malcolm Parlett in Britain, and Robert E. Stake, Louis Smith and Elliot Eisner in the United States, naturalistic evaluations have achieved some legitimacy. In Britain, in fact, this may be the dominant mode of evaluation. In the United States the overwhelming number of evaluations are still quantitative and formal, reflecting the strong positive science tradition of American social science. However, naturalistic evaluation has made inroads even in the United States.

Some of the differences between quantitative and naturalistic advocates arise over the different role that evaluation is expected to play in educational change. In the following chapter Stake presents the most comprehensive explication yet of his view of the role naturalistic evaluation is to serve. Stake sees educational change as fundamentally dependent upon the beliefs of educational practitioners. Unless they are persuaded to change, not much change will occur. Practitioner change will necessarily be gradual and evolutionary in developing, with practitioners modifying their practice over time based upon their own perceptions of what is the correct thing to do.

Traditional research which provides only general propositional knowledge statements has little relevance for practitioners. They are more interested in their own particular situation. What they will respond to, according to Stake, is vicarious experiences from which they can draw naturalistic generalizations about what to do. Hence, naturalistic evaluation should supply vicarious experiences that practitioners can understand and relate to. Through this new personal understanding, practitioners will be persuaded to act differently in their practice. Stake's view is quite different from that guiding most evaluation research, as for example that of Weiss in the next section of the book, who questions whether evaluation has anything to offer the practitioner. Stake would say that evaluation is useful only if it can relate to the practitioner's personal experience.

Rob Walker's chapter presents some of the difficulties he has encountered in conducting naturalistic studies. First, naturalistic case studies are highly interventionist in effect if not in intent. Interviewing and observing people greatly affect what people do. And sharing one's observations and conclusions with those people can cause intense reactions, as Walker illustrates. Second, naturalistic case studies often present distorted views of the world one is trying to portray. These distortions enter for a number of reasons and with sufficient power to transform the reality of the situation significantly. Finally, naturalistic studies are conservative in that they portray current practices and fix them in time although the reality of the actual situation changes even before the case study is written. Walker offers no panaceas for these problems of naturalistic research but suggests some ethical cautions the researcher/evaluator should attend to.

The last chapter in this section is by Stephen Kemmis. Kemmis was trained and apprenticed in the naturalistic tradition but the principles he explicates should apply to all evaluations in his view. He sees the role of evaluation as feeding information into a critical debate among program participants as to what that specific program should do. His account strongly emphasizes the rationality and autonomy of each participant, very much in the tradition of naturalistic evaluators. Kemmis also tries to go beyond individuals, however, and work towards the development of community. One of the difficulties of liberal theory has been that maximizing everyone's individual autonomy destroys the sense of community and the public interest. Kemmis tries to balance individualism by the development of community through self-critical debate. Thus action research by and for participants becomes a preferred method of investigation. In a sense with Kemmis's principles one begins to leave naturalistic evaluation and enter the realm of participatory evaluation, to move from an epistemological position to a political one.

An Evolutionary View of Educational Improvement[1]

Robert E. Stake
University of Illinois

As educational researchers and program evaluators, we are interested in improving instructional practice. In this chapter I will present an argument that naturalistic enquiry has been a *neglected element* in facilitating change and improvement in practice. In Brazil, as around the world, there is great desire to improve education, but also a reluctance to use our national treasuries for doing so. We need make the most of our research effort. And we need to realize the special need for an evolutionary style of correction, avoiding the implantation of devices and techniques into systems which cannot adapt to them.

Almost 200 years ago Immanuel Kant observed:

> ... the whole mechanism of education has no coherence if it is not designed in agreement with a well-weighed plan, ... it might behoove the state likewise to reform itself from time to time and, attempting evolution instead of revolution, progress perpetually toward the better.[2]

Evolutionary change is gradual, internally 'planned,' in harmony with the organic system, and adaptive to the habitat. I want to draw special attention to the choice between evolutionary change and 'creationist' change. The Moral Majority creationists sometimes call it 'cataclysmic' change. It is the kind of change exemplified by switching suddenly from traditional teaching to *Man: A Course of Study* or to 'competency based education.' Much of our course development work is based on a creationist notion of change. I prefer an evolutionary change, or at least, for any one organization, finding a better balance between evolutionary change and creationist change.

Later in the chapter I will present a schematic theory of action. I will connect naturalism and evolutionary change to teaching and administrative practice.

We researchers-evaluators-developers-consultants engage in serious business. We deal with people's lives — not only the lives of young people, but of teachers and other adults. We deliberately try to *change* them, and seldom exactly as they would change themselves. We interfere with their lives, convinced we are helping them toward something better. We are opposed to coercion, yet unattentive to the moral complexity of entice-ment. In the process of change how much should we give people opportunity to approve, to participate in controlling, the changes we would make in their lives? Contemplating, we will recognize that an evolutionary point of view (though of course not an assurance of it) can bolster self-determination.

In this chapter I will allude to a recurring science-education controversy in public schools in the United States involving the teaching of evolution of the species.

Anyone who examines the instructional technology literature and the operations research literature on 'planned change'[3] might come to the conclusion that there are only two ways to progress to the better: one way being to obtain *better information* and use it more rationally; the other way being to come to deeper *understanding of one's 'self'* and to find better ways of relating to and communicating with one's associates.

In the first way, the required better information is assumed to come from scientific studies which approximate — as nearly as conditions allow — the experiments of the natural sciences. A more rational use of this information requires carefully drawn plans with clearly stated goals and schedules. The second commonly recognized path to improvement in-volves self-analysis by individuals or groups, often guided by psycho-therapeutic expertise, and usually under conditions removing constraint on expression of personal feeling. There is merit to each of these remedies, and each can be carried to excess.

Almost absent from mention in the 'change literature' is the *common* way in which improvement *is* accomplished, a way followed intuitively by the greatest, and the least, of our thinkers. It is the experiential way, an evolutionary way, recognized particularly by John Dewey.[4] One may change practice when *new experience* causes re-examination of problems: Intuitively we start thinking of alternative solutions.

I observe that this third method of planned change regularly occurs, and that it is at least as important as the other two. I believe that program improvement efforts should more often rely upon the experiences and intuitions of the practitioners involved. I am *not*, on this occasion, advocating 'action research', which is research carried on by practit-ioners.[5] I *am* urging the design of studies to be carried out by trained researchers, carried out in such a way as to provide vicarious experience to the readers, done so that they easily combine new experience with old. One might say it is buying into the 'case method' of instruction. The role of the program evaluator or educational researcher on these occasions is to assist practitioners in reaching new experiential understandings, which in previous writing[6] I have called 'naturalistic generalization.'

One would expect this approach usually to lead to *evolutionary change* rather than to a replacement kind of change. In the literature on reform of social and educational practice it is regularly implied that problems are better dealt with by implanting new parts externally-created than by correcting practice. Here I call for aid to the *self*-correction of practice.

Before discussing evolutionary change and naturalistic generalization further, let me reflect on efforts to change educational practice in the United States. Most actual change continues to occur by the action of the individual instructor. But 'planned change' is usually thought of as an institutional or government responsibility. We have a thirty-year history of federal involvement in projects aimed at creating change in schools. These projects have ranged from the writing of new curricular materials, to creation of new programs for teacher education, to devizing new models for administering educational programs. Reviewing federal project rationales, Charles Lindblom and David Cohen[7] noted a heavy reliance on the aggregation of *new knowledge*. Researchers, developers, and evaluators were commissioned to produce new knowledge which was 'supposed to replace the ordinary and presumably deficient knowledge of local practitioners.'[8]

Concurrently with these federal projects, the schools and colleges felt pressures generated by a society facing serious dislocations. Professional people found their training insufficient, academics found old knowledge challenged. Even without external pressure almost all educational practitioners have felt needs for change. Many have wanted a greater opportunity to teach what they are good at teaching; many have wanted a greater security from overexpectation. Education is a presumptious profession. Often a practitioner never learns a task's ending. That needed feeling of accomplishment and completion is often lacking. A student's literacy is a life-long reaching. A faculty introduces a new curriculum but never finds out how far beyond nominal acceptance the teaching is changed. A teacher's time-tested exercises become of doubtful value, especially with changing ethnicities in the classroom.

Into uncertainty the educator plunges, clutching textbook or management plan, hoping to survive, hoping to help others survive. There is no way such a professional can be successful — however she defines success — with all problems, perhaps not even with the majority of them. Such a professional lives with the niggling sensation that she could do more, ought to do more. For most educational practitioners in my world, there exists an internal pressure to change, to improve, to do better next time.

During these thirty years we had across the country major federal projects and institutional pressures aimed at producing new knowledge to improve our universities and schools; *and* within their faculties a desire to change. One might expect this combination to assure a significant change. Lay observers and professionals alike, including Tom Hastings, David Cohen and John Goodlad, concluded, however, that it did not happen.

For one thing, within faculties there has not been a consensus as to needed direction and degree of change. The federal programs resulted in much less desired change than hoped for. I think the dominant research and development model was partly at fault.

Overemphasis on Knowledge-Based Change

It was curriculum specialist Madeleine Grumet[9] who said,

> What is most fundamental to our lives as men and women sharing a moment on this planet is the process of reproducing ourselves.

She was speaking of teachers and professors as well as parents. But she saw us parents and teachers as I do, more as builders of the nest, arrangers of cognitive furniture, actors in the same play — with a hand occasionally on the sculptor's chisel, but never as the *'creators'* of education. Enablers sometimes, but not creators. All important, yes, but not creators.

[Let me insert here that I think that it makes just as little sense to talk about *student learnings* as 'created' or 'produced'. Some of us in our technological roles get carried away by the notions of Genesis, expectations that we control what registers in a learner's mind. Learning is no more the creation of educationists than is the Atlantic Ocean the creation of the Amazon River.]

I am distressed by curriculum-builders who see curricula *created* by authors of guidebooks, textbooks, objectives lists, and by those who see the curriculum *created* by teachers. As is manifestly apparent in the extensive classroom studies of John Goodlad[10], the curriculum is not created — it exists.

It exists ever-changing, even in the most traditional schools, ever-changing — little because formal knowledges advance, changing more because learners create new images of themselves, with each group of youngsters forcefully different from last year's. The curriculum is ever-changing, more with the change in our social technology, changing only in some small degree by educators who strive to make it better.

It is true of course that:

Research can evoke Knowledge which leads to Improved Practice

But perhaps because education is so 'knowledge-oriented' many of us have a tenacious expectation that KNOWLEDGE can make sick education well, or primitive education modern. In a review of the impact of curriculum research a few years ago Edmund Short of Penn State said:

a number of researchers have redefined the scope of the phenomena and have conceived it, not as a problem of 'research into
practice,' but as one of 'knowledge production and utilization.'[11]

In my mind appears the image of two towering enterprises,
KNOWLEDGE PRODUCTION and KNOWLEDGE UTILIZA-
TION, rising high, reaching out to one another, perhaps to form a golden
arch. It is an attractive image, particularly to someone justifying a research
budget or planning the implementation of a newly-written curriculum.
Certainly, this is sometimes the right model for managing research,
attempting to maximize the production of knowledge that would facilitate
a new consideration of practice. (And certainly, in retrospect, changes in
practice can almost always be described in terms of changes of
knowledge.)

But according to Short's findings, backed up more recently by
Lindblom and Cohen[12] and Carol Weiss[13], knowledge production and
knowledge utilization are seldom enjoined. Teachers and administrators
have little use for most research reports, and for the new knowledge
produced by large-scale change projects.

A frequent response to this situation is to assume people just do not
know how to understand research findings. Allen Schmieder, an official in
Washington, once commented:

> Very few people are professionally trained to build on research
> findings, or to market good educational ideas.[14]

What is needed — it seemed — was still another enterprise, *Knowledge
Dissemination*, to provide a scaffolding to connect our two towers.

It is a dream that distracts from the task at hand.

Directing attention to knowledge production and dissemination
diminishes attention to practice. Building the ERIC system and other
information services in the US appears to have increased the orientation to
researcher constructs and diminished emphasis on practice. Some policy
studies should continue to ask, 'Research into practice — how?'. But those
enquiries are unlikely to succeed in changing practice. The research
enterprise will be insufficiently useful as long as researchers have little
interest in studying the entwining, personalistic, and crisis-like problems
of daily practice. Unfortunately, researchers tend to conceptualize new
systems as ones that would operate in orderly circumstances and with
dispassionate practitioners. Planners have been fascinated with
schemata[15], with sophisticating technology. Unlike practitioners, and the
helpers of practitioners, the dissemination researcher's goal has not been
the well-being of daily practice.

Sometimes the well-being of daily practice requires changed practice,
sometimes preserved practice, but always an emphasis on practice. The
end-product desired is not knowledge-about-practice or any of the formal

generalizations most researchers strive for. Formal knowledge is *not* necessarily a stepping stone to improved practice. Such knowledge may be helpful in the long run, but for *each* educational situation the importance of formal knowledge about teaching or about administration remains to be demonstrated.[16]

According to Michael Polanyi[17] and Donald Schon[18] practice is guided largely by personal knowings, based on and gleaned from personal experience. And change in pedagogical or administrative practice, or resistance to change, is often rooted in a sense of personal protection, even survival. Because of this personal aspect it will sometimes be more useful for research itself to be designed so that:

Research can evoke Vicarious Experience which leads to Improved Practice.

You in my audience may prefer to define vicarious experience as just another form of knowledge, so that this latter statement does not conflict with the one before. But as spelled out by Polanyi the kind of knowings generated by experiencing, whether direct or vicarious, are different from the knowings which come from encounter with articulated statements of knowledge. The knowings which arise from experience are more tacit, contextual, personalistic. These are self-generated knowings, *naturalistic generalizations*, that come when, individually for each person, for each practitioner, new experience is added to old.

Formal research reports *may* contain the detailed description necessary to generate vicarious experience for readers, thereby modifying the reader's ever-developing naturalistic generalizations. But the author of the formal research report seldom assumes a commitment to facilitate this vicarious experience. Naturalistic case studies[19] *are* impelled by this commitment. The naturalistic researcher presents an exhibit of raw data — portrayals of actual teaching and learning problems, witnessing of observers who understand the reality of the classroom, words of the people involved. These raw data provide readers with vicarious experiences which interact with existing naturalistic generalizations formed from previous experience. Naturalistic research leads to vicarious experience.

Vicarious Experience

The vicar is a substitute, performing a service for those not well-placed to perform for themselves. The naturalistic researcher observes and records what readers are not placed to observe for themselves, but who, when reading the descriptive account, can experience vicariously the various perplexities and efforts to remedy. Mary Lee Smith, one of the 'vicars' of our *Case Studies in Science Education,* quoted a science teacher in Colorado:

> Teachers are extension of the parent and as such should teach the value system that is consistent with the community. The community has a vested interest in the schools, and has a right to demand that certain values be taught and certain others not to be taught.[20]

And a teacher in rural Illinois told field-researcher Alan Peshkin:

> I've been accused of being a Communist and an atheist. Once the science teacher and I brought two classes together to discuss Darwin. We were studying the twenties in history and talking about the Scopes trial. A few periods later a kid came by and asked if I was an atheist. These students are riled by a discussion of evolution.[21]

Situations such as these of high school science teaching can be studied by researchers either in knowledge-producing *or* experience-producing ways.[22] A researcher whose aim is to create formal generalizations, propositional generalizations, would probably do a content analysis of these quotations, attending to a few key variables such as 'curriculum authenticity' and 'teacher sensitivity.' Such a researcher seldom presents personal testimony as evidence. The data to be collected are more directly representative of the stated hypotheses, more in the form of pre-selected variables. Situational and contextual information often are considered irrelevant.

For the experience-evoking kind of research, for naturalistic-generalization-inviting research, a wider net is cast — gathering direct testimony, 'thick descriptions,'[23] time-bound, place-bound, personality-bound information, data of a phenomenological bent. The naturalistic researcher chooses the most coherent and immediately relevant information and puts it — in more-or-less natural state — into the resulting report.

Certainly, naturalistic researchers must focus and delimit their study, attending to one or a few major issues. But naturalistic researchers will present the data in more, rather than less, natural form, leaving in the richness and ambiguity and conflict which are part of ordinary experience. The readers then can weigh the given data against their own experience and perhaps confront previous interpretations and temper convictions formerly held. Changes affecting the naturalistic generalizations of each reader may relate to the interpretations of the researcher, but they may be in response to aspects of the data not considered by the researcher. Consider, for example, the nuances and suggestions which come to mind because of the quoted teacher's concern about being called an 'atheist.' An administrator's naturalistic generalization might be: 'I can't leave the teachers alone to work out such sensitive issues with the public.' A teacher's might be: 'Most students are terribly dependent on a teacher to deal rationally with the science-religion controversy.' Such contextualized vignettes inform the practitioner much differently than do comparisons of groups on variables.

If the classroom practice of a teacher becomes something tomorrow it otherwise would not have been, convictions may have been altered by such vicarious experience as a naturalistic research report evokes. More of our research should be objective study serving the teacher's subjective experience. To quote Thomas Flanagan in *The Year of the French*:

> We possess ideas, but we are possessed by feelings. They lie too deep for understanding, astir with their own secret life, and carrying us with them.[24]

The Determinants of Action

Evoking vicarious experience may be useful — you might say — but is it really the place to make our investment? To consider the alternative investments of educational research let us survey the various ways a researcher might facilitate practice. Let us carefully analyze the determinants of action. Keep in mind the outcome is action — or more specifically, professional practice.

Action

The practitioner or actor, for example, a teacher or administrator, is someone responsible, in part, for an educational 'system,' for example, a classroom, a state department of education. This person is moved to act, to change an activity, to refrain from acting, or to resist acting, only when sufficient external demand or internal conviction arises. Otherwise inertia keeps her doing the same as before.

Most efforts to change educational action, certainly most of those supported by state and federal agencies in the USA, have been authoritarian in orientation. An 'order' to change is issued from higher administrative level, often as a condition for receiving certain funding. The literature on program innovation discusses the problems of such mandates. Some of these external demands come softened and sweetened with attractive workshops or fellowships for practitioners.

Figure 1.

But still, practitioners consistently reject (often by non-acknowledgement) new approaches, reorganizations, or curriculum reforms, even when use is mandated. For good or bad, the supervisory system is just too weak to guarantee compliance. External demand is weaker than most people think, and almost no demand can be impressed by the research community. If research is to influence, usually it will be via change in the practitioner's convictions.

In our *Case Studies in Science Education* we found that reforms were rejected in secondary school classrooms mostly because the new teaching styles did not leave teachers in command of responsibilities they considered critical, including those of fostering student obedience and seeing adolescence as a time of preparation.[25] These organized change-efforts fell short in part because personal experience and conviction were not accommodated. A practitioner's convictions are influenced by *understanding* and *voluntarism*. Voluntarism is a basis of action rooted in faith and personal feeling — conation ranging from momentary impulse to abiding devotion. The research community tries to influence practitioners' feelings, especially about rationality and technology, but its opportunities to influence understanding are much greater than its opportunities to influence feeling.

Figure 2.

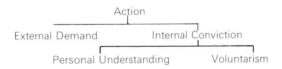

In his book *Explanation and Understanding*[26] Finnish philosopher George Henrik von Wright stressed that understanding is arrived at through dialogue and rumination, drawing from pools of knowledge both experiential and propositional. Or as I indicate in the schematic, personal understanding comes from both naturalistic and formalistic generalizations.

Figure 3.

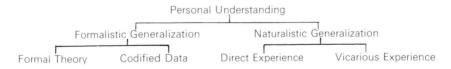

Continuing the analysis, we might say that theory and codified data are the main constituents of our formal, verbalized generalizations — whereas experience, real and vicarious, is the main constituent of the naturalistic generalizations. The interaction of determinants of action of course is

much more complex and turbulent than shown here; yet these representations should help us identify points at which there may be infusion from
research. In the first half of this chapter I argued that our efforts to
provide formalistic generalization through theory and empirical data have
had too little impact on practitioners. Little, on the other hand, has been
tried by researchers to influence practitioner *experience*.

Here now is my combined schematic diagram of the determinants of
action. If we consider every entry point, if we consider every major
leverage available to the researcher to influence practice, *one* stands out as
neglected, an undercultivated category of knowledge. It is the disciplined
collection of that experiential knowledge that might lead a reader
vicariously to naturalistic generalization.

Figure 4.

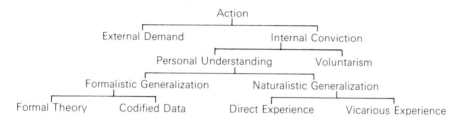

I note again that in their reports and research designs, educational
researchers emphasize formal generalizations, explanations. Those knowings are indeed essential to communication and in a complex world,
essential to practice, but they are too exclusively relied on by researchers
and educational authorities, too regularly presumed to be preferable
messages.

The intention of most educational research is to provide formalistic
generalization. A typical research report might highlight the correlation
between time spent on team projects *and* gain in scores on an achievement
test. The report might identify personality, affective and demographic
variables. Even with little emphasis on causation this report is part of the
grand explanation of student learning. It provides one way of knowing
about educational practice.

A more naturalistic research report might deal with the same topic,
perhaps with the same teachers and pupils, yet reflecting a different
epistemology. The naturalistic data would describe the actual interactions
within student teams. The report would probably portray project work —
conveying style, context, and evolution. A person would be described as
an individual, with uniqueness not just in deviant scores, but as a key to
understanding the interactions. A reader senses the experience of team-
work in this particular situation. It is a *unique* situation in some respects,
but ordinary in other respects. Readers recognize similarities with

situations of their own. Perhaps they are stimulated to think of old problems in a new way.

Curriculum evaluation and instructional research *can* be organized, by intent and with sophistication, to provide the raw data to furnish vicarious experience which should help the reader/practitioner develop new naturalistic generalizations to guide practice.

In this chapter I have *not* suggested that teachers and administrators are impervious to change suggested by formal knowledge. Some will respond, for example, to the essay of a curriculum specialist, others to an article documenting student attitude scores. Some instructors respond well to logic, codified data, and regulatory statement — but usually too few of them to satisfy campuswide and nationwide need for change.

Practitioners can be moved by what fellow practitioners elsewhere are experiencing, by what community residents expect, and by how their students respond. In one of our rural secondary schools the science teacher said:

> Evolution has never come up as an issue. I don't know. My personal view is probably 'safe.' I don't see any divergence between the theory of evolution and a religious viewpoint. I suppose I'm not really radical. Maybe that's the reason I haven't had any 'feedback.' If I were an atheist, I suppose *that* might present a problem. And the students don't make it a problematic discussion either. Never had any one do that. Here again, our students are pretty much of one mind. They're pretty 'closed' in the ideas they have. I've barely had any 'feedback' from the community.[27]

Now think again of the teacher quoted by Peshkin a few pages back. She too was moved-to-act by student response, but her reaction was quite different from that of this teacher. Each decision as to how to treat 'Evolution' in science class is influenced by particular experiences. Teachers will react, but not always of course in the way that specialists in 'planned-change' desire. Providing more opportunity for naturalistic generalization is not likely to increase the uniformity of practice. But improvement and standardization are separate and different goals, of course.

Research which attends to the complexity and contextuality of daily practice can reasonably aspire to provide the best possible knowledge for in-service education, i.e., for modifying practice. According to Lawrence Stenhouse, a British curriculum specialist:

> ... in-service development needs curriculum development and research in teaching. The error has been to see in-service education as the servant of curriculum reform rather than curriculum as a research field to serve in-service education.[28]

My argument that vicarious-experience data are neglected knowledge for the understanding and improvement of practice has a political side effect — which I should mention again. To emphasize the uniqueness of each classroom is to support autonomy for the classroom teacher.

But the argument for 'naturalistics' is not primarily political, nor humanistic. It is pragmatic. Even in situations where teachers are pleading, as were CSSE teachers, for someone else to specify their curricular responsibilities[29], it is likely that neither parent nor state will be served if external demands on the teacher are inconsistent with their convictions. We cannot expect a substantial change in practice if teachers and administrators lack understanding of new problems and new needs.

In the science classes of the United States and in the rural schools of Brazil we find few teachers expecting that researchers can provide either formal generalizations or vicarious experience capable of helping them solve their problems. Substantive change often will require arrangement of circumstances in which teachers engage in solitary and mutual self-study, i.e., action research. But action research needs more than first-hand knowledge and immediate experience. It needs problem representations and experiential descriptions that disciplinary-based researchers can provide[30]. To generate that back-up research is the plea of this article.

Our assistance of course needs to accommodate career-long investments-in-practice the teachers have already made. They cannot be expected to sacrifice much in the way of technical readiness or social standing in the adventitious hope that students would learn better. But vicarious experience, if relevant and interesting, is widely accepted by teachers and other practitioners. Thus this rationale that new vicarious experience might mix with old, and lead to evolutionary changes in conviction and practice.

To summarize then: we have seen that many efforts to produce change in the schools have failed to do so, frequently despite practitioner desire to change. It appears this is partly because the major ways of implementing planned change have been rejected by practitioners. Among researchers the dominant belief is that formal generalizations are the essential ingredient of improved practice. Too often they have designed new, perhaps theory-based, programs rather than modifying practice within its relatively fixed context. Researchers should have a stronger sense of both the appetite for change *and* the survival instincts of our teachers and administrators.

My argument has been that practice is largely guided by tacit knowing, by naturalistic generalization, formed from experiencing, often implicit. Formative evaluation and other change-effort research has often failed to honor naturalistic generalization. Too seldom has it presented practitioners with the vicarious experience which helps alter conviction and practice. Evolutionary change is slow, but it can capitalize on a still remaining abundance of fitness, uniqueness, personal understanding and a universal desire to survive.

Notes

1 This chapter was the keynote presentation at the National Symposium on Evaluation, Federal University of Espirito Santo, Vitoria, Brazil, August 1984. Earlier versions had appeared as 'Naturalistic generalizations' by myself and Deborah Trumbell in the *Review Journal of Philosophy and Social Science*, VII, 1982 and as 'Generalizations', a paper presented at the Annual Meeting of the American Educational Research Association, April 1980. My interest in an evolutionary approach was first awakened by Tom Hastings' ideas of the role of program evaluation in instructional research and nursed along by Stephen Kemmis' 1976 University of Illinois dissertation, 'Evaluation and the evolution of knowledge about educational programs'.

2 From a 1798 essay entitled 'An old question raised again: Is the human race constantly progressing?' and quoted here from translations edited by BECK, L.W. (1963) *On History*, Indianapolis, Bobbs-Merrill, p. 152.

3 See for example the summative review by FULLAN, M. (1982) *The Meaning of Educational Change*, NYC, Teachers College Press; and management science literature emphasizing group dynamics since Kurt Lewin.

4 DEWEY, J. (1916) *Democracy and Education*, NYC, Macmillan.

5 As usually defined, action research has *practitioners* planning, changing practice, observing and reflecting. See for example, 'Action research: notes on the national seminar' by BROWN, L., HENRY, C., HENRY, J.A. and McTAGGART, R. (1982) in *Classroom Action Research Network Bulletin*, 5, Cambridge Institute of Education.

6 STAKE, R.E. (1978) 'The case study method in social inquiry', *Educational Researcher*, 7, 2, February, pp. 5–8.

7 LINDBLOM, C.E. and COHEN, D.K. (1979) *Usable Knowledge: Social Science and Social Problem Solving*, New Haven, Yale University Press.

8 Quoted in COWDEN, P. and COHEN, D.K. (1979) *Divergent Words of Practice: The Federal Reform of Local School in the Experimental Schools Program*, Cambridge, Mass, Center for the Study of Public Policy, summer.

9 GRUMET, M. (1980) 'Conception, contradiction and curriculum', paper presented at the Annual Meeting of the American Educational Research Association, Boston, April.

10 See GOODLAD, J. (1984) *A Place Called School*, NYC, McGraw Hill.

11 SHORT, E.C. (1973) 'Status of knowledge production and utilization in curriculum', paper presented at the Annual Meeting of the American Educational Research Association, New Orleans, February.

12 *Ibid.*

13 WEISS, C. (Ed.) (1977) *Using Social Research in Public Policy Making*, Lexington, Mass, Lexington Heath.

14 SCHMIEDER, A.A. (1975) *Journal of Teacher Education*, spring, pp. 18–23.

15 THORNDYKE, P.W. (1981) *Schema Theory as a Guide for Educational Research: White Knight or White Elephant?*, Rand Paper Series, March 1981. Invited address presented at the Annual Meeting of the American Educational Research Association, Los Angeles, April.

16 See ATKIN, J.M. (1973) 'Practice-oriented inquiry: A third approach to research in education, *Educational Researcher*, 2, pp. 3–4.

17 POLANYI, M. (1958) *Personal Knowledge*, Chicago, University of Chicago Press.
18 SCHON, D. (1982) *The Reflective Practitioner: How Professionals Think in Action*, NYC, Basic Books.
19 See my entry 'Case study' in NISBET, J. (Ed.) (1985) *World Yearbook of Education*.
20 In STAKE, R. and EASLEY, J (Eds) (1978) *Case Studies in Science Education*, Urbana, Ill, CIRCE, University of Illinois, Booklet II, Volume I, pp. 2–13.
21 *Ibid*, STAKE, R.E. and EASLEY, J., Booklet IV, Volume I, pp. 4–51.
22 This is not quite the distinction made by Cronbach and Suppes between conclusion-based and decision-based research. Both they and I have been attentive to: whose thinking is climatic, researchers or practitioners? But they accentuated differences in 'problems' pursued in research and practice, whereas I am accentuating differences in epistemological structure between formalized abstraction and informal experience. See their (1969) *Research for Tomorrow's Schools: Disciplined Inquiry for Education*, New York, Macmillan.
23 See GEERTZ, G. (1973) *The Interpretation of Culture*, NYC, Basic Books.
24 FLANAGAN, T. (1979) *The Year of the French*, New York, Holt, Rinehart and Winston.
25 STAKE, R.E. and EASLEY, J. (Eds) XIII, 16–3.
26 Von WRIGHT, G.H. (1971) *Explanation and Understanding*, London, Routledge and Kegan Paul.
27 STAKE, R.E. and EASLEY, J., *op cit.*, Booklet IV, Volume I, pp. 4–11.
28 STENHOUSE, L. 'Review of the status of precollege science, mathematics, and social studies educational practice in US schools', Norwich, England, Centre for Applied Research in Education, University of East Anglia, unpublished manuscript.
29 STAKE, R.E. and EASLEY, J. *op cit.*, XII, pp. 14–22.
30 In his theory of action Jurgen Habermas presupposed a 'real relationship of communicating (and cooperating) investigators, where each of the sub-systems is part of the surrounding social systems, which in turn are the result of the sociocultural evolution of the human race', (1974) *Theory and Practice*, (translated by John Viertel), London, Heinemann, p. 14.

Three Good Reasons for Not Doing Case Studies in Curriculum Research

Rob Walker
Deakin University, Australia

While case-study methods of research have a long history of use in educational enquiry, they have a particular attraction for those with an interest in curriculum for, in curriculum research, case studies offer a means of integration across the disciplines of the social sciences. They also offer an emphasis on synthesis rather than on analysis and a means of approaching hidden curriculum, informal social structures and unintended consequences of action on the same terms as formal curriculum, social, and management structures. In other words, those who share a view of the curriculum field as organized around issues rather than around theories, find in case study an empirical genre appropriately flexible, eclectic and capable of creating surprises.

The view of curriculum studies as organized around analysis of issues has undoubtedly been stimulated by the experience of the curriculum development movement and, perhaps curiously, in no way diminished by its demise. The past ten years has, therefore, seen the development of increased interest in case-study research,[1,2] an interest often associated with a particular view of curriculum research as 'process',[3] for this view lends itself least easily to conventional research approaches.

The attraction of case-study research also derives from a central dilemma in the curriculum field, for in recent years (in Britain, Australasia and the USA at least) we have seen a number of attempts to centralize and to standardize what is taught in schools at specified age and grade levels. Paradoxically, this growing tendency toward centralization has been accomplished by an apparent growth of diversity in the curriculum practice of individual schools and individual classrooms. In this context, case studies offer both some measure of diversity, and of the processes which give rise to it (and so to the administrator and the politician they may appear to promise some measure of control). To those at the periphery, case studies seem to celebrate diversity and so to endorse it, often when other avenues to legitimacy offer less promise of progress.

It will be clear from what I have written that I have a view of case-study research in curriculum as marked by the attempt to get beyond illustrative examples of more general phenomena to the particularities and idiosyncracies of the instance, though not necessarily to turn to social science theory in the process. Case studies are, to me, primarily documentary and descriptive in character, but are marked by the attempt to reach across from the experience of those who are the subjects of study to those who are the audience. As so conceived, case studies are not limited to an illustrative role in relation to current theorizing, but may be one step ahead of it.

One of the incidental qualities of case studies is that they usually reveal that the person writing them is, to an extent, changed by doing the research and this is reflected in the present chapter, which draws on my own attempts to try and do case-study research. It is written less for those who are looking for a justification for case-study research, than it is for those who, like me, feel the end is justifiable but who have difficulties with the means. Its focus is on what some might call methodology; it is about the practical, and it is written in the hope that it might help others be successful where I have failed.

A Common Problem

Given the aspirations of the kind of case-study research I have outlined, a common problem is how to get beyond routine data to the stories that make the case come to life. This is an especially common problem in interviewing, where people often find it hard to break out of the constraint of telling you what they think you want (or ought) to know in order to tell you what you want to hear. Most of us more or less consciously adopt tactics for trying to close down one line of discussion in order to open up other, quite different lines. Barry MacDonald, for example, has a favourite question. When the interviewee is in full flight in what to the interviewer is a wrong direction, Barry will pause, look hard at the interviewee, and ask; 'But what keeps you *awake* at night?' This sharp break in formal discourse allows people to recollect their thoughts and to set out in the direction of a more personal and intimate discussion. It is an effective question. So effective I find myself asking the same question in relation to research. Like many of those who write in what loosely is called the 'naturalistic tradition' I tend to talk and write a lot about methods of research; but what keeps me awake at night? The truth is, very little, but over the years there have been a number of occasions when things have gone wrong in the course of carrying out case studies and this paper started out simply as a list of the events that have troubled me to the point where I lay awake worrying about them. As I thought about them and talked about them the list narrowed to three headings: three good reasons for not doing case-study research. They are that:

(a) Case-study research is an intervention, and often an uncontrolled intervention, in the lives of others.
(b) Case-study research provides a biased view, a distorted picture of the way things are.
(c) Case-study research is essentially conservative.

In the rest of the chapter I shall fill out each of these headings with examples before asking myself if three good reasons for not doing case-study research are in fact enough to stop me doing it.

An Uncontrolled Intervention in the Lives of Others

It is something of a paradox that, while we tend to fret at our failure as researchers/evaluators to get the messages through to those in policy-forming positions (see, for instance, Jenkins *et al.*[4]), we simultaneously face the problem that research/evaluation is highly intrusive in the lives of those who are its subjects. Indeed one of the main reasons why so much of the literature is taken up with pursuing questions of a methodological kind is in order to find ways of reducing the threat of intervention.

To take the simplest examples, to interview someone, to observe someone teaching, to talk with teachers about the head, or with pupils about teaching, are each potentially undermining of the façades which individuals and institutions construct in order to make the management of schooling possible. Those who have done research in schools will know and recognize the power of the interview as a means of intervention in the lives of others; an intervention often denied but no less real for that. And it is important to stress that intervention does not need to be an aspiration on the part of the interviewer in order for its effect to be felt. It is in the nature of the situation that power is vested in the questioner. The *kinds* of questions that are asked are usually enough to set trains of thought going in the interviewee's head that do not stop when the interview ends. Those who have been interviewed will know that it is quite common, for some hours, or even days after the interview has ended to keep rethinking lines of thought that first came to light in the interview itself. The question is a powerful tool for change, sometimes more powerful than the recommendation or the conclusion.

The same is true of being observed. The fact of being observed alone is enough to heighten some self-perceptions and sensitivities at the cost of others, even when the observer gives little clue as to what is being looked for. And while the literature often reports the problem of access and acclimatization (which are essentially researchers' problems), other problems are associated with the processes of exit and withdrawal, especially when the observation takes place over long periods of time.

This much is perhaps common knowledge, but when I think about the things that have gone wrong in research studies I have done, a number of them fall into the category of uncontrolled intervention. An example might help.

Some time ago I did a school case-study in order to try out the notion of 'condensed fieldwork' which Barry MacDonald and I devized as a key method for use in applying naturalistic approaches within evaluation studies (see MacDonald and Walker[5]). The plan was that I should make a one-day visit to the school in order to explain the study and return sometime later to make a three-day data-collection field visit; then I would write up the first draft of the 'case study', take it back to the school for comment and spend a further three days collecting responses and further data as directed by the school. The final case study would be a rewrite of the first draft taking into account all that this account stimulated by way of a response.

Compared to conventional 'ethnographic' field studies, the model here was intentionally interventive in character, but the intention of the design was to control the intervention by use of an extensive set of procedures for the uses made of information. Each of the subjects was promised total confidentiality during the initial fieldwork phase, in the sense that any information that was to go into the first draft of the case study would be sent to them so that they could examine it for relevance, fairness and accuracy, and so that they had an opportunity to edit and to censor any parts they did not want to be seen by their colleagues. At the second stage, the school as a whole was offered the opportunity to make similar changes to the draft before it was seen by anyone outside.

The first phase went reasonably well. I spent three days in the school, mainly tape-recording interviews with teachers. I returned to the University and spent three weeks writing up the first draft of the study from the transcripts, organizing the report in such a way that I could take the sections back to the individuals concerned before collating a version for the school to see. Past experience had though led me to some worries about this kind of design. As David Jenkins has pointed out, although the design makes it sound as though a lot of power is being handed to the subjects of the study, in practice, because the researcher/evaluator actually holds the information, all kinds of ploys and suspicions can come into play.[6] The effect can be to feed the power of the researcher, perhaps to an even greater extent than in a conventional participant-observation study, where the subjects have greater freedom to withhold commitment to the research enterprise.

In the early phase of the study one problem that worried me particularly was that, in condensing the interview material into a case-study format, I was free to commit all kinds of methodological violence on the data which was difficult for the subjects to control. Simply in translating from the spoken to the written word, in editing out sections and in rearranging the text, it is possible to arrive at meanings that go beyond what the speaker intended. Aware of this problem (and of my penchant for dramatic reconstruction), I duplicated all the tapes and left copies with each of the subjects. As I left the school at the end of day three of the field-work period, I said 'I am going away to write the first draft of the study, but I am taking away with me no more than I have left you. We have equal access to the data. If you are unhappy with what I write for whatever reason, if you think I have misquoted you, misunderstood or misrepresented you, you and I can both return to the tapes to check what has happened and to correct it'.

I admit I felt rather pleased with myself. Because I was aspiring to make the relationship between researchers and their subjects more 'democratic' (see MacDonald and Walker[7]), I felt this device of sharing access to the data was rather a neat one, especially as some of David Jenkins's criticism was still rattling around between my ears. I was also pleased with the idea because it put pressure on me to push past the data into interpretation. The way I saw it, as each teacher already had the data, I had to do more than regurgitate it if I was to retain their interest in the study. I wanted them to read the study and to be surprised by it, and as they already had the data I felt I would have to really work on it to produce accounts they found insightful and interesting. As someone who needs a sense of competition in order to generate motivation, I found this a good device for stimulating my own enthusiasm. I should add that I went to great lengths to stress to each of the teachers that it was important that they keep their tapes to themselves. I said that even if they felt quite happy to share their tapes with their colleagues, I would not want a situation to arise where someone who wanted to suppress what they had said found it difficult to resist staff-room social pressure to pre-release the data. Everybody accepted this as reasonable and agreed to wait until the written reports were available.

When I returned to the school some four weeks later I knew something was wrong. People who had been friendly during the earlier visit ignored me or paid me the minimum of attention. When I started to show people the written reports they were off-hand and dismissive. They did not seem to want to know anything about them. I was puzzled, but by mid-morning the story broke. One of the teachers took me on one side and told me that immediately after my previous visit the head had asked each of them to hand over their tapes. Some refused but eventually gave in. Within a few days the head had all the tapes but one, and locked them in his office.

My response was one of disbelief, followed quickly by confusion. What should I do? Should I confront the head and demand an explanation? Should I wait and see what happened, pretending I didn't know? How could I best rescue the study? Later that day I managed to talk to the head, and to let him know that I knew what had happened without actually confronting him with a sense of anger or disappointment. His explanation was a good one. He had been the last person I had interviewed during the previous visit. He claimed it was only when I talked to him that he realized some of the implications of the questions I had asked other teachers. While he did not object to being asked such things he realized that the total set of the data was potentially explosive. 'But I had promised you I would not show it to anyone until you had a chance to see it, as individuals and as a school', I protested. 'I think I trust you', he said, 'but I am not sure I trust everyone else involved'. The way he saw it there were teachers who might get together and share their tapes and find ways of using them that were not in what he saw as the interest of the school. As head, he did not feel he could take the risk of having such information loose in the school while I was 'away in the university'. If something went wrong, he argued, he had to be in control of the situation. If information leaked to the local press or to the office, he had to know what was happening. He realized he had broken the procedures of the research, but claimed that he had a greater responsibility for the running of the school, which overrode any agreements he might have with me.

It was a direct collision between the 'democratic' model built-in to the design of the research, and a bureaucratic model built-in to the organization of the school. It caused me some anguish and loss of sleep. I recovered the situation enough to be able to complete the study. I don't think that any of the teachers suffered as a result of what happened or the school was in any way changed by the events I had precipitated, though whether the school let any later researchers through the door I don't know. I certainly haven't left any tapes behind anywhere since.

There is another kind of intervention that case-study research can make into people's lives, and that is intervention that cuts the other way, across the researcher's side of the counter. I have recently completed a case study of the work of a local authority advisory team. My interest is in the observational work of advisers and inspectors. What kind of opportunities do they get to observe schools and classes? What do they look for? What kinds of infomation do they collect? What do they do with the information when they have got it? For two years I followed one team of advisers around schools, into meetings and into the office in order to understand better how those in a field role in a large social service organization function as the 'eyes and ears' of the Authority.[8]

Before I began, people warned me I would have a lot of problems with access and with the release of data, partly because the area is a sensitive one and partly because advisers constitute a relatively high-status occupational group. With this in mind I again designed the research to maximize the control that the subjects had over the use of the data. Part way through the study I became worried about the situation I was in, and in an annual progress report I wrote to the sponsors that, while I was collecting a lot of interesting material, I could not promise to make it available either in the period of the grant or in the final report, because, given its sensitivity, the advisers were unlikely to give me permission to use it. No researcher likes to hide good data, any more than journalists like to sit on a good story. But I was going further still. I was telling a funding agency whose good (tax-payers') money I had spent, that I was unlikely to deliver the goods I promised in the proposal. No-one likes offending funding agencies, especially at the present time, though perhaps tenured members of university faculty should feel free to take such risks. What is more worrying is the consequence of my loss of credibility in the research community among those of my colleagues who may be looking to me for their next contract. Among researchers I am in a privileged position, but I feel a keen sense of responsibility to those who do not share it. Case-study research carries some high risks, one of which is apparently just this kind of intervention in the life of researchers, especially those unprotected by regular jobs.

Case Studies Give a Distorted View of the World

Most case studies in education rely heavily on interview material and concentrate their focus on the immediate workings of organizations, particularly schools. As I have already indicated, the interview is a powerful and interventive research tool but it is also highly productive in that it allows you to cover a lot of ground at speed and, given modern recording technology, to emerge with a lot of data from a short field visit. The dangers of relying too heavily on interview data, from the problem of who you select to interview, to what they select to tell you, to how you select what to write, are well rehearsed in the social-science fieldwork literature. They are no less real or important for that, but they are problems well documented elsewhere.

Whatever the recommendations to be found in the standard textbooks in case-study research it is not always as easy to balance interview data against observations as it might seem, especially when the subjects of the study have some control over the process of assembling the study. I recently ran into a classic case of this problem in a case study I worked on with Saville Kushner and Clem Adelman. Part of this study involved a 'portrayal' of a school which served the Spanish-speaking community in an American city: the portrayal being assembled from interviews with the teachers, observations of teaching, and 'field-time' spent in the school. We chose to write up the study using, at one point, a series of transcripts from lessons taught to different classes in order to give some sense of variation within the school; variation in teaching approach, in age/grade/level of the children, in subject area and in bilingual competence.[9]

One of the teachers who taught younger children let us record her lessons and we emerged with a set of transcripts which revealed a competent teacher who strongly emphasized a didactic, instructional approach. Our reading of the transcript was that she did not come over from the transcript alone as very warm or sympathetic, as compared with some of the other teachers. But set against this observational data we had some interview data which showed her in a very different light. She was a nun who had devoted her life to the immigrant community, not just as a teacher, but as a social worker, friend and advocate. She was acutely aware of the problems faced by the children in her class and their families, and highly respected in the community and in the school system. We tried to write around the transcript some of the biographical material we collected in order to give the reader a means of seeing beyond the limited image presented in the transcript. The teacher was distressed by what we did, mainly on a question of principle. As a Catholic she resented any implication that she had worked for any self-serving purpose. At one point in the account we wrote I quoted one of her one-time colleagues describing her as the 'Mother Theresa of the school system'. She wanted this comment removed from the study, in fact she wanted everything removed except the transcript. We tried to persuade her that, to an outsider, the transcript showed her in an unsympathetic light; she was well aware of this, but wanted it that way. 'That is the way I am', she said, 'I can't deny that'. If people misrepresented her because they lacked access to the information that the pupils, parents and other teachers had, which meant they saw her in a different light, she said she felt that was their problem and she had limited sympathy for them.

It was a difficult situation to find a way through. I got locked into it without an escape route, and it was left to Clem and Saville to negotiate some kind of compromise, but it caused me to worry about the consequences of selection. It caused me to worry too about research as an intervention in the lives of others. It was one of those research relationships I mishandled, and it was fortunate that others were involved to resolve it. Usually we work on our own and that route is not available.

When I have told this story as a moral tale it has disturbed those who take a strong view of the sense of responsibility that the researcher owes to the research enterprise. A good deal of the freedom we have, they argue, is contingent on our ability to find the truth and to tell it without fear. In arguing for the need to compromise 'the truth' with the need to protect the subject they say I am not making a methodological point, but one which cuts through to an assumption that is fundamental to the whole enterprise.

As often happens with arguments of this kind I find myself persuaded by the rhetoric, but find the working of its practice less clear-cut than might appear. In the case of the story I have just told it would seem that the end result was a compromise of 'the truth' in order to soften the intervention of the research in the lives of the subjects. But this in itself is only part of the story, for when I look at the final report I have to admit that it is a much better depiction of reality than the overdrawn stereotype I first had in my head of an apparent paradox between the person the teacher is and the way in which she teaches. That paradox was primarily a feature of *my* perception of the reality, and not a good account of the reality itself. As I got to know it better, to think about what I saw, and to talk to others about it, I realized that it was inadequate. So, in the end, it was not just a question of being talked out of a strongly held belief about what was 'true', but of coming to realize that my interpretation was partial and limited and that it did not serve the case study well to make too much of it.

There is a problem of distortion at another level that stems from the heavy emphasis case studies tend to place on what teachers say. As such studies accumulate the interview responses of teachers come to loom large in the image that builds up of the way the system operates. It can be argued that this is no bad thing, and that such a perspective is long overdue, but the problem of balance remains. How much emphasis should be placed on the reports given by teachers as opposed to those given by pupils, by parents, by chief education officers, by civil servants . . .? What often happens, I think, is that those who figure most fully in case studies are those who have, or who are given, most power in the negotiation process that lies behind the writing and release of the study. Those who have little power (for example the pupils) tend not to figure centre stage. Those who have a lot (teachers and head teachers) tend to occupy a lot of space and often to use their position to influence the way they are presented.

In evaluation this is often not a problem, for the evaluation may see itself as providing opportunities for those in schools to make just that kind of use of the studies. Distortion is significant and balance important, but there is little sense of responsibility for any conception of a level of truth that lies behind it. In practice the process of negotiating the account often *is* the process of evaluation.

The distortion problem is more worrying for the case-study worker writing to a research audience, especially when a situation arises where there are two accounts; a public account the school agrees to release, and a private account that it requires the researcher to keep private. Evaluators may be prepared to sign away their right to contribute their own viewpoint within the study so long as they can maintain a position of independence in relation to some overall conception of balance. Researchers, however, usually feel the need, not just to maintain an independent stance, but also for an opportunity to promote what they see as independent view.

If evaluation case studies tend to rely too heavily on interview data, observational research studies often underestimate the significance of what people say, and make too much of what the researcher claims to observe. Either way we end up with very distorted pictures of the way the system works. In the first case we make too much of the perspective of those who are located within the system at certain selected points. In the second we get a view of the way schools and classrooms work which minimizes the significance of the human actors in the situation.

It is difficult to make this criticism as specific as I would like to, because what I am talking about is an image built up from the accumulation of studies and experiences rather than the characteristics of particular studies. But if I can fall back on personal experience again, I worked for several years in what has become known as 'classroom research'. I spent a lot of time closely observing what I had selected as being classrooms with distinctive pupil-teacher relationships, a particular approach to the use of resources, and a learning philosophy that might be typified as 'exploratory' or 'discovery', or 'creative'. I certainly do not regret the time I gave to that research. I learnt an enormous amount and I think it was important research to do. After some time, though, I did begin to get a feeling of unease about the effects of what I was doing. When I asked myself what the purpose of the research was, the answer I gave myself was that it was to understand better what was happening in those classrooms. Here, I told myself, were teachers devizing ways of teaching that marked a break with the way they had been taught, and a break very often with what else was going on in their schools. Set alongside the writings of radical innovators, what was happening in these classrooms had a complexity that made the writings look inadequate. Rather than write polemic that might influence teachers I thought that a strong justification for the research I was doing was that it would both help the teachers I was studying push further along the lines of their own development, and provide others with more valuable 'case studies' than I could find elsewhere in the literature.

That argument sustained my enthusiasm for several years, but there came a time when it looked inadequate. As I began to piece the case studies together I realized that, while it was true they depicted rather well what was happening in the classrooms I had observed and filmed, they also made them extremely vulnerable. I found it harder and harder to write about them because I began to realize that you don't need to assume a conspiracy against innovation in order to locate its enemies: providing an adequate description is enough. I had committed the classic error of what Gouldner rather brutally calls, 'underdog sociology'.

The only way I could 'balance' the account I gave was to pursue the process of documentation throughout the system. The classes I had studied needed to be balanced by equally penetrating studies of locations I hadn't studied. It is not enough to reveal what happens in classrooms if you do not at the same time reveal what is happening in staff meetings, in the head's office, in the local education authority and perhaps in the Department of Education and Science (DES). To be fair you almost need a requirement specifying what would count as 'equal exposure'. This is in part what I mean when I say that case studies give a distorted view of the world. The view they give *always* emphasizes one set of views rather than another; in fact the very power of the case study comes from just that selective bias, especially when the view taken is not one shared by the reader. But when we look at what we have case studied, it seems to me it has nearly always been vulnerable areas of the system: innovations, teachers, classrooms, and schools. Where are the really penetrating case-studies of the DES, of the National Union of Teachers, of local authorities, of examination boards, or of influential academics? The only ones I can find have been suppressed, remain unpublished or are awaiting transformation into history. Most of those academics who have an interest in these areas are too concerned with acting on the stage to risk observing what is happening, and the rest of us tend to leave that responsibility to journalists, who are inevitably limited by time, space and the editor's scissors.

Case Studies are Conservative

I have reached a point where my categories are beginning to merge, as part of what I have said already points to a conservatism built-in to the notion of case-study research. Certainly, in the recent literature what has been case studied has been the margins of the system, and that is particularly true of educational innovations. Not, I hasten to add, that those who have done the studies have wished particularly to increase the vulnerability of innovations to the political process, in fact the contrary is almost certainly true. But that has often been their effect: the unintended consequence of their publication.

Case studies are, though, conservative in a deeper sense than this. It is not simply that case studies of innovations have been used to bring them under control, but that it is in the nature of the case study to embalm what is established practice simply by describing it. The very process of conceiving, writing and publishing a case study solidifies and crystallizes a reality in the minds of readers and writer which is, initially tenuous, fluid and dissolved in another medium. The act of case study (and perhaps of any research) is to describe reality in order to create it. The implicit is made explicit, the intuitive is made self evident and the abstract is made concrete. Once fixed, the case study changes little, but the situations and the people caught in it have moved even before the image is available. The case study is therefore 'conservative' in much the same way that a photograph is conservative. It captures an instant in time and space which can then be held against a moving changing reality. As readers we can turn to Louis Smith's account of Kensington School,[10] Hargreaves' case study,[11] Shipman's account of the Keele Project[12] or MacDonald's studies of Rosehill or of Canon Roberts Schools[13] and read them as though those schools and projects exist now as they did then. The case study freezes something of their vitality for later readers. Yet none of these studies reveal the situations they describe as they are now, they live only in the literature and the minds of their readers.[14]

I have written of this 'conservatism' as though it was a limitation in case-study research. That is because my theme has been to link up aspects of the research that have caused me concern, and one of the aspects of case study that has worried me on several occasions in the past has been a feeling of being overtaken by events. For example, having worked hard to portray the state of a number of curriculum issues in a school, to be told by the school at the fifth draft of the report, 'You've got it. That is right. That is an accurate account of the way things were a year ago. But since then everything has changed'. And while I know it cannot have changed that much, I know in many respects the school is right, and even that the process of writing the case study has contributed to its own redundancy. Even in evaluation, with a strong emphasis placed on fast reporting, we deal in models and images, and even in history, more often than we allow.

Looked at another way this 'conservatism' has more positive aspects, though it involves rethinking the purposes and the possibilities of the enterprise. Just as the still photograph has value as a record, as a point of identification, and as an image in its own right; so the case study has more uses than I think we often allow. The mistake is to assume that the case study is a mirror, rather than to acknowledge that it is analogous to a cumbersome and primitive plate camera that we have scarcely learnt to handle. To continue exploring the potential of case-study method requires enthusiasm and a degree of trust. We are experimenting with a method we do not fully understand (and it is a method related to, but very different from the field methods developed in the social sciences).

It is that sense of potential that provides my main excuse for continuing to work in the area of case-study research, despite awareness of mistakes I have made in the past, and certain knowledge that I will make others in the future. It is not easy to make yourself relive those things that have gone wrong, especially where they involve relationships with others, but when opportunities occur for doing further studies my enthusiasm always gets the better of my sense of caution. The important lesson to be learned is, I think, to make every effort to learn from our mistakes.

What resolutions should be carried through from the mistakes I have recounted here?

(a) First, not to underestimate the interventive power of the case study and its methods. Where possible to make use of multiple observers, to act to protect the lives of participants, and to hold to procedures which build in countervailing forces in order to strengthen the position of those who are subjects of, and to, such research.

(b) Second, to take care not to neglect the fact that the conduct of research is a social process, a temporary system, which has to find space for itself and so to be accommodated by other interests. Case-study research is not simply interventive as a process, but as the presence of people and relationships impinging on existing patterns of authority and of social relations. In the academic world we tend to lay great stress on the value of information for understanding, and to stress democratic rights of free access to information. In the worlds we study, research information is often conceived as the currency of power, and right of access to it controlled by bureaucratic boundaries. The interaction of these two sets of conflicting assumptions is frequently a more significant part of the research process than we admit or allow. It is not simply noise in the system, or the consequence of poor designs, but marks a fundamental discontinuity between the worlds of the researcher and of the subject.

(c) Third, where possible to design studies such that those with power over the lives of others included in the scope of the study are required by the design to see the nature of their responsibilities. In particular, to design studies that give those at different levels of the system equal access to, and control over, the resources that the research provides.

(d) Fourth, we should constantly look for ways of underlining the fact that case studies tell *a* truth but not *the* truth. They may offer certain claims to truth, depending on the nature of the evidence they provide, but they are always partial accounts; constructions of reality; representations. Though, as I have argued here, they may well become part of the culture they describe, in that they provide shared memories and perceptions for their subjects, and so are likely to become a part of institutional mythology.

Acknowledgement

This paper was written during a period as visiting lecturer at Monash University. I am grateful to Lawrence Ingvarson, Stephen Kemmis, Colin Power, Don Hogben and their students for discussions on its themes.

Notes

1 WALKER, R. (1982) 'The use of case studies in applied research and evaluation', in HARTNETT, A. (Ed.) *The Social Sciences in Educational Studies*, London, Heinemann.

2 SHAW, K.E. (1978) 'Understanding the curriculum: the approach through case studies', *Journal of Curriculum Studies*, 10, 1, January–March.

3 STENHOUSE, L. (1975) *An Introduction to Curriculum Research*, London, Heinemann.

4 JENKINS, D. *et al.* (1981) 'Thou nature art my goddess', *Cambridge Journal of Education*, 11, 3.
5 MacDONALD, B. and WALKER, R. (Eds) (1974) *Innovation, Evaluation, Research and the Problem of Control*, SAFARI Interim papers, Norwich, Centre for Applied Research in Education, University of East Anglia.
6 JENKINS, D. (1980) 'An adversary's account of SAFARI's ethics of case study' in SIMONS, H. (Ed.) *Towards a Science of the Singular*, occasional publication 10, Norwich, Centre for Applied Research in Education, University of East Anglia.
7 MacDONALD, B. and WALKER, R. (Eds) (1974) *op cit.*
8 WALKER, R. (1981) *The Observational Work of LEA Inspectors and Advisors*, final report to the SSRC, copies available from the Centre for Applied Research in Education, University of East Anglia.
9 MacDONALD, B. *et al.* (1982) *A Study of Bilingual Education in the USA*, Norwich, Centre for Applied Research in Education, University of East Anglia.
10 SMITH, L. and KEITH, P. (1971) *Anatomy of Educational Innovation*, New York, Wiley.
11 HARGREAVES, D. (1967) *Social Relations in a Secondary School*, London, Routledge and Kegan Paul.
12 SHIPMAN, M. (1974) *Inside a Curriculum Project*, London, Methuen.
13 MacDONALD, B. (1978) *The Experience of Innovation*, occasional publication 6, Norwich, Centre for Applied Research in Education, University of East Anglia.
14 SMITH is, however, currently writing *Kensington Revisited* (to be published by the Falmer Press), a revised view of the school and of those who taught there at the time of the first study.

Seven Principles for Programme Evaluation in Curriculum Development and Innovation

Stephen Kemmis
Deakin University

Different definitions of evaluation abound. The Australian Curriculum Development Centre (CDC) Study Group on curriculum evaluation reviewed a variety of definitions with currency in the evaluation literature and adopted the following one as the most useful guide for the evaluation of CDC's own projects and programmes and for curriculum evaluation more generally: 'Evaluation is the process of delineating, obtaining and providing information useful for making decisions and judgments about educational programs and curricula'.[1]

This definition highlights the function of evaluative information in assisting decision-making. It reflects a fairly widespread agreement among evaluation theorists[2] about the role of evaluation in informing action at discrete decision-points. But it is important to recognize that a curriculum programme and its evaluation are highly interactive, not only in 'summative' decisions, but throughout the process of curriculum development. In short, the discrete decision points are few and far between and evaluation permeates development: the two processes are not discontinuous. Accordingly, a desirable definition of evaluation will acknowledge the mutuality of the relationship between evaluation and curriculum development and its continuous, organic and reflexive contribution to thought and action about a curriculum. Other definitions of evaluation, while more general than the one adopted by the CDC Study Group seem more likely to recognize the pervasiveness of the evaluation function, and less likely to treat it as discontinuous and separate from development. Stake and Denny (1969), for example, have this to say:

> Considered broadly, evaluation is the discovery of the nature and worth of something. In relation to education, we may evaluate students, teachers, curriculums, administrators, systems, programs and nations. The purposes for evaluation may be many, but always evaluation attempts to describe something and to indicate its perceived merits and shortcomings ... Evaluation is not a

117

search for cause and effect, an inventory of present status, or a prediction of future success. It is something of all of these but only as they contribute to understanding substance, function and worth.[3]

This definition, emphasizing 'nature and worth', 'perceived merits and shortcomings' and 'understanding', goes further towards acknowledging evaluation as an ever-present aspect of considered action. One might quibble over the use of the word 'discovery', suggesting as it does that the nature and worth of the thing evaluated antedate the evaluative search for them, but the force of the term is mitigated by the notion that merit and shortcomings are 'perceived' rather than intrinsic or imminent.

It is critical in deciding upon a definition to guide evaluation efforts to give due importance to the pervasiveness of the evaluative dimension of all human activity, and to the fact that it is present in a range of individual and public judgment processes which exist whether or not an evaluation is formally commissioned or expected of project and programme participants. Indeed, when evaluations of particular programmes *are* commissioned, they should approximate (and focus and sharpen) these informal critical processes, not ignore or supplant them. Though the formality of commissioning or requiring an evaluation imposes certain obligations to formalize and discipline the individual and public judgment processes which occur naturally in considered activity, formal evaluations should attempt deliberately to preserve something of the conviviality of the informal processes.

Preserving conviviality is no easy task. These principles attempt to provide a framework within which conviviality can be preserved by emphasizing the continuity and mutuality of concern between programme participants, a programme sponsor, an evaluation sponsor and an evaluator. They also attempt to emphasize that evaluation forms a natural part of the critical thinking that guides the development process. This is not to say that formal evaluations can lack rigour, discipline or honesty; rather, it is to assert that their critical edge should be tempered with humane values rather than narrowly technocratic or bureaucratic concerns.

Accordingly, the definition of evaluation which has informed and guided the development of these principles is this: *Evaluation is the process of marshalling information and arguments which enable interested individuals and groups to participate in the critical debate about a specific programme.* So construed, evaluation consists in harnessing and refining the ubiquitous processes of individual and public judgment, not in resolving or replacing them with a technology of judgment.

There is a certain kind of seduction in discussing principles: one is often inclined to share the aspirations they embody simply because they seem worthy ones or because the rhetoric of principles is lofty and stirring.

For this reason, the discussion of each principle includes a reference to two alternative principles. Each of the three resulting sets of principles (the set advocated here and the two alternative sets) are more or less self-consistent.[4]

The reader is invited to choose between the three sets and to consider in choosing that the choice may be a revealing one: it will indicate a preference for the interests and concerns of one group over another when evaluator, sponsor and programme participants interact in the evaluation process.

1 The Principle of Rationality as Reasonableness

Programme participants act reasonably in the light of their circumstances and opportunities. It is the task of an evaluation to illuminate the reasoning which guides programme development and evolution, to identify the contextual and historical factors which influence it and to facilitate critical examination of these matters in and around the programme community.

Evaluation is always guided by the impulse to understand and to act on the basis of understanding. It thus has a major role to play in articulating justifications of action. Properly speaking, the justification of action is not merely a backward-looking enterprise, to be equated with post-rationalization. On the contrary, it is concerned with demonstrating both *how* things have come to be as they are (that is, with illuminating the reasoning which has guided the activities of those associated with a programme and identifying the circumstances which shaped and constrained them) and with providing information and arguments which can justify contemplated action.

In evaluating an educational programme it is critical to explicate the reasoning which has guided the activities of those associated with it. Unless there are very good reasons for assuming otherwise, the evaluator and the evaluation sponsor should assume that persons will act reasonably in the light of their current circumstances and the available opportunities. That is to say, it should be assumed that those associated with a programme are committed to acting with understanding; in ways informed by their values and beliefs; wisely and prudently. By explicating the reasoning of those in and around a programme, an evaluation may therefore share the understandings of those who are deeply concerned with it. It may help to disclose the nature of the programme and the values it embraces and give those associated with it an opportunity to have their perspectives on it represented.

The truths to be told about educational programmes are social truths. They are negotiated among those who claim to know it and those who want to know better. The principle of 'rationality as reasonableness'[5] draws attention to this negotiation process. Claims about the programme are defended and challenged in a process of critical debate or conversation. What will count as the truths to be told about the programme will depend upon the quality of the debate. Rational debate consists in giving reasons and defending reasoning with information and arguments.

An evaluation may make a substantial contribution to this critical process. It can gather evidence relevant to programme aims and claims, and subject it to critical cross-examination. It can elicit, articulate and share understandings about why the course of development, implementation and dissemination is as it is by reference to the purposes of participants, the constraints of circumstance and the available opportunities, and reflect on these understandings in the light of the wider context and experience of the programme as a whole. Likewise, it can subject the views of programme audiences — supporters, detractors and those who have not yet a basis for making judgments about it — to critical scrutiny so a 'conversation' between the perspectives of those associated with it can be created and maintained.

The implication of the principle of rationality as reasonableness is that evaluators will attend to a wide variety of perspectives on a programme, to the diverse claims made about it, to its context and to its history. They will thus be in a position to harness and refine the individual and public judgment processes by which the programme comes to be understood and by which its value is determined. The quality of the evaluation may be judged by the quality of its contribution to informing and improving the critical debate about the programme.

Evaluation should thus aim to contribute to programme improvement both directly and indirectly: by its direct interaction with programme participants and by feeding and refining the interaction between programme praticipants and their audiences.

An alternative principle to the principle of rationality as reasonableness, and one which is not advocated here, is that of 'rationality as rulefollowing', Stake's (1975) label of 'preordinate'[6] fits evaluation approaches which have prior rules for judging a programme and which do not respond to immediate value-perspectives, information-needs and circumstances. For example, some evaluation approaches are based on the notion of rational consumption and set out criteria and standards which must be met before a programme can be considered a 'good buy'. Scriven's 'product evaluation checklist'[7] is perhaps the best example of this. It lists thirteen considerations in the evaluation of products, producers and proposals, and sets standards of adequacy for each. They are: (1) need; (2) market; (3) performance: true field trials; (4) performance: true consumer; (5) performance: critical comparisons; (6) performance: long term; (7) performance: side-effects; (8) performance: process; (9) performance: causation; (10) performance: statistical significance; (11) performance: educational significance; (12) cost-effectiveness; and (13) extended support.

These are powerful considerations and the model provides a useful set of questions to be asked of a programme or product. But the criteria are subject to interpretation in application and they do not respond sufficiently to the nature of the critical debate which actually attends a programme. How would such an evaluation model account for the controversy over SEMP (the Curriculum Development Centre's Social Education Materials Project), for example, where different value premises underlie the opposing positions which cannot be resolved on the basis of a common criterion test? Furthermore, the criteria are extremely stringent in practice and few curriculum developments are able to justify themselves in terms of the standards Scriven sets. Rhetorically, one might claim that these standards should always be met, but since they cannot be met in real curriculum development how can what actually happens be justified? It must be by appeal to something else, that is, by something other than the criteria the checklist proposes.

There are other forms of rationality as rule-following. Evaluations guided only by considerations of testing and measurement are rule-following, drawing their rules from psychometrics. Cronbach[8] has pointed out their limitations for real curriculum evaluation which depends on more information than simply data about student performance on carefully-designed tests. More generally, Hastings[9] has drawn attention to the fact that research methods, inspired by their own rational models (for their own purposes) often distort evaluation problems by twisting them to fit the methods they employ. Clearly, methods which are designed to handle closely-defined, special problems are of limited help in handling poorly-defined, multiform programme realities. The problem about specifying the rules for rational justification in curriculum is that the rules are likely to be limited; rationality as reasonableness makes no such prescription about what particular rules must be applied, though it recognizes the usefulness of such rules as far as they seem relevant.

A second alternative principle, also not advocated here, is the view of rationality implied in 'rational planning'. This view sees justification as based on the notion of satisfaction of needs. If a need can be identified and regarded as an urgent one, then programmes can be designed to satisfy it. Relatively few educational programmes can be said to satisfy urgent needs, though education as a whole responds to a general social need. But the rational planning approach tends also to take a contractual view of programmes: to see them in terms of the obligations imposed on those brave or foolish enough to accept grants to develop programmes. Within such a view, measurements of need-reduction or aims-achievement, coupled with fulfilment of contractual obligations, are sufficient to demonstrate that a programme is successful.

Potential grantees exploit the invitation this approach suggests, 'manufacturing' needs, over-promising, and using limited or biased measures. The exploitations are not always deliberate; rather, they are inspired by a cultural tendency towards legalism and concepts of exchange rooted in economics. Such values have their place, of course, and programme evaluations which do not attend to the contractual obligations of grantees may fail to take account of important aspects of the programmes.

But the 'rational planning' approach to evaluation may treat educational programmes in a bureaucratized way which does not do justice to the organic and reflective character of social and educational life. Programme objectives change, as they should, in response to changing circumstances and opportunities; educational programmes rarely specify the sole means by which goals can be achieved; 'needs' are usually relative in education, not absolute. The 'rationality as reasonableness' approach is likely to take a more open-minded view of programme justification which is sensitive to the relativity of educational values and their adaptation to social contexts.

To adopt the principle of rationality as reasonableness is thus to take the view that social truths are socially-negotiated and historically- and culturally-relative. It is to reject the notion that any discrete set of rules can be formulated which will provide universal criteria of programme adequacy. Similarly, it is to reject the notion that programmes can be justified solely by reference to their own goals, objectives and obligations or by reference solely to needs-reduction. Evaluations based on either of these alternative perspectives are likely to be limited and partial, providing an inadequate basis of information and argument for those who want to enter the critical debate about a programme.

2   The Principle of Autonomy and Responsibility

Moral responsibility for an outcome can only be ascribed to a person to the degree that his or her free choice of action as an autonomous moral agent was a cause of that outcome. Curriculum development projects and programmes are co-operative enterprises. Evaluators must illuminate the interactive character of accountability for a programme.

Just as the evaluator may assume that those involved with a programme act rationally in the sense that they are open to arguments based on reason, so it may be assumed that those involved with the programme are autonomous and responsible moral agents. This has implications for the way programme participants, evaluators, evaluation sponsors and programme sponsors view accountability issues in evaluation.

Most programme sponsors use or distribute public funds for programme development and implementation. They are publicly accountable for their use of these funds; programme participants must also account for their use of the resources allocated to them. Financial and management procedures usually accompany development project fundings to ensure that accountability demands are met. A 'maximalist' view of accountability requires programme participants to justify every decision about the use of resources by reference to programme goals, social needs and the consequences of each decision (especially in terms of programme outcomes for students and teachers). But it is sufficient to adopt a 'minimalist' view of accountability as keeping financial and other records which show that programmes have operated within their budgets and according to their terms of reference, and to make these records open to view.[10]

More generally, the minimalist view of accountability is based on the principle of autonomy and responsibility. According to this principle, moral responsibility for an outcome can only be ascribed to a person to the degree that his or her free choice of action as an autonomous moral agent was a cause of that outcome. To the degree that the person's choices were constrained by others, or by circumstances outside his control, then to that degree the person cannot be held responsible (or at least not solely responsible) for the outcomes.

In a climate where the accountability dragon has reared its head and begun to roar in education, it is as well to be clear about these issues. Any programme sponsor is always implicated in the accountability issue. By constraining the choices open to those who carry out its work, it reduces their autonomy as agents. It must therefore accept a part of the responsibility for the outcomes. Accountability is always bilateral: it concerns provision as well as performance.

Accountability is not a matter of the distribution of praise and blame. Curriculum development is a co-operative enterprise between programme sponsors and participants; the co-actors share responsibility just as they jointly constrain one another's opportunities. Nor will it do to take an overly-personalized view of responsibility. Structural constraints of programme design and organization impose constraints on free action whose effects are sometimes difficult to predict; circumstances which surround development are often beyond the control of participants and may restrict free action in unanticipated ways. One task of programme evaluation is to identify such structural constraints and to determine their effects. A programme evaluation should therefore be highly sensitive to historical and contextual issues so that the work of the programme can be seen against its background of constraints and opportunities.

One alternative principle concerning accountability not advocated here would be one based on ideals of truth and justice. According to such a principle, an evaluator or programme sponsor might adopt some view of what constituted true and just work, perhaps spelling out criteria for truth and justice. These would then constitute a view of what 'the good' (or best) in curriculum development might be. Programme participants could be held accountable for deviations from this ideal.

This sort of principle is clearly unsuitable given the commitment already declared to the notion that social truths are socially-negotiated. And it is unsuitable in a pluralist society where different value-perspectives, with different patterns of coherence and legitimacy, coexist. Curriculum development always expresses social and educational values and it is proper that they be critically analyzed and examined in each case. Far from asserting what values are proper for a programme and then judging it according to those values alone, evaluations should attempt to explore the diverse values and value-perspectives expressed in a programme and the work of those involved in developing it, setting these in a context of the diverse values of the wider society beyond the development group.

A principle concerning accountability based on ideals of truth and justice and concerned with attributing blame for deviations from these ideals thus seems both inappropriate and unworkable. The principle of autonomy and responsibility allows for interaction among value-perspectives; it does not close off critical debate by imposing an ideal because this happens to be the ideal of the evaluator or the programme sponsor. Programme sponsors will no doubt have their own curriculum values and hope to express them through their work, but they should not assume that these values can be imposed unilaterally — they must stand up to the test of critical debate among a plurality of value-perspectives.

A second alternative view of accountability, likewise not advocated here, might be one based on the notion of contractual obligation. Such a view would seem to be based more on notions of prudence and expedience than on principle. Nevertheless, it is worth exploring briefly. The accountability issue as it has been aired in education has frequently been discussed in these terms. According to this view, there is a chain of obligations from the classroom teacher through education systems to ministers of education and ultimately through parliaments to the people. Each superordinate agency is seen as totally responsible for the actions of all subordinates. This view is based on a notion of management which might be described as highly positivistic, that is, the notion that management causes events to occur. This managerialism is contrary to the facts of development, of course: subordinates are not mere operators whose every action is determined by job specification. It is also contrary to the values of professionalism in education: teachers are not operatives but relatively autonomous professionals. (This value reaches its peak in the notion of academic freedom; it is moderated by notions of social responsibility.)

If a programme sponsor were to adopt this contractual and manager-ialistic view of accountability it might present itself as a 'responsible' authority yet preserve the capacity to disavow responsibility when things go wrong, claiming that operatives in its projects and programmes stepped outside their specified tasks and responsibilities. Naturally, it cannot do so: the principle of autonomy and responsibility embodies an acknowl-

bear in shaping the overall common interest. At the same time, these diverse individuals are capable of disinterest, suspending their own values and interests as they try to understand and develop the common work. The notion of a community of self-interests is an important one simply because it emphasizes these 'internal' and 'external' negotiations. Programmes are cooperative efforts among participants and thus sponsors cannot disavow their involvement when commissioning evaluation studies.

The foregoing paragraphs have emphasized the sponsor's involvement in the cooperatives formed in project and programme work, primarily because it should be clear both to project workers and to evaluators that the work *is* cooperative. Naturally, the same might be said of all other participants in the cooperative: all are bound by it unless they withdraw for some other overriding reason.

Two alternative principles to the principle of community self-interest could be proposed, based on the one hand on the notion of 'the public interest' (defined outside the interests of participating individuals and agencies), or, on the other, on the notion of the sponsor's self-interest. The first might depend on some definition of what is supposed to be in the public good and specify criteria by which programmes might be judged; the second might assert a narrow definition of value according to the sponsor's own perspective. For reasons already outlined in the discussion of earlier principles (social negotiation of social truths, pluralism, the importance of contributing to the critical debate about a programme), neither of these approaches is a reasonable option. Since the sponsoring agency is a participant in the development process along with other groups and agencies, it is interested in improving the quality of critical debate about curriculum. To do so, it requires evaluations which share information among those involved in the process (with due regard for the protection of the rights of individuals) rather than evaluations which serve only its own purposes or only those of other particular groups within the cooperative. (Equally, it is not interested in evaluations which serve only the purposes of those outside the communities of self-interests it forms.)

4   The Principle of Plurality of Value-perspectives

A range of different value-perspectives becomes relevant in judging a programme. An evaluation should identify these different perspectives and be responsive to the different concerns they imply.

Programme participants' values and interests are served by their participation in curriculum development. The particular individuals and agencies cooperating in a project or programme have their own values and interests which may be independently justified. Other audiences for the work of a project or programme will likewise judge it by reference to their own values and interests. A programme sponsor can claim no monopoly on the values or criteria by which a programme is to be evaluated.

According to the principle of plurality of value perspectives, programme evaluators should recognize that a range of perspectives may be relevant in making a judgment of it. Any judgment of the value of a project or programme will be made in the light of the value commitments of the judge; programme evaluators should therefore inform themselves and their audiences about the value perspectives of relevant judges, be responsive to their concerns, and provide information which is appropriate (and valued most highly) as evidence according to their criteria of judgment. If the information and arguments collected in the course of the evaluative study are relevant and significant to the audiences of the evaluation, there is a greater likelihood that they will be used in the critical debate about the programme.

As an alternative to this principle, the view could be taken that judgments of a programme should be the prerogative of those best-equipped to judge: for example, competent authorities in curriculum as a field, curriculum development processes, the subject-matter of the programme, or teaching and learning processes. While these specialists may well be able to provide valuable information and insights into the programme, they are not the only ones entitled to judge it. An evaluation should embrace such perspectives but should go beyond them to take into account the perspectives of other interested parties (for example, students, parents, community groups or employers). The mature judgment of specialists may be of great value to audiences less familiar with specialist debates about the nature and worth of a programme, but lay concerns demand attention too: as clients or observers of the programme, laymen must have their questions treated seriously in an evaluation study, have specialist issues made accessible to them, and see how these specialist issues fit into the broader context of the issues concerning the programme as a whole.

Still another principle which could be adopted would concern a sponsor's own right to judge, and the primacy of its right as a sponsor of development to have its own questions answered. To be sure, a programme evaluation should address questions which the sponsor regards as important. But such a principle, pursued single-mindedly, would have a conservative and defensive effect. It would make the evaluation a service for the sponsor at the expense of other audiences with legitimate rights to be heard. In order to feed the critical debate about the programme and to refine it, an evaluation must engage the perspectives of a variety of audiences.

5   The Principle of the Self-critical Community: Internal Evaluation, Evaluation Consultancy, Meta-evaluation, External and Independent Evaluation

> Critical debate about the nature and worth of a programme already exists within and around its programme community. It is the task of programme evaluation to refine this debate and improve its bearing on programme action. Evaluation consultancy may provide additional tools for this purpose. Meta-evaluation efforts may help to improve the quality of the contribution of programme evaluation. An external evaluation may contribute to the critical debate by increasing awareness of a particular set of values and interests relevant to a programme; it should not be thought of as an alternative to the self-critical process. An independent evaluation may help to harness programme self-criticism where the programme community is diffuse or divided by controversy. Self-criticism by the programme community is the primary basis for programme evaluation; other evaluation efforts extend it in different ways but do not supplant it.

The community of self-interests formed by a curriculum project or programme is likely to embrace a variety of value-perspectives which, through their interaction in its life and work, create a continuing conversation about its nature and worth. This conversation provides a basis for systematic self-criticism within the community; it is nourished by contact with perspectives from the wider social and educational communities outside.

A major task for programme evaluation is to harness this self-critical conversation: to collect the perspectives and judgments of those associated with a programme, to reclaim meanings and concerns from the flux of programme experience, and to make this store of understandings available to participants and other audiences. Describing the programme, formulating issues regarded as significant by those associated with it, collecting judgments and portraying these in ways which are accessible to evaluation audiences — these are activities through which the evaluator can contribute to the critical debate about a programme and improve the quality of the critique.

Such activities acknowledge that critical debate already exists independently of the evaluation of a programme, within and between programme staff and interested observers. Far from attempting to supersede 'natural' critical debate, an evaluation should attempt to capitalize on it, harness it and refine it. In doing so, it can engage the perspectives and concerns of those within and outside the programme (without imposing perspectives which are regarded as 'foreign' by those within). By bringing these perspectives in contact with one another and opening up interaction across the borders of the programme, the evaluation may generate authentic knowledge about the programme — that is, knowledge grounded in the life-circumstances of participants and understood as experience. Authentic knowledge is the only sure basis for programme improvement and for improvement of critical debate because it reflects personal understandings which will express themselves as free commitments in the actions of participants.

The implication for evaluators is that evaluations should be responsive to audience concerns and the real, experienced issues which surround a programme. The evaluation task is thus an educative one, informing and developing the understandings of those associated with the programme. The evaluation may accept as its primary task the formulation of programme issues in ways which clarify them for programme participants and audiences. It may report frequently rather than just towards the end of the evaluation, so that the perspectives of participants and audiences can be engaged more or less continually rather than in a single confrontation of perspectives. The recurring 'reports' of the evaluator can be regarded as a conversation which develops the points of view of those it engages. In this conversational process, interim reports should be less formal and regarded as ephemeral (rather than highly authoritative) by participants and audiences. A final report should reflect the evolution or history of the critical debate in and around the programme. Evaluation reporting should be regarded as a dynamic process rather than static or discontinuous; the evaluation findings as contributory and reflexive rather than confrontational or inert; the evaluator as a facilitator of debate rather than as an 'objective' outsider who represents truth against one-sidedness or complete understanding against the partial understandings of participants.

Regarding the programme as a self-critical community does not mean that it is an insular group feeding only on its own perspectives; using the self-critical debate within the programme as a basis for the evaluation does not mean that the evaluation becomes simply a kind of self-report. Through the evaluation (as well as through programme initiatives), participants should be brought into contact with the perspectives of other relevant judges and audiences, some of whom may be quite distant from the programme. The self-critical community of the programme can incorporate the perspectives of 'outsiders' by creating a conversation with them through which both sides can learn each other's perspectives. This can occur if the programme and the evaluation create opportunities for outsiders to see the work (or portrayals of the work), to consider it, to judge it, and to explain their judgments.

The principle of the self-critical community establishes self-criticism as the cornerstone of programme evaluation. All participants in the community of self-interests formed by the programme have a right to be heard in the critical process. As already indicated, the value of self-criticism does not preclude external judgment, rather, it attempts to create mechanisms whereby external judgments can be incorporated into project or programme thinking. To emphasize the value of self-criticism is not to advocate programme insularity; on the contrary, it is to emphasize the value of authentic knowledge as a basis for development and debate and to encourage participants to take a broad, critical view of the programme in its wider historical context. But it is also to stress that once a programme surrenders self-knowledge to external authority as a basis for development, it loses its autonomy as an intellectual community.

As a corollary to this principle it follows that each participant agency in the cooperative enterprise of a programme regards itself as a self-critical community, and evaluates its own activities in a spirit of self-criticism.

The primary implication of the principle of the self-critical community is that curriculum projects and programmes should establish 'internal' evaluation mechanisms which can systematically record and develop the critical debate about their work. These 'internal' evaluations may be augmented in four ways: by evaluation consultancy; by meta-evaluation; by external evaluation; and by independent evaluation.

(a)   Evaluation consultancy

Where specialist evaluation expertise is available, programme participants and evaluation sponsors may want to take advantage of it. Using such advice is by no means precluded under the principle of the self-critical community. For many evaluation tasks (like interview techniques, questionnaire design, planning and sampling), technical assistance is highly desirable. But this advice should not be thought of as definitive, finally authoritative or legitimating. As Hastings pointed out[12] the nature and scope of an evaluation can all too easily be limited to the capacity of the particular evaluation methods, techniques or instruments with which an evaluation specialist is familiar. Programme participants should consider the extent to which the advice of specialists and the evaluation processes and findings they propose will contribute to the critical debate about the programme and 'programme decision-making' (that is, whether the information and arguments collected will help in guiding and refining action in the programme.)

In short, evaluation consultancy can help considerably in the planning and execution of a self-critical evaluation. But programme participants should consider who is helped and how and when they will be helped by particular evaluation methods and techniques. In the end, the community of participants bears responsibility for the programme, so evaluation plans must be judged by reference to their impact in the community of participants and on those who interact with it.

(b)   Meta-evaluation

A programme sponsor is a co-participant in the community of self-interests formed by a programme. But as an agency authority accountable for the expenditure of its resources, it will generally need to be satisfied that the evaluation arrangements proposed for a project or programme are adequate and appropriate. Programme sponsors therefore have an interest in meta-evaluation (the evaluation of evaluation), to determine whether a programme evaluation can meet the demands of the critical debate to which the programme is subject. This is in part an internal management question, but it will naturally include an interactive element through which project or programme evaluators confer with programme sponsors (who are often also sponsors of programme evaluations). In exceptional cases, programme evaluations may be formally evaluated by evaluation sponsors, but most often the meta-evaluation process will be in the nature of informal monitoring and interaction.

According to the principle of the self-critical community, the primary responsibility for programme evaluation is 'internal' to the programme. Programme or programme evaluation sponsors may want to ensure, however, that adequate evaluation consultancy is available to the programme community, and they may want to encourage some form of meta-evaluation which can monitor the responsiveness of evaluation efforts to the concerns of the programme community and interested observers. Like the programme evaluation function, the meta-evaluation function can be 'devolved' from the sponsor to the programme community in order to ensure that the range of concerns, perspectives and interests present in the programme community is being considered in the critical debate about the programme. It is possible that a meta-evaluation will guarantee that sponsors' interests in the evaluation are met at the expense of other interests in the same way that evaluation consultancy can serve some interests at the expense of others; thus, a meta-evaluation must be judged by reference to the same criterion as the primary programme evaluation: How does it contribute to the improvement of the critical debate about the programme as a whole, for the whole community of programme participants and interested observers?

(c)   External evaluation

Following negotiation with other participants in the community of self-interests of a project or programme, a programme sponsor may sponsor distinct evaluation studies which are outside (or in addition to) the self-critical evaluation of the programme. These evaluations will take two forms: external evaluation and independent evaluation.

External evaluation studies may be commissioned when the community of self-interest of a programme wants advice, critical review or validation from substantive specialists, or when the judgment of recognized authorities in a field is necessary for a project, programme or evaluation to be regarded as credible. In such cases, care should be taken in negotiating an evaluation contract with potential external evaluators to see that the evaluation study respects the interests of the programme community as a whole (as expressed in these principles). Most programme evaluations undertaken today are of this form. Regrettably, they tend not to take account of the values embodied in these principles (for example, rationality as reasonableness, autonomy and responsibility, community of self-interest, etc.). In consequence, they may further some interests in a programme at the expense of others, impose a 'foreign' perspective on its work, or deny the authentic knowledge of participants. We should not be too xenophobic about this state of affairs, though: often such perspectives prefigure the views of the wider community outside the programme (indeed, they often shape outside views). A healthy self-critical community should incorporate these external perspectives and, where necessary, correct them by reference to the concerns and circumstances of the programme as a community with particular goals, terms of reference and contexts.

Just as it is a mistake to assume that an external evaluation represents the 'true' perspective on a programme (though it may aspire to objectivity, its very purpose will align it with particular interests in or around the programme at the expense of other interests), it is a mistake to think of a self-critical evaluation as a complete amalgam or synthesis of relevant perspectives. Both kinds of evaluation are fluid and interactive, not susceptible of completeness or ruling definitively on the worth of a programme. A self-critical evaluation aspires to awareness of the diversity of values and interests in and around a programme and more conscious negotiated control of programme development and evolution; an external evaluation aspires to awareness of particular values and interests, and to influencing programme development or evolution in the light of these particular values and interests. The mistake is to think that either represents a unified or complete perspective on the programme which can form the basis of an unequivocal plan for action.

(d)   Independent evaluation

Sometimes a project or programme will be so large or diffuse that its sense of being a community of self-interests or a self-critical community is sharply attenuated. It may be able to develop only a very poor sense of itself as a whole. In other cases, programme participants may prefer a 'specialization of function' in evaluation, so that one person or a small group take responsibility for the conduct of the evaluation (though programme participants will naturallly continue to participate in the critical debate). In such cases, an independent evaluator may be appointed or commissioned in order to harness and refine the critical process on behalf of the programme. Such an evaluator may prefer to be regarded as an evaluation 'facilitator'.

Moreover, when the community of a programme embraces a wide variety of viewpoints which must be articulated and explored before a joint perspective can be reached about the value and meaning of the work, an independent evaluation will be appropriate. Similarly, an independent evaluation will be appropriate when the work of a programme is particularly controversial and a variety of value perspectives within or outside a programme must be considered before an evaluation can be regarded as relevant and credible by audiences with differing value commitments.

Independent evaluations will often require the services of evaluation specialists capable of dealing with conflicting value perspectives, political pressure, complex theoretical conceptualizations, and the real and difficult issues of curriculum associated with a particular programme. They may need to adopt refined evaluation procedures capable of generating and maintaining negotiation among the conflicting theoretical, practical, and organizational interests of those in and around the programme. It is necessary to take great care in negotiating evaluation contracts with potential independent evaluators in order to ensure that the contract (as much as the evaluation) respects the values and interests of the range of participants in the community of the programme.

The principle of the self-critical community is a recognition of the natural existence of self-reflection within a programme, on the one hand, and the natural critical debate around it, on the other. Such a principle may encourage those involved in project and programme evaluation to be 'responsive' in the sense that Stake (1975)[13] uses the term. He says:

> An educational evaluation is *responsive evaluation* if it orients more directly to program activities than to program intents; responds to audience requirements of information; and if the different value-perspectives present are referred to in reporting the success and failure of the program (p. 14).

But in addition to this, such a principle may encourage evaluators to see their work as part of a naturally-occurring process of evaluative activity in a programme, not distinct from it.

It would be possible to adopt alternative principles to this one. On the one hand, curriculum programmes could be evaluated solely by teams of expert external evaluators, thus putting the validation function of evaluation before all others. Or programme sponsors could adopt a form of evaluative activity based on their own perspectives of what projects and programmes should be, thus establishing the primacy of their own value-frameworks (as seals of approval) in every programme evaluation. But neither of these principles will suffice. The cooperative nature of curriculum development and the diffuse control of educational organizations (with different participants having different sources of legitimacy — teachers' professionalism, schools' autonomy, ministerial responsibility for state systems, parents' and community roles in school councils, students' rights etc.) mean that curriculum evaluations must encompass wider views than those of substantive experts or programme sponsors' particular predilections. Programme evaluators simply cannot afford to ignore the wider debate about a programme in its social and educational context.

Current trends in the history of evaluation have been significantly influenced by the demands of project evaluation, where outside groups of evaluators have been called in to observe and evaluate curriculum development work in order to provide external validation of the quality of development. As a consequence, much recent evaluation literature reflects an expectation that evaluations will be 'objective', disinterested, expert and validatory. But external evaluation cannot provide unilateral validation. There is an older trend in evaluation based on school accreditation, inspection and appraisal which is more organically related to school curriculum work. But the techniques these purposes generated are not well suited to the evaluation of innovative curriculum projects or programmes. The older tradition stabilized itself around the organization of a school rather than around the organization of a new curricular activity or product.

Project or programme evaluation must be able to negotiate between the demands for curriculum validation and the conditions of schooling in different systems. Programme evaluation cannot treat curricula as discrete products, to be considered as if they existed independently of their contexts of application, nor can it focus all its attention on the conditions in schools adopting particular innovations. The principle of the self-critical community recognizes that innovations enter adopting systems by a process of negotiation; evaluation should facilitate negotiation by refining the critical debate.

The people who work on, use and sponsor a particular programme form a natural focus for its evaluation activities; their work provides a natural forum for critical thinking about it. The principle of the self-critical community may encourage those associated with innovative programmes to regard their natural evaluative work as a primary, not a secondary, evaluation function; accordingly, it is proper to expect that 'internal', self-critical evaluations will provide the primary basis for judgments about the nature and worth of programmes. Evaluation should not be regarded as a specialist activity tagged on to development to monitor and observe from a position of privilege (the outside observer) as if the interests which guided evaluation work were unrelated to the interests of those which guide the developers (that is, that there are no confluences or conflicts among their values and interests). Evaluation is interactive and reactive; it should not be construed as 'objective' and outside the whole system of social relationships which constitute curriculum development programmes in practice.

6 The Principle of Propriety in the Production and Distribution of Information

Evaluation processes inevitably affect the political economy of information in a programme (the production and distribution of information about it). Because information and arguments justify or legitimize decisions, evaluation affects the distribution of power and resources in programme situations. Programme participants and interested observers live with the consequences of the use and abuse of evaluation information. An evaluation should have explicit principles of procedure which govern its conduct and its processes of information production and distribution.

As suggested in the introduction to these principles, evaluation is often defined as 'delineating, obtaining and providing information for making decisions and judgments about educational programs'. Indeed, formal evaluation efforts may well be included among the management and decision-making processes of a project or programme. Though it has been an explicit purpose of these principles to widen that definition, it would be naïve to assert that evaluation was not normally regarded as an important management and decision-making tool. Evaluation processes thus link the generation of information and arguments about a programme with the power to decide: those responsible for deciding the shape and conduct of a programme, whether it should be implemented, or even whether it should be continued or discontinued will look to evaluation studies as sources of information and arguments when they make their decisions. Evaluation is thus inevitably a political process, affecting the flows of information in a situation and having life-consequences for those who inhabit it.

The point was made dramatically by ethnographer Harry Wolcott in a throwaway line at the Annual Meeting of the American Educational Research Association in 1976. Discussing several papers on ethics and methodology in fieldwork, he remarked: 'Some people define evaluation as the collection of data to guide decisions to continue, revise or terminate programmes. If you were an ethnographer, how would you like your material to be used to continue, revise or terminate another culture?'

The production and distribution of information about people, projects and programmes through evaluation must be regulated according to a principle of propriety capable of taking into account the moral, social and political consequences of information use and abuse. The evaluator must find procedures appropriate to each context by which he or she can negotiate the disputed territory between the public's 'right to know', management's 'right to relevant information', and the individual's 'right to discretion'. Even in cases where innovators are anxious to have their work more widely known, or where teachers regard their work as exemplary, there may be consequences of the release of information which may jeopardize their future opportunities. Evaluators must treat seriously the problems raised by the political economy of information production and distribution — the role of evaluation in the distribution of power in particular settings and in the support or denial of already-existing power-structures. It is not sufficient to take a moralistic stance on open information, on privacy or on the rights of sponsors: the production and distribution of information inevitably affects the politics of the programme situation and it is up to the evaluator to find procedures which are defensible within the particular context and technically feasible given the constraints of time and resources.

The principle of propriety in the production and distribution of information implies that evaluators must set out their intended procedures for information control in the form of an evaluation contract or a statement of procedural aspirations so that everyone who becomes involved in the evaluation process knows how the information is to be produced and distributed, what risks are involved in cooperating with the evaluator, and what safeguards exist against the misuse of evaluative information. Such procedures should specify how information is to be collected, analyzed, interpreted and reported. It should indicate the status of the evaluator's interpretations *vis-à-vis* the interpretations of programme participants (including programme sponsors). The contract should make clear who will come to know what about whom as a result of the evaluative process and its products. (The process is just as important as the product in shaping the views of participants in the evaluation.) It should make it clear what procedures will govern access to 'data-sources' (people, records, events), the conduct of the evaluation and the determination of its boundaries, the ownership of the evaluation data and findings, the release of information, rights to publication, confidentiality rules and mechanisms for accountability of the evaluation. It may also be possible to specify safeguards against abuse of the intended procedures (like rights of appeal or the sanction of denying the evaluator further access to the situation).

Alternative principles can hardly be framed in terms of 'impropriety': no-one could accept the notion that an evaluation should use information improperly. The principle of propriety presented here does specify the rights of participants in a programme to know how the information is to be used and controlled. It attempts to set up a model of equitable distribution of information based on the rights and obligations of all those involved in an evaluation study. Evaluations would operate in a spirit contrary to the present principle if they were an exclusive information service for evaluation sponsors rather than a service to a range of audiences associated with the programme, if they used secret reporting, if they failed to take into account the diverse perspectives and interpretations of participants and evaluation audiences, or if they published reports in forms suitable only for research audiences. The principle thus establishes a view of evaluation opposed both to the view that evaluation is an arm of the educational research industry serving some general ideal of truth or 'the public interest', and to the view that it is a tool to be used in the service of bureaucratic responsibility.[14]

Furthermore, the principle of propriety in the production and distribution of information establishes the view that evaluators have the responsibility to be aware of the consequences of information production and distribution and to respond in defensible ways by developing appropriate procedures for information control.

7 The Principle of Appropriateness

Evaluation design is a practical matter. An evaluation must be appropriate to the programme setting, responsive to programme issues, and relevant to the programme community and interested observers. An evaluation design must be renegotiated as the study progresses in the light of changing circumstances, issues and interests, and in the light of its own consequences (as they become apparent).

The contemporary scene in evaluation theory and research abounds with evaluation models and approaches with a bewildering variety of foci and employing a diversity of specific techniques. While this variety and diversity must be acknowledged, evaluators and evaluation sponsors should not adopt an unconstrained eclecticism with respect to evaluation just because no dominant orthodoxy has emerged in the field. These principles, and the value commitments they embody, identify some forms of evaluation as unacceptable. To be acceptable, particular evaluations should embody the six principles previously presented, but they must also be appropriate to their objects. That is to say, evaluation studies must suit the curriculum projects, programmes, processes or products to be evaluated and the contexts in which they appear. The design of an evaluation is a practical matter, depending on considerations of purposes; audiences; substantive issues raised by programme theory, aspirations, organization and practice; resources; issues of information control in the particular political economy of the programme and its evaluation; relevant evidence; methods for data-collection; issues and approaches to analysis and interpretation; and modes of reporting.

Evaluators and participants in curriculum projects and programmes must take all of these topics into account in designing or commissioning evaluation studies. The appropriateness of evaluation designs is a practical matter, not a technical or theoretical one. Decisions about the form an evaluation should take cannot be made by reference to the 'internal logics' of evaluation models and approaches alone; such decisions must take into account the needs, preferences, obligations, circumstances and opportunities of those who will be most closely involved in the evaluation process (as evaluators, programme participants, sponsors, evaluation audiences).

As in the case of the sixth principle, it is hardly possible to propose an alternative principle of 'inappropriateness'. But inappropriate evaluation designs are often proposed for the evaluation of curriculum projects and programmes. Such designs are ones which suffer from 'methodological tunnel vision', employing evaluation models dogmatically or inflexibly when more sensitive attention to the critical debate about a programme or the circumstances of its operation would suggest a different approach. Evaluation designs are also inappropriate when they fail to serve those most closely involved in the work of a programme, reporting instead only to sponsors or research audiences. These audiences have a legitimate claim for evaluative information, to be sure, but evaluations frequently fail to serve the needs and interests of those most directly affected by the work.

If the evaluators of curriculum projects and programmes take seriously the thrust of the definition of evaluation proposed at the beginning of this chapter — that it is the process of marshalling information and arguments which enable interested individuals and groups to participate in the critical debate about a specific programme — then it is less likely that they will err on the side of inappropriateness. Appropriate evaluations will take into account the social and contextual conditions under which educational programmes operate and include a meta-evaluation component: the evaluation will thus include an element of self-reflection which allows those involved with the evaluation and the programme to monitor its effects on programme development and evolution and on the social life of the programme as a community. The aim of this self-reflection is to treat the appropriateness of the evaluation as problematic and dynamic, not as something which can be decided once and for all at the design stage. It is to recognize that evaluation programmes, like curriculum programmes, are negotiated between interested individuals in the light of their consequences.

Stephen Kemmis

Acknowledgements

The author wishes to acknowledge the contribution of those people who offered criticism and commentary on earlier drafts of these principles; Max Angus, Ed Davis, Ernest R. House, Caroline Hueneke, Clare Hughes, Neil Russell, Malcolm Skilbeck and Ralph Straton. In particular he wishes to thank Barry MacDonald for many valuable discussions about principles of procedure in evaluation.

He is also grateful for the support of the Australian Curriculum Development Centre to which he was evaluation consultant at the time when the first draft of the principles was prepared.

Notes

1 *Curriculum Evaluation: A CDC Study Group Report* (1977) CDC professional series, Curriculum Development Centre, Canberra, p. 24.
2 See for example CRONBACH, L.J. (1963) 'Course improvement through evaluation', *Teachers College Record*, 64, pp. 672–93; MACDONALD, B. (1973) 'Briefing decision-makers' in HOUSE, E.R. (Ed.) *School Evaluation: The Politics and Process*, Berkeley, Calif, McCutchan; STUFFLEBEAM, D.L. *et al*. (1971) *Educational Evaluation and Decision Making in Education*, Itasca, Ill., Peacock.
3 STAKE, R.E. and DENNY, T. (1969) 'Needed concepts and techniques for utilizing more fully the potential of evaluation', *National Society for the Study of Education Yearbook*, LXVIII, Pt II, Chicago, University of Chicago Press, p. 370.
4 The two 'alternative' sets may be somewhat less internally-consistent since they parallel the first set.
5 See WEIR, E. (1976) *Rationality as Reasonableness*, University of Illinois at Urbana-Champaign, Office for Instructional Research.
6 STAKE, R.E. (1975) 'To evaluate an arts program' in STAKE, R.E. (Ed.) *Evaluating the Arts in Education: A Responsive Approach*, Columbus, Ohio, Charles E. Merrill.
7 SCRIVEN, M. (1974) 'Evaluation perspectives and procedures' in POPHAM, W.J. (Ed.) *Evaluation in Education: Current Applications*, Berkeley, Calif., McCutchan.
8 CRONBACH, L.J. (1963) *op. cit.*
9 HASTINGS, J.T. (1969) 'The kith and kin of educational measures', *Journal of Educational Measurement*, 6, pp. 127–30.
10 See STAKE, R.E. (1973) 'School accountability laws', *Evaluation Comment*, 4, pp. 1–3. The present definition is based upon Stake's.
11 HOUSE, E.R. and CARE, N.S. (1977) *Fair Evaluation Agreement*, University of Illinois at Urbana-Champaign, Center for Instructional Research and Curriculum Evaluation, mimeo.
12 HASTINGS, J.T. (1969) *op. cit.*
13 STAKE, R.E. (1975) 'To evaluate an arts program' in STAKE, R.E. (Ed.) *Evaluating the Arts in Education: A Responsive Approach*, Columbus, Ohio, Charles E. Merrill.
14 See MACDONALD, B. (1976) 'Evaluation and the control of education' in TAWNEY, D.A. (Ed.) *Curriculum Evaluation Today: Trends and Implications*, Schools Council Research Studies, London, Macmillan; MacDonald distinguishes 'autocratic', 'bureaucratic' and 'democratic' forms of evaluation in his political classification.

5
Participatory Evaluation: The Stakeholder Approach

Introduction

By the late seventies the extensive evaluation activities of the federal government in the United States had been roundly criticized by a large number of people. The National Institute of Education decided to try a significantly different approach to evaluation that might address some of the strongest criticisms. The fundamental idea was to have others participate in the evaluation itself, and this participatory attempt was called the stakeholder approach because these who were to participate were those who had a stake in the program. The story of this particular attempt to democratize evaluation is encapsulated in this section of the book. It is not an entirely happy story.

In her first chapter in this section, Carol Weiss traces the criticisms and government action that led to the development of the stakeholder approach. Critics had contended that program evaluation was unrealistic, in that it held programs to standards of success impossible to attain; irrelevant, in that much evaluation information had no connection to the people involved; unfair, in that the powerless were held accountable by the powerful; and unused, in that the evaluation results seldom influenced decisions about the programs.

Responding to these criticisms federal officials within the National Institute of Education thought that involving stakeholders in the evaluation would sensitize evaluators to local needs, give the information requests of the local stakeholders high priority, and provide some local control over the evaluation itself. Hence, the local stakeholders would be empowered by the evaluation, thus improving the evaluation's realism, relevance, fairness, and utility. Evaluation was recognized as partly a political process, and the stakeholder approach was a political solution to evaluation problems.

As Weiss notes, there was perhaps another motivation working as well. Some evaluations had been hotly contested politically. By sharing control of the evaluation with local stakeholders, the federal bureaucrats could partially defuse the political fall-out and criticisms directed at them by critics of past evaluations.

The first two programs chosen to employ the stakeholder approach were intensely political. One was the Cities-in-Schools program, a favorite of Rosalyn Carter and strongly supported by the Carter White House. The other was PUSH/Excel, the educational program of the Reverend Jesse Jackson, the highly charismatic leader of the black minority in America and possibly the most controversial person in the United States. Both programs were clearly politically loaded. The stakeholder approach was tried with these two.

The chapter by Farrar and House relates what happened when the stakeholder notion was applied to PUSH/Excel. Essentially, the contractors who won the bid to do the evaluation did not engage the stakeholders in any meaningful way. Although calling the study a stakeholder evaluation, the evaluators actually employed a more traditional, technocratic approach to the evaluation. The evaluators claimed that they tried but could achieve no meaningful participation from the stakeholder groups. Farrar and House claim the evaluators' efforts to involve the stakeholders were minimal and inept. In any case, the PUSH/Excel program could not meet the standards imposed by the evaluators and was called a failure. The evaluation results were widely reported in the mass media and eventually had an effect upon Jesse Jackson's campaign for the presidency. The high promise of the stakeholder approach was converted into something quite different in the course of events.

In reassessing the stakeholder approach to evaluation in the light of the experiences of the Cities-in-Schools and PUSH/Excel evaluations, Weiss concludes that the stakeholder approach holds modest promise. It can improve the fairness of the evaluation, democratize access to data, and equalize whatever power knowledge provides. However, it will not ensure that appropriate, relevant information is collected nor increase the use of the evaluation results, she concludes. Weiss wonders whether the planning of evaluations is the proper place to redress the inequitable distribution of influence and authority.

Weiss also contends that several smaller studies by different groups would have been preferable to one 'blockbuster' study. The single blockbuster study places too much weight upon one group of evaluators. A group of studies, perhaps each examining the program from the perspective of one stakeholder group, might have several advantages. Finally, Weiss speculates that qualitative designs would be better for involving stakeholders than the quantitative design employed in these evaluations.

Overall, the stakeholder evaluations of Cities-in-Schools and PUSH/Excel were not satisfying experiences for anyone involved. They remain controversial and hotly contested. In my opinion these two evaluations were badly done, and the stakeholder notion never truly employed. In general, evaluators have a very difficult time including broad public participation in what they conceive as a technical act.

The Stakeholder Approach to Evaluation: Origins and Promise

Carol H. Weiss
Harvard Graduate School of Education

The National Institute of Education's advocacy of the stakeholder approach resulted from decades of criticism of evaluation practice. For more than twenty years, observers have noted serious shortcomings in the manner in which evaluations were conducted. Almost everyone associated with the evaluation of social programs seems to have written a critique of some aspect of the enterprise. Indeed, it sometimes seems that more papers have been published criticizing evaluation practices and procedures than reporting the results of studies conducted. Educational evaluators have been in the forefront of the criticism industry. For example, with dramatic sweep, Guba (1969) titled one early paper 'The Failure of Educational Evaluation.'

Many critiques have centered on methodological inadequacies. In addition, there have been complaints about the lack of fit between evaluation and the sociopolitical context of the program world. Critics charge that evaluation is narrow because it focuses on only a small subset of questions of importance to program people; unrealistic because it measures the success of programs against unreasonably high standards; irrelevant because it provides answers to questions that no one really cares about; unfair because it is responsive to the concerns of influential people, such as bureaucratic sponsors, but blind to the wants of others lower in the hierarchy, such as front-line staff and clients; and unused in councils of action where decision are made. These concerns motivated NIE to develop the stakeholder approach. Because they provide the intellectual underpinning for the stakeholder notion, we will examine them briefly to try to discern where critics lay the blame for shortcomings.

Narrow

Of necessity, evaluations select a limited number of issues for examination. No study can encompass all the issues that come up in the hurly-burly world in which programs function. Inevitably, arbitrary limits are set, and some of the things that turn out to be crucial to program people are not addressed by evaluators.

Critics claim that evaluators too often select for attention the issues that are easy to study with available social-scientific tools, not the issues that are important. Evaluators, they contend, choose their issues and variables for reasons that have little to do with the needs of people who make decisions about the program (Berk and Rossi, 1976; Patton, 1978).

One of the ways in which evaluators narrow their focus is by concen. trating on measurement of program outcomes. In doing so, critics claim, evaluators give insufficient attention to what goes on inside the program. Thus, they ignore issues of operation that program people can do something about (Williams, 1971). Further, even when it is appropriate to limit attention to outcome indicators, evaluators tend to select a narrow set of indicators (Stake, 1978). In education, for example, the standard measures are student scores on standardized tests. Yet, many programs have much broader goals than improved test scores, and these other goals (improvements in social competence, health, persistence in school, and so on) are often disregarded. Some programs that aim only peripherally at educational improvement, such as changes in school governance, still find themselves evaluated by the available standby-tests.

Unrealistic

Evaluators, it is claimed, often choose outcome measures that are difficult to budge. As a result, if the program is a relatively modest effort, it is unlikely that changes will be of sufficient size to move the indicators into the zone of statistical significance (Caro, 1971; Schwarz, 1980). To expect a reading program that meets two hours a week to affect reading scores significantly or to expect a counselling program for delinquents to prevent all further delinquent behavior is to impose standards of success that are unreasonable. By the choice of such measures, the evaluator almost dooms the program to a judgment of failure.

Irrelevant

Critics contend that much of the data that evaluators collect and analyze is unresponsive to the real needs of people involved in the program (Cochran, 1980; Datta, 1981; Parlett and Hamilton, 1976). For example, data on program outcomes do not give program staff much information about what they can do to improve the program. Program staff may want to know why they are not attracting more people, which strategies of programming are more helpful, why people drop out, what kinds of staff are more successful, and how long the program should run. An evaluation that relies on test scores provides data that can be useful for summative decisions, but these data give program people little insight into the operational issues with which they must deal every day.

Unfair

Evaluations, critics allege, usually address questions that concern federal staff or program managers. They rarely consider the needs and wants of less powerful groups such as program recipients (Coleman, 1980; House, 1980). It is possible for clients to enter a program with expectations that differ in important ways from the official goals of the program. Yet, the evaluator rarely takes such expectations into account or judges the program from the clients' perspective.

Similarly, evaluators usually report study results to superordinate groups — the Congress, the sponsoring federal agency, managers of the local agency. They seldom report findings to line staff members who actually give services and even less often to clients whose lives are affected by what the program does and does not accomplish. Evaluation addresses the concerns at the top levels of the hierarchy, while the people whose lives are affected most deeply by the program's success or failure are bypassed.

Even when federal staff do not try to dictate the scope and dimensions of the evaluation, evaluators tend to be responsive to what they perceive as federal priorities. They have a vested interest in satisfying the office that funds evaluations. If they are to receive further evaluation contracts, they see their role as one of responding to the concerns of the sponsoring body. Thus, even when the federal presence is not active, evaluators tend to ignore issues of moment to other actors in the program context.

Unused

Critics allege that evaluation results seldom influence decisions about the course of the program (Rutman, 1980; Scott and Shore, 1979; Weiss, 1972). The evaluator conducts the study, completes the report, and leaves. Program managers take comfort from the findings that are positive and bury or forget the findings that suggest a need for major reform. At policy levels, there are few examples of evaluations that lead decision makers to expand a successful program or to terminate a program that shows few beneficial effects. Despite all the rhetoric about the utility of evaluative evidence for improving the rationality of decision making, evaluation often seems to leave the situation unchanged.

Early Reform Attempts

NIE was not the first federal agency to become exercised about the shortcomings of evaluation practice. Other federal agencies have made efforts to improve the craft. The President's Committee on Juvenile Delinquency, the Office of Economic Opportunity, the Model Cities Administration, the Office of Education, and the National Institute of Mental Health, among others, have all attempted to respond to the criticisms. Over the years, they have tried to institute three types of reforms.

Sensitizing Evaluators to Local Needs

Repeatedly, evaluators have been advised to involve user groups in the development and conduct of evaluation studies (Glaser and Backer, 1972; Windle and Ochberg, 1975). Drawing on the array of traditions that advocate user involvement as a means of increasing commitment to study results, staff in several agencies promoted active participation by program people in the design of studies. They urged evaluators to provide periodic feedback on study results to participant groups and to devote a major effort to the dissemination of results (Davis and Salasin, 1975; Zweig and Marvin, 1981).

Such advice was frequently heeded. Sensitive evaluators immersed themselves in the local situation and came to understand the concerns of various parties. They shaped their studies to respond to local needs and to represent the diversity of local issues. When they had information to report, they made strenuous efforts to bring it to the attention of the people involved and to interpret it in ways that were meaningful. Many other evaluators paid no attention. Their primary commitment was to the canons of social science. Whether they satisfied program people was of secondary concern. They had been trained in proper methodology, and they were not willing to sacrifice their standards in order to satisfy the whims of people who knew little about validity and causality and who cared even less.

Evaluators who worked for local agencies were more likely to attend to local issues, although not necessarily to the concerns of people far down in the hierarchy such as teachers, students, and parents. Evaluators who conducted nationwide studies rarely had the motivation to involve themselves in concerns below the federal level.

Funding Separate Evaluations for Different User Groups

A number of agencies officially recognized the divergent information needs of federal policy makers and local program managers. In evaluations of ESEA Title I, school districts were expected to do their own evaluations for their own purposes, while federal staff sponsored nationwide studies. The Office of Economic Opportunity recognized and funded three different types of evaluation. Type I evaluations were designed to assess the overall effectiveness of a national program. Type II evaluations inquired into the relative effectiveness of different strategies of programming. Type III evaluations, which monitored the performance of individual projects, placed the emphasis on assessment of operational efficiency (Wholey and others, 1970; Williams, 1971).

A few adventurous agencies provided funding to client groups to do their own evaluations of the programs in which they participated. The Model Cities Administration, for example, funded neighborhood participant groups in a few cities to evaluate the programs in their neighborhoods. The funds were meant to enable these groups to study the program from their own perspective and thereby satisfy their own interests, information needs, and criteria of success.

Separate evaluations for purposes of federal policy making and local program management tended to have reasonable success, although the quality of local evaluations was erratic. Experience with the funding of client groups to conduct evaluations was less satisfactory. Most client groups were not convinced that evaluation was useful. They tended to be more interested in changing conditions than in studying them. Even when money was available for study, these groups rarely followed through on the laborious and time-consuming process of evaluation. Information was not their priority. They wanted action. They believed that they understood the problems and the types of interventions that would make headway against them, without all the rigmarole that evaluation seemed to entail.

Systematic Canvass of User Group Values and Information Priorities

Another way to see that evaluation addresses the full range of issues that matter to participants is to undertake a systematic canvass of each group's concerns and criteria for success. Such procedures as multiattribute utility scaling were developed to collect data about the program features that each group valued and the relative weight that they assigned to these features. Once evaluators knew which goals were important and how important they were, they could collect information on matters of concern to each group of actors, and they could use the utility weights assigned by the different groups to assess the program's success (Edwards, 1971; Guttentag, 1973).

Evaluators who use this procedure have generally used it to learn about each group's goals for the program, rather than any broader set of concerns. They report that systematic weighting of participants' definitions of goals provides a useful basis for evaluation (Edwards, Guttentag, and Snapper, 1975; Snapper and Seaver, 1978). However, the process demands large amounts of time and considerable input from participants, and the final results do not always satisfy participants. When they see the numbers attached to their preferences by the process of assemblage, iteration, and calculation, they frequently find that the aggregate does not represent what they meant to convey (Guttentag and Snapper, 1974). And when the evaluator recommends the alternative that scores highest on their utility weightings, participants sometimes reject it in favor of an alternative that is intuitively more acceptable (Lock, 1982).

The stakeholder approach to evaluation attempted to build on much of this experience. It took the several pieces — involvement of people holding different positions in the social structure of programs, attention to their interests and utilities, representation of their priorities, emphasis on feedback and dissemination — and tried to shape them into a coherent package. Stakeholder-oriented evaluation was to remedy the assorted ills of old-style evaluation without running afoul of the pitfalls of some of the newer ventures.

Development of the Stakeholder Model

As it matured through staff discussions within NIE in the mid 1970s, the stakeholder approach to evaluation was designed explicitly both to increase the use of evaluation results for decision making and to bring a wider variety of people into active participation in the evaluation process. The former aim, increased use, was to be accomplished in large part by achievement of the latter aim, involvement of a diversity of prospective users in the design and conduct of the study.

How well does the stakeholder approach deal with the complaints leveled at evaluation practice? First, it addresses the issue of fairness directly. By empowering an array of concerned groups to play an active part in the evaluation, the stakeholder approach makes fairness a central tenet. Since it gives high priority to their definitions of information requirements and to timely feedback of the information that they want, it democratizes the evaluation process.

The stakeholder approach should also improve the relevance of information, because it gives stakeholders a strong voice in deciding what information shall be collected. In the process, and by their very diversity, stakeholders will help to avoid the narrowness of measurement that occasioned many complaints.

The unrealistic character of evaluation measures is not quite so easily disposed of. Gold (1981) notes that newly enfranchised groups can have their own unrealistic expectations about the size and scope of program effects. He devotes considerable attention to procedures for continual 'reality testing.' The evaluator is charged with responsibility for reviewing the developmental history of the program and other programs of similar type and for helping stakeholders to understand from the outset which expectations are reasonable. At a number of points during the evaluation, the evaluator is to provide information on the progress of program implementation. All parties to the evaluation are expected to become more realistic as the evaluation provides successive readings on indicators of program success and as stakeholders and evaluators learn to regard program development as an evolving process.

Wider and more immediate use of evaluation results is the driving force behind the stakeholder model. It assumes that giving people the information that they want when they want it and in a form that makes sense to them will increase their commitment to its use. When people have decisions to make, they will have relevant information that they had a say in developing and that responds to their interests.

There is a delicious flavor to the concept. It tackles some of the pervasive problems that have plagued evaluation, and it addresses them with high-minded intent and plausible strategies of action. However, many of its operating features are not well specified. There is ambiguity about a number of central concepts, and evaluators who are expected to implement the stakeholder approach confront a series of unresolved issues. This was true in 1977, when the first attempt to implement stakeholder-oriented evaluation began, and it still seems true today.

Some Unresolved Issues

Definition of Stakeholders

Who exactly are stakeholders? NIE documents sometimes describe them as people who make decisions about the program. However, the same documents also describe them as all the people whose lives are affected by the program and its evaluation. Thus, groups identified as stakeholders in these documents include teachers, school administrators, students, parents, school board members, the mayor's office, the Congress, the research community, the Department of Education, state officials, national program managers, and community organizations. Wide latitude for interpretation remains.

The research community is included in NIE's list of stakeholders because one of NIE's abiding aims is to use evaluations to build a body of generalized knowledge about what does and does not work in education. Are the interests of this community — primarily in valid, generalizable knowledge — compatible with the concerns of people engaged with the program? Can a single evaluation study satisfy such disparate needs? Can any team of evaluators, however skilful, provide information of immediate utility for various sets of program participants and at the same time conduct an adequate test of a replicable program model?

The justification for stakeholder involvement relies heavily on the idea that it can increase the use of evaluation results in decision making. But not all the groups associated with or affected by a program have program decisions to make. Students, parents, and community groups all have little say in the future of the program. Teachers, principals, youth workers, counselors, and other direct service staff do make decisions, but their decisions are generally about issues for which evaluations give little guidance.

Having a stake in a program is not the same thing as having a stake in an evaluation of the program. The kind of information that many people who have a stake in the program want is data that prove their worth. They want program vindicators, not program indicators. Even clients, who probably should want to know whether the program is likely to do them any good and whether they should participate, usually make up their mind on the basis of firsthand experience, not evaluative data. If they enjoy the program and the special attention it gives them, they, too, are likely to want data that justify its continuation.

Another question that arises is: Who defines which groups are stakeholders and which groups are not? Does NIE make the determination, or do evaluators? And does the right to decide who is in and who is out reduce the efficacy of stakeholder evaluation as an instrument of democratization? Since the concept arose from above, in the rarified halls of NIE — not from demands for inclusion from below, can a truly representative orientation be sustained?

Compatibility with Traditional Evaluation Procedures

Another unresolved issue is the extent to which the stakeholder approach is compatible with conventional evaluation practice, particularly with goal-oriented summative evaluation. The stakeholder approach puts a premium on flexibility and on the ability to respond to emergent information needs. Traditional evaluations develop indicators of program effectiveness in advance, so that they can take before and after measures on the same variable. Does the stakeholder approach make demands that conventionally trained evaluators cannot fulfill? Can evaluators integrate formative and summative concerns within a single study, at a level of competence and with a degree of richness that satisfy their varied audiences?

The stakeholder approach requires time for negotiation. NIE foresaw the additional demands and tried to accommodate them in the schedule.

Did they make ample allowance? Or did they underestimate the time and resources necessary to keep the elaborate process moving along?

The stakeholder approach changes the role of evaluators. They are asked not only to be technical experts who do competent research. They are required to become political managers who orchestrate the involvement of diverse interest groups. They must be negotiators, weighing one set of information requests against others and coming to amicable agreements about priorities. They must be skilful educators, sharing their knowledge about appropriate expectations for program development and program success while giving participants a sense of ownership of the study. Are the expectations for evaluators unreasonably high?

Finally, the stakeholder approach marks a change in evaluation priorities. The salience of quantitative, summative assessment of the value of the program concept is reduced. People still care about outcomes. NIE continues to care, as do stakeholders who have to make decisions about whether to support the program in their school district and with their funds. They retain — or they should retain — a concern for the technical quality of the research and for the validity of its results. But such interests are jostled for dominance by demands from other stakeholders for current information on a barrage of practical questions. Can evaluators juggle the competing demands?

These were some of the issues left unresolved when the stakeholder concept was launched. Still, all things considered, the concept was worth a trial. Important evaluations were coming up, and NIE decided to put the idea into practice. Experience would help to flesh out the concept. The potential benefits seemed promising enough to warrant taking the stakeholder approach into the field.

Promise of the Stakeholder Approach

In many ways, the idea marks a decided advance in awareness of the purposes and potential of program evaluation. Above all, it represents a recognition of the political nature of the evaluation process. Unlike early formulations of the mission of evaluation, it does not cast evaluation as the impartial, objective judge of a program's worth. It does not claim that scientific research methods can reveal a single unvarnished truth that, by the sheer force of its verity, can lead decision makers to the right course of action.

The stakeholder concept represents an appreciation that each program affects many groups, which have divergent and even incompatible concerns. It realizes — and legitimizes — the diversity of interests at play in the program world. It recognizes the multiple perspectives that these interests bring to judgment and understanding. It takes evaluation down from the pedestal and places it in the midst of the fray. It aims to make evaluation a conveyor of information, not a deliverer of truth; an aid, not a judge. Realization of the legitimacy of competing interests and the multiplicity of perspectives and willingness to place evaluation at the service of diverse groups are important intellectual advances.

Furthermore, the stakeholder approach represents an awareness of the developmental nature of large-scale social programming. It does not assume that programs are laboratory-like interventions — clearly formulated and replicable entities whose effects can be judged once and for all. Embedded in the concept is a realistic sense of the growing, changing, shifting course that programs follow and of the variety of information needed in the development process. The concept emphasizes quick response to emerging questions and quick feedback to aid in program design and redesign.

One of its most engaging characteristics is the shift in power that it signals. No longer is the federal agency to have a monopoly on control. The concept enfranchises a diverse array of groups, each of which is to have a voice in the planning and conduct of studies. Local as well as national concerns are to be addressed. Issues specific to individual sites and generic issues common across sites receive attention.

The reasons for NIE's willingness to cede authority were not all altruistic. As it had learned through sorry experience, full responsibility for the evaluation of programs could put the agency on the hot seat, particularly when the program being studied was a pet project of an influential political figure and evaluation found it wanting. The stakeholder approach could spread the responsibility. Several observers have suggested that a reduction in NIE's political vulnerability was a significant if unstated goal of the stakeholder approach. By sharing control over the direction of evaluations and therefore over the findings that emerged, NIE was trying to defuse political pressures on itself, on the evaluators, and on the program agencies.

However, the means with which NIE chose to share its responsibility was slightly incongruous. The stakeholder approach imposed a bureaucratic procedure on participation. Stakeholders were to be identified, convened, given set tasks, and required to participate in scheduled and routinized activities. The procedure was a far cry from the disorderly contest of ordinary interest group politics. The potential for conflict among groups was recognized, but it was to be constrained by orderly proceduralism. NIE appears to have assumed that harmony could be achieved by focusing on the definition of the information needs of different groups and by restricting attention to the issue of who needed to know what and when.

Implicitly, NIE seems also to have expected the stakeholder approach to reduce the level of conflict in decision making about the program. Multi-lateral participation in the evaluation process would help the several groups involved in the program to develop mutual understanding and to appreciate one another's viewpoints. Even more important, since they had to agree on the design of the evaluation they would all have to accept its results. The facts would be settled. In later discussions, they could discuss divergence in the values that they attached to the facts, but they could not argue about what the facts were. The area of contentiousness would be bounded.

Furthermore, the federal program office would be removed from the conflict. NIE was no longer judging local performance through evaluation, not weighing or criticizing. Local people were shaping the evaluation themselves. Thus, relations between local and federal authorities should be more relaxed and collegial.

The stakeholder approach was expected to build support for and commitment to the findings that evaluations produced. People who had helped to plan and design an evaluation would have bought in. They would take the results seriously. If and when they took part in subsequent decision making, they were expected to use the data that evaluation provided. At the very least, they could hardly say that the evaluators had studied the wrong things or that they had ignored the effects that mattered. Thus, the stakeholder approach was expected to increase the use of evaluation results in decision making. This had been the stimulus for reform in the first place, and its attainment would represent the real test of the efficacy of the concept.

The Stakeholder Approach in Action

The stakeholder approach received its first trials in evaluations of the Cities-in-Schools and Push/Excel programs. Both programs were highly complex, and both had politically sensitive connections with important people. That the stakeholder approach should be tested in connection with these two programs was partly due to chance; they were the evaluations that happened to come along as the stakeholder approach reached maturity. In another way, however, the concatenation was not at all accidental. NIE had developed the stakeholder approach in part to deal with just such contingencies — politicized program, diverse constituencies, the incipient risk to NIE of an evaluation that might antagonize powerful people. The stakeholder approach would yield an evaluation that was responsive to multiple concerns, and it would protect NIE's bureaucratic interests.

It is relevant, however, that both programs were very difficult to evaluate. They tended to be inchoate, emergent, characterized by high levels of ambiguity. Their activities differed from day to day and from site to site. The programs were administered not by orderly school bureaucracies according to predictable sets of rules but by outside, movement-like groups. They depended in considerable part on the dedication of committed workers and the charisma of leaders. To evaluate such programs as these with conventional evaluation techniques appeared to be courting trouble. Yet, if the programs were to receive federal money, the rules said that they had to be evaluated. Thus, they became the first tests of the stakeholder approach.

References

BERK, R.A. and ROSSI, P.H. (1976) 'Doing good or worse: evaluation research politically re-examined', *Social Problems*, 3, pp. 337–49.

CARO, F.G. (Ed.) (1971) *Readings in Evaluation Research*, New York, Russell Sage Foundation.

COCHRAN, N. (1980) 'Society as emergent and more than rational: An essay on the inappropriateness of program evalution', *Policy Sciences*, 12, 2, pp. 113–29.

COLEMAN, J.S. (1980) 'Policy research and political theory', *University of Chicago Record*, 14, 2.

DATTA, L.E. (Ed.) (1981) *Evaluation in Change*, Beverly Hills, Calif., Sage.

DAVIS, H.R. and SALASIN, S. (1975) 'The utilization of evaluation' in STRUENING, E. and GUTTENTAG, M. (Eds) *Handbook of Evaluation Research*, Beverly Hills, Calif., Sage.

EDWARDS, W. (1971) 'Social utilities', *The Engineering Economist*, summer, symposium series.

EDWARDS, W., GUTTENTAG, M. and SNAPPER, K.J. (1975) 'Effective evaluation: A decision-theoretic approach' in STRUENING, E.L. and GUTTENTAG, M. (Eds) *Handbook of Evaluation Research*, Beverly Hills, Calif., Sage.

GLASER, E.M. and BACKER, T.E. (1972) 'A clinical approach to program evaluation', *Evaluation*, 1, pp. 54–9.

GOLD, N. (1981) *The Stakeholder Process in Educational Program Evaluation*, Washington DC, National Institute of Education.

GUBA, E.G. (1969) 'The failure of educational evaluation', *Educational Technology*, 9, 5, pp. 29–38.

GUTTENTAG, M. (1973) 'Subjectivity and its use in evaluation research', *Evaluation*, 1, 2, pp. 60–5.

GUTTENTAG, M. and SNAPPER, K. (1974) 'Plans, evaluations, and decisions', *Evaluation*, 2, 1, pp. 58–64 and 73–4.

HOUSE, E.R. (1980) *Evaluating with Validity*, Beverly Hills, Calif., Sage.

LOCK, A.R. (1982) 'A strategic business decision with multiple criteria: the Bally men's shoe problem', *Journal of Operational Research Society*, 33, pp. 327–32.

PARLETT, M. and HAMILTON, D. (1976) 'Evaluation as illumination: a new approach to the study of innovatory programs' in GLASS, G.V. (Ed.) *Evaluation Studies Review Annual 1979*, Beverly Hills, Calif., Sage.

PATTON, M.Q. (1978) *Utilization-Focused Evaluation*, Beverly Hills, Calif., Sage.

RUTMAN, L. (1980) *Planning Useful Evaluations*, Beverly Hills, Calif., Sage.

SCHWARZ, P.A. (1980) 'Program devaluation: Can the experiment reform?' in LOVELAND, E. (Ed.) *Measuring the Hard-to-Measure*, New Directions for Program Evaluation, no 6, San Francisco, Jossey-Bass.

SCOTT, R.A. and SHORE, A.R. (1979) *Why Sociology Does Not Apply: A Study of the Use of Sociology in Public Policy*, New York, Elsevier.

SNAPPER, K.J. and SEAVER, D.A. (1978) *Application of Decision Analysis to Program Planning and Evaluation: Technical Report*, Falls Church, Va, Decision Science Consortium.

STAKE, R.E. (1978) 'Responsive education' in HAMILTON, D. and others (Eds) *Beyond the Numbers Game*, Berkeley, Calif., McCutchan.

WEISS, C.H. (1972) 'Utilization of evaluation: Toward comparative study' in WEISS, C.H. (Ed.) *Evaluating Action Programs: Readings in Social Action and Evaluation*, Boston, Allyn and Bacon.

WHOLEY, J.S. and others (1970) *Federal Evaluation Policy*, Washington, DC Urban Institute.

WILLIAMS, W. (1971) *Social Policy Research and Analysis*, New York, Elsevier.

WINDLE, C. and OCHBERG, F.M. (1975) 'Enhancing program evaluation in the community mental health centers program', *Evaluation*, 2, 2, pp. 30–6.

ZWEIG, F.M. and MARVIN, K.E. (Eds) (1981) *Educating Policy Makers for Evaluation*, Beverly Hills, Calif., Sage.

The Evaluation of Push/Excel: A Case Study

Eleanor Farrar and Ernest House
Huron Research Institute and University of Illinois

Jesse Jackson, interviewed on the CBS television program *Sixty Minutes* on 4 December 1977, said: 'Now, the challenge is upward mobility, and that is why the focus on not only getting in school but producing in school becomes a new kind of challenge ... We must struggle to excel because competition is keener, because doors that once opened are now closing in our faces. It's my judgment we need a massive revolution in our attitude.

'But we cannot do it alone ... Many other people must get involved ... We pulled together a group of ministers [and] massive parent involvement. We've begun to mobilize disc jockeys and key athletes and artists and entertainers ... So, in a real sense, what we're doing is not operating alone; we're simply using our talent and energy to mobilize involvement to take on a massive problem.'

Hubert Humphrey was watching *Sixty Minutes* from his hospital bed in Minneapolis on that night, and he heard Jesse Jackson speak of the need for a movement to convince black youth to excel in school. He watched Jackson's impassioned appeal to a stadium full of wildly applauding teenagers in Los Angeles; he heard Jackson's call to the black community to join in the endeavor. The next day, Humphrey called his old friend Joseph Califano, Secretary of Health, Education, and Welfare. Califano (1981) reports: 'In a weak voice, his strength consumed by his battle with cancer, [Humphrey] asked me if I had seen the *Sixty Minutes* program. When I responded, he said, "Well, then, you saw what I saw. I want you to talk to Jesse Jackson and help him. He's doing something for those kids. I've talked to him this morning and told him I'll talk to you. Now, you get him down to your office and help him. Will you do that for me?" I told him I would.' (p. 294)

This case study was supported in part by the National Institute of Education (NIE), but the study presents the views of the authors, for which the NIE is not responsible. This case reflects AIR's account of Push/Excel's early history. The authors are indebted to Maria Sachs and Stephen Raudenbush for proof that the story can be told at a fraction of its original length.

Thus began the federal government's involvement in Push/Excel, a motivational program for black youth started by Jackson two years earlier and supported by individual, corporate, and foundation contributions. One month later, the National Institute of Education awarded two grants to the Push Foundation: a $25,000 grant to plan a Push/Excel conference and a $20,000 grant for preliminary program evaluation and project design. Five months later, NIE awarded another $400,000 for the design of projects in Chicago, Kansas City, and Los Angeles and for expansion to additional sites. Next, the US Office of Education began planning for a $3 million demonstration project to begin in January 1979. By early May 1978, more than twenty local education agencies had expressed interest in taking part in the demonstration.

Not long after, at Califano's request, NIE began to plan a national evaluation of Push/Excel. For some observers, the government's involvement, although uninvited, seemed to be a big boost for Push/Excel. But was it? An editorial in the *Washington Star* ('A Shove Comes to Push, 1978) expressed reservations: 'We must admit that HEW Secretary Joe Califano's announcement that his department is giving two modest grants to the Reverend Jesse Jackson's Push program strikes us as a good news/bad news event. Our delight, accordingly, is not unmixed with worry. With even modest federal grants, especially from HEW, come bureaucratic intruders; and with bureaucratic intruders come "guidelines"; and with guidelines come stale, meddlesome orthodoxies and ideologies that are quite capable of rubbing the sharp edge off the best ideas. Jesse Jackson's movement is, we think, one of the most hopeful things that has happened to this country in years and has been so because he marches to his own drummer. The last thing we need is the federalization of Jesse Jackson.'

The editorialist's worry was prophetic: Less than five years later, Push/Excel was struggling to survive. Budgets and staff had been reduced, and federal and philanthropic support had shifted to other interests. The few remaining local programs had severed connections with the national office, abandoned the Push/Excel name, and reduced Jackson's crusade for total community involvement to familiar school programs for underachieving black youth.

The story of Push/Excel's demise is complex. It involves shifting political winds and straitened school finances, Jackson's unpredictability and insensitivity to school politics, and struggles between various groups of program participants. The national Push/Excel staff sought to persuade local districts and schools to share program control and decision making. It was a reasonable goal, but it failed to allow for school politics and the need of local Excel staffs for central direction. The federally sponsored evaluation of Push/Excel and its press coverage are also part of the story. Government support required Excel to undergo an evaluation, and despite all evidence that it was a movement, it was evaluated as a program. The evaluators tried to help it to become one, but for three years, as they guided and advised Excel staff, their reports documented Excel's inability to produce the desired effect on students and the community. These findings were widely reported in the national and local press, and in less than three years, before the final report appeared, the verdict was in: Jesse Jackson's inspirational movement had failed.

This is a case study of the federally sponsored evaluation of Push/Excel. The authors of this chapter had no involvement with Push/Excel prior to this case study. In the course of our work, we interviewed staff and participants in two local Excel programs and made several trips to NIE, the Department of Education, and the evaluators' offices. We reviewed documents, press articles, and program files, and we were generously granted hours of interviews by NIE and AIR. Their views of Push/Excel and its evaluation are, we hope, fairly represented, but those of the national program office are not: Our requests to meet with Push/Excel national staff and with Jesse Jackson remained unanswered.

The story begins with the federal government's involvement in Push/Excel two years after Jackson began the movement, and it concludes with publication of the final evaluation report some fifty-two months later. The study was commissioned by the National Institute of Education as part of an examination of the utility and productivity of urban secondary school program evaluation. To ensure that the evaluation would be useful to Push/Excel stakeholders, NIE sought to involve them in the evaluation process. Stakeholders included federal officials and national Push/Excel staff and sponsors as well as local participants — students, parents, school people, churches, funding sources, and other community segments. The evaluation was to show not only how Push/Excel affected students, schools, and communities but also how these groups influenced the evaluation.

The Federal Involvement

Not everyone shared Humphrey's enthusiasm for a federal role in Push/Excel. A few days after Humphrey's conversation with Califano, Califano called Patricia Albjerg Graham, director of NIE, to ask about funding for Excel. According to Graham (personal interview, June 1981), 'I called [various] people and said, ... "Should we put money into [Jackson's] operation? It seems to me that the basic question is 'Can you bottle charisma and organize it?'" And people said, "Well, yes." And they said he'd also had trouble keeping his books straight. [Subsequently, I told Jackson], "There's money for you to plan a program ... which we will evaluate ... If you take federal cash, then you have to ... account for how [it] is spent and specify what it is you're going to do with [it]. And the gist of the evaluation is whether or not you did [that]" ... This is shortened, of course. It was about an eight-month discussion.'

Mary Berry, Assistant Secretary of HEW, recalled (personal interview, July 1982) that, after speaking with Humphrey, Califano offered to fund Push/Excel. However, Jackson refused the money, saying, 'No, I have no program.' Califano told Jackson that was not important; he could hire a writer to prepare a proposal to HEW, and the government would provide technical help to develop a program. Jackson accepted.

Several weeks later, Jackson met with a group that included Mary Berry, Ernest Boyer, US Commissioner of Education; Jeff Schiller and Patricia Graham from NIE; and James Comer of Yale, who was completing an evaluation of Excel funded by the Ford Foundation. They discussed the evaluation, including the possibility that it would attempt 'to show that Jesse was no good and that Push/Excel was no good' (Graham, personal interview, June 1981). Some of those present argued that there should be no evaluation. As Graham recalls this meeting, 'I said [that] the gist of evaluation is not to figure out whether the program meets the evaluator's goals, but for the evaluator to figure out what your goals are, which means that you've got to figure out what your goals are.' According to Graham, an evaluation had to be done. How extensive it should be and what form it should take were arguable, but some form of accounting, both substantial and financial, was required.

NIE decided to use the stakeholder approach in the evaluation of Push/Excel. There was little discussion of other possibilities. According to Jeff Schiller, assistant director of NIE's Teaching and Learning Program, this was due to a concern for evaluation utility. Conflict between evaluators and program staff had frequently undermined the credibility and usefulness of evaluation for decision makers. The NIE group, and particularly Norman Gold, believed that stakeholder involvement could prevent such problems. NIE had contracted with the American Institutes for Research (AIR) to use the stakeholder approach in evaluating the Cities-in-Schools Program under Gold's direction, and NIE wished to explore it further. Push/Excel was selected for the same treatment — chiefly, as Schiller remembers it (personal interview, July 1982), 'because it was there.' According to Schiller, 'The stakeholder notion was a good one to try with Cities-in-Schools and Push/Excel anyway. We knew there'd never be any federal policy in this area. [Excel] would always be locally modified, implemented, and supported, and it had to be evaluated against their goals. Also, it was very developmental. The stakeholder approach would improve the implementation process and [evaluation] utility.'

Norman Gold was responsible for drafting the request for proposals for evaluation of Push/Excel (National Institute of Education, 1978). Gold, who has been described as 'handling all the politically sensitive evaluations at NIE,' gave potential bidders considerable latitude. Since the evaluation would have several audiences — parents, teachers, community members, policy makers, and evaluators — the contractor was to consult with panels representing these groups during the design and implementation of the evaluation. Noting that this approach implied no 'technical compromises which will satisfy consumers but [lack] methodological rigor and clarity,' the request for proposals outlined seven questions that the contractor was to address (National Institute of Education, 1978):

1 To what extent have the programs been implemented; what implementation problems were there, and how were they addressed; and how does the implementation vary within and between cities?

2 How have students benefited from the program both in and out of school in terms of long- and short-term gains?

3 How have participating schools been affected by the Excel program and support? What were the effects on the delivery of educational services, staff morale, and the general climate of the schools?

4 Excel stresses close involvement of parents, families, and the community in schools. What has been the impact of the program upon these groups?

5 What has been the impact of Reverend Jackson, Push, and other unique aspects of Excel upon programmatic outcomes?

6 What are the marginal extra costs of schooling attributable to Excel? How much of these are start-up costs and how much ongoing costs?

7 To what extent can the processes, structures, and costs of Excel be accommodated within normal school administrative procedures and budgets? (pp. 8–9)

The intention was that other stakeholders would add to this list. According to Norman Gold (personal interview, January 1982), '[I was attempting to] set up a process by which the evaluators would not dominate the evaluation as much as they had in the past, [nor would] the federal government; . . . [one in which] we would empower others to have more say.'

The work was to proceed in two phases: four months to design the evaluation and thirty-two months to carry it out. The total level of effort was 12.5 FTE/person-years. The first phase would familiarize the contractor with the programs, the expectations of stakeholders, and the basis for decisions about continuing support. This phase had the explicit aim of increasing the evaluation's usefulness by enabling stakeholders' information needs to be incorporated into the final design.

Award of the contract was swift. The request for proposals was issued in September 1978, proposals were due in October, and the contract was signed in January 1979. The budget was $750,000. NIE received seven proposals. According to Gold (personal interviews, October 1980 and July 1982), it was 'not a hot competition. The proposals weren't great.' AIR was chosen because 'they understood what the stakeholder concept was all about,' although NIE was uneasy about relying on the same principal investigator for two similar evaluations, and although the stakeholder approach was not prominent in AIR's proposal.

The wisdom and the appropriateness of formal evaluation of Jesse Jackson's movement had been questioned, but evaluation had to accompany the serendipitous federal involvement in Push/Excel. The stakeholder approach was selected because NIE was exploring it as a way of reducing conflicts and of increasing the utility of evaluations. NIE's information about the program was sketchy: Since most Excel documents were designed for promotion, the request for proposals relied heavily on Jackson's proposal to the Department of Health, Education, and Welfare, which had been developed at Califano's urging with HEW help and funding (National Institute of Education, 1978, p. 3). NIE staff had visited the Los Angeles site, where they had been impressed by reports of improved attendance and by the student activities that they found (personal interview with Jeff Schiller, July 1982). NIE concluded that, while the program was still loose and unstructured, it made sense to begin collecting 'a data base around some [useful] conceptual structure for evaluation' (personal interview with Norman Gold, July 1982). The evaluators were to develop the structure after investigation of program activities and objectives at five sites. Armed with NIE's impressions of Excel and its possibilities, AIR began its three-year study.

Push/Excel: A Movement and a Program

The evaluation of Push/Excel was not destined to be straightforward. Excel had been launched as a movement — a grass-roots, self-help effort to achieve a broad set of goals through personal and community commitment. It was not a structured education reform with an implementation blueprint, and Excel's national staff were not educators or program developers. Their experience lay in the civil rights movement and its strategy and tactics. They lacked the skills and the perspective needed to develop a school program. The fact that program objectives and activities differed across schools was a further complication, which ruled out the usual methods of multisite evaluation. When the evaluation contract was awarded, what existed was an eloquent, charismatic leader of national reputation who had attracted a staff of committed followers, considerable public and private funding, and several school districts willing to make an attempt to translate a self-help ideology into a school program that could regenerate black youth — an unlikely subject for scrutiny by social science.

Eleanor Farrar and Ernest R. House

The Origins of Excel

Push/Excel was the offspring of Operation Push, a social action organization founded by Jesse Jackson in 1971 after his break with the Southern Christian Leadership Conference. It grew out of a demonstration staged at the White House on 15 January 1975, for full-time employment and jobs for blacks. The demonstration ended abruptly when Reverend Jackson told the marchers to go home. Subsequently, a letter from the Push/Excel board of directors to potential donors explained Jackson's decision: 'Walking through file after file of protesters, a tall, athletic young black minister — a man who had been in the vanguard of the civil rights movement for years — was shocked to see that a great many of the youths were drunk or on drugs, visibly out of control. That man, the Reverend Jesse Jackson, realized then that the time had come for him to change his target for reform. As he painfully said: "The door of opportunity is open for our people, but they are too drunk, too unconscious to walk through the door"' (Reverend O. Moss, Jr., letter, n.d., cited in Murray and others, 1982, p. 12).

Ten months later, Jackson appeared before a student assembly in Chicago's predominantly black Martin Luther King High School. His message was blunt: It was up to blacks to ensure that they did not waste the opportunities that they had. Or, as Jackson put it, 'No one will save us for us but us.' It was the first stop on a cross-country tour that the *Washington Post* later described as Jesse Jackson's 'crusade' (Murray and others, 1982, p. 12).

The Movement

Jackson's crusade carried a timeless message: that hard work, self-discipline, delayed gratification, and persistence were qualities that youth needed in order to succeed. Jackson believed that black youths in particular blamed society for their failures and that they expected society to provide redress. He hoped to replace this futile aspiration with one based on sacrifice and commitment to a larger personal goal.

Jackson believed that the resources of the entire community had to be mobilized. He urged parents to take an interest in their children's schooling, to establish regular study hours at home, and to pick up report cards at school. Schools were admonished to raise their standards for behavior and academic performance. The community was urged to participate in program events, to contribute time and money, and to offer rewards and opportunities. In brief, Jackson celebrated a striving toward solid middle-class virtues through total involvement by students and communities, especially the church. The prominence that Jackson assigned to the church reflected his Southern background and the origins of his movement. He elaborated his beliefs in ten 'commandments,' later renamed *the ten principles* (Push for Excellence, Inc., n.d.):

1 It is essential that a public institution clearly define itself, to say unequivocally what it believes in and stands for.
2 The development of responsible adults is a task requiring community commitment. It cannot be left solely to the public schools.
3 The principal tasks of the public schools cannot be achieved if a disproportionate amount of time and resources must be given to maintaining order. Public schools are not obligated to serve students who persistently disrupt schools and violate the rights of others.
4 The full responsibility for learning cannot be transferred from the student to the teacher.
5 Parents must consistently support the proposition that students have responsibilities as well as rights and that the schools have an obligation to insist upon both.
6 High performance takes place in a framework of expectation.
7 There is nothing inherently undemocratic in requiring students to do things that are demonstrably beneficial to them.
8 Involvement in and commitment to meaningful activities which give one a sense of identity and worth are essential to all human beings and are especially critical to adolescents.
9 The practice of convenience leads to collapse, but the laws of sacrifice lead to greatness. This applies to students, teachers, parents, administrators, and community leaders.
10 A sound *ethical* climate must be established for a school system as a whole and for each individual school, because the death of ethics is the sabotage of excellence. Politicians, school board members, superintendents, central office staff, principals, teachers, parents, and ministers have the obligation to take an aggressive lead in setting such ethical standards. (pp. 4–5)

Jackson's message of self-help and high standards of achievement struck responsive chords wherever he went. Stadiums were filled. Television and newspapers recorded his successes. Editorials praised the wisdom of his pronouncements, and appearances on nationally televised talk shows followed. A rally in the New Orleans Superdome drew more than 65,000 people; 20,000 watched Jackson, joined by entertainers Marlon Brando and Aretha Franklin, in Los Angeles. Education editor Art Bronscombe (1979) described the Denver rally in the 12 September 1979, issue of the *Denver Post:* 'Leading about 4,000 students in chants of "I am somebody . . . Down with dope, up with hope," the Reverend Jesse Jackson opened his Push for Excellence program in the Denver public schools Tuesday.

The slim, dynamic Chicago Baptist minister ... told the multiracial throng that his generation has largely conquered the mountain of equal opportunity ... "The mountain you must conquer is ... the mountain of effort." "The Lord makes oranges grow on trees," he shouted, "but you've got to squeeze the juice yourselves." He paused frequently to demand that the students join him in such chants as "Nobody can save us from us, for us, but us." And he told them, "There is nothing more powerful in the world than development of the mind and a strong character."'

In spring 1976, the Chicago Board of Education agreed to initiate Excel activities in ten schools, and a year later preliminary Excel activities began in Kansas City, Los Angeles, Washington, DC, and Chattanooga, Tennessee. Other cities made inquiries and began planning. In 1977 alone, Jackson made more than forty personal appearances at colleges, high schools, and educational conferences. These activities were supported largely by corporate and philanthropic contributions: Illinois Bell, the Joe Drown and Piton Foundations, the Ford Foundation, Lilly Foundation, Rockefeller Brothers Fund, and Chicago Community Trust. In record time, Jesse Jackson's crusade had become an educational movement of national proportions.

Jackson's base was Operation Push, of which he had been President since 1971. Push considered itself a 'civil economics' organization, aimed at achieving economic parity for blacks by using strategies that had proved so effective in the civil rights movement: selective patronage, boycotts of specific businesses, and the mass rally. The structure and modus operandi of Operation Push were reflected in the practices of the fledgling movement. As AIR later described it (Murray and others, 1982) '[The] Push organizational structure ... adapted continually to accommodate the issues and funds at hand. Programs and departments came and went, along with the ... staff that conducted them. Through it all, Jackson took the lead ... When he decided to seek reform among youth, the organization accommodated once more and added a new box to its organization chart — this time labeled *Push for Excellence*.' (p. 14) Push/Excel was a modest part of the Operation Push enterprise, which was a strong pressure in the black and third-world political scene, but for a time, Push/Excel was a source of national visibility for both the organization and its peripatetic leader.

The Program

If Jackson's movement caught on overnight, efforts to translate it into an organization that could implement his message proceeded slowly. Originally, Operation Push was to take care of fund raising and promotion, while local staff were to develop and manage local operations. But, it quickly became apparent that most local staff were inexperienced in community organization and unable to deal effectively with top-level school bureaucrats. They needed and expected help from a national office, which Operation Push finally established in spring 1977. A Push/Excel national director and administrative aide were hired to design program components, coordinate activities, develop a structured approach to Excel, and expand its resource base. But, almost from the start, they spent more time helping Jackson to spread his message than they did developing implementation tools for local staff.

Gradually, program descriptions became available. One of the first, an illustrated booklet providing 'just a few starter ideas,' suggested activities to involve community members and sustain student commitment: reward and incentive programs, career day forums, 'witness for excellence' meetings. It also recommended media campaigns, school plays emphasizing excellence, and field trips. A second publication (Push for Excellence, Inc., n.d.) was more specific. It discussed Excel's objectives, described activities to make the program work (teachers must 'expect quality work,' while churches must 'begin tutoring programs,' 'adopt schools,' and so on), and provided tips on how to begin local Excel programs.

Jackson placed six activities at the core of an Excel program (Push for Excellence, Inc., n.d.)

1 *State of the School Address.* At the start of each school year, the principal should give a state of the school address, setting the climate and the goals for the year. The principal must be the moral authority, teach discipline and academic achievement; and development will be the by-product.

2 *Student Pledges.* Students must pledge to commit themselves to study every school-day night a minimum of two hours from 7 to 9 P.M., with the television, radio, and record player off and no telephone interruptions. If we match our effort and discipline in athletics in the academic arena, we will achieve the same results.

3 *Parent Pledges.* Parents must pledge to accept the responsibility to monitor their child's study hours and agree to go to school to pick up their child's report card each grading period.

4 *Teacher Pledges.* Teachers must pledge to make meaningful homework assignments; to collect, grade, and return homework to students; and call the parent if a student is absent two days in a row or is doing poorly in school — all of which reflects increased expectations of students on the part of teachers.

5 *Written Ethical Code of Conduct.* A written ethical code of

conduct, which presents alternative life-styles to drugs, al-
cohol, violence, teenage pregnancy, and other forms of decadence that detract from an educational atmosphere, must be
implemented.

6 *Voter Registration.* On graduation day, all eligible seniors
would receive a diploma in one hand (symbolizing knowledge
and wisdom) and a voter registration card in the other
(symbolizing power and responsibility), as well as ... nonpart-
isan information on how to vote and operate a voting machine.
(p. 2)

But, the methods that schools used to get the activities under way and to
increase participation were left to local invention.

The early Push/Excel material portrays signing the pledge as the
main event and the suggested activities as ancillary ways of keeping people
involved, of expressing the pledged commitments. The pledge appeared to
be critical to Excel — perhaps because it was viewed almost as a religious
experience, a commitment analogous to coming forward in the church and
pledging one's life to Christ. Underlying this commitment was the notion
of change as a conversion process. One converts and thereby changes one's
life forever in one swift action; subsequent activities are devices to
reinforce commitment. In its early efforts, Push/Excel seemed driven by
the belief that demonstrable change would naturally follow the pledge.

The AIR evaluators did not believe that change must follow conversion or that Excel activities were sufficient for demonstrated change to
occur. In commenting on program development at that time, AIR noted
(Murray and others, 1982): 'These [activities] were more in the nature of a
good place to start than a prescription for how to apply the Push/Excel
message concretely. The fledgling programs . . . had been struggling with
the next steps . . . Now, with the availability of federal money [and] the
flood of new requests for help, the need for a concrete, describable
program of activities became urgent. But, who was to produce it? Not
Jackson, who explicitly saw his role as catalyst, not program designer or
implementor. Not the existing Push/Excel staff, who at this point
consisted of a national director and a secretary. Program development was
a major job, calling . . . for expertise in a variety of skills, a sizable staff,
and time.' (p. 25)

The development of an organizational model for local Excel programs
was the next step. (The national Push/Excel office takes credit for the
model, but the Chattanooga program director said that it originated in Los
Angeles and that it was refined in Chattanooga.) The model called for
close collaboration between school districts and local Push/Excel staff. A
Push/Excel site director hired by the national office was responsible for
local fund raising, liaison with the national office, coordinating activities,

and assisting program staff. Community liaison persons, employed by the national staff but based in schools, worked to involve the community. Each school had a teacher-adviser for recruiting and counseling, who, jointly with the community liaison, selected the advisory council, comprised of students, teachers, parents, and community members. A district administrator was named Push/Excel program director. Working with his Excel counterpart, he was to coordinate decision making and share responsibility for program operations. This organization presumed that school districts would be willing to give nondistrict personnel a major voice in school affairs and to commit resources to implementation of the concept of total community involvement.

The national office expected local staff to use this structure in devising a program and activities suited to the local context. Jackson's ten principles and six core activities gave them a place to start, and the mass rally provided an audience. It was then up to them to develop a Push/Excel program that would build and sustain commitment to the broad movement objectives.

Excel's Early Implementation

In practice, early implementation of the Push/Excel program model and activities varied from site to site. Frequently, it was problematic. When the NIE evaluation contract was awarded in 1979, six programs were affiliated with Push/Excel: the original pilot program sites in Chicago, Los Angeles, and Kansas City and sites in Memphis, Denver, and Chattanooga where programs were about to begin. Financial woes and political turmoil in other districts that adopted Push/Excel left few still operating after the first two years.

The Chicago program was initiated in ten high schools. Although local philanthropy and national office funds provided resources for start-up, district support was halting, and the program was never fully implemented. Kansas City had programs in two high schools, but only one was endorsed by the district. Local infighting followed, and the district eventually lost confidence in the program.

In Los Angeles, Push/Excel had the support of district administrators. First-year funding was adequate for the full complement of staff, but the second year coincided with the passage of Proposition 13, which resulted in a budget reduction of nearly 30 per cent. The program was finally terminated.

Despite difficulties and controversies at the older sites, there were high hopes for the future of the three new programs. Then, Jesse Jackson went to the Middle East.

Eleanor Farrar and Ernest R. House

Jackson's Trip to the Middle East

Days before the evaluation contract was signed, Jackson made front-page news when he was photographed arm in arm with PLO leader Yasir Arafat. The story sent shock waves reverberating through local Push/Excel communities. Jackson had intended to encourage links between third-world oil-exporting nations and black U.S. businesses, but his debut in international politics was unanimously censured by American public opinion and the press. Although his action was unrelated to Excel, it created serious problems for the program and for the evaluation. Support died in Memphis and wavered elsewhere, and the trip abruptly terminated Excel's prospects in Louisiana. Only in Chattanooga did the program survive essentially undamaged — in large part due to the efforts of Excel board member Ruth Homberg, publisher of the *Chattanooga Times* and an important part of the Chattanooga power structure.

Whatever the reasons for Jackson's trip, its consequences for the program were far-reaching. Local staff had not felt much support from the national office in their struggle to establish working relationships with school districts, and the estrangement deepened, setting the stage for a formal break. The AIR evaluation may also have been affected: The publicity — most of it negative — made Push/Excel and the evaluation highly visible and highly vulnerable.

Summary

As the AIR evaluation got under way, both it and Push/Excel faced several problems. First, Excel was less a program than a movement whose success depended on a charismatic leader. This was not the familiar terrain of evaluation studies. Second, the national staff lacked the inclination and skills needed to transform the movement into a structured school program. By failing to provide sufficient guidance to local programs already beset with political problems and weak management, they encouraged even greater program diversity. Third, Push/Excel was riddled with dissension. Although committed students and staff worked creatively together in many Excel schools, administrative conflict among national, district, and local levels was often the rule. Fourth, Jesse Jackson's credibility had been tarnished. His trip angered many and raised serious questions about his politics and judgment. This deflected energy and attention from program activities and increased local stakes in the evaluation's outcome.

Still another problem soon to confront Push/Excel was that the evaluators, in trying to provide constructive criticism to aid program development, in fact drew negative publicity that undermined the morale of the movement just as it faced a most difficult task: translating great potential into a sustained program at the grassroots level.

Evaluation Design

Preliminary Activities

AIR's proposal was for an 'incremental evaluation,' a new approach that AIR president Paul A. Schwarz had been working on. Schwarz (1980) noted that evaluations were commonly treated as scientific experiments, as a result of which they posed the question, Did A (the activities) result in Y (the outcome)? But, program outcomes could occur long after the activities that were supposed to produce them, and although these distal effects were considered valuable, they were hard to detect and to attribute to program activities; there were other possible explanations. Proximal effects, though less robust, were easier to demonstrate and provided better diagnostic information. Thus, according to Schwarz, the real question is, Given Y, does A' lead to Y?

Schwarz viewed the choice of outcomes as critical. Measuring more proximal effects would show whether the program was on track. If it was not, it could be modified piecemeal — a process Schwarz labeled *incremental*. These increments and their relationship were defined in terms of the program rationale: 'The blueprint for building solutions.' If the program had no rationale, the evaluator had to develop one.

Charles A. Murray and Saundra R. Murray (no relation), AIR's proposed principal investigator and project director respectively, drafted the evaluation proposal in that spirit. Noting that 'the core of [the] evaluation ... is to establish causality: to document the impact of Excel,' they rejected the classical experimental design, proposing instead to 'split the causality question into a number of ... components,' in each of which 'The problem of controls and extraneous effects can be managed adequately' (Murray and others, 1978). Over thirty-two months, the proposal states, '*it is possible to trace presumed linkages contemporaneously.*'

In agreement with Excel's assertion that student achievement was not the basic program objective, AIR proposed to measure Excel's effectiveness by examining change in student and community behavior ('investment behavior') as a precondition of the desired effects, which included improved achievement. These changes would be broken down into increments, each leading to the next and ultimately to the outcome. Some incremental objectives would be identified at the outset to obtain a data base for assessing change; others would be identified along the way. Since the interpretation of Excel would vary across sites, this implied that the data bases could be site specific. It was an ambitious plan.

The four-month design phase involved several tasks. One was to develop a program rationale. Another concerned the role of stakeholders in the study. AIR defined stakeholders as program staff and national users of the evaluation for program planning and decision making. But, where

NIE had envisioned stakeholders as active participants in the evaluation, the role that AIR conceived was limited to one of providing details about program operations and reacting to AIR's list of plausible outcomes. Also, AIR refused to convene the national users, whose hidden agendas might affect the developing program. Although stakeholders were to participate to some degree, no serious attention was given to making the evaluation useful to them.

Thus, the emphasis shifted from summative assessments for decision-making stakeholders to diagnostic appraisal. The shift was due both to AIR's skepticism about involving stakeholders and to its eagerness to test the incremental approach, which would provide local sites with feedback for formative purposes — a particular strength with Excel, where the evaluation could help to shape an ill-defined program. For AIR, this formative function outweighed the evaluation's increased usefulness to stakeholders that NIE had hoped for. Although Jesse Jackson's crusade was a movement, to allow incremental evaluation, it had to be treated as a program that had identifiable proximate steps. Thus, a major task of the evaluation would be to help Excel to develop into a program.

Stakeholder Participation

The principal parties to the evaluation met over a soul food dinner at Jesse Jackson's home in March 1979 to arrange for AIR-Excel staff briefings and visits to the three prototype sites, so that program descriptions could be developed and stakeholder needs assessed. After the site visits, panels were convened in Chicago and Kansas City. (The Los Angeles meeting was canceled by the site director.) AIR asked the twenty-five stakeholder groups — program and district staff, funding agencies, parents, clergy, and business and community organizations — to rank-order five evaluation questions and their preferred ways of receiving evaluation information. Interestingly, the top-ranked question in both cities was, 'What political considerations affect program success or failure?' Low on the list was whether the Push/Excel concept of total involvement had the desired effects. As ways of presenting information, Kansas City chose press releases, newsletters, and annual reports, while Chicago chose information briefings. AIR noted that 'the diversity in expectation reflects the many interpretations . . . of Push/Excel. We are confident that we have engaged our users for future interactions and increased the likelihood that evaluation products will be used' (American Institute for Research, 1979, p. 17).

Charles Murray had a less sanguine reaction (personal interview, December 1980): 'The program people [believed] that there were certain things they had to say: "We are going to raise grades, we are going to improve test scores." . . . I said, "Well, . . . this is not what you're really trying to do!" ... And [they replied], "We don't think we are either, but we have to [say that] in order to make ourselves plausible." ... [I said], "We want you to help us design this evaluation, ... to hear your priorities and adapt the evaluation to that ...." The [subsequent] discussions were generally very forced, very artificial.'

Norman Gold recalled much squabbling about role definitions, while AIR's proposed indicators were not discussed (personal interview, October 1980). All in all, the stakeholders contributed little to the evaluation design or to the plan for disseminating findings. For its part, AIR discussed methods and what the evaluation could and could not accomplish and pointed out why local information needs were implausible or impracticable. According to Gold, the meetings helped people to understand the evaluation but largely failed to elicit what people wanted to know or when. The final design was not the result of joint planning by AIR and Excel, and neither NIE nor AIR was pleased. Norman Gold's view was that the stakeholder notion was not well used, and Charles Murray shared Gold's dissatisfaction (personal interview, December 1980): 'We don't really have it right yet ... You do want people who are going to make decisions about a program to be involved in the evaluation ... but too much of the way we were going about it ... is a charade. Now, the technical review panel for Cities-in-Schools said, ... 'You could have gotten these folks to talk about what they wanted [and] to contribute much more to your design." ... I don't think we [did] it better for Excel. And, it was not for lack of trying. It was because we didn't have much better ideas than we had the first time around.'

If the stakeholder meetings did not produce the collaboration that NIE had intended, one reason was stakeholder naiveté about what evaluations can accomplish. Program staff knew what they wanted to learn about Excel, such as its effect on test scores, but many stakeholders did not know about the attendant political and methodological problems or the limits of evaluation science for studying certain questions that AIR rejected as unresearchable. And, although stakeholders supported the program's laudable aims, they often knew little about its local operation and goals. They thought of Excel much as they thought of the poverty program or the civil rights movement. One day, Excel's success or failure would be self-evident, not because of the pronouncements of sponsored studies. But, collaboration also fell short because AIR was not squarely behind it. Stakeholders were concerned with political issues, which did not interest AIR, not with community involvement, which was the chief interest of AIR and NIE. Furthermore, the evaluators had preferred ways of reporting information, and when the stakeholders' ideas diverged they were rejected.

The inclusion of stakeholders' preferences was precisely what NIE had in mind in requesting a stakeholder-based study. The evaluation process was to be reformed by examining what stakeholders wanted to know, making the evaluation more useful and precluding arguments about program effects. But, the study was conceived and developed in the mainstream of applied science, and unorthodoxy was not taken seriously. In this context, where stakeholders lacked sophistication in evaluation research, program objectives were unclear, and the evaluator was luke-warm about stakeholder involvement, it is not surprising that AIR's preferences prevailed.

The Evaluation Design

In the design of the evaluation, Schwarz's incremental approach took pride of place. AIR's program rationale defined various proximal goals as preludes to achievement, the most distal outcome. Each of the proximal goals would be affected by student, parent, and community involvement. But, the evaluators cautioned, '[We] must recognize that Push/Excel has a route to impact that bypasses all of the usual trappings of a social action program: Impact can occur simply because someone has listened to the Reverend Jackson's speeches and has been motivated to act' (Murray and others, 1979, p. 8).

According to the program rationale developed by AIR, national and local efforts would lead to parent, school, and community involvement, which in turn would lead to student involvement. This would engender motivation, responsibility, atmosphere, and opportunity, which would lead to 'investments': the expenditure of time, effort, or money for a future return. AIR hoped to document results for each sequence of steps to an outcome. These 'knowledge modules' would be fed back to program developers for possible modification. Only when cause and effect had been established would resources be devoted to the next link.

Most outcome measures would be collected through interviews. Other information, such as attendance, could be gleaned from school records and from Push/Excel activities. Program personnel would be interviewed three times a year, and students and parents would be interviewed twice. At six sites, 100 tenth graders from each of twelve schools would be interviewed. Detailed two-year case histories would be constructed for half. Not until page fifty-nine of the *Evaluation Design* was the stakeholder notion discussed: Stakeholders would be assembled to review the evaluation design (Murray and others, 1979).

Reactions of National and Federal Stakeholders

A draft evaluation design was ready by the annual Push/Excel national convention in Cleveland in May 1979, when Saundra Murray reviewed it with Excel personnel. But, it was not distributed until two days later.

program was to be based on their program rationale, which had evolved from their reading of Jackson's speeches and national office promotion material. But, because each local program had developed its own distinctive characteristics and because each local program had different goals and priorities, the evaluators' plans met resistance and claims that their concept was not consonant with local goals. Even when the goals were identical, the evaluation findings on progress toward attaining them did not help local staff to make improvements. The evaluation helped to identify shortcomings but not to rectify them. Although AIR offered suggestions, they were more in the nature of guesses or hunches than prescriptions based on experience. The evaluators, after all, were not program developers.

Another consequence of the evaluators' definition of program was that the student impact study was very poorly designed. The Push/Excel operation started in Denver and Chattanooga in fall 1979, but the predata on students, parents, and teachers were not collected until the following spring, well into the second half of the program's first operating year. A great number of Push/Excel activities had occurred much earlier. Data were collected months after the initial rallies, Jackson's speeches, and student-parent pledging. Perhaps these events did not affect student and parent attitudes — an assumption apparently made by the evaluators. But, it is entirely plausible, even likely, that this public fanfare did have significant effects that were reflected in the preindicators of program impact, which were quite high. Since the evaluators believed that that there was no program, they ignored this possibility in comparing their pre and postdata. Combined with the extraordinarily low response rate from the student sample, this makes their conclusions about the program's impact highly suspect. Given the study design, even a program that met their specifications would have found it difficult to show student impact.

One lesson of the Push/Excel evaluation is that charisma and social science do not mix well. This point may be painfully obvious, but the lack of fit is greater than commonly believed. First, there is the bureaucratically imposed proposal writing, funding, scheduling, and reporting, which hampered the Push/Excel program from the outset. For example, a report was to appear every six months; yet even with great effort, the Push/Excel organization, hardly a smooth-running machine at best, could not remedy the deficiencies noted in one report before the next report was upon them. And, once having invested in a particular evaluation approach, the federal bureaucracy could not change course without admitting to miscalculation, which it was unwilling to do.

Perhaps even more damaging was the imposition of technical rationality on Push/Excel. AIR's incremental approach to evaluation was based upon activity-outcome, cause-effect, means-ends reasoning. Each outcome, effect, and end should be measurable. Once discovered and ·documented, these 'knowledge modules' could be transplanted from

Denver to Chattanooga or anywhere else. The notion of social technology underlying this approach was better suited to the manufacture of television sets or computers than to the development of a movement. And, it was not at all the way in which Jesse Jackson and his people thought of their role; their sense of mission could not be neatly systematized in this way.

A final point concerning the mismatch between charisma and social science involves the different notions of social change held by the two. The technocratic view of evaluators and bureaucrats suggests that change is — or should be — produced by incremental changes, which are facilitated by immediate feedback for correction, modification, reinforcement, and retrial. An extreme version of this view is stimulus response theory, in which all change is trial and error modified by reinforcement. By contrast, the charismatic view of social change embodied in Push/Excel is that of change by conversion. Through a single event, one can commit oneself to a different course of behavior that will change one's life, and perhaps society, forever. This event can occur at a mass rally of the sort held by Push/Excel, which resembled the religious meeting at which a convert steps forward to pledge himself or herself to a life for Christ. Without such mass conversions, there would be no Christianity, no Russian revolution, no civil rights movement.

One of the embarrassments of social science is that it presumes to understand and explain social events in the way that the natural sciences explain physical events. In truth, social science is far more parochial than it claims; its concepts and viewpoints are narrow. In many instances of applied social research, a charismatic event has been viewed through a technocratic lens, and the results benefit no one. In the re-examination now under way of what social science is and what it can do, perhaps social scientists will keep this in mind.

Acknowledgements

This case study was supported in part by the National Institute of Education (NIE), but the study presents the views of the authors, for which the NIE is not responsible. This case reflects AIR's account of Push/Excel's early history. The authors are indebted to Maria Sachs and Stephen Raudenbush for proof that the story can be told at a fraction of its original length.

References

'A Shove Comes to Push', *Washington Star*, 8 January 1978.
American Institute for Research (1979) *Assessment of Stakeholders' Needs*, Washington, DC, American Institute for Research, July.

BRONSCOMBE, A. (1979) '"Sermon" by Jackson opens Push/Excel', *Denver Post*, 12 September.

CALIFANO, J.A. Jr. (1981) *Governing America*, New York, Simon and Schuster.

MURRAY, C. and others (1978) *Proposal to NIE*, Washington, DC, American Institute for Research, October.

MURRAY, C. and others (1979) *Evaluation Design*, Washington DC, American Institute for Research, July.

MURRAY, C. and others (1980a) *The Evolution of a Program*, Technical Report No. 1, March, Washington, DC, American Institute for Research.

MURRAY, C. and others (1980b) *Implementation Guide*, Technical Report No. 2, September, Washington, DC, American Institute for Research.

MURRAY, C. and others (1980c) *The Program, the School, and the Students*, Technical Report No. 3, April, Washington DC, American Institute for Research.

MURRAY, C. and others (1982) *Final Report*, Washington, DC, American Institute for Research, March.

National Institute of Education (1978) 'Evaluation of project Excel', FRP-NIE-R-78-0026, Washington, DC, National Institute of Education, 5 September.

Push for Excellence (nd) *Push for Excellence: The Developing Process of Implementation*, Chicago, Push for Excellence Inc.

RICH, S. (1980a) 'US study faults Jesse Jackson's school program', *Washington Post*, 22 April, p. 1.

RICH, S. (1980b) 'US study faults Jackson's Push school plan', *Washington Post*, 5 October, p. 5.

ROSSI, P.H. (1979) Personal communication to Norman Gold, National Institute of Education, 23 July.

SCHWARZ, P.A. (1980) 'Program devaluation: can the experiment reform?' in LOVE LAND, E (Ed.) *Measuring the Hard-to-Measure*, New Directions for Program Evaluation, No. 6, San Francisco, Jossey-Bass.

WORTMAN, P.M. (nd) Memo to Norman Gold, National Institute of Education 'Comments on the AIR draft evaluation design of the Push for Excellence program'.

Toward the Future of Stakeholder Approaches in Evaluation

Carol H. Weiss,
Harvard Graduate
School of Education

Given the very special situation in the Cities-in-Schools (CIS) and Push/Excel (Excel) programs, the stakeholder approach to evaluation has hardly received a fair test. In fact, some people argue that it was implemented with such a minimalist interpretation of its scope that its potential benefits inevitably went unrealized. So many other difficulties beset the evaluation — primarily as a result of the attempt to apply formal quantitative assessment to shifting (and, in the case of Push/Excel, inchoate) programs — that the stakeholder approach did not have much chance to affect the course of events. On the positive side, perhaps it engaged the attention of actors who might otherwise have ignored it entirely, particularly people at the local sites. On the negative side, it probably diverted a fair amount of evaluators' time from strictly evaluative functions. But the turbulent nature of the programs and the mismatch with standard outcome evaluation procedures were probably the critical elements in both cases.

The inability to attain the expected benefits in these cases may have been the result of extraneous factors (incomplete implementation of the stakeholder concept, inappropriate evaluation strategies, fluidity of programs, and so on). Is it possible that stakeholder-oriented evaluation would work in other, more congenial settings? Or are there basic flaws in its underlying assumptions that inevitably limit its capacity to deliver what it promises?

Conversations with colleagues on this project — Robert Stake, Ernest House, Eleanor Farrar, Anthony Bryk, and David Cohen — have encouraged me to see the intentions of stakeholder-oriented evaluation as fundamentally threefold: first, to increase the use of evaluation results in decision making; second, to empower a wider assortment of groups to determine evaluation priorities; and third, to shift governance of evaluation from sole control by NIE to shared control, thereby reducing NIE's responsibility. Partisans of the approach may have had other expectations, such as providing greater legitimacy for evaluations in general, for NIE's evaluations in particular, and for NIE as the evaluation agency. But the three aims listed here appear to represent the nub of the stakeholder argument.

I interpret the term *stakeholders* to mean either the members of groups that are palpably affected by the program and who therefore will conceivably be affected by evaluative conclusions about the program or the members of groups that make decisions about the future of the program, such as decisions to continue or discontinue funding or to alter modes of program operation. These are quite distinct categories of people, although there is some overlap. I include them both as stakeholders, because that is my reading of NIE's intent.

Perhaps it would be useful to maintain and elaborate the distinctions. Analytically, stakeholders can be divided into four categories, depending on the kinds of information that are likely to be valuable to them (Figure 1).

Assumptions

With these prefatory remarks, let us try to disentangle the expectations inherent in the stakeholder notion. As developed at NIE, the approach makes a series of assumptions about the involvement of stakeholders in the evaluation process.

1   Stakeholder groups can be identified in advance of the start of evaluation.
   (a)   The sponsor, the evaluator, or both can figure out whose interests are at stake.
   (b)   The sponsor and/or the evaluator will select a representative set of groups to participate in the evaluation.
2   Stakeholders want an evaluation of the program with which they are associated.
   (a)   They want to have evaluative information available about the program.
   (b)   They are willing to participate in the evaluation process.
3   They want specific kinds of information to help them make plans and choices.
   (a)   They can identify their information needs in advance.
   (b)   The kinds of information they want are the kinds that evaluation studies produce.
   (c)   The kinds of information that different stakeholder groups want can be reconciled with one another.
4   Evaluators will respond to stakeholder requests for information.
   (a)   They have the requisite time, resources, interest, and commitment to the process.

    (b) They have the interpersonal skills to solicit realistic information requests from groups, even from those for whom evaluative information is not salient.

    (c) They have the political skills to negotiate accommodations in priorities among competing stakeholder groups.

    (d) They have the technical proficiency to design and conduct a study that produces valid data to satisfy diverse information requests.

    (e) They will report back promptly, responsively, using forms of presentation that are appropriate to various audiences.

5 Stakeholders who have participated in an evaluation will develop pride of ownership in the conclusions.

    (a) They will accept them as true.

    (b) They will take them seriously.

6 Stakeholders who have decisions to make (mainly federal policy makers, school-district administrators, outside philanthropists, and program directors) will use evaluation results as a basis for decision making.

    (a) Information in and of itself is a decisive component in decision making.

    (b) The stakeholder approach makes a wide assortment of information available.

    (c) The information is relevant to the situation that exists when decisions are being made. If circumstances have changed since the study was planned, the information collected remains appropriate to changed conditions and sufficient to answer current questions.

    (d) Stakeholders who do not have program-wide decisions to make (principals, teachers, students, parents, community organizations) know that at least their criteria and concerns were taken into account in the evaluation and that information of importance to them was considered in decision making. They will therefore, perhaps, accord the decisions greater legitimacy.

7 (A revisionist assumption) Even if evaluation results do not sway specific decisions, they will enrich discussions about future programming and illuminate undertakings of program actors.

Analyzing the Assumptions

A number of these assumptions look perfectly reasonable — at least under reasonable conditions. Of course, if we push any one of them too far, we

Figure 1. Categories of Stakeholders

Category	Types of Decisions to be Made	Types of Evaluation Results That Are Relevant
Policy maker (the Congress, the secretary of the Department of Education, local philanthropists, school board members)	Shall we continue to fund the program? Is it achieving the desired results? Shall we expand it or reduce it?	Outcomes of program for participants, causally linked to the intervention.
Program manager (national program staff, program directors in cities, program designers)	How can we improve the program? Should we recruit different staff, serve different kids, use different techniques?	Differential outcomes for different types of students, by types of service received, by type of staff, and so forth. Qualitative information on what is going well and poorly during implementation.
Practitioner	What shall I do to help Joan and Pedro? How can I get Elsie to try harder?	Usually not much, except perhaps for some overview of how the whole project is going. Practitioner's own knowledge and experience are more relevant and salient.
Clients and citizen organizations (students, parents, community groups)	Shall we keep attending the program (assuming we have the choice) and supporting it?	Not much. Outcomes of the program for previous participants should be relevant, but often the evaluation has not gone on long enough to provide such data. In any event, clients' own experiences are more salient.

can find situations under which it will break down. Let us see which assumptions seem generally viable and which depend on images of orderliness and rationality that rarely prevail in the program world.

The first assumption, that stakeholder groups can be identified in advance, looks feasible. The CIS and Excel evaluations seemed to have encountered little difficulty on this score. We could ask whether the groups that AIR identified and assembled were truly representative of all important stakeholder interests. For example, how actively represented were teacher, student, and parent concerns? How long did representatives of these groups continue to participate? There is also a perennial question about the representation of potential users of program information. Groups that are not actively associated with the program now can have a real stake in the information that evaluators will produce, such as school districts that would want to adopt the program if it proved successful. No procedural mechanisms appear capable of identifying, let alone representing, the entire set of potential users of evaluation results or the questions that they will raise. But in the normal course of events, adequate representation of stakeholders seems feasible.

The second assumption, that people want evaluations and that they will participate in them, probably holds good for some groups some of the time. Given a choice, however, it seems likely that many groups would forgo evaluation entirely. These groups have learned over past decades that evaluations are more likely to be the bearers of bad tidings than good. When results are circulated, they often pose a threat to the program rather than support and guidance. Information is a minor benefit compared to the questions and criticisms that it can provoke. Only when federal beneficence is contingent upon evaluation do many groups accept it as inevitable and come on board.

The third assumption, that people can specify their information needs in advance, has the same 'maybe/maybe not' quality, although it lists toward 'maybe not.' As cognitive psychologists have demonstrated and as decision theorists have learned to their regret, people do not always know in advance what they will need to know in order to make a decision (Slovic, Fischhoff, and Lichtenstein, 1977; Slovic and Lichtenstein, 1971). Unless situations are routine and repetitive, the human cognitive apparatus is not always up to the task of foreseeing which information will be critical. Moreover, the assumption that evaluation requests can be defined early in the study relies on a vision of an orderly and predictable environment. It assumes that organizations can schedule their choices and calculate their information needs with confidence that things will go as planned. In fact, neither the political environment nor the organizational milieu is stable. Program decision making is beset by unexpected occurrences from inside and outside the organization. Long experience with the development of management information systems and with managers' inability to specify their needs correctly is instructive here (AAACMIS, 1974; Ackoff, 1967; Grudnitski, 1981).

The capacity to define information needs far ahead of time is limited by individual, organizational, and political constraints. Many people will make an effort to tell what they need to know, but much of what they say is a learned, stereotypical response. People in schools, for example, almost always say that they want to know test scores. Whether or not test scores are relevant to the program or useful in decision making, people have been indoctrinated to the notion that achievement is the central mission of schools and that neglect of test scores would therefore be unprofessional conduct.

Not uncommonly, people do not actually want to know anything. If you define these people as stakeholders and ask them to describe their information needs, they will generally give an answer. In today's information society, saying that they do not need data is tantamount to branding themselves as illiterates. So, lacking any clear need, they can take the opportunity to ask for information that they know will cast the program in a good light, such as data on the number of hours of service provided or on parents' satisfaction with the program. Another strategy is to ask for something, without regard for exactly what it is, because information is a scarce resource and therefore worth fighting for. If stakeholders are competitive groups in a competitive environment and if information is the counter in the game, then information is what groups play for — almost regardless of its content.

Thus, the assumption that stakeholders are reliable sources of information priorities is not a very good one if specification is required far in advance, as in most pre post designs. It is much more plausible if the evaluation is a qualitative, illuminative investigation of program operation. In most qualitative evaluations, evaluators have ample opportunity to shift direction and to follow new questions as they emerge. They are not locked in to a set of measures that can prove to be irrelevant when the 'post' time rolls around.

The fourth assumption, that evaluators will respond to stakeholder requests for information, needs to confront the fact that it takes a variety of skills and considerable dedication to be responsive. Under some circumstances, responsiveness might prove to be impossible. If stakeholders press demands for a great deal of information or if their demands are incompatible, the evaluators may be battered in the effort to satisfy all parties. Later or sooner, they may give up the effort to be responsive and assume unilateral control. The CIS and Excel evaluations demonstrate that being a responsive evaluator is an arduous task. Both evaluations also suggest, I think, that the task can be managed under favorable conditions.

The fifth assumption, that stakeholders who participate in a stakeholder-oriented evaluation develop a sense of ownership in the study, is open to considerable question. There is a good deal of experience with this particular strategy, since involvement of potential users in evaluations has long been a staple prescription (Eidell and Kitchel, 1968; Flanagan, 1961; Havelock, 1969; Joly, 1967). Many efforts have been made in the past to conduct evaluations in this style. Some have been successful in giving prospective users a stake in the findings, particularly when users are few in number and when there is relative agreement on most significant issues (Conway and others, 1976; Rothman, 1980). But even under these favorable conditions, many well-intentioned researchers have been unable to secure acceptance of the validity and usability of study results (Berg and others, 1978; Lazarsfeld and others, 1967; Rich, 1977).

It is when disagreement is rife that user involvement is expected to be especially important for winning the allegiance of discordant groups. If each group believes that it has had a say in designing the evaluation, and if each group believes that it has gotten the information that it wants, then presumably all groups will have common commitment to consideration of findings. But when disagreement is rife, the evaluators are caught in a bind. They have to resolve discrepant requests and conflicting advice, and it seems inevitable that they will disappoint one or another of the parties. Groups whose requests are disregarded will lose interest in the study and its findings; on occasion they may become overtly hostile.

Another concomitant of involving users in the planning and conduct of studies is that it gives users an inside look at how the study is done. A close view can engender disenchantment as well as commitment. Insiders know the weaknesses as well as the strengths of the research — the shortcuts, unreliabilities, missing data, contradictions in sources. Some develop considerable skepticism about the worth of the final report (Berg and others, 1978), and they have less allegiance to it than outsiders who were not privy to the compromises in data and method that were made.

Some stakeholders are likely to be happy with evaluation results and to feel a sense of pride, but their happiness can derive more from the support that the evaluation gives to their stake than from the part they played in the study. Groups that find their positions threatened by evaluation results can revoke their support if they see their crucial interests endangered, even if they did participate in the evaluation process.

In sum, experience suggests that participation in a study can increase support for the study, but only if certain conditions are met: One's advice has to be given due attention, one has to see the study as being appropriately and reputably conducted, and results must not threaten significant personal or organizational interests.

The sixth assumption, that people who take part in an evaluation will use the results as a basis for decisions, is constrained by the fact, noted earlier, that not all stakeholders have decisions to make — at least, decisions of the kind for which evaluation has much evidence to offer. But for those people who do make decisions, is it reasonable to expect that those who participate in the evaluation process will be more likely to base their decisions on evaluation results? On the positive side, it is safe to say that these people know more about the study than they would have if they had not taken part. In that sense, there is a better chance that they will absorb the information and use it. Not to use it takes a conscious decision. They can hardly remain oblivious.

The stakeholder approach also assumes that the results are relevant. Several factors already noted limit the generality of this assumption — for example, the common inability to predict information requests accurately, calls from different groups for inconsistent evaluation designs and inform-ation items, the possibility that one group's advice will be disregarded or overruled. Still, the notion that participation will improve relevance remains plausible. For example, when local groups take an active part in the evaluation, the study is much more likely to address the concerns that exercise them.

The rub comes at the point of applying results to a decision. The usual expectation is that decision makers will use evaluation results to choose between alternative A and alternative B. Unless A and B are minor matters, evaluation evidence is not likely to be the decisive element. Decision making about issues of import, such as whether to continue funding a project, is basically a political process. In making such a decision, people have to consider a wide range of factors — who supports the program and how much clout the supporters have, what alternatives there are that can serve clients if the program is terminated, whether alternative programs are likely to be more successful, whose jobs are in jeopardy if the program ends, how clients will feel and how they will fare without the program, what community reaction will be, what costs will be involved, and so on. Evaluation results provide evidence on only a small number of relevant issues. Thus, even if the evaluation is conducted with the broadly inclusive sweep anticipated for the stakeholder strategy, it never addresses all the issues that have to be considered. Nor does it settle the issues that it does address in a conclusive way. Therefore, evaluative evidence about program operations and outcomes goes into the hopper together with an array of other concerns, information, allegiances, ideological proclivities, and interests. Decision makers have to reach an accommodation that satisfies many people on many dimensions. While evidence of program effectiveness is important, it probably never will be the sole determinant — or even the most powerful determinant — of political choice.

If NIE or anyone else expects the stakeholder approach or any other reform in evaluation practice to make research information the major basis for decision making, they are destined for disappointment. Too many other factors must be considered, too many other conditions must be accommodated, for information to play such a stellar role (Lindbloom, 1968; March, 1982; Weiss, 1973).

The seventh, revisionist, assumption is that the stakeholder orientation can increase the use of evaluation for purposes of enlightenment (Caplan, 1977; Pelz, 1978; Weiss, 1977). Responsive, relevant, well-circulated evaluation results can provide information that keeps people well informed about a range of programmatic issues. Evaluation results can provide evidence about what works well and what does not, about the kinds of problems that arise, and about the reactions of staff and students. They can challenge prevailing assumptions about a program and the theories of behavior that underlie it. They can suggest reinterpretations of past experience and help to make retrospective sense about what the program has been doing. Without dictating specific decisions, they can permeate people's understanding of program potentials and limits. Over time, such understanding can have significant influence on the aims that people set, the alternatives that they consider, and the directions that they take in future programming (Weiss, 1980). Use in this sense seems to be a realistic goal for stakeholder-oriented evaluation.

In its early presentations, the stakeholder approach resembled many of the educational and social programs of the past generation. Its high-minded intentions were yoked to untested practices, and it promised too much. Its advocates expected a relatively minor reform to accomplish grand objectives. As evaluation of social programs have demonstrated time and again, changing behavior is not a simple task. More temperate expectations for stakeholder evaluation would put the idea in perspective.

A Tentative Balance Sheet

Our review of assumptions inherent in the stakeholder approach suggests that none of them is open-and-shut. There is leakage at every step along the way. The chances that any one step will be fully realized are less than one — often considerably less — and the cumulative chances of achieving expected benefits decline multiplicatively. Prospects for significant gains in evaluation utility do not seem especially bright unless collateral changes are made in the substance of evaluations and in the structure of the programs. Simply pasting the stakeholder process alongside current practice involves acceptance of many existing constraints.

Over all, the stakeholder approach seems to hold modest promise for achieving modest aims. It can improve the fairness of the evaluation process. It can probably make marginal improvements in the range of information collected and in the responsiveness of data to participant requests. It can counter the federal tilt of many previous evaluations and give more say to local groups. It can democratize access to evaluative information. If stakeholder groups take an active role, it can make them more knowledgeable about evaluation results and equalize whatever power knowledge provides. When many groups know the results of a study, the likelihood increases that the information will be absorbed and drawn upon in later deliberations.

However, the stakeholder approach will not ensure that appropriate information is collected. Stakeholders will not usually be able to specify the kinds of data that matter to them with much accuracy, and even when they can, program conditions and outside events will probably change before the data become available. By the time that stakeholders confront decisions, the evaluation will be able to provide evidence on only a fraction of the questions at current issue.

The stakeholder approach will probably not visibly increase the use of results in the making of specific decisions. For example, a philanthropist who sees a report of no success for a program that he supports may find that his participation in the evaluation process makes little difference to his decision about whether to continue support. He still has to think about the implications of his position on many dimensions. Nor will stakeholder evaluation bring harmony to contentious program arenas. It can elicit diverse views, but it cannot contain them. In fact, if differences are wide, the opportunity to stake out turf during the evaluation process can make people more aware of the conflicts that exist. Even if they can work out accommodations over evaluation priorities, accommodations over program issues will be no easier to arrange.

If the stakeholder approach has potential for improving evaluations, it also makes new demands. It increases the burden on evaluators, and it demands time and attention from groups associated with the program as policy makers, managers, planners, practitioners, and clients. Some of these groups — including, perhaps, evaluators — will find the experience illuminating and worthwhile, but it is likely that others will not. The approach will trade some people's heightened satisfaction of others' annoyance or frustration.

Questions for the Future

Some conditions of stakeholder participation can profit from further thinking. I nominate three issues for consideration: the definition of participation, the competing claims of a single study and several independent studies, and the mode of study design.

Participation

Which groups should be involved? Does it make sense to limit participation to groups that face decisions and care about information, such as funders, managers, and planners? Other groups have interests in the program that deserve consideration, but it is the program and its future that concern them, not information about the program. They want a voice in what happens, not in what data shall be collected. Evaluation planning is not necessarily the best forum to engage them. Participation with a more specifically programmatic focus could effectively attract their participation and profit from their perspectives.

The inclusion of multiple groups in the evaluation process is an attempt to redress the inequitable distribution of influence and authority. But evaluation planning is a strange avenue for such redress. The stakeholder approach could be construed as a way of deflecting stakeholder attention from decisions that more directly affect them. Indeed, it almost appears to be a substitute for involving stakeholders in the making of policy. A Machiavellian mind could conceive of the stakeholder approach as a way to mire stakeholder groups (particularly powerless groups) in the details of criteria definition and item wording, while the powers that be go blithely on with decisions as usual.

Of course, no such demonic scheme is at work. The reasons for involving stakeholders in evaluation is that NIE has control of evaluation, whereas it has little voice in program decision making. NIE is taking advantage of the opportunity to broaden representation in the one domain over which it has authority. The intent is high-minded. But the actuality is that participation takes place at some remove from the center circle of program decision making. Whether a reduction of inequities in the evaluation process results in net gains for all stakeholders is a matter that deserves attention.

One Study or Several

In the first two stakeholder-oriented evaluations a single contract was let. Placing the responsibility for an entire evaluation on a single team of evaluators lays a heavy burden on its members, particularly when they have to cope with all the extra demands that the stakeholder approach entails. It makes them the arbiter of the only game in town. It gives them the responsibility for adjudicating among rival interests (including their own interests) and for deciding the direction that the study shall follow.

There is nothing intrinsic to the stakeholder approach that requires the funding of a single study to accommodate the interests of all parties to the program. The single blockbuster study appears to be an unthinking carryover from previous evaluation practice. For some time, it was assumed that one large study was better than several smaller studies, because the large study would have larger sample sizes, use more consistent measures, and therefore produce more precise estimates of effect. The stakeholder approach was tacked on to existing contracting practice.

As recent critics have noted, the blockbuster study suffers from severe limitations. It provides only one set of readings on one set of indicators, and the results depend on the particular operationalization employed. Cronbach and his associates (1980) have advocated 'a fleet of studies' using different methods and different measures, done by different teams of investigators. If separate studies converge on results, the pattern of evidence is much more convincing than the results of a single study.

For the stakeholder approach, does it make more sense to fund several small studies? Each study could examine the program from the perspective of one set of stakeholders. The separate studies would be able to use the criteria of the separate groups and follow the issues that mattered to them. From the series of separate studies, a multidimensional view of reality would be more likely to emerge. The various pieces of evidence would illuminate the varied viewpoints.

It remains to be seen whether multiple studies would enrich understanding of the program, or whether they would create more conflict as each group pressed the evidence that supported its own case. It seems possible that multiple studies could do both. But they might enable interested groups of stakeholders to focus on issues that they defined as important without overloading traffic in a single study.

A sequence of studies could also explore diverse facets of programming. As new issues arose, new studies could pursue them. Since no one can foresee all contingencies in advance, sequential evaluations would be more likely to keep pace with shifting conditions. They could follow the variety of issues that a program encounters over the course of its life. Of course, there might be problems in maintaining continuity. A government funding agency like NIE would have to maintain its commitment to the exploration of a program's implementation and outcomes over a period of time. If early results proved disappointing, would the agency be under pressure to divert evaluation resources elsewhere, or could it continue to support study of the program, its problems, and its achievements?

Qualitative or Quantitative

What kinds of evaluation designs are compatible with the stakeholder approach? Does it fit best with qualitative, illuminative, ethnographic, process-oriented evaluation? The two case studies included in this volume seem to suggest so. Is that an idiosyncrasy of the particular programs, or is it inherent in the stakeholder idea? Can the approach ever be linked successfully with quantitative before-and-after evaluation? Could it work if the program under study had stabilized and settled down?

Are there ways that a stakeholder-oriented evaluation can serve both formative and summative purposes? Past experience suggests that studies that attempt the dual task tend either to scant one function or the other, or else they are swamped by floods of data, much of which usually goes unanalyzed. Can modifications in design overcome these problems, or should formative-qualitative and summative-quantitative studies routinely be separate undertakings?

As an attempt to cope with recognized shortcomings in evaluation practice, stakeholder-oriented evaluation retains modest promise. It has been tested with two particularly difficult programs, where its achievements were limited. Clearly, it cannot right all past wrongs or attain the nirvana that its advocates hoped for. At this point, I think it deserves further testing. As experience accumulates and if we conscientiously learn from that experience, we should be able to specify the conditions under which the stakeholder approach is likely to prove useful and to probe the realistic limits of its potential.

References

ACKOFF, R.L. (1967) 'Management misinformation systems', *Management Science*, B147–B156.
American Accounting Association Committee on Management Information Systems (AAACMIS) (1974) 'Current accounting issues in the area of management information systems', *The Accounting Review*, supplement.

BERG, M.R. and others (1978) *Factors Affecting Utilization of Technology Assessment Studies in Policy Making*, Ann Arbor, Mich, Center for Research on Utilization of Scientific Knowledge.

CAPLAN, N. (1977) 'A minimal set of conditions necessary for the utilization of social science knowledge in policy formulation at the national level' in WEISS, C. (Ed.) *Using Social Research in Public Policy Making*, Lexington, Mass, Lexington Books.

CONWAY, R. and others (1976) 'Promoting knowledge utilization through clinically oriented research: the benchmark program', *Policy Studies Journal*, 4, 3, pp. 264–9.

CRONBACH, L.J. and Associates (1980) *Toward Reform of Program Evaluation*, San Francisco, Jossey-Bass.

EIDELL, T.L. and KITCHELL, J.M. (Eds) (1968) (Eds) *Knowledge Production and Utilization in Educational Administration*, Eugene, Ore, Center for the Advanced Study of Educational Administration, University of Oregon.

FLANAGAN, J.C. (1961) 'Case studies on the utilization of behavioural science research' in *Case Studies in Bringing Behavioural Science into Use, Studies, in the Utilization of Behavioural Science*, Vol 1, Stanford, Calif., Institute for Communication Research.

GRUDNITSKI, G. (1981) 'A methodology for a listening information relevant to decision makers' in Ross, C.A. (Ed.) *Proceedings of the Second International Conference on Information Systems*, Cambridge, Mass, Second Internatonal Conference on Information Systems.

HAVELOCK, R.G. (1969) *Planning for Innovation Through Dissemination and Utilization of Knowledge*, Ann Arbor, Mich, Center for Research on Utilization of Scientific Knowledge.

JOLY, J.M. (1967) 'Research and innovation: two solitudes?', *Canadian Education and Research Digest*, 2, pp. 184–94.

LAZARSFIELD, P.F., SEWELL, W.H. and WILENSKY, H.L. (Eds) (1967) *The Uses of Sociology*, New York, Basic Books.

LINDBLOOM, C.E. (1986) *The Policy-Making Process*, Englewood Cliffs, NJ, Prentice Hall.

MARCH, J.G. (1982) 'Theories of choice and making decisions', *Society*, 20, 1, pp. 29–39.

PELZ, D.C. (1978) 'Some expanded perspectives on use of social science in public policy' in YINGER, J.M. and CUTLER, S.J. (Eds) *Major Social Issues*, New York, Free Press.

RICH, R.F. (1977) 'Uses of social science information by federal bureaucrats: Knowledge for action versus knowledge for understanding' in WEISS, C. (Ed.) *Using Social Research in Public Policy Making*, Lexington, Mass, Lexington Books.

ROTHMAN, J. (1980) *Social R & D: Research and Development in the Human Services*, Englewood Cliffs, NJ, Prentice Hall.

SLOVIC, P., FISCHHOFF, B. and LICHTENSTEIN, S. (1977) 'Behavioural decision theory', *Annual Review of Psychology*, 28, pp. 1–39.

SLOVIC, P. and LICHTENSTEIN, S. (1971) 'Comparison of bayesian and regression approaches to the study of information procession in judgement', *Organizational Behaviour and Human Performance*, 6, pp. 649–744.

WEISS, C.H. (1973) 'Where politics and evaluation meet', *Evaluation*, 1, 3, pp. 37–45.

WEISS, C.H. (Ed.) (1977) *Using Social Research in Public Policy Making*, Lexington, Mass, Lexington Books.

WEISS, C.H. with BUCUVALAS, M.J. (1980) *Social Science Research and Decision Making*, New York, Columbia University Press.

6
Teachers and Evaluation:
Learning to Labor

Introduction

One of the strongest current movements in the United States is the effort to evaluate teachers in various ways, presumably as a step towards improving the educational system. A number of teacher evaluation schemes have been proposed and most of them involve the testing of teachers directly or the testing of students and holding the teachers accountable for the student gains. Hence, various states and municipalities have employed tests to measure what prospective teachers know before they enter teacher training and tests to assess what they know after teacher training, often with a minimum test score the teacher must attain before being allowed to teach. Teacher evaluation is also linked to merit pay plans to differentially reward teachers for performance and to dismissal procedures for incompetent teachers. Needless to say, there is a lack of public confidence in teachers and the schools, a lack of confidence inspired and expressed by the highest political figures and the mass media.

In the chapter reprinted here Darling-Hammond and her colleagues have reviewed the current research literature on teacher evaluation and sorted it out according to fundamental perspective one holds about the nature of teaching itself. In their view one may conceive of teaching as labor, as craft, as profession, or as art. Teaching as labor conceives of teaching as a set of standard operating procedures rationally planned and programmed by administrators. Evaluation then consists of a direct inspection of the teacher's work by the supervisor to see if the work is being properly performed. This includes monitoring lesson plans, classroom performance, and performance results.

Teaching as craft means seeing teaching as requiring a repertoire of specialized techniques and rules for the application of those techniques. Evaluation does not require direct inspection but rather ascertaining whether the teachers possess the requisite skills. Teaching as profession requires not only specialized techniques and skills but also theoretical knowledge as well. Standards for performance are developed by peers. Finally, teaching as art requires personalized and creative problem-solving unique to each individual. Evaluation could involve self-assessment and perhaps critical assessment of one's work by others.

Most current reform activity in American education is based upon the notion of teaching as labor, or occasionally teaching as craft. Control is placed outside the teachers themselves, vested in tests and assessment procedures operated by administrators. The pressures are strong and we are likely to see intense conflicts over the issue of teacher evaluation in the next several years.

Teacher Evaluation in the Organizational Context: A Review of the Literature

Linda Darling-Hammond, Arthur E. Wise, and Sara R. Pease
The Rand Corporation

ABSTRACT. This article presents a conceptual framework for examining the design and implementation of teacher evaluation processes in school organizations. Research on teaching, organizational behavior, and policy implementation suggests that different educational and organizational theories underlie various teacher evaluation models. The conceptions of teaching work and of change processes reflected in teacher evaluation methods must be made explicit if educational goals, organizational needs, and evaluation purposes are to be consonant and well served.

Over the last decade teacher evaluation has assumed increasing importance. The demand for accountability in education has shifted from broad issues of finance and program management to specific concerns about the quality of classroom teaching and teachers. These concerns have led to a resurgence of interest in evaluating teachers and to the development of new systems for teacher evaluation.

As in other areas of education, the theory and practice of teacher evaluation diverge. In this chapter, we explore the reasons for this divergence by reviewing and integrating the findings of two distinct streams of research. The first is research on teaching effectiveness, its measurement, and development of models for teacher evaluation. The second area consists of organizational and implementation research. This literature treats organizational control and authority; management of internal and external demands for organizational maintenance and accountability; processes of decision-making, communication, and implementation in school organizations; and problems of achieving consensus among various actors in the organizational context.

There is a growing realization that the development of successful teacher evaluation systems requires attention to both these sets of issues (Knapp, 1982; Natriello, Hoag, Deal and Dornbusch, 1977). We suggest in this chapter that knowledge and practice can be advanced by making explicit the educational and organizational theories underlying different conceptions of teaching work and of teacher evaluation. We examine how external demands for accountability are at odds with internal organizational needs for stability and trust; how loosely coupled organizations like school systems handle these competing demands; and how teacher evaluation may affect organizational operations and teaching work. We synthesize educational and organizational theories about the nature and control of teaching work to examine the implications of teacher evaluation processes for organizational sorting functions, instructional improvement efforts, and maintenance of productive working relationships. Finally, we argue that successful teacher evaluation requires consistent and shared views of the teaching-learning process and of the organizational context in which teacher evaluation takes place.

This chapter develops a conceptual framework for understanding teacher evaluation in the organizational context. We do not present a detailed synopsis of all the literature that pertains to teacher evaluation techniques, methods, instruments, and processes. Some excellent compilations of this literature have been published recently (for example, Lewis, 1982; Millman, 1981a; Peterson and Kauchak, 1982; Stiggins and Bridgeford, 1982), and we refer readers to them for information on teacher evaluation practices. Instead we show how diverse areas of research on teaching and schools can be brought to bear on the question of designing and implementing successful teacher evaluation systems. We attempt to broaden the conceptual base for teacher evaluation research by adopting an organizational process framework for evaluating teacher evaluation.

Policy Context

The public has come to believe that the key to educational improvement lies in upgrading the quality of teachers rather than in changing school structure or curriculum. Improving teacher quality was the most frequent response to the 1979 Gallup poll's question on what public schools could do to earn an 'A' grade, beating by large margins such reforms as emphasizing the basics, improving school management, lowering class size, or updating the curriculum (Gallup, 1979). In response to these perceptions, states and local school districts have initiated a wide range of policy changes affecting the certification, evaluation, and tenure of both prospective and currently employed teachers (Gudridge, 1980; Vlaanderen, 1980).

Several states have adopted teacher competency tests, such as the National Teacher Examinations, for teacher certification; others are considering licensure, which would include statewide teacher examinations prior to certification along with the establishment of a professional standards and practices board (Lewis, 1979; McNeil, 1981; Southern

Regional Education Board, 1979; Vlaanderen, 1980). Some, like Oklahoma, are adopting comprehensive programs that include higher admission standards for colleges of education, competency tests for certification and recertification, evaluation of performance, and continuing teacher education (Kleine and Wisniewski, 1981). Most states have legislated requirements for teacher performance evaluation (Beckham, 1981), and some of the more recent statutes specify which testing instruments or evaluation procedures are acceptable.

Not surprisingly, teacher evaluation processes increasingly have become the subject of collective bargaining agreements. A Rand Corporation study found that between 1970 and 1975, the percentage of contracts examined that contained teacher evaluation provisions increased from 42 to 65 (McDonnell and Pascal, 1979). Contracts often specify methods of information gathering, frequency of observations and evaluation, processes for communicating evaluation criteria and results, opportunities for teacher response and remediation in the case of negative evaluations, and due process procedures (Strike and Bull, 1981).

Mitchell and Kerchner (1983) argue that because of collective bargaining, teacher evaluation has become an increasingly rule-based process, linked less to judgments of competence than to evidence about whether teachers have adhered to clearly specified minimum work standards. 'The objectification of evaluation standards,' they state, 'has had the effect of discoupling the relationship between teaching performance and the behaviors on which teachers are held subject to discipline and discharge' (pp. 19–20). Their observation reflects the difficulty in using teacher evaluation results for both formative (improvement-oriented) and summative (personnel decisionmaking) purposes.

Although a survey by the American Association of School Administrators (Lewis, 1982) found that few school districts were using evaluation results as the basis for layoff decisions, there is growing literature on the legal requirements for using evaluation results for dismissal (Beckham, 1981; Peterson and Kauchak, 1982; Strike and Bull, 1981). Courts have generally required that a school system strictly apply an established formal dismissal procedure with due process safeguards. Further, the school authorities must determine minimum acceptable teaching standards in advance, inform the staff of these standards, and, finally, document for the court how a teacher's performance violates these standards (Beckham, 1981). Beckham recommends that to withstand judicial scrutiny an evaluation policy must include: (a) a predetermined standard of teacher knowledge, competencies, and skills; (b) an evaluation system capable of detecting and preventing teacher incompetencies; and (c) a system for informing teachers of the required standards and according them an opportunity to correct teaching deficiencies.

Each of these criteria poses some problems for the design and implementation of a teacher evaluation system. There are particular difficulties in integrating the requirements of an evaluation policy geared toward job status decisions with those of a policy aimed at improving teaching. The most obvious problem is that developing a predetermined standard of teacher knowledge, competencies, or skills poses nontrivial controversies about the content and specificity of the standards. Furthermore, where standardized tests or performance assessments are used to make job status decisions, courts generally require that they have a demonstrable, direct relationship to effective job performance, that is, they must have proven validity. We explore the difficulties of such a demonstration in a later section of this chapter.

Detecting teacher incompetencies involves the development and careful application of reliable, generalizable measures of teaching knowledge or behavior. The state-of-the-art of measurement for teacher evaluation may not be adequate. *Preventing* incompetency implies the development of either a fool-proof approach to teacher training or a teacher-proof approach to instruction; we leave that to utopians. *Correcting* deficiencies seems a more approachable objective; however, this is the point at which research on teaching effectiveness leaves off and where summative and formative evaluation approaches collide.

It is one thing to define and measure teacher competence in a standardized fashion; it is quite another to change teacher performance. Research on individual and organizational behavior suggests that first-order solutions are unlikely to effect change, and, further, that successful approaches involve processes that may be inconsistent with those used to derive summative evaluation judgments. That is, the context-free generalization necessary for implementing a uniform evaluation system may counteract the context-specific processes needed to effect change in individual or organizational behaviors.

Policy Conflicts and Tensions

Many observers have pointed out that public pressures for summative evaluation affecting teacher job status — selection and promotion, dismissal, and reduction in force decisions — may make formative evaluation much more difficult (Knapp, 1982; Peterson and Kauchak, 1982; Feldvebel, 1980). Increasing the prescriptiveness and specificity of evaluation procedures, particularly the need for extensive documentation of all negative findings, generates anxiety among teachers and inhibits the principal's role as instructional leader or staff developer (Munnelly, 1979). Summative evaluation criteria must be more narrowly defined if they are to be applied uniformly, thus limiting their use for formative purposes. Furthermore, constraints on classroom behavior intended to weed out incompetent teachers may prevent good teachers from exercising their talents fully (Darling-Hammond and Wise, 1981). Knapp (1982) concludes

> The net result of these pressures for more careful summative judgments of teachers is to put administrators under particular strain. Though 'better' performance evaluation may appear to make the issues explicit and decisions objective, it may also generate as much heat as light, particularly where the various constituents to the design of evaluation do not agree. The pressure to improve teaching performance may foster more elaborate evaluation systems, but with summative thrusts getting in the way of formative efforts. (p. 10)

This tension between evaluation goals is in part a reflection of the differences among evaluation constituencies. These stakeholders have divergent views on the primary purpose of teacher evaluation and, hence, of what constitutes a successful evaluation system. Knapp's (1982) articulation of various stakeholders' perspectives is useful. Teachers have a stake in maintaining their jobs, their self-respect, and their sense of efficacy. They want a teacher evaluation system that encourages self-improvement, appreciates the complexity of their work, and protects their rights. Principals have a stake in maintaining stability in their organizations, allowing them to respond to parental and bureaucratic concerns for accountability while keeping staff morale intact. They want an evaluation system that is objective, not overly time-consuming, and feasible in the organizational context. Parents and public officials have a stake in the 'bottom line' — the effects of teaching on student outcomes. They want an evaluation system that relates teacher performance to teacher effectiveness, and that guarantees appropriate treatment of children in classrooms.

These differing views make choices about teacher evaluation processes difficult. They also affect implementation, because even after a policy is adopted, its terms and emphases are renegotiated at every level in the implementation system (Berman and McLaughlin, 1973–1978; Elmore, 1979). This renegotiation may not occur in a formal way, but practices at the school district, school, and classroom levels will be a function of cross pressures that may alter the formal process in important ways.

All these factors argue for understanding teacher evaluation plans in the context of organizational behaviors and processes. In the succeeding sections of this chapter we examine the educational and organizational concepts underlying different views of teacher evaluation, we describe the teacher evaluation processes and models currently in use, and we discuss implementation of teacher evaluation in the organizational context.

Educational and Organizational Concepts

The newly emerging policy thrusts in the area of teacher evaluation reflect diverse perspectives on the role of teachers in the educational enterprise, the nature of teaching work, the organization and operations of schools, and even the purposes of schooling. Different theories of learning and of the operation of educational organizations are embodied in different models for teacher evaluation, and any attempt to identify the components of 'successful' evaluation procedures must explicitly recognize their underlying assumptions.

Perhaps most problematic is the definition of teacher knowledge, skills, and competencies in a fashion useful for a *policy system*. Policies rely on generalizations that can be uniformly applied and administered according to rules. The further away policy development occurs from the implementation level, the more uniformly applicable generalizations and prescriptions for practice must be. They must rely on context-free assumptions linking theory to results.

As Darling-Hammond and Wise (1981) point out, many current policies are 'rationalistic' — they seek to rationalize the actions of teachers by specifying curricular objectives, by prescribing instructional methods for attaining the objectives, and by evaluating the extent to which the objectives are attained. They assume a direct link between teacher behavior and student learning, as well as a close match between external goals and classroom activities.

Yet, other theories of education are possible. Various theories differ significantly in their explanations of the nature of teaching and learning, the processes of schooling, and the ways in which educational organizations operate. We cannot here develop a full exposition of the range of educational theories; a few examples must suffice. At the heart of the rationalistic theory stand the policymaker and the administrator who rationalize the operations of the school through deliberate decision-making and procedure-setting. In the spontaneous theory, the teacher is the central figure. 'The rest of the vast educational enterprise chiefly serves the purpose of permitting the teacher to give spontaneous expression to the educated man he finds within himself — and in so doing, to foster useful intellectual growth in his pupils' (Stephens, 1976, pp. 140–1). The individual child is the focal point for the humanistic theory, and the schooling system revolves around his needs and interests in providing an environment to facilitate his development.

The distinguishing elements of these and other theories of education include differences concerning how goals for education are set (and by whom), what the goals in fact are, how they are to be transmitted among and operationalized by the various actors in the schooling process. The actors are variously viewed as active or passive, deliberate and rational or spontaneous and instinctive. The components of the educational system are variously perceived as autonomous or interdependent, tightly or loosely couple, vertically or horizontally integrated, consensual or individualistic in their perceptions of values, norms, and objectives. De facto power may be perceived as centralized at various hierarchical levels or relatively decentralized.

Depending on which theory of education one subscribes to and which model of the educational process seems most aptly to describe what one observes, the appropriate roles and tasks of policymakers, school administrators, teachers, and students will appear quite different. Certainly if policymakers and practitioners view the reality of schooling in vastly different ways, policies and practices will be dissonant, and intended policy outcomes will be unlikely to occur. Furthermore, whether a particular evaluation approach meets its proximate and ultimate goals will depend on the specific organizational context in which it is used, as well as the implementation processes that take place at each level of the operating system — that is, how the procedures are carried out within the classroom, school district, and, where relevant, the state.

Much of the existing literature on teacher evaluation examines instruments and techniques for evaluation without reference to their theoretical underpinnings or to the organizational contexts in which they are to be used. Without such reference, potential users cannot easily assess whether a particular approach will be well suited to their aims, conceptions of education, or organizational characteristics. Nor can they evaluate the implementation processes necessary to successfully use a given instrument or technique. Our approach seeks to place existing teacher evaluation procedures within a conceptual framework that explicitly links the various types of procedures to the models of learning and school organization which they reflect and to the organizational contexts in which they can best be used.

Conceptions of Teaching Work

Evaluation involves collecting and using information to judge the worth of something. It is an activity that teachers themselves engage in, though often informally (Shavelson, 1976). As we will argue, different conceptions of teaching work imply different ways by which information is collected and judgments of worth are made. Implied in these different conceptions of teaching work are different notions of educational goals, teacher planning activities, interactive teaching behavior, and self or other evaluation activities. The evaluation of teaching — collecting and using information to judge worth — will vary depending on one's conception of teaching work.

One way to illuminate a complex subject is through comparison. Teachers have been compared to craftspersons and professionals (Broudy, 1956; Lortie, 1975), bureaucrats (Wise, 1979), managers (Berliner, 1982), laborers (Mitchell and Kerchner, 1983), and artists (Eisner, 1978). Here we will use four ways of looking at teaching work: labor, craft, profession, or art (Mitchell and Kerchner, 1983). These ways of viewing teaching work provide a theoretical framework for analyzing teacher evaluation, because they sharply reveal the assumptions that lie behind different techniques for evaluating teachers. In incorporating this typology into our conceptual framework, we describe 'pure' conceptions of teaching work, recognizing in reality that pure prototypes do not exist. Nevertheless, as a heuristic device, we will see that every technique implicitly rests on assumptions about teaching work and the relation of the teacher to the administrative structure of the school.

Every teacher evaluation system must embody a definition of the teaching task and a mechanism to evaluate the teacher. Under the conception of teaching as *labor*, teaching activities are 'rationally planned, programmatically organized, and routinized in the form of standard operating procedures' by administrators (Mitchell and Kerchner, 1983, p. 35). The teacher is responsible for implementing the instructional program in the prescribed manner and for adhering to the specified routines and procedures. The evaluation system involves direct inspection of the teachers' work — monitoring lesson plans, classroom performance, and performance results; the school administrator is seen as the teachers' *supervisor*. This view of teaching work assumes that effective practices can be determined and specified in concrete ways, and that adherence to these practices will be sufficient to produce the desired results.

Under the conception of teaching as *craft*, teaching is seen as requiring a repertoire of specialized techniques. Knowledge of these techniques also includes knowledge of generalized rules for their application. In this conception, once the teaching assignment has been made, the teacher is expected to carry it out without detailed instructions or close supervision. Evaluation is indirect and involves ascertaining that the teacher has the requisite skills. The school administrator is seen as a *manager* whose job is to hold teachers to general performance standards. This view of teaching work assumes that general rules for applying specific techniques can be developed, and that proper use of the rules combined with knowledge of the techniques will produce the desired outcomes.

Under the conception of teaching as *profession*, teaching is seen as not only requiring a repertoire of specialized techniques but also as requiring the exercise of judgment about when those techniques should be applied (Shavelson, 1976; Shavelson and Stern, 1981). To exercise sound professional judgment, the teacher is expected to master a body of theoretical knowledge as well as a range of techniques. Broudy (1956) makes the distinction between craft and profession in this way: 'We ask the professional to diagnose difficulties, appraise solutions, and to choose among them. We ask him to take total responsibility for both strategy and tactics . . . From the craftsman, by contrast, we expect a standard diagnosis, correct performance of procedures, and nothing else' (p. 182). Standards for evaluating professionals are developed by peers, and evaluation focuses on the degree to which teachers are competent at professional problem-solving; the school administrator is seen as an *administrator* whose task it is to ensure that teachers have the resources necessary to carry out their work. This view of teaching work assumes that standards of professional knowledge and practice can be developed and assessed, and that their enforcement will ensure competent teaching.

Under the conception of teaching as *art*, teaching techniques and their application may be novel, unconventional, or unpredictable. This is not to say that techniques or standards of practice are ignored, but that their form and use are personalized rather than standardized. As Gage (1978) explains, the teaching art involves 'a process that calls for intuition, creativity, improvisation, and expressiveness — a process that leaves room for departures from what is implied by rules, formulas, and algorithms' (p. 15). He argues that teaching *uses* science but cannot itself *be* a science because the teaching environment is not predictable. In this view, the teacher must draw upon not only a body of professional knowledge and skill, but also a set of personal resources that are uniquely defined and expressed by the personality of the teacher and his or her individual and collective interactions with students.

Because teaching viewed as an art encompasses elements of personal insight (as well as theoretically grounded professional insight), the teacher as artist is expected to exercise considerable autonomy in the performance of his or her work. Evaluation involves both self-assessment and critical assessment by others. Such evaluation would entail 'the study of holistic qualities rather than analytically derived quantities, the use of "inside" rather than externally objective points of view' (Gage, 1978, p. 15). It would rely on high-inference rather than low-inference variables, on observation of patterns of events rather than counts of specific, discrete behaviors (Eisner, 1978; Gage, 1978). In this view, the school administrator is seen as a *leader* whose work it is to encourage the teacher's efforts. The view assumes that teaching patterns (i.e., holistic qualities that pervade a teacher's approach) can be recognized and assessed by using both internal and external referents of validity.

Obviously, these four conceptions of teaching work are ideal types that will not be found in pure form in the real world. In fact, various components of teachers' work embody different ideal types (for example, motivating students, performing hall duty, presenting factual information, establishing and maintaining classroom relationships). Nonetheless, the conceptions of teaching work signal different definitions of success in a teacher evaluation system.

The disparity in implicit views cannot be ignored. McNeil and Popham (1973), for example, make a strong case for evaluating teachers by their contribution to the performance of students rather than by the use of teacher process criteria. Millman also argues that 'criteria and techniques for the fair use of student achievement in both the formative and summative roles of teacher evaluation can be devised' (Millman, 1981b). This view presupposes that students' learning as measured by their test performance is a direct function of teaching ability; it seeks to measure the worth of teachers by reference to the *product* or output of their work, thus it envisions teaching work as labor and the student as raw material. However, only 11 per cent of teachers believe that scores on standardized achievement tests are valid measures of teacher effectiveness (NEA, 1979). Implicit in the view of most teachers is the notion that other factors or dynamics of the teaching and learning process are at least as important in determining learning outcomes as the ability of the teacher. These other factors are a combination of those school conditions not under the teacher's control and the unpredictable elements inherent in human interaction that give rise to a conception of teaching work as profession or art.

Conceptions of Teaching in Teaching Research

Although the various conceptions of teaching work are distinct along several dimensions, they can be usefully viewed on a continuum that incorporates increasing ambiguity or complexity in the performance of teaching tasks as one moves from labor at one extreme to art at the other. The role of the teaching environment in determining teacher behavior also increases in importance as one moves along the continuum. The more variable or unpredictable one views the teaching environment as being, the more one is impelled toward a conception of teaching as a profession or art. Gage (1978) uses the distinction between teaching as science or art to describe how the elements of predictability and environmental control differentiate the two. A science of teaching is unattainable, he observes, because it 'implies that good teaching will some day be attainable by closely following rigorous laws that yield high predictability and control' (p. 17). Using science to achieve practical ends, he argues, requires artistry — the use of judgment, intuition, and insight in handling the unpredicted, knowledge of when to apply which laws and generalizations and when not to, the ability to make clinical assessments of how multiple variables affect the solution to a problem.

Research on teaching parallels these conceptions of teaching work in the degree to which predictability and environmental controls are assumed or even considered in the design and goals of the research. Some efforts to link specific teacher characteristics or teaching behaviors to student outcomes have sought context-free generalizations about what leads to or constitutes effective teaching. Although this line of research strongly suggests that what teachers do in the classroom does affect students, claims that discrete sets of behaviors consistently lead to increased student performance (for example, Medley, 1979; Rosenshine and Furst, 1971; Stallings, 1977) have been countered by inconsistent and often contradictory findings that undermine faith in the outcomes of simple process-product research (for example, Doyle, 1978; Dunkin and Biddle, 1974; Shavelson and Dempsey-Atwood, 1976). The most extensive process-product study of teacher effectiveness, the Beginning Teacher Evaluation Study, conducted for California's Commission for Teacher Preparation and Licensing, contributed to the discomforts associated with linking teacher behaviors to student learning. After that monumental effort, '[t]he researchers ., , concluded that linking precise and specific teacher behavior to precise and specific learning of pupils (the original goal of the inquiry) is not possible at this time ... These findings suggest that the legal requirement for a license probably cannot be well stated in precise behavioral terms' (Bush, 1979, p. 15; see also McDonald and Elias, 1976).

At best, the teaching performances advanced as having consistently positive effects on student achievement are relatively broad constructs rather than discrete, specific actions of teachers. The Beginning Teacher Evaluation Study found little evidence that single teaching performance variables can be identified as essential for effective teaching, but found that differences in *patterns* of teaching performances contribute to learning. However, even these broader patterns are not uniformly applicable to all grade levels, subject areas, and teaching situations (McDonald and Elias, 1976). Similarly, the often cited variables identified by Rosenshine and Furst (1971) as consistently related to student achievement are best characterized as high-inference variables; that is, they do not readily break down into easily tabulated, discrete teaching actions. As Centra and Potter (1980) note, these variables — clarity, variability, enthusiasm, task-oriented or business-like behaviors, student opportunity to learn criterion material, use of student ideas and general indirectness, criticism, use of structuring comments, types of questions, probing, and instructional difficulty level — are undoubtedly important, 'but few of them could be usefully considered "basic teaching tasks"' (Centra and Potter, 1980, p. 282).

Furthermore, subsequent research on these variables, variously measured to be sure, has produced inconsistent findings that seem due to more than mere measurement differences. Rosenshine, for example, now finds that 'indirectness,' one of the effective teaching variables identified in his earlier review, is to be discouraged in classroom teaching as it detracts from student achievement (Rosenshine, 1979). The status of research on 'direct instruction' and its companion concept, 'academic learning time' bears special mention because of the eagerness with which it has been accepted as state-of-the-art knowledge by many researchers and practitioners concerned not only with the development of teacher evaluation systems but also with educational quality improvement more generally.

This line of research also highlights many of the dilemmas that confront those who must define criteria for effective teaching.

Direct instruction is generally proposed as the vehicle for increasing the amount of time students spend actively engaged in appropriate learning activities (see, for example, Berliner, 1977; Bruner, 1976; Rosenshine, 1977). Berliner (1977) defines academic learning time as 'on task or engaged time by students, interacting with materials or participating in activities of intermediate level difficulty that are academically focused' (p. 3). Following Wiley and Harnischfeger's (1974) not surprising finding that the amount of time students spend in school is related to their achievement, others have found that time spent on academic subjects is related to achievement in those subject areas (Fisher *et al.*, 1978; Stallings, 1977), although the strength and consistency of the relationship has been found to vary considerably (Gage, 1978, p. 75). Further refinements in the concept have sought to measure active student engagement in learning activities as related to achievement, but with equivocal success. McDonald and Elias (1976) reported mixed results for academic learning time as a predictor of achievement, and, surprisingly, found time allocated for instruction a generally better predictor than student engagement rate. McDonald (1976) also reported that more class-as-a-whole teaching, while leading to greater pupil attentiveness (i.e., engagement), had negative effects on achievement.

Assuming, nonetheless, that engaged time may positively affect achievement, what are the teaching behaviors that increase engaged time? The most common answer is direct instruction,[1] defined by Rosenshine (1979) as referring to,

> academically focused, teacher-directed classrooms using sequenced and structured materials. It refers to teaching activities where goals are clear to students, time allocated for instruction is sufficient and continuous, coverage of content is extensive, the performance of students is monitored, questions are at a low cognitive level ..., and feedback to students is immediate and academically oriented. In direct instruction, the teacher controls instructional goals, chooses materials appropriate for the student's ability, and paces the instructional episode. The goal is to move the students through a sequenced set of materials or tasks. Such materials are common across classrooms and have a relatively strong congruence with the tasks on achievement tests. (p. 38)[2]

In terms of teaching behaviors, Rosenshine's explication reveals that direct instruction is characterized by frequency of single-answer questions and drill, large-group instruction, and opportunities for 'controlled practice.' Teaching behaviors that are discouraged include the use of higher order, divergent, or open-ended questions, exploration of student's ideas, student-initiated discourse or choice of activities, conversation about personal experience or about subject matter tangential to the immediate objectives of the lesson at hand. In this sense, direct instruction contrasts with 'teacher indirectness' (Flanders, 1970) and with approaches generally ascribed to 'open' rather than 'traditional' instruction (Horwitz, 1979; Peterson, 1979).

Elements of the direct instructional approach have been investigated in several studies. Support for various elements of the approach in terms of effects on student achievement on standardized tests has been reported by Soar (1972); Evertson and Brophy (1973); Wright (1975); Bell, Sipursky, and Switzer (1976); Ward and Barcher (1975), especially for high-ability children; and Röhr (1976), especially for low-ability children. On the other hand, teacher *indirectness* has been found to have positive effects on student achievement in a review of research by Glass *et al.* (1977), especially for secondary school students, and in many of the studies reviewed by Dunkin and Biddle (1974) and Horwitz (1979). Thus, while we may concede that teachers ought to do something to engage their students in active learning, we are still left with serious questions about what that something is.

Some researchers have addressed the problem of inconsistent research findings by reference to interaction effects and attention to other situation-specific variables. This line of research finds that effective teaching behaviors vary for students of different socioeconomic, mental, and psychological characteristics (for example, Brophy and Evertson, 1974, 1977; Cronbach and Snow, 1977; Peterson, 1976) and for different grade levels and subject areas (Gage, 1978; McDonald and Elias, 1976). Nonetheless, given the particular teaching context, many infer from this research that appropriate behaviors can be specified to increase student achievement.

Problems have been identified even with this more limited approach to linking teaching behaviors with student outcomes. First, interaction effects that may be identified from teaching research are not confined to easily translatable two- or even three-way interactions. Thus, their generalizability for establishing rules of practice is severely constrained (Knapp, 1982; Shavelson, 1973). Cronbach (1975) questioned the application of the line of aptitude-treatment interaction (ATI) research that he helped initiate twenty years earlier when he observed:

> An ATI result can be taken as a general conclusion only if it is not in turn moderated by further variables ... Once we attend to interactions, we enter a hall of mirrors that extends to infinity. However far we carry our analysis — to third order or fifth order or any other — untested interactions of a still higher order can be envisioned. (p. 119)

With respect to teaching research, Cronbach has concluded that established empirical generalizations 'in a world in which most effects are interactive' might no longer be a fruitful strategy for research. Instead, he proposes that researchers pursue a course of short-run empiricism that is 'response sensitive,' one that takes exceptions as the rule, and that makes continual adjustments on the basis of individual, context-specific responses (pp. 121–2).

A related finding is that teaching behaviors that have sometimes been found to be effective often bear a distinctly curvilinear relation to achievement. That is, a behavior that is effective when used in moderation can produce significant and negative results when used too much (Peterson and Kauchak, 1982; Soar, 1972), or, as others have found, when applied in the wrong circumstances (see, for example, Coker, Medley and Soar, 1980; McDonald and Elias, 1976). This kind of finding also makes it difficult to develop rules for teaching behaviors that can be applied generally.

A more problematic finding is that the effectiveness of the two very distinct sets of teaching behaviors described above varies depending on the goals of instruction. Many of the behaviors that seem to result in increased achievement on standardized tests and factual examinations are dissimilar, indeed nearly opposite, from those that seem to increase complex cognitive learning, problem-solving ability, and creativity (McKeachie and Kulik, 1975; Peterson, 1979; Soar, 1977; Soar and Soar, 1976). As Centra and Potter (1980) observe,

> Higher order skills (for example, inferential reasoning) are not particularly likely to be acquired (and certainly will not be demonstrated) by students whose teachers ask only lower-order questions ... When the measure of student achievement is a multiple-choice, factually oriented test, it is not possible to assess the effects of teachers' higher-order questions, and no conclusions regarding the effectiveness of teacher questioning should be drawn from such studies. (p. 285)

Furthermore, some research suggests that desirable affective outcomes of education — independence, curiosity, and positive attitudes toward school, teacher, and self — seem to result from teaching behaviors that are different from those prescribed for increasing student achievement on standardized tests of cognitive skills (Horwitz, 1979; McKeachie and Kulik, 1975; Peterson, 1979; Traub *et al.*, 1973). To confound matters further, these effects also seem to vary by type of student (Peterson, 1979).

We say that this finding related to goals is 'problematic' because it raises more fundamental difficulties to agreement on effective teaching than does the identification of interaction effects or even the recognition of contextual factors. These variables complicate matters, but they do not entirely derail the effective teaching train. Attention to intervening variables can still, theoretically at least, lead to specifications of appropriate teaching behaviors. Goal specification, however, is not the province of educational researchers. If markedly different teaching behaviors lead to divergent results that can be deemed equally desirable, there is no way to identify a single construct called effective teaching, much less delimit its component parts. One can, at best, pursue alternative models of effective teaching, making explicit the goals underlying each. This has yet to become part of the empirical research base on teaching effects, although educational philosophers and organizational theorists have treated the issues of goal specification in more explicit terms (see, for example, Eisner and Vallance, 1974; Weick, 1976; Fenstermacher, 1978). As Fenstermacher (1978) notes:

> The process-product research on teacher effectiveness lacks a normative theory of education; this research does not incorporate a conception or justification of what is ultimately worth knowing or doing, it includes no view or defense of right conduct or moral integrity, nor does it give consideration to or argument for the ethical obligations and reasonable expectations of persons who act in specific historical, social, political, and economic settings. The lack of such a theory is not necessarily a fault of this research, except when its results are converted from theorems to rules for teachers to follow. (p. 175)

Questions of educational goals are clearly critical for the design of teacher evaluation systems, but, as we have noted, not central to teaching effects research. Putting such questions aside for the moment, we observe that, as the various lines of research on teacher effectiveness ascribe different degrees of generalizability to effective teaching behaviors and different weights to context-specific variables, they embody different conceptions of teaching work. The more complex and variable the educational environment is seen as being, the more one must rely on teacher judgment or even insight to guide the activities of classroom life, and the less one relies on generalized rules for teacher behavior.

The conversion of teacher effects research findings to rules for teacher behavior is a cornerstone of many performance-based teacher evaluation models. These models implicitly assume that the rules are generalizable because student outcomes are determined primarily by particular uniform teaching behaviors. By implication, the models assume either that other contextual influences on student outcomes are relatively unimportant, or that these other influences do not call for different teaching behaviors for teaching to be effective. Research on nonteaching variables in the educational environment calls into question the view of teaching as technological in nature, or at the least limits the generalizability of this view. This line of research constrains the application of process-product approaches to teacher evaluation in two ways: (a) it indicates that many factors other than teaching behaviors have profound effects on student learning; and (b) it suggests that effective teaching must be responsive to a number of student, classroom, and school variables in ways that preclude the application of predetermined approaches to teaching.

In a review of research on school and teacher effects on student learning, Centra and Potter (1980) observed that 'student achievement is affected by a considerable number of variables, of which teacher behavior is but one' (p. 287). Although they reject the extreme view that teachers have no effect on student outcomes, they conclude that 'teacher effects are likely to be small when compared with the totality of the effects of the other variables affecting student achievement, [and] . . . the effects of any one of the variables . . . are likely to be small when compared with the combined interactive effect of all the other variables' (p. 287). Anderson's (1982) review of research on school climate also indicates that many organizational and social system variables interact to influence teacher performance, student behavior, and student learning, and that these dependent variables simultaneously influence each other. Factors like school size, program characteristics and resources, administrative organization, incentive structures, and others mediate teacher and pupil performance both by imposing constraints and by presenting divergent models for successful teaching (Joyce and Weil, 1972; Mckenna, 1981).

Researchers who adopt an ecological perspective for investigating teaching also point out that reciprocal causality, particularly with respect to teacher and student behaviors, limits the applicability of process-product research findings (Doyle, 1979). Research grounded in this perspective finds that what students do affects teachers' behaviors and that the complexity of classroom life calls for teaching strategies responsive to environmental demands. As Doyle (1979) notes,

> Traditionally, research on teaching has been viewed as a process of isolating a set of effective teaching practices to be used by individual teachers to improve student learning or by policy makers to design teacher education and teacher evaluation programs. The emphasis in this tradition has been on predicting which methods or teacher behaviors have the highest general success rate, and much of the controversy over the productivity of research on teaching has centered on the legitimacy of propositions derived from available studies . . . [The ecological approach] would seem to call into question the very possibility of achieving a substantial number of highly generalizable statements about teaching effectiveness. (pp. 203–4)

Doyle contends that the process-product paradigm for research leads us to focus on behaviors that promise to be 'context-proof, teacher-proof, and even student-proof' even though they may not be the most important behaviors in bringing about learning (Doyle, 1978, p. 169). He proposes instead the use of a 'mediating process' paradigm that takes into account the students' responses and the psychological processes that govern learning. Ecological analysis of teaching, as Doyle describes it, encompasses three basic features that are consonant with the research strategy advocated by Cronbach (1975). They are (a) a vigorously naturalistic approach, (b) a direct focus on environment-behavior relationships, and (c) a concern for the functional value or adaptive significance of behaviors in an environment (Doyle, 1979, pp. 188–9).

This approach is consistent with the interactionist view of teaching neatly capsulized by Brophy and Evertson (1976):

> [E]ffective teaching requires the ability to implement a very large number of diagnostic, instructional, managerial, and therapeutic skills, tailoring behavior in specific contexts and situations to the specific needs of the moment. Effective teachers not only must be able to do a large number of things; they also must be able to recognize which of the many things they know how to do applies at a given moment and be able to follow through by performing the behavior effectively. (p. 139)

The approach is also consonant with an intentionalist thesis for studying teaching that examines teachers' *reasons* for adopting particular behaviors in different classroom situations rather than simply examining behaviors (Fenstermacher, 1978; Shavelson and Stern, 1981).

Research on the stability and generalizability of measures of teaching behaviors lends support to a context-specific view of teaching. Stability refers to the extent that a teacher's behavior as measured at one point in time correlates with measures taken at another point in time. Generalizability refers to the extent that such measures are stable across different teaching situations (for example, different subject areas, grade levels, student ability levels, etc.). The bottom-line question is, Does a given teacher exhibit the same kinds of behavior at different points in time and within different teaching contexts? In general, the answer is 'no', especially with regard to measures of specific, discrete teaching behaviors (Shavelson and Dempsey-Atwood, 1976).[3] While this finding may be due to poor measurement instruments, it may also be due to the fact that teachers adjust their behaviors to the changing needs of the teaching context.

Some have suggested that teaching process research ought to account for this possibility by examining the variability or flexibility of teaching acts. Research on teacher characteristics has found that, of teacher characteristic variables, measures of teacher flexibility, adaptability, or creativity exhibit the most consistent relationship with ratings of teacher performance and effectiveness (McDonald and Elias, 1976; Schalock, 1979.) The implications for teacher evaluation of this view of teaching work are markedly different from those inherent in a view of teaching behaviors as stable or a view of the teaching environment as largely unrelated to effective teaching acts.

⁷e see the manifestations of these different points of view in teacher
tion systems that are based on divergent premises. On one hand,
many states are considering or beginning to implement systems of
competency-based certification or recertification and performance-based
evaluation (Vlaanderen, 1980). These systems assume the validity, stability, and generalizability of effective teaching behaviors. On the other
hand, teacher evaluation systems that rely heavily on approaches like
clinical supervision, self-assessment, and interactive evaluation processes
have been developed on the premise that situation-specific elements and
teacher intentionality must play a role in assessing teacher performance.
In the next section, we explore how choices of teacher evaluation systems
also depend on views of schooling processes and of schools as
organizations.

Theories of Schools as Organizations

The four conceptions of teaching work we have discussed can be divided
into those which presuppose a more rationalistic school organization —
labor and craft — and those which presuppose less rationalistic school
organizations — profession and art. Teacher evaluation processes must
operate within a school system's organization. General beliefs about how
schools as organizations operate may influence choices of evaluation
procedures (for example, hierarchical procedures vs. more lateral processes like self-assessment or peer review). The implementation of those
procedures will depend not only on policymakers' implicit theories, but
also on the realities of the organizational context. For example, is the
organization really closed to environmental influence? Can it really
operate as a tightly coupled bureaucracy? Below we discuss two models of
school organization that are ideal types representing dramatically different
organizational theories. Many other models exist in theory and can be
found, at least in hybrid form, in the real world. We discuss these two to
illustrate how radically different assumptions can result in divergent
approaches to teacher evaluation.

The rationalistic model of school organization. Those who apply a
rationalistic approach to education assume that the processes of teaching
and learning rest on an underlying order. In the most simplified terms, the
assumption of predictability requires a view that students are essentially
passive objects, hence each student of X, Y and Z characteristics will react
in the same way when a given stimulus or treatment is applied by the
teacher. Outcomes are predictable; all that remains for decisionmakers to
devise is a correct specification of inputs or processes. Results are achieved
by the deliberate application of rationally conceived practices. Students
will learn in direct proportion to the amount and kind of deliberate effort
exerted by the teacher.

A rationalistic view of teaching presumes that once the goals of education are decided upon by external authorities, administrators will define behavioral objectives and teachers will teach to those objectives. Teacher and pupil performance can be tested; these assessments will yield meaningful measures of the success of the educational enterprise. The tests will give a clear picture of student and, by implication, teacher competencies. Objectively measured student competencies can be linked to other objectively measured teacher competencies because the student is an empty organism to be shaped in deliberate ways by the teacher-trainer. The teacher is to deliver a product which fits the specifications described by the goals and objectives.

The schooling process in the rationalistic model is characteristic of bureaucracies. It entails (a) a functional division of labor; (b) the definition of staff roles as offices which are distinguished by functional specificity of performance and universalistic, affectively neutral interaction with clients; (c) the hierarchic ordering of offices; and (d) operation according to rules of procedure which set limits to the discretionary performance of officers by specifying both the aims and the modes of official action (Bidwell, 1965). By conceiving of the teacher as bureaucrat, laborer, or craftsperson, the model gives little play for variations in teacher or student temperament, interests, or styles. It also ignores the importance of organizational context — the fact that in different situations teachers and students will perform differently. Finally, it ignores intervening variables between teacher competencies and teacher effectiveness by assuming tight coupling throughout the system and existence of environmental controls. A belief in this model might lead a school system to choose teacher evaluation processes that emphasized evaluation by superordinate specialists, material rewards and sanctions, precise ordering of tasks and/or specification of outcomes, the specification of processes, adherence to rules, and hierarchical relationships (Fuller, Wood, Rapoport, and Dornbusch, 1982).

The natural systems model of school organization. A less rationalistic model of school organization is based on the idea that effective teaching does not depend on deliberate, rational planning by superordinates (Stephens, 1976). The teacher as professional or artist is to be given an environment in which his or her profession or art can be practiced. The organizational model underlying this view is the natural systems model employed by some social scientists to look at organizations. This model posits loose coupling of organizational elements. If one believes that schools function as natural systems, then one will not try to impose bureaucratic procedures inappropriately. Bureaucratic procedures may still be employed, but their limits will be acknowledged and attention will be paid to teacher- and context-specific variables. Thus, viewing the school as a natural system *may* be conducive to a professional structure for teaching work. Suppose, for example, that policymakers think of the school system as a bureaucracy but it really functions as a natural system. The model tells us that certain rationalistic procedures may not be successful. A belief in this model does not tell us that teachers will, in fact, be treated as professionals or artists. It does, however, allow for that possibility.

> In the natural systems model, organization 'policy' accumulates crescively and in an unplanned manner ... [T]he model implies that power is dispersed, partly because of 'slippage' that can occur between the levels at which policies are formulated and those at which they are implemented ... Also the hierarchy accentuates communication problems; the longer the hierarchy the more distortion that can take place at each successive lower level, due to misinterpretations as well as to conflicts of interest between subordinate and superordinate groups.(Corwin, 1974, pp. 255–6)

The assumptions of the natural systems model differ from those of the rationalistic model in important ways. The natural systems model assumes the following organizational characteristics:

1 Absence of consensus among the membership on values, norms, and objectives;
2 Functional autonomy of the parts of the organization;
3 Bargaining and compromise to decide the terms of the relationship in the absence of consensus;
4 De facto decentralization of power;
5 Incomplete information for making decisions; and
6 Lack of coordination in planning and policymaking.

Corwin (1974) reasons that this model most accurately describes organizations with long hierarchies where the higher levels are directly linked to the political system and the organization is susceptible to outside influences. In school organizations thus conceived, teachers will maintain their own values and pursue their own objectives despite edicts from higher authorities. Because they are functionally autonomous and de facto power is decentralized, and because planning and policymaking are not highly coordinated, teachers may not govern their routine actions with reference to the deliberate decisions made by others in the hierarchy (see also Weick, 1976). They may accede to some rationalistic procedures through a process of bargaining and compromise, but these will not completely override the teachers' own conceptions of teaching work.

This view of school organizations also allows for the notion that teacher autonomy may be desirable in order for teachers to serve their clients in the way they judge best, based on more intimate knowledge of specific client needs (Lipsky, 1980). Similarly, Lewin's (1938) efficacy model suggests that less bureaucratic forms of organization may enhance workers' motivation and self-efficacy (Fuller *et al.*, 1982). What Fuller calls the 'humanistic views' of organizations sees hierarchical control and routinization of work tasks as undermining workers' efficacy by limiting their responsibility and their participation in problem-solving (*cf*. Bacharach and Aiken, 1979; French and Raven, 1977; Lawler, 1973; Mobley, Griffeth, Hand, and Meglino, 1979). In this view, the routinization or standardization that a rational-bureaucratic model imposes on teaching work may be seen as counterproductive to the extent that it constrains teachers in using their professional or personal judgment.

The degree to which these educational and organizational theories are reflected in teacher evaluation processes is examined in the succeeding sections of this paper.

Approaches to Teacher Evaluation

The choice of a teacher evaluation process is, as we have observed, associated with views of teaching work and of the school as an organization, although quite often these associations are made only implicitly in evaluation decisionmaking. A more explicit choice factor is the use to which the evaluation results are to be put.

Purposes for Teacher Evaluation

As indicated in Figure I, teacher evaluation may serve four basic purposes. The figure's cells artificially represent these purposes and levels of decisionmaking as distinct. In fact, teacher evaluation may be directed at small or large groups of teachers (rather than simply individuals or whole schools), and may represent degrees of hybrid improvement and accountability concerns (as when promotion decisions are linked to improvement efforts).

Many teacher evaluation systems are nominally intended to accomplish all four of these purposes, but different processes and methods are better suited to one or another of these objectives. In particular, improvement and accountability may require different standards of adequacy and of evidence. Focusing on individual or organizational concerns also leads to different processes, for example, bottom-up or top-down approaches to change, unstandardized or standardized remedies for problems identified. Berliner and Fenstermacher illuminate these differences with respect to staff development (our improvement dimension), although their observations are applicable to accountability purposes as well. Their definition of staff development encompasses four scales along which approaches may differ:

Figure 1. Four basic purposes of teacher evaluation.

Purpose/Level	Individual	Organizational
Improvement (formative information)	Individual staff development	School improvement
Accountability (summative information)	Individual personnel (job status) decisions	School status (for example, certification) decisions

> Staff development activities may be [a] internally proposed or externally imposed, in order to [b] effect compliance, remediate deficiencies, or enrich the knowledge and skills of [c] individual teachers or groups of teachers, who [d] may or may not have a choice to participate in the activities. (Fenstermacher and Berliner, in press, p. 6)

They note that as more differentiation occurs between participant roles and organizational levels, the profile of a staff development activity tends to shift from internal to external initiation, from an enrichment to a compliance focus, from participation by individuals or small groups to standardized programs for large groups, and from voluntary to involuntary participation. As the profile of a staff development activity shifts, so does its usefulness for a variety of purposes.

Staff development may be a vehicle for training teachers as technicians to implement policies devised by someone else (Floden and Feiman, 1981). Teacher evaluation in this case would focus on how faithfully the prescribed procedures or curricula are adhered to. This approach is most useful for organizational improvement or accountability purposes. Alternatively, staff development may be viewed as a means for helping teachers move from the acquisition of particular skills to applications of their judgment in order for them to play an analytic role in developing curricula and methods. Or staff development may be designed to help the teacher move to higher developmental stages in order to enable him or her to develop multiple perspectives about teaching and learning, to become more flexible, adaptive, and creative (Floden and Feiman, 1981). Teacher evaluation in these views would focus on teachers' personal stages of development and areas of confidence and would be most suited for individual improvement purposes.

In general, teacher evaluation processes most suited to accountability purposes must be capable of yielding fairly objective, standardized, and externally defensible information about teacher performance. Evaluation processes useful for improvement objectives must yield rich, descriptive information that illuminates sources of difficulty as well as viable courses for change. Teacher evaluation methods designed to inform organizational decisions must be hierarchically administered and controlled to ensure credibility and uniformity. Evaluation methods designed to assist decisionmaking about individuals must consider the context in which individual performance occurs to ensure appropriateness and sufficiency of data.

Although these purposes and the approaches most compatible with them are not necessarily mutually exclusive, an emphasis on one may tend to limit the pursuit of another. Similarly, while multiple methods for evaluating teachers can be used — and many argue, should be used — it is important to consider what purposes are best served by each if teacher evaluation goals and processes are to be consonant. Furthermore, some processes are distinctly inconsistent with others and with some purposes for evaluation. These disjunctures should be recognized before a teacher evaluation system is adopted and put in place.

Teacher Evaluation Processes and Methods

There have been several recent reviews of teacher evaluation processes in which the authors identified from six to twelve general approaches to teacher evaluation (Ellett, Capie and Johnson, 1980; Haefele, 1980; Lewis, 1982; Millman, 1981a; Peterson and Kauchak, 1982). They reveal that the approaches used to evaluate teachers seek to measure very different aspects of teaching and the teacher. They rely on different conceptions of what demontrates adequacy and on diverse notions of how to recognize or measure adequacy. Some seek to assess the quality of the *teacher* (teacher competence); others seek to assess the quality of *teaching* (teacher performance). Other approaches claim to assess the teacher or his or her teaching by reference to student outcomes (teacher effectiveness). Medley (1982) offers useful definitions of four terms often treated as synonyms:

- *Teacher competency* refers to any single knowledge, skill, or professional value position, the possession of which is believed to be relevant to the successful practice of teaching. Competencies refer to specific things that teachers know, do, or believe but not to the effects of these attributes on others.
- *Teacher competence* refers to the repertoire of competencies a teacher possesses. Overall competence is a matter of the degree to which a teacher has mastered a set of individual competencies, some of which are more critical to a judgment of overall competence than others.
- *Teacher performance* refers to what the teacher *does* on the job rather than to what she or he *can* do (that is, how competent she or he is). Teacher performance is specific to the job situation; it depends on the competence of the teacher, the context in which the teacher works, and the teacher's ability to apply his or her competencies at any given point in time.
- *Teacher effectiveness* refers to the effect that the teacher's performance has on pupils. Teacher effectiveness depends not only on com-

petence and performance, but also on the responses pupils make. Just as competence cannot predict performance under different situations, teacher performance cannot predict outcomes under different situations.

The tools and processes that are used to assess teacher competence, performance, or effectiveness are based on assumptions about how these qualities are linked to one another, how they may be measured, and how the measurements may be used to make decisions. There is substantial debate on all these questions. In this section, we will briefly describe the tools and processes currently used for evaluating school personnel and summarize the issues raised by each.

Teacher Interviews. Teacher interviews or conferences have been a prevalent evaluation method in the past and are a cornerstone of some of the more recent evaluation strategies. Haefele (1981, p. 49) has identified two uses for teacher interviews: for the purpose of hiring decisions and for communicating performance appraisals to a practicing teacher. Teacher selection interviews in the past have been generally informal and un-structured. One standardized interview method developed and used more recently is the Teacher Perceiver Interview. The instrument, which poses hypothetical questions or situations to the candidate, purportedly assesses noncognitive traits and reduces the possible interviewer bias of un-structured interviews. However, there is no empirical research regarding the ability of such instruments to predict the effectiveness of teachers.

In the past, the teacher appraisal interview and classroom observation represented the totality of the evaluation process. After the principal or evaluator observed a teacher's performance in the classroom, a conference was convened to communicate the evaluation results. In the conference, teaching performance standards were established, teaching performance was motivated, assessments were made, warnings were issued, guidance was given, and superior performance was recognized. Recently, however, the interview has been viewed as an important element of a broader evaluation procedure. In particular, a preobservation conference has been recognized as useful for the involvement of teachers in their own professional development and for a more regularized exchange of feedback from superiors (Garawski, 1980; Gudridge, 1980; Redfern, 1980). Hunter (in Gudridge, 1980, pp. 39–40) on the other hand, believes the preobserv-ation conference, which determines what behaviors the evaluator is looking for, locks a teacher into those behaviors during the observation, inhibiting individual teaching styles.

Competency Tests. There is a strong trend toward the use of standardized tests for initial certification and hiring. This trend is based partly on the belief that teachers should be able to demonstrate cognitive competence as a prerequisite to a teaching position and partly on the public's suspicion about the effectiveness of teacher education and training (Harris, 1981). There is also a growing belief that such tests can be used for recertification and dismissal decisions.

By far the most widely used competency test is the National Teacher Examination (NTE). Harris estimated that 75,000 teacher candidates in 24 states and 311 school districts take the exam each year. In some states and school districts, passing the NTE is a condition of employment (Harris, 1981, pp. 63–4). The examination measures academic achievement and preparation in areas of general education, professional education, and specialized subject areas. The assumption is that test performance accurately reflects at least one determinant of successful teaching — cognitive competence. However, a review of studies that have examined the relationship between NTE scores and measures of teacher performance found no consistent relationships (Quirk, Witten and Weinberg, 1973).

There are also a number of state and locally developed teacher examinations. Most prominent in the literature is the Georgia Teacher Area Criterion Referenced Test,[4] which assesses a prospective teacher's knowledge of a specific curriculum area. Passing this exam is a precondition of certification throughout the state (Ellett *et al.*, 1980; Harris, 1981; Hathaway, 1980; Lewis, 1982). Similar tests have been developed in Florida, South Carolina, Dallas and Houston, Texas, and Montgomery County, Maryland.

Proponents of standardized teacher tests maintain that tests guarantee a minimum standard of knowledge on the part of prospective teachers, eliminate interviewer bias, and are legally defensible. However, critics claim that tests obviously cannot assess the classroom performance of a teacher (Haefele, 1980; Harris, 1981). Further, past studies (Coleman *et al.*, 1966; Guthrie, 1970) indicate that higher knowledge levels are not clearly translated into more effective teaching.

Indirect Measures. J.A. King (1981) has examined the possible use of indirect measures of teacher competence. She reviews the research literature on teacher personality and characteristics and concludes that 'no single set of skills, attitudes, interests, and abilities' has been found to discriminate between effective and ineffective teachers (p. 174; see also Gage, 1963). Despite this finding, she argues that indirect measures, especially professional commitment as expressed in extra-classroom activities, ought to be a supplementary source of evaluation data. Schalock (1979) identifies two promising lines of research on teacher characteristics. One finds relationships between teacher flexibility or adaptability and teacher effectiveness. The other finds that some teacher characteristics are more effective in some teaching contexts than in others. These findings have not yet found their way into the practice of teacher evaluation.

Traditionally, indirect measures such as training and experience are those linked to teacher salary and promotion opportunities and, implicitly, to teacher evaluation.

Classroom Observation. This method, usually coupled with teacher interviews or conferences, is the mainstay of most teacher evaluations. It involves direct observation of the teacher performing in the classroom. To the extent that observation can capture what the teacher knows and does in interaction with a class of students, it can result in measures of performance. Classroom observation reveals 'a view of the climate, rapport, interaction, and functioning of the classroom available from no other source' (Evertson and Holley, 1981, p. 90). Classroom observation techniques vary significantly in structure and methodology. Although the school principal acts as the observer in most cases, trained evaluators, school system administrators, other teachers, or students may observe and rate teachers. Increasingly, observations by supervisors are preceded by a preobservation conference (Garawski, 1980; Redfern, 1980). Frequency of observation and the length of each observation period vary according to time constraints and school board policies regarding evaluation. Finally, the observer may use a number of standardized observation instruments to guide him or her in the assessment.

This evaluation method has the advantages of seeing teachers in action and within the context of their schools. However, even proponents of classroom observation recognize its limitations. Observer bias, insufficient sampling of performance, and poor measurement instruments can threaten the reliability and validity of results (Evertson and Holley, 1981; Haefele, 1980; Lewis, 1982; Peterson and Kauchak, 1982). Supervisory ratings have generally been found to lack interrater reliability and validity (Medley, 1982; Peterson and Kauchak, 1982). Performance ratings have also shown limited stability and generalizability, particularly when low-inference measures of discrete teaching behaviors are used (Shavelson and Dempsey-Atwood, 1976).

Student Ratings. The potential use of student ratings for teachers has attracted a great deal of attention in the literature. Student ratings are another form of 'classroom observation' — they measure observed performance from the student's rather than the administrator's point of view. Although usually applied at the college level, several authors (Aleamoni, 1981; Haefele, 1980; McNeil and Popham, 1973; Peterson and Kauchak, 1982) believe that student ratings could be applied in secondary and, in some cases, elementary schools. The use of student ratings in evaluation assumes that: (a) the student knows when he has been motivated; (b) it is the student whose behavior is to be changed; (c) student rating is feedback to the teacher; and (d) student recognition may motivate good teaching. This method is inexpensive with a high degree of reliability, usually ranging from .8 to .9 and above (Peterson and Kauchak, 1982), with some studies finding a modest degree of correlation between student ratings of teachers and student achievement. On the other hand, questions about the validity and utility of student ratings limit their acceptance as primary policy instruments for teacher evaluation (Aleamoni, 1981; Haefele, 1980).

Peer Review. In this process, a committee of peers evaluates teaching through an examination of such documents as lesson plans, examinations, examples of graded examinations, and classroom observations. This process covers a broader spectrum of performance, encompassing not only performance in the classroom, but also intentionality (what the teacher intends to have happen) and other teaching behavior as exhibited by assignment and grading practices. Although seldom used in formal teaching evaluations, the literature identifies many potential advantages to peer evaluation. The assumption underlying this approach is that peers are in the best position to assess competence, thus it suggests a professional conception of teaching work. Also, evaluators who are familiar with the classroom experience, subject matter, and demands on a teacher can render specific and practical suggestions for improvement.

Peer evaluation in practice has received mixed reviews. Although a three year experiment including peer review was enthusiastically supported by the teaching staff in one district (Lewis, 1982), another school district found that teachers lacked respect for evaluations by their peers and that the evaluations resulted in staff tension (Lewis, 1982). Because the method is more open to divergent criteria for assessing performance and is not subject to direct administrative control, it is not generally recommended for use as the basis of personnel decisions (Haefele, 1980; Peterson and Kauchak, 1982; Thomas, 1979).

Student Achievement. In education, the ultimate concern is the student's learning. For some this means that student achievement is the only true indicator of teacher effectiveness. In an educational management system like teacher evaluation, student achievement must be measured in a manner consonant with the outcomes held to be important. Student achievement can be measured in many ways: comparing student test scores to a national norm; comparing test score gains with those of a comparable class; net gains over time, and so forth (Haefele, 1980). Such scores, while representing legitimate and understandable indicators for many audiences, nonetheless require that numerous assumptions be made to link them to teacher competence or even teacher performance.

Studies of the reliability of student test scores as a measure of teaching effectiveness consistently indicate that reliability is quite low, that is, that the same teacher produces markedly different results in different situations, calling into question the use of such teacher effectiveness scores as an indicator of teacher competence (Brophy, 1973; Rosen-shine, 1970; Shavelson and Russo, 1977; Veldman and Brophy, 1974). Further, the use of tests to measure teaching performance may inhibit curriculum innovation since teachers will tend to teach to the test (Shine and Goldman, 1980), and may ignore or counteract the effects of teacher behaviors on other desirable outcomes (Centra and Potter, 1980; Peterson, 1979).

Some researchers recommend a variation of this method in which a teacher is assessed while teaching students a lesson in an unfamiliar subject. However, such teaching simulations are relatively time-consuming and very expensive evaluation methods. Moreover, samples of behavior in an artificial setting run the risk of simplifying the complexity of teaching work, thus rendering the method invalid (Medley, 1982).

Faculty Self-evaluations. Self-evaluation has recently joined other sources of assessment as a technique in teacher evaluation. The combination of self-evaluation and individual goal-setting may promote self-reflection and motivation toward change and growth. A teacher can use data derived form any technique — student or peer ratings, self-assessment measures of student achievement, and so forth, to make judgments about his or her own teaching. Externally developed 'objective' data may permit the teacher to assess his or her own strengths and weaknesses against both personal and organizational standards and reinforce a teacher's professionalism.

This process, less formal than the others, while obviously not suitable for accountability decisions, can be used for individual and collective staff development. In particular, both Redfern (1980) and Manatt (Lewis, 1982) consider self-evaluation an essential component of their cooperative evaluation models discussed below. Thus, self-evaluation should be regarded not as an evaluation process in itself, but as an important source of information and motivation in a broader evaluation program.

Conclusion. In the literature on evaluation processes and tools, some papers rely heavily on research for reaching their conclusions; others do not. It is safe to say that research has not identified a teacher evaluation method which is unvaryingly 'successful.' (A similar conclusion was reached by Ornstein and Levine, 1981.) This is not a surprising finding.

A judgment of success depends on the purposes for which a technique is used as well as its ability to measure what it purports to measure. Some of these approaches seek to measure competence while others, that rely on direct observation, seek to measure performance. Still others rely on student performance as a measure of teacher effectiveness, and by implication, teacher competence and performance. The generally low levels of reliability, generalizability, and validity attributed to teacher evaluation methods suggest that unidimensional approaches for assessing competence, performance, or effectiveness are unlikely to capture enough information about teaching attributes to completely satisfy any of the purposes for teacher evaluation.

Teacher evaluation methods are but one part of a broader process of goal-setting, standard-setting, assessment, and decision making that occurs within the organizational context. For any method, the criteria used for evaluation may vary, along with the instruments for assessing performance and the means for implementing the approach (for example, frequency of assessments, uses made of results). In the next section, we present some specific configurations of evaluation processes and methods that have been proposed as models for teacher evaluation.

Teacher Evaluation Models

Approaches to teacher evaluation and improvement vary depending on:

- What teacher attributes (for example, professional training, teaching competencies, etc.) are believed to be important for effective teaching;
- Which aspect of the instructional process the district hopes to affect (for example, assurance of teacher quality; improved teaching techniques; learning outcomes, etc.); and
- What will be the criteria for evaluating success (for example, demonstration by the teacher of desired behaviors or competencies, teacher or student test scores, etc.).

Because we cannot here provide a comprehensive list of teacher evaluation models, we will describe a few of the more widely reported models.

Two of the most widely discussed evaluation models[5] are Manatt's (Manatt, Palmer and Hidlebaugh, 1976) 'Mutual Benefit Evaluation' and Redfern's (1980) 'Management by Objectives Evaluation.' Both models have been implemented in a number of school districts,[6] and both models are characterized by (a) goal-setting; (b) teacher involvement in the evaluation process; and (c) centralized teaching standards and criteria. The major difference between them is the point at which a teacher is brought into the evaluation process.

Manatt describes his model as a system in which teachers, administrators, and the educational program itself may be objectively evaluated (Gudridge, 1980). Although Manatt insists that the model is designed primarily to improve teacher performance rather than to ferret out incompetent teachers, he nevertheless stresses points needed to withstand court scrutiny of resulting dismissals (for example, evaluation criteria must be 'legally' discriminating; must adhere to procedural due process).

There are four steps in the model:

1   The school board and administration (or whoever is responsible for evaluation development) must determine criteria for minimum

> acceptable teaching standards. For example, Manatt suggests that these might include productive teaching techniques, positive interpersonal relations, organized class management, intellectual stimulation, and out-of-class behavior (Gudridge, 1980, pp. 36–8).

2   A diagnostic evaluation is performed to assess each teacher's present status *vis-à-vis* the standards. Although Manatt does not prescribe specific measurement instruments, he suggests that evaluation processes should include a preobservation conference with the teacher, a teacher self-evaluation, classroom observations, and postobservation conferences.

3   With the cooperation of the teacher, the evaluator sets job targets (three to five are recommended) for the teacher's performance improvement. Manatt suggests that the targets be specific and objectively measurable.

4   After a specified time, the teacher is reevaluated and new job targets are set.

Redfern borrowed the 'management-by-objectives' model from business and applied it to teacher evaluation. Like the Manatt model, a teacher's responsibilities and learning goals are set by the responsible school authority. However, before any evaluation takes place, the evaluator and teacher *jointly* establish individual objectives, an action plan, and measurable progress indicators (Haefele, 1980; Lewis, 1982; Redfern, 1980). The teacher's action plan is monitored through diagnostic rather than summative observations. The observation results are assessed by the evaluators who then meet with the teacher to discuss progress and to set additional objectives. Redfern does not prescribe monitoring or measurement processes because each action plan would call for different methods and tools (Redfern, 1980). The collegial nature of the model makes teacher self-evaluation essential (Iwanicki, 1981).

These models are intended to promote the professional growth of the individual teacher and the integration of individual performance objectives with school board policies. They also establish, with the teacher's participation, a structured set of evaluation goals intended to reduce uncertainties and misunderstandings between the teacher and evaluator. On the other hand, critics charge that the goal-setting models place too much emphasis on measurable objectives. Further, they argue, to be properly implemented the models may require large investments in time and money (Iwanicki, 1981).

Both models straddle the competency-based and outcomes-based evaluation philosophies. The models are 'results-oriented' but allow for various definitions of 'results.' In some cases, it would appear that results may be measurable increases in learning; in others, a positive result may be the demonstration of a new teaching competency. However, the

Redfern model seems to allow more input from the teacher, thus fostering the image of professionalism, while Manatt's model seems to delegate professional decisions to supervisors.

The evaluation program in Salt Lake City, Utah, also widely discussed, is more explicitly responsive to accountability demands. The school superintendent and principal establish building unit performance standards. In turn, the principal and teacher establish performance goals that support school board goals. Personal goals may also be set. Teacher performance is assessed annually using student test scores, classroom observation, and other means (Thomas, 1979). The remediation system is pivotal. A teacher may be 'placed on remediation' as the result of an annual evaluation or by a formal complaint lodged by a student, peer, or parent. If the complaint seems justified, a four-member, shared governance committee works with the teacher and, after five months, the teacher is dismissed or retained, based on the committee's recommendation. The Salt Lake approach may have survived in part because the local teacher organization is involved in the process — recommending two governance committee members — and the district has no mandatory tenure law (Thomas, 1979).

The Georgia evaluation system is also receiving considerable attention, especially among southern states. In essence, the Georgia system requires each teacher to possess professional knowledge and training and to demonstrate mastery of fourteen teaching competencies. Each prospective teacher must pass a criterion-referenced test as a precondition to receiving a three year non-renewable certificate. To receive recertification, sometime within three years a teacher must prepare a portfolio of lesson plans, test papers, and other teaching documents for a team of trained evaluators. In addition, he or she must pass a classroom assessment based on the Teacher Performance Assessment Instrument (TPAI). The instrument is used by three independent observers to rate the teacher's classroom performance in terms of demonstration of the specific competencies. If a teacher fails the evaluation, she or he may take it again. Georgia officials believe that the TPAI will withstand court challenges, in part, because the University of Georgia researchers believe they have found a connection between the TPAI's 14 teaching competencies and student learning gains (Ellett *et al.*, 1980; Lewis, 1982).

The program used in Salem, Oregon, is also based on the belief that certain teacher behaviors influence student learning; therefore, mastery of these behaviors by all teachers will result in more effective teaching. The slate of desired behaviors and competencies is determined by the administration. In fact, the administration presents the competency program to the teachers in a taped presentation to ensure standard communication of evaluation expectations and uniformity among schools. For those who fail to demonstrate mastery of all the competencies, retraining is provided by district 'master teachers' who have received fifteen to twenty hours of training in evaluation. The program calls for frequent classroom observation: four times annually for new teachers; three times for experienced teachers (DuBois, 1980; Lewis, 1982). The model is intended to 'reduc[e] the stress [and] trauma . . . of change . . . [by] controlling goals to assure a high rate of success' (Lewis, 1982, p. 55).

Finally, we cite two models that adhere to the belief that a teacher's professional needs vary over the course of his or her career and that each teacher is a professional even an artistic, individual (Lewis, 1982). The evaluation program used in Bedford, Ohio, is intended to evolve throughout a teacher's career. This model assures that criteria for evaluating an experienced teacher will be different from those used to make the original employment decision or for evaluating new teachers. This evolving model is unstructured and highly dependent on teacher self-evaluation and joint efforts between teacher and evaluator. Similarly, the New Hampton, Iowa, evaluation program is based on a belief that 'no single model [of instruction] will result in effective learning . . .' and that 'an evaluation system must respect the uniqueness of each individual staff member' (Lewis, 1982, p. 22).

An approach that seems consonant with flexible, multigoal models such as these is the clinical supervision approach, a process often compared to the Manatt and Redfern models (Lewis, 1982, p. 31). While the components are structurally similar, the clinical supervision approach is more informal in setting performance goals and generally involves more one-to-one interaction between the teacher and the evaluator. Ideally, areas of improvement and concern are mutually identified, and professional goals evolve during a systematic plan of classroom observations. As Manatt notes, without specific school board guidelines or evaluation criteria, 'supervisor and teacher are both assumed to be instructional experts, with the teacher identifying his concerns and the supervisor assisting . . .' (Lewis, 1982, p. 42). Clinical supervision is highly interactive and may promote professionalism and a sense of efficacy among teachers. However, it is also a time-consuming process, and the data gathered during the observations may be uninterpretable to those outside the supervisor-teacher relationship. Thus, clinical supervision approaches may prove to be of limited use for accountability purposes.

Application of the Models

Most of the above models can be characterized as having a decisionistic orientation (Floden and Weiner, 1978). They reflect a view of evaluation as an activity which functions to inform decisions about the pursuit of stable, consensual programmatic, and instructional goals. Other models of evaluation, such as the last two briefly described above, start from the premise that instructional goals are neither stable nor entirely consensual.

Such models include multiple goals for and functions of evaluation including, for example, conflict resolution and complacency reduction (Floden and Weiner, 1978; Chen and Rossi, 1980), as well as empowerment of the individual teacher.

The application of research-based teacher evaluation models to real-life settings must overcome the gap that exists between technically defensible specifications of criteria or methods and politically viable solutions to organizational problems. There is a growing recognition that any kind of evaluation activity involves value choices — and conflicts — at all levels of the operating system (Rein, 1976; Rossi, Freeman and Wright, 1979; Sroufe, 1977). Evaluation is political because it serves as a tool in a larger policymaking process and because it is inherently directed at making a judgment of worth about something. Any such judgment ultimately rearranges or reaffirms an existing constellation of stakes that individuals or groups have in what is being evaluated (Englert, Kean and Scribner, 1977). Furthermore, the *process* of evaluation must be understood as encompassing a continual process of bargaining and goal modification that occurs 'because the conditions and effective constituency surrounding goal setting are different from the conditions and effective constituency surrounding implementation' (Stone, 1980, pp. 23–24).

Knapp (1982) describes the divergence existing between many teacher evaluation models and actual practices in terms of the differing standards applied by researchers and practitioners to ultimately political value choices.

> Value choices are nowhere more clearly at issue than in decisions about the aspects of the teacher and teaching to be evaluated. Scholars have tended to make these value choices on scientific grounds: in effect, they are arguing that evaluation systems should be focused on whatever can be operationally defined and demonstrated to contribute to student learning ... A number of proposals for improved teacher appraisal systems have been advanced, but a 'better' system tends to be defined in terms of accuracy and links to an established base of teacher effects research. Such systems rest on an idealized image of school management, that ignores the powerful effects of organizational and contextual forces on management activity. (pp. 4–5)

In actual practice, he finds that schools follow 'the lines of least resistance,' evaluating aspects of teachers and teaching in more vague terms so as to simultaneously satisfy diverse constituencies. A defensible teacher evaluation process is one that allows them to balance several goals at once:

- Sorting teachers;

- Maintaining staff morale and collegiality;
- Maintaining organizational distance from environmental demands (for example, for accountability); and
- Devising improvements that require modest, incremental change.

This does not mean that research-based teacher evaluation models cannot succeed in the real world, only that adaptations to the organizational context must be explicitly considered and sought if the processes are to be implemented successfully.

Implementing Teacher Evaluation in the Organizational Context

The major findings of Rand's Change Agent Study (Berman and McLaughlin, 1978), which examined the local outcomes of federal program initiatives for innovation, are relevant to our discussion of teacher evaluation in the local context. The study found that

- Implementation dominated the outcome of planned change efforts.
- The process of implementation is shaped by local factors — rather than by adopting a particular technology, the availability of information, funding level, or particular type of program.
- Effective implementation is characterized by a process of mutual adaptation, in which both the project and participants change over time.

While the Change Agent Study concerned the implementation of selected federal programs, its findings are relevant since we are concerned with the implementation of teacher evaluation processes in specific schools and school systems. Numerous other studies have also established the importance of the local organizational context and its implementation processes in determining the outcomes of planned change efforts (see, for example, Lipsky, 1976; Milstein, 1980; Selznick, 1966; Stone, 1980). These studies have pointed to the importance of recognizing local participants in change efforts as purposive agents and to the need for adaptations of change strategies by those who actually implement them.

Research on individual and organizational change indicates that the degree of control and autonomy characterizing participants' roles in the implementation process is critical to success of a planned change effort. Although the literatures are distinct, their respective findings argue powerfully for an approach emphasizing 'transformation' rather than 'conversion' to new methods, techniques, or principles of behavior (Fenstermacher, 1978).

The transformation approach starts from the assumption that participants in any change process hold subjectively reasonable beliefs that direct their actions. The actions informed by these beliefs are unlikely to change substantially if change strategies are converted to rules for behavior without attention to transforming the belief structure underlying the existing behavior patterns. The objectively reasonable beliefs encompassed by a change proposal are offered as evidence for consideration by participants rather than as rules for them to follow (Fenstermacher, 1978). This evidence *empowers* people to change their own behaviors rather than forcing them to adhere superficially to rules that have no intrinsic meaning for them. A transformation approach allows for policy adaptation and for situation-specific responses where internal and external perspectives converge.

Changing Teacher Behavior

One of the primary goals of teacher evaluation is the improvement of individual and collective teaching performance in schools. Effectively changing the behavior of another person requires enlisting the cooperation and motivation of that person, in addition to providing guidance on the steps needed for improvement to occur. At the individual level, change relies on the development of two important conditions within the individual: knowledge that a course of action is the correct one and a sense of empowerment or efficacy, that is, a perception that pursuing a given course of action is both worthwhile and possible.

Most teacher evaluation processes attend to questions of how to identify effective teaching without addressing questions of how to bring about changes in teaching behavior, assuming that having discovered what ought to be done, implementation of recommended actions will naturally follow. Gage's (1978) translation of research findings into a series of 'teachers should' statements is representative of the externally oriented approach to effecting change. However, Fenstermacher (1978) argues that 'if our purpose and intent are to change the practices of those who teach, it is necessary to come to grips with the subjectively reasonable beliefs of teachers' (p. 174). This process entails the creation of internally verifiable knowledge rather than the imposition of rules for behavior. It incorporates an intentionalist thesis for observing and influencing teaching behaviors, one that gives full weight to teachers' beliefs and intentions in assessing what they do and in guiding them in the formation of alternative beliefs about useful courses of action.

The intentionalist view assumes (a) that teachers are rational professionals who make judgments and carry out decisions in an uncertain, complex environment; and (b) that teachers' behaviors are guided by their thoughts, judgments, and decisions (Shavelson and Stern, 1981). Thus behavior change requires transformation of belief structures and knowledge in a manner that allows for situation-specific applications.

Effective change requires knowledge control on the part of the teacher. Not only is information-processing reliant on the teachers' beliefs, but the ways in which new knowledge or transformed beliefs are applied must be under the teacher's control. Good and Power (1976) apply this notion to the effective use of teaching theory for changing teaching practice:

> [A]t best, generalizations about teaching derived from research act as guides to assessing the likely consequences of alternative strategies in complex educational situations. Such generalizations must necessarily be indeterminate since they cannot predict precisely what will happen in a particular case. But this does not decrease their value for the teacher ... Theories can be of value in specifying those dimensions which are relevant to the understanding of classroom phenomena, can extend the range of hypotheses (alternative strategies) considered, and *sensitize* the teacher to the possible consequences of his actions. Indeed, ultimately, the validity and usefulness of theory may rest in the hands of teachers ... that is, whether it sensitizes them to the classroom context, helps them make more informed decisions, and to monitor their own behavior. (p. 58)

This concept entails the development of an internally verifiable knowledge base that empowers the teacher to apply internal against external referents of validity and to engage in appropriate self-assessment and self-improvement activities.

An understanding of how empowerment enables change is further informed by a substantial body of psychological research on self-efficacy. Perceptions of self-efficacy are an important element of the link between knowledge and behaviors. As Bandura (1982) notes:

> Knowledge, transformational operations, and component skills are necessary but insufficient for accomplished performances. Indeed, people often do not behave optimally, even though they know full well what to do. This is because self-referent thought also mediates the relationship between knowledge and action ... Self-appraisals of operative capabilities function as one set of proximal determinants of how people behave, their thought patterns, and the emotional reactions they experience ... Social environments may place constraints on what people do or may aid them to behave optimally. Whether their endeavors are socially impeded or supported will depend, in part, on how efficacious they are perceived to be. (p. 122–3 and 131)

In this conception, self-perceptions of efficacy both affect performance and are affected by others' perceptions of a person's efficaciousness. Research on this topic indicates that perceived self-efficacy better predicts subsequent behavior than does actual performance attainment, and that it influences coping behaviors, self-regulation of refractory behaviors, perseverance, responses to failure experiences, growth of intrinsic interest and motivation, achievement strivings, and career pursuits (Bandura, 1982; Bandura and Schunk, 1981; Bandura, Adams, Hardy and Howells, 1980; Betz and Hackett, 1981; Brown and Inouye, 1978; Kazdin, 1979; Collins, 1982; DiClemente, 1981).

The relevance of teachers' self-perceptions of efficacy to their performance has been demonstrated in several studies. Berman and McLaughlin's study on implementation of innovative projects found that the teacher's sense of efficacy had stronger positive effects on the percent of project goals achieved, the amount of teacher change, and improved student performance than did teacher experience or verbal ability (Berman and McLaughlin, 1977, pp. 136–9). Armor (1976) found that teachers' self-perceptions of efficacy were strongly and positively related to students' reading achievement, unlike teacher education, experience, or other background characteristics. Other studies have reported similar positive relationships between teachers' sense of self-efficacy and student achievement (Brookover, 1977; Rutter *et al.*, 1979).

More important, substantial research also suggests that an individual's sense of efficacy can be influenced by interactions with others as well as by organizational factors. Individual perceptions of self-efficacy and motivation are influenced by the value of rewards and the expectancy of achieving objectives (Vroom, 1964). Self-efficacy is not an entirely internal construct; it requires a responsive environment that allows for and rewards performance attainment (Bandura, 1982, p. 140). However, the goals must be personally valued and must present a challenge to the individual, or the task performance will be devalued (Lewin, 1938; Lewin, Dembo, Festinger and Sears, 1944). Furthermore, role designations can enhance or underline self-efficacy.

> Situational factors that often accompany poor performance can in themselves instill a sense of incompetence that is unwarranted ...
> [W]hen people are cast in subordinate roles or are assigned inferior labels, implying limited competence, they perform activities at which they are skilled less well than when they do not bear the negative labels or the subordinate role designations. (Bandura, 1982 p. 142)

A review by Fuller, Wood, Rapoport and Dornbusch (1982) of the research on individual efficacy in the context of organizations suggests that increased performance and organizational efficacy for teachers will result from:

• Convergence between teachers and administrators in accepting the goals and means for task performance (Ouchi, 1980);

- Higher levels of personalized interaction and resource exchange between teachers and administrators (Talbert, 1980);
- Lower prescriptiveness of work tasks (Anderson, 1973);
- Teachers' perceptions that evaluation is soundly based and that evaluation is linked to rewards or sanctions; and
- Teacher input into evaluation criteria, along with diversity of evaluation criteria (Pfeffer, Salancik and Leblebici, 1976; Rosenholtz and Wilson, 1980).

These findings converge markedly with those of Natriello and Dornbusch (1980–81) on determinants of teachers' satisfaction with teacher evaluation systems. They found that teacher satisfaction is strongly related to (a) perceptions that all evaluators share the same criteria for evaluation; (b) more frequent samplings of teacher performance; (c) more frequent communication and feedback; and (d) teachers' ability to affect the criteria for evaluation. Furthermore, frequency of negative feedback did not cause dissatisfaction, but infrequency of evaluation did. Teacher satisfaction with evaluation, then, seems to be based on perceptions that evaluation is soundly based, that is, that the teacher has some control over both task performance and its assessment. These perceptions influence the teacher's sense of performance efficacy (Fuller *et al.*, 1982, p. 24).

Finally, opportunities for self-assessment and for reference to personal standards of performance strongly influence self-efficacy and motivation. As Bandura (1982) observes:

> In social learning theory an important cognitively based source of motivation operates through the intervening processes of goal setting and self-evaluative reactions. This form of self-motivation, which involves internal comparison processes, requires personal standards against which to evaluate performance.

The importance of self-assessment has begun to achieve recognition in the teacher evaluation literature (Bodine, 1973; Bushman, 1974; Riley and Schaffer, 1979), as has the importance of allowing teacher input into the determination of evaluation criteria and standards (Knapp, 1982).

Individual change relies on knowledge, self-referent thought, and motivation. These are, in turn, profoundly influenced by the signals and opportunities provided within the organizational environment. The transformatory character of individual change is equally applicable at the organizational level. Thus the success of change efforts is influenced by implementation processes that define opportunities for developing shared knowledge, diagnosing and designing strategies, and promoting collective efficacy.

Teacher Evaluation in the Organizational Context

The recent evolution of policy analysis and program evaluation has led to a recognition of the importance of including organizational considerations as an integral part of research that attempts to understand policy effects (Sabatier and Mazmanian, 1979; Sproull, 1979; Wildavsky, 1980). Formal policies and procedures, it has been found, may constrain, but do not construct, the final outcomes of any institutional endeavor. The local implementation process and organizational characteristics — such as institutional climate, organizational structures and incentives, local political processes, expertise, and leadership style — are critical elements in determining the ultimate success of a policy at achieving its intended effects (Berman and McLaughlin, 1978; Mann, 1978; Weatherley and Lipsky, 1977). Effective change requires a process of mutual adaptation in which change agents at all levels can shape policies to meet their needs — one in which both the participants and the policy are transformed by the convergence of internal and external reference points.

Implementation of any school policy, including a teacher evaluation policy, represents a continuous interplay among diverse policy goals, established rules and procedures (concerning both the policy in question and other aspects of the school's operations), intergroup bargaining and value choices, and the local institutional context. Teacher evaluation procedures, for example, will be influenced by the political climate that exists within a school system, by the relationship of the teachers' organization to district management, by the nature of other educational policies and operating programs in the district, and by the very size and structure of the system and its bureaucracy. These variables and others are equally potent at the school level.

Many organizational theorists have advanced the notion that school systems are loosely coupled. That is, they do not conform to the rational-bureaucratic model, which assumes consensus on organizational goals and technologies, tight links between vertical and horizontal functions and actors, frequent inspection of work tasks, and consistent and unambiguous lines of communication and authority (Deal, Meyer and Scott, 1974; March, 1976; Weick, 1976). Weick (1982) goes so far as to suggest that 'the task of educating is simply not the kind of task that can be performed in a tightly coupled system' (p. 674). He argues that it is wrong to treat evidence of loose coupling as the result of improper management or indecisiveness. Because of the nature of teaching work, the diversity of school constituencies, and the changing nature of demands on the educational system, tightly coupled, standardized responses to identified problems may reduce the organization's capability to respond to future needs or problems, and may set in motion actions that conflict with other educational and organizational goals.

This perception is supported by research on the effects of implementing performance-based teacher evaluation processes in local school systems. The results of four case studies of the implementation of performance-based staff layoff policies led Johnson (1980) to conclude that the existence of such policies does not guarantee automatic implementation. Furthermore, unintended consequences at the school site call into question the educational worth of top-down implementation processes, which 'compromise the autonomy of the local school; alter the role of the principal as protector, provider, and instructional leader; jeopardize the cooperative and collegial relations among staff; and diminish the effectiveness of teacher supervision' (p. 216). The inability of principals to adapt teacher evaluation practices to changing supervisory needs, combined with a decrease in the principal's overall autonomy in shaping school programs, seemed to diminish the principals' capacities to serve as advocates and leaders for their staff, programs, and schools. Ironically, the growing body of 'school effects' research suggests that strong leadership from principals is a key component in shaping successful schools (see for example Brookover, 1977). It appears possible that some kinds of tightly coupled teacher evaluation processes may jeopardize the effective functioning of the school organization to the extent that standardization from above inhibits the capacity of the principal for exerting school-level decision-making authority.

Meyer and Rowan (1978) reinforce this view of school operations by suggesting that school organizations must maintain a 'logic of confidence' to survive in a constantly changing, plural environment. They assert that the relative lack of direct inspection of teaching work is a sensible way of buffering the organization from conflicting external demands and from the uncertainties of teacher and pupil performance in educational settings. Standardized evaluation of teachers aimed at accountability purposes may undercut the logic of confidence that binds the school together and permits it to function. Among the propositions they advance to help understand educational organizations are the following:

- The more bureaucratically organized the educational system, the less actual control is exercised over instruction and the more the logic of confidence prevails. In such systems, more control is exercised over formal educational categories and definitions (for example, program definition, staff certification, pupil classification, etc.) than instructional processes.
- Loosely coupled educational organizations respond more effectively to environmental pressures. Instruction adapts more quickly to the informal pressures of parents and the desires of teachers. Programs adapt more quickly to institutional changes in environmental categories.
- Educational organizations respond to external institutional pressures with programmatic or categorical change ... They respond to local changes in teacher or parent preference with activity change ... Each part or level of the system responds relatively independently to its environment. Thus, the greatest part of organizationally planned change in instruction is never really implemented, and the greatest part of change in instruction is not organizationally planned.

If these observations are true, as the body of implementation research suggests they may be, we must ask what change strategies can be effective in such a seemingly confused and confusing milieu. Fortunately, organizational theorists do not stop short of suggesting some approaches that are plausible in loosely coupled, nonconsensual organizations like schools.

The first general area for attention concerns the nature and frequency of communications. Weick (1982) contends that one of the most important jobs of administrators in a loosely coupled system is 'symbol management'; that is, the articulation of general themes and directions 'with eloquence, persistence, and detail' (p. 675). He distinguishes symbols from goals: Symbols tell people what they are doing and why; goals tell people when and how well they are doing it. Because problems, hence goals, change constantly, symbols are the glue that holds the organization together.

> The administrator who manages symbols does not sit in his or her office mouthing clever slogans. Eloquence must be disseminated. And since channels are unpredictable, administrators must get out of the office and spend lots of time one on one — both to remind people of central visions and to assist them in applying these visions to their own activities. The administrator teaches people to interpret what they are doing in a common language. (Weick, 1982 p. 676)

Sproull's (1979) implementation research also directs our attention to the importance of communications and symbol management. The implementation processes that greatly affect policy outcomes include: (a) the processes by which the policy is made visible enough to capture the attention of the organization's members; (b) the processes by which it is made meaningful to the members, that is, how it is understood and interpreted at various levels of the operating system; (c) the processes by which response repertoires (standard operating procedures and practices) are invoked; and (d) the processes by which behavioral directives or guides for action are conveyed from the central office to school sites. Successful implementation processes rely on the existence of cognitive 'consistency-producing mechanisms' that relate the policy to interpretations of the organization's history and current work. Providing that mechanism is the province of the symbol manager.

The importance for teacher evaluation of frequent communication and shared understanding between administrators and teachers is supported in several empirical studies reported by Natriello and Dornbusch (1980–1981). Their findings, like those of other implementation researchers (for example, Cohen, 1976; Deal *et al.* 1974), reflect differences in perception between superordinates and subordinates regarding the frequency and substance of communications. Teachers report that they do not know what the criteria are for teacher evaluation, that they are rarely observed, and that evaluation feedback is scarce, while their principals report just the opposite.[7] More important, frequency of observation and feedback — even negative feedback — is strongly correlated with teacher satisfaction with the evaluation system. Furthermore, teachers are more satisfied with evaluation systems in which they can affect the criteria on which they are judged.

This brings us to the second area of concern: the development of a sense of efficacy among those at whom improvement efforts are directed. Earlier, we reviewed the psychological literature suggesting the importance of self-efficacy for change and the school effects literature suggesting that improved performance actually results from this quality. Theories on the exercise of authority in organizations also suggest that recognition of task complexity and preservation of some autonomy for personnel encourage a sense of self-efficacy (Dornbusch and Scott, 1975; Thompson, Dornbusch and Scott, 1975). In addition, motivation by intrinsic incentives through evaluations that allow self-assessment is more powerful than motivation that relies on external assessment and reward (Deci, 1976; Meyer, 1975).

Finally, the nature of decisionmaking and policy formulation processes, which are closely tied to communications and empowerment, is critical to successful implementation of a teacher evaluation system. These processes involve coalitions of stakeholders interacting to define problems and solutions under conditions of ambiguity (Cohen and March, 1974). Resolving ambiguity by attempts at tight coupling may not necessarily be as productive as indirect change efforts that preserve the ability of smaller units to adapt to local conditions (Deal and Celotti, 1980; March, 1976). As Knapp (1982) comments:

> The process of developing evaluation systems is an occasion for many things in an organization such as the interaction of constituencies, celebration of important values, and the joint recognition of problems. Whether or not performance objectives are met by a specified proportion of a school district's teachers, the *indirect* results of such efforts may have considerable impact on staff enthusiasm, beliefs, or behavior, with ultimate benefits for students. (p. 18)

These propositions lead us to hypothesize four minimal conditions for the successful operation of a teacher evaluation system:

- All actors in the system have a shared understanding of the criteria and processes for teacher evaluation;
- All actors understand how these criteria and processes relate to the dominant symbols of the organization, that is, there is a shared sense that they capture the most important aspects of teaching, that the evaluation system is consonant with educational goals and conceptions of teaching work;

- Teachers perceive that the evaluation procedure enables and motivates them to improve their performance; and principals perceive that the procedure enables them to provide instructional leadership;
- All actors in the system perceive that the evaluation procedure allows them to strike a balance 'between adaptation and adaptability, between stability to handle present demands and flexibility to handle unanticipated demands' (Weick, 1982, p. 674); that is, that the procedure achieves a balance between control and autonomy for the various actors in the system.

Conclusion

Teacher evaluation is an activity that must satisfy competing individual and organizational needs. The imperative of uniform treatment for personnel decisions may result in standardized definitions of acceptable teaching behavior. However, research on teacher performance and teaching effectiveness does not lead to a stable list of measurable teaching behaviors effective in all teaching contexts. Moreover, research on individual and organizational behavior indicates the need for context-specific strategies for improving teaching rather than systemwide hierarchical efforts. If teacher evaluation is to be a useful tool for teacher improvement, the process must strike a careful balance between standardized, centrally administered performance expectations and teacher-specific approaches to evaluation and professional development.

Acknowledgements

This review was prepared as part of a study of teacher evaluation practices sponsored by the National Institute of Education (Contract No. 400–82–0007). The empirical phase and the project will be completed in late 1983.

The authors wish to acknowledge the intellectual fuel and insightful criticism supplied by Milbrey McLaughlin and Rich Shavelson of the Rand Corporation at early stages of the chapter's development. The project is advised by a Stakeholder's Panel whose members contributed useful comments on the first draft. However, the chapter does not necessarily reflect the views of the panel, the National Institute of Education, or the Rand Corporation.

Notes

1 Direct instruction as we discuss it here is by no means the only way to increase academic learning time. Other school policies (for example, longer school days,

fewer interruptions, different curriculum and program requirements) and teaching practices are equally plausible means for pursuing this objective. However, the literature generally treats these two as companion concepts, and so we treat them here, though we observe that their marriage in the literature may be the result of the researchers' focus on teacher behavior, rather than on the total context of the classroom.

2 The congruence between what is taught and what is tested may, of course, contribute to the apparent success of direct instruction.

3 However, high-inference, global ratings that rely on patterns of overall teacher behavior are somewhat more stable than other measures (Shavelson and Dempsey-Atwood, 1976).

4 This test should not be confused with Georgia's Teacher Performance Assessment Instrument, which assesses actual teaching performance of a teacher and is necessary for recertification.

5 We use the word 'model' here because it is widely used in the field; we do not use it either in a judgmental sense or in the social science sense of a theoretically based exposition of interrelated assumptions.

6 Gudridge reported that the Manatt model has been used in five districts in Iowa and Illinois (Gudridge, 1980, p. 42). Between 1975 and 1980, Redfern assisted sixteen school districts across the country to develop an 'MBO' program (Redfern, 1980, pp. 159–61).

7 A principal may engage in evaluation behavior a great deal of the time; that behavior will be visible to a given teacher only a fraction of the time.

References

ALEAMONI, L.M. (1981) 'Student ratings of instruction' in MILLMAN, J. (Ed.) *Handbook of Teacher Evaluation*, Beverly Hills, Calif., Sage.

ANDERSON, B.D. (1973) 'School bureaucratization and alienation from high school', *Sociology of Education*, 46, 2, pp. 315–34.

ANDERSON, C.S. (1982) 'The search for school climate: A review of the research', *Review of Educational Research*, 52, 3, pp. 368–420.

ARMOR, D., CONRY-OSEGUERA, P., COX, M., KING, N., McDONNELL, L., PASCAL, A., PAULY, E. and ZELLMAN, G., (1976) *Analysis of the School Preferred Reading Program in Selected Los Angeles Minority Schools*, R-2007-LAUSD, Santa Monica, Calif., The Rand Corporation.

BACHARACH, S. and AIKEN, M. (1979) 'The impact of alienation, meaninglessness, and meritocracy on supervisor and subordinate satisfaction, *Social Forces*, 57, pp. 853–71.

BANDURA, A. (1982) 'Self-efficacy mechanism in human agency', *American Psychologist*, 37, 2, pp. 122–47.

BANDURA, A. and SCHUNK, D.H. (1981) 'Cultivating competence, self-efficacy, and intrinsic interest through proximal self-motivation', *Journal of Personality and Social Psychology*, 41, pp. 586–98.

BANDURA, A., ADAMS, N.E., HARDY, A.B. and HOWELLS, G.N. (1980) 'Tests of the generality of self-efficacy theory', *Cognitive Therapy and Research*, 4, pp. 39–66.

BEKHAM, J.C. (1981) *Legal Aspects of Teacher Evaluation*, Topeka, Kans, National Organization on Legal Problems of Education.

BELL, A.E., SIPURSKY, M.A. and SWITZER, F. (1976) 'Informal or open-area education in relation to achievement and personality', *British Journal of Educational Psychology*, 46, pp. 235–43.

BERLINER, D.C. (1982) 'The Executive Functions of Teaching', paper presented at the Annual Meeting of the American Educational Research Association, New York, March.

BERLINER, D.C. (1977) *Instructional Time in Research on Research on Teaching*, San Francisco, Far West Laboratory for Educational Research and Development.

BERMAN, P. and McLAUGHLIN, M.W. (1973–78) *Federal Programs Supporting Educational Change*, R-1589-HEW, Santa Monica, Calif., The Rand Corporation.

BERMAN, P. and McLAUGHLIN, M.W. (1977) *Federal Programs Supporting Educational Change, Vol. 7: Factors affecting implementation and continuation*, Santa Monica, Calif., The Rand Corporation.

BETZ, N.E. and HACKETT, G. (1981) 'The relationships of career-related self-efficacy expectations to perceived career options in college women and men, *Journal of Counseling Psychology*, 28, pp. 399–410.

BIDWELL, C.E. (1965) 'The school as a formal organization' in March, J.G. (Ed.) *Handbook of Organizations*, Chicago, Rand McNally.

BODINE, R. (1973) 'Teachers' self-assessment' in HOUSE, E.R. (Ed.) *School Evaluation*, Berkeley, Calif., McCutchan.

BROOKOVER, W. (1977) *Schools Can Make a Difference*, East Lansing, College of Urban Development, Michigan State University.

BROPHY, J.E. (1973) 'Stability of teacher effectiveness', *American Educational Research Journal*, 10, pp. 245–52.

BROPHY, J.E. and EVERTSON, C.M. (1976) *Learning from Teaching: A Developmental Perspective*, Boston, Allyn and Bacon.

BROPHY, J.E. and EVERTSON, C. (1974) *Process-product Correlations in the Texas Teacher Effectiveness Study: Final Report*, Austin, Texas, Research and Development Center for Teacher Education.

BROPHY, J.E. and EVERTSON, C.M. (1977) 'Teacher behavior and student learning in second and third grades', in BORICH, G.D. (Ed.) *The Appraisal of Teaching: Concepts and Process*, Reading, Mass, Addison-Wesley.

BROUDY, H.S. (1956) 'Teaching — craft or profession?', *The Educational Forum*, January pp. 175–84.

BROWN, I.JR. and INOUYE, D.K. (1978) 'Learned helplessness through modeling: The role of perceived similarity in competence', *Journal of Personality and Social Psychology*, 36, pp. 900–8.

BRUNER, J.S. (1976) 'Foreword' in BENNETT, N., JORDAN, J., LONG, G. and WADE, B. (Eds) *Teaching Styles and Pupil Progress*, Cambridge, Mass, Harvard University Press.

BUSH, R.N. (1979) 'Implications of the BTES', *The Generator*, 9, 1, pp. 13–15.

BUSHMAN, J.H. (1974) 'Are teachers playing "statue' in the classroom?" *NASSP Bulletin*, 58, p. 386.

CENTRA, J.A. and POTTER, D.A. (1980) 'School and teacher effects: An interrelational model', *Review of Educational Research*, 50, 2, pp. 273–91.

CHEN, H. and ROSSI, P.H. (1980) 'The multi-goal, theory-driven approach to evaluation: A model linking basic and applied social sciences', *Social Forces*, 59, 1, pp. 106–22.

COHEN, E. (1976) *Organization and Instruction in Elementary Schools*, Stanford, Calif., Stanford Center for Research and Development in Teaching.

COHEN, M. and MARCH, J. (1974) *Leadership and Ambiguity: The American College President*, New York, McGraw Hill.

COKER, H., MEDLEY, D. and SOAR, R. (1980) 'How valid are expert opinions about effective teaching?', *Phi Delta Kappan*, 62, 2, pp. 131–4 and 149.

COLEMAN, J., CAMPBELL, E.A., HOBSON, C.J., McPARTLAND, J., MOOD, A., WEINFELD, F.D. and YORK, R.L. (1966) *Equality of Education Opportunity*, Washington, DC, US Government Printing Office.

COLLINS, J. (1982) *Self-efficacy and Ability in Achievement Behavior*, unpublished doctoral dissertation, Stanford University.

CORWIN, R.G. (1974) 'Models of educational organizations' in KERLINGER, F.N. *Review of Research in Education Vol. 2*, Itasca, Ill., F.E. PEACOCK.

CRONBACH, L.J. 'Beyond the two disciplines of scientific psychology', *American Psychologist*, 30, pp. 116–27.

CRONBACH, L.J. and SNOW, R.E. (1977) *Aptitudes and Instructional Methods: A Handbook for Research on Interactions*, New York, Irvington.

DARLING-HAMMOND, L. and WISE, A.E. (1981) *A Conceptual Framework for Examining Teachers' Views of Teaching and Educational Policies*, N-1668-FF, Santa Monica, Calif., The Rand Corporation.

DEAL, T.E. and CELOTTI, L.D. (1980) 'How much influence do (and can) educational administration have on classrooms?', *Phi Delta Kappan*, 61, 7, pp. 471–3.

DEAL, T., MEYER, J. and SCOTT, R. (1974) 'Organizational support for innovative instructional programs: district and school levels', paper presented at the Annual Meeting of the American Educational Research Association, Chicago, April.

DECI, E.L. (1976) 'The hidden costs of rewards' , *Organizational Dynamics*, 4, 3, pp. 61–72.

DICLEMENTE, C.C. (1981) 'Self-efficacy and smoking cessation maintenance: A preliminary report', *Cognitive Therapy and Research*, 5, pp. 175–87.

DORNBUSCH, S.M. and SCOTT, W.R. (1975) *Evaluation and the Exercise of Authority*, San Francisco, Jossey-Bass.

DOYLE, W. (1978) 'Paradigms for research on teacher effectiveness' in SHULMAN, L.S. (Ed.) *Review of Research in Education*, Vol. 5, Itasca, Ill., F.E. PEACOCK.

DOYLE, W. (1979) 'Classroom tasks and students' abilities' in PETERSON, P.L. and WALBERG, H.J. (Eds) *Research on Teaching*, Berkeley, Calif., McCutchan.

DUBOIS, D.W. (1980) 'Teacher evaluation: the Salem public schools model', *OSSC Bulletin*, 24, 3.

DUNKIN, M.J. and BIDDLE, B.J. (1974) *The Study of Teaching*, New York, Holt, Rinehart and Winston.

EISNER, E.W. (1978) 'On the uses of educational connoisseurship and criticism for evaluating classroom life', *Teachers College Record*, 78, pp. 345–58.

EISNER, E.W. and VALLANCE, E. (1974) 'Five conceptions of curriculum: Their roots and implications for curriculum planning' in EISNER, E.W. and VALLANCE, E. (Eds) *Conflicting Conceptions of Curriculum*, Berkeley, Calif., McCutchan.

ELLETT, C.D., CAPIE, W. and JOHNSON, C.E. (1980) 'Assessing teaching performance', *Educational Leadership*, 38, 3, pp. 219–20.

ELMORE, R.T. (1979) *Complexity and Control: What Legislators and Administrators Can Do About Implementation*, Seattle, Wash, Institute of Governmental Research.

ENGLERT, R.M. KEAN, M.H. and SCRIBNER, J.D. (1977) 'Politics of program evaluation in large city school districts', *Education and Urban Society*, 9, pp. 425–50.

EVERTSON, C.M. and BROPHY, J.E. (1973) *High Inference Behavioral Ratings and Correlates of Teaching Effectiveness*, Austin, Tex, Research and Development Center for Teacher Education, University of Texas.

EVERTSON, C.M. and HOLLEY, F.M. (1981) 'Classroom observation' in MILLMAN, J. (Ed.) *Handbook of Teacher Evaluation*, Beverly Hills, Calif., Sage.

FELDVEBEL, A.M. (1980) 'Teacher evaluation: Ingredients of a credible model', *Clearing House*, 53, 9, pp. 415–20.

FENSTERMACHER, G.D. and BERLINER, D.C. (in press) *On Determining the Value of Staff Development*, Santa Monica, Calif., The Rand Corporation.

FENSTERMACHER, G.D. (1978) 'A philosophical consideration of recent research on teacher effectiveness' in SHULMAN, L.S. (Ed.) *Review of Research in Education*, Vol. 6, Itasca, Ill., F.E. Peacock.

FISHER, C.W., FILBY, N. MARLIAVE, R., CAHEN, L., DISHAW, M., MOORE, J. and BERLINER, D. (1978) *Teaching Behaviors, Academic Learning Time and Student Achievement: Final Report of Phase III-B, Beginning Teacher Evaluation Study*, San Francisco, Far West Laboratory for Educational Research and Development.

FLANDERS, N.A. (1970) *Analyzing Teacher Behavior*, Reading, Mass, Addison-Wesley.

FLODEN, R.E. and FEIMAN, S. (1981) *A Consumer's Guide to Teacher Development*, East Lansing, Mich., Institute for Research on Teaching, Michigan State University.

FLODEN, R.E. and WINER, S.S. (1978) 'Rationality to ritual: The multiple roles of evaluation in governmental process', *Policy Sciences*, 9, pp. 9–18.

FRENCH, J.JR. and RAVEN, B. (1977) 'The bases of social power' in STRAW, B. (Ed.) *Psychological Foundations of Organizational Behavior*, Santa Monica, Calif., Goodyear.

FULLER, B., WOOD, K., RAPOPORT, T. and DORNBUSCH, S.M. (1982) 'The organizational context of individual efficacy', *Review of Educational Research*, 52, 1, pp. 7–30.

GAGE, N.L. (1963) 'Paradigms for research on teaching' in GAGE, N.L. (Ed.) *Handbook for Research on Teaching*, Chicago, Rand McNally.

GAGE, N.L. (1978) *The Scientific Basis of the Art of Teaching*, New York, Teachers College Press.

GALLUP, G.H. (1979) 'The eleventh annual Gallup poll of the public's attitudes toward the public schools', *Phi Delta Kappan*, 60, pp. 33–45.

GARAWSKI, R.A. (1980) 'The eleventh annual Gallup poll of the public's attitudes toward the public schools', *Phi Delta Kappan*, 60, pp. 33–45.

GLASS, G.V., COULTER, D., HARTLEY, S., HEAROLD, S., KAHL, S., KALK, J. and SHERRETZ, L. (1977) *Teacher 'Indirectness' and Pupil Achievement: An Integration of Findings*, Boulder, Col, Laboratory of Educational Research, University of Colorado.

GOOD, T.L. and POWER, C.N. (1976) 'Designing successful classroom environments for different types of students', *Journal of Curriculum Studies*, 8, 1, pp. 45–60.

GUDRIDGE, B.M. (1980) *Teacher Competency: Problems and Solutions*, Arlington, Va, American Association of School Administrators.

GUTHRIE, J. (1970) 'Survey of school effectiveness studies', in MOOD, A. (Ed.) *Do Teachers Make a Difference?*, Washington DC, US Government Printing Office.

HAEFELE, D.L. (1980) 'How to evaluate thee, teacher — let me count the ways', *Phi Delta Kappan*, 61, 5, pp. 349–52.

HAEFELE, D.L. (1981) 'Teacher Interviews' in MILLMAN, J. (Ed.) *Handbook of Teacher Evaluations*, Beverly Hills, Calif., Sage.

HARRIS, W.U. (1981) 'Teacher command of subject matter' in MILLMAN, J. (Ed.) *Handbook of Teacher Evaluations*, Beverly Hills, Calif., Sage.

HATHAWAY, W.E. (1980) 'Testing teachers', *Educational Leadership*, 38, 3, pp. 210–15.

HORWITZ, R.A. (1979) 'Effects of the "open classroom"' in WALBERG, H.J. (Ed.) *Educational Environments and Effects: Evaluation, Policy and Productivity*, Berkeley, Calif., McCutchan.

IWANICKI, E.F. (1981) 'Contract plans: A professional growth-oriented approach to evaluating teacher performance' in MILLMAN, J. (Ed.) *Handbook of Teacher Evaluation*, Beverly Hills, Calif., Sage.

JOHNSON, S.M. (1980) 'Performance-based staff layoffs in the public schools: Implementation and outcomes', *Harvard Educational Review*, 50, 2, pp. 214–33.

JOYCE, B.R. and WEIL, M. (1982) *Models of Teaching*, Englewood Cliffs, NJ, Prentice Hall.

KAZDIN, A.E. (1979) 'Imagery elaboration and self-efficacy in the covert modeling treatment of unassertive behavior', *Journal of Consulting and Clinical Psychology*, 47, pp. 725–33.

KING, J.A. (1981) 'Beyond classroom walls: Indirect measures of teacher competence' in MILLMAN, J. (Ed.) *Handbook of Teacher Evaluation*, Beverly Hills, Calif., Sage.

KLEINE, P.E. and WISNIEWSKI, R. (1981) 'Bill 1706: A forward step for Oklahoma', *Phi Delta Kappan*, 63, 2, pp. 115–17.

KNAPP, M.S. (1982) *Toward the Study of Teacher Evaluation as an Organizational Process: A Review of Current Research and Practice*, Menlo Park, Calif., Educational and Human Services Research Center, SRI International.

LAWLER, E. (1973) *Motivation in Work Organizations*, Monterey, Calif., Brooks-Cole.

LEWIN, K. (1938) *The Conceptual Representation and the Measurement of Psychological Forces*, Durham, N.C., Duke University Press.

LEWIN, K., DEMBO, T., FESTINGER, L. and SEARS, P. (1944) 'Level of aspiration' in HUNT, J. (Ed.) *Personality and Behavioral Disorders*, Vol. 2, New York, Ronald Press.

LEWIS, A. (1982) *Evaluating Educational Personnel*, Arlington, Va, American Association of School Administrators.

LEWIS, D.M. (1979) 'Certifying functional literacy: Competency testing and implications for due process and equal educational opportunity', *Journal of Law and Education*, 8, 2, p. 145.

LIPSKY, M. (1976) 'Toward a theory of street-level bureaucracy' in HAWLEY, W. and LIPSKY, M. (Eds) *Theoretical Perspectives on Urban Politics*, Englewood Cliffs, NJ, Prentice Hall.

LIPSKY, M. (1980) *Street-level Bureaucracy*, New York, Russell Sage.

LORTIE, D. (1975) *Schoolteacher*, Chicago, University of Chicago Press.

McDONALD, F.J. (1976) *Summary Report: Beginning Teacher Evaluation Study*, Phase II, Princeton, NJ, Educational Testing Service.

McDONALD, F.J. and ELIAS, P. (1976) *Executive Summary Report: Beginning Teacher Evaluation Study, Phase II*, Princeton, NJ, Educational Testing Service.

McDONNELL, L. and PASCAL, A. (1979) *Organized Teachers in American Schools*, R-2407-NIE, Santa Monica, Calif., The Rand Corporation.

McKEACHIE, W.J. and KULIK, J.A. (1975) 'Effective college teaching' in KERLINGER, F.N. (Ed.) *Review of Research in Education*, Vol. 3, Itasca, Ill., F.E. Peacock.

McKENNA (1981) 'Context/environment effects in teacher evaluation' in MILLMAN, J. (Ed.) *Handbook on Teacher Evaluation*, Beverly Hills, Calif., Sage.

McNEIL, J.D. (1981) 'The politics of teacher evaluation' in MILLMAN, J. (Ed.) *Handbook of Teacher Evaluation*, Beverly Hills, Calif., Sage.

McNEIL, J. and POPHAM, W. (1973) 'The assessment of teacher competence' in TRAVERS, R.M. (Ed.) *Second Handbook of Research on Teaching*, Chicago, Rand McNally.

MANATT, R.P., PALMER, K.L. and HIDLEBAUGH, E. (1976) 'Evaluating teacher performance with improved rating scales', *NASSP Bulletin*, 60, 401, pp. 21–3.

MANN, D. (Ed.) (1978) *Making Change Happen?*, New York, Teachers College Press.

MARCH, J.G. (1976) 'The technology of foolishness' in MARCH, J.G. and OLSEN, J.P. (Eds) *Ambiguity and Choice in Organizations*, Bergen, Norway, Universitetsforlaget.

MEDLEY, D.M. (1979) 'The effectiveness of teachers' in PETERSON, P.L. and WALBERG, H.J. (Eds) *Research on Teaching*, Berkeley, Calif, McCutchan.

MEDLEY, D.M. (1982) *Teacher Competency Testing and the Teacher Educator*, Charlottesville, Virginia, Association of Teacher Educators and the Bureau of Educational Research, University of Virginia.

MEYER, H.H. (1975) 'The pay-for-performance dillemma' *Organizational Dynamics*, 3, 3, pp. 39–50.

MEYER, J. and ROWAN, B. (1978) 'Structure of educational organizations', in MEYER, M.W. (Ed.) *Environments and Organizations*, San Francisco, Jossey-Bass.

MILLMAN, J. (Ed.) (1981a) *Handbook of Teacher Evaluation*, Beverly Hills, Calif., Sage.

MILLMAN, J. (1981b) 'Student achievement as a measure of teacher competence' in MILLMAN, J. (Eds) *Handbook of Teacher Evaluation*, Beverly Hills, Calif., Sage.

MILSTEIN, M.M. (Ed.) (1980) *Schools, Conflict and Change*, New York, Teachers College Press.

MITCHELL, D.E. and KERCHNER, C.T. (1983) 'Collective bargaining and teacher policy' in SHULMAN, L.S. and SYKES, G. (Eds) *Handbook of Teaching and Policy*, New York, Longman.

MOBLEY, W., GRIFFETH, W. HAND, H. and MEGLINO, B. (1979) 'Review and conceptual analysis of the employee turnover process', *Psychological Bulletin*, 86, 3, pp. 493–522.

MUNNELLY, R.J. (1979) 'Dealing with teacher incompetence: Supervision and evaluation in a due process framework', *Contemporary Education*, 50, 4, pp. 221–5.

National Education Association (1979) *Teacher Opinion Poll*, Washington, DC, National Education Association.

NATRIELLO, G. and DORNBUSCH, S.M. (1980–81) 'Pitfalls in the evaluation of teachers by principals', *Administrator's Notebook*, 29, 6.

NATRIELLO, G., HOAG., M., DEAL., T.E. and DORNBUSCH, S.M. (1977) *A Summary of the Recent Literature on the Evaluation of Principals, Teachers, and Students*, occasional paper no. 18, Stanford, Calif., Stanford Center for R & D in Teaching, Stanford University.

ORNSTEIN, A.C. and LEVINE, D.V. (1981) 'Teacher behavior research: Overview and outlook', *Phi Delta Kappan*, 62, 8, pp. 592–6.

OUCHI, W.G. (1980) 'Markets, bureaucracies, and clans', *Administrative Science Quarterly*, 25, 1, pp. 129–41.

PETERSON, K. and KAUCHAK, D. (1982) *Teacher Evaluation: Perspectives, Practices and Promises*, Salt Lake City, Utah, Center for Educational Practice, University of Utah.

PETERSON, P.L. (1976) *Interactive Effects of Student Anxiety, Achievement Orientation, and Teacher Behavior on Student Achievement and Attitude*, unpublished doctoral dissertation, Stanford University.

PETERSON, P.L. (1979) 'Direct instruction reconsidered' in PETERSON, P.L. and WALBERG, H.J. (Eds) *Research on Teaching*, Berkeley, Calif., McCutchan.

PFEFFER, J., SALANCIK, G. and LEBLEBICI, H. (1976) 'The effect of uncertainty on the use of social influence in organizational decision making', *Administrative Science Quarterly*, 21, 2, pp. 227–48.

QUIRK, T.J., WITTEN, B.J. and WEINBERG, S.F. (1973) 'Review of studies of the concurrent and predictive validity of the National Teacher Examination', *Review of Educational Research*, 43, pp. 89–114.

REDFERN, G.B. (1980) *Evaluating Teachers and Administrators: A Performance Objectives Approach*, Boulder, Colo, Westview Press.

REIN, M. (1976) *Social Science and Public Policy*, New York, Penguin Books.

RILEY, R.D. and SCHAFFER, E.C. (1979) 'Self-certification: Accounting to oneself', *Journal of Teacher Education*, 30, 2, pp. 23–6.

ROHR, G. (1976) 'Results on standardized achievement tests for students in grades 3 and 6: A comparative study of some open-plan schools and traditionally built schools in Malmo', *Didakometry and Sociometry*, 8, 1, p. 12.

ROSENHOLTZ, S.J. and WILSON, B. (1980) 'The effect of classroom structure on shared perceptions of ability', *American Educational Research Journal*, 17, pp. 75–82.

ROSENSHINE, B. (1970) 'The stability of teacher effects upon student achievement', *Review of Educational Research*, 40, pp. 647–62.

ROSENSHINE, B. (1977) 'Review of teaching variables and student achievement' in BORICH, G.D. (Ed.) *The Appraisal of Teaching: Concepts and Process*, Reading, Mass, Addison-Wesley.

ROSENSHINE, B.V. (1979) 'Content, time, and director instruction' in PETERSON, P.L.

and WALBERG, H.H. (Eds) *Research on Teaching*, Berkeley, Calif., McCutchan.

ROSENSHINE, B. and FURST, N. (1971) 'Research on teacher performance criteria' in SMITH, B.O. (Ed.) *Research in Teacher Education: A Symposium*, Englewood Cliffs, NJ, Prentice Hall.

ROSSI, P.H., FREEMAN, H.E. and WRIGHT, S.R. (1979) *Evaluation: A Systematic Approach*, Beverly Hills, Calif., Sage.

RUTTER, M., MAUGHAN, B., MORTIMORE, P., OUSTON, J., and SMITH, A. (1979) *Fifteen Thousand Hours: Secondary Schools and Their Effects on Children*, Cambridge, Mass, Harvard University Press.

SABATIER, P. and MAXMANIAN, D. (1979) *The Implementation of Regulatory Policy: A Framework of Analysis*, Davis, Calif., Institute of Governmental Affairs.

SCHALOCK, D. (1979) 'Research on teacher selection' in BERLINER, D.C. (Ed.) *Review of Research in Education*, Vol. 7, Washington, DC, American Educational Research Association.

SELZNICK, P. (1966) *TVA and the Grass Roots*, New York, Harper and Row.

SHAVELSON, R. (1973) 'What is the basic teaching skill?', *Journal of Teacher Education*, 14, pp. 144–51.

SHAVELSON, R. and DEMPSEY-ATWOOD, N. (1976) 'Generalizability of measures of teacher behavior', *Review of Educational Research*, 46, pp. 553–612.

SHAVELSON, R. and RUSSO, N.A. (1977) 'Generalizability of measures of teacher effectiveness', *Educational Research*, 19, 3, pp. 171–83.

SHAVELSON, R. and STERN, P. (1981) 'Research on teachers' pedagogical thoughts, judgments, decisions and behavior', *Review of Educational Research*, 51, 4, pp. 455–98.

SHINE, W.A. and GOLDMAN, N. (1980) reply to Fred G. Burke, *Educational Leadership*, 38, 3, p. 201.

SOAR, R.S. (1972) *Follow Through Classroom Process Measurement and Pupil Growth*, Gainesville, Flo, Institute for Development of Human Resources, University of Florida.

SOAR, R.S. (1977) 'An integration of findings from four studies on teacher effectiveness' in BORICH, G.D. (Ed.) *The Appraisal of Teaching: Concepts and Process*, Reading, Mass, Addison-Wesley.

SOAR, R.S. and SOAR, R.M. (1976) 'An attempt to identify measures of teacher effectiveness from four studies', *Journal of Teacher Education*, 27, pp. 261–7.

Southern Regional Education Board (1979) *Teacher Education and Certification: State Actions in the South*, Atlanta, Georgia, Southern Regional Education Board.

SPROULL, L.S. (1979) *Response to Regulation: An Organizational Process Framework*, Pittsburgh, Pa, Carnegie-Mellon University.

SROUFE, G.E. (1977) 'Evaluation and politics' in SCRIBNER, J. (Ed.) *The Politics of Education*, Chicago, University of Chicago Press.

STALLINGS, J.A. (1977) 'How instructional processes relate to child outcomes' in BORICH, G.D. (Ed.) *The Appraisal of Teaching: Concepts and Process*, Reading Mass, Addison-Wesley.

STEPHENS, J.M. (1976) *The Process of Schooling*, New York, Holt, Rinehart and Winston.

STIGGINS, R.J. and BRIDGEFORD, N.J. (1982) *Performance Assessment for Teacher Development*, Portland, Ore, Center for Performance Assessment.

STONE, C.N. (1980) 'The implementation of social programs: Two perspectives', *Journal of Social Issues*, 36, 4, pp. 13–34.

STRIKE, K. and BULL, B. (1981) 'Fairness and the legal context of teacher evaluation' in MILLMAN, J. (Ed.) *Handbook of Teacher Evaluation*, Beverly Hills, Calif., Sage.

TALBERT, J. (1980) *School Organization and Institutional Changes: Exchange and Power in Loosely-Coupled Systems*, Stanford, Calif., Institute for Research on Educational Finance and Governance, Stanford University.

THOMAS, M.D. (1979) *Evaluation of Educational Personnel*, Bloomington, Ill., Phi Delta Kappa Educational Foundation.

THOMPSON, J.E., DORNBUSCH, S.M. and SCOTT, W.R. (1975) *Failures of Communication in the Evaluation of Teachers by Principals*, no. 43, Stanford, Calif., Stanford Center for Research and Development in Teaching.

TRAUB, R., WEISS, J., FISHER, C., USELLA, D. and KHAN, S. (1973) *Openness in Schools: An Evaluation of the Wentworth County Roman Catholic School Board Schools*, Toronto, Ont., Educational Evaluation Center, Ontario Institute for Studies in Education.

VELDMAN, D.J. and BROPHY, J.E. (1974) 'Measuring teacher effects on pupil achievement', *Journal of Educational Psychology*, 66, pp. 319–24.

VLAANDEREN, R. (1980) *Trends in Competency-based Teacher Certification*, Denver, Colo, Education Commission of the States.

VROOM, V. (1964) *Work and Motivation*, New York, Wiley.

WARD, W.D. and BARCHER, P.R. (1975) 'Reading achievement and creativity as related to open classroom experience', *Journal of Educational Psychology*, 67, pp. 683–91.

WEATHERLEY, R. and LIPSKY, M. (1977) 'Street-level bureaucrats and institutional innovation: Implementating special education reform', *Harvard Educational Review*, 47, 2, pp.171–97.

WEICK, K.E. (1976) 'Educational organizations as loosely-coupled systems', *Adminstrative Science, Quarterly*, 21, pp. 1–19.

WEICK, K.E. (1982) 'Administering education in loosely coupled schools', *Phi Delta Kappan*, 63, 10, pp. 673–6.

WILDAVSKY, A. (1980) *Speaking Truth to Power: The Art and Craft of Policy Analysis*, Boston, Little, Brown and Company.

WILEY, D.E. and HARNISCHFEGER, A. (1974) 'Explosion of a myth: Quantity of schooling and exposure to instruction, major educational vehicles', *Educational Researcher*, 3, pp. 7–12.

WISE, A.E. (1979) *Legislated Learning*, Berkeley, University of California Press.

WRIGHT, R.J. (1975) 'The affective and cognitive consequences of an open education elementary school', *American Educational Research Journal*, 12, pp. 449–568.

Contributors

Linda Darling-Hammond is a social scientist with the Rand Corporation and specializes in educational policy analysis, law and governance of education and research into teaching.

Eleanor Farrar is Senior Research Associate at the Huron Research Institute and specializes in the study of the implementation of federal programs.

Ernest House is Professor of Administration, Higher and Continuing Education, and Educational Psychology in the Center for Instructional Research and Curriculum Evaluation at the University of Illinois at Urbana, USA.

Stephen Kemmis is Associate Professor of Curriculum Studies at Deakin University, Victoria, Australia. He specializes in educational research and evaluation methodology.

Gill Kirkup is a Lecturer at the Institute of Educational Technology at the Open University, UK, and specializes in course development and evaluation and particularly in women's studies.

David Nevo is a Senior Lecturer in the School of Education at Tel-Aviv University in Israel. He specializes in evaluation theory, educational measurement and research.

Sara Pease is a Research Assistant with the Rand Corporation specializing in domestic federal policy, legal and regulatory analysis.

Michael Scriven is Professor of Education at the University of Western Australia.

Robert Stake is Professor of Educational Psychology in the Center for Instructional Research and Curriculum Evaluation at the University of Illinois at Urbana, Illinois.

Rob Walker spent many years at the Centre for Applied Educational Research and the University of East Anglia, UK, and is now at Deakin University, Victoria, Australia. He specializes in evaluation studies.

Carol Weiss is Senior Lecturer at the Harvard Graduate School of Education and specializes in evaluation theory and practice. She was winner of the Evaluation Research Society's Myrdal Award for Science

Arthur Wise is a Senior Social Scientist with the Rand Corporation specializing in educational policy analysis, law and governance of education and research on teaching.

Index